DESIGNING THE USER INTERFACE

DESIGNING THE USER INTERFACE

Strategies for Effective Human-Computer Interaction / 5th Edition

Ben Shneiderman & Catherine Plaisant

University of Maryland, College Park

Addison-Wesley

Boston   San Francisco   New York

London   Toronto   Sydney   Tokyo   Singapore   Madrid

Mexico City   Munich   Paris   Cape Town   Hong Kong   Montreal

Editor-in-Chief: Michael Hirsch
Editorial Assistant: Stephanie Sellinger
Managing Editor: Jeff Holcomb
Senior Manufacturing Buyer: Carol Melville
Art Director: Linda Knowles
Senior Media Producer: Bethany Tidd
Director of Marketing: Margaret Waples
Marketing Manager: Erin Davis
Marketing Coordinator: Kathryn Ferranti
Director of Marketing Services: Stacey Abraham
Online Product Manager: Bethany Tidd
Manager, Rights and Permissions: Diann Korta
Permissions Project Manager: Shannon W. Barbe
Text Permission Coordinator: Dana Weightman
Visual Research Manager: Beth Brenzel

Image Permission Coordinator: Ang'john Ferreri
Full-Service Project Management: Rose Kernan,
   Nesbitt Graphics, Inc.
Composition and Illustrations:
   Nesbitt Graphics, Inc.
Text Designer: Jerilyn Bockorick,
   Nesbitt Graphics, Inc.
Cover Designer: Joyce Cosentino Wells
Cover Photos: (clockwise, from top left) © Jeff
   Savage; © Alan Becker/The Image Bank/Getty
   images; © Bob Daemmrich/The Image Works;
   © Michael DeYoung/Aurora/Getty Images;
   AISPIX/Shutterstock; © Mel Yates/Cultura/
   Getty Images. Background: © Jason Reed/Pho-
   todisc/Getty Images

Access the latest information about Addison-Wesley titles from our World Wide Web site:
http://www.pearsonhighered.com/cs

Credits and acknowledgments borrowed from other sources and reproduced, with permission, in this textbook appear in the Acknowledgments section in the endmatter of this book.

Many of the designations by manufacturers and sellers to distinguish their products are claimed as trademarks. Where those designations appear in this book, and the publisher was aware of a trademark claim, the designations have been printed in initial caps or all caps.

Microsoft® and Windows® are registered trademarks of the Microsoft Corporation in the U.S.A. and other countries. Screen shots and icons reprinted with permission from the Microsoft Corporation. This book is not sponsored or endorsed by or affiliated with the Microsoft Corporation.

The programs and applications presented in this book have been included for their instructional value. They have been tested with care, but are not guaranteed for any particular purpose. The publisher does not offer any warranties or representations, nor does it accept any liabilities with respect to the programs or applications.

Library of Congress Cataloging-in-Publication Data
Shneiderman, Ben.
   Designing the user interface / Ben Shneiderman, Catherine Plaisant; contributors, Maxine Cohen, Steven Jacobs. -- 5th ed.
      p. cm.
   Includes bibliographical references and index.
   ISBN 0-321-53735-1 (alk. paper)
   1. Human-computer interaction. 2. User interfaces (Computer systems) I.Plaisant, Catherine. II. Title.
QA76.9.H85S54 2009
005.4'37--dc22
                            2009003477

Addison Wesley
is an imprint of

ISBN-13: 978-0-321-53735-5
ISBN-10: 0-321-53735-1
10 9 8 7 6 5 4 3 —CRK—13 12

To Jenny and Peter;
Anna, Sara, and Thomas

Preface

Designing the User Interface is written for students, researchers, designers, managers, and evaluators of interactive systems. It presents a broad survey of how to develop high-quality user interfaces for interactive systems. Readers with backgrounds in computer science, psychology, sociology, industrial engineering, information science/studies/systems, business, education, and communications should all find fresh and valuable material. Our goals are to encourage greater attention to usability issues and to promote further scientific study of human-computer interaction, including the rapidly emerging topic of social media participation.

Since the publication of the first four editions of this book in 1986, 1992, 1998, and 2005, HCI practitioners and researchers have grown more numerous and influential. The quality of interfaces has improved greatly, while the community of users and its diversity have grown dramatically. Researchers and designers could claim success, but today user expectations are higher, applications are more demanding, and platforms are more varied. In addition to desktop computers, designers now must accommodate web-based services and an increasingly diverse set of mobile devices. User interface designers are moving in new directions: some innovators provoke us with virtual and augmented realities, whereas others offer alluring scenarios for ubiquitous computing, embedded devices, and tangible user interfaces.

These innovations are important, but much work remains to be done to improve the experiences of novice and expert users who still struggle with too many frustrations. These problems must be resolved if we are to achieve the goal of universal usability, enabling all citizens in every country to enjoy the benefits of these new technologies. This book is meant to inspire students, guide designers, and provoke researchers to seek those solutions.

Keeping up with the innovations in human-computer interaction is a demanding task, and requests for an update begin arriving soon after the publication of each edition. The expansion of the field led the single author of the first three editions, Ben Shneiderman, to turn to Catherine Plaisant, a long-time valued research partner, for coauthoring help with the fourth and fifth editions. In addition, two contributing authors lent their able support to this fifth edition: Maxine S. Cohen and Steven M. Jacobs have long experience teaching with earlier editions of the book and provided fresh perspectives that improved the quality for all readers and instructors. In preparing for this edition, we harvested information from books and journals, scanned the World Wide Web, attended conferences, and consulted with colleagues. Then we returned to our keyboards to write, producing first drafts that served as a starting point to generate feedback from colleagues, HCI practitioners, and students. The work that went into the final product was intense, but satisfying. We hope you, the readers, will put these ideas to good use and produce more innovations for us to report in future editions.

New in the Fifth Edition

Readers will see the dynamism of human-computer interaction reflected in the substantial changes to this fifth edition. The good news is that most universities now offer courses in this area, and some require it in computer science, information schools (iSchools), or other disciplines. Courses and degree programs in human-computer interaction, human-centered computing, interaction design, etc. are a growing worldwide phenomenon at every educational level. Although many usability practitioners must still fight to be heard, corporate and government commitments to usability engineering grow stronger daily. The business case for usability has been made repeatedly, and dedicated web sites describe scores of studies demonstrating strong return on investment for usability efforts.

Comments from instructors who used the previous editions were influential in our revisions. The main change was to dramatically expand our coverage of social media participation and user-generated content, especially from mobile devices. We deleted the chapter on software tools, as these change so rapidly and deserve more attention than we could give them in a single chapter. Every remaining chapter has been updated with fresh ideas, examples, figures, and references. At the same time, some topics have become less relevant; they, together with older references, have been removed.

The opening chapter addresses the growing issue of ensuring universal usability for increasingly diverse users of interactive systems. The second chapter presents design guidelines, principles, and theories that have been substantially updated to reflect new ways of thinking. Part 2 covers refinements to development methodologies and evaluation techniques. Part 3 explores progress in direct manipulation and its extensions such as virtual and augmented reality, as well as changes to menus, form fill-in, and command languages brought about by the new platforms (especially mobile devices). Since collaboration and social media participation have become so central, the final chapter in this part of the book has been heavily expanded and updated. Part 4 emphasizes Quality of Service and a series of important design issues. Chapter 12 has been thoroughly revised to reflect the vitality of user documentation and online help in serving the goal of universal usability. Finally, information search and visualization now have their own chapters, since we believe that these topics have grown dramatically in importance.

We strive to give balanced presentations on controversial topics such as 3D, speech, and natural-language interfaces. Philosophical controversies such as the degree of human control and the role of animated characters are treated carefully to present fairly the viewpoints that differ from our own. We gave colleagues a chance to comment on these sections and made a special effort to provide a balanced presentation while making our own opinions clear, especially in the Afterword. Readers will have to judge for themselves whether we succeeded.

Instructors wanted guidelines and summary tables; these elements are shown in boxes throughout the book. The Practitioner Summaries and Researcher Agendas remain popular; they have been updated. The references have been expanded and freshened with many new sources, with classic papers still included. We worked hard to select references that were widely available and often web-accessible. Figures, especially those showing screen designs, age quickly, so many new user interfaces are shown. Printing in full color makes these figures valuable as a record of contemporary design styles.

Ways to Use This Book

We hope that practitioners and researchers who read this book will want to keep it on their shelves to consult when they are working on new topics or seeking pointers to the literature.

Instructors may choose to assign the full text in the order that we present it or to make selections from it. The opening chapter is a good starting point for most students, but instructors may take different paths depending on their disciplines. For example, instructors might emphasize the following chapters, listed by area:

- Computer science: 2, 5, 6, 7, 8, 9, 10, 13, 14
- Psychology and sociology: 2, 4, 5, 9, 10, 11, 12
- Industrial engineering: 2, 4, 5, 10, 11, 13, 14
- Library and information studies: 2, 4, 9, 11, 12, 13, 14
- Business and information systems: 3, 4, 5, 9, 10, 12, 13, 14
- Education technology: 2, 4, 9, 12, 13, 14
- Communication arts and media studies: 4, 5, 9, 11, 12
- Technical writing and graphic design: 3, 4, 5, 11, 12

Companion Website (www.aw.com/DTUI)

The presence of the World Wide Web has a profound effect on researchers, designers, educators, and students. We want to encourage intense use of the Web by members of all these groups, but the volatility of the Web is not in harmony with the permanence of printed books. Publishing numerous web site URLs in the book would have been risky, because changes are made daily. For these and other reasons, we have established a Companion Website to accompany this book. We hope that every reader will visit the site, and that you will not hesitate to send us ideas for improving it.

In addition to pointers to current web resources, a variety of supplemental materials for this text are available at the book's Companion Website. The following are accessible to all readers who register using the prepaid access card in the front of this book:

- Links to hundreds of human-computer interaction resources, examples, and research studies that enhance and expand on the material in each chapter
- Chapter/section summaries
- Self-test questions and discussion questions for each chapter
- Homework assignments and projects

PowerPoint lecture slides are also available from Addison-Wesley's Instructor Resource Center (http://www.pearsonhighered.com/irc/). For information about accessing these instructor's supplements, visit the Instructor Resource Center or send an e-mail to *computing@aw.com*.

Acknowledgments

Writing is a lonely process; revising is a social one. We are grateful to the many colleagues and students who have made suggestions for improvements to prior editions. We particularly appreciate the strong contributions from Maxine S. Cohen to Chapters 4, 5, 9, and 12 and Steven M. Jacobs to Chapters 3, 7, 10, and 11, as well as their help throughout the book. Their experiences both in industry and in teaching with the earlier editions of the book over the course of many years added valuable perspectives to this fifth edition. After one two-day kickoff meeting, we collaborated smoothly by using e-mail, LiveSync for draft documents, and Skype for hour-long phone calls every one to three weeks. Cooperative personalities, hard work, and appropriate tools made this massive project possible even with tight time constraints. We look forward to a continuing partnership on the Companion Website and future editions.

Our close daily collaborators at the University of Maryland have a profound influence on our work: many thanks to Ben Bederson, Allison Druin, François Guimbretière, Kent Norman, Doug Oard, Jennifer Preece, Anne Rose, and Vibha Sazawal. We also appreciate the undergraduate and graduate students who provide encouraging feedback and challenging questions, plus the motivation to keep updating this book.

Extensive comments from the review panel played a strong role in our revisions. These individuals made numerous constructive suggestions:

Harry Hochheiser, *Towson University*

Juan Pablo Hourcade, *University of Iowa*

Richard D. Manning, *Nova Southeastern University*

Chris North, *Virginia Tech*

Jeff Offutt, *George Mason University*

In addition, several colleagues responded to requests or commented generously on certain chapters or sections about which they were especially knowledgeable: thanks to Christopher Andrews, Patrick Baudisch, Justine Cassell, Nick Chen, David Doermann, Cody Dunne, Jean-Daniel Fekete, Dennis Galletta, Jennifer Golbeck, Art Graesser, Chang Hu, Bonnie John, Lewis Johnson, Matt Kirschenbaum, Kari Kraus, Alex Quinn, Kiki Schneider, Hyunyoung Song, Michael Twidale and Bo Xie.

Thanks also to Jonathan Feinberg, creator of the clever and free Wordle (http://www.wordle.net/), which we used to make the chapter opening graphics. These graphics are based on word frequencies in each chapter and are used per the terms of the Creative Commons Attribution 3.0 United States License.

The publisher's editorial and production staff were actively involved in this book from the start. We appreciate the contributions of Michael Hirsch, Jeffrey Holcomb, Stephanie Sellinger, Bethany Tidd, Linda Knowles, and Joyce Cosentino Wells. At Nesbitt Graphics, we thank Rose Kernan, Paul Fennessy, Risa Clow, and Jerilyn Bockorick. The copyeditor for the fourth and fifth editions, Rachel Head, taught us a lot about lucid and informative writing. We apologize if we have left out any other contributors. Finally, a further thanks goes to the students and professionals from around the world who have sent us comments and suggestions. Their provocative questions about our growing discipline and profession encourage us daily.

Ben Shneiderman (ben@cs.umd.edu)
Catherine Plaisant (plaisant@cs.umd.edu)

Brief Contents

Contents

PART 1

INTRODUCTION

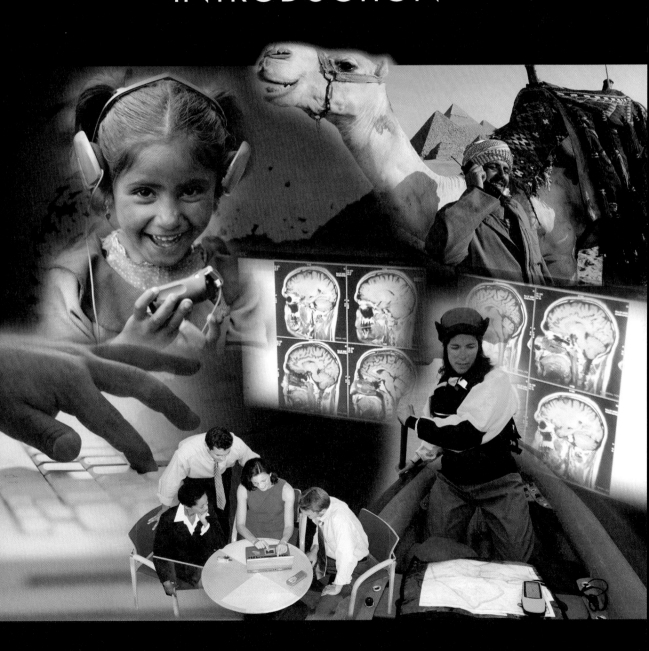

CHAPTER 1

Usability of Interactive Systems

> 66 Designing an object to be simple and clear takes at least twice as long as the usual way. It requires concentration at the outset on how a clear and simple system would work, followed by the steps required to make it come out that way—steps which are often much harder and more complex than the ordinary ones. It also requires relentless pursuit of that simplicity even when obstacles appear which would seem to stand in the way of that simplicity. 99

T. H. Nelson
The Home Computer Revolution, 1977

1.1 Introduction

User-interface designers are becoming the heroes of a profound transformation. Their work has turned the personal computer into the social computer, enabling users to communicate and collaborate in remarkable ways. The desktop applications that once served the needs of professionals are now enabling broad communities of users to prepare user-generated content that can be shared with millions of World Wide Web users. And now the web-based social networking and social media applications that were once available only to desktop users are accessible through billions of cellphones and other mobile devices.

These dramatic shifts are possible because researchers and user-interface designers have harnessed the advancing technologies to serve human needs. Researchers created the interdisciplinary design science of *human-computer interaction* by applying the methods of experimental psychology to the powerful tools of computer science. Then they integrated lessons from educational and industrial psychologists, instructional and graphic designers, technical writers, experts in human factors or ergonomics, information architects, and adventuresome anthropologists and sociologists. The payoff is seen in the success of increasingly powerful social media, which might be called *social-computer interaction*. As the impact of these social tools and services spreads, researchers and designers are gathering fresh insights from policy analysts, intellectual property defenders, privacy protectors, consumer advocates, and ethicists.

User interfaces help produce business success stories and Wall Street sensations. They also produce intense competition, copyright-infringement suits, intellectual-property battles, mega-mergers, and international partnerships. Crusading Internet visionaries promote a world with free access to information and entertainment, while equally devoted protectors of creative artists argue for fair payments.

User interfaces are also controversial because of their central role in personal identification, national defense, crime fighting, electronic health records, and so on. In the aftermath of the September 11, 2001 terrorist attacks, some members of the U.S. Congress blamed the inadequacies of user interfaces for the failure to detect the terrorists.

At an individual level, user interfaces change many people's lives: effective user interfaces for professionals mean that doctors can make more accurate diagnoses and pilots can fly airplanes more safely; at the same time, children can learn more effectively, users with disabilities can lead productive lives, and graphic artists can explore creative possibilities more fluidly. Some changes, however, are disruptive. Too often, users must cope with frustration, fear, and failure when they encounter excessively complex menus, incomprehensible terminology, or chaotic navigation paths. What user wouldn't be disturbed by receiving a message such as "Illegal Memory Exception: Severe Failure" with no guidance about what to do next?

FIGURE 1.1

Apple® Mac OS X®. The top-left corner shows a Windows XP virtual machine and the Facebook social networking web site (http://www.facebook.com/). The top right is a Unix Terminal, and the bottom-right window shows eBay (http://www.ebay.com/), a popular online auction site. The bottom of the screen also shows the Dock, a menu of frequently accessed items whose icons grow larger on mouse-over.

The steadily growing interest in user-interface design stems from designers' desire to improve the users' computing experience (Figs. 1.1 and 1.2 show some popular operating systems). In business settings, better decision-support and document-sharing tools support entrepreneurs, while in home settings digital photo libraries and videoconferencing enhance family relationships. Millions of people take advantage of the World Wide Web's extraordinary educational and cultural heritage resources, which provide access to everything from outstanding art objects from China, music from Indonesia, sports from Brazil, and entertainment from Hollywood or Bollywood (Figs. 1.3 to 1.7 show some popular web sites). Mobile devices enrich daily life for many users, including those with disabilities, limited literacy, and low incomes (Fig. 1.8 shows some mobile

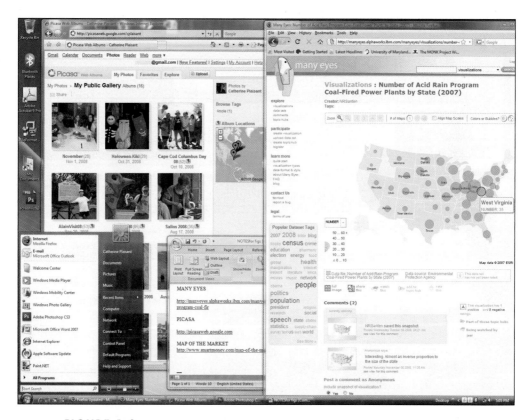

FIGURE 1.2

Microsoft® Windows Vista®, showing icons at the top left and the Start menu at the bottom left. Transparency reveals the window underneath the menu. The main window on the left is Google's picture sharing application Picasa™. On the right side IBM's Many Eyes™ application lets users post and visualize data (here showing the distribution of coal power plants on a US map). Other users can then post comments or add tags.

FIGURE 1.3

Apple's iTunes® interface (http://www.apple.com/itunes/) allows PC and Macintosh® users to shop for music, videos, and much more, then manage their media and synchronize their collections with music players like the iPod® and iPhone™.

devices). On a worldwide scale, promoters and opponents of globalization debate the role of technology in international development, while activists work to attain the United Nations Millennium Development Goals.

The transition away from desktop web-based applications is accelerating, encouraged by the explosive growth of mobile devices (especially cellphones) that support personal communication. The proliferation of such devices in developed as well as developing nations has been astonishing. Some analysts see a close linkage between economic growth and cellphone dissemination, since communications facilitate commerce and stimulate entrepreneurial ventures. Mobile devices also enrich family and friend relationships, enable timely medical care, and provide life-saving disaster response services to professionals and residents.

Explosive growth is also the appropriate description for what's happening in the realms of social networking and user-generated content. While older media,

FIGURE 1.4

The Amazon.com web site (http://www.amazon.com/) will make book and product recommendations based on a user's personal history with the site.

such as newspapers and television, have sought to increase their audiences through new media, their audiences have dwindled in favor of social networking sites such as MySpace and Facebook and user-generated content presented by sites like YouTube and Wikipedia (all of which are among the top ten most visited web sites). These early leaders are just a taste of what is to come, as entrepreneurs generate ever more clever social media participation accessible through web-based applications and mobile devices.

Designers are enabling users to create, edit, and distribute three-dimensional representations, animations, music, voice, video recordings. The result is ever-richer multimedia experiences on web sites and a creative outpouring of user-generated content available on mobile devices.

Sociologists, anthropologists, policymakers, and managers are studying how social media participation is changing education, family life, personal relationships,

FIGURE 1.5

YouTube (http://www.youtube.com/) became a top-ten web site by offering free uploads and downloads of millions of videos, encouraging a creative outpouring of hilarious and serious short (2–10 minute) videos. This example shows a demonstration of the game *Untold Legends*™ on a Sony™ PlayStation®3.

and services such as medical care, financial advice, and political organizations. They are also dealing with issues of organizational impact, job redesign, distributed team-work, work-at-home scenarios, and long-term societal changes. As face-to-face interaction gives way to screen-to-screen, how can personal trust and organizational loyalty be preserved?

Designers face the challenge of providing services on small-, wall-, and mall-sized displays, ranging from mobile devices such as cellphones to large plasma panels and projected displays. The *plasticity* of their designs must ensure smooth conversion across different display sizes, delivery by

FIGURE 1.6

The Library of Congress web site (http://www.loc.gov/) provides access to primary sources from over 200 collections that cover diverse topics ranging from the American Civil War to Yiddish Theater in the 1920s.

way of desktop web browsers or pocket-sized cellphones, translation into multiple languages, and compatibility with accessibility-support devices for disabled users.

Some innovators promise that desktop computers and their user interfaces will disappear, while new interfaces will become ubiquitous, pervasive, invisible, and embedded in the surrounding environment. They believe that novel

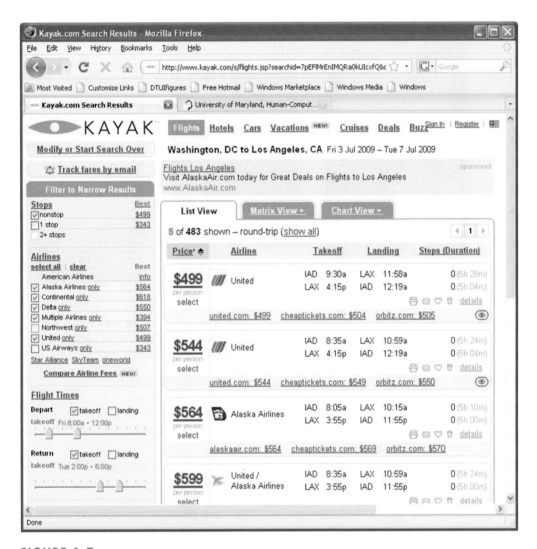

FIGURE 1.7

Firefox® 3.0 showing the Kayak travel search web site (http://www.kayak.com/) with check boxes to select nonstop flights and specific airlines. This user has also specified a range of flight times using double-box range sliders.

devices will be context-aware, attentive, and perceptive, sensing users' needs and providing feedback through ambient displays that glow, hum, change shape, or blow air. Some visionaries foresee advanced mobile devices that are wearable, or even implanted under the skin. The individual sensors that track users entering buildings or FedEx packages arriving at destinations will give way to elaborate sensor nets that follow crowds, epidemics, and pollution.

FIGURE 1.8

Advanced cellphones, like the Blackberry Curve® smartphone, Apple iPhone, and T-Mobile G1™ using Android™, have larger displays, provide Internet connections, and support a growing variety of applications.

Other designers promote persuasive technologies that change users' behavior, multi-modal or gestural interfaces that facilitate use, and affective interfaces that respond to the user's emotional state.

We are living in an exciting time for designers of user interfaces. The inspirational pronouncements from technology prophets can be thrilling, but rapid progress is more likely to come from those who do the hard work of tuning designs to genuine human needs. These designers will rigorously evaluate actual use with eager early adopters, as well as reluctant late adopters, and seriously study the resistant non-users. This book's authors believe that the next phase of human-computer interaction will be strongly influenced by those who are devoted to broadening the community of users by consciously promoting universal usability and highlighting social media participation.

This first chapter gives a broad overview of human-computer interaction from practitioners' and researchers' perspectives. It lays out usability goals, measures, and motivations in Sections 1.2 and 1.3, takes on the large topic of universal usability in Section 1.4, and closes with a statement of goals for our profession. Specific references cited in the chapter appear on page 42, and a set of general references begins on page 46: lists of relevant books, guideline documents, journals, video collections, and professional organizations give readers starting points for further study.

The second chapter reviews the guidelines, principles, and theories that will be drawn on and refined throughout the book. Chapters 3–4 introduce development processes and evaluation methods, while Chapters 5–9 cover interaction styles that range from graphical direct manipulation to textual commands and their implementation using common interaction devices. Collaboration is included in this part to emphasize the need for every designer to go beyond the personal computer and consider the many forms of social computing. Chapters 10–14 address the critical design decisions that often determine the success or failure of products and that may lead to breakthroughs that open the way to new possibilities. The Afterword reflects on the societal and individual impacts of technology.

1.2 Usability Goals and Measures

Every designer wants to build high-quality interfaces that are admired by colleagues, celebrated by users, and imitated by competitors. But getting such attention takes more than flamboyant promises and stylish advertising; it's earned by providing quality features such as usability, universality, and usefulness. These goals are achieved by thoughtful planning, sensitivity to user needs, devotion to requirements analysis, and diligent testing, all while keeping within budget and on schedule.

Managers who pursue user-interface excellence first select experienced designers and then prepare realistic schedules that include time for guidelines preparation and repeated testing. The designers begin by determining user needs, generating multiple design alternatives, and conducting extensive evaluations (Chapters 3 and 4). Modern user-interface-building tools then enable implementers to quickly build working systems for further testing.

Successful designers go beyond vague notions of "user friendliness," doing more than simply making checklists of subjective guidelines. They have a thorough understanding of the diverse community of users and the tasks that must be accomplished. They study evidence-based guidelines and pursue the research literature when necessary. Great designers are deeply committed to serving the users, which strengthens their resolve when they face difficult choices, time pressures, and tight budgets.

When managers and designers have done their jobs well, their effective interfaces generate positive feelings of success, competence, and mastery in the user community. The users have a clear mental model of the interface that enables them to confidently predict what will happen in response to their actions. In the best cases, the interface almost disappears, enabling users to concentrate on their work, exploration, or pleasure. This kind of calming environment gives users the feeling that they are "in the flow," operating at their peak, while attaining their goals.

Close interaction with the user community leads to a well-chosen set of benchmark tasks that is the basis for usability goals and measures. For each user type and each task, precise measurable objectives guide the designer through the testing process. The ISO 9241 standard *Ergonomics of Human-System Interaction* (ISO, 2008) focuses on admirable goals—*effectiveness*, *efficiency*, and *satisfaction*—but the following usability measures, which focus on the latter two goals, lead more directly to practical evaluation:

1. *Time to learn*. How long does it take for typical members of the user community to learn how to use the actions relevant to a set of tasks?

2. *Speed of performance*. How long does it take to carry out the benchmark tasks?

3. *Rate of errors by users*. How many and what kinds of errors do people make in carrying out the benchmark tasks? Although time to make and correct errors might be incorporated into the speed of performance, error handling is such a critical component of interface usage that it deserves extensive study.

4. *Retention over time*. How well do users maintain their knowledge after an hour, a day, or a week? Retention may be linked closely to time to learn, and frequency of use plays an important role.

5. *Subjective satisfaction*. How much did users like using various aspects of the interface? The answer can be ascertained by interviews or by written surveys that include satisfaction scales and space for free-form comments.

Every designer would like to succeed in every measure, but there are often forced tradeoffs. If lengthy learning is permitted, task-performance times may be reduced by use of complex abbreviations, macros, and shortcuts. If the rate of errors is to be kept extremely low, speed of performance may have to be sacrificed. In some applications, subjective satisfaction may be the key determinant of success; in others, short learning times or rapid performance may be paramount. Project managers and designers who are aware of the tradeoffs can be more effective if they make their choices explicit and public. Requirements documents and marketing brochures that make clear which goals are primary are more likely to be valued.

After multiple design alternatives have been raised, the leading possibilities should be reviewed by designers and users. Low-fidelity paper mock-ups are useful, but high-fidelity online prototypes create a more realistic environment for expert reviews and usability testing. The user documentation and the online help can be written before the implementation, to provide another review and a new perspective on the design. Next, the implementation can be carried out with proper software tools; this task should be a modest one if the design is complete and precise. Finally, the acceptance test certifies that the delivered interface meets the goals of the designers and customers. These development processes and software tools are described more fully in Chapters 3 and 4.

BOX 1.1
Goals for requirements analysis.

1. Ascertain the users' needs.
2. Ensure proper reliability.
3. Promote appropriate standardization, integration, consistency, and portability.
4. Complete projects on schedule and within budget.

The business case for usability is strong and has been made repeatedly (Landauer, 1995; Norman, 2000; Bias and Mayhew, 2005). User-interface design success stories can also be managerial success stories, for projects that are on budget and on schedule. A thoroughly documented set of user needs clarifies the design process, and a carefully tested prototype generates fewer changes during implementation while avoiding costly updates after release. Thorough acceptance testing of the implementation produces robust interfaces that are aligned with user needs.

1.3 Usability Motivations

The enormous interest in interface usability arises from the growing recognition of the benefits well-designed interfaces bring to users. This increased motivation emanates from designers and managers of life-critical systems; industrial and commercial systems; home and entertainment applications; exploratory, creative, and collaborative interfaces; and sociotechnical systems.

1.3.1 Life-critical systems

Life-critical systems include those that control air traffic, nuclear reactors, power utilities, police or fire dispatch, military operations, and medical instruments. In these applications, high costs are expected, but they should yield high reliability and effectiveness. Lengthy training periods are acceptable to obtain rapid, error-free performance, even when the users are under stress. Subjective satisfaction is less of an issue because the users are well-motivated professionals. Retention is obtained by frequent use of common functions and practice sessions for emergency actions.

1.3.2 Industrial and commercial uses

Typical industrial and commercial uses include interfaces for banking, insurance, order entry, production management, airline and hotel reservations (Fig. 1.7), utility billing, and point-of-sales terminals. In these cases, costs shape many judgments. Operator training time is expensive, so ease of learning is important. Since many businesses are international, translation to multiple languages and adaptations to local cultures are necessary. The tradeoffs between speed of performance and error rates are governed by the total cost over the system's lifetime (Chapter 10). Subjective satisfaction is of modest importance; retention is obtained by frequent use. Speed of performance is central for most of these applications because of the high volume of transactions, but operator fatigue, stress, and burnout are legitimate concerns. Trimming 10% off the mean transaction time could mean 10% fewer operators, 10% fewer workstations, and a 10% reduction in hardware costs.

1.3.3 Home and entertainment applications

The rapid expansion of home and entertainment applications is a further source of interest in usability. Personal-computing applications include e-mail clients, search engines, cellphones (Fig. 1.8), digital cameras, and music players. Entertainment applications have flourished, making computer games a larger industry than Hollywood, while novel game input devices like the Nintendo® Wii™ (Fig. 1.9) and *Guitar Hero*™'s simplified musical instrument (Fig. 1.10) open up entirely new possibilities in areas ranging from sports to education to rehabilitation. The social media applications include social networking (MySpace, Facebook), virtual environments (*Second Life*®, *EverQuest*®), and user-generated content (YouTube, Flickr). For these interfaces, ease of learning, low error rates, and subjective satisfaction are paramount because use is discretionary and competition is fierce. If the users cannot succeed quickly, they will give up or try a competing supplier.

Choosing the right functionality while keeping costs low is difficult. Novices are best served by a constrained, simple set of actions, but as users' experience increases, so does their desire for more extensive functionality and rapid performance. A layered or level-structured design is one approach to facilitating graceful evolution from novice to expert usage: Users can move up to higher layers when they need additional features or have time to learn them. A simple example is the design of search engines, which almost always have basic and advanced interfaces (Chapter 13). Another approach to winning novice users is to carefully trim the features to make a simple device, such as the highly successful Blackberry or iPhone.

1.3.4 Exploratory, creative, and collaborative interfaces

An increasing fraction of computer use is dedicated to supporting human creativity. Exploratory applications include World Wide Web browsers and

FIGURE 1.9

The Nintendo Wii controller has been a huge success with sports games such as tennis or golf, character animation games such as *Mario*™, and fitness software that helps with balance, stretching, muscle tone, etc.

FIGURE 1.10

Guitar Hero, a highly successful music playing game in which users learn to play popular songs and earn points for how well they keep up. The web site shows potential users how the provided special small guitar functions and how people use it; it also hosts a community for discussions and runs contests.

search engines (Figs. 1.11 to 1.13), scientific, and business team collaborations support. Creative applications include architectural design environments (Fig. 1.14), music-composition tools, and video-editing systems. Collaborative interfaces enable two or more people to work together (even if the users are separated by time and space) through use of text, voice, and video mail; through electronic meeting systems that facilitate face-to-face meetings; or through groupware that enables remote collaborators to work concurrently on a document, map, spreadsheet, or image.

FIGURE 1.11

The Yahoo! portal (http://www.yahoo.com/) gives users access to e-mail, weather, healthcare, banking, and personal photo services. It provides a search window (near top, center); 20 categories for browsing (left); plus news, shopping, and entertainment links.

FIGURE 1.12A

The Google search engine (http://www.google.com/). This window shows the simple user interface for searching.

In these systems, the users may be knowledgeable in the task domains but novices in the underlying computer concepts. Their motivation is often high, but so are their expectations. Benchmark tasks are more difficult to describe because of the exploratory nature of these applications, and usage can range from occasional to frequent. In short, it is difficult to design and evaluate these systems. Designers can pursue the goal of having the computer "vanish" as users become completely absorbed in their task domains. This goal seems to be met most effectively when the computer provides a direct-manipulation representation of the world of action (Chapter 5), supplemented by keyboard shortcuts. Then, tasks are carried out by rapid familiar selections or gestures, with immediate feedback and new sets of choices. Users can keep their focus on the task, with minimal distraction caused by operating the interface.

1.3.5 Sociotechnical systems

A growing domain for usability is in complex systems that involve many people over long time periods, such as systems for health support, identity verification, disaster response, and crime reporting. Interfaces for these systems, often created by governmental organizations, have to deal with trust, privacy, and responsibility, as well as limiting the harmful effects of malicious tampering, deception, and incorrect information. Users will want to know who to turn to when things go wrong, and maybe who to thank when things go right (Whitworth and de Moor, 2009).

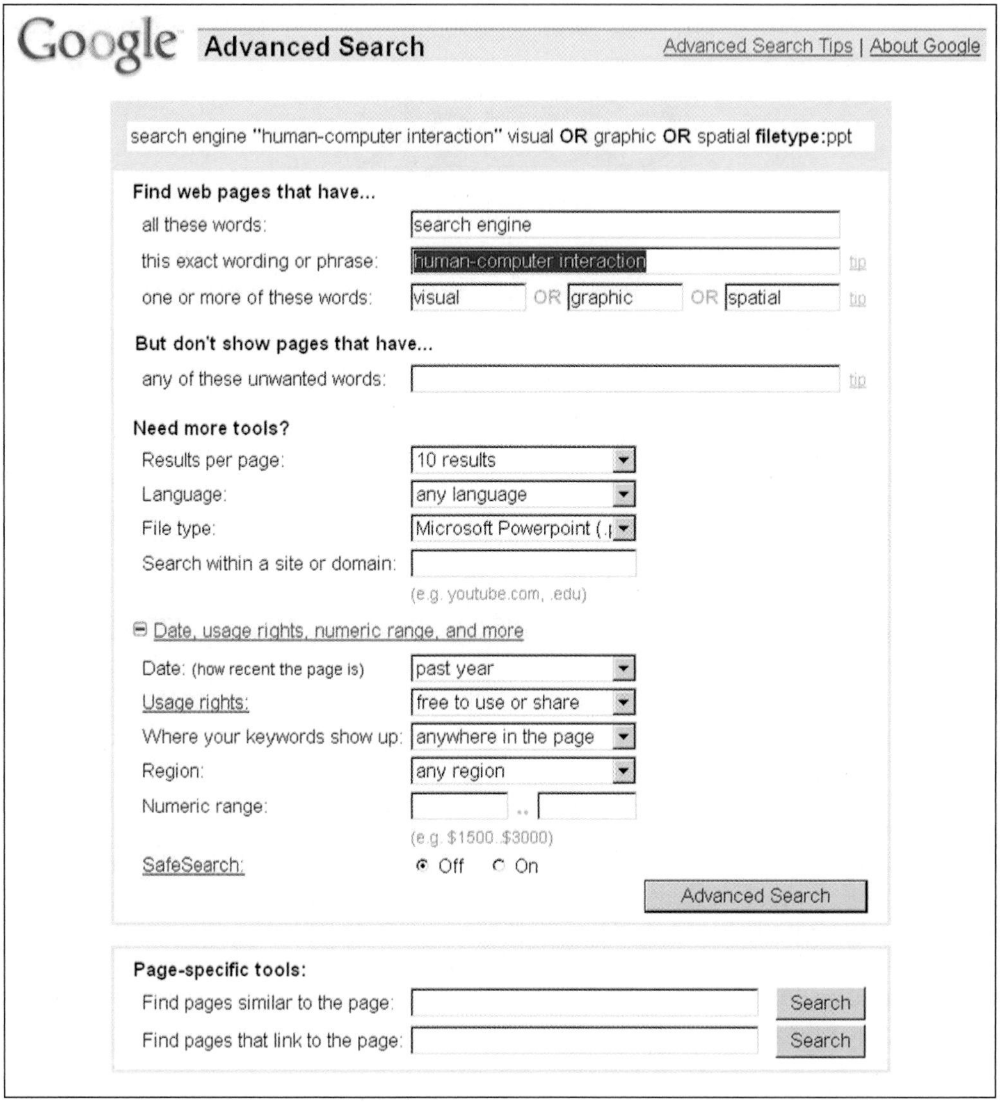

Google **Advanced Search**   Advanced Search Tips | About Google

search engine "human-computer interaction" visual **OR** graphic **OR** spatial **filetype**:ppt

Find web pages that have...

all these words: | search engine |

this exact wording or phrase: | human-computer interaction | tip

one or more of these words: | visual | OR | graphic | OR | spatial | tip

But don't show pages that have...

any of these unwanted words: | | tip

Need more tools?

Results per page: | 10 results   ▼ |

Language: | any language   ▼ |

File type: | Microsoft Powerpoint (.; ▼ |

Search within a site or domain: | |

(e.g. youtube.com, .edu)

⊟ Date, usage rights, numeric range, and more

Date: (how recent the page is) | past year   ▼ |

Usage rights: | free to use or share ▼ |

Where your keywords show up: | anywhere in the page ▼ |

Region: | any region   ▼ |

Numeric range: | | .. | |

(e.g. $1500..$3000)

SafeSearch: ⊙ Off   ○ On

[Advanced Search]

Page-specific tools:

Find pages similar to the page: | | [Search]

Find pages that link to the page: | | [Search]

FIGURE 1.12B

This window shows the advanced user interface for searching, providing more ways to focus the search.

For example, in electronic voting systems (Herrnson et al., 2008) citizens need to have reassuring feedback that their votes were correctly recorded, possibly by having a printed receipt. In addition, government officials and professional observers from opposing parties need to have ways of verifying that the votes from each district and regional aggregations are correctly

FIGURE 1.13

The Google search engine showing the results of a search on "human-computer interaction."

reported. If complaints are registered, investigators need tools to review procedures at every stage.

Designers of sociotechnical systems have to take into consideration the diverse levels of expertise of users with different roles. Successful designs for the large number of novice and first-time users emphasize ease of learning and provide the feedback that builds trust. Designs for professional administrators and seasoned investigators enable rapid performance of complex procedures, perhaps with visualization tools to spot unusual patterns or detect fraud in usage logs.

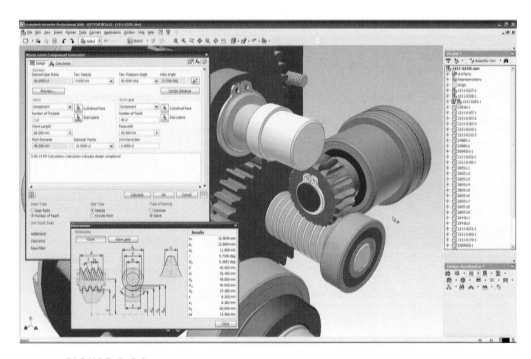

FIGURE 1.14

Using the Autodesk® Inventor® software for engineering tasks such as shaft design, gear design, and bearing selection, engineers at Stork Townsend, Inc. were able to create a custom gearbox with confidence that the unit would perform to expectations in a harsh environment. Shown here: The Worm Gear Component Generator is used to create matched sets of paired gears used in this gearbox design. All mating assembly constraints are automatically added, and an additional benefit to users is that this same interface is used for any edits to the gear pairs. (Courtesy of Autodesk and Stork Townsend, Inc.)

1.4 Universal Usability

The remarkable diversity of human abilities, backgrounds, motivations, personalities, cultures, and work styles challenges interface designers. A right-handed female designer in India with computer training and a desire for rapid interaction using densely packed screens may have a hard time designing a successful interface for left-handed male artists in France with a more leisurely and free-form work style. Understanding the physical, intellectual, and personality differences between users is vital for expanding market share, supporting required government services, and enabling creative participation by the broadest possible set of users. As a profession, we will be remembered for how well we meet our users' needs. That's the ultimate goal: addressing the needs of all users (Shneiderman, 2000; Lazar, 2007).

The huge international consumer market in mobile devices, especially cellphones, is already raising the pressure for designs that are universally usable. While skeptics suggest that accommodating diversity requires dumbing-down or lowest-common-denominator strategies, our experience is that rethinking interface designs for differing situations often results in a better product for all users. Measures to accommodate the special needs of one group, such as curb cuts in sidewalks for wheelchair users, often have payoffs for many groups, such as parents with baby strollers, skateboard riders, travelers with wheeled luggage, and delivery people with handcarts. With this in mind, this section introduces the challenges posed by physical, cognitive, perceptual, personality, and cultural differences. It covers considerations for users with disabilities, older adults, and young users, ending with a discussion of hardware and software diversity. The important issues of different usage profiles (novice, intermittent, and expert), wide-ranging task profiles, and multiple interaction styles are covered in Section 2.3.3.

1.4.1 Variations in physical abilities and physical workplaces

Accommodating diverse human perceptual, cognitive, and motor abilities is a challenge to every designer. Fortunately, *ergonomics* researchers and practitioners have gained substantial experience from design projects with automobiles, aircraft, cellphones, and so on. This experience can be applied to the design of interactive computer systems and mobile devices.

Basic data about human dimensions comes from research in *anthropometry* (Dreyfuss, 1967; Pheasant, 1996). Thousands of measures of hundreds of features of people—male and female, young and adult, European and Asian, underweight and overweight, tall and short—provide data to construct 5- to 95-percentile design ranges. Head, mouth, nose, neck, shoulder, chest, arm, hand, finger, leg, and foot sizes have been carefully cataloged for a variety of populations. The great diversity in these static measures reminds us that there can be no image of an "average" user and that compromises must be made or multiple versions of a system must be constructed.

Cellphone keypad design parameters—distance between keys, size of keys, and required pressure (Section 8.2)—evolved to accommodate differences in users' physical abilities. People with especially large or small hands may have difficulty using standard cellphones or keyboards, but a substantial fraction of the population is well served by one design. On the other hand, since screen-brightness preferences vary substantially, designers often enable users to control this parameter. Similarly, controls for chair seat and back heights and for display angles allow individual adjustment. When a single design cannot accommodate a large fraction of the population, multiple versions or adjustment controls are helpful.

Physical measures of static human dimensions are not enough, though. Measures of dynamic actions—such as reach distance while seated, speed of finger presses, or strength of lifting—are also necessary (Bailey, 1996).

Since so much of work is related to perception, designers need to be aware of the ranges of human perceptual abilities, especially with regard to vision (Ware, 2004). For example, researchers consider human response time to varying visual stimuli or time to adapt to low or bright light. They examine human capacity to identify an object in context or to determine the velocity or direction of a moving point. The visual system responds differently to various colors, and some people are color-deficient, either permanently or temporarily (due to illness or medication). People's spectral range and sensitivity vary, and peripheral vision is quite different from the perception of images in the fovea (the central part of the retina). Designers need to study flicker, contrast, motion sensitivity, and depth perception, as well as the impact of glare and visual fatigue. Finally, designers must consider the needs of people who have eye disorders, damage, or disease, or who wear corrective lenses.

Other senses are also important: for example, touch for keyboard or touchscreen entry and hearing for audible cues, tones, and speech input or output (Chapter 8). Pain, temperature sensitivity, taste, and smell are rarely used for input or output in interactive systems, but there is room for imaginative applications.

These physical abilities influence elements of the interactive-system design. They also play a prominent role in the design of the workplace or workstation (or playstation). The *Human Factors Engineering of Computer Workstations* standard (HFES, 2007) lists these concerns:

- Work-surface and display-support height
- Clearance under work surface for legs
- Work-surface width and depth
- Adjustability of heights and angles for chairs and work surfaces
- Posture—seating depth and angle, backrest height, and lumbar support
- Availability of armrests, footrests, and palmrests
- Use of chair casters

Workplace design is important in ensuring high job satisfaction, good performance, and low error rates. Incorrect table heights, uncomfortable chairs, or inadequate space to place documents can substantially impede work. The standards document also addresses such issues as illumination levels (200 to 500 lux); glare reduction (antiglare coatings, baffles, mesh, positioning); luminance balance and flicker; equipment reflectivity; acoustic noise and vibration; air temperature, movement, and humidity; and equipment temperature.

The most elegant screen design can be compromised by a noisy environment, poor lighting, or a stuffy room, and that compromise will eventually lower performance, raise error rates, and discourage even motivated users. Thoughtful designs, such as workstations that provide wheelchair access and good lighting, will be even more appreciated by users with disabilities and older adults.

Another physical-environment consideration involves room layout and the sociology of human interaction. With multiple workstations in a classroom or office, different layouts can encourage or limit social interaction, cooperative work, and assistance with problems. Because users can often quickly help one another with minor problems, there may be an advantage to layouts that group several terminals close together or that enable supervisors or teachers to view all screens at once from behind. On the other hand, programmers, reservations clerks, or artists may appreciate the quiet and privacy of their own workspaces.

Mobile devices are increasingly being used while walking or driving and in public spaces, such as restaurants or trains where lighting, noise, movement, and vibration are part of the user experience. Designing for these more fluid environments presents opportunities for design researchers and entrepreneurs.

1.4.2 Diverse cognitive and perceptual abilities

A vital foundation for interactive-systems designers is an understanding of the cognitive and perceptual abilities of the users (Ashcraft, 2005). The journal *Ergonomics Abstracts* offers this classification of human cognitive processes:

• Short-term and working memory
• Long-term and semantic memory
• Problem solving and reasoning
• Decision making and risk assessment
• Language communication and comprehension
• Search, imagery, and sensory memory
• Learning, skill development, knowledge acquisition, and concept attainment

   It also suggests this set of factors affecting perceptual and motor performance:

• Arousal and vigilance
• Fatigue and sleep deprivation

- Perceptual (mental) load
- Knowledge of results and feedback
- Monotony and boredom
- Sensory deprivation
- Nutrition and diet
- Fear, anxiety, mood, and emotion
- Drugs, smoking, and alcohol
- Physiological rhythms

These vital issues are not discussed in depth in this book, but they have a profound influence on the design of interactive systems. The term *intelligence* is not included in this list, because its nature is controversial and measuring pure intelligence is difficult.

In any application, background experience and knowledge in the task and interface domains play key roles in learning and performance. Task- or computer-skill inventories can be helpful in predicting performance.

1.4.3 Personality differences

Some people are eager to use computers, while others find them frustrating. Even people who enjoy using computers may have very different preferences for interaction styles, pace of interaction, graphics versus tabular presentations, dense versus sparse data presentation, and so on. A clear understanding of personality and cognitive styles can be helpful in designing interfaces for diverse communities of users.

One evident difference is between men and women, but no clear pattern of gender-related preferences in interfaces has been documented. While the majority of video-game players and designers are young males, some games (such as *The Sims*™ and *Guitar Hero*) draw ample numbers of female players. Designers can get into lively debates about why women prefer certain games, often speculating that women prefer less violent action and quieter soundtracks. Other conjectures are that women prefer social games, characters with appealing personalities, softer color patterns, and a sense of closure and completeness. Can these informal conjectures be converted to measurable criteria and then validated?

Turning from games to productivity tools, the largely male designers may not realize the effects on women users when command names require the users to KILL a process or ABORT a program. These and other potentially unfortunate mismatches between the user interface and the users might be avoided by more thoughtful attention to individual differences among users (Beckwith et al., 2006).

Unfortunately, there is no simple taxonomy of user personality types. A popular, but controversial, technique is to use the Myers-Briggs Type Indicator, or MBTI (Keirsey, 1998), which is based on Carl Jung's theories of personality types. Jung conjectured that there were four dichotomies:

- *Extroversion versus introversion.* Extroverts focus on external stimuli and like variety and action, whereas introverts prefer familiar patterns, rely on their inner ideas, and work alone contentedly.

- *Sensing versus intuition.* Sensing types are attracted to established routines, are good at precise work, and enjoy applying known skills, whereas intuitive types like solving new problems and discovering new relations but dislike taking time for precision.

- *Perceptive versus judging.* Perceptive types like to learn about new situations but may have trouble making decisions, whereas judging types like to make a careful plan and will seek to carry through the plan even if new facts change the goal.

- *Feeling versus thinking.* Feeling types are aware of other people's feelings, seek to please others, and relate well to most people, whereas thinking types are unemotional, may treat people impersonally, and like to put things in logical order.

The theory behind the MBTI provides portraits of the relationships between professions and personality types and between people of different personality types. It has been applied to testing user communities and has provided guidance for designers, but the linkage between personality types and interface features is weak.

Successors to the MBTI include the Big Five Test, based on the OCEAN model: Openness to Experience/Intellect (closed/open), Conscientiousness (disorganized/organized), Extraversion (introverted/extraverted), Agreeableness (disagreeable/agreeable), and Neuroticism (calm/nervous). There are hundreds of other psychological scales, including risk taking versus risk avoidance; internal versus external locus of control; reflective versus impulsive behavior; convergent versus divergent thinking; high versus low anxiety; tolerance for stress; tolerance for ambiguity, motivation, or compulsiveness; field dependence versus independence; assertive versus passive personality; and left- versus right-brain orientation. As designers explore computer applications for the home, education, art, music, and entertainment, they may benefit from paying greater attention to personality types.

Another approach to personality assessment is by studying user behavior. For example, some users file thousands of e-mails in a well-organized hierarchy of folders, while others keep them all in the inbox, using search strategies to find what they want later. These distinct approaches may well relate to personality variables, and for the designer, the message of dual requirements is clear.

1.4.4 Cultural and international diversity

Another perspective on individual differences has to do with cultural, ethnic, racial, or linguistic background (Fernandes, 1995; Marcus and Gould, 2000). Users who were raised learning to read Japanese or Chinese will scan a screen differently from users who were raised learning to read English or French. Users from reflective or traditional cultures may prefer interfaces with stable displays from which they select a single item, while users from action-oriented or novelty-based cultures may prefer animated screens and multiple clicks. Preferred content of web pages also varies; for example, university home pages in some cultures emphasize their impressive buildings and respected professors lecturing to students, while others highlight student team projects and a lively social life. Mobile device preferences also vary across cultures and have rapidly changing styles—for example, the thin and sharp-edged RAZR™ phone from Motorola® was a great success, but it then gave way to the rounded corners of iPhones and other competitors.

More and more is being learned about computer users from different cultures, but designers are still struggling to establish guidelines for designing for multiple languages and cultures. The growth of a worldwide computer market (many U.S. companies have more than half of their sales in overseas markets) means that designers must prepare for internationalization. Software architectures that facilitate customization of local versions of user interfaces offer a competitive advantage. For example, if all text (instructions, help, error messages, labels, and so on) is stored in files, versions in other languages can be generated with little or no additional programming. Hardware issues include character sets, keyboards, and special input devices. User-interface design concerns for internationalization include the following:

- Characters, numerals, special characters, and diacriticals
- Left-to-right versus right-to-left versus vertical input and reading
- Date and time formats
- Numeric and currency formats
- Weights and measures
- Telephone numbers and addresses
- Names and titles (Mr., Ms., Mme., M., Dr.)
- Social security, national identification, and passport numbers
- Capitalization and punctuation
- Sorting sequences
- Icons, buttons, and colors
- Pluralization, grammar, and spelling
- Etiquette, policies, tone, formality, and metaphors

The list is long and yet incomplete. Whereas early designers were often excused from cultural and linguistic slips, the current highly competitive atmosphere means that more effective localization may produce a strong advantage. To develop effective designs, companies run usability studies with users from different countries, cultures, and language communities.

The role of information technology in international development is steadily growing, but much needs to be done to accommodate the diverse needs of users with vastly different language skills and technology access. To promote international efforts to foster successful implementation of information technologies, representatives from around the world met for the 2003 and 2005 United Nations World Summit on the Information Society. They declared their

> desire and commitment to build a people-centered, inclusive and development-oriented Information Society, where everyone can create, access, utilize and share information and knowledge, enabling individuals, communities and peoples to achieve their full potential in promoting their sustainable development and improving their quality of life, premised on the purposes and principles of the Charter of the United Nations and respecting fully and upholding the Universal Declaration of Human Rights.

The plan called for applications to be "accessible to all, affordable, adapted to local needs in languages and culture, and [to] support sustainable development." The UN Millennium Development Goals, which are hoped to be achieved by 2015, include: eradicate extreme poverty and hunger; reduce child mortality; combat HIV/AIDS, malaria and other diseases; and ensure environmental sustainability. Information and communications technologies can play important roles in developing the infrastructure that is needed to achieve these goals.

1.4.5 Users with disabilities

The flexibility of desktop, web, and mobile devices makes it possible for designers to provide special services to users who have disabilities (Vanderheiden, 2000; Stephanidis, 2001; Horton, 2005; Thatcher et al., 2006). In the United States, the Amendment to Section 508 of the Rehabilitation Act requires federal agencies to ensure access to information technology, including computers and web sites, by employees and the public (http://www.access-board.gov/508.htm). The Access Board spells out the guidelines for vision-impaired, hearing-impaired, and mobility-impaired users; these include keyboard or mouse alternatives, color-coding, font-size settings, contrast settings, textual alternatives to images, and web features such as frames, links, and plug-ins. Similar legislation has stimulated activity in many countries, and tool developers have responded by making web-page authoring tools that guarantee compliance in most circumstances and web-page code checkers that provide feedback about needed changes.

Screen magnification to enlarge portions of a display and text-to-speech conversion can be done with hardware and software supplied by many vendors (Blenkhorn et al., 2003). Text-to-speech conversion can help blind users to receive e-mail or to read text files, and speech-recognition devices permit voice-controlled operation of some user interfaces. Graphical user interfaces were a setback for vision-impaired users, but technology innovations such as Freedom Scientific's JAWS®, GW Micro's Window-Eyes™, or Dolphin's Hal™ screen reader facilitate conversion of spatial information into spoken text (Thatcher et al., 2006). Similarly, IBM®'s Home Page Reader™ and Conversa®'s voice-enabled web browser enable access to web-based information and services. Speech generation and auditory interfaces are also appreciated by sighted users under difficult conditions, such as when driving an automobile, riding a bicycle, or working in bright sunshine.

Users with hearing impairments generally can use computers with only simple changes (conversion of tones to visual signals is often easy to accomplish) and can benefit from office environments that make heavy use of e-mail and fac-simile (fax) transmissions. Telecommunications devices for the deaf (TDD or TTY) enable telephone access to information, such as train or airplane schedules, and services (federal agencies and many companies offer TDD or TTY access). Numerous special input devices for users with physical disabilities are available, depending on the specific impairment; speech recognition and eye-gaze control devices, head-mounted optical mice, and many other innovative devices (even the telephone) were pioneered for the needs of disabled users (Chapter 8).

Designers can benefit by planning early to accommodate users who have disabilities, since at this point substantial improvements can be made at low or no cost. For example, moving the on/off switch to the front of a computer adds a minimal charge, if any, to the cost of manufacturing, but it improves ease of use for all users, and especially for the mobility-impaired. Other examples are the addition of closed captions to television programs for deaf viewers, which can be useful for hearing viewers as well, and the use of ALT tags to describe web graphics for blind users, which improves search capabilities for all users.

The motivation to accommodate users who have visual, auditory, and motor disabilities has increased since the enactment of U.S. Public Laws 99–506 and 100–542, which require U.S. government agencies to establish accessible infor-mation environments for employees and citizens. Any company wishing to sell products to the U.S. government should adhere to these requirements. Further information about accommodation in workplaces, schools, and the home is available from many sources:

- Private foundations (e.g., the American Foundation for the Blind and the National Federation of the Blind)

- Associations (e.g., the Alexander Graham Bell Association for the Deaf, the National Association for the Deaf, and the Blinded Veterans Association)

- Government agencies (e.g., the National Library Service for the Blind and Physically Handicapped of the Library of Congress and the Center for Technology in Human Disabilities at the Maryland Rehabilitation Center)
- University groups (e.g., the TRACE Research and Development Center at the University of Wisconsin, Web Accessibility in Mind at Utah State University, and the Web Accessibility Initiative at MIT)
- Manufacturers (e.g., Apple, IBM, Microsoft, and Sun Microsystems™)

The potential for benefit to people with disabilities is one of the gifts of computing; it brings dividends in the increased capacity for learning, gainful employment, social participation, and community contribution. In addition, many users are temporarily disabled: they may forget their glasses, be unable to read while driving, or struggle to hear in a noisy environment. The University of Wisconsin's TRACE Center and Utah State University's Web Accessibility in Mind (WebAIM) organization have web sites that provide guidelines and resources for designers who are addressing universal usability. WebAIM covers cognitive disabilities, such as memory loss, dementia, aphasia, and attention disorders, as well as reading, linguistic, and visual comprehension difficulties. It offers specific guidance to designers, such as ways to clearly structure sequences of operations, highlight key information, and make the structure explicit. The Web Accessibility Initiative at MIT's World Wide Web Consortium produces consensus guidelines and tools to help developers promote web accessibility.

Improving designs for users with disabilities is an international concern. The United Nations Enable web site (http://www.un.org/disabilities/) promotes awareness, while country-specific web sites, such as AccessiWeb in France (http://www.accessiweb.org/), describe legal requirements and language-specific software tools.

1.4.6 Older adult users

Seniority offers many pleasures and all the benefits of experience, but aging can also have negative physical, cognitive, and social consequences. Understanding the human factors of aging can help designers to create user interfaces that facilitate access by older adult users. The benefits to senior citizens include improved chances for productive employment and opportunities to use writing, e-mail, and other computer tools, plus the satisfactions of education, entertainment, social interaction, and challenge (Furlong and Kearsley, 1990; Hart et al., 2008). Older adults are particularly active participants in health support groups (Xie, 2008). The benefits to society include increased access to seniors, which is valuable for their experience and the emotional support they can provide to others.

The National Research Council's report *Human Factors Research Needs for an Aging Population* describes aging as

> a nonuniform set of progressive changes in physiological and psychological functioning. . . . Average visual and auditory acuity decline considerably with age, as do average strength and speed of response. . . . [People experience] loss of at least some kinds of memory function, declines in perceptual flexibility, slowing of "stimulus encoding," and increased difficulty in the acquisition of complex mental skills, . . . visual functions such as static visual acuity, dark adaptation, accommodation, contrast sensitivity, and peripheral vision decline, on average, with age. (Czaja, 1990)

This list has its discouraging side, but many people experience only moderate effects and continue participating in many activities, even throughout their nineties.

The further good news is that interface designers can do much to accommodate older adult users and, thus, to give older adults access to the beneficial aspects of computing and network communication. How many young people's lives might be enriched by e-mail access to grandparents or great-grandparents? How many businesses might benefit from electronic consultations with experienced senior citizens? How many government agencies, universities, medical centers, or law firms could advance their goals from easily available contact with knowledgeable, older adult citizens? As a society, how might we all benefit from the continued creative work of senior citizens in literature, art, music, science, or philosophy?

As the world's population ages, designers in many fields are adapting their work to serve older adults. Baby boomers have already begun to push for larger street signs, brighter traffic lights, and better nighttime lighting to make driving safer for drivers and pedestrians. Similarly, desktop, web, and mobile devices can be improved for all users by providing users with control over font sizes, display contrast, and audio levels. Interfaces can also be designed with easier-to-use pointing devices, clearer navigation paths, consistent layouts, and simpler command languages to improve access for older adults and every user (Czaja and Lee, 2002; Hart et al., 2008). Researchers and designers are beginning to work on improving interfaces to golden-age software (Czaja et al., 2006). Let's do it *before* Bill Gates turns 65! In the United States, the AARP's Older Wiser Wired initiatives provide education for older adults and guidance for designers. The European Union also has multiple initiatives and research support for computing for older adults.

Networking projects, such as the San Francisco–based SeniorNet, are providing adults over the age of 50 with access to and education about computing and the Internet "to enhance their lives and enable them to share their knowledge and wisdom" (http://www.seniornet.org/). Computer games are attractive for older adults, as shown by the surprising success of Nintendo's Wii, because they stimulate social interaction, provide practice in sensorimotor skills such as eye–to–hand coordination, enhance dexterity, and improve reaction time. In addition, meeting a challenge and gaining a sense of accomplishment and mastery are helpful in improving self-image for anyone.

In our experiences in bringing computing to two residences for older adults, we also encountered residents' fear of computers and belief that they were incapable of using computers. These fears gave way quickly after a few positive experiences. The older adults, who explored e-mail, photo sharing, and educational games, felt quite satisfied with themselves and were eager to learn more. Their newfound enthusiasm encouraged them to try automated bank machines and supermarket touchscreen kiosks. Suggestions for redesigns to meet the needs of older adults (and possibly other users) also emerged—for example, the appeal of high-precision touchscreens compared with the mouse was highlighted (Chapter 8).

In summary, making computing more attractive and accessible to older adults enables them to take advantage of technology and enables others to benefit from their participation. For more information on this topic, check out the Human Factors & Ergonomics Society, which has an Aging Technical Group that publishes a newsletter and organizes sessions at conferences.

1.4.7 Children

Another lively community of users is children, whose uses emphasize entertainment and education. Even pre-readers can use computer-controlled toys, music generators, and art tools (Fig. 1.15). As they mature, begin reading, and gain limited keyboard skills, they can use a wider array of desktop applications, web services, and mobile devices. When they become teenagers, they may become highly proficient users who often help their parents or other adults. This idealized growth path is followed by many children who have easy access to technology and supportive parents and peers. However, many children without financial resources or supportive learning environments struggle to gain access to technology. They are often frustrated with its use and are endangered by threats surrounding privacy, alienation, pornography, unhelpful peers, and malevolent strangers.

The noble aspirations of designers of children's software include educational acceleration, facilitating socialization with peers, and fostering the self-confidence that comes from skill mastery. Advocates of educational games promote intrinsic motivation and constructive activities as goals, but opponents often complain about the harmful effects of antisocial and violent games.

For teenagers, the opportunities for empowerment are substantial. They often take the lead in employing new modes of communication, such as instant messaging and text messaging on cellphones, and in creating cultural or fashion trends that surprise even the designers (for example, playing with simulations and fantasy games and participating in web-based virtual worlds).

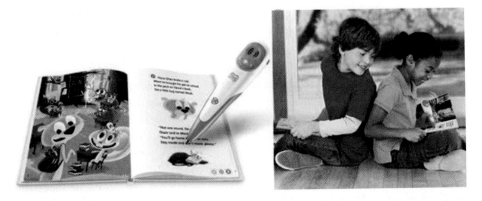

FIGURE 1.15

Two children using an educational package (LeapFrog®'s Tag™ Reading Basics) that has books and a pen that children can use for learning to read, learning letter sounds, and playing games (http://www.leapfrog.com).

Appropriate design principles for children's software recognize young people's intense desire for the kind of interactive engagement that gives them control with appropriate feedback and supports their social engagement with peers (Druin and Inkpen, 2001; Bruckman et al., 2007). Designers also have to find the balance between children's desire for challenge and parents' requirements for safety. Children can deal with some frustrations and with threatening stories, but they also want to know that they can clear the screen, start over, and try again without severe penalties. They don't easily tolerate patronizing comments or inappropriate humor, but they like familiar characters, exploratory environments, and the capacity for repetition. Younger children will sometimes replay a game, reread a story, or replay a music sequence dozens of times, even after adults have tired of it. Some designers work by observing children and testing software with children, while the innovative approach of "children as our technology-design partners" engages them in a long-term process of cooperative inquiry during which children and adults jointly design novel products and services. A notable successful product of working with children as design partners is the International Children's Digital Library (Fig. 1.16), which offers 2500+ of the world's best children's books in 40+ languages using an interface in 15 languages while supporting low- and high-speed networks (Druin et al., 2007).

Designing for younger children requires attention to their limitations. Their evolving dexterity means that mouse dragging, double-clicking, and small targets cannot always be used; their emerging literacy means that written instructions and error messages are not effective; and their low capacity for abstraction

FIGURE 1.16
Children using the International Children's Digital Library on the XO device from the One Laptop Per Child project. Courtesy of International Children's Digital Library Foundation (http://www.childrenslibrary.org/).

means that complex sequences must be avoided unless an adult is involved. Other concerns are short attention spans and limited capacity to work with multiple concepts simultaneously. Designers of children's software also have a responsibility to attend to dangers, especially in web-based environments, where parental control over access to violent, racist, or pornographic materials is unfortunately necessary. Appropriate information for the education of children about privacy issues and threats from strangers is also a requirement.

The capacity for playful creativity in art, music, and writing and the value of educational activities in science and math remain potent reasons to pursue children's software. Enabling them to make high-quality images, photos, songs, or poems and then share them with friends and family can accelerate children's personal and social development. Offering access to educational materials from libraries, museums, government agencies, schools, and commercial sources enriches their learning experiences and serves as a basis for children to construct their own web resources, participate in collaborative efforts, and contribute to community-service projects. Providing programming and simulation-building tools enables older children to take on complex cognitive challenges and construct ambitious artifacts for others to use. These and other opportunities have motivated efforts (such as One Laptop Per Child) to bring low-cost computers to children around the world—hopefully coupled with rich content, parental guidance materials, and effective teacher training.

1.4.8 Accommodating hardware and software diversity

In addition to accommodating different classes of users and skill levels, designers need to support a wide range of hardware and software platforms. The rapid progress of technology means that newer systems may have a hundred or a thousand times greater storage capacity, faster processors, and higher-bandwidth networks. However, designers need to accommodate older devices and deal with newer mobile devices that may have low-bandwidth connections and small screens.

The challenge of accommodating diverse hardware is coupled with the need to ensure access through many generations of software. New operating systems, web browsers, e-mail clients, and application programs should provide backward compatibility in terms of their user-interface design and file structures. Skeptics will say that this requirement can slow innovation, but designers who plan ahead carefully to support flexible interfaces and self-defining files will be rewarded with larger market shares (Shneiderman, 2000).

For at least the next decade, three of the main technical challenges will be:

- *Producing satisfying and effective Internet interaction on high-speed (broadband) and slower (dial-up and some wireless) connections.* Some technological breakthroughs have already been made in compression algorithms to reduce file sizes for images, music, animations, and even video, but more are needed. New technologies are needed to enable pre-fetching or scheduled downloads. User control of the amount of material downloaded for each request could also prove beneficial (for example, allowing users to specify that a large image should be reduced to a smaller size, sent with fewer colors, converted to a simplified line drawing, replaced with just a text description, or downloaded at night when Internet charges are lower).

- *Enabling access to web services from large displays (1200 × 1600 pixels or larger) and smaller mobile devices (640 × 480 and smaller).* Rewriting each web page for different display sizes may produce the best quality, but this approach is probably too costly and time-consuming for most web providers. New software-tool breakthroughs are needed to allow web-site designers to specify their content in a way that enables automatic conversions for an increasing range of display sizes.

- *Supporting easy maintenance of or automatic conversion to multiple languages.* Commercial operators recognize that they can expand their markets if they can provide access in multiple languages and across multiple countries. This means isolating text to allow easy substitution, choosing appropriate metaphors and colors, and addressing the needs of diverse cultures (Section 1.4.4).

The good news is that rethinking designs to accommodate these diverse needs can improve the quality for all users. As for costs, with appropriate software tools, e-commerce providers are finding that a small additional effort can expand markets by 20% or more.

1.5 Goals for Our Profession

Clear goals are useful not only for interface development but also for educational and professional enterprises. Three broad goals seem attainable: (1) influencing academic and industrial researchers; (2) providing tools, techniques, and knowledge for commercial designers; and (3) raising the computer consciousness of the general public.

1.5.1 Influencing academic and industrial researchers

Early research in human-computer interaction was done largely by introspection and intuition, but this approach suffered from a lack of validity, generality, and precision. The techniques of psychologically oriented, controlled experimentation can lead to a deeper understanding of the fundamental principles of human interaction with computers. The scientific method for interface research, which is based on controlled experimentation, has this basic outline:

- Understanding of a practical problem and related theory
- Lucid statement of a testable hypothesis
- Manipulation of a small number of independent variables
- Measurement of specific dependent variables
- Careful selection and assignment of subjects
- Control for bias in subjects, procedures, and materials
- Application of statistical tests
- Interpretation of results, refinement of theory, and guidance for experimenters

Materials and methods must be tested by pilot experiments, and results must be validated by replication in various situations.

Of course, the scientific method based on controlled experimentation has its weaknesses. It may be difficult or expensive to find adequate subjects, and laboratory conditions may distort the situation so much that the conclusions have no application. Controlled experiments typically deal with short-term usage, so understanding long-term consumer behavior or experienced user strategies is difficult. Since controlled experiments emphasize statistical aggregation, extremely good or poor performance by individuals may be overlooked. Furthermore, anecdotal evidence or individual insights may be given too little emphasis because of the authoritative influence of statistics.

Because of these concerns, controlled experimentation is balanced by ethnographic observation methods. Anecdotal experiences and subjective reactions are recorded, thinking aloud or protocol approaches are employed, and field or case studies can be carried out. Other research methods include automated logging of user behavior, surveys, focus groups, and interviews.

Within computer science, there is a growing awareness of the need for greater attention to usability issues. Courses on human-computer interaction are required for some undergraduate degrees, and interface-design issues are being added to many courses. Researchers who propose new programming languages, privacy-protection schemes, or network services are more aware of the need to match human cognitive skills. Designers of advanced graphics systems, agile manufacturing equipment, or consumer products increasingly recognize that the success of their proposals depends on the construction of a suitable human interface.

There is a grand opportunity to apply the knowledge and techniques of traditional psychology (and of subfields such as cognitive psychology) to the study of human-computer interaction. Psychologists are investigating human problem solving and creativity with computers to gain an understanding of cognitive processes. The benefit to psychology is great, but psychologists also have a golden opportunity to dramatically influence an important and widely used technology.

Researchers in information science, business and management, education, sociology, anthropology, and other disciplines are benefiting from and contributing to the study of human-computer interaction. There are so many fruitful directions for research that any list can be a provocative starting point. Here are a few:

- *Reduced anxiety and fear of computer usage.* Although computers are widely used, some otherwise competent people resist using e-mail and engaging in e-commerce because they are anxious about—or even fearful of—breaking the computer, making an embarrassing mistake, or having their privacy violated. Fear of scams and frustration with e-mail spam could also be reduced by improved designs that promote security and privacy while increasing the users' control over their experiences.

- *Graceful evolution.* Although novices may begin their interactions with a computer by using just a few features, they may later wish to move up to more powerful facilities. Refined multi-layer interface designs and training materials are needed to smooth the transition from novice to knowledgeable user to expert. The differing requirements of novices and experts in terms of prompting, error messages, online assistance, display complexity, locus of control, pacing, and informative feedback all need investigation. Users may be allowed to customize their interfaces far beyond changing backgrounds and ring tones, but methods for guiding users through such a process are an open topic.

- *Social media participation.* The recent remarkable spread of social media and social networking is just an early indicator of larger changes to come. Enabling web-based sharing of user-generated content, especially from mobile devices, is just beginning; much work remains to be done in raising the quality of what is produced, enabling effective annotations, making these materials accessible, and facilitating reuse in ways that protect users' desires for privacy or profit.

- *Input devices.* The plethora of input devices presents opportunities and challenges to interface designers (Chapter 5). There are heated discussions about the relative merits of multi-touch screens; voice, eye-gaze, and gestural input; and haptic devices. Such conflicts could be resolved through experimentation with multiple tasks and users. Underlying issues include speed, accuracy, fatigue, error correction, and subjective satisfaction.

- *Online help.* Although many interfaces offer help text and video tutorials online, we have only limited understanding of what constitutes effective instruction for novices, knowledgeable users, and experts (Chapter 12). The role of these aids and of online user communities could be studied to assess user success and satisfaction, even on the small screens found on mobile devices.

- *Information exploration.* As navigation, browsing, and searching in multimedia digital libraries and the World Wide Web become more common, the pressure for more effective strategies and tools will increase (Chapter 13). Users will want to filter, select, and restructure their information rapidly with minimum effort and without fear of getting lost or finding misleading information. Large databases of text, images, graphics, sound, and scientific data will become easier to explore with emerging information-visualization and visual analytic tools.

1.5.2 Providing tools, techniques, and knowledge for commercial designers

User-interface design and development are hot topics, and international competition is lively. Employers who used to see usability as a secondary topic are increasingly hiring user-interface designers, information architects, user-interface implementers, and usability testers. These employers recognize the competitive advantage from high-quality consumer interfaces and from improving the performance of their employees. There is a great thirst for knowledge about software tools, design guidelines, and testing techniques. User-interface–building tools provide support for rapid prototyping and interface development while aiding design consistency, supporting universal usability, and simplifying evolutionary refinement.

Guidelines documents have been written for general and specific audiences (see the list at end of this chapter). Many projects are taking the productive route of writing their own guidelines, which are tied to the problems of their application environments. These guidelines are constructed from experimental results, experience with existing interfaces, and knowledgeable guesswork.

Iterative usability studies and acceptance testing are appropriate during interface development. Once the initial interface is available, refinements can be made on the basis of online or printed surveys, individual or group interviews, or more controlled empirical tests of novel strategies (Chapter 4).

Feedback from users during the development process and for evolutionary refinement can provide useful insights and guidance. E-mail facilities allow users to send comments directly to the designers. Online user consultants and fellow users can provide prompt assistance and supportive encouragement.

1.5.3 Raising the computer consciousness of the general public

The media are so filled with stories about computers that raising public consciousness of these tools may seem unnecessary. However, many people are still uncomfortable with computers. When they do finally use a bank machine, a cell phone, or e-mail, they may feel fearful of making mistakes, anxious about damaging the equipment, worried about feeling incompetent, or threatened by the computer "being smarter than I am." These fears are generated, in part, by poor designs that have complex commands, hostile and vague error messages, tortuous and unfamiliar sequences of actions, or a deceptive anthropomorphic style.

One of our goals is to encourage users to translate their internal fears into outraged action (Shneiderman, 2002). Instead of feeling guilty when they get a message such as SYNTAX ERROR, users should express their anger at the interface designer who was so inconsiderate and thoughtless. Instead of feeling inadequate or foolish because they cannot remember a complex sequence of actions, they should complain to the designer who did not provide a more convenient mechanism or should seek another product that does.

Usability ultimately becomes a question of national priorities. Advocates of electronic voting and other services, promoters of e-healthcare, and visionaries of e-learning increasingly recognize the need to influence allocation of government resources and commercial research agendas. Policymakers and industry leaders become heroes when they facilitate access and promote quality, but they become villains when failures threaten children, disrupt travel, or menace consumers.

As examples of successful and satisfying interfaces become more visible, the crude designs will begin to appear archaic and will become commercial failures. As designers improve interactive systems, some users' fears will recede, and the positive experiences of their competence, mastery, and satisfaction will flow in. Then, the images of computer scientists and interface designers will change in the public's view: The machine-oriented and technical image will give way to one of personal warmth, sensitivity, and concern for the users.

Practitioner's Summary

If you are designing an interactive system, thorough user and task analyses can provide the information for a proper functional design. A positive outcome is more likely if you pay attention to reliability, availability, security, integrity, standardization, portability, integration, and the administrative issues of schedules and budgets. As design alternatives are proposed, they can be evaluated for their role in providing short learning times, rapid task performance, low error rates, ease of retention, and high user satisfaction. Designs that accommodate the needs of children, older adults, and users with disabilities can improve the quality for all users. As your design is refined and implemented, evaluation by pilot studies, expert reviews, usability tests, user observations, and acceptance tests can accelerate improvement. Success in product development is increasingly being measured in terms of hard evidence that universal usability is being attained, (rather than testimonials from a few enthusiastic users). The rapidly proliferating literature and sets of evidence-based guidelines may be of assistance in designing your project while accommodating the increasingly diverse and growing community of users.

Researcher's Agenda

The criteria for success in research favor innovations that work for broad communities of users performing useful tasks over longer time periods. At the same time, researchers are struggling to understand what kinds of imaginative consumer products will attract, engage, and satisfy diverse populations. The opportunities for researchers are unlimited. There are so many interesting, important, and doable projects that it may be hard to choose a direction. The goal of universal usability through plasticity of interface designs will keep researchers busy for years. Getting past vague promises and measuring user performance with alternate interfaces will be central to rapid progress. Each experiment has two parents: the practical problems facing designers, and the fundamental theories based on principles of human behavior and interface design. Begin by proposing a lucid, testable hypothesis. Then consider the appropriate research methodology, conduct the experiment, collect the data, and analyze the results. Each experiment also has three children: specific recommendations for the practical problem, refinements of theories, and guidance for future experimenters. Each chapter of this book ends with specific research proposals.

WORLD WIDE WEB RESOURCES

http://www.aw.com/DTUI/

This book is accompanied by a web site (http://www.aw.com/DTUI/) that includes pointers to additional resources tied to the contents of each chapter. In addition, this web site contains information for instructors, students, practitioners, and researchers. The links for Chapter 1 include pointers to general resources on human-computer interaction, such as professional societies, government agencies, companies, bibliographies, and guideline documents.

Readers seeking references to scientific journals and conferences can consult the online searchable bibliography for human-computer interaction (http://www.hcibib.org/). Built under the heroic leadership of Gary Perlman, it makes available more than 40,000 journal, conference, and book abstracts, plus link collections on many topics, including consulting companies, history, and international development.

Some wonderful World Wide Web resources are:

1. The HCI Index (http://degraaff.org/hci/)
2. Diamond Bullet Design (http://www.usabilityfirst.com/)
3. Usability.gov, a great resource on usability methods and guidelines for the U.S. government (http://www.usability.gov/)
4. IBM's extensive guide to user-centered design methods (https://www-306.ibm.com/software/ucd/)

E-mail lists for announcements and discussion lists are maintained by ACM SIGCHI (http://www.acm.org/sigchi/) and by the British HCI Group (http://www.bcs-hci.org.uk/), which also sponsors the frequently updated Usability News (http://www.usabilitynews.com/).

References

Specialized references for this chapter appear here; general information resources are listed in the following section.

Beckwith, L. Burnett, M., Grigoreanu, V., and Wiedenbeck, S., Gender HCI: What about the software? *IEEE Computer* 39, 11 (2006), 97–101.

Blenkhorn, Paul, Evans, Gareth, King, Alasdair, Kurniawan, Sri Hastuti, and Sutcliffe, Alistair, Screen magnifiers: Evolution and evaluation, *IEEE Computer Graphics and Applications* 23, 5 (Sept/Oct 2003), 54–61.

Bruckman, Amy, Forte, Andrea, and Bandlow, Alisa, HCI for kids, in Jacko, Julie and Sears, Andrew (Editors), *The Human-Computer Interaction Handbook, Second Edition*, Lawrence Erlbaum Associates, Hillsdale, NJ (2008), 793–810.

Center for Information Technology Accommodation, Section 508: The road to accessibility, General Services Administration, Washington, DC (2002). Available at http://www.section508.gov/.

Czaja, S. J. (Editor), *Human Factors Research Needs for an Aging Population*, National Academy Press, Washington, DC (1990).

Czaja, S. J., Charness, N., Fisk, A. D., Hertzog, C., Nair, S. N., Rogers, W. A., and Sharit, J., Factors predicting the use of technology: Findings from the Center for Research and Education on Aging and Technology Enhancement (CREATE), *Psychology and Aging* 21, 2 (2006), 333–352.

Czaja, S. J. and Lee, C. C., Designing computer systems for older adults, in Jacko, Julie and Sears, Andrew (Editors), *The Human-Computer Interaction Handbook*, Lawrence Erlbaum Associates, Hillsdale, NJ (2003), 413–427.

Dickinson, Anna, Smith, Michael J., Arnott, John L., Newell, Alan F., and Hill, Robin L., Approaches to web search and navigation for older computer novices, *Proc. SIGCHI Conference on Human Factors in Computing Systems*, ACM Press, New York (2007), 281–290.

Druin, Allison and Inkpen, Kori, When are personal technologies for children?, *Personal Technologies* 5, 3 (2001), 191–194.

Druin, A., Weeks, A., Massey, S., and Bederson, B. B., Children's interests and concerns when using the International Children's Digital Library: A four country case study, *Proc. Joint Conference on Digital Libraries (JCDL 2007)*, ACM Press, New York (2007), 167–176.

Furlong, Mary and Kearsley, Greg, *Computers for Kids Over 60*, SeniorNet, San Francisco, CA (1990).

Hart, T. A., Chaparro, B. S., and Halcomb, C. G., Evaluating websites for older adults: adherence to 'senior-friendly' guidelines and end-user performance, *Behavior & Information Technology* 27, 3 (May 2008), 191–199.

Herrnson, P.S., Niemi, R.G., Hanmer, M.J., Bederson, B.B., Conrad, F.G., and Traugott, M., *Voting Technology and the Not-So-Simple Act of Casting a Ballot*, Brookings Institute Press, Washington, DC (2008).

Keirsey, David, *Please Understand Me II: Temperament, Character, Intelligence*, Prometheus Nemesis Books, Del Mar, CA (1998).

Marcus, Aaron and Gould, Emile West, Cultural dimensions and global user-interface design: What? So what? Now what?, *Proc. 6th Conference on Human Factors and the Web* (2000). Available at http://www.tri.c.com/hfweb/.

Pheasant, Stephen, *Bodyspace: Anthropometry, Ergonomics and the Design of the Work, Second Edition*, CRC Press, Boca Raton, FL (1996).

Shneiderman, B., Universal usability: Pushing human-computer interaction research to empower every citizen, *Communications of the ACM* 43, 5 (May 2000), 84–91.

Vanderheiden, Greg, Fundamental principles and priority setting for universal usability, *Proc. ACM Conference on Universal Usability*, ACM Press, New York (2000), 32–38.

Xie, Bo, Older adults, health information, and the Internet, *ACM interactions* 15, 4 (2008), 44–46.

General information resources

Primary journals include the following:

ACM interactions: A Magazine for User Interface Designers, ACM Press, New York

ACM Transactions on Accessible Computing, ACM Press, New York

ACM Transactions on Computer-Human Interaction, ACM Press, New York

AIS Transactions on Human-Computer Interaction, AIS, Atlanta, GA

Behaviour & Information Technology (BIT), Taylor & Francis Ltd., London, U.K.

Computer Supported Cooperative Work, Springer, Berlin, Germany

Human-Computer Interaction, Taylor & Francis Ltd., London, U.K.

Information Visualization, Palgrave Macmillan, Houndmills, Basingstoke, U.K.

Interacting with Computers, Elsevier, London, U.K.

International Journal of Human-Computer Interaction, Taylor & Francis Ltd., London, U.K.

International Journal of Human-Computer Studies, Elsevier, London, U.K.

Journal of Organizational Computing and Electronic Commerce, Taylor & Francis Ltd., London, U.K.

Journal of Usability Studies, Usability Professionals Assn., Bloomington, IL

New Review of Hypermedia and Multimedia, Taylor & Francis Ltd., London, U.K.

Universal Access in the Information Society, Springer, Berlin, Germany

Other journals that regularly carry articles of interest include:

ACM: Communications of the ACM (CACM)

ACM Computers in Entertainment

ACM Computing Surveys

ACM Transactions on Graphics

ACM Transactions on Information Systems

AIS: Communications of the Association for Information Systems

Cognitive Science

Computers in Human Behavior

Ergonomics

Human Factors (HF)

IEEE Computer

IEEE Computer Graphics and Applications

IEEE Multimedia

IEEE Software

IEEE Transactions on Systems, Man, and Cybernetics (IEEE SMC)

IEEE Transactions on Visualization and Computer Graphics (IEEE TVCG)

Journal of Computer-Mediated Communication

Journal of Visual Languages and Computing

Personal and Ubiquitous Computing

Presence

Technical Communication

UMUAI: User Modeling and User-Adapted Interaction

World Wide Web: Internet and Web Information Systems

The Association for Computing Machinery (ACM) has a Special Interest Group on Computer & Human Interaction (SIGCHI), which publishes a newsletter and holds regularly scheduled conferences. ACM also publishes the highly regarded *Transactions on Human-Computer Interaction* and the lively magazine *interactions*. Other ACM Special Interest Groups, such as Graphics and Interactive Techniques (SIGGRAPH), Accessible Computing (SIGACCESS), Multimedia (SIGMM), and Hypertext, Hypermedia, and Web (SIGWEB), also produce conferences and newsletters. Other relevant ACM groups are Computers and Society (SIGCAS), Design of Communication (SIGDOC), Groupware (SIGGROUP), Information Retrieval (SIGIR), and Mobility of Systems, Users, Data, and Computing (SIGMOBILE).

The IEEE Computer Society, through its many conferences, transactions, and magazines, covers user-interface issues. The American Society for Information Science & Technology (ASIST) has a Special Interest Group on Human-Computer Interaction (SIGHCI) that publishes a newsletter and organizes sessions at the annual ASIST convention. Similarly, the business-oriented Association for Information Systems (AIS) has a SIGHCI that publishes a newsletter and a journal and runs sessions at several conferences. The long-established Human Factors & Ergonomics Society also runs annual conferences and has a Computer Systems Technical Group with a newsletter. Additionally, the Society for Technical Communications (STC), the American Institute of Graphic Arts (AIGA), the International Ergonomics Association, and the Ergonomics Society increasingly focus on user interfaces. The influential business-oriented Usability Professionals Association (UPA) publishes the *UX - User Experience* magazine and the online *Journal of Usability Studies*. The UPA also spawned the annual World Usability Day with hundreds of events around the world each November.

The International Federation for Information Processing has a Technical Committee (TC.13) and Working Groups on Human-Computer Interaction. The British Computer Society Human-Computer Interaction Group has held an international conference since 1985 and published *Interfaces* magazine. The French Association Francophone pour l'Interaction Homme-Machine (AFIHM), the Spanish Asociación Interacción Persona-Ordenador (AIPO), and other associations promote HCI within their language communities. Other groups conduct important events in South Africa, Australia/New Zealand, Scandinavia, Asia, Latin America, etc.

Conferences—such as the ones held by the ACM (especially SIGCHI and SIGGRAPH), IEEE, ASIST, Human Factors & Ergonomics Society, and IFIP—often have relevant papers presented and published in the proceedings. INTERACT, Human-Computer Interaction International, and Work with Computing Systems are conference series that cover user-interface issues broadly. Many specialized conferences may also be of interest: for example, User Interfaces Software and Technology, Hypertext, Computer-Supported Cooperative Work, Intelligent User Interfaces, Computers and Accessibility, Ubiquituous Computing, Wearable, Computers and Cognition, Designing Interactive Systems, and more.

Brad Myers's brief history of HCI (*ACM interactions*, March 1998) is one starting point for those who want to study the emergence and evolution of this field. James Martin provided a thoughtful and useful survey of interactive systems in his 1973 book, *Design of Man-Computer Dialogues*. Ben Shneiderman's 1980 book, *Software Psychology: Human Factors in Computer and Information Systems*, promoted the use of controlled experimental techniques and scientific research methods. Rubinstein and Hersh's *The Human Factor: Designing Computer Systems for People* (1984) offered an appealing introduction to computer-system design and many useful guidelines. The first edition of this book, published in 1987, reviewed critical issues, offered guidelines for designers, and suggested research directions.

A steady flow of influential books have stimulated widespread media and public attention about usability issues, including Nielsen's *Usability Engineering* (1993), Landauer's *The Trouble with Computers* (1995), and Nielsen's *Designing Web Usability* (1999). Don Norman's 1988 book *The Psychology of Everyday Things* (reprinted as *The Design of Everyday Things*) is a refreshing look at the psychological issues involved in the design of the everyday technology that surrounds us.

As the field matures, subgroups and publications centered around specialized topics emerge; this is happening with mobile computing, web design, online communities, information visualization, virtual environments, and so on. The following list of guidelines documents and books is a starting point to an exploration of the large and growing literature.

Guidelines documents

Apple Computer, Inc., *Apple Human Interface Guidelines*, Apple, Cupertino, CA (June 2008). Available at http://developer.apple.com/.

—Explains how to design consistent visual and behaviorial properties for Mac OS X with the Aqua user interface.

Apple Computer, Inc., *iPhone Human Interface Guidelines for Web Applications* (2008). Available at http://developer.apple.com/.

—Explains how to design applications for the iPhone mobile web platform.

Dept. of Defense, *Human Engineering Design Criteria for Military Systems, Equipment and Facilities*, Military Standard MIL-STD–1472F, U.S. Government Printing Office, Washington, DC (1999).

—Covers traditional ergonomic and anthropometric issues. Later editions pay increasing attention to user-computer interfaces. Interesting and thought-provoking reminder of many human-factors issues.

Federal Aviation Administration, *The Human Factors Design Standard*, Atlantic City, NJ (updated July 2007). Available at http://hf.tc.faa.gov/hfds/.

—Extensive compilation of human-factors standards for contractors to follow, especially relevant to aircraft and air-traffic control.

Human Factors & Ergonomics Society, *ANSI/HFES 100-2007 Human Factors Engineering of Computer Workstations*, Santa Monica, CA (2007).

—Carefully considered revised standards for the design, installation, and use of computer workstations. Emphasizes ergonomics and anthropometrics.

International Organization for Standardization, *ISO 9241 Ergonomics of Human-System Interaction*, Geneva, Switzerland (updated 2008). Available at http://www.iso.org/.

—Thorough general introduction, covering dialog principles, guidance on usability, presentation of information, user guidance, menu dialogs, command dialogs, direct-manipulation dialogs, form-filling dialogs, and much more. This is an important source for many countries and companies.

Microsoft, Inc., *The Microsoft Windows User Experience*, Microsoft Press, Redmond, WA (1999).

—Provides thoughtful analyses of usability principles (user in control, directness, consistency, forgiveness, aesthetics, and simplicity) and gives detailed guidance for Windows software developers.

Microsoft, Inc., *Windows Vista User Experience Guidelines* (2008). Available at http://msdn.microsoft.com/en-us/library/aa511258.aspx.

—Describes design principles, controls, commands, text, interaction, windows, and aesthetics.

NASA, *NASA.gov Standards and Guidelines*, Washington, DC (2005). Available at http://www.hq.nasa.gov/pao/portal/usability/.

—Describes the information architecture and user-interface design for the NASA portal.

National Cancer Institute, *Research-based Web Design and Usability Guidelines*, Dept. of Health & Human Services, National Institutes of Health (updated edition 2006). Available at http://www.usability.gov/pdfs/guidelines.html.

—Authoritative and packed with numerous full-color examples of information-oriented web sites.

Sun Microsystems, Inc., *Java Look and Feel Design Guidelines, Second Edition*, Addison-Wesley, Reading, MA (2001). Available at http://java.sun.com/products/jlf/.

—Shows designers how to create visual design and behaviors in a consistent, compatible, and aesthetic manner.

United Kingdom Ministry of Defence, *Human Factors for Designers of Systems*, Defence Standard 00-250, Issue 1 (23 May 2008). Available at http://www.dstan.mod.uk/data/00/250/00000100.pdf.

—Describes human factors integration processes, requirements, and acceptance testing.

World Wide Web Consortium's Web Accessibility Initiative, *Web Content Accessibility Guidelines 2.0*, Geneva, Switzerland (2008). Available at http://www.w3.org/WAI/.

—Practical, implementable three-level prioritization of web design guidelines for users with disabilities. The Web Accessibility Initiative (WAI) develops strategies, guidelines, and resources to help make the Web accessible to people with disabilities. Four principles are offered: Perceivable, Operable, Understandable, and Robust.

World Wide Web Consortium, *Web Accessibility Evaluation Tools*, Geneva, Switzerland (2008). Available at http://www.w3.org/WAI/ER/existingtools.html.

—An occasionally updated list of software tools related to accessibility; demonstrates lively activity.

Books

Classic books

Bailey, Robert W., *Human Performance Engineering: Using Human Factors/Ergonomics to Achieve Computer Usability, Third Edition*, Prentice-Hall, Englewood Cliffs, NJ (1996).

Beyer, Hugh and Holtzblatt, Karen, *Contextual Design: Defining Customer-Centered Systems*, Morgan Kaufmann, San Francisco, CA (1998).

Cakir, A., Hart, D. J., and Stewart, T. F. M., *Visual Display Terminals: A Manual Covering Ergonomics, Workplace Design, Health and Safety, Task Organization*, John Wiley & Sons, New York (1980).

Card, Stuart K., Moran, Thomas P., and Newell, Allen, *The Psychology of Human-Computer Interaction*, Lawrence Erlbaum Associates, Hillsdale, NJ (1983).

Carroll, John M., *Making Use: Scenario-Based Design of Human-Computer Interactions*, MIT Press, Cambridge, MA (2000).

Dreyfuss, H., *The Measure of Man: Human Factors in Design, Second Edition*, Whitney Library of Design, New York (1967).

Dumas, Joseph S. and Redish, Janice C., *A Practical Guide to Usability Testing*, Ablex, Norwood, NJ (1999, revised edition).

Fernandes, Tony, *Global Interface Design: A Guide to Designing International User Interfaces*, Academic Press Professional, Boston, MA (1995).

Foley, James D., van Dam, Andries, Feiner, Steven K., and Hughes, John F., *Computer Graphics: Principles and Practice in C, Second Edition*, Addison-Wesley, Reading, MA (1995).

Hiltz, Starr Roxanne and Turoff, Murray, *The Network Nation: Human Communication via Computer*, Addison-Wesley, Reading, MA (1978, revised edition 1998).

Krueger, Myron, *Artificial Reality II*, Addison-Wesley, Reading, MA (1991).

Landauer, Thomas K., *The Trouble with Computers: Usefulness, Usability, and Productivity*, MIT Press, Cambridge, MA (1995).

Laurel, Brenda, *Computers as Theater*, Addison-Wesley, Reading, MA (1991).

Marchionini, Gary, *Information Seeking in Electronic Environments*, Cambridge University Press, Cambridge, U.K. (1995).

Marcus, Aaron, *Graphic Design for Electronic Documents and User Interfaces*, ACM Press, New York (1992).

Martin, James, *Design of Man-Computer Dialogues*, Prentice-Hall, Englewood Cliffs, NJ (1973).

Mullet, Kevin and Sano, Darrell, *Designing Visual Interfaces: Communication Oriented Techniques*, Sunsoft Press, Englewood Cliffs, NJ (1995).

Mumford, Enid, *Designing Human Systems for New Technology*, Manchester Business School, Manchester, U.K. (1983).

National Research Council, Committee on Human Factors, *Research Needs for Human Factors*, National Academies Press, Washington, DC (1983).

Nielsen, Jakob, *Usability Engineering*, Academic Press, Boston, MA (1993).

Norman, Donald A., *The Psychology of Everyday Things*, Basic Books, New York (1988).

Norman, Donald A., *The Invisible Computer: Why Good Products Can Fail, the Personal Computer Is So Complex, and Information Appliances Are the Solution*, MIT Press, Cambridge, MA (2000).

Preece, Jenny, *Online Communities: Designing Usability and Supporting Sociability*, John Wiley & Sons, New York (2000).

Raskin, Jef, *Humane Interface: New Directions for Designing Interactive Systems*, Addison-Wesley, Reading, MA (2000).

Rubinstein, Richard and Hersh, Harry, *The Human Factor: Designing Computer Systems for People*, Digital Press, Maynard, MA (1984).

Sheridan, T. B. and Ferrel, W. R., *Man-Machine Systems: Information, Control, and Decision Models of Human Performance*, MIT Press, Cambridge, MA (1974).

Shneiderman, Ben, *Software Psychology: Human Factors in Computer and Information Systems*, Little, Brown, Boston, MA (1980).

Shneiderman, Ben and Kearsley, Greg, *Hypertext Hands-On! An Introduction to a New Way of Organizing and Accessing Information*, Addison-Wesley, Reading, MA (1989).

Turkle, Sherry, *The Second Self: Computers and the Human Spirit*, Simon and Schuster, New York (1984).

Weizenbaum, Joseph, *Computer Power and Human Reason: From Judgment to Calculation*, W. H. Freeman, San Francisco, CA (1976).

Winograd, Terry and Flores, Fernando, *Understanding Computers and Cognition*, Ablex, Norwood, NJ (1986).

Recent books

Ashcraft, Mark H., *Cognition, Fourth Edition*, Prentice-Hall, Englewood Cliffs, NJ (2005).

Ballard, Barbara, *Designing the Mobile User Experience*, John Wiley & Sons, New York (2007).

Benyon, David, Turner, Phil, and Turner, Susan, *Designing Interactive Systems: People, Activities, Contexts, Technologies*, Addison-Wesley, Reading, MA (2005).

Buxton, Bill, *Sketching User Experiences: Getting the Design Right and the Right Design*, Morgan Kaufmann, San Francisco, CA (2007).

Cooper, Alan, Reimann, Robert, and Cronin, David, *About Face 3: The Essentials of Interaction Design*, John Wiley & Sons, New York (2007).

Dix, Alan, Finlay, Janet, Abowd, Gregory, and Beale, Russell, *Human-Computer Interaction, Third Edition*, Prentice-Hall, Englewood Cliffs, NJ (2003).

Dourish, Paul, *Where the Action Is*, MIT Press, Cambridge, MA (2002).

Dumas, Joseph S. and Loring, Beth A., *Moderating Usability Tests: Principles and Practices for Interacting*, Morgan Kaufmann, San Francisco, CA (2008).

Fogg, B.J., *Persuasive Technology: Using Computers to Change What We Think and Do*, Morgan Kaufmann, San Francisco, CA (2002).

Galitz, Wilbert O., *The Essential Guide to User Interface Design: An Introduction to GUI Design Principles and Techniques, Third Edition*, John Wiley & Sons, New York (2007).

Holtzblatt, Karen, Wendell, Jessamyn Burns, and Wood, Shelley, *Rapid Contextual Design: A How-to Guide to Key Techniques for User-Centered Design*, Morgan Kaufmann, San Francisco, CA (2004).

Johnson, Jeff, *GUI Bloopers 2.0: Common User Interface Design Don'ts and Dos*, Morgan Kaufmann, San Francisco, CA (2007).

Jones, Matt and Marsden, Gary, *Mobile Interaction Design*, John Wiley & Sons, New York (2006).

Jones, William, *Keeping Found Things Found: The Study and Practice of Personal Information Management*, Morgan Kaufmann, San Francisco, CA (2008).

Keates, Simeon, *Designing for Accessibility: A Business Guide to Countering Design Exclusion*, CRC Press, Boca Raton, FL (2006).

Kortum, Philip, *HCI Beyond the GUI: Design for Haptic, Speech, Olfactory and Other Nontraditional Interfaces*, Morgan Kaufmann, San Francisco, CA (2008).

Love, Steve, *Understanding Mobile Human-Computer Interaction*, Morgan Kaufmann, San Francisco, CA (2005).

Löwgren, J. and Stolterman, E., *Thoughtful Interaction Design: A Design Perspective on Information Technology*, MIT Press, Cambridge, MA (2004).

Ludlow, P. and Wallace, M., *The Second Life Herald: The Virtual Tabloid That Witnessed the Dawn of the Metaverse*, MIT Press, Cambridge, MA (2007).

Markopoulos, Panos, Read, Janet, MacFarlane, Stuart, and Hoysniemi, Johanna, *Evaluating Children's Interactive Products: Principles and Practices for Interaction Designers*, Morgan Kaufmann, San Francisco, CA (2008).

Moggridge, Bill, *Designing Interaction*, MIT Press, Cambridge, MA (2006).

Norman, D., *Emotional Design: Why We Love (or Hate) Everyday Things*, Basic Books, New York (2004).

Norman, K. L., *Cyberpsychology: An Introduction to the Psychology of Human-Computer Interaction*, Cambridge University Press, New York (2008).

Pirolli, Peter, *Information Foraging Theory: Adaptive Interaction with Information*, Oxford University Press, New York (2007).

Rubin, Jeffrey and Chisnell, Dana, *Handbook of Usability Testing: How to Plan, Design, and Conduct Effective Tests, Second Edition*, John Wiley & Sons, New York (2008).

Saffer, Dan, *Designing for Interaction*: *Creating Smart Applications and Clever Devices*, New Riders, Indianapolis, IN (2006).

Schummer, Till and Lukosch, Stephan, *Patterns for Computer-Mediated Interaction*, John Wiley & Sons, New York (2007).

Sharp, Helen, Rogers, Yvonne, and Preece, Jenny, *Interaction Design: Beyond Human-Computer Interaction, Second Edition*, John Wiley & Sons, West Sussex, England (2007).

Shneiderman, Ben, *Leonardo's Laptop: Human Needs and the New Computing Technologies*, MIT Press, Cambridge, MA (2002).

Sieckenius de Souza, C., *Semiotic Engineering of Human-Computer Interaction*, MIT Press, Cambridge, MA (2005).

Stone, Debbie, Jarrett, Caroline, Woodroffe, Mark, and Minocha, Shailey, *User Interface Design and Evaluation*, Morgan Kaufmann, San Francisco, CA (2005).

Te'eni, Dov, Carey, Jane, and Zhang, Ping, *Human-Computer Interaction: Developing Effective Organizational Information Systems*, John Wiley & Sons, New York (2007).

Thackara, John, *In the Bubble: Designing in a Complex World*, MIT Press, Cambridge, MA (2005).

Tullis, Thomas and Albert, William, *Measuring the User Experience: Collecting, Analyzing, and Presenting Usability Metrics*, Morgan Kaufmann, San Francisco, CA (2008).

Ware, Colin, *Information Visualization: Perception for Design, Second Edition*, Morgan Kaufmann, San Francisco, CA (2004).

Ware, Colin, *Visual Thinking for Design*, Morgan Kaufmann, San Francisco, CA (2008).

Web design resources

Alliance for Technology Access, *Computer and Web Resources for People with Disabilities: A Guide to Exploring Today's Assistive Technology*, Hunter House, Alameda, CA (2000).

Horton, Sarah, *Access by Design: A Guide to Universal Usability for Web Designers*, New Riders, Indianapolis, IN (2005).

Lazar, Jonathan, *User-Centered Web Development*, Jones & Bartlett Publishers, Boston, MA (2001).

Lynch, Patrick J. and Horton, Sarah, *Web Style Guide: Basic Design Principles for Creating Web Sites, Third Edition*, Yale University Press, New Haven, CT (2008).

King, Andrew B., *Website Optimization: Speed, Search Engine & Conversion Rate Secrets*, O'Reilly Media, Sebastopol, CA (2008).

Krug, Steve, *Don't Make Me Think!: A Common Sense Approach to Web Usability, Second Edition*, New Riders, Indianapolis, IN (2005).

Nielsen, Jakob, *Designing Web Usability: The Practice of Simplicity*, New Riders, Indianapolis, IN (1999).

Nielsen, Jakob and Loranger, Hoa, *Prioritizing Web Usability*, New Riders, Indianapolis, IN (2006).

Nielsen, Jakob and Tahir, Marie, *Homepage Usability: 50 Websites Deconstructed*, New Riders, Indianapolis, IN (2002).

Porter, Josh, *Designing for the Social Web*, New Riders, Indianapolis, IN (2008).

Redish, Janice, *Letting Go of the Words: Writing Web Content that Works*, Morgan Kaufmann, San Francisco, CA (2007).

Rosenfeld, Louis and Morville, Peter, *Information Architecture for the World Wide Web, Second Edition*, O'Reilly Media, Sebastopol, CA (2002).

Spool, Jared M., Scanlon, Tara, Schroeder, Will, Snyder, Carolyn, and DeAngelo, Terri, *Web Site Usability: A Designer's Guide*, Morgan Kaufmann, San Francisco, CA (1999).

Thatcher, Jim et al., *Web Accessibility: Web Standards and Regulatory Compliance*, friends of ED (2006).

Van Duyne, Douglas K., Landay, James A., and Hong, Jason I., *The Design of Sites: Patterns, Principles, and Processes for Crafting a Customer-Centered Web Experience*, Addison-Wesley, Reading, MA (2002).

Wroblewski, Luke, *Web Form Design: Filling in the Blanks*, Rosenfeld Media, Brooklyn, NY (2008).

Collections

Classic collections

Baecker, R., Grudin, J., Buxton, W., and Greenberg, S. (Editors), *Readings in Human-Computer Interaction: Towards the Year 2000*, Morgan Kaufmann, San Francisco, CA (1995).

Badre, Albert and Shneiderman, Ben (Editors), *Directions in Human-Computer Interaction*, Ablex, Norwood, NJ (1980).

Bergman, Eric, *Information Appliances and Beyond*, Morgan Kaufmann, San Francisco, CA (2000).

Carey, Jane (Editor), *Human Factors in Management Information Systems*, Ablex, Norwood, NJ (1988).

Carroll, John M. (Editor), *Designing Interaction: Psychology at the Human-Computer Interface*, Cambridge University Press, Cambridge, U.K. (1991).

Druin, Allison (Editor), *The Design of Children's Software: How We Design, What We Design and Why*, Morgan Kaufmann, San Francisco, CA (1999).

Hartson, H. Rex (Editor), *Advances in Human-Computer Interaction, Volume 1*, Ablex, Norwood, NJ (1985).

Helander, Martin, Landauer, Thomas K., and Prabhu, Prasad V. (Editors), *Handbook of Human-Computer Interaction*, North-Holland Elsevier Science, Amsterdam, The Netherlands (1997).

Laurel, Brenda (Editor), *The Art of Human-Computer Interface Design*, Addison-Wesley, Reading, MA (1990).

Nielsen, Jakob (Editor), *Advances in Human-Computer Interaction, Volume 5*, Ablex, Norwood, NJ (1993).

Norman, Donald A. and Draper, Stephen W. (Editors), *User Centered System Design: New Perspectives on Human-Computer Interaction*, Lawrence Erlbaum Associates, Hillsdale, NJ (1986).

Shneiderman, Ben (Editor), *Sparks of Innovation in Human-Computer Interaction*, Ablex, Norwood, NJ (1993).

Thomas, John C. and Schneider, Michael L. (Editors), *Human Factors in Computer Systems*, Ablex, Norwood, NJ (1984).

Van Cott, H. P. and Kinkade, R. G. (Editors), *Human Engineering Guide to Equipment Design*, U.S. Superintendent of Documents, Washington, DC (1972).

Winograd, Terry (Editor), *Bringing Design to Software*, ACM Press, New York, and Addison-Wesley, Reading, MA (1996).

Recent collections

Bias, Randolph and Mayhew, Deborah (Editors), *Cost-Justifying Usability: An Update for the Internet Age, Second Edition*, Morgan Kaufmann, San Francisco, CA (2005).

Branaghan, Russell J. (Editor), *Design by People for People: Essays on Usability*, Usability Professionals' Association, Bloomingdale, IL (2001).

Carroll, John M. (Editor), *Human-Computer Interaction in the New Millennium*, Addison-Wesley, Reading, MA (2002).

Carroll, Johh M. (Editor), *HCI Models, Theories, and Frameworks: Toward a Multidisciplinary Science*, Morgan Kaufmann, San Francisco, CA (2003).

Earnshaw, Rae, Guedj, Richard, van Dam, Andries, and Vince, John (Editors), *Frontiers in Human-Centred Computing, Online Communities and Virtual Environments*, Springer-Verlag, London, U.K. (2001).

Erickson, Thomas and McDonald, David W. (Editors), *HCI Remixed: Essays on Works That Have Influenced the HCI Community*, MIT Press, Cambridge, MA (2008).

Jacko, Julie and Sears, Andrew (Editors), *The Human-Computer Interaction Handbook: Second Edition*, Lawrence Erlbaum Associates, Hillsdale, NJ (2008).

Kaptelinin, V. and Nardi, B., *Acting with Technology: Activity Theory and Interaction Design*, MIT Press, Cambridge, MA (2006).

Lazar, J. (Editor), *Universal Usability: Designing User Interfaces for Diverse Users,* John Wiley & Sons, New York (2007).

Lumsden, Joanna (Editor), *Handbook of Research on User Interface Design and Evaluation for Mobile Technology,* IGI Publishing, Hershey, PA (2008).

Nahl, Diane and Bilal, Dania (Editors), *Information and Emotion: The Emergent Affective Paradigm in Information Behavior Research and Theory,* Information Today, Medford, NJ (2007).

Proctor, Robert (Editor), *Handbook of Human Factors in Web Design,* Routledge, New York (2004).

Salvendy, Gavriel (Editor), *Handbook of Human Factors, Third Edition,* John Wiley & Sons, New York (2006).

Stephanidis, Constantine (Editor), *User Interfaces for All: Concepts, Methods, and Tools,* Lawrence Erlbaum Associates, Hillsdale, NJ (2001).

Streitz, Norbert, Kameas, Achilles, and Mavrommati, Irene (Editors), *The Disappearing Computer: Interaction Design, System Infrastructures and Applications for Smart Environments, Lecture Notes in Computer Science* 4500, Springer, Heidelberg, Germany (2007).

Whitworth, Brian and De Moor, Aldo (Editors), *Handbook of Research on Socio-Technical Design and Social Networking Systems,* IGI Global, Hershey, PA (2009).

Zhang, P. and Galletta, D. (Editors), *Human-Computer Interaction and Management Information Systems – Foundations,* M. E. Sharpe, Inc., Armonk, NY (2006).

Video Recordings

Video is an effective medium for presenting the dynamic, graphical, and interactive nature of modern user interfaces. The Technical Video Program of the ACM SIGCHI conferences presents excellent demonstrations of often-cited but seldom-seen systems. Many CHI videos are available from the Open Video project, at http://www.open-video.org/. The brief videos from the Human-Computer Interaction Lab at the University of Maryland, dating back to 1991, are online at http://www.cs.umd.edu/hcil/pubs/videoreports.shtml, and a selection are also on the Open Video project. A wonderful set of lectures from Stanford University's CS547 Human-Computer Interaction Seminar can be found at http://scpd.stanford.edu/scpd/students/cs547archive.htm. A Georgia Tech team produces a Human-Centered Computing Education Digital Library with videos, lectures, slides, and other materials, available at http://hcc.cc.gatech.edu/.

Inspirational videos from the annual Technology, Entertainment & Design Conference, which covers a wide range of topics including visionary user-interface themes, are found at http://www.ted.com/index.php/talks/. Another exceptional resource is YouTube (http://www.youtube.com/), where a search on "user interfaces" produces a list of hundreds of recent product demonstrations, research reports, and some clever and funny technology demonstrations.

2

Guidelines, Principles, and Theories

> 66 We want principles, not only developed—the work of the closet—but applied, which is the work of life. 99

Horace Mann
Thoughts, 1867

> 66 There never comes a point where a theory can be said to be true. The most that anyone can claim for any theory is that it has shared the successes of all its rivals and that it has passed at least one test which they have failed. 99

A. J. Ayer
Philosophy in the Twentieth Century, 1982

2.1 Introduction

User-interface designers have accumulated a wealth of experience and researchers have produced a growing body of empirical evidence and theories, all of which can be organized into:

1. Specific and practical guidelines that prescribe good practices and caution against dangers.
2. Middle-level principles to analyze and compare design alternatives.
3. High-level theories and models that describe objects and actions with consistent terminology so that comprehensible explanations can be made to support communication and teaching. Other theories are predictive, such as those for reading, typing, or pointing times.

In many contemporary systems, there is a grand opportunity to improve the user interface. Cluttered displays, complex procedures, inconsistent layouts, and insufficient informative feedback can generate debilitating stress. It is understandable that users whose network connections drop as they are completing lengthy online purchase orders may become frustrated and even angry. Stress and frustration can lead to poorer performance, minor slips, and serious errors, all contributing to job dissatisfaction and consumer resistance.

Guidelines, principles, and theories—which can provide preventive medicine and remedies for these problems—have matured in recent years. Reliable methods for predicting pointing and input times (Chapter 8), helpful cognitive theories (Chapter 10), and better training methods (Chapter 12) now shape research and guide design.

This chapter begins with a sampling of guidelines for navigating, organizing displays, getting user attention, and facilitating data entry (Section 2.2). Then Section 2.3 covers some fundamental principles of interface design, such as coping with user skill levels, task profiles, and interaction styles. It presents the Eight Golden Rules of interface design, explores ways of preventing user errors, and closes with a section on ensuring human control while increasing automation. Section 2.4 reviews several theories of interface design.

2.2 Guidelines

From the earliest days of computing, interface designers have written down guidelines to record their insights and to try to guide the efforts of future designers. The early Apple and Microsoft guidelines, which were influential for desktop-interface designers, have been followed by dozens of guidelines documents for the Web and mobile devices (see the list at the end of Chapter 1). A guidelines document helps by developing a shared language and then promoting consistency among multiple designers in terminology usage, appearance, and action sequences. It records best practices derived from practical experience or empirical studies, with appropriate examples and counterexamples. The creation of a guidelines document engages the design community in lively discussions about input and output formats, action sequences, terminology, and hardware devices (Galitz, 2007; Lynch and Horton, 2008).

Critics complain that guidelines can be too specific, incomplete, hard to apply, and sometimes wrong. Proponents argue that building on experience from design leaders contributes to steady improvements. Both groups recognize the value of lively discussions in promoting awareness.

The following four sections provide examples of guidelines, and Section 3.3.2 discusses how they can be integrated into the design process. The examples address some key topics, but they merely sample the thousands of guidelines that have been written.

2.2.1 Navigating the interface

Since navigation can be difficult for many users, providing clear rules is helpful. The sample guidelines presented here come from the National Cancer Institute's effort to assist government agencies with the design of informative web pages (NCI, 2006), but these guidelines have widespread application. Most are stated positively ("reduce the user's workload"), but some are negative ("do not display unsolicited windows or graphics"). The NCI's 388 guidelines, which offer cogent examples and impressive research support, cover the design process, general principles, and specific rules. This sample of the guidelines gives useful advice and a taste of their style:

- *Standardize task sequences*. Allow users to perform tasks in the same sequence and manner across similar conditions.

- *Ensure that embedded links are descriptive.* When using embedded links, the link text should accurately describe the link's destination.

- *Use unique and descriptive headings.* Use headings that are distinct from one another and conceptually related to the content they describe.

- *Use radio buttons for mutually exclusive choices.* Provide a radio button control when users need to choose one response from a list of mutually exclusive options.

- *Develop pages that will print properly.* If users are likely to print one or more pages, develop pages with widths that print properly.

- *Use thumbnail images to preview larger images.* When viewing full-size images is not critical, first provide a thumbnail of the image.

Guidelines to promote accessibility for users with disabilities were included in the U.S. Rehabilitation Act. Its Section 508, with guidelines for web design, is published by the Access Board (http://www.access-board.gov/508.htm), an independent U.S. government agency devoted to accessibility for people with disabilities. The World Wide Web Consortium (W3C) adapted these guidelines (http://www.w3.org/TR/WCAG20/) and organized them into three priority levels, for which it has provided automated checking tools. A few of the accessibility guidelines are:

- *Text alternatives.* Provide text alternatives for any non-text content so that it can be changed into other forms people need, such as large print, braille, speech, symbols, or simpler language.

- *Time-based media.* Provide alternatives for time-based media (e.g., movies or animations). Synchronize equivalent alternatives (such as captions or auditory descriptions of the visual track) with the presentation.

- *Distinguishable.* Make it easier for users to see and hear content, including separating foreground from background. Color is not used as the only visual means of conveying information, indicating an action, prompting a response, or distinguishing a visual element.

- *Predictable.* Make Web pages appear and operate in predictable ways.

The goal of these guidelines is to have web-page designers use features that permit users with disabilities to employ screen readers or other special technologies to give them access to web-page content.

2.2.2 Organizing the display

Display design is a large topic with many special cases. Smith and Mosier (1986) offer five high-level goals as part of their guidelines for data display:

1. *Consistency of data display.* During the design process, the terminology, abbreviations, formats, colors, capitalization, and so on should all be standardized and controlled by use of a dictionary of these items.

2. *Efficient information assimilation by the user.* The format should be familiar to the operator and should be related to the tasks required to be performed with the data. This objective is served by rules for neat columns of data, left justification for alphanumeric data, right justification of integers, lining up of decimal points, proper spacing, use of comprehensible labels, and appropriate measurement units and numbers of decimal digits.

3. *Minimal memory load on the user.* Users should not be required to remember information from one screen for use on another screen. Tasks should be arranged such that completion occurs with few actions, minimizing the chance of forgetting to perform a step. Labels and common formats should be provided for novice or intermittent users.

4. *Compatibility of data display with data entry.* The format of displayed information should be linked clearly to the format of the data entry. Where possible and appropriate, the output fields should also act as editable input fields.

5. *Flexibility for user control of data display.* Users should be able to get the information from the display in the form most convenient for the task on which they are working. For example, the order of columns and sorting of rows should be easily changeable by the users.

This compact set of high-level objectives is a useful starting point, but each project needs to expand these into application-specific and hardware-dependent standards and practices. For example, these generic guidelines, which emerged from a report on design of control rooms for electric-power utilities (Lockheed, 1981), remain valid:

- Be consistent in labeling and graphic conventions.
- Standardize abbreviations.
- Use consistent formatting in all displays (headers, footers, paging, menus, and so on).
- Present data only if they assist the operator.
- Present information graphically where appropriate by using widths of lines, positions of markers on scales, and other techniques that relieve the need to read and interpret alphanumeric data.
- Present digital values only when knowledge of numerical values is necessary and useful.
- Use high-resolution monitors and maintain them to provide maximum display quality.
- Design a display in monochromatic form using spacing and arrangement for organization and then judiciously add color where it will aid the operator.
- Involve users in the development of new displays and procedures.

Chapter 11 further discusses data-display issues.

2.2.3 Getting the user's attention

Since substantial information may be presented to users for the normal performance of their work, exceptional conditions or time-dependent information must be presented so as to attract attention (Wickens and Hollands, 2000). These guidelines detail several techniques for getting the user's attention:

- *Intensity*. Use two levels only, with limited use of high intensity to draw attention.
- *Marking*. Underline the item, enclose it in a box, point to it with an arrow, or use an indicator such as an asterisk, bullet, dash, plus sign, or X.
- *Size*. Use up to four sizes, with larger sizes attracting more attention.
- *Choice of fonts*. Use up to three fonts.
- *Inverse video*. Use inverse coloring.
- *Blinking*. Use blinking displays (2–4 Hz) or blinking color changes with great care and in limited areas.
- *Color*. Use up to four standard colors, with additional colors reserved for occasional use.
- *Audio*. Use soft tones for regular positive feedback and harsh sounds for rare emergency conditions.

A few words of caution are necessary. There is a danger of creating cluttered displays by overusing these techniques. Some web designers use blinking advertisements or animated icons to attract attention, but users almost universally disapprove. Animation is appreciated primarily when it provides meaningful information, such as for a progress indicator. Novices need simple, logically organized, and well-labeled displays that guide their actions. Expert users prefer limited labels on fields so data values are easier to extract; subtle highlighting of changed values or positional presentation is sufficient. Display formats must be tested with users for comprehensibility.

Similarly highlighted items will be perceived as being related. Color-coding is especially powerful in linking related items, but this use makes it more difficult to cluster items across color codes (Section 11.6). User control over highlighting—for example, allowing cell phone users to select the color for contacts that are close family members and friends or for meetings that are of high importance—may provide a useful resolution to concerns about personal preferences.

Audio tones, like the clicks in keyboards or ringing sounds in telephones, can provide informative feedback about progress. Alarms for emergency conditions do alert users rapidly, but a mechanism to suppress alarms must be provided. If several types of alarms are used, testing is necessary to ensure that users can distinguish between the alarm levels. Prerecorded or synthesized voice messages are a useful alternative, but since they may interfere with communications between operators, they should be used cautiously (Section 8.4).

2.2.4 Facilitating data entry

Data-entry tasks can occupy a substantial fraction of users' time and can be the source of frustrating and potentially dangerous errors. Smith and Mosier (1986) offer five high-level objectives as part of their guidelines for data entry (Courtesy of MITRE Corporate Archives: Bedford, MA):

1. *Consistency of data-entry transactions*. Similar sequences of actions should be used under all conditions; similar delimiters, abbreviations, and so on should be used.

2. *Minimal input actions by user*. Fewer input actions mean greater operator productivity and—usually—fewer chances for error. Making a choice by a single keystroke, mouse selection, or finger press, rather than by typing in a lengthy string of characters, is potentially advantageous. Selecting from a list of choices eliminates the need for memorization, structures the decision-making task, and eliminates the possibility of typographic errors. However, if users must move their hands from a keyboard to a separate input device, the advantage is negated, because home-row position is lost. Expert users often prefer to type six to eight characters instead of moving to a mouse, joystick, or other selection device.

   A second aspect of this guideline is that redundant data entry should be avoided. It is annoying for users to enter the same information in two locations, since the double entry is perceived as a waste of effort and an opportunity for error. When the same information is required in two places, the system should copy the information for the user, who should still have the option of overriding it by retyping.

3. *Minimal memory load on users*. When doing data entry, users should not be required to remember lengthy lists of codes and complex syntactic command strings.

4. *Compatibility of data entry with data display*. The format of data-entry information should be linked closely to the format of displayed information.

5. *Flexibility for user control of data entry*. Experienced data-entry operators may prefer to enter information in a sequence that they can control. For example, on some occasions in an air-traffic–control environment, the arrival time is the prime field in the controller's mind; on other occasions, the altitude is the prime field. However, flexibility should be used cautiously, since it goes against the consistency principle.

Guidelines documents are a wonderful starting point to give designers the benefit of experience, but they will always need management processes to facilitate education, enforcement, exemption, and enhancement (Section 3.3.2).

2.3 Principles

While guidelines are narrowly focused, principles tend to be more fundamental, widely applicable, and enduring. However, they also tend to need more clarification. For example, the principle of recognizing user diversity makes sense to every designer, but it must be thoughtfully interpreted. A preschooler playing an animated computer game is a long way from a reference librarian doing bibliographic searches for anxious and hurried patrons. Similarly, a grandmother sending a text message is a long way from a highly trained and experienced air-traffic controller. These sketches highlight the differences in users' background knowledge, training in the use of the system, frequency of use, and goals, as well as in the impact of user errors. Since no single design would be ideal for all of these users and situations, successful designers must characterize their users and the context in which their products will be used as precisely and completely as possible.

Section 1.4 offered an introduction to the variety of individual differences that designers must address in pursuing universal usability. This section focuses on a few fundamental principles, beginning with accommodating user skill levels and profiling tasks and user needs. It discusses the five primary interaction styles (direct manipulation, menu selection, form fill-in, command language, and natural language) and the Eight Golden Rules of interface design, followed by a section on error prevention. Finally, it covers controversial strategies for ensuring human control while increasing automation.

2.3.1 Determine users' skill levels

Learning about the users is a simple idea but a difficult and, unfortunately, often undervalued goal. No one would argue against this principle, but many designers simply assume that they understand the users and the users' tasks. Successful designers are aware that people learn, think, and solve problems in different ways: Some users prefer to deal with tables rather than graphs, with words instead of numbers, or with rigid structures rather than open-ended forms.

All design should begin with an understanding of the intended users, including population profiles that reflect their age, gender, physical and cognitive abilities, education, cultural or ethnic backgrounds, training, motivation, goals, and personality. There are often several communities of users for an interface, especially for web applications and mobile devices, so the design effort is multiplied. Typical user communities—such as nurses, doctors, storekeepers, high-school students, or librarians—can be expected to have various combinations of knowledge and usage patterns. User groups from different countries may each deserve special attention, and regional differences often exist within countries. Other variables that characterize users include location (for example, urban versus rural), economic profile, disabilities, and attitudes towards using technology. Users with poor reading skills, limited education, and low motivation require special attention.

In addition to these profiles, an understanding of users' skills with interfaces and with the application domain is important. Users might be tested for their familiarity with interface features, such as traversing hierarchical menus or drawing tools. Other tests might cover domain-specific abilities, such as knowledge of airport city codes, stockbrokerage terminology, insurance-claims concepts, or map icons.

The process of getting to know the users is never-ending, because there is so much to know and because the users keep changing. However, every step towards understanding the users and recognizing them as individuals with outlooks different from the designer's own is likely to be a step closer to a successful design.

For example, a generic separation into novice or first-time, knowledgeable intermittent, and expert frequent users might lead to these differing design goals:

- *Novice or first-time users.* True novice users—for example, grandparents sending their first e-mail to a grandchild—are assumed to know little of the task or interface concepts. By contrast, first-time users are often professionals who know the task concepts well but have shallow knowledge of the interface concepts (for example, a business traveler using a new rental car's navigation system). Both groups of users may arrive with learning-inhibiting anxiety about using computers. Overcoming these limitations, via instructions, dialog boxes, and online help, is a serious challenge to the designer of the interface. Restricting vocabulary to a small number of familiar, consistently used concept terms is essential to begin developing the user's knowledge. The number of actions should also be small so that novice and first-time users can carry out simple tasks successfully, which reduces anxiety, builds confidence, and provides positive reinforcement. Informative feedback about the accomplishment of each task is helpful, and constructive, specific error messages should be provided when users make mistakes. Carefully designed user documentation, video demonstrations, and task-oriented online tutorials may be effective.

- *Knowledgeable intermittent users.* Many people are knowledgeable but intermittent users of a variety of systems (for example, corporate managers using word processors to create templates for travel reimbursements). They have stable task concepts and broad knowledge of interface concepts, but they may have difficulty retaining the structure of menus or the location of features. The burden on their memories will be lightened by orderly structure in the menus, consistent terminology, and high interface apparency, which emphasizes recognition rather than recall. Consistent sequences of actions, meaningful messages, and guides to frequent patterns of usage will help these users to rediscover how to perform their tasks properly. These features will also help novices and some experts, but the major beneficiaries are knowledgeable intermittent users. Protection from danger is necessary to support relaxed exploration of features and usage of partially forgotten action sequences. These users will benefit from context-dependent help to fill in missing pieces of task or interface knowledge. Well-organized reference manuals with search capabilities are also useful.

- *Expert frequent users.* Expert "power" users are thoroughly familiar with the task and interface concepts and seek to get their work done quickly. They demand rapid response times, brief and nondistracting feedback, and the shortcuts to carry out actions with just a few keystrokes or selections. When a sequence of three or four actions is performed regularly, frequent users are willing to create a *macro* or other abbreviated form to reduce the number of required steps. Strings of commands, shortcuts through menus, abbreviations, and other accelerators are requirements.

The characteristics of these three classes of usage must be refined for each environment. Designing for one class is easy; designing for several is much more difficult.

When multiple user classes must be accommodated in one system, the basic strategy is to permit a *multi-layer* (sometimes called *level-structured* or *spiral*) approach to learning. Novices can be taught a minimal subset of objects and actions with which to get started. They are most likely to make correct choices when they have only a few options and are protected from making mistakes—that is, when they are given a *training-wheels* interface. After gaining confidence from hands-on experience, these users can choose to progress to ever-greater levels of task concepts and the accompanying interface concepts. The learning plan should be governed by the users' progress through the task concepts, with new interface concepts being chosen when they are needed to support more complex tasks. For users with strong knowledge of the task and interface concepts, rapid progress is possible.

For example, novice users of a cell phone can quickly learn to make/receive calls first, then to use the menus, and later to store numbers for frequent callees. Their progress is governed by the task domain, rather than by an alphabetical list of commands that are difficult to relate to the tasks. The multi-layer approach must be applied in the design of not only the software, but also the user manuals, help screens, error messages, and tutorials. (Shneiderman, 2003). Multi-layer designs seem to be the most promising approach to promoting universal usability.

Another option for accommodating different usage classes is to permit users to personalize the menu contents, which has proven to be advantageous in a word processor study (McGrenere et al., 2007). A third option is to permit users to control the density of informative feedback that the system provides. Novices want more informative feedback to confirm their actions, whereas frequent users want less distracting feedback. Similarly, it seems that frequent users like displays to be more densely packed than do novices. Finally, the pace of interaction may be varied from slow for novices to fast for frequent users.

2.3.2 Identify the tasks

After carefully drawing the user profile, the developers must identify the tasks to be carried out. Every designer would agree that the set of tasks must be determined before design can proceed, but too often, the task analysis is done informally or incompletely. Task analysis has a long history (Bailey, 1996; Hackos and Redish, 1998), but successful strategies usually involve long hours of observing and interviewing users. This helps designers to understand task frequencies and sequences and make the tough decisions about what tasks to support. Some implementers prefer to include all possible actions in the hope that some users will find them helpful, but this causes clutter. The PalmPilot's designers were dramatically successful because they ruthlessly limited functionality (calendar, contacts, to-do list, and notes) to guarantee simplicity.

High-level task actions can be decomposed into multiple middle-level task actions, which can be further refined into atomic actions that users execute with a single command, menu selection, or other action. Choosing the most appropriate set of atomic actions is a difficult task. If the atomic actions are too small, the users will become frustrated by the large number of actions necessary to accomplish a higher-level task. If the atomic actions are too large and elaborate, the users will need many such actions with special options, or they will not be able to get exactly what they want from the system.

The relative task frequencies are important in shaping, for example, a set of commands or a menu tree. Frequent tasks should be simple and quick to carry out, even at the expense of lengthening some infrequent tasks. Relative frequency of use is one of the bases for making architectural design decisions. For example, in a word processor:

- Frequent actions might be performed by pressing special keys, such as the four arrow keys, Insert, and Delete.
- Less frequent actions might be performed by pressing a single letter plus the Ctrl key, or by a selection from a pull-down menu—examples include underscore, bold, or save.
- Infrequent actions or complex actions might require going through a sequence of menu selections or form fill-ins—for example, to change the printing format or to revise network-protocol parameters.

Similarly, cell phone users can assign their close friends and family members to speed-dial numbers so that frequent calls can be made easily by pressing a single key.

Job Title	TASK				
	Query by Patient	Update Data	Query Across Patients	Add Relations	Evaluate System
Nurse	0.14	0.11			
Physician	0.06	0.04			
Supervisor	0.01	0.01	0.04		
Appointment personnel	0.26				
Medical-record maintainer	0.07	0.04	0.04	0.01	
Clinical researcher			0.08		
Database programmer		0.02	0.02	0.05	

FIGURE 2.1

FREQUENCY OF TASK BY JOB TITLE
Hypothetical frequency-of-use data for a medical clinic information system.
Answering queries from appointments personnel about individual patients is the
highest-frequency task.

Creating a matrix of users and tasks can help designers sort out these issues
(Fig. 2.1). In each box, the designer can put a check mark to indicate that this
user carries out this task. A more precise analysis would include frequencies
instead of just simple check marks. Such user-needs assessment clarifies what
tasks are essential for the design and which ones could be left out to preserve
system simplicity and ease of learning.

2.3.3 Choose an interaction style

When the task analysis is complete and the task objects and actions have been
identified, the designer can choose from these primary interaction styles: direct
manipulation, menu selection, form fill-in, command language, and natural language (Box 2.1 and Box 2.2). Chapters 5 through 7 explore these styles in detail;
this summary gives a brief comparative overview.

Direct manipulation   When a clever designer can create a visual representation of the world of action, the users' tasks can be greatly simplified because
direct manipulation of familiar objects is possible. Examples of such systems
include the desktop metaphor, drawing tools, air-traffic control systems, and
games. By pointing at visual representations of objects and actions, users can
carry out tasks rapidly and can observe the results immediately (for example,

BOX 2.1
Advantages and disadvantages of the five primary interaction styles.

Advantages	Disadvantages
Direct manipulation	
Visually presents task concepts	May be hard to program
Allows easy learning	May require graphics display and pointing devices
Allows easy retention	
Allows errors to be avoided	
Encourages exploration	
Affords high subjective satisfaction	
Menu selection	
Shortens learning	Presents danger of many menus
Reduces keystrokes	May slow frequent users
Structures decision making	Consumes screen space
Permits use of dialog-management tools	Requires rapid display rate
Allows easy support of error handling	
Form fill-in	
Simplifies data entry	Consumes screen space
Requires modest training	
Gives convenient assistance	
Permits use of form-management tools	
Command language	
Flexible	Poor error handling
Appeals to "power" users	Requires substantial training and memorization
Supports user initiative	
Allows convenient creation of user-defined macros	
Natural language	
Relieves burden of learning syntax	Requires clarification dialog
	May not show context
	May require more keystrokes
	Unpredictable

BOX 2.2
Spectrum of directness.

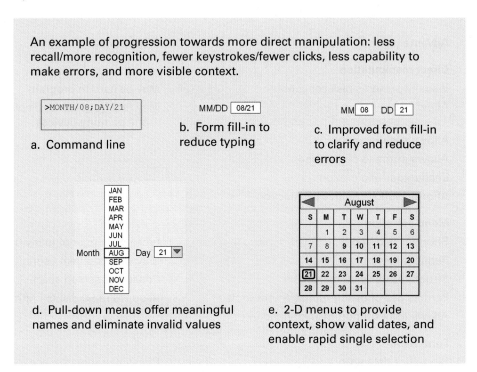

An example of progression towards more direct manipulation: less recall/more recognition, fewer keystrokes/fewer clicks, less capability to make errors, and more visible context.

>MONTH/08;DAY/21

a. Command line

MM/DD 08/21

b. Form fill-in to reduce typing

MM 08 DD 21

c. Improved form fill-in to clarify and reduce errors

d. Pull-down menus offer meaningful names and eliminate invalid values

e. 2-D menus to provide context, show valid dates, and enable rapid single selection

dragging and dropping an icon into a trash can). Keyboard entry of commands and menu selections are replaced by the use of pointing devices to select from a visible set of objects and actions. Direct manipulation is appealing to novices, is easy to remember for intermittent users, and, with careful design, can be rapid for frequent users. Chapter 5 describes direct manipulation and its application.

Menu selection   In menu-selection systems, users read a list of items, select the one most appropriate to their task, and observe the effect. If the terminology and the meaning of the items are understandable and distinct, users can accomplish their tasks with little learning or memorization and just a few actions. The greatest benefit may be that there is a clear structure to decision making, since all possible choices are presented at one time. This interaction style is appropriate for novice and intermittent users and can be appealing to frequent users if the display and selection mechanisms are rapid. For designers, menu-selection systems require careful task analysis to ensure that all functions are supported conveniently and that terminology is chosen carefully and used consistently. User interface-building tools that support menu selection provide an enormous benefit by ensuring consistent screen design, validating completeness, and supporting maintenance. Menu selection is discussed in Chapter 6.

Form fill-in When data entry is required, menu selection alone usually becomes cumbersome, and form fill-in (also called *fill in the blanks*) is appropriate. Users see a display of related fields, move a cursor among the fields, and enter data where desired. With the form fill-in interaction style, users must understand the field labels, know the permissible values and the data-entry method, and be capable of responding to error messages. Since knowledge of the keyboard, labels, and permissible fields is required, some training may be necessary. This interaction style is most appropriate for knowledgeable intermittent users or frequent users. Chapter 6 provides a thorough treatment of form fill-in.

Command language For frequent users, command languages (discussed in Chapter 7) provide a strong feeling of being in control. Users learn the syntax and can often express complex possibilities rapidly, without having to read distracting prompts. However, error rates are typically high, training is necessary, and retention may be poor. Error messages and online assistance are hard to provide because of the diversity of possibilities and the complexity of mapping from tasks to interface concepts and syntax. Command languages and lengthier query or programming languages are the domain of expert frequent users, who often derive great satisfaction from mastering a complex set of semantics and syntax. Powerful advantages include easy history keeping and simple macro creation.

Natural language The hope that computers will respond properly to arbitrary natural-language sentences or phrases engages many researchers and system developers, in spite of limited success thus far. Natural-language interaction usually provides little context for issuing the next command, frequently requires clarification dialog, and may be slower and more cumbersome than selecting from a well-organized menu. Still, when users are knowledgeable about a task domain whose scope is limited and where intermittent use inhibits command-language training, there exist opportunities for natural-language interfaces (discussed at the end of Chapter 7).

Blending several interaction styles may be appropriate when the required tasks and users are diverse. For example, a form fill-in interface for shopping check-out can include menus for items such as accepted credit cards, and a direct-manipulation environment can allow a right-click that produces a pop-up menu with color choices. Also, keyboard commands can provide shortcuts for experts who seek more rapid performance than mouse selection. Chapters 5–7 expand on the constructive guidance for using the different interaction styles outlined here, and Chapter 8 describes how input and output devices influence these interaction styles. Chapter 9 deals with interaction when using collaborative interfaces and participating in social media.

2.3.4 The Eight Golden Rules of interface design

This section focuses attention on eight principles, called "Golden Rules," that are applicable in most interactive systems. These principles, derived from experience and refined over three decades, require validation and tuning for specific design domains. No list such as this can be complete, but it has been well received as a useful guide to students and designers. The Eight Golden Rules are:

1. *Strive for consistency.* Consistent sequences of actions should be required in similar situations; identical terminology should be used in prompts, menus, and help screens; and consistent color, layout, capitalization, fonts, and so on should be employed throughout. Exceptions, such as required confirmation of the delete command or no echoing of passwords, should be comprehensible and limited in number.

2. *Cater to universal usability.* Recognize the needs of diverse users and design for *plasticity*, facilitating transformation of content. Novice to expert differences, age ranges, disabilities, and technological diversity each enrich the spectrum of requirements that guides design. Adding features for novices, such as explanations, and features for experts, such as shortcuts and faster pacing, can enrich the interface design and improve perceived system quality.

3. *Offer informative feedback.* For every user action, there should be system feedback. For frequent and minor actions, the response can be modest, whereas for infrequent and major actions, the response should be more substantial. Visual presentation of the objects of interest provides a convenient environment for showing changes explicitly (see the discussion of direct manipulation in Chapter 5).

4. *Design dialogs to yield closure.* Sequences of actions should be organized into groups with a beginning, middle, and end. Informative feedback at the completion of a group of actions gives operators the satisfaction of accomplishment, a sense of relief, a signal to drop contingency plans from their minds, and an indicator to prepare for the next group of actions. For example, e-commerce web sites move users from selecting products to the checkout, ending with a clear confirmation page that completes the transaction.

5. *Prevent errors.* As much as possible, design the system such that users cannot make serious errors; for example, gray out menu items that are not appropriate and do not allow alphabetic characters in numeric entry fields (Section 2.3.5). If a user makes an error, the interface should detect the error and offer simple, constructive, and specific instructions for recovery. For example, users should not have to retype an entire name-address form if they enter an invalid zip code, but rather should be guided to repair only the faulty part. Erroneous actions should leave the system state unchanged, or the interface should give instructions about restoring the state.

6. *Permit easy reversal of actions*. As much as possible, actions should be reversible. This feature relieves anxiety, since the user knows that errors can be undone, and encourages exploration of unfamiliar options. The units of reversibility may be a single action, a data-entry task, or a complete group of actions, such as entry of a name-address block.

7. *Support internal locus of control*. Experienced users strongly desire the sense that they are in charge of the interface and that the interface responds to their actions. They don't want surprises or changes in familiar behavior, and they are annoyed by tedious data-entry sequences, difficulty in obtaining necessary information, and inability to produce their desired result.

8. *Reduce short-term memory load*. Humans' limited capacity for information processing in short-term memory (the rule of thumb is that we can remember "seven plus or minus two chunks" of information) requires that designers avoid interfaces in which users must remember information from one screen and then use that information on another screen. It means that cell phones should not require re-entry of phone numbers, web-site locations should remain visible, multiple-page displays should be consolidated, and sufficient training time should be allotted for complex sequences of actions.

These underlying principles must be interpreted, refined, and extended for each environment. They have their limitations, but they provide a good starting point for mobile, desktop, and web designers. The principles presented in the ensuing sections focus on increasing users' productivity by providing simplified data-entry procedures, comprehensible displays, and rapid informative feedback to increase feelings of competence, mastery, and control over the system.

2.3.5 Prevent errors

66 There is no medicine against death, and against error no rule has been found. 99

Sigmund Freud
(inscription he wrote on his portrait)

The importance of error prevention (the fifth golden rule) is so strong that it deserves its own section. Users of cell phones, e-mail, spreadsheets, air-traffic control systems, and other interactive systems make mistakes far more frequently than might be expected. Experienced analysts make errors in almost half their spreadsheets, even when the spreadsheets are used in making important business decisions (Panko, 2008).

One way to reduce the loss in productivity due to errors is to improve the error messages provided by the interface. Better error messages can raise success rates in repairing the errors, lower future error rates, and increase subjective satisfaction (Shneiderman, 1982). Superior error messages are more specific, positive in tone, and constructive (telling the user what to do, rather than merely reporting the problem). Rather than using vague ("?" or "What?") or hostile ("Illegal Operation" or "Syntax Error") messages, designers are encouraged to use informative messages, such as "Printer is off, please turn it on" or "Months range from 1 to 12".

Improved error messages, however, are only helpful medicine. A more effective approach is to prevent the errors from occurring. This goal is more attainable than it may seem in many interfaces.

The first step is to understand the nature of errors. One perspective is that people make mistakes or "slips" (Norman, 1983) that designers can help them to avoid by organizing screens and menus functionally, designing commands and menu choices to be distinctive, and making it difficult for users to take irreversible actions. Norman also offers other guidelines, such as providing feedback about the state of the interface (e.g., changing the cursor to show whether a map interface is in zoom-in or select mode) and designing for consistency of actions (e.g., ensuring that Yes/No buttons are always displayed in the same order). Norman's analysis provides practical examples and a useful theory. Additional design techniques to reduce errors include the following:

Correct actions. Industrial designers recognize that successful products must be safe and must prevent users from dangerously incorrect usage of the products. Airplane engines cannot be put into reverse until the landing gear has touched down, and cars cannot be put into reverse while traveling forward at faster than five miles per hour. Similar principles can be applied to interactive systems—for example, inappropriate menu items can be grayed out so they can't be inadvertently selected, and web users can be allowed to simply click on the date on a calendar instead of having to type in a month and day for a desired airline flight departure. Likewise, instead of having to enter a 10-digit phone number, cell phone users can scroll through a list of frequently or recently dialed numbers and select one with a single button press. Another option used by some systems, such as the Visual Basic® programming environment, is offering automatic command completion to reduce the likelihood of user errors: The user types the first few letters of a command and the computer completes it as soon as the input is sufficient to distinguish the command from others. Techniques such as these do some of the work for the user, thereby reducing opportunities for user errors.

Complete sequences. Sometimes an action requires several steps to reach completion. Since people may forget to complete every step of an action, designers may attempt to offer a sequence of steps as a single action. In an automobile, the driver does not have to set two switches to signal a left turn; a single switch causes both (front and rear) turn-signal lights on the left side of the car to flash. Likewise, when a pilot throws a switch to lower the landing gear, hundreds of mechanical steps and checks are invoked automatically. This same concept can be applied to interactive uses of computers.

As another example, users of a word processor can indicate that all section titles are to be centered, set in uppercase letters, and underlined, without having to issue a series of commands each time they enter a section title. Then, if users want to change the title style—for example, to eliminate underlining—a single command will guarantee that all section titles are revised consistently. As a final example, an air-traffic controller may formulate plans to change the altitude of a plane from 14,000 feet to 18,000 feet in two increments; after raising the plane to 16,000 feet, however, the controller may get distracted and fail to complete the action. The controller should be able to record the plan and then have the computer prompt for completion. The notion of complete sequences of actions may be difficult to implement because users may need to issue atomic actions as well as complete sequences. In this case, users should be allowed to define sequences of their own; the macro or subroutine concept should be available at every level of usage. Designers can gather information about potential complete sequences by studying sequences of commands that people actually issue and the patterns of errors that people actually make.

Thinking about universal usability also contributes to reducing errors—for example, a design with too many small buttons may cause unacceptably high error rates among older users or others with limited motor control, but enlarging the buttons will benefit all users. Section 4.6.2 addresses the idea of logging user errors so designers can continuously improve designs.

2.3.6 Ensuring human control while increasing automation

The guidelines and principles described in the previous sections are often devoted to simplifying the users' tasks. Users can then avoid routine, tedious, and error-prone actions and can concentrate on making critical decisions, coping with unexpected situations, and planning future actions (Sanders and McCormick, 1993). (Box 2.3 provides a detailed comparison of human and machine capabilities.)

The degree of automation increases over time as procedures become more standardized and the pressure for productivity grows. With routine tasks, automation is desirable, since it reduces the potential for errors and the users' workload. However, even with increased automation, designers can still offer the predictable and controllable interfaces that users usually prefer. The human supervisory role needs to be maintained because the real world is an *open system* (that is, a nondenumerable number of unpredictable events and system failures

BOX 2.3

Relative capabilities of humans and machines. *Sources*: Compiled from Brown, 1988; Sanders and McCormick, 1993.

Humans Generally Better	Machines Generally Better
Sense low-level stimuli	Sense stimuli outside human's range
Detect stimuli in noisy background	Count or measure physical quantities
Recognize constant patterns in varying situations	Store quantities of coded information accurately
Sense unusual and unexpected events	Monitor prespecified events, especially infrequent ones
Remember principles and strategies	Make rapid and consistent responses to input signals
Retrieve pertinent details without *a priori* connection	Recall quantities of detailed information accurately
Draw on experience and adapt decisions to situation	Process quantitative data in prespecified ways
Select alternatives if original approach fails	Reason deductively: infer from a general principle
Reason inductively: generalize from observations	Perform repetitive preprogrammed actions reliably
Act in unanticipated emergencies and novel situations	Exert great, highly controlled physical force
Apply principles to solve varied problems	Perform several activities simultaneously
Make subjective evaluations	Maintain operations under heavy information load
Develop new solutions	Maintain performance over extended periods of time
Concentrate on important tasks when overload occurs	
Adapt physical response to changes in situation	

are possible). By contrast, computers constitute a *closed system* (only a denumerable number of normal and failure situations can be accommodated in hardware and software). Human judgment is necessary for the unpredictable events in which some action must be taken to preserve safety, to avoid expensive failures, or to increase product quality (Hancock and Scallen, 1996).

For example, in air-traffic control, common actions include changes to a plane's altitude, heading, or speed. These actions are well understood and potentially can be automated by a scheduling and route-allocation algorithm, but the controllers must be present to deal with the highly variable and unpredictable emergency situations. An automated system might deal successfully with high volumes of traffic, but what would happen if the airport manager closed runways because of turbulent weather? The controllers would have to reroute planes quickly. Now suppose that one pilot requests clearance for an emergency landing because of a failed engine, while another pilot reports a passenger with chest pains who needs prompt medical attention. Human judgment is necessary to decide which plane should land first, and how much costly and risky diversion of normal traffic is appropriate. Air-traffic controllers cannot just jump into an emergency; they must be intensely involved in the situation as it develops if they are to make informed and rapid decisions. In short, many real-world situations are so complex that it is impossible to anticipate and program for every contingency; human judgment and values are necessary in the decision-making process.

Another example of the complexity of life-critical situations in air-traffic control was illustrated by an incident on a plane that had a fire on board. The controller cleared other traffic from the flight path and began to guide the plane in for a landing, but the smoke was so thick that the pilot had trouble reading his instruments. Then the onboard transponder burned out, so the air-traffic controller could no longer read the plane's altitude from the situation display. In spite of these multiple failures, the controller and the pilot managed to bring down the plane quickly enough to save the lives of many—but not all—of the passengers. A computer could not have been programmed to deal with this particular unexpected series of events.

A tragic outcome of excess of automation occurred during a flight to Cali, Colombia. The pilots relied on the automatic pilot and failed to realize that the plane was making a wide turn to return to a location that they had already passed. When the ground-collision alarm sounded, the pilots were too disoriented to pull up in time; they crashed 200 feet below a mountain peak, killing all but four people on board.

The goal of system design in many applications is to give operators sufficient information about current status and activities to ensure that, when intervention is necessary, they have the knowledge and the capacity to perform correctly, even under partial failures (Sheridan, 1997; Billings, 1997). The U.S. Federal Aviation Agency stresses that designs should place the user in control and automate only to "improve system performance, without reducing human involvement" (FAA, 2007). These standards also encourage managers to "train users when to question automation."

The entire system must be designed and tested, not only for normal situations, but also for as wide a range of anomalous situations as can be anticipated. An extensive set of test conditions might be included as part of the requirements document. Operators need to have enough information that they can take responsibility for their actions. Beyond supervision of decision making and handling of failures, the role of the human operator is to improve the design of the system.

Questions about integrating automation with human control also emerge in systems for home and office automation. Many designers are eager to create an autonomous agent that knows people's likes and dislikes, makes proper inferences, responds to novel situations, and performs competently with little guidance. They believe that human-human interaction is a good model for human-computer interaction, and they seek to create computer-based partners, assistants, or agents (Berners-Lee et al., 2001).

The controversy is over whether to create tool-like interfaces or to pursue autonomous, adaptive, or anthropomorphic agents that carry out the users' intents and anticipate needs (Gratch et al., 2002). The agent scenarios often show a responsive, butler-like human—like the bow-tied, helpful young man in Apple Computer's famous 1987 video on the *Knowledge Navigator*. Microsoft's 1995 BOB program, which used cartoon characters to create onscreen partners, was unsuccessful; its much-criticized Clippit, nicknamed Clippy, character was also withdrawn. Web-based characters to read the news, such as Ananova™, have also faded to obscurity (although the news site itself is still operational). On the other hand, avatars representing users, not computers, in game-playing and three-dimensional social environments (for example, *Second Life*) have remained popular; users appear to enjoy the theatrical experience of creating a new identity with sometimes exotic appearances (Section 5.6).

To succeed with anthropomorphic representations of computers (Section 11.3), promoters will have to understand and overcome the history of their unsuccessful application in the products just mentioned, as well as in bank terminals, computer-assisted instruction, talking cars, and postal-service stations. Hopeful scenarios include anthropomorphic pedagogical agents whose talking faces instruct, respond to, or guide students using natural-language interaction (D'Mello et al., 2007). The voice instruction may be helpful, but there is less evidence of the benefit of a talking face (Moreno and Mayer, 2007; Section 7.6.5).

A variant of the agent scenario, which does not include an anthropomorphic realization, is that the computer employs a *user model* to guide an adaptive interface. The system keeps track of user performance and adapts the interface to suit the users' needs. For example, when users begin to make menu selections rapidly, indicating proficiency, advanced menu items may appear. Automatic adaptations have been proposed for interface features such as the content of menus, order of menu items (Section 6.5.2), type of feedback (graphic or tabular), and content of help screens. Advocates point to video games that increase the speed or number of dangers as users progress though stages of the game. However, games are notably different from most work situations, where users have goals and motivations to accomplish their tasks.

There are some opportunities for adaptive user models to tailor system designs (such as for e-mail spam filters or Google search results ranking), but even occasional unexpected behavior can have serious negative effects that discourage use. If adaptive systems make surprising changes, users must pause to see what has happened. They may then become anxious, because they may not be able to predict the next change, interpret what has happened, or restore the system to the previous state. Consulting users before a change is made might be helpful, but such intrusions may still disrupt problem-solving processes and annoy users. Empirical evidence has begun to clarify that the more acceptable direction to take is user-controlled content adaptation, such as allowing users to specify that more sports stories be shown in a newspaper web site (Kobsa, 2004).

An extension of user modeling is the notion of recommender systems or collaborative filtering in distributed World Wide Web applications. In this case, there is no agent or adaptation in the interface, but the system aggregates information from multiple sources in some (often proprietary) way. Such approaches have great entertainment and practical value for uses such as selecting movies, books, or music; users are often intrigued and amused to see what suggestions emerge from aggregated patterns of preferences or purchases (Konstan and Riedl, 2003). Amazon.com has shown success by suggesting to users that "customers who bought X also bought Y."

FIGURE 2.2

Mac OS X system preferences for Universal Access features which allow options to help vision-impaired users to see or hear what is on the screen. Zoom can magnify the contents of the screen, and the White on Black option gives the display higher contrast. The system can speak selected text and text underneath the mouse, and speech recognition allows users to launch applications as well as to execute application commands by simply speaking.

The philosophical alternative to agents and user modeling is to design comprehensible systems that provide consistent interfaces, user control, and predictable behavior. Designers who emphasize a direct-manipulation style believe that users have a strong desire to be in control and to gain mastery over the system, which allows them to accept responsibility for their actions and derive feelings of accomplishment (Shneiderman, 2007). Historical evidence suggests that users seek comprehensible and predictable systems and shy away from those that are complex or unpredictable; for example, pilots may disengage automatic piloting devices if they perceive that these systems are not performing as they expect.

Another resolution of the controversy is to accept user control at the interface, but consider agent-like or multi-agent programming to automate internal processes such as disk-space allocation or network routing based on current loads. However, these are adaptations based on system features, not user profiles.

Agent advocates promote autonomy, but this means they must take on the issue of responsibility for failures. Who is responsible when an agent violates copyright, invades privacy, or destroys data? Agent designs might be better received if they supported performance monitoring while allowing users to examine and revise the current user model.

An alternative to agents with user models may be to expand the control-panel model. Computer control panels, like automobile cruise-control mechanisms and television remote controls, are designed to convey the sense of control that users seem to expect. Users employ control panels to set physical parameters, such as the cursor blinking speed or speaker volume, and to establish personal preferences such as time/date formats or color schemes (Figs. 2.2 and 2.3). Some software packages allow users to set parameters such as the speed of play in games. Users start at layer 1 and can then choose when to progress to higher

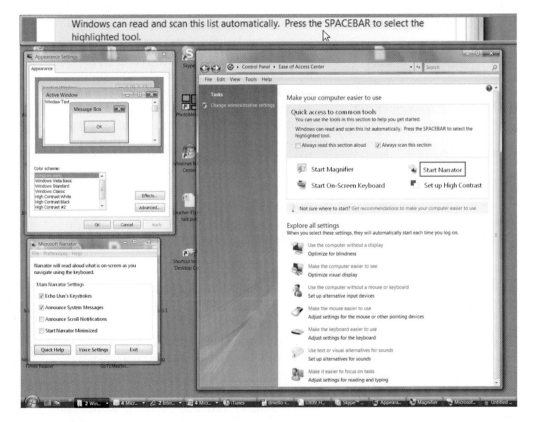

FIGURE 2.3

Microsoft Windows Vista Control Panel showing the Appearance Setting dialog box (upper left), the Narrator (lower left), and the Ease of Access Center with a screen magnifier and other features to help users with disabilities.

levels; often they are content remaining experts at layer 1 of a complex interface rather than dealing with the uncertainties of higher layers. More elaborate control panels exist in style sheets of word processors, specification boxes of query facilities, and information-visualization tools. Similarly, scheduling software may have elaborate controls to allow users to execute planned procedures at regular intervals or when triggered by events.

2.4 Theories

One goal for the discipline of human-computer interaction is to go beyond the specifics of guidelines and build on the breadth of principles to develop tested, reliable, and broadly useful *theories*. Of course, for a topic as large as user-interface design, many theories are needed.

Some theories are *descriptive*; these are helpful in developing consistent terminology for objects and actions, thereby supporting collaboration and training. Other theories are *explanatory*, describing sequences of events and, where possible, cause and effect, making interventions possible. Still other theories are *prescriptive*, giving designers clear guidance for their choices. Finally, the most precise theories are *predictive*, enabling designers to compare proposed designs for execution time, error rates, conversion rates, or trust levels.

Another way to group theories is according to the types of skills involved, such as *motor* (pointing with a mouse), *perceptual* (finding an item on a display), or *cognitive* (planning the sequence of steps needed to pay a bill) skills. Motor skill performance predictions are well established and accurate for predicting keystroking or pointing times (see Fitts's Law, Section 8.3.5). Perceptual theories have been successful in predicting reading times for free text, lists, formatted displays, and other visual or auditory tasks. Cognitive theories, involving short-term, working, and long-term memory, are central to problem solving and play a key role in understanding productivity as a function of response time (Chapter 10). However, predicting performance on complex cognitive tasks (combinations of subtasks) is especially difficult because of the many strategies that might be employed and the many opportunities for going astray. The ratio of times required to perform complex tasks between novices and experts or between first-time and frequent users can be as high as 100 to 1. Actually, the contrast is even more dramatic, because novices and first-time users often are unable to complete the tasks.

Web designers have emphasized information-architecture theories with navigation as the key to user success. Web users can be considered as *foraging* for information, and therefore the effectiveness of the *information scent* of links is the issue (Pirolli, 2003). A high-quality link, relative to a specific task, gives users a good scent (or indication) of what is at the destination. For example, if users are trying to find an executable demonstration of a software package, a link with the text "download demo" has a good scent. The challenge to designers is to understand user tasks well enough to design a large web site such that users will be able to find their way successfully from a home page to the right destination, even if it is three or four clicks away. Information-foraging theory attempts to predict user success rates given a set of tasks and a web site, so as to guide refinements.

Taxonomies can be an important part of descriptive and explanatory theories. A taxonomy imposes order by classifying a complex set of phenomena into understandable categories. For example, a taxonomy might be created for different kinds of input devices: direct versus indirect, linear versus rotary, 1-, 2-, 3- or higher-dimensional, and so on (Card et al., 1990). Other taxonomies might cover tasks (structured versus unstructured, novel versus regular) or user-interface styles (menus, form fill-in, commands). An important class of taxonomies (Norman, 2008) has to do with the individual differences among users, such as personality styles (convergent versus divergent, field-dependent versus independent), technical aptitudes (spatial visualization, reasoning), and user experience levels (novice, knowledgeable, expert). Taxonomies facilitate useful comparisons, organize topics for newcomers, guide designers, and often indicate opportunities for novel products—for example, a task by type taxonomy organizes the information visualizations in Chapter 14.

Any theory that might help designers to predict performance for even a limited range of users, tasks, or designs is a contribution. At the moment, the field is filled with hundreds of theories competing for attention while being refined by their promoters, extended by critics, and applied by eager and hopeful—but skeptical—designers (Carroll, 2003). This development is healthy for the emerging discipline of human-computer interaction, but it means that practitioners must keep up with the rapid developments not only in software tools and design guidelines, but also in theories. Critics raise two challenges:

- *Theories should be more central to research and practice.* A good theory should guide researchers in understanding relationships between concepts and generalizing results. It should also guide practitioners when making design tradeoffs for products. The power of theories to shape design is most apparent in focused theories such as GOMS (described in Section 2.4.1) or Fitts's Law; it is more difficult to demonstrate for explanatory theories, whose main impact may be in educating the next generation of designers or guiding research.

- *Theories should lead rather than lag behind practice.* Critics remark that too often a theory is used to explain what has been produced by commercial product designers. A robust theory should predict or at least guide practitioners in designing new products. Effective theories should suggest novel products and help refine existing ones.

Another direction for theoreticians is to predict the subjective satisfaction or emotional reactions of users. Researchers in media and advertising have recognized the difficulty of predicting emotional reactions, so they complement theoretical predictions with their intuitive judgments and extensive market testing (Nahl and Bilal, 2007).

Broader theories of small-group behavior, organizational dynamics, and sociology are proving to be useful in understanding social media and collaborative interfaces (Chapter 9). Similarly, the methods of anthropology or social psychology may be helpful in understanding technology adoption and overcoming barriers to new technology that cause resistance to change.

There may be "nothing so practical as a good theory," but coming up with an effective theory is often difficult. By definition, a theory, taxonomy, or model is an abstraction of reality and therefore must be incomplete. However, a good theory should at least be understandable, produce similar conclusions for all who use it, and help to solve specific practical problems. This section reviews a range of descriptive and explanatory theories.

2.4.1 Design-by-levels

One approach to developing descriptive theories is to separate concepts according to levels. Such theories have been helpful in software engineering and network design. An appealing and easily comprehensible model for interfaces is the four-level conceptual, semantic, syntactic, and lexical model (Foley et al., 1995):

1. The *conceptual level* is the user's "mental model" of the interactive system. Two mental models for image creation are paint programs that manipulate pixels and drawing programs that operate on objects. Users of paint programs think in terms of sequences of actions on pixels and groups of pixels, while users of drawing programs think in terms of sequences of actions on objects and groups of objects. Decisions about mental models affect each of the lower levels.

2. The *semantic level* describes the meanings conveyed by the user's input and by the computer's output display. For example, deleting an object in a drawing program could be accomplished by undoing a recent action or by invoking a delete-object action. Either action should eliminate only a single object and leave the rest untouched.

3. The *syntactic level* defines how the user actions that convey semantics are assembled into complete sentences that instruct the computer to perform certain tasks. For example, the delete-files action could be invoked by dragging an object to a trash can, followed by a click in a confirmation dialog box.

4. The *lexical level* deals with device dependencies and with the precise mechanisms by which users specify the syntax (for example, a function key or a mouse double-click within 200 milliseconds).

This four-level approach is convenient for designers because its top-down nature is easy to explain, matches the software architecture, and allows for useful modularity during design. Over the years, the success of graphical direct-manipulation interfaces has shifted attention up to the conceptual level, which is closest to the task domain. For example, designers of personal financial interfaces have shifted from using command-line interfaces to direct-manipulation interfaces. These interfaces build on the users' mental model of writing checks by showing the image of a check for users to fill in. The same image of a check serves as the query template, so users can specify dates, payees, or amounts.

The check is a natural object to show users, but actions can be given visual representations as well (for example, a trash can for deletion or a play button to start playing a video). Users have to learn the semantics (e.g., that they can recover a file by opening up the trash can or stop a video by clicking on the pause button), but if the designers choose familiar objects to associate with the actions, users can quickly acquire the correct mental model for operating the user interface. Of course, users also have to learn the syntax of dragging objects or clicking to initiate the actions, but these mechanisms are commonly used and have become well known.

The idea of design-by-levels is successful even in more complex systems with many objects and actions. For example, the human body can be discussed in terms of neural, muscular, skeletal, reproductive, digestive, circulatory, and other subsystems, which in turn might be described in terms of organs, tissues, and cells. Most real-world objects have similar decompositions: buildings into floors, floors into rooms, rooms into doors/walls/windows, and so on. Similarly, movies can be decomposed into scenes, scenes into shots, and shots into dialog, images, and sounds. Since most objects can be decomposed in many ways, the designer's job is to create comprehensible and memorable levels of objects.

In parallel with the decomposition of objects, designers need to decompose complex actions into several smaller actions. For example, a baseball game has innings, pitches, runs, and outs, and a building-construction plan can be reduced to a series of steps such as surveying the property, laying the foundation, building the frame, raising the roof, and completing the interior. Most actions can also be decomposed in many ways, so again the designer's job here is to create comprehensible and memorable levels of actions. The goal of simplifying interface concepts while presenting visual representations of the objects and actions involved is at the heart of the direct-manipulation approach to design (Chapter 5).

When a complete user-interface design has been made, the user tasks can be described by series of actions. These precise descriptions can serve as a basis for predicting the time required to perform tasks, by simply counting up the number of milliseconds needed to complete all the steps. For example, resizing a photo may require several mouse drags, selections of menu items, clicks on dialog box buttons, and typing of dimensions, but each of these actions takes a predictable amount of time. Several researchers have successfully predicted the time required for complex tasks by adding up the times required for each component action. This predictive approach, based on *goals, operators, methods,* and *selection rules* (GOMS), decomposes goals into many operators (actions), and then into methods. Users apply selection rules to choose among alternate methods for achieving goals (Card, et al., 1983; Baumeister, et al., 2000).

The GOMS approach works best when the users are expert and frequent users who are fully focused on the task and make no mistakes. Advocates of GOMS have developed software tools to simplify and speed up the modeling process in the hope of increasing usage (John et al., 2004). Critics complain that broader theories are needed to predict novice user behavior, the transition to proficiency, the rate of errors, performance under stress, and retention over time.

Designers can apply design-by-level strategies by starting with clear definitions of the high-level objects and actions, which are taken from language used in the task domain. Music can be thought of as songs, organized by artists, albums, and genres. Users can find a song, then play it, or add it to a playlist. The clarity of this conceptual structure earned it a patent and has stimulated multiple commercial successes.

Applying the GOMS approach might enable designers to choose between alternate designs by predicting performance times for expert users carrying out benchmark tasks. But of course, there is much more to do with regard to designing the semantics of these concepts, the visual displays (with comprehensible controls), and the syntax of how the actions are carried out.

2.4.2 Stages-of-action models

Another approach to forming explanatory theories is to portray the stages of action that users go through in trying to use interactive products such as information appliances, web interfaces, or mobile devices (e.g., music players). Norman (1988) offers seven stages of action, arranged in a cyclic pattern, as an explanatory model of human-computer interaction:

1. Forming the goal
2. Forming the intention
3. Specifying the action
4. Executing the action
5. Perceiving the system state

6. Interpreting the system state

7. Evaluating the outcome

Some of Norman's stages correspond roughly to Foley et al.'s (1995) separation of concerns; that is, the user forms a conceptual intention, reformulates it into the semantics of several commands, constructs the required syntax, and eventually produces the lexical token by the action of moving the mouse to select a point on the screen. Norman makes a contribution by placing his stages in the context of *cycles of action* and *evaluation*. This dynamic process of action distinguishes Norman's approach from the other models, which deal mainly with knowledge that must be in the user's mind. Furthermore, the seven-stages model leads naturally to identification of the *gulf of execution* (the mismatch between the user's intentions and the allowable actions) and the *gulf of evaluation* (the mismatch between the system's representation and the user's expectations).

This model leads Norman to suggest four principles of good design. First, the state and the action alternatives should be visible. Second, there should be a good conceptual model with a consistent system image. Third, the interface should include good mappings that reveal the relationships between stages. Fourth, users should receive continuous feedback. Norman places a heavy emphasis on studying errors, describing how errors often occur in moving from goals to intentions to actions and to executions.

A stages-of-action model helps us to describe user exploration of an interface (Polson and Lewis, 1990). As users try to accomplish their goals, there are four critical points where user failures can occur: (1) users may form inadequate goals, (2) users might not find the correct interface object because of an incomprehensible label or icon, (3) users may not know how to specify or execute a desired action, and (4) users may receive inappropriate or misleading feedback. The latter three failures may be prevented by improved design or overcome by time-consuming experience with the interface (Franzke, 1995).

Refinements of the stages-of-action model have been developed for other domains. For example, information-seeking has been characterized by these stages: (1) recognize, (2) accept the information problem, (3) formulate and (4) express the query, then (5) examine the results, (6) reformulate the problem, and (7) use the results (Marchionini and White, 2007). Of course, there are variations with users skipping stages or going back to earlier stages, but the model helps guide designers and users.

Commercial web-site designers know the benefit of a clear stages-of-action model in guiding anxious users through a complex process. The Amazon.com web site converts the potentially confusing checkout process into a comprehensible four-stage process: (1) Sign-in, (2) Shipping & Payment, (3) Gift-Wrap, and (4) Place Order. Users can simply move through these four stages or back up to previous stages to make changes.

Participants in online communities and user-generated content sites also move through stages as they gain confidence and a greater sense of responsibility for quality. There are many paths, but a study of Wikipedia contributors (Bryant et al., 2005) suggests at least these stages: (1) reader of articles related to personal interests, (2) fixer of mistakes and omissions in familiar topics, (3) registered user and caretaker for collection of articles, (4) author for new articles, (5) participant in community of authors, and (6) administrator who is active in governance and future directions.

Designers can apply stages-of-action models by thinking deeply about the beginning, middle, and end stages to ensure that they cover a wide enough scope of usage. Many new products emerge as a result of adding novel features to what was considered a well-defined process; for example, expanding the music-playing process to include the earlier stages of music purchase or composition and the later stages of music sharing or reviewing/rating.

2.4.3 Consistency

An important goal for designers is a *consistent* user interface. The argument for consistency is that if terminology for objects and actions is orderly and describable by a few rules, users will be able to learn and retain them easily. This example illustrates consistency and two kinds of inconsistency (**A** illustrates lack of consistency, and **B** shows consistency except for a single violation):

Consistent	Inconsistent A	Inconsistent B
delete/insert table	delete/insert table	delete/insert table
delete/insert column	remove/add column	remove/insert column
delete/insert row	destroy/create row	delete/insert row
delete/insert border	erase/draw border	delete/insert border

Each of the actions in the consistent version is the same, whereas the actions vary for inconsistent version A. The inconsistent action verbs are all acceptable, but their variety suggests that they will take longer to learn, will cause more errors, will slow down users, and will be harder for users to remember. Inconsistent version B is somehow more startling, because there is a single unpredictable inconsistency; it stands out so dramatically that this language is likely to be remembered for its peculiar inconsistency.

Consistency for objects and actions is a good starting point, but there are many other forms of consistency that require careful thought by designers. Consistent use of color, layout, icons, fonts, font sizes, button sizes, and much more is vital in giving users a clear understanding of the interface. Inconsistency in elements such as the positioning of buttons or colors will slow users down by 5–10%, while changes to terminology slow users by 20–25%.

Consistency is an important goal, but there may be conflicting forms of consistency, and sometimes inconsistency is a virtue (for example, to draw attention to a dangerous operation). Competing forms of consistency require designers to make difficult choices or invent new strategies. For example, while automobile interface designers have agreed to always place the accelerator pedal to the right of the brake pedal, there's no agreement about whether turn signal controls should be to the right or left of the steering wheel.

Consistency issues are critical in the design of mobile devices. In successful products, users get accustomed to consistent patterns, such as initiating actions with a left-side button while terminating actions with a right-side button. Similarly, up and down scrolling actions should be done consistently using buttons that are vertically aligned. A frequent problem is the inconsistent placement of the Q and Z characters on phone buttons.

Designers can enforce consistency by developing detailed guidelines documents for their designs (Section 3.3.2) that spell out all of the consistency requirements. Expert reviewers of user interfaces can then verify the consistency of the design. This requires a careful eye and thoughtful attention to how each screen is laid out, each action sequence is carried out, and each sound is played.

2.4.4 Contextual theories

While the scientific methods of experimental and cognitive psychology were a profound influence on early work in human-computer interaction, a growing awareness of the special needs of this new discipline led to the rise of alternative theories. Complaints against tightly controlled laboratory studies of isolated phenomena were raised by researchers and practitioners. Investigators of workplace and home computing identified the critical role of users' complex interactions with other people, electronic devices, and paper resources. For example, successful users of interfaces often have colleagues nearby that they can ask for help, or require diverse documents to complete their tasks. Unexpected interruptions are a regular part of life, and sticky notes attached to the sides of computer monitors are often consulted for vital information. In short, the physical and social environments are inextricably intertwined with use of information and communications technologies. Design cannot be separated from patterns of use.

Suchman's (1987) analysis in her book *Plans and Situated Action* is often credited with launching this reconsideration of human-computer interaction. She argued that the cognitive model of orderly human plans that were executed when needed was insufficient to describe the richer and livelier world of work or personal usage. She proposed that users' actions were situated in time and place, making user behavior highly responsive to other people and to environmental contingencies. If users got stuck in using an interface, they might ask for help, depending on who was around, or consult a manual, if one were available. If they were pressed for time they might risk some shortcuts, but if the work was life-critical they would be extra cautious. Rather than having fixed plans, users constantly changed their plans in response to the circumstances. The argument of distributed cognition is that knowledge is not only in the users' minds, but distributed in their environments—some knowledge is stored on paper documents, while other knowledge is maintained by computers or available from colleagues.

Physical space was an important consideration for those who began to think more about ubiquitous, pervasive, and embedded devices. However, they sought to shift attention from "place" to "space," implying that the social/psychological space had to be considered in addition to the physical place (Dourish, 2001). These notions are likely to become still more important as varied sensors become more common. Sensors to activate doors in supermarkets or faucets and hand-dryers in bathrooms are first steps, but newer sensors that detect and monitor human activity seem likely to proliferate. The goals of these developments are often positive (e.g., safety, security, or healthcare), but threats to privacy, dangers of errors, and the need to preserve human control will have to be considered carefully.

Alternative models of technological use emphasize the social environment, the motivations of users, or the role of experience. Innovators believe that the turbulence of actual usage (as opposed to idealized task specifications) means that users have to be more than test subjects—they have to be participants in design processes (Greenbaum and Kyng, 1991). Breakdowns are often seen as sources of insight about design, and users are encouraged to become reflective practitioners who are continuously engaged in the process of design refinement. Understanding the transition from novice to expert and the differences in skill levels has become a focus of attention, further calling into question the utility of hour-long laboratory or half-day usability-testing studies as a guide to the behavior of users after a month or more of experience. These movements encourage greater attention to detailed ethnographic observation, longitudinal case studies, and action research by participant observers (Nardi, 1997; Redmiles, 2002).

Contextual theories are especially relevant to mobile devices and ubiquitous computing innovations. Such devices are portable or installed in a physical space, and they are often designed specifically to provide place-specific information (for example, a city guide on a portable computer or a museum guide that gives information on a nearby painting). A taxonomy of mobile device applications could guide innovators:

- *Monitor* blood pressure, stock prices, or air quality and give *alerts* when normal ranges are exceeded.

- *Gather* information from meeting attendees or rescue team members and *spread* the action list or current status to all.

- *Participate* in a large group activity by voting and *relate* to specific individuals by sending private messages.

- *Locate* the nearest restaurant or waterfall and *identify* the details of the current location.

- *Capture* information or photos left by others and *share* yours with future visitors.

These five pairs of actions could be tied to a variety of objects (such as photos, annotations, or documents), suggesting new mobile devices and services. They also suggest that one way of thinking about user interfaces is by way of the objects that users encounter and the actions that they take. A more ambitious use of mobile devices might be to aggregate information from thousands of cell-phones to determine where there is highway congestion or which rides at an amusement park have the longest waiting lines.

Designers can apply contextual theories by observing users in their own environments as they carry out their work, engage socially, or participate in sports or play. A detailed record of how tasks are chosen and carried out, including collaborations with others, internal or external interruptions, and errors that occur would lay the basis for interface design. Contextual theories are about how people form intentions, how aspirations crystalize, how empathy is encouraged, and how trust shapes behavior; they are also about emotional states of excitement or frustration, the joy of attaining goals, and the disappointment of failure. These strong reactions are hard to capture in predictive mathematical equations, but it is important to study and understand them. To that end, many researchers are shifting their methods from controlled experiments to ethnographic observation, focus group discussions, and long-term case studies. Survey and interview data can provide quantitative data for much-needed theories of how design variables affect users' levels of satisfaction, fear, trust, and cooperativeness.

Practitioner's Summary

Design principles and guidelines are emerging from practical experience and empirical studies. Managers can benefit by reviewing available guidelines documents and then constructing local versions. These documents record organizational policies, support consistency, and record the results of practical and experimental testing. Guidelines documents also stimulate discussion of user-interface issues and help train new designers. More established principles—such as recognizing user diversity, striving for consistency, and preventing errors—have become widely accepted, but they require fresh interpretation as technology and applications evolve. Automation is increasing for many tasks, but preserving human control is still a beneficial goal.

In spite of the growing set of guidelines, principles, and theories, user-interface design is a complex and highly creative process. Successful designers begin with thorough requirements, task analysis, and specifications of the user communities. For expert users with established sequences of actions, predictive models that guide designers to reduce the time required for each step are valuable. For novel applications and novice users, focusing on task objects and actions (for example, songs and albums that can be played or added to playlists) can lead to easily learned designs that promote user confidence. For every design, extensive testing and iterative refinement are necessary parts of the development process.

Researcher's Agenda

The central problem for human-computer–interaction researchers is developing adequate theories and models. Traditional psychological theories must be extended and refined to accommodate the complex human learning, memory, and problem solving required in user interfaces. Useful goals include descriptive taxonomies, explanatory theories, and predictive models. When predictions can be made for learning times, performance speeds, error rates, subjective satisfaction, or human retention over time, designers can more easily choose among competing designs.

Theories in human-computer interaction can be grouped into four families: those that focus on design by levels, stages of action, consistency, and contextual awareness. Theories can be useful even if they are narrowly focused on a specific task, such as choosing a video from a database of a million videos, and a specific user, such as a proficient teenaged female. However, theories become more valuable when they apply to a wider range of tasks, such as any selection task, and to a wider range of users. Even more powerful are theories that apply to diverse tasks such as e-mailing, web searching, or cell phone data entry. Applied research problems are suggested by each of the hundreds of design principles or guidelines that have been proposed. Each validation of these principles and clarification of the breadth of applicability is a small but useful contribution to the emerging mosaic of human performance with interactive systems.

```
WORLD WIDE WEB RESOURCES
http://www.aw.com/DTUI/
```

Many web sites include guidelines documents for desktop, web, and mobile device interfaces and recommendations for universal usability strategies to accommodate users with disabilities or other special needs. Theories are proliferating, and the Web is a good place to keep up with the latest ones. Debates over hot topics can be found in relevant blogs and newsgroups, which are searchable from many standard services such as Yahoo! or Google.

References

Anderson, J. R. and Lebiere, C., *The Atomic Components of Thought*, Lawrence Erlbaum Associates, Mahwah, NJ (1998).

Bailey, Robert W., *Human Performance Engineering: Using Human Factors/Ergonomics to Achieve Computer Usability, Third Edition*, Prentice-Hall, Englewood Cliffs, NJ (1996).

Baumeister, L., John, B. E., and Byrne, M., A comparison of tools for building GOMS models, *Proc. CHI 2000 Conference: Human Factors in Computing Systems*, ACM Press, New York (2000), 502–509.

Berners-Lee, Tim, Hendler, James, and Lassila, Ora, Semantic web, *Scientific American* 284, 5 (May 2001).

Billings, Charles E., *Animation Automation: The Search for a Human-Centered Approach*, Lawrence Erlbaum Associates, Hillsdale, NJ (1997).

Bridger, R. S., *Introduction to Ergonomics*, McGraw-Hill, New York (1995).

Brown, C. Marlin, *Human-Computer Interface Design Guidelines*, Ablex, Norwood, NJ (1988).

Bryant, Susan, Forte, Andrea, and Bruckman, Amy, Becoming Wikipedian: Transformation of participation in a collaborative online encyclopedia, *Proc. ACM SIGGROUP International Conference on Supporting Group Work*, ACM Press, New York (2005), 1–10.

Card, Stuart K., Mackinlay, Jock D., and Robertson, George G., The design space of input devices, *Proc. CHI '90 Conference: Human Factors in Computing Systems*, ACM Press, New York (1990), 117–124.

Card, Stuart, Moran, Thomas P., and Newell, Allen, *The Psychology of Human-Computer Interaction*, Lawrence Erlbaum Associates, Hillsdale, NJ (1983).

Carroll, John M. (Editor), *HCI Models, Theories, and Frameworks: Toward a Multidisciplinary Science*, Morgan Kaufmann, San Francisco, CA (2003).

D'Mello, Sidney, Picard, Rosalind, and Graesser, Arthur, Toward an affect-sensitive AutoTutor, *IEEE Intelligent Systems, 22* (2007), 53–61.

Dourish, Paul, *Where the Action Is: The Foundations of Embodied Interaction*, MIT Press, Cambridge, MA (2001).

Federal Aviation Administration, *The Human Factors Design Standard*, Atlantic City, NJ (updated 2007). Available at   http://acb220.tc.faa.gov/hfds/.

Foley, James D., van Dam, Andries, Feiner, Steven K., and Hughes, John F., *Computer Graphics: Principles and Practice in C, Second Edition*, Addison-Wesley, Reading, MA (1995).

Franzke, Marita, Turning research into practice: Characteristics of display-based interaction, *Proc. CHI '95 Conference: Human Factors in Computing Systems*, ACM Press, New York (1995), 421–428.

Galitz, Wilbert O., *The Essential Guide to User Interface Design: An Introduction to GUI Design Principles and Techniques, Third Edition*, John Wiley & Sons, New York (2007).

Gilbert, Steven W., Information technology, intellectual property, and education, *EDUCOM Review* 25 (1990), 14–20.

Graesser, Arthur C., VanLehn, Kurt, Rose, Carolyn P., Jordan, Pamela W., and Harter, Derek, Intelligent tutoring systems with conversational dialogue, *AI Magazine* 22, 4 (Winter 2001), 39–52.

Gratch, J., Rickel, J., Andre, E., Badler, N., Cassell, J., and Petajan, E., Creating interactive virtual humans: Some assembly required, *IEEE Intelligent Systems* 17, 4 (2002), 54–63.

Greenbaum, Joan and Kyng, Morten, *Design at Work: Cooperative Design of Computer Systems*, Lawrence Erlbaum Associates, Hillsdale, NJ (1991).

Hackos, JoAnn T. and Redish, Janice C., *User and Task Analysis for Interface Design*, John Wiley & Sons, New York (1998).

Hancock, P. A. and Scallen, S. F., The future of function allocation, *Ergonomics in Design* 4, 4 (October 1996), 24–29.

John, B. E., Prevas, K., Salvucci, D. D., and Koedinger, K., Predictive human performance modeling made easy, *Proc. CHI 2004 Conference: Human Factors in Computing Systems*, ACM Press, New York (2004), 455–462.

John, Bonnie and Kieras, David E., Using GOMS for user interface design and evaluation: Which technique?, *ACM Transactions on Computer-Human Interaction* 3, 4 (December 1996a), 287–319.

John, Bonnie and Kieras, David E., The GOMS family of user interface analysis techniques: Comparison and contrast, *ACM Transactions on Computer-Human Interaction* 3, 4 (December 1996b), 320–351.

Kobsa, Alfred, Adaptive interfaces, in Bainbridge, W. S. (Editor), *Encyclopedia of Human-Computer Interaction*, Berkshire Publishing, Great Barrington, MA (2004).

Konstan, Jospeh and Riedl, John, *Word of Mouse: The Marketing Power of Collaborative Filtering*, TimeWarner, New York (2003).

Lockheed Missiles and Space Company, *Human Factors Review of Electric Power Dispatch Control Centers, Volume 2: Detailed Survey Results*, (prepared for) Electric Power Research Institute, Palo Alto, CA (1981).

Lynch, Patrick J. and Horton, Sarah, *Web Style Guide: Basic Design Principles for Creating Web Sites, Third Edition*, Yale University Press, New Haven, CT (2008).

Marchionini, G. and White, R. W., Find what you need, understand what you find, *International Journal of Human-Computer Interaction* 23, 3 (2007), 205–237.

McGrenere, Joanna, Baecker, Ronald M., and Booth, Kellogg S., A field evaluation of an adaptable two-interface design for feature-rich software, *ACM Trans. on Computer-Human Interaction* 14, 1 (May 2007), Article 3.

Moreno, R. and Mayer, R. E., Interactive multimodal learning environments, *Educational Psychology Review* 19 (2007), 309–326.

Mullet, Kevin and Sano, Darrell, *Designing Visual Interfaces: Communication Oriented Techniques*, Sunsoft Press, Englewood Cliffs, NJ (1995).

Nahl, Diane and Bilal, Dania (Editors), *Information and Emotion: The Emergent Affective Paradigm in Information Behavior Research and Theory*, Information Today, Medford, NJ (2007).

Nardi, Bonnie A., *Context and Consciousness: Activity Theory and Human-Computer Interaction*, MIT Press, Cambridge, MA (1997).

National Cancer Institute, *Research-based Web Design and Usability Guidelines*, Dept of Health & Human Services, National Institutes of Health (updated edition 2006).

National Research Council, *Intellectual Property Issues in Software*, National Academy Press, Washington, DC (1991).

Norman, Donald A., Design rules based on analyses of human error, *Communications of the ACM* 26, 4 (1983), 254–258.

Norman, Donald A., *The Psychology of Everyday Things*, Basic Books, New York (1988).

Norman, Kent L., Models of the mind and machine: Information flow and control between humans and computers, *Advances in Computers* 32 (1991), 119–172.

Norman, Kent L. Cyberpsychology: *An Introduction to the Psychology of Human-Computer Interaction*, Cambridge University Press, New York (2008), Chapter 9.

Panko, Raymond, What we know about spreadsheet errors, *Journal of End User Computing* 10, 2 (Spring 1998), 15–21. Revised May 2008, available at http://panko.shidler.hawaii.edu/ssr/Mypapers/whatknow.htm.

Payne, S. J. and Green, T. R. G., Task-action grammars: A model of the mental representation of task languages, *Human-Computer Interaction* 2 (1986), 93–133.

Pew, R. W. and Gluck, K. A. (Editors), *Modeling Human Behavior with Integrated Cognitive Architectures: Comparison, Evaluation, and Validation*, Lawrence Erlbaum Associates, Mahwah, NJ (2004).

Pirolli, Peter, Exploring and finding information, in Carroll, John M. (Editor), *HCI Models, Theories, and Frameworks: Toward a Multidisciplinary Science*, Morgan Kaufmann, San Francisco, CA (2003).

Polson, Peter and Lewis, Clayton, Theory-based design for easily learned interfaces, *Human-Computer Interaction* 5 (1990), 191–220.

Redmiles, David (Editor), Special issue on activity theory and the practice of design, *Computer Supported Cooperative Work* 11(2002), 1–2.

Reeves, Byron and Nass, Clifford, *The Media Equation: How People Treat Computers, Television, and New Media Like Real People and Places*, Cambridge University Press, Cambridge, U.K. (1996).

Sanders, M. S. and McCormick, E. J., *Human Factors in Engineering and Design, Seventh Edition*, McGraw-Hill, New York (1993).

Sheridan, Thomas B., Supervisory control, in Salvendy, Gavriel (Editor), *Handbook of Human Factors, Second Edition*, John Wiley & Sons, New York (1997), 1295–1327.

Shneiderman, Ben, System message design: Guidelines and experimental results, in Badre, A. and Shneiderman, B. (Editors), *Directions in Human-Computer Interaction*, Ablex, Norwood, NJ (1982), 55–78.

Shneiderman, Ben, Direct manipulation: A step beyond programming languages, *IEEE Computer* 16, 8 (1983), 57–69.

Shneiderman, Ben, Promoting universal usability with multi-layer interface design, *ACM Conference on Universal Usability*, ACM Press, New York (2003), 1–8.

Shneiderman, Ben, Human responsibility for autonomous agents, *IEEE Intelligent Systems* 22, 2 (March/April 2007), 60–61.

Smith, Sid L. and Mosier, Jane N., *Guidelines for Designing User Interface Software*, Report ESD-TR–86–278, Electronic Systems Division, MITRE Corporation, Bedford, MA (1986). Available from National Technical Information Service, Springfield, VA.

Suchman, Lucy A., *Plans and Situated Actions: The Problem of Human-Machine Communication*, Cambridge University Press, Cambridge, U.K. (1987).

Wickens, Christopher D. and Hollands, Justin G., *Engineering Psychology and Human Performance*, Prentice-Hall, Englewood Cliffs, NJ (2000).

PART 2

DEVELOPMENT PROCESSES

CHAPTER 3

Managing Design Processes

> 66 Just as we can assert that no product has ever been created in a single moment
> of inspiration . . . nobody has ever produced a set of requirements for any
> product in a similarly miraculous manner. These requirements may well
> begin with an inspirational moment but, almost certainly, the emergent
> bright idea will be developed by iterative processes of evaluation until it
> is thought to be worth starting to put pencil to paper. Especially when
> the product is entirely new, the development of a set of requirements
> may well depend upon testing initial ideas in some depth. 99

W. H. Mayall
Principles in Design, 1979

> 66 The Plan is the generator. Without a plan, you have lack of order
> and willfulness. The Plan holds in itself the essence of sensation. 99

Le Corbusier
Towards a New Architecture, 1931

Written in collaboration with Steven M. Jacobs

3.1 Introduction

In the first decades of computer-software development, technically oriented programmers designed text editors, programming languages, and applications for themselves and their peers. The substantial experience and motivation of these users meant that complex interfaces were accepted and even appreciated. Now, the user population for mobile devices, instant messaging, e-business, and digital libraries is so vastly different from the original that programmers' intuitions may be inappropriate. Current users are not dedicated to the technology; their background is more tied to their work needs and the work tasks they perform, while their use of computers for entertainment has increased. Designers who carefully observe current users, refine their prototypes by thoughtful analysis of task frequencies and sequences, and validate through early usability and thorough acceptance tests are likely to produce high-quality interfaces.

In the best organizations, the technocentric style of the past is yielding to a genuine desire to accommodate the users' skills, goals, and preferences. Designers seek direct interaction with users during requirements and feature definition, the design phase, the development process, and throughout the system lifecycle. Iterative design methods that allow early testing of low-fidelity prototypes, revisions based on feedback from users, and incremental refinements suggested by usability-test administrators are catalysts for high-quality systems.

Around the world, *usability engineering* has evolved into a recognized discipline with maturing practices and a growing set of standards. The Usability Professionals Association (UPA) has become a respected community with active participation from large corporations and numerous small design, test, and build firms. The UPA's annual "World Usability Day" sponsors hundreds of lectures plus visits to policy makers and industrial research decision makers. There is a movement to certify usability professionals based on a body of knowledge published by the UPA (Usability Professionals Assn., 2008). Also, usability test reports are becoming standardized (for example, via the Common Industry Format), so that buyers of software can compare products across suppliers.

The variety of design situations precludes a comprehensive strategy. Managers will have to adapt the strategies offered in this chapter (Section 3.2) to suit their organizations, projects, schedules, and budgets. These strategies begin with the organizational design that gives appropriate emphasis to support usability.

As a goal, we should push tools and development capabilities closer towards end users, particularly in the web domain. For examples, check out the tools for building Amazon.com "wish lists," the Google Mashup Editor, or Many Eyes shared visualizations. A willingness to be flexible and open in the development process and to offer some of these tailoring capabilities to the end user can increase the chances for successful user-interface development.

There are four pillars of successful user-interface development: user-interface requirements, guidelines documents and processes, user-interface software tools, and expert reviews and usability testing. These elements are introduced in Section 3.3. Then, in Section 3.4, development methodologies for successful user-interface development are discussed, and contextual inquiry and rapid contextual design are addressed as a framework for user-centered design (Holtzblatt et al., 2005).

Ethnographic observation (Section 3.5) is a proven enabler to the successful development process. Participatory design (Section 3.6) and scenario development (Section 3.7) are also critical to success. Social impact statements should be produced early in the design review (Section 3.8), and legal concerns should be addressed during the design process (Section 3.9).

3.2 Organizational Design to Support Usability

Corporate marketing and customer-assistance departments are becoming more aware of the importance of usability and are a source of constructive encouragement. When competitive products provide similar functionality, usability engineering is vital for product acceptance. Many organizations have created usability laboratories to provide expert reviews and to conduct usability tests of products during development. Outside experts can provide fresh insights, while usability-test subjects perform benchmark tasks in carefully supervised conditions (Rubin and Chisnell, 2008; Dumas and Redish, 1999). These and other evaluation strategies are covered in Chapter 4.

Companies may not yet have chief usability officers (CUOs) or vice presidents for usability, but they often have user-interface architects and usability engineering managers. High-level commitment helps to promote attention at every level. Organizational awareness can be stimulated by Usability Day presentations, internal seminars, newsletters, and awards. However, resistance to new techniques and changing roles for software engineers can cause problems in organizations.

Organizational change is difficult, but creative leaders blend inspiration and provocation. The high road is to appeal to the desire for quality that most professionals share. When they are shown data on shortened learning times, faster performance, or lower error rates on well-designed interfaces, managers are likely to be more sympathetic to applying usability-engineering methods. Even more compelling for e-commerce managers is evidence of higher rates of conversion, enlarged market share, and increased customer retention. For managers of consumer products, the goals include fewer returns/complaints, increased brand loyalty, and more referrals. The low road is to point out the frustration, confusion, and high error rates caused by current complex designs, while citing the successes of competitors who apply usability-engineering methods.

Return on investment (ROI) for usability engineering in major corporations is almost always questioned. However, there have been numerous white papers citing awareness and evidence that usability testing can pay dividends (Nielsen, 2008; Bias and Mayhew, 2005). Most large and many small organizations maintain a centralized human-factors group or usability laboratory as a source of expertise in design and testing techniques (Perfetti, 2006). However, each project should have its own user-interface architect who develops the necessary skills, manages the work of other people, prepares budgets and schedules, and coordinates with internal and external human-factors professionals when further expertise, references to the literature, or usability tests are required. This dual strategy balances the needs for centralized expertise and decentralized application. It enables professional growth in the user-interface area and in the application domain (for example, in geographic information or web-based product catalogs).

Some industries, such as in aerospace, are often required to address Human Systems Integration (HSI) requirements that deal with a combination of human factors, usability, display design, navigation, and so on, while meeting customer requirements for the same (National Research Council, 2007; Defense Acquisition University, 2004).

As the field of user-interface design has matured, projects have grown in complexity, size, and importance. Role specialization is emerging, as it has in fields such as architecture, aerospace, and book design. User-interface design takes on new perspectives when writing web, mobile, or desktop applications, with an emerging discipline in translating the same information across each of these media. Eventually, individuals will become highly skilled in specific problem areas, such as user-interface–building tools, graphic-display strategies, voice and audio tone design, shortcuts, navigation, and online tutorial writing. Consultation with graphic artists, book designers, advertising copywriters, instructional-textbook authors, game designers, or film-animation creators is expected. Perceptive system developers recognize the need to employ psychologists for conducting experimental tests, sociologists for evaluating organizational impact, educational psychologists for refining training procedures, and social workers for guiding customer-service personnel.

As design moves to implementation, the choice of user-interface–building tools is vital to success. These rapidly emerging tools enable designers to build novel systems quickly and support the iterative design/test/refine cycle.

Guidelines documents were originally seen as the answer to usability questions, but they are now appreciated as a broader social process in which the initial compilation is only the first step. Management strategies for the "four Es" presented here—education, enforcement, exemption, and enhancement—are just beginning to emerge and to become institutionalized.

The business case for focusing on usability has been made powerfully and repeatedly (Nielsen 2008; Bias and Mayhew, 2005; Marcus, 2002; Karat, 1994). It apparently needs frequent repetition, because traditional managers and engineers are often resistant to changes that would bring increased attention to the users' needs. Claire-Marie Karat's business-like reports within IBM (Karat, 1994) became influential documents when they were published externally. She reported up to $100 payoffs for each dollar spent on usability, with identifiable benefits in reduced program-development costs, reduced program-maintenance costs, increased revenue due to higher customer satisfaction, and improved user efficiency and productivity. Other economic analyses showed fundamental changes in organizational productivity (with improvements of as much as 720%) when designers kept usability in mind from the beginning of development projects (Landauer, 1995). Even minimal application of usability testing followed by correction of 20 of the easiest-to-repair faults improved user success rates from 19% to as much as 80%.

It is important to note that there are interface-development activities where the ROI for usability analysis during the development cycle is not immediately apparent, but true usability of the delivered system is crucial for success. One familiar example is voting machines. An end result of confused, misinterpreted voting results would be catastrophic and counter to the best interests of the voting population, but the usability analysis and associated development costs should be manageable by the government contractor building the electronic voting booth system.

Usability engineers and *user-interface architects*, sometimes called the user experience (UX) team, are gaining experience in managing organizational change. As attention shifts away from software engineering or management-information systems, battles for control and power manifest themselves in budget and personnel allocations. Well-prepared managers who have a concrete organizational plan, defensible cost/benefit analyses, and practical development methodologies are most likely to be winners.

Design is inherently creative and unpredictable. Interactive system designers must blend a thorough knowledge of technical feasibility with a mystical esthetic sense of what attracts users. One method to characterize design (Rosson and Carroll, 2002) is:

- Design is a *process*; it is not a state and it cannot be adequately represented statically.
- The design process is *nonhierarchical*; it is neither strictly bottom-up nor strictly top-down.
- The process is *radically transformational*; it involves the development of partial and interim solutions that may ultimately play no role in the final design.
- Design intrinsically involves the *discovery of new goals*.

These characterizations of design convey the dynamic nature of the process. But in every creative domain, there can also be discipline, refined techniques, wrong and right methods, and measures of success. Once the early data collection is done and preliminary requirements are established, more detailed design and early development can begin. This chapter covers strategies for managing early stages of projects and presents design methodologies. Chapter 4 focuses on evaluation methods.

3.3 The Four Pillars of Design

66 If standardization can be humanized and made flexible in design and the economics brought to the home owner, the greatest service will be rendered to our modern way of life. It may be really born—this democracy, I mean. 99

Frank Lloyd Wright
The Natural House, 1954

The four pillars described in this section can help user-interface architects to turn good ideas into successful systems (Fig. 3.1). They are not guaranteed to work flawlessly, but experience has shown that each pillar can produce an order-of-magnitude speed-up in the process and can facilitate the creation of excellent systems.

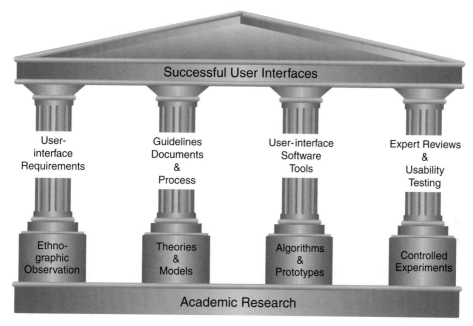

FIGURE 3.1

The four pillars of successful user-interface development.

3.3.1 User interface requirements

Soliciting and clearly specifying user requirements is a major key to success in any development activity (Selby, 2007). Methods to elicit and reach agreement upon user-interface requirements differ across organizations and industries, but the end result is the same: a clear specification of the user community and the tasks the users perform. Laying out the user-interface requirements is part of the overall requirements development and management process; the system requirements (hardware, software, system performance, reliability, etc.) must be clearly stated, and any requirements dealing with the user interface (input/output devices, functionality, interfaces, range of users, etc.) must be specified and agreed upon.

The success or failure of software projects often depends on the precision and completeness of the understanding among all the users and implementers. What happens without adequate requirements definition? You are not sure what problem you are solving, and you do not know when you are done.

Be careful not to impose human operator actions (requirements) onto the user-interface requirements (Box 3.1). For example, *do not* specify a requirement like this: "The user shall decide how much to withdraw from the ATM within

BOX 3.1
Examples of user-interface requirements regarding system behavior.

- Performance requirements:

  "The web site shall give users the ability to update their user profiles, e.g., name, mail address, e-mail address, phone."

  "The system shall permit the ATM customer 15 seconds to make a selection. The customer shall be warned that the session will be ended if no selection is made."

  "The mobile device shall be able to save draft text messages when out of the service area."

- Functional requirements:

  "The system shall ensure that the PIN entered matches the one on file."

  "The web site shall provide other, related purchase options based on past visits to the web site."

  "The credit card transaction must be approved prior to displaying a confirmation number."

- Interface requirements:

  "The web site shall permit ordering stamps online."

  "Kiosk screen styles shall conform to existing print media guidelines."

  "The mobile device shall permit downloading of ring tones."

five seconds." Rather, allocate that same requirement to the computer system: "The ATM shall permit a user five seconds to select a withdrawal amount . . . before prompting for a response."

One successful method for determining user-interface requirements is to use ethnographic observation (discussed in Section 3.5), monitoring the context and environment of real users in action. Tradeoffs between what functions are done best by computers versus humans in human-computer interaction (Section 2.3.6) should also be discussed at this point in the development process.

3.3.2 Guidelines documents and processes

Early in the design process, the user-interface architect should generate, or require other people to generate, a set of working guidelines. Two people might work for one week to produce a 10-page document, or a dozen people might work for two years to produce a 300-page document. One component of Apple's success with the Macintosh was the machine's early and readable guidelines document, which provided a clear set of principles for the many application developers to follow and thus ensured harmony in design across products. Microsoft's *Windows Vista User Experience Guidelines*, which have been refined over the years, also provide a good starting point and an educational experience for many programmers. These and other guidelines documents are referenced and described briefly in the general reference section at the end of Chapter 1.

Each project has different needs, but guidelines should be considered for:

- Words, icons, and graphics
  - Terminology (objects and actions), abbreviations, and capitalization
  - Character set, fonts, font sizes, and styles (bold, italic, underline)
  - Icons, buttons, graphics, and line thickness
  - Use of color, backgrounds, highlighting, and blinking
- Screen-layout issues
  - Menu selection, form fill-in, and dialog-box formats
  - Wording of prompts, feedback, and error messages
  - Justification, whitespace, and margins
  - Data entry and display formats for items and lists
  - Use and contents of headers and footers
  - Strategies for adapting to small and large displays
- Input and output devices
  - Keyboard, display, cursor control, and pointing devices
  - Audible sounds, voice feedback, speech I/O, touch input, and other special input modes or devices
  - Response times for a variety of tasks
  - Alternatives for users with disabilities
- Action sequences
  - Direct-manipulation clicking, dragging, dropping, and gestures
  - Command syntax, semantics, and sequences
  - Shortcuts and programmed function keys
  - Touchscreen navigation for devices such as the Apple iPhone and tabletop systems such as Microsoft Surface™
  - Error handling and recovery procedures
- Training
  - Online help, tutorials, and support groups
  - Training and reference materials

Guidelines creation (Box 3.2) should be a social process within an organization to help it gain visibility and build support. Controversial guidelines (for example,

BOX 3.2
Recommendations for guidelines documents.

- Provides a social process for developers
- Records decisions for all parties to see
- Promotes consistency and completeness
- Facilitates automation of design
- Allows multiple levels:
    Rigid standards
    Accepted practices
    Flexible guidelines
- Announces policies for:
    Education: How to get it?
    Enforcement: Who reviews?
    Exemption: Who decides?
    Enhancement: How often?

on when to use voice alerts) should be reviewed by colleagues or tested empirically. Procedures should be established to distribute the guidelines, to ensure enforcement, to allow exemptions, and to permit enhancements. Guidelines documents must be living texts that are adapted to changing needs and refined through experience. Acceptance may be increased by a three-level approach of rigid standards, accepted practices, and flexible guidelines. This approach clarifies which items are firmer and which items are susceptible to change.

The creation of a guidelines document at the beginning of an implementation project focuses attention on the interface design and provides an opportunity for discussion of controversial issues. When the development team adopts the guidelines, the implementation proceeds quickly and with few design changes. For large organizations there may be two or more levels of guidelines, to provide organizational identity while allowing projects to have distinctive styles and local control of terminology. Some organizations develop "style guides" to capture this (see, for example, Microsoft, 2008).

The "four Es" provide a basis for creating a living document and a lively process:

- *Education*. Users need training and a chance to discuss the guidelines. Developers must be trained in the resultant guidelines.

- *Enforcement*. A timely and clear process is necessary to verify that an interface adheres to the guidelines.

- *Exemption.* When creative ideas or new technologies are used, a rapid process for gaining exemption is needed.

- *Enhancement.* A predictable process for review, possibly annually, will help keep the guidelines up-to-date.

3.3.3 User-interface software tools

One difficulty in designing interactive systems is that customers and users may not have a clear idea of what the system will look like when it is done. Since interactive systems are novel in many situations, users may not realize the implications of design decisions. Unfortunately, it is difficult, costly, and time-consuming to make major changes to systems once those systems have been implemented.

Although this problem has no complete solution, some of the more serious difficulties can be avoided if, at an early stage, the customers and users can be given a realistic impression of what the final system will look like (Gould and Lewis, 1985). A printed version of the proposed displays is helpful for pilot tests, but an onscreen display with an active keyboard and mouse is more realistic. The prototype of a menu system may have only one or two paths active, instead of the thousands of paths envisioned for the final system. For a form-fill-in system, the prototype may simply show the fields but not actually process them. Prototypes have been developed with simple drawing or word-processing tools or even PowerPoint® presentations of screen drawings manipulated with PowerPoint slide shows and other animation. Flash® and Ajax can also be used. Flash is a multimedia authoring and delivery platform for embedded web content. Building an interface in Flash is comparable to using other tools. Ajax is a combination of technologies for interactive web pages, much closer to a development environment. Other design tools that can be used are Adobe® PageMaker® or Illustrator®.

Development environments such as Microsoft's Visual Basic/C++ are easy to get started with yet have an excellent set of features. Visual Studio®, as well as C# and the .NET Framework, certainly can be evaluated for your user-interface development project. Make sure to evaluate tool capabilities, ease of use, ease to learn, cost, and performance. Tailor your tool choices for the size of the job. Building a software architecture that supports your user-interface development project is just as important as it is for any other (particularly large-scale) software development activity.

Sophisticated tools such as Sun's Java™ provide cross-platform development capabilities and a variety of services. People who want to write their own Java programs can use the Java Development Kit™ (JDK). The *Java Look and Feel Design Guidelines* (Sun Microsystems, 2001) is a terrific reference on the user-interface style for Java developers writing with Java Foundation Classes

(JFC). As an example of how rapidly this field is changing, at the time of this writing, Java released the LightWeight User Interface Toolkit (LWUIT), billed as "a versatile and compact API for creating attractive application mobile user interfaces."

Although they are not the focus of this book, there are many web sites offering insight into current user-interface software tools; one of the authors' favorites is the Web Developers Journal.

3.3.4 Expert reviews and usability testing

Theatrical producers know that extensive rehearsals and previews for critics are necessary to ensure a successful opening night. Early rehearsals may involve only the key performers wearing street clothes, but as opening night approaches, dress rehearsals with the full cast, props, and lighting are required. Aircraft designers carry out wind-tunnel tests, build plywood mock-ups of the cabin layout, construct complete simulations of the cockpit, and thoroughly flight-test the first prototype. Similarly, web-site designers now recognize that they must carry out many small and some large pilot tests of components before release to customers (Dumas and Redish, 1999). In addition to a variety of expert review methods, tests with the intended users, surveys, and automated analysis tools are proving to be valuable. Procedures vary greatly depending on the goals of the usability study, the number of expected users, the danger of errors, and the level of investment. Chapter 4 covers expert reviews, usability testing, and other evaluation methods in depth.

3.4 Development Methodologies

Many software development projects fail to achieve their goals. Some estimates of the failure rate put it as high as 50% (Jones, 2005). Much of this problem can be traced to poor communication between developers and their business clients or between developers and their users.

Successful developers work carefully to understand the business's needs it and refine their skills in eliciting accurate requirements from nontechnical business managers. In addition, since business managers may lack the technical knowledge to understand proposals made by the developers, dialog is necessary to reduce confusion about the organizational implications of design decisions.

Successful developers also know that careful attention to user-centered design issues during the early stages of software development dramatically reduces both development time and cost. User-centered design leads to systems that generate fewer problems during development and have lower maintenance costs over their lifetimes. They are easier to learn, result in faster performance, reduce user errors substantially, and encourage users to explore features that go beyond the minimum required to get by. In addition, user-centered design practices help organizations align system functionality with their business needs and priorities.

Software developers have learned that consistently following established development methodologies can help them meet budgets and schedules (Sommerville, 2006; Pfleeger, 2005). But while software-engineering methodologies are effective in facilitating the software development process, they have not always provided clear processes for studying the users, understanding their needs, and creating usable interfaces. Small consulting firms that specialize in user-centered design have created innovative design methodologies to guide developers, such as rapid contextual design (Holtzblatt et al., 2005), which is based on the approach of contextual inquiry (Beyer and Holtzblatt, 1998). Some large corporations have also integrated user-centered design into their practices; for example, IBM's Ease of Use method fits with its existing corporate methods (Fig. 3.2). Agile technologies and methodologies provide

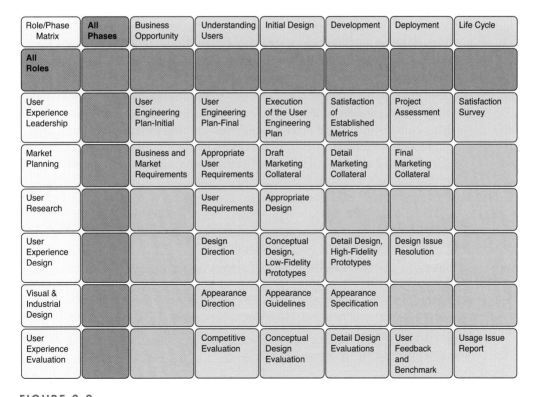

Role/Phase Matrix	All Phases	Business Opportunity	Understanding Users	Initial Design	Development	Deployment	Life Cycle
All Roles							
User Experience Leadership		User Engineering Plan-Initial	User Engineering Plan-Final	Execution of the User Engineering Plan	Satisfaction of Established Metrics	Project Assessment	Satisfaction Survey
Market Planning		Business and Market Requirements	Appropriate User Requirements	Draft Marketing Collateral	Detail Marketing Collateral	Final Marketing Collateral	
User Research			User Requirements	Appropriate Design			
User Experience Design			Design Direction	Conceptual Design, Low-Fidelity Prototypes	Detail Design, High-Fidelity Prototypes	Design Issue Resolution	
Visual & Industrial Design			Appearance Direction	Appearance Guidelines	Appearance Specification		
User Experience Evaluation			Competitive Evaluation	Conceptual Design Evaluation	Detail Design Evaluations	User Feedback and Benchmark	Usage Issue Report

FIGURE 3.2

IBM's Ease of Use development methodology, which specifies activities by roles and phases.

the room to be responsive to user-interface development and usability needs (Boehm and Turner, 2004).

These business-oriented approaches specify detailed deliverables for the various stages of design and incorporate cost/benefit and return-on-investment analyses to facilitate decision making. They may also offer management strategies to keep projects on track and to facilitate effective collaboration among teams that include both business and technical participants. Since user-centered design is only a part of the overall development process, these methodologies must also mesh with the various software-engineering methodologies that are used in industry today.

There are dozens of advertised development methods (such as GUIDE, STUDIO, and OVID), but the focus here is on Holtzblatt et al.'s rapid contextual design, summarized below. There are tools for contextual design and managing the data (Holtzblatt and Beyer, 2008), and there are other recent, excellent sources for usability engineering processes and interaction design (Heim, 2008; Sears and Jacko, 2008; Leventhal and Barnes, 2007; Sharp et al., 2007). The rapid contextual design method (Table 3.1) involves the following steps:

1. *Contextual inquiry*. Plan for, prepare, and then conduct field interviews to observe and understand the work tasks being performed. Review business practices.

2. *Interpretation sessions and work modeling*. Hold team discussions to draw conclusions based on the contextual inquiry, including gaining an understanding of the workflow processes in the organization as well as cultural and policy impacts on work performed. Capture key points (affinity notes).

Contextual inquiry
Interpretation sessions and work modeling
Model consolidation and affinity diagram building
Personas
Visioning
Storyboarding
User environment design
Paper prototypes and mock-up interviews

TABLE 3.1

Rapid contextual design from *Rapid Contextual Design: A How-To Guide to Key Techniques for User-Centered Design*, Morgan Kaufmann, San Francisco, CA (2005).

3. *Model consolidation and affinity diagram building.* Present the data gathered to date from users and the interpretation and work modeling to a larger, targeted population to gain insight and concurrence. Consolidate the work models to illustrate common work patterns and processes and create *affinity diagrams* (hierarchical representations of the issues to address user needs).

4. *Persona development.* Develop personas (fictitious characters) to represent the different user types within a targeted demographic that might use a site or product (Cooper, 2004). This aids the team in communicating the needs of the users and bringing those user needs to fruition. Examples of personas, at a high level, are: 1) 22-year-old male with 5+ years of video game playing experience, or 2) 70-year-old female using computer only for e-mail and digital photo sharing.

5. *Visioning.* Review and "walk" the consolidated data, sharing the personas created. The visioning session helps define how the system will streamline and transform the work of the users. Capture key issues and ideas using flipcharts or any media that will facilitate expressing the vision of the revised business processes.

6. *Storyboarding.* The vision guides the detailed redesign of user tasks using pictures and graphs to describe the initial user-interface concepts, business rules, and automation assumptions. Storyboarding defines and illustrates the "to be built" assumptions.

7. *User environment design.* The single, coherent representation of the users and the work to be performed is expressed in the user environment design (UED). The UED is built from the storyboards.

8. *Interviews and evaluations with paper prototypes and mock-ups.* Conduct interviews and tests with actual users, beginning with paper prototypes and then moving on to higher-fidelity prototypes. Capturing the results of the interviews aids in ensuring that the systems will meet end-user requirements.

3.5 Ethnographic Observation

The early stages of most methodologies include observation of users. Since interface users form a unique culture, ethnographic methods for observing them in the workplace are becoming increasingly important (Fig. 3.3). Ethnographers join

FIGURE 3.3
Preteen researchers with the University of Baltimore's KidsTeam observe children's reading habits in the home (left). Researchers in Paris brainstorm ideas for new family technologies with families from France, Sweden, and the United States (right).

work or home environments to listen and observe carefully, sometimes stepping forward to ask questions and participate in activities (Fetterman, 1998; Harper, 2000; Millen, 2000). As ethnographers, user-interface designers gain insight into individual behavior and the organizational context. However, they differ from traditional ethnographers in that, in addition to seeking understanding of their subjects, user-interface designers focus on interfaces for the purpose of changing and improving those interfaces. Also, whereas traditional ethnographers immerse themselves in cultures for weeks or months, user-interface designers usually need to limit this process to a period of days or even hours to obtain the relevant data needed to influence a redesign (Hughes et al., 1997). Ethnographic methods have been applied to office work (Suchman, 1987), air-traffic control (Bentley et al., 1992), and other domains (Marcus, 2005).

The goal of this observation is to obtain the necessary data to influence interface redesign. Unfortunately, it is easy to misinterpret observations, to disrupt normal practice, and to overlook important information. Following a validated ethnographic process reduces the likelihood of these problems. Examples of ethnographic observation research include: 1) how cultural probes have been adopted and adapted by the HCI community (Boehner et al., 2007), 2) development of an interactive location-based service for supporting distributed mobile collaboration for home healthcare (Christensen et al., 2007), and 3) social dynamics influencing technological solutions in developing regions (Ramachandran et al., 2007). Guidelines for preparing for the evaluation, performing the field study, analyzing the data, and reporting the findings might include the following:

- Preparation
  - Understand policies in work environments and family values in homes.
  - Familiarize yourself with the existing interface and its history.
  - Set initial goals and prepare questions.
  - Gain access and permission to observe or interview.

- Field study
  - Establish a rapport with all users.
  - Observe or interview users in their setting, and collect subjective and objective quantitative and qualitative data.
  - Follow any leads that emerge from the visits.
  - Record your visits.

- Analysis
  - Compile the collected data in numerical, textual, and multimedia databases.
  - Quantify data and compile statistics.
  - Reduce and interpret the data.
  - Refine the goals and the process used.

- Reporting
  - Consider multiple audiences and goals.
  - Prepare a report and present the findings.

These notions seem obvious when stated, but they require interpretation and attention in each situation. For example, understanding the differing perceptions that managers and users have about the efficacy of the current interface will alert you to the varying frustrations of each group. Managers may complain about the unwillingness of staff to update information promptly, but staff may be resistant to using the interface because the log-in process takes six to eight minutes. Respecting the rules of the workplace is important for building rapport: In preparing for one observation, we appreciated that the manager called to warn us that graduate students should not wear jeans because the users were prohibited from doing so. Learning the technical language of the users is also vital for establishing rapport. It is useful to prepare a long list of questions that you can then filter down by focusing on the proposed goals. Awareness of the differences between user communities, such as those mentioned in Section 1.4, will help to make the observation and interview process more effective.

Data collection can include a wide range of subjective impressions that are qualitative or of subjective reactions that are quantitative, such as rating scales or rankings. Objective data can consist of qualitative anecdotes or critical incidents that capture user experiences, or can be quantitative reports about, for example, the number of errors that occur during a one-hour observation of six users. Deciding in advance what to capture is highly beneficial, but remaining alert to unexpected happenings is also valuable. Written report summaries have proved to be valuable, far beyond expectations; in most cases, raw transcripts of every conversation are too voluminous to be useful.

Making the process explicit and planning carefully may seem awkward to many people whose training stems from computing and information technology. However, a thoughtfully applied ethnographic process has proved to have many benefits. It can increase trustworthiness and credibility, since designers learn about the complexities of the intended environment by visits to the workplace, school, home, or other environment where the eventual system will be deployed. Personal presence allows designers to develop working relationships with several end users to discuss ideas, and, most importantly, the users may consent to be active participants in the design of their new interface.

3.6 Participatory Design

Many authors have urged participatory design strategies, but the concept is controversial. *Participatory design* is the direct involvement of people in the collaborative design of the things and technologies they use. The arguments in favor suggest that more user involvement brings more accurate information about tasks and an opportunity for users to influence design decisions.

However, the sense of participation that builds users' ego investment in successful implementation may be the biggest influence on increased user acceptance of the final system (Kujala, 2003; Muller, 2002; Damodaran, 1996).

On the other hand, extensive user involvement may be costly and may lengthen the implementation period. It may also generate antagonism from people who are not involved or whose suggestions are rejected, and potentially force designers to compromise their designs to satisfy incompetent participants (Ives and Olson, 1984).

Participatory design experiences are usually positive, however, and advocates can point to many important contributions that would have been missed without user participation. People who are resistant might appreciate the somewhat formalized multiple-case-studies *plastic interface for collaborative technology initiatives through video exploration* (PICTIVE) approach (Rosson and Carroll, 2006; Muller, 1992). Users sketch interfaces, then use slips of paper, pieces of plastic, and tape to create low-fidelity early prototypes. A scenario walkthrough is then recorded on videotape for presentation to managers, users, or other designers. With the right leadership, the PICTIVE approach can effectively elicit new ideas and be fun for all involved (Muller et al., 1993). Many variations of participatory design have been proposed that engage participants to create dramatic performances, photography exhibits, games, or merely sketches and written scenarios. High-fidelity prototypes and simulations can also be key in eliciting user requirements.

Careful selection of users helps to build a successful participatory design experience. A competitive selection increases participants' sense of importance and emphasizes the seriousness of the project. Participants may be asked to commit to repeated meetings and should be told what to expect about their roles and their influence. They may have to learn about the technology and business plans of the organization and be asked to act as a communication channel to the larger group of users that they represent.

The social and political environment surrounding the implementation of complex interfaces is not amenable to study by rigidly defined methods or controlled experimentation. Social and industrial psychologists are interested in these issues, but dependable research and implementation strategies may never emerge. The sensitive project leader must judge each case on its merits and must decide what is the right level of user involvement. The personalities of the participatory design team members are such critical determinants that experts in group dynamics and social psychology may be useful as consultants. Many questions remain to be studied, such as whether homogeneous or diverse groups are more successful, how to tailor processes for small and large groups, and how to balance decision-making control between typical users and professional designers.

Socio-technical system (STS) developers, who work on complex systems for applications such as transportation security, voting, online auctions, e-learning, and healthcare delivery, are increasingly aware of the value of participatory design. They seek user input from stakeholders at every stage to understand sensitive issues such as privacy protection, damage from errors, costs of delays, and legal constraints, as well as ethical issues, such as bias that favors one user group or exclusion that raises barriers for another user group (Whitworth and De Moore, 2009).

The experienced user-interface architect knows that organizational politics and the preferences of individuals may be more important than technical issues in governing the success of an interactive system. For example, warehouse managers who see their positions threatened by an interactive system that provides senior managers with up-to-date information through desktop displays may try to ensure that the system fails by delaying data entry or by being less than diligent in guaranteeing data accuracy. The interface designer should take into account the system's effect on users and should solicit their participation to ensure that all concerns are made explicit early enough to avoid counterproductive efforts and resistance to change. Novelty is threatening to many people, so clear statements about what to expect can be helpful in reducing anxiety.

Ideas about participatory design are being refined with diverse users, ranging from children to older adults. Arranging for participation is difficult for some users, such as those with cognitive disabilities or those whose time is precious (for example, surgeons). The levels of participation are becoming clearer; one taxonomy describes the roles of children in developing interfaces for children, older adults in developing interfaces whose typical users will be other older adults, and so on, with roles varying from testers to informants to partners (Druin, 2002; Fig. 3.4). Testers are merely observed as they try out novel designs, while informants comment to designers through interviews and focus groups. Design partners are active members of a design team, which in the case of children's software will naturally involve participants of many ages—the intergenerational team.

Further research in this area is published at Participatory Design Conferences (PDCs), held biennially since 1990. The PDC conferences are sponsored by Computer Professionals for Social Responsibility (CPSR). For ethnographic observation and participatory design, developers and project managers who regularly strive to get buy-ins from diverse participants are more likely to succeed.

3.7 Scenario Development

When a current interface is being redesigned or a well-polished manual system is being automated, reliable data about the distribution of task frequencies and

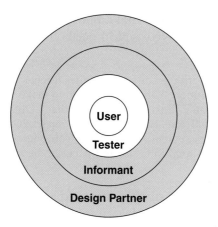

FIGURE 3.4

Druin's model of the four levels of user participation. The blue areas (informant and design partner) represent stages of participatory design.

sequences is an enormous asset. If current data do not exist, usage logs can quickly provide insight.

A table with user communities listed across the top and tasks listed down the side is helpful. Each box can then be filled in with the relative frequency with which each user performs each task. Another representation tool is a table of task sequences, indicating which tasks follow other tasks. Often, a flowchart or transition diagram helps designers to record and convey the sequences of possible actions; the thickness of the connecting lines indicates the frequency of the transitions.

In less well-defined projects, many designers have found day-in-the-life scenarios helpful to characterize what happens when users perform typical tasks. During the early design stages, data about current performance should be collected to provide a baseline. Information about similar systems helps, and interviews can be conducted with stakeholders, such as users and managers (Rosson and Carroll, 2002; Bodker, 2000; Carroll, 2000).

An early and easy way to describe a novel system is to write scenarios of usage and then, if possible, to act them out as a form of theater. This technique can be especially effective when multiple users must cooperate (for example, in control rooms, cockpits, or financial trading rooms) or multiple physical devices are used (for example, at customer-service desks, medical laboratories, or hotel check-in areas). Scenarios can represent common or emergency situations with both novice and expert users. Personas can also be included in scenario generation.

In developing the National Digital Library, the design team began by writing 81 scenarios that portrayed typical needs of potential users. Here is an example:

> *K–16 Users*: A seventh-grade social-studies teacher is teaching a unit on the Industrial Revolution. The teacher wants to make use of primary source material that would illustrate the factors that facilitated industrialization, the manner in which it occurred, and the impact that it had on society and on the built environment. Given the teaching load, the teacher only has about four hours total to locate and package the supplementary material for classroom use.

Other scenarios might describe how users explore a system, such as this optimistic vision, written for the U.S. Holocaust Museum and Education Center:

> A grandmother and her 10- and 12-year old grandsons have visited the museum before. They have returned this time to the Learning Center to explore what life was like in her shtetl in Poland in the 1930s. One grandson eagerly touches the buttons on the welcome screen, and they watch the 45-second video introduction by the museum director. They then select the button on "History before the Holocaust" and choose to view a list of towns. Her small town is not on the list, but she identifies the larger nearby city, and they get a brief textual description, a map of the region, and a photograph of the marketplace. They read about the history of the town and view 15-second videos of the marketplace activity and a Yiddish theater production. They bypass descriptions of key buildings and institutions, choosing instead to read biographies of a famous community leader and a poet. Finally, they select "GuestBook" and add their names to the list of people who have indicated an affiliation with this town. Further up on the list, the grandmother notices the name of a childhood friend from whom she has not heard in 60 years—fortunately, the earlier visitor has left an address.

This scenario was written to give nontechnical museum planners and the Board of Directors an idea of what could be built if funding were provided. Such scenarios are easy for most people to grasp, and they convey design issues such as physical installation (room and seats for three or more patrons with sound isolation) and development requirements (video production for the director's introduction and conversion of archival films to video).

An elaborate scenario development process was also conducted to help U.S. statistical agencies formulate a vision for a Statistical Knowledge Network. Patterns of citizen requests were combined with agency proposals to develop 15 brief scenarios, using the first-person format, such as these two that were the basis of empirical tests of proposed interfaces:

> I'm a social activist in the Raleigh-Durham, North Carolina area and have become increasingly concerned about urban sprawl and the loss of rural

areas for both farming and recreation. I need statistics to support my claim that significant differences occur when urban development occurs in rural and/or farming areas.

I would like to open a grocery store specializing in organic products in the greater Seattle metropolitan area. What are the trends in production and consumption of organic food products? Would the Seattle area be a good place to locate?

Some scenario writers take a further step and produce videotapes to convey their intentions. There have been several famous future scenarios, including Apple's *Knowledge Navigator* (1987), which produced numerous controversies. It portrayed a professor using voice commands to talk with a bow-tied preppie character on the screen and touch commands to develop ecological simulations. Many viewers enjoyed the tape, but thought that it stepped over the bounds of reality by having the preppie agent recognize the professor's facial expressions, verbal hesitations, and emotional reactions. Another example is Bruce Tognazzini's *Starfire* scenario for Sun Microsystems (1994), which gave his elaborate but realistic impression of a large-screen work environment that supported rich collaborations with remote colleagues.

By 2003, cell-phone developers were producing scenarios about how personal, family, and commercial relationships would change due to mobile video communications—an appealing example is the Japanese NTT DoCoMo's *Vision 2010: Beyond the Mobile Frontier*, which shows how a family can realize its goal of remaining in close contact while children go to study far away from home. NTT DoCoMo has produced several other scenarios worth viewing, including *Mobile Life Story "Concert" version*, *Vision 2010: Old School Friends*, and *The Road to Hokusai's Waterfall*. The DoCoMo videos all portray a wonderful, technology-enhanced future, with easy-to-use interfaces on reliable mobile devices that are accessible to all ages. The video scenarios enforce our need for secure, private data communication to enhance our personal security, health, and safety.

Another scenario of note is Microsoft's *Health Future Vision*, a futuristic look at interconnected mobile communications technology in healthcare. Concepts that are illustrated include: remote transmittal of personal health status information; hospital communications and collaboration tools; advanced, accessible user interfaces using mobile, touchscreen technology; controls for secure patient health and identification information; environments (walls and furniture) that serve seamlessly as input/output devices; and more.

3.8 Social Impact Statement for Early Design Review

Interactive systems often have a dramatic impact on large numbers of users. To minimize risks, a thoughtful statement of anticipated impacts circulated among stakeholders can be a useful process for eliciting productive suggestions early in the development, when changes are easiest.

Governments, utilities, and publicly regulated industries increasingly require information systems to provide services. However, some critics have strong negative attitudes towards modern technologies and see only a hopeless technological determinism: "Technopoly eliminates alternatives to itself. It consists in the deification of technology, which means that the culture seeks its authorization in technology, finds its satisfactions in technology, and takes its orders from technology" (Postman, 1993).

Postman's endless fears do not help us to shape more effective technology or to prevent damage from technology failures. However, constructive criticism and guidelines for design could be helpful in reversing the long history of incorrect credit histories, dislocation through de-skilling or layoffs, and deaths from flawed medical instruments. Current concerns focus on privacy invasion from surveillance systems, government attempts to restrict access to information, and voting fraud because of poor security. While guarantees of perfection are not possible, policies and processes can be developed that will more often than not lead to satisfying outcomes.

A *social impact statement*, similar to an environmental impact statement, might help to promote high-quality systems in government-related applications (reviews for private-sector corporate projects would be optional and self-administered). Early and widespread discussion can uncover concerns and enable stakeholders to state their positions openly. Of course, there is the danger that these discussions will elevate fears or force designers to make unreasonable compromises, but these risks seem reasonable in a well-managed project. An outline for a social impact statement might include these sections (Shneiderman and Rose, 1996):

- Describe the new system and its benefits.
  - Convey the high-level goals of the new system.
  - Identify the stakeholders.
  - Identify specific benefits.
- Address concerns and potential barriers.
  - Anticipate changes in job functions and potential layoffs.
  - Address security and privacy issues.
  - Discuss accountability and responsibility for system misuse and failure.
  - Avoid potential biases.
  - Weigh individual rights versus societal benefits.

- Assess tradeoffs between centralization and decentralization.
- Preserve democratic principles.
- Ensure diverse access.
- Promote simplicity and preserve what works.
- Outline the development process.
  - Present an estimated project schedule.
  - Propose a process for making decisions.
  - Discuss expectations of how stakeholders will be involved.
  - Recognize needs for more staff, training, and hardware.
  - Propose a plan for backups of data and equipment.
  - Outline a plan for migrating to the new system.
  - Describe a plan for measuring the success of the new system.

A social impact statement should be produced early enough in the development process to influence the project schedule, system requirements, and budget. It can be developed by the system design team, which might include end users, managers, internal or external software developers, and possibly clients. Even for large systems, the social impact statement should be of a size and complexity that make it accessible to users with relevant backgrounds.

After the social impact statement is written, it should be evaluated by the appropriate review panel as well as by managers, other designers, end users, and anyone else who will be affected by the proposed system. Potential review panels include federal government units (for example, the General Accounting Organization or Office of Personnel Management), state legislatures, regulatory agencies (for example, the Securities and Exchange Commission or the Federal Aviation Administration), professional societies, and labor unions. The review panel will receive the written report, hold public hearings, and request modifications. Citizen groups also should be given the opportunity to present their concerns and to suggest alternatives.

Once the social impact statement is adopted, it must be enforced. A social impact statement documents the intentions for the new system, and the stakeholders need to see that those intentions are backed up by actions. Typically, the review panel is the proper authority for enforcement.

The effort, cost, and time involved should be appropriate to the project, while facilitating a thoughtful review. The process can offer large improvements by preventing problems that could be expensive to repair, improving privacy protection, minimizing legal challenges, and creating more satisfying work environments. Information-system designers take no Hippocratic Oath, but pledge themselves to strive for the noble goal of excellence in design can win respect and inspire others.

3.9 Legal Issues

As user interfaces have become more prominent, serious legal issues have emerged. Every developer of software and information should review legal issues that may affect design, implementation, or marketing.

Privacy is always a concern whenever computers are used to store data or to monitor activity. Medical, legal, financial, and other data often have to be protected to prevent unapproved access, illegal tampering, inadvertent loss, or malicious mischief. Recently implemented privacy assurance laws such as those imposed on the medical and financial communities can lead to complicated, hard-to-understand policies and procedures. Physical security measures to prohibit access are fundamental; in addition, privacy protection can involve user-interface mechanisms for controlling password access, identity checking, and data verification. Effective protection provides a high degree of privacy with a minimum of confusion and intrusion into work. Website developers should provide easily accessible and understandable privacy policies.

A second concern encompasses safety and reliability. User interfaces for aircraft, automobiles, medical equipment, military systems, utility control rooms, and the like can affect life-or-death decisions. If air-traffic controllers are confused by the situation display, they can make fatal errors. If the user interface for such a system is demonstrated to be difficult to understand, it could leave the designer, developer, and operator open to a lawsuit alleging improper design. Designers should strive to make high-quality and well-tested interfaces that adhere to state-of-the-art design guidelines. Accurate records documenting testing and usage will protect designers in case problems arise.

A third issue is copyright or patent protection for software (Samuelson, 2007; Lessig, 2006). Software developers who have spent time and money developing a package are frustrated in their attempts to recover their costs and to make a profit if potential users make illegal copies of the package, rather than buying it. Technical schemes have been tried to prevent copying, but clever hackers can usually circumvent the barriers. It is unusual for a company to sue an individual for copying a program, but cases have been brought against corporations and universities. There is also a vocal community of developers, led by the League for Programming Freedom, that opposes software copyright and patents, believing that broad dissemination is the best policy. An innovative legal approach, Creative Commons™, enables authors to specify more liberal terms for others to use their works. The open-source software movement has enlivened these controversies. The Open Source Initiative describes the movement as follows: "When programmers can read, redistribute, and modify the source code for a piece of software, the software evolves. People improve it, people adapt it, people fix bugs. And this can happen at a speed that, if one is used to the slow pace of conventional software development, seems astonishing." Some open-source products, such as the Linux® operating system and the Apache™ web server, have become successful enough to capture a substantial fraction of the market share.

A fourth concern is with copyright protection for online information, images, or music. If customers access an online resource, do they have the right to store the information electronically for later use? Can the customer send an electronic copy to a colleague or friend? Who owns the "friends" list and other shared data in social networking sites? Do individuals, their employers, or network operators own the information contained in e-mail messages? The expansion of the World Wide Web, with its vast digital libraries, has raised the temperature and pace of copyright discussions. Publishers seek to protect their intellectual assets, while librarians are torn between their desire to serve patrons and their obligations to publishers. If copyrighted works are disseminated freely, what incentives will there be for publishers and authors? If it is illegal to transmit any copyrighted work without permission or payment, science, education, and other fields will suffer. The fair-use doctrine of limited copying for personal and educational purposes helped cope with the questions raised by photocopying technologies. However, the perfect rapid copying and broad dissemination permitted by the Internet demand a thoughtful update (Lessig, 2001; Samuelson, 2003).

A fifth issue is freedom of speech in electronic environments. Do users have a right to make controversial or potentially offensive statements through e-mail or listservers? Are such statements protected by the First Amendment? Are networks like street corners, where freedom of speech is guaranteed, or are networks like television broadcasting, where community standards must be protected? Should network operators be responsible for or prohibited from eliminating offensive or obscene jokes, stories, or images? Controversy has raged over whether Internet service providers have a right to prohibit e-mail messages that are used to organize consumer rebellions against themselves. Another controversy emerged over whether a network operator has a duty to suppress racist e-mail remarks or postings to a bulletin board. If libelous statements are transmitted, can a person sue the network operator as well as the source? Should designers build systems where the default is to "opt out" of lists, and users have to explicity "opt in" by making a selection from a dialog box?

Other legal concerns include adherence to laws requiring equal access for disabled users and attention to changing laws in countries around the world. Do Yahoo! and eBay have to enforce the laws of every country in which they have customers? These and other issues mean that developers of online services must be sure to consider all the legal implications of their design decisions.

NetCoalition is a collective public policy organization that monitors many of the legal issues raised here; its web site is an excellent source for information about privacy legislation and related issues. There are also many other legal issues to be aware of today, including anti-terrorism, counterfeiting, spam, spyware, liability, Internet taxation, and others. These issues certainly require your attention, and legislation may eventually be needed.

Practitioner's Summary

Usability engineering is maturing rapidly, with once-novel ideas becoming standard practices. Usability has increasingly taken center stage in organizational and product planning. Development methodologies such as contextual design help by offering validated processes with predictable schedules and meaningful deliverables. Ethnographic observation can provide information to guide task analysis and to complement carefully supervised participatory design processes. Logs of usage provide valuable data about task frequencies and sequences. Scenario writing helps to bring common understanding of design goals, is useful for managerial and customer presentations, and helps to plan usability tests. For interfaces developed by governments, public utilities, and regulated industries, an early social impact statement can elicit public discussion that is likely to identify problems and produce interfaces that have high overall societal benefits. Designers and managers should obtain legal advice to ensure adherence to laws and protection of intellectual property.

Researcher's Agenda

Human-interface guidelines are often based on best-guess judgments rather than on empirical data. More research could lead to refined standards that are more complete and dependable, and to more precise knowledge of how much improvement can be expected from a design change. Because technology is continually changing, we will never have a stable and complete set of guidelines, but scientific studies will have enormous benefits in terms of reliability and the quality of decision making about user interfaces. Design processes, ethnographic methods, participatory design activities, scenario writing, and social impact statements are evolving. Variations are needed to address international diversity, special populations such as children or older adults, and long-term studies of actual usage. Thoughtful case studies of design processes would lead to their refinement and promote more widespread application. Creative processes are notoriously difficult to study, but well-documented examples of success stories will inform and inspire.

WORLD WIDE WEB RESOURCES

http://www.aw.com/DTUI/

Design processes promoted by companies and professional standards organizations, with information on how to develop style guidelines, are available online. References to guidelines documents are included in Chapter 1.

References

Bentley, R., Hughes, J., Randall, D., Rodden, T., Sawyer, P., Shapiro, D., and Sommerville, I., Ethnographically-informed systems design for air traffic control, *Proc. CSCW '92 Conference: Sharing Perspectives*, ACM Press, New York (1992), 123–129.

Beyer, Hugh and Holtzblatt, Karen, *Contextual Design: Defining Customer-Centered Systems*, Morgan Kaufmann, San Francisco, CA (1998).

Bias, Randolph and Mayhew, Deborah (Editors), *Cost-Justifying Usability: An Update for the Internet Age, Second Edition*, Morgan Kaufmann, San Francisco, CA (2005).

Bodker, Susan, Scenarios in user-centered design – Setting the stage for reflection and action, *Interacting with Computers* 13, 1 (2000), 61–76.

Boehm, Barry and Turner, Richard, *Balancing Agility and Discipline: A Guide for the Perplexed*, Addison-Wesley, Reading, MA (2004).

Boehner, Kirsten, Vertesi, Janet, Sengers, Phoebe, and Dourish, Paul, How HCI interprets the probes, *Proc. Conference on Human Factors in Computing Systems (ACM CHI 2007)*, ACM Press, New York (2007), 1077–1086.

Carroll, John M. (Editor), *Making Use: Scenario-Based Design of Human-Computer Interactions*, MIT Press, Cambridge, MA (2000).

Christensen, Claus M., Kjeldskov, Jesper, and Rasmussen, Klaus K., GeoHealth: A location-based service for nomadic home healthcare workers, *Proc. 2007 Conference of the Computer-Human Interaction Special Interest Group (CHISIG) of Australia on Computer-Human Interaction: Design: Activities, Artifacts and Environments*, ACM Press, New York (2007), 273–281.

Cooper, Alan, *The Inmates are Running the Asylum*, Sams, New York (2004).

Damodaran, Leela, User involvement in the systems design process – A practical guide for users, *Behaviour & Information Technology* 15, 6 (1996), 363–377.

Defense Acquisition University, *Defense Acquisition Guidebook – Chapter 6, Human Systems Integration (HSI)* (2004). Available at https://akss.dau.mil/dag/welcome.asp.

Druin, Allison, The role of children in the design of new technology, *Behaviour & Information Technology* 21, 1 (2002), 1–25.

Dumas, Joseph and Redish, Janice, *A Practical Guide to Usability Testing, Revised Edition*, Intellect Books, Bristol, U.K. (1999).

Fetterman, D. M., *Ethnography: Step by Step, Second Edition*, Sage, Thousand Oaks, CA (1998).

Gould, John D. and Lewis, Clayton, Designing for usability: Key principles and what designers think, *Communications of the ACM* 28, 3 (March 1985), 300–311.

Harper, R., The organization of ethnography, *Proc. CSCW 2000*, ACM Press, New York (2000), 239–264.

Heim, Steven, *The Resonant Interface: HCI Foundations for Interaction Design*, Addison-Wesley, Reading, MA (2008).

Holtzblatt, Karen and Beyer, Hugh, CDTools, InContext Enterprises, Inc., http://www.incontextdesign.com/cdtools/index.html (2008).

Holtzblatt, Karen, Wendell, Jessamyn Burns, and Wood, Shelley, *Rapid Contextual Design: A How-To Guide to Key Techniques for User-Centered Design*, Morgan Kaufmann, San Francisco, CA (2005).

Hughes, J., O'Brien, J., Rodden, T., and Rouncefield, M., Design with ethnography: A presentation framework for design, *Proc. ACM Symposium on Designing Interactive Systems*, ACM Press, New York (1997), 147–159.

Ives, Blake and Olson, Margrethe H., User involvement and MIS success: A review of research, *Management Science* 30, 5 (May 1984), 586–603.

Jones, Capers, A CAI State of the Practice Interview, Computer Aid, Inc., http://web.ecs.baylor.edu/faculty/grabow/Fall2007/COMMON/Secure/Refs/capersjonesinterview1.pdf (July 2005)

Karat, Claire-Marie, A business case approach to usability, in Bias, Randolph and Mayhew, Deborah (Editors), *Cost-Justifying Usability*, Academic Press, New York (1994), 45–70.

Kujala, Sari, User involvement: A review of the benefits and challenges, *Behaviour & Information Technology* 22, 1 (2003), 1–16.

Landauer, Thomas K., *The Trouble with Computers: Usefulness, Usability, and Productivity*, MIT Press, Cambridge, MA (1995).

Lessig, Lawrence, *The Future of Ideas: The Fate of the Commons in a Connected World*, Random House, New York (2001).

Lessig, Lawrence, *Code and Other Laws of Cyberspace, Version 2.0*, Basic Books, New York (2006).

Leventhal, Laura and Barnes, Julie, *Usability Engineering: Process, Products, and Examples*, Prentice Hall, Upper Saddle River, NJ (2007).

Marcus, Aaron, Return on investment for usable user-interface design: Examples and statistics (2002). Available at http://www.amanda.com/resources/ROI/AMA_ROIWhitePaper_28Feb02.pdf.

Marcus, Aaron, A practical set of culture dimensions for global user-interface development (2005). Available at http://www.amanda.com/resources/articles_f.html.

Mayhew, Deborah J., *The Usability Engineering Lifecycle: A Practitioner's Guide to User Interface Design*, Morgan Kaufmann, San Francisco, CA (1999).

Microsoft, Inc., *Microsoft's Windows Vista User Experience Guidelines* (2008). Available at http://www.procontext.com/en/guidelines/style-guides.html#microsoft.

Millen, David, Rapid ethnography: Time deepening strategies for HCI field research, *Proc. ACM Symposium on Designing Interactive Systems*, ACM Press, New York (2000), 280–286.

Muller, Michael, Retrospective on a year of participatory design using the PICTIVE technique, *Proc. CHI '92: Human Factors in Computing Systems*, ACM Press, New York (1992), 455–462.

Muller, Michael, Participatory design, in Jacko, Julie and Sears, Andrew (Editors), *The Human-Computer Interaction Handbook*, Lawrence Erlbaum Associates, Hillsdale, NJ (2003), 1051–1068.

Muller, M., Wildman, D., and White, E., Taxonomy of PD practices: A brief practitioner's guide, *Communications of the ACM* 36, 4 (1993), 26–27.

Myers, Brad, Hudson, Scott E., and Pausch, Randy, Past, present and future of user interface software tools, in Carroll, John M. (Editor), *HCI in the New Millennium*, ACM Press, New York (2001), 213–233.

National Research Council, Committee on Human Factors, Committee on Human-System Design Support for Changing Technology, Pew, Richard W. and Mavor, Anne S. (Editors), *Human-System Integration in the System Development Process: A New Look*, National Academies Press, Washington, DC (2007).

NetCoalition, http://www.NetCoalition.com/ (2008).

Nielsen, Jakob, *Designing Web Usability: The Practice of Simplicity*, New Riders, Indianapolis, IN (1999).

Nielsen, Jakob, Usability ROI declining, but still strong (2008). Available at http://www.useit.com/alertbox/roi.html.

Perfetti, Christine, Building and managing a successful user experience team (2006). Available at http://www.uie.com/events/uiconf/2006/articles/bloomer_wolfe_interview/.

Pfleeger, Shari Lawrence and Atlee, Joanne, *Software Engineering: Theory and Practice, Fourth Edition*, Prentice-Hall, Englewood Cliffs, NJ (2009).

Postman, Neil, *Technopoly: The Surrender of Culture to Technology*, Vintage Books, New York (1993).

Ramachandran, Divya, Kam, Matthew, Chiu, Jane, Canny, John, and Frankel, James F., Social dynamics of early stage co-design in developing regions, *Proc. Conference on Human Factors in Computing Systems (ACM CHI 2007)*, ACM Press, New York (2007), 1087–1096.

Rose, Anne, Plaisant, Catherine, and Shneiderman, Ben, Using ethnographic methods in user interface re-engineering, *Proc. ACM Symposium on Designing Interactive Systems*, ACM Press, New York (1995), 115–122.

Rosson, Mary Beth, *Usability Engineering: Scenario-Based Development of Human Computer Interaction*, Morgan Kaufmann, San Francisco, CA (2002).

Rosson, Mary Beth and Carroll, John M., *Usability Engineering: Scenario-Based Development of Human Computer Interaction*, Morgan Kaufmann, San Francisco, CA (2002).

Rosson, Mary Beth and Carroll, John M., Dimensions of participation in information system design, in Zhang, Ping and Galletta, Dennis F. (Editors), *Human-computer Interaction and Management Information Systems: Applications*, M.E. Sharpe, Armonk, NY (2006), 337–352.

Rubin, Jeffrey and Chisnell, Dana, *Handbook of Usability Testing: How to Plan, Design, and Conduct Effective Tests, Second Edition*, John Wiley & Sons, New York (2008).

Samuelson, Pamela, Digital rights management {and, or, vs.} the law, *Communications of the ACM* 46, 4 (April 2003), 41–45.

Samuelson, Pamela and Schultz, Jason, Should copyright owners have to give notice about their use of technical protection measures?, *Journal of Telecommunications & High Technology Law* 6 (2007), 41–76. Republication forthcoming in *Digital Rights Management Technologies* (ICFAI 2008).

Samuelson, Pamela, Intellectual property for an information age: How to balance the public interest, traditional legal principles, and the emerging digital reality, *Communications of the ACM* 44, 2 (February 2001), 67–68.

Sears, Andrew and Jacko, Julie A., *The Human-Computer Interaction Handbook: Fundamentals, Evolving Technologies and Emerging Applications, Second Edition*, CRC Press, Boca Raton, FL (2008).

Selby, Richard W. (Editor), *Software Engineering: Barry W. Boehm's Lifetime Contributions to Software Development, Management, and Research*, John Wiley & Sons, New York (2007), 663–685.

Sharp, Helen, Rogers, Yvonne, and Preece, Jenny, *Interaction Design: Beyond Human-Computer Interaction, Second Edition*, John Wiley & Sons, New York (2007).

Shneiderman, Ben and Rose, Anne, Social impact statements: Engaging public participation in information technology design, *Proc. CQL '96: ACM SIGCAS Symposium on Computers and the Quality of Life*, ACM Press, New York (1996), 90–96.

Sommerville, Ian, *Software Engineering, Eighth Edition*, Addison-Wesley, Reading, MA (2006).

Suchman, Lucy A., *Plans and Situated Actions: The Problem of Human-Machine Communication*, Cambridge University Press, Cambridge, U.K. (1987).

Sun Microsystems, Inc., *Java Look and Feel Design Guidelines, Second Edition*, http://java.sun.com/products/jlf/ed2/book/ (2001).

Usability Professionals Association, Usability body of knowledge, http://www.usabilitybok.org/ (2008).

Web Developers Journal, http://webdevelopersjournal.com/software/webtools.html (2008).

Whitworth, Brian and De Moore, Aldo (Editors), *Handbook of Research on Socio-Technical Design and Social Networking Systems*, IGI Global, Hershey, PA (2009).

Evaluating Interface Designs

66 The test of what is real is
that it is hard and rough. . . .
What is pleasant belongs in dreams. 99

Simone Weil
Gravity and Grace, 1947

Written in collaboration with Maxine S. Cohen

4.1 Introduction

Designers can become so entranced with their creations that they may fail to evaluate them adequately. Experienced designers have attained the wisdom and humility to know that extensive testing is a necessity. If feedback is the "breakfast of champions," then testing is the "dinner of the gods." However, careful choices must be made from the large menu of evaluation possibilities to create a balanced meal.

There are many factors that influence when and where evaluation is performed within the development cycle. For instance, the determinants of the evaluation plan (Nielsen, 1993; Dumas and Redish, 1999; Sharp, et al., 2007) include at least:

- Stage of design (early, middle, late)
- Novelty of the project (well defined versus exploratory)
- Number of expected users
- Criticality of the interface (for example, life-critical medical system versus museum-exhibit support system)
- Costs of the product and finances allocated for testing
- Time available
- Experience of the design and evaluation team

The range of evaluation plans might be anywhere from an ambitious two-year test with multiple phases for a new national air-traffic–control system to a three-day test with six users for a small internal web site. The range of costs might be from 20% of a project to 5%. Testing should occur at different times in the evaluation cycle, ranging from early to just before release.

A few years ago, focusing on usability and doing testing was just considered a good idea that might help you get ahead of the competition. However, the rapid growth of interest in usability means that failing to test is now risky indeed. Not only has the competition strengthened, but customary engineering practice now requires adequate testing and follow-through with recommended changes, as appropriate and time and budgeting permit. Failure to perform and document testing as well as not heeding the changes recommended from the testing process could lead to failed contract propoals or malpractice lawsuits from users where errors arise that may have been avoided, if the changes were made.

One troubling aspect of testing is the uncertainty that remains even after exhaustive testing by multiple methods. Perfection is not possible in complex human endeavors, so planning must include continuing methods to assess and repair problems during the lifecycle of an interface. Second, even though problems may continue to be found, at some point a decision has to be made about completing prototype testing and delivering the product. Third, most testing methods will account appropriately for normal usage, but performance in unpredictable situations or times with high levels of input, such as nuclear-reactor–control or air-traffic–control emergencies or heavily subscribed voting times (e.g., presidential elections), is extremely difficult to test. Development of testing methods to deal with stressful situations and even with partial equipment failures will have to be undertaken as user interfaces are developed for an increasing number of life-critical applications. Traditional lab testing (Section 4.3) may not accurately and with sufficient fidelity represent the high-stress and often hostile environments in which systems developed for health care providers, first responders, or the military are employed. Likewise, testing a global-positioning driving system will not work in a laboratory or other stationary location; it can only be tested out in the field. Some special medical devices may also need to be tested in their natural environments, such as a hospital, an assisted living facility, or even a private home. Many mobile devices are better evaluated in their natural contexts as well.

Discussions abound about the best ways to do usability testing and to report the results. The choice of evaluation methodology must be appropriate for the problem or research question under consideration (Greenberg and Buxton, 2008). Usability evaluators must broaden their methods and be open to non-empirical methods, such as user sketches (Tohidi et al., 2006a), consideration of design alternatives (Tohidi et al., 2006b), and ethnographic studies (Section 3.5). Producing sketches of possible user-interface designs, similar to the design sketches used by architects, is one interesting approach. This allows more alternatives to be explored in the early stage, before the design becomes so permanent.

Usability is about more than just ease of use, but there needs to be some measure of usefulness (Dicks, 2002). Today, complex systems that are hard to test with simple controlled experiments abound (Olsen, 2007). There is quite a bit of discussion concerning the number of users that participate in a usability study. Instead of focusing on the number of users, studies should focus on common tasks and task coverage (Lingdaard and Chattratichart, 2007). Usability must be viewed as a multidimensional concept (Koohang, 2004). Testing novel devices, such as tabletops using surface computing, may require some special consideration. Usability inspection techniques may have to be modified to take into account the concept of shared and personal spaces on a table: Table-CUA (T-CUA) is a groupware evaluation technique that extends Collaboration Usability Analysis (CUA) to the desktop, taking into consideration the group activity dimension (Pinelle and Gutwin, 2008).

Usability testing has become an established and accepted part of the design process, but it needs to be broadened and understood in the context of highly sophisticated systems, experienced users with high expectations, mobile and other innovative devices (such as gaming systems and controllers), and competition in the marketplace. A series of usability evaluations and related analyses have been conducted over the years, referred to as the Comparative Usability Evaluation (CUE) studies. The most recent study (CUE-4) showed some surprising results: Usability testing may overlook some problems, even critical ones (Molich and Dumas, 2008). Spool (2007) suggests three radical changes to the usability evaluation process: (1) stop making recommendations, and instead present observational findings; (2) stop conducting evaluations, and push the research onto the design team; and (3) seek out new techniques, because new tools are needed. This is an exciting and provocative time in usability evaluation; practitioners should heed this advice, look closely at current procedures, and perhaps make some revolutionary changes.

4.2 Expert Reviews

A natural starting point for evaluating new or revised interfaces is to present them to colleagues or customers and ask for their opinions. Such informal demos with test subjects can provide some useful feedback, but more formal expert reviews have proven to be far more effective (Stone et al., 2005; Nielsen and Mack, 1994). These methods depend on having experts (whose expertise may be in the application or user-interface domain) available on staff or as consultants. Expert reviews can then be conducted on short notice and rapidly.

Expert reviews can occur early or late in the design phase. The outcome may be a formal report with problems identified or recommendations for changes. Alternatively, the expert review may culminate in a discussion with or presentation to designers or managers. Expert reviewers should be sensitive to the design team's ego, involvement, and professional skill; suggestions should be made cautiously, in recognition of the fact that it is difficult for someone freshly inspecting an interface to fully understand the design rationale and development history. When reviewing some interfaces, such as gaming applications, domain expertise can be a critical component. The reviewers can note possible problems to discuss with the designers, but development of solutions generally should be left to the designers.

Expert reviews usually take from half a day to one week, although a lengthy training period may be required to explain the task domain or operational procedures. It may be useful to have the same as well as fresh expert reviewers as the project progresses. There are a variety of expert-review methods from which to choose:

- *Heuristic evaluation.* The expert reviewers critique an interface to determine conformance with a short list of design heuristics, such as the Eight Golden Rules (Section 2.3.4). It makes an enormous difference if the experts are familiar with the rules and are able to interpret and apply them. Today, there are many different types of devices that may be subject to a heuristic evaluation, and it is important that the heuristics match the application. Box 4.1 lists some heuristics developed specifically for the gaming environment. A similar set of 29 *playability heuristics* is also under development. This set splits the heuristics into three categories: game usability, mobility heuristics, and gameplay heuristics (Korhonen and Koivisto, 2006). Gameplay heuristics are the most difficult to evaluate because familiarity with all aspects of the game is required. Using the heuristics to follow good interaction design principles while maintaining the challenge and suspense of the game is a difficult balance.

BOX 4.1
Heuristics for the gaming environment.

1. Provide consistent responses to user's actions.
2. Allow users to customize video and audio setting, difficulty, and game speed.
3. Provide predictable and reasonable behavior for computer controlled units.
4. Provide unobstructed views that are appropriate for the user's current actions.
5. Allow users to skip non-playable and frequently repeated content.
6. Provide intuitive and customizable input mappings.
7. Provide controls that are easy to manage and that have an appropriate level of sensitivity and responsiveness.
8. Provide users with information on game status.
9. Provide instructions, training, and help.
10. Provide visual representations that are easy to interpret and that minimize the need for micromanagement.

From Pinelle et al., 2008.

- *Guidelines review.* The interface is checked for conformance with the organizational or other guidelines document (see Chapter 1 for a list of organizational guidelines documents and Section 2.2 for more on creating your own). Because guidelines documents may contain a thousand items or more, it may take the expert reviewers some time to absorb them and days or weeks to review a large interface.

- *Consistency inspection.* The experts verify consistency across a family of interfaces, checking the terminology, fonts, color schemes, layout, input and output formats, and so on within the interfaces as well as in the documentation and online help. Software tools can help automate the process, as well as produce concordances of words and abbreviations.

- *Cognitive walkthrough.* The experts simulate users walking through the interface to carry out typical tasks. High-frequency tasks are a starting point, but rare critical tasks, such as error recovery, also should be walked through. Some form of simulating a day in the life of a user should be part of the expert review process. Cognitive walkthroughs were developed for interfaces that can be learned by exploratory browsing (Wharton et al., 1994), but they are useful even for interfaces that require substantial training. An expert might try the walkthrough privately and explore the system, but there also should be a group meeting with designers, users, or managers to conduct a walkthrough and provoke discussion. Extensions to cover web-site navigation incorporate richer descriptions of users and their goals, plus linguistic-analysis programs to estimate the similarity of link labels and destinations (Blackmon et al., 2002).

- *Metaphors of human thinking (MOT).* The experts conduct an inspection that focuses on how users think when interacting with an interface. They consider metaphors for five aspects of human thinking: habit, the stream of thought, awareness and associations, the relation between utterances and thought, and knowing. In experimental settings, this technique seems to perform better (in terms of evaluators identifying more problems and problems that are more complex and therefore bigger issues for expert users than for novices) than cognitive walkthough and heuristic evaluation (Frøkjær and Hornbæk, 2008).

- *Formal usability inspection.* The experts hold a courtroom-style meeting, with a moderator or judge, to present the interface and to discuss its merits and weaknesses. Design-team members may rebut the evidence about problems in an adversarial format. Formal usability inspections can be educational experiences for novice designers and managers, but they may take longer to prepare and more personnel to carry out than do other types of review.

Expert reviews can be scheduled at several points in the development process, when experts are available and when the design team is ready for feedback.

The number of expert reviews will depend on the magnitude of the project and on the amount of resources allocated.

An expert-review report should aspire to comprehensiveness, rather than making opportunistic comments about specific features or presenting a random collection of suggested improvements. The evaluators might use a guidelines document to structure the report, then comment on novice, intermittent, and expert features and review consistency across all displays, paying attention to ensure that the usability recommendations are both useful and usable. Some suggestions for writing effective usability recommendations can be found in Box 4.2.

If the report ranks recommendations by importance and expected effort level, managers are more likely to implement them (or at least, the high-payoff, low-cost ones). In one expert review, the highest priority was to shorten a three-to-five-minute login procedure that required eight dialog boxes and passwords on two networks. The obvious benefit to already over-busy users was apparent, and they were delighted with the improvement. Common middle-level recommendations include reordering the sequence of displays, providing improved instructions or feedback, and removing nonessential actions. Expert reviews should also include required small fixes such as spelling mistakes, poorly aligned data-entry fields, or inconsistent button placement. A final category includes less vital fixes and novel features that can be addressed in the next version of the interface.

Expert reviewers should be placed in a situation as similar as possible to the one that intended users will experience. They should take training courses, read the documentation, take tutorials, and try the interface in as close as possible to a realistic work environment, complete with noise and distractions. However,

BOX 4.2
Making usability recommendations useful and usable.

- Communicate each recommendation clearly at the conceptual level.
- Ensure that the recommendation improves the overall usability of the application.
- Be aware of the business or technical constraints.
- Show respect for the product team's constraints.
- Solve the whole problem, not just a special case.
- Make recommendations specific and clear.
- Avoid vagueness by including specific examples in your recommendations.

From Molich et al., 2007.

expert reviewers may also retreat to a quieter environment for a detailed review of each screen.

Another approach, getting a *bird's-eye view* of an interface by studying a full set of printed screens laid out on the floor or pinned to walls, has proved to be enormously fruitful in detecting inconsistencies and spotting unusual patterns. The bird's-eye view enables reviewers to quickly see if the fonts, colors, and terminology are consistent and whether the multiple developers have adhered to a common style.

Expert reviewers may also use software tools (e.g., WebTango) to speed their analyses, especially with large interfaces (Ivory, 2003). Sometimes string searches on design documents, help text, or program code can be valuable, but more specific interface-design analyses—such as web-accessibility validation, privacy-policy checks, and download-time reduction—are growing more effective. Some sample tools that are used for web-accessibility violations include IBM's Rational Policy Tester Accessibility Edition Software (formerly Bobby™ or WebXAct™), InFocus™, Resource Allocation Methodology Project (RAMP), and LIFT™. These tools usually provide specific instructions for improvements. A further discussion of automated tools can be found in Section 4.6.5.

The danger with expert reviews is that the experts may not have an adequate understanding of the task domain or user communities. Different experts tend to find different problems in an interface, so three to five expert reviewers can be highly productive, as can complementary usability testing. Experts come in many flavors, and conflicting advice can further confuse the situation (cynics say, "For every Ph.D., there is an equal and opposite Ph.D."). To strengthen the possibility of successful expert review, it helps to choose knowledgeable experts who are familiar with the project and who have a long-term relationship with the organization. These people can be called back to see the results of their intervention, and they can be held accountable. However, even experienced expert reviewers have difficulty knowing how typical users—especially first-time users—will behave.

4.3 Usability Testing and Laboratories

The emergence of usability testing and laboratories since the early 1980s is an indicator of the profound shift in attention towards user needs. Traditional managers and developers resisted at first, saying that usability testing seemed like a nice idea, but that time pressures or limited resources prevented them from trying it. As experience grew and successful projects gave credit to the testing process, demand swelled and design teams began to compete for the scarce resource of the usability-laboratory staff. Managers came to realize that having a usability test on the schedule was a powerful incentive to complete a design phase. The usability-test report provided supportive confirmation of progress and specific recommendations for changes. Designers sought the bright light of evaluative feedback to guide their work, and managers saw fewer disasters as projects approached delivery dates. The remarkable surprise was that usability testing not only sped up many projects, but also produced dramatic cost savings (Rubin and Chisnell, 2008; Sherman, 2006; Dumas and Redish, 1999).

Usability-laboratory advocates split from their academic roots as these practitioners developed innovative approaches that were influenced by advertising and market research. While academics were developing controlled experiments to test hypotheses and support theories, practitioners developed usability-testing methods to refine user interfaces rapidly. Controlled experiments (Section 4.7) have at least two treatments and seek to show statistically significant differences; usability tests are designed to find flaws in user interfaces. Both strategies use a carefully prepared set of tasks, but usability tests have fewer participants (maybe as few as three), and their outcome is a report with recommended changes, as opposed to validation or rejection of a hypothesis. Of course, there is a useful spectrum of possibilities between rigid controls and informal testing, and sometimes a combination of approaches is appropriate.

4.3.1 Usability labs

The movement towards usability testing stimulated the construction of usability laboratories (Rubin and Chisnell, 2008; Dumas and Redish, 1999; Nielsen, 1993). Having a physical laboratory makes an organization's commitment to usability clear to employees, customers, and users. A typical modest usability laboratory would have two 10-by-10-foot areas, divided by a half-silvered mirror (Fig. 4.1): one for the participants to do their work and another for the testers and observers (designers, managers, and customers). IBM was an early leader in developing usability laboratories. Microsoft started later but embraced the idea with more than 25 usability-test labs. Hundreds of software-development companies have followed suit, and a consulting community that will do usability testing for hire also has emerged.

Usability laboratories are typically staffed by one or more people with expertise in testing and user-interface design, who may serve 10 to 15 projects per year throughout an organization. The laboratory staff meet with the user-interface architect or manager at the start of the project to make a test plan with scheduled dates and budget allocations. Usability-laboratory staff members participate in early task analysis or design reviews, provide information on software tools or literature references, and help to develop the set of tasks for the usability test. Two to six weeks before the usability test, the detailed test plan is developed; it contains the list of tasks plus subjective satisfaction and debriefing questions. The number, types, and sources of participants are also identified—sources might be customer sites, temporary personnel agencies,

FIGURE 4.1

Usability lab test with participant and observer seated at a workstation. Recording devices capture the user's actions and the contents of the screens, while microphones capture thinking-aloud comments. The test monitor sits in another room with a one-way mirror so the participant is visible. At the test monitor's control station, there are various consoles collecting data, displaying what is shown on the participant's screen (http://www.cure.at/controlrooms).

or advertisements placed in newspapers. A pilot test of the procedures, tasks, and questionnaires with one to three participants is conducted one week before the test, while there is still time for changes. This typical preparation process can be modified in many ways to suit each project's unique needs. Figure 4.2 provides a detailed breakdown of steps to follow when conducting usability assessments.

After changes are approved, participants are chosen to represent the intended user communities, with attention to their backgrounds in computing, experience with the task, motivation, education, and ability with the natural language used in the interface. Usability-laboratory staff also must control for physical concerns (such as eyesight, left- versus right-handedness, age, gender, education, and computer experience) and for other experimental conditions (such as time of day, day of week, physical surroundings, noise, room temperature, and level of distractions).

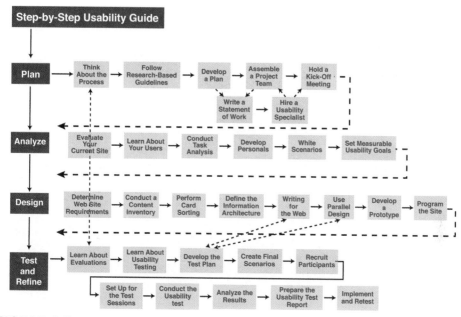

FIGURE 4.2

Usability.gov Step by Step Usability Guide. This guide shows all the steps from planning a usability test to performing the actual test and reporting the results.

Recording participants performing tasks is often valuable for later review and for showing designers or managers the problems that users encounter. Reviewing the recordings is a tedious job, so careful logging and annotation during the test is vital to reduce the time spent finding critical incidents. Most usability laboratories have acquired or developed software to facilitate logging of user activities (typing, mousing, reading screens, reading manuals, and so on) by observers with automatic timestamping. Some of the more popular data-logging tools include Live Logger, Morae from TechSmith®, Spectator, LogSquare from Mangold, and VisualMarker. Participants may be anxious about the cameras at the start of the test, but within minutes they usually focus on the tasks and ignore the recording process. The reactions of designers to seeing the actual recordings of users failing with their interfaces are sometimes powerful and may be highly motivating. When designers see participants repeatedly picking the wrong menu item, they often realize that the label or placement needs to be changed.

Another relatively new technique available to the usability-evaluation professional is *eye-tracking* software (Fig. 4.3). The eye-tracking data can show where participants gazed at the screen and for how long. The results are displayed

FIGURE 4.3

In this eye-tracking setup, the participant wears a helmet that monitors and records where on the screen the participant is looking (http://www.cure.at/eyetracking/).

in color-coded heat maps (Fig. 12.4) that clearly demonstrate which areas of the screen are viewed and which areas are ignored. Up until recently, this software was rather expensive, but now it can be supplied as a simple add-on to a personal computer (Fig. 4.4). When testing with small mobile devices like cellphones, special equipment may be needed to capture the user's screen and associated activities (Fig. 4.5).

At each design stage, the interface can be refined iteratively and the improved version can be tested. It is important to fix even small flaws (such as spelling errors or inconsistent layout) quickly, since they influence user expectations.

4.3.2 Handling participants and the Institutional Review Board (IRB)

Participants should always be treated with respect and should be informed that it is not *they* who are being tested; rather, it is the software and user interface that are under study. They should be told about what they will be doing (for example, finding products on a web site, creating a diagram using a mouse, or

FIGURE 4.4

Portable lab with eye tracking (http://www.mangold-international.com/en.html).

studying a restaurant guide on a touchscreen kiosk) and how long they will be expected to stay. Participation should always be voluntary, and *informed consent* should be obtained (Box 4.3).

In most places, an Institutional Review Board (IRB) governs any research performed with human subjects. There are different levels of review and precise procedures that must be followed. Special populations may also have unique considerations that need to be attended to. Most universities have an IRB representative that can explain these procedures in detail.

4.3.3 Think aloud and related techniques

An effective technique during usability testing is to invite users to *think aloud* (sometimes referred to as *concurrent think aloud*) about what they are doing as they are performing the task. The designer or tester should be supportive of the participants, not taking over or giving instructions, but prompting and listening for clues about how they are dealing with the interface. Think-aloud protocols yield interesting clues for the observant usability tester; for example, they may

FIGURE 4.5

Special mobile camera to track and record activities on the screen of a hand-held device (http://www.tracksys.co.uk/product-details.php?id=9).

hear comments such as "This web page text is too small . . . so I'm looking for something on the menus to make the text bigger . . . maybe it's on the top in the icons . . . I can't find it . . . so I'll just carry on."

After a suitable time period for accomplishing the task list—usually one to three hours—the participants can be invited to make general comments or suggestions or to respond to specific questions. The informal atmosphere of a think-aloud session is pleasant and often leads to many spontaneous suggestions for improvements. In their efforts to encourage thinking aloud, some usability laboratories have found that having two participants working together produces more talking, as one participant explains procedures and decisions to the other.

Another related technique is called *retrospective think aloud*. With this technique, after completing a task users are asked what they were thinking as they performed the task. The drawback is that the users may not be able to wholly and accurately recall their thoughts after completing the task; however, this approach allows users to focus all their attention on the tasks they are performing and generates more accurate timings.

It's important to consider timing when using think-aloud techniques. The standard think-aloud procedure may alter the true task time, as verbalizing

BOX 4.3

Informed consent guidelines.

Each informed consent statement should contain:

- The purpose of the study (an explanation of why the study is being done).
- The procedure being used for the study. This section should also include a time expectation for the participant and the protocol for requesting a break.
- If there will be any video or audio recording, who will see the recordings, and what happens to the recording material when the testing is completed (not all studies involve recordings).
- A statement of confidentiality and how the anonymity of the participant is preserved.
- Any risks to the participant (in most usability studies there is minimal risk).
- The fact that participation is voluntary and that the participant can withdraw at any time with no penalty.
- Whom to contact with questions and for any further information after the study, and a statement that initial questions about the testing have been answered satisfactorily.

The informed consent statement should be signed prior to the start of any testing.

From Dumas and Loring, 2008.

the thought process creates additional cognitive load, and the users may pause the task activity as they vocalize their thoughts. Retrospective think-aloud procedures will not alter the task timings themselves, but because the users need to perform the tasks and then reflect on and review them again, their overall time commitment may be doubled. Also, be aware that using the think-aloud technique along with eye tracking may generate invalid results: Users' eyes may wander while they are speaking, causing spurious data to be generated.

4.3.4 The spectrum of usability testing

Usability testing comes in many different flavors and formats. Most of the current research demonstrates the importance of testing often and at varied times during the design cycle. The purpose of the test and the type of data that is needed are important considerations. Testing may be done at the exploratory stage, when the designers are trying to conceive the correct design, or as a validation effort to ensure that certain requirements were met. The following is a list of the various types of usability testing. Testing can be performed using combinations of these methods as well.

- *Paper mockups and prototyping.* Early usability studies can be conducted using paper mockups of screen displays to assess user reactions to wording, layout, and sequencing. A test administrator plays the role of the computer by flipping the pages while asking a participant user to carry out typical tasks. This informal testing is inexpensive, rapid, and usually productive. Typically designers create *low-fidelity* paper prototypes of the design, but today there are computer programs (e.g., Visio™) that can allow designers to create more detailed *high-fidelity* prototypes with minimal effort. Interestingly enough, though, users have been shown to respond more openly to the lower-fidelity designs (Snyder, 2003).

- *Discount usability testing.* This quick-and-dirty approach to task analysis, prototype development, and testing has been widely influential because it lowers the barriers to newcomers (Nielsen, 1993). A controversial aspect is the recommendation to use only three to six test participants. Advocates point out that most serious problems are found with only a few participants, enabling prompt revision and repeated testing, while critics hold that a broader subject pool is required to thoroughly test more complex systems. One resolution to the controversy is to use discount usability testing as a *formative evaluation* (while designs are changing substantially) and more extensive usability testing as a *summative evaluation* (near the end of the design process). The formative evaluation identifies problems that guide redesign, while the summative evaluation provides evidence for product announcements ("94% of our 120 testers completed their shopping tasks without assistance") and clarifies training needs ("with four minutes of instruction, every participant successfully programmed the videorecorder").

- *Competitive usability testing.* Competitive testing compares a new interface to previous versions or to similar products from competitors. This approach is close to a controlled experimental study (Section 4.7), and staff must be careful to construct parallel sets of tasks and to counterbalance the order of presentation of the interfaces. Within-subjects designs seem the most powerful, because participants can make comparisons between the competing interfaces—fewer participants are needed, although each is needed for a longer time period.

- *Universal usability testing.* This approach tests interfaces with highly diverse users, hardware, software platforms, and networks. When a wide range of international users are anticipated, such as for consumer electronics products, web-based information services, or e-government services, ambitious testing is necessary to clean up problems and thereby help ensure success. Trials with small and large displays, slow and fast networks, and a range of operating systems or Internet browsers will do much to raise the rate of customer success. Being aware of any perceptual or physical limitations of the users (e.g., vision impairments, hearing difficulties, motor or mobility impairments) and modifying the testing to accommodate these limitations will result in the creation of products that can be used by a wider variety of users.

- *Field tests and portable labs.* This testing method puts new interfaces to work in realistic environments or in a more naturalistic environment in the field for a fixed trial period. Field tests can be made more fruitful if logging software is used to capture error, command, and help frequencies, as well as productivity measures. Portable usability laboratories with recording and logging facilities have been developed to support more thorough field-testing (Fig. 4.6). A different kind of field testing involves supplying users with test versions of new software or consumer products; tens or even thousands of users might receive beta versions and be asked to comment. Some companies that provide this service include Noldus, UserWorks, Ovo Studios, and Experience Dynamics.

- *Remote usability testing.* Since web-based applications are available internationally, it is tempting to conduct usability tests online, avoiding the complexity and cost of bringing participants to a lab. This makes it possible to have larger numbers of participants with more diverse backgrounds, and it may add to the realism, since participants do their tests in their own environments and use their own equipment. Participants can be recruited by e-mail from customer

FIGURE 4.6

An example of a portable usability lab setup (http://www.userworks.com).

lists or through online communities. This opens the pool of participants to sophisticated users that, perhaps because of their remote locations or other physical challenges, could not otherwise get to a lab location. The downside is that there is less control over user behavior and diminished ability to observe their reactions, although usage logs and phone interviews are useful supplements. These tests can be performed both synchronously (users do tasks at the same time while the evaluator observes) and asynchronously (users perform tasks independently and the evaluator looks at the results later). Some studies have shown remote usability testing to find more problems than traditional usability testing. Synchronous remote usability testing is a valid evaluation technique. Software that supports this type of testing includes NetMeeting™, WebEx™, and Lotus® Sametime®.

- *Can-you-break-this tests.* Game designers pioneered the *can-you-break-this* approach to usability testing by providing energetic teenagers with the challenge of trying to beat new games. This destructive testing approach, in which the users try to find fatal flaws in the system or otherwise destroy it, has been used in other types of projects as well and should be considered seriously. Software purchasers have little patience with flawed products, and the cost of sending out thousands of replacement disks is high. Furthermore, the loss of goodwill when customers have to download and install revised versions is one that few companies can bear.

For all its success, usability testing does have at least two serious limitations: it emphasizes first-time usage and provides limited coverage of the interface features. Since usability tests are usually only one to three hours long, it is difficult to ascertain how performance will be after a week or a month of regular usage. Within the short time of a usability test, the participants may get to use only a small fraction of the system's features, menus, dialog boxes, or help screens. These and other concerns have led design teams to supplement usability testing with varied forms of expert reviews.

Further criticisms of usability-lab testing come from proponents of activity theory and those who believe that realistic test environments are necessary to evaluate information appliances, ambient technologies, and consumer-oriented mobile devices. They argue that longer-term testing, such as a six-month trial for a home TV interface, is necessary to understand adoption and learning processes (Petersen et al., 2002). Furthermore, tests of interfaces used in high-stress situations and mission-critical domains such as military combat, law enforcement, first response, and similar situations often cannot be conducted in traditional usability-lab settings. Creating a realistic environment is critical to adequately test such interfaces, but not always possible. When under high stress, the user may have trouble processing all the information being generated and displayed and be able to process only a subset of the information (Rahman, 2007).

Usability testing with mobile devices also needs special attention. Some issues to be aware of include availability of extra batteries and chargers, signal strength issues, ensuring that the user is focusing on the interface when using paper prototypes, and having users tap on the interface with a stylus because a finger may block the observer from seeing what was tapped (Schultz, 2006).

The current interest in usability testing is apparent from the assortment of recent books devoted to the topic. These sources (Dumas and Loring, 2008; Rubin and Chisnell, 2008; Dumas and Fox, 2008; Stone et al., 2005; Barnum, 2002) discuss setting up usability labs, the role of the usability monitor, the collection and reporting of the test data, and other information needed to run professional usability tests. Additional information on cost savings and return on investment due to usability testing can be found in other sources (Sherman, 2006; Bias and Mayhew, 2005).

4.3.5 Usability test reports

The U.S. National Institute for Standards and Technology took a major step towards standardizing usability-test reports in 1997, when it convened a group of software manufacturers and large purchasers to work for several years to produce the Common Industry Format for summative usability testing results. The format describes the testing environment, tasks, participants, and results in a standard way, so as to enable consumers to make comparisons. The group's work (http://www.nist.gov/iusr/) is ongoing; the participants are developing guidelines for formative usability test reports and some best practice guidelines are emerging. Key points are that it is important to understand the audience (who will be reading the report) and to keep the report short (Theofanos and Quesenbery, 2005). Another guide published by the U.S. Department of Health and Human Services provides helpful and easy to follow web design and usability guidelines (National Cancer Institute, 2006).

4.4 Survey Instruments

User surveys (written or online) are a familiar, inexpensive, and generally acceptable companion for usability tests and expert reviews. Managers and users can easily grasp the notion of surveys, and the typically large numbers of respondents (hundreds to thousands of users) confer a sense of authority compared to the potentially biased and highly variable results from small numbers of usability-test participants or expert reviewers. The keys to successful surveys are clear goals in advance and development of focused items that help to attain those goals. Experienced surveyors know that care is also needed during design, administration, and data analysis (de Leeuw et al., 2008).

4.4.1 Preparing and designing survey questions

A survey form should be prepared, reviewed by colleagues, and tested with a small sample of users before a large-scale survey is conducted. Methods of statistical analysis (beyond means and standard deviations) and presentation (histograms, scatterplots, and so on) should also be developed before the final survey is distributed. In short, directed activities are more successful than unplanned statistics-gathering expeditions. Our experience is that directed activities also provide the most fertile frameworks for unanticipated discoveries. Since biased samples of respondents can produce erroneous results, survey planners need to build in methods to verify that respondents represent the population in terms of age, gender, experience, and so on.

It is important to pre-test or pilot-test any survey instrument prior to actual use. Users can be asked for their subjective impressions about specific aspects of the interface, such as the representation of:

- Task domain objects and actions
- Interface domain metaphors and action handles
- Syntax of inputs and design of displays

It may also be useful to ascertain certain characteristics about the users, including:

- Background *demographics* (age, gender, origins, native language, education, income)
- Experience with computers (specific applications or software packages, length of time, depth of knowledge, whether knowledge was acquired through formal training or self-teaching)
- Job responsibilities (decision-making influence, managerial roles, motivation)
- Personality style (introvert versus extrovert, risk taking versus risk averse, early versus late adopter, systematic versus opportunistic)
- Reasons for not using an interface (inadequate services, too complex, too slow, afraid)
- Familiarity with features (printing, macros, shortcuts, tutorials)
- Feelings after using an interface (confused versus clear, frustrated versus in control, bored versus excited)

Online and web-based surveys avoid the cost and effort of printing, distributing, and collecting paper forms. Many people prefer to answer a brief survey displayed on a screen instead of filling in and returning a printed form, although there is a potential bias in the self-selected sample. Some surveys of World Wide Web utilization include more than 50,000 respondents.

In one survey (Gefen and Straub, 2000), e-commerce users were asked to respond to five statements according to the following commonly used *Likert* scale:

Strongly agree   Agree   Neutral   Disagree   Strongly disagree

The items in the survey were these:

- Improves my performance in book searching and buying
- Enables me to search and buy books faster
- Enhances my effectiveness in book searching and buying
- Makes it easier to search for and purchase books
- Increases my productivity in searching and purchasing books

Such a list of questions can help designers to identify problems users are having and to demonstrate improvements to the interface as changes are made in training, online assistance, command structures, and so on; progress is demonstrated by improved scores on subsequent surveys.

Coleman and Williges (1985) developed a set of bipolar semantically anchored items (pleasing versus irritating, simple versus complicated, concise versus redundant) that asked users to describe their reactions to using a word processor. In one of our pilot studies of error messages in text-editor usage, users had to rate the messages on 1-to-7 scales:

Hostile	1	2	3	4	5	6	7	Friendly
Vague	1	2	3	4	5	6	7	Specific
Misleading	1	2	3	4	5	6	7	Beneficial
Discouraging	1	2	3	4	5	6	7	Encouraging

Another approach is to ask users to evaluate aspects of the interface design, such as the readability of characters, the meaningfulness of command names, or the helpfulness of error messages. If users rate as poor one aspect of the interactive system, the designers have a clear indication of what needs to be redone. If precise—as opposed to general—questions are used in surveys, there is a greater chance that the results will provide useful guidance for taking action.

Additional attention may be needed when dealing with special populations. For example, questionnaires for children must be in age-appropriate language, questionnaires for international users may need to be translated, larger fonts may be needed for older adults, and special accommodations may need to be made for users with disabilities.

4.4.2 Sample questionnaires

Questionnaires and surveys are commonly used in usability evaluation. Several instruments and scales have been developed and refined over time. The early questionnaires concentrated on elements such as clarity of fonts, appearance on the screen, and keyboard configurations. Later questionnaires deal with multimedia components, videoconferencing, and other current interface designs. Here is some information on a few (most use a Likert-like scale):

> The *Questionnaire for User Interaction Satisfaction* (QUIS). Developed by Shneiderman and refined by Chin et al. (1988). The QUIS (http://lap. umd.edu/quis/) has been applied in many projects with thousands of users, and new versions have been created that include items relating to web-site design and videoconferencing. The University of Maryland's Office of Technology Commercialization licenses QUIS in electronic and paper forms to hundreds of organizations internationally, with special licensing terms for student researchers. The licensees sometimes use only parts of the QUIS or extend its domain-specific items. Table 4.1 contains a portion of the QUIS, including an example for collecting computer experience data.

> The *System Usability Scale* (SUS). Developed by John Brooke when he worked for Digital Equipment Corporation; sometimes referred to as the "quick and dirty" scale (Brooke, 1996). The SUS consists of 10 statements with which users rate their agreement (on a 5-point scale). Half of the questions are positively worded and the other half are negatively worded.

PART 1: System Experience

1.1   How long have you worked on this system?
     ___ less than 1 hour   ___ 6 months to less than 1 year
     ___ 1 hour to less than 1 day   ___ 1 year to less than 2 years
     ___ 1 day to less than 1 week   ___ 2 years to less than 3 years
     ___ 1 week to less than 1 month   ___ 3 years or more
     ___ 1 month to less than 6 months

PART 6: Learning

6.1   Learning to operate the system   difficult   easy
         1 2 3 4 5 6 7 8 9   NA

     6.1.1 Getting started   difficult   easy
         1 2 3 4 5 6 7 8 9   NA

     6.1.2 Learning advanced features   difficult   easy
         1 2 3 4 5 6 7 8 9   NA

     6.1.3 Time to learn to use the system   difficult   easy
         1 2 3 4 5 6 7 8 9   NA

TABLE 4.1

Questionnaire for User Interaction Satisfaction (QUIS) (© University of Maryland, 1997)

	Strongly disagree				Strongly agree
1 I think that I would like to use this system frequently	1	2	3	4	5
2 I found the system unnecessarily complex	1	2	3	4	5

TABLE 4.2

System Usability Scale (SUS) example

A score is computed that can be viewed as a percentage. Table 4.2 contains a sample from the SUS.

The *Post-Study System Usability Questionnaire* (PSSUQ). Developed by IBM; has 48 items that focus on system usefulness, information quality, and interface quality (Lewis, 1995).

The *Computer System Usability Questionnaire* (CSUQ). A later development by IBM that contains 19 statements to which participants respond using a 7-point scale. Table 4.3 contains a sample from the CSUQ.

The *Software Usability Measurement Inventory* (SUMI). Developed by the Human Factors Research Group (HFRG); this contains 50 items designed to measure users' perceptions of their affect (emotional response), efficiency, and control and of the learnability and helpfulness of the interface (Kirakowski and Corbett, 1993). Table 4.4 contains a sample from the SUMI.

The Website Analysis and MeasureMent Inventory *(WAMMI) questionnaire.* Does web-based evaluations and is available in more than a dozen languages.

Although many of these questionnaires were developed a while ago, they still serve as reliable and valid instruments. Some have been transformed by changing the focus of the items asked about. Specialized questionnaires have

		1 2 3 4 5 6 7		NA
1 Overall, I am satisfied with how easy it is to use this system.	Strongly disagree	○ ○ ○ ○ ○ ○ ○	Strongly agree	○
2 I can effectively complete my work using this system.	Strongly disagree	○ ○ ○ ○ ○ ○ ○	Strongly agree	○

TABLE 4.3

Computer System Usability Questionnaire (CSUQ) example

	Agree	Undecided	Disagree
1 This software responds too slowly to inputs.	❑	❑	❑
2 I would recommend this software to my colleagues.	❑	❑	❑

TABLE 4.4

Software Usability Measurement Inventory (SUMI) example

been developed and tested based on these proven instruments. One example is the Mobile Phone Usability Questionnaire (MPUQ), which consists of 72 items broken down into six factors: ease of learning and use, helpfulness and problem-solving capabilities, affective aspect and multimedia properties, commands and minimal memory load, control and efficiency, and typical tasks for mobile phones (Ryu and Smith-Jackson, 2006). The SUS has also been used with cell phones as well as interactive voice systems, web-based interfaces, and other interfaces and has been shown to be a robust and versatile tool (Bangor et al., 2008). As with any metric, any score should not be used in isolation. The best testing procedure, leading to the most confidence-inspiring results, would include triangulating the data from multiple methods, such as observations, interviews, logging of interface usage, and so on (Shneiderman and Plaisant, 2006).

More details on questionnaires can be found at Gary Perlman's web site (http://oldwww.acm.org/perlman/question.html) and Jurek Kirakowski's web site (http://www.ucc.ie/hfrg/resources/qfaq1.html). Writing and designing good questionnaires is an art as well as a science. Several books (Tullis and Albert, 2008; Rubin and Chisnell, 2008) and articles (Tullis and Stetson, 2004) provide further reading on use, validity, and development of good and valid questionnaires. In addition to the standard type measures of satisfaction, specialized devices (e.g., mobile devices) and gaming interfaces may require unique measures such as pleasure, joy, affect, challenge, or realism.

4.5 Acceptance Tests

For large implementation projects, the customer or manager usually sets objective and measurable goals for hardware and software performance. Many authors of requirements documents are even so bold as to specify the mean time between failures, as well as the mean time to repair for hardware and, in some cases, software failures. More typically, a set of test cases is specified for the software, with possible response-time requirements for the hardware/software combination. If the completed product fails to meet these acceptance criteria, the system must be reworked until success is demonstrated.

These notions can be neatly extended to the human interface. Explicit acceptance criteria should be established when the requirements document is written or when a contract is offered. Rather than use the vague and misleading criterion of "user friendliness," measurable criteria for the user interface can be established for the following:

- Time for users to learn specific functions
- Speed of task performance
- Rate of errors by users
- User retention of commands over time
- Subjective user satisfaction

An acceptance test for a food-shopping web site might specify the following:

> The participants will be 35 adults (25–45 years old), native speakers with no disabilities, hired from an employment agency. They will have moderate web-use experience: 1–5 hours/week for at least a year. They will be given a 5-minute demonstration on the basic features. At least 30 of the 35 adults should be able to complete the benchmark tasks within 30 minutes.

Another testable requirement for the same interface might be this:

> Special participants in three categories will also be tested: (a) 10 older adults aged 55–65; (b) 10 adult users with varying motor, visual, and auditory disabilities; and (c) 10 adult users who are recent immigrants and use English as a second language.

Since the choice of the benchmark tasks is critical, pilot testing must be done to refine the materials and procedures used. A third item in the acceptance test plan might focus on retention:

> Ten participants will be recalled after one week and asked to carry out a new set of benchmark tasks. In 20 minutes, at least eight of the participants should be able to complete the tasks correctly.

In a large interface, there may be 8 or 10 such tests to carry out different components of the interface and with different user communities. Other criteria, such as subjective satisfaction, output comprehensibility, system response time, installation procedures, printed documentation, or graphics appeal, may also be considered in acceptance tests of complete commercial products.

If precise acceptance criteria are established, both the customer and the interface developer can benefit. Arguments about user friendliness are avoided, and contractual fulfillment can be demonstrated objectively. Acceptance tests differ from usability tests in that the atmosphere may be adversarial, so outside testing organizations are often appropriate to ensure neutrality. The central goal of acceptance testing is not to detect flaws, but rather to verify adherence to requirements.

After successful acceptance testing, there may be a period of field testing before national or international distribution. In addition to further refining the user interface, field tests can improve training methods, tutorial materials, telephone-help procedures, marketing methods, and publicity strategies.

The goal of early expert reviews, usability testing, surveys, acceptance testing, and field testing is to force as much as possible of the evolutionary development into the prerelease phase, when change is relatively easy and inexpensive to accomplish.

4.6 Evaluation During Active Use

A carefully designed and thoroughly tested interface is a wonderful asset, but successful active use requires constant attention from dedicated managers, user-service personnel, and maintenance staff. Everyone involved in supporting the user community can contribute to interface refinements that provide ever-higher levels of service. You cannot please all of the users all of the time, but earnest effort will be rewarded by the appreciation of a grateful user community. Perfection is not attainable, but percentage improvements are possible and are worth pursuing.

Gradual interface dissemination is useful so that problems can be repaired with minimal disruption. As user numbers grow, major changes to the interface should be limited to an announced annual or semiannual revision. If interface users can anticipate the changes, resistance will be reduced, especially if they have positive expectations of improvement. More frequent changes are expected in the rapidly developing World Wide Web environment, but stable access to key resources even as novel services are added may be the winning policy.

4.6.1 Interviews and focus-group discussions

Interviews with individual users can be productive because the interviewer can pursue specific issues of concern. After a series of individual discussions, focus-group discussions are valuable to ascertain the universality of the users' comments (Kuhn, 2000). Interviewing can be costly and time-consuming, so usually only a small fraction of the user community is involved. On the other hand, direct contact with users often leads to specific, constructive suggestions. Professionally led focus groups can elicit surprising patterns of usage or hidden problems, which can be quickly explored and confirmed by participants. On the other hand, outspoken individuals can sway the group or dismiss comments from weaker participants. Interviews and focus groups can be arranged to target specific sets of users, such as experienced or long-term users of a product, generating different sets of issues than would be raised with novice users.

A large corporation conducted 45-minute interviews with 66 of the 4,300 users of an internal message system. The interviews revealed that the users were happy with some aspects of the functionality, such as the capacity to pick up messages at any site, the legibility of printed messages, and the convenience of after-hours access. However, the interviews also revealed that 23.6% of the users had concerns about reliability, 20.2% thought that using the system was confusing, and 18.2% said convenience and accessibility could be improved, whereas only 16.0% expressed no concerns. Later questions in the interview explored specific features. As a result of this interview project, a set of 42 enhancements to the interface was proposed and implemented. The designers of the interface had earlier proposed an alternate set of enhancements, but the results of the interviews led to a changed set of priorities that more closely reflected the users' needs.

4.6.2 Continuous user-performance data logging

The software architecture should make it easy for system managers to collect data about the patterns of interface usage, speed of user performance, rate of errors, and/or frequency of requests for online assistance. Logging data provide guidance in the acquisition of new hardware, changes in operating procedures, improvements to training, plans for system expansion, and so on.

For example, if the frequency of each error message is recorded, the highest-frequency error is a candidate for attention. The message could be rewritten, training materials could be revised, the software could be changed to provide more specific information, or the command syntax could be simplified. Without specific logging data, however, the system-maintenance staff has no way of knowing which of the many hundreds of error-message situations is the biggest problem for users. Similarly, staff should examine messages that never appear, to see whether there is an error in the code or whether users are avoiding use of some facility.

If logging data are available for each command, each help screen, and each database record, changes to the human-computer interface can be made to simplify access to frequently used features. Managers also should examine unused or rarely used facilities to understand why users are avoiding those features. A major benefit of usage-frequency data is the guidance that they provide to system maintainers in optimizing performance and in reducing costs for all participants. This latter argument may yield the clearest advantage to cost-conscious managers, whereas the increased quality of the interface is an attraction to service-oriented managers.

Logging may be well intentioned, but users' rights to privacy deserve to be protected. Links to specific user names should not be collected unless necessary. When logging aggregate performance crosses over to monitoring individual activity, managers must inform users of what is being monitored and how the gathered information will be used. Although organizations may have a right to measure workers' performance levels, workers should be able to view the results and to discuss the implications. If monitoring is surreptitious and is later discovered, resulting worker mistrust of management could be more damaging than the benefits of the collected data. Manager and worker cooperation to improve productivity, and worker participation in the process and benefits, are advised.

With the huge impact of the Internet on e-commerce, many companies are interested in tracking hits on their sites, page views, etc. There has been an explosion of companies (Google, Microsoft, Yahoo!, and others) that offer such services, referred to as *web analytics*. They provide the companies with detailed tracking information on their web sites, including graphic displays and calculations and computations to demonstrate the impact on return on investment changes.

Commercial services such as Nielsen® NetRatings™ and Knowledge Networks™ are making a success of providing clients with log data and analyses of web visits from their panels of users. These users have provided their demographic information and are paid to answer surveys or allow their web-visitation patterns to be logged. A similar effort with mobile devices is provided by M:Metrics™ (now part of comScore™). The purchasers of the data are interested in knowing what kinds of people buy books, visit news sites, or seek healthcare information to guide their marketing, product development, and web-site design efforts.

4.6.3 Online or telephone consultants, e-mail, and online suggestion boxes

Online or telephone consultants can provide extremely effective and personal assistance to users who are experiencing difficulties. Many users feel reassured if they know that there is a human being to whom they can turn when problems arise. These consultants are an excellent source of information about problems users are having and can suggest improvements and potential extensions.

Many organizations offer toll-free numbers through which the users can reach a knowledgeable consultant; others charge for consultation by the minute or offer support only to elite or premium customers. On some network systems, the consultants can monitor the user's computer and see the same displays that the user sees while maintaining telephone voice contact. This service can be extremely reassuring, because users know that someone can walk them through the correct sequence of displays to complete their tasks. When users want service, they typically want it immediately. In recognition of that, Netflix™ has created a staff of 375 customer service representatives that can handle calls from its 8.4 million customers, replacing online support with phone support (not offshore). Netflix is proud to say that this approach has paid off, with Nielsen Online and ForeSee Results reporting top ratings in customer satisfaction for the company (Stross, 2008).

Organizations often also (or alternatively) maintain a standard e-mail address of *staff@<organization>* or offer instant messaging or real-time chat facilities that allow users to get help from whomever is online. Sometimes these

FIGURE 4.7
Bug report using Google's Chrome browser (http://www.google.com/chrome/).

services are staffed by software agents supplemented by actual people. Such services help users, build customer loyalty, and provide insights that can lead to design refinements as well as novel product extensions.

Suggestion boxes and complaint facilities are becoming common in web sites for organizations that are eager to provide high levels of customer support. Google's Chrome™ browser provides a bug-reporting facility (Fig. 4.7). User bug reports have also gained popularity in the open-source community with web-based tools such as Bugzilla™.

4.6.4 Discussion groups, wikis, and newsgroups

Some users may have questions about the suitability of a software package for their application, or may be seeking someone who has had experience using an interface feature. They are not likely to have a particular individual in mind, so e-mail does not serve their needs. Furthermore, with the international use of software products and the 7-days-a-week, 24-hours-a-day computing environment, users may encounter issues outside of traditional working hours. Many interface designers and web-site managers offer users discussion groups, newsgroups, or even wikis (Section 9.3) to permit posting of open messages and questions. More independent (and controversial) discussion groups are also hosted by various services and can easily be found using today's powerful search engines.

Discussion groups usually offer lists of item headlines, allowing users to scan for relevant topics. User-generated content fuels these discussion groups. Anyone can add new items, but usually someone moderates the discussion to ensure that offensive, useless, or repetitive items are removed. When there are a substantial number of users who are geographically dispersed, moderators may have to work hard to create a sense of community.

Personal relationships established by face-to-face meetings increase the sense of community among users. Ultimately, it is the people who matter, and human needs for social interaction should be satisfied. Every technical system is also a social system that needs to be encouraged and nurtured.

By soliciting user feedback in any of these ways, managers can gauge user attitudes and elicit useful suggestions. Furthermore, users may have more positive attitudes towards interfaces or web services if they see that the managers genuinely desire comments and suggestions.

4.6.5 Tools for automated evaluation

Software tools can be effective in evaluating user interfaces for desktop applications, web sites, and mobile devices. Even straightforward tools to check spelling or concordance of terms benefit interface designers. Simple metrics that report numbers of displays, widgets, or links between displays capture the size of a user-interface project, but the inclusion of more sophisticated evaluation procedures can allow interface designers to assess whether a menu tree is too deep or contains redundancies, whether widget labels have been used consistently, whether all buttons have proper transitions associated with them, and so on.

An early example is Tullis's (1988) Display Analysis Program, which takes alphanumeric screen designs (no color, highlighting, separator lines, or graphics) and produces display-complexity metrics plus some advice, such as this:

```
Upper-case letters: 77% The percentage of upper-case letters
is high.
     Consider using more lower-case letters, since text printed
     in normal upper- and lower-case letters is read about 13%
     faster than text in all upper case. Reserve all upper-case
     for items that need to attract attention.
Maximum local density = 89.9% at row 9, column 8.
Average local density = 67.0%
     The area with the highest local density is identified
     . . . you can reduce local density by distributing the
     characters as evenly as feasible over the entire screen.
Total layout complexity = 8.02 bits
Layout complexity is high.
This means that the display items (labels and data) are not well
aligned with each other . . . Horizontal complexity can be
reduced by starting items in fewer different columns on the
screen (that is, by aligning them vertically).
```

The movement towards graphical user interfaces with richer fonts and layout possibilities has reduced interest in Tullis's metrics, but better measures for analyzing web-based layouts are emerging. These include analyses of grouping, alignment, symmetry, and consistency, as well as evaluations of more vague notions such as whether the layout is clean, sophisticated, or creative (Parush et al., 2005; Lavie and Tractinsky, 2004).

The World Wide Web Consortium provides a Markup Validation Service (http://validator.w3.org/) for HTML checking that pinpoints problems and delivers feedback such as this:

```
Line 13, Column 8: required attribute "TYPE" not specified.
Line 68, Column 29: document type does not allow element
"BODY" here.
Line 848, Column 23: required attribute "ACTION" not specified.
```

The U.S. National Institute of Standards and Technology (NIST) Web Metrics Testbed (http://zing.ncsl.nist.gov/WebTools/) provides extensive testing tools, such as a static analyzer (WebSAT) for web pages or sites, a categorical analyzer (WebCAT) to check whether categories extracted from web pages fit the designers' intents, an "instrumenter" (WebVIP) to quickly instrument existing web pages to capture logs of interactive use, a 2D visualization of the user's path through a web site (VISVIP), and other tools to guide web designers. Tools for checking your web site for adherence to Section 508 requirements for accessibility (http://www.section508.info/) offer guidance about fixes to specific lines of code, such as:

```
A text equivalent for every non-text element shall be provided
(e.g., via "alt", "longdesc", or in element content). Please add
a description via the alt or/and longdesc element.
Web pages shall be designed so that all information conveyed
with color is also available without color, for example from
context or markup.
```

To guide designers seeking to make appealing web pages, researchers correlated site ratings with 141 layout metrics (Ivory and Hearst, 2002). The ratings were assigned by Internet professionals, acting as judges for the Webby Awards. The researchers analyzed the informational, navigational, and graphical aspects of 5,300 web pages to build statistical models that can predict, with over 90% accuracy in most cases, the scores assigned to the web sites. The resulting predictive models, collectively labeled WebTango (Ivory, 2003), were then examined to determine which design features they recommend. The results were complex—for instance, showing interactions between the functional types and sizes of web pages. Some of the easily applicable results for page design were that high ratings were assigned when large pages had columnar organization, headings were used in proportion to the amount of text, and animated graphical ads were limited. Other recommendations for text design included keeping average link text to two to three words, using sans-serif fonts for body text, and applying colors to highlight headings. One intriguing finding was that preferred web sites did not always have the fastest user performance, suggesting that in e-commerce and entertainment applications attractiveness may be more important than rapid task execution. Further analysis of the results could lead to conjectures about the design goals that bring about high preference. For example, users may prefer designs that are comprehensible, predictable, and visually appealing and that incorporate relevant content.

Download speeds for web pages can be improved by using web-site optimization services that count the number of items in a page, the number of bytes in each image, and the size of the source code. These services also provide suggestions for how to revise web pages for faster performance.

Another family of tools is *run-time logging software*, which captures the users' patterns of activity. Simple reports—such as the frequency of each error message, menu-item selection, dialog-box appearance, help invocation, form-field usage, or web-page access—are of great benefit to maintenance personnel and to revisers of the initial design. Experimental researchers can also capture performance data for alternative designs to guide their decision making. Software to analyze and summarize the performance data (e.g., ergoBrowser™) is improving steadily.

When evaluating mobile devices in the field, unobtrusive methods to gather data may be needed. A log-file-recording tool that captures clicks with associated timestamps and positions on the screen, keeping track of items selected and screen changes, capturing the screen shots, and recording when a user is finished can provide valuable information for analysis. In one study with 30 users, such an analysis identified five problems that were not detected by reviewing video recordings or using the think-aloud method (Kawalek et al., 2008).

Of course, gathering the data from a usability evaluation is only the beginning. Making sense of the data, identifying patterns, and reaching a better understanding of what the data show are difficult and tedious tasks. ExperiScope is an automated tool that makes use of visualization techniques and other models (keystroke-level and GOMS) to find patterns in the data (Guimbretière et al., 2007). This tool is flexible and supports two-handed and pressure-based interactions. The output visualization (Fig. 4.8) is a graphic that shows elapsed time along the horizontal axis and other characteristics of the interaction on the vertical axis.

4.7 Controlled Psychologically Oriented Experiments

Scientific and engineering progress is often stimulated by improved techniques for precise measurement. Rapid progress in the designs of interfaces will be stimulated as researchers and practitioners evolve suitable human-performance measures and techniques. We have come to expect that automobiles will have

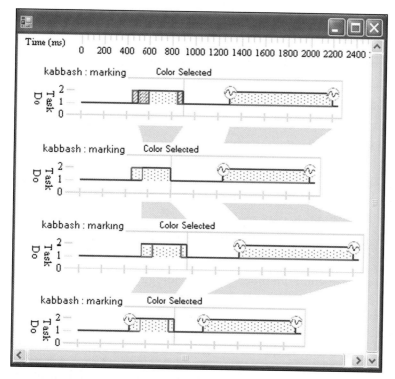

FIGURE 4.8

The output from ExperiScope showing time across the horizontal axis. The vertical axis displays multiple patterns. The top pattern is the aggregate view of the bottom patterns using hatching where the patterns disagree. The purple line is the activity of the pen tip. The green line is the activity of the pen button. The grey bands between the patterns are to simplify the reading of the graphic (Guimbretière et al., 2007).

miles-per-gallon reports pasted to their windows, appliances will have energy-efficiency ratings, and textbooks will be given grade-level designations; soon, we will expect software packages to show learning-time estimates and user-satisfaction indices from appropriate evaluation sources.

4.7.1 Experimental approaches

Academic and industrial researchers are discovering that the power of the traditional scientific method can be fruitfully employed in the study of interfaces. They are conducting numerous experiments that are uncovering basic design principles. The outline of the scientific method as applied to human-computer interaction might include these tasks:

- Deal with a practical problem and consider the theoretical framework.
- State a lucid and testable hypothesis.
- Identify a small number of independent variables that are to be manipulated.
- Carefully choose the dependent variables that will be measured.
- Judiciously select participants, and carefully or randomly assign participants to groups.
- Control for biasing factors (nonrepresentative sample of participants or selection of tasks, inconsistent testing procedures).
- Apply statistical methods to data analysis.
- Resolve the practical problem, refine the theory, and give advice to future researchers.

The classic experimental methods of psychology are being enhanced to deal with the complex cognitive tasks of human performance with information and computer systems. The transformation from Aristotelian introspection to Galilean experimentation that took two millennia in physics is being accomplished in just over two decades in the study of human-computer interaction.

The reductionist approach required for controlled experimentation yields narrow but reliable results. Through multiple replications with similar tasks, participants, and experimental conditions, reliability and validity can be enhanced. Each small experimental result acts like a tile in the mosaic of human performance with computer-based information systems.

Managers of actively used systems are also coming to recognize the power of controlled experiments in fine-tuning the human-computer interface. As proposals are made for new menu structures, novel cursor-control devices, and reorganized display formats, a carefully controlled experiment can provide data to support a management decision. Fractions of the user population can be given proposed improvements for a limited time, and then performance can be compared with the control group. Dependent measures may include performance times, user-subjective satisfaction, error rates, and user retention over time.

For example, the competition over mobile device-input methods has led to numerous experimental studies of keyboard arrangements with similar training methods, standard benchmark tasks, common dependent measures that account for error rates, and strategies for testing frequent users. Such careful controls are necessary because a 10-minute reduction in learning time, a 10% speed increase, or 10 fewer errors could be a vital advantage in a competitive consumer market.

4.7.2 Experimental design

A full discussion of experimental design is outside the scope of this book. Experimental design and statistical analysis are complex topics (Lazar et al., 2009; Cozby, 2006; Elmes et al., 2005). We will cover some very basic terminology and methodologies here, but novice experimenters would be well advised to collaborate with experienced social scientists and statisticians to glean the details.

In a tightly controlled experimental study, selecting the appropriate participants is important. Since conclusions and inferences are often made from the data, it is important that the sample is *representative* of the target users for the interface. Users are frequently grouped or categorized by some sort of *demographic*, such as age, gender, computer experience, etc. When selecting participants from a population to create the sample, the *sampling technique* needs to be considered. Are people selected *randomly*? Is there a *stratified* subsample that should be used? Novice researchers may want to use their friends and family members, creating a *convenience* sample, but such a sample is not typically representative, may be biased, and therefore can compromise the confidence and validity of the results. The sample size is another consideration. It is important to define a *confidence level* that needs to be met for the study. A full discussion of sample sizes and confidence levels can be found in most statistics books.

Basic experimental design comes in two flavors: *between-subjects* or *within-subjects*. In a *between-subjects* design, the groups are relatively similar in makeup, and each group is given a different treatment. To have a powerful effect, this design approach needs to have a relatively large number of users in each group. The large sample size usually ensures that the groups (if selected appropriately) are similar in nature, so the differences can be attributed primarily to the different treatments. If the groups are too small, the results may be related to the individual characteristics of each group. In a *within-subjects* design, each participant performs the same tasks, and the data being recorded is compared across participants. Although the sample size can be smaller, there may still be concerns about fatigue (causing performance to decrease) or practice and familiarity (causing performance to increase). It is important to *counterbalance* the tasks, since the order of the tasks can impact the results. If the variable being measured is ease of use, earlier tasks may artificially seem more difficult since the user is not yet familiar with the system; likewise, later tasks may be seen as easier not because the tasks themselves are less complex, but because of the familiarity with the system that the user has acquired.

In the design of an experimental study, there are different types of variables that need to be considered and understood. The *independent variable* is something that is being manipulated. For example, you may have two different interface designs: one that provides access to a help system and one that does not. The *dependent variable* is something that happens as a result of the experiment and is usually measured. Examples of dependent variables include time to complete the task, number of errors, and user satisfaction. Experimental design needs to be carefully controlled so the main differences found in the dependent variables can be contributed to the independent variables, not other outside sources or confounding variables.

Practitioner's Summary

Interface developers evaluate their designs by conducting expert reviews, usability tests (in lab settings and in the field), surveys, and rigorous acceptance tests. Once interfaces are released, developers carry out continuous performance evaluations by interviews or surveys, or by logging users' performance in a way that respects their privacy. If you are not measuring user performance, you are not focusing on usability!

Successful interface project managers understand that they must work hard to establish a relationship of trust with the user community. As markets are opened (for example, in another country or vertical market segment), managers have to start fresh in gaining recognition and customer loyalty. Special attention may need to be devoted to novice users, users with disabilities, and other special populations (children, older adults). In addition to providing a properly functioning system, successful managers recognize the need to offer social mechanisms for feedback, such as online surveys, interviews, discussion groups, consultants, suggestion boxes, newsletters, and conferences.

Researcher's Agenda

Researchers can contribute their experience with experimentation to develop improved techniques for interface evaluation. Guidance in conducting pilot studies, acceptance tests, surveys, interviews, and discussions would benefit commercial development groups. Strategies are needed to cope with evaluation for the numerous specific populations of users and the diverse forms of disabilities that users may have. Experts in constructing psychological tests can help in preparing validated and reliable test instruments for subjective evaluation of web-based, desktop, and mobile interfaces, including specialized gaming interfaces. Such standardized tests would allow independent groups to compare the acceptability of interfaces. Would benchmark data sets and task libraries help standardize evaluation? How useful can researchers make automated testing against requirements documents? How many users are needed to generate valid recommendations? How can we better explain the differences between users' perceptions of a task and the objective measures? How do we select the best measure for a task? How can life-critical applications for experienced professionals be tested reliably? Is there a single usability metric that can be used and compared across types of interfaces? Can we combine performance data and subjective data and create a single meaningful result? Is there a theory to explain and understand the relationship between measures?

Psychotherapists and social workers could contribute to training online or telephone consultants—after all, helping troubled users is a human-relationships issue. Finally, more input from experimental, cognitive, and clinical psychologists would help computer specialists to recognize the importance of the human aspects of computer use. Can psychological principles be applied to reduce novice users' anxiety or expert users' frustration? Could profiles of users' skill levels with interfaces be helpful in job-placement and training programs? How can good usability practices be applied to the gaming environment while preserving the challenge and excitement of the game itself?

Additional work is also needed on the appropriate choice of evaluation methodology. Some of the traditional methodologies need to be expanded, and non-empirical methods, such as sketches and other design alternatives, should be considered. Changes are needed to make usability reports that are understandable, readable, and useful. Additional work on developing automated tools is needed, with attention paid to the specialized systems (mobile devices, games, personal devices) that are available today. The standardized usability instruments need modification and validation as they deal with different criteria and different environments. What happens if testing cannot take place in a usability lab? Perhaps the testing must be done in a field setting to ensure validity. How can we effectively simulate the high-stress situations that users encounter in hostile environments? Satisfaction may be more broadly defined including characteristics such as fun, pleasure, and challenge.

WORLD WIDE WEB RESOURCES

http://www.aw.com/DTUI/

Additional information on usability testing and questionnaires is available on the companion web site.

References

Bangor, Aaron, Kortum, Philip T., and Miller, James, An empirical evaluation of the system usability scale, *International Journal of Human-Computer Interaction* 24, 6 (2008), 574–594.

Barnum, Carol M., *Usability Testing and Research*, Longman, New York, NY (2002).

Bias, Randolph G. and Mayhew, Deborah J. (Editors), *Cost-Justifying Usability, Second Edition*, Morgan Kaufmann, San Francisco, CA (2005).

Blackmon, M.H., Polson, P.G., Kitajima, M., and Lewis, C., Design methods: Cognitive walkthrough for the Web, *Proc. CHI 2002 Conference: Human Factors in Computing Systems*, ACM Press, New York (2002), 463–470.

Brooke, John, SUS: A quick and dirty usability scale, in Jordan, P.W., Thomas, B., Weerdmeester, B.A., and McClelland, I.L. (Editors), *Usability Evaluation in Industry*, Taylor and Francis, London, U.K. (1996).

Chin, John P., Diehl, Virginia A., and Norman, Kent L., Development of an instrument measuring user satisfaction of the human-computer interface, *Proc. CHI '88 Conference: Human Factors in Computing Systems*, ACM Press, New York (1988), 213–218.

Coleman, William D. and Williges, Robert C., Collecting detailed user evaluations of software interfaces, *Proc. Human Factors Society, Twenty-Ninth Annual Meeting*, Santa Monica, CA (1985), 204–244.

Cozby, Paul C., *Methods in Behavioral Research, Ninth Edition*, McGraw-Hill, New York (2006).

de Leeuw, Edith D., Hox, Joop J., and Dillman, Don A., *International Handbook of Survey Methodology*, Lawrence Erlbaum Associates, New York (2008).

Dicks, R. Stanley, Mis-usability: On the uses and misuses of usability testing, *Proc. SIGDOC '02 Conference*, ACM Press, New York (2002), 26–30.

Dumas, Joseph and Fox, Jean, Usability testing: Current practice and future directions, in Sears, Andrew and Jacko, Julie (Editors), *The Human-Computer Interaction Handbook, Second Edition*, Lawrence Erlbaum Associates, Hillsdale, NJ (2008), 1129–1149.

Dumas, Joseph and Loring, Beth, *Moderating Usability Tests: Principles and Practices for Interacting*, Morgan Kaufmann, Burlington, MA (2008).

Dumas, Joseph and Redish, Janice, *A Practical Guide to Usability Testing, Revised Edition*, Intellect Books, Bristol, U.K. (1999).

Elmes, David G., Kantowitz, Barry H., and Roediger, Henry L., *Research Methods in Psychology, Eighth Edition*, Wadsworth Publishing, Belmont, CA (2005).

Frøkjær, Erik and Hornbæk, Kasper, Metaphors of human thinking for usability inspection and design, *ACM Transactions on Computer-Human Interaction* 14, 4 (2008), 20.1–20.33.

Gefen, David and Straub, Detmar, The relative importance of perceived ease of use in IS adoption: A study of e-commerce adoption, *Journal of the Association for Information Systems* 1, 8 (October 2000). Available at http://jais.isworld.org/articles/default.asp?vol=1&art=8.

Greenberg, Saul and Buxton, Bill, Usability evaluation considered harmful (some of the time), *Proc. CHI 2008 Conference: Human Factors in Computing Systems*, ACM Press, New York (2008), 111–119.

Guimbretière, François, Dixon, Morgan, and Hinckley, Ken, ExperiScope: An analysis tool for interaction data, *Proc. CHI 2007 Conference: Human Factors in Computing Systems*, ACM Press, New York (2007), 1333–1342.

Ivory, Melody Y., *Automated Web Site Evaluation: Researchers' and Practitioners' Perspectives*, Kluwer Academic Publishers, Dordrecht, The Netherlands (2003).

Ivory, Melody Y. and Hearst, Marti A., Statistical profiles of highly-rated web site interfaces, *Proc. CHI 2002 Conference: Human Factors in Computing Systems*, ACM Press, New York (2002), 367–374.

Kawalek, Jurgen, Stark, Annegret, and Riebeck, Marcel, A new approach to analyze human-mobile computer interaction, *Journal of Usability Studies* 3, 2 (February 2008), 90–98.

Kirakowski, J. and Corbett, M., SUMI: The Software Usability Measurement Inventory, *British Journal of Educational Technology* 24, 3 (1993), 210–212.

Koohang, Alex, Expanding the concept of usability, *Informing Science Journal* 7 (2004), 129–141.

Korhonen, Hannu and Koivisto, Elina M.I., Playability heuristics for mobile games, *Proc. MobileHCI '06 Conference*, ACM Press, New York (2006), 9–15.

Kuhn, Klaus, Problems and benefits of requirements gathering with focus groups: A case study, *International Journal of Human-Computer Interaction* 12, 3/4 (2000), 309–325.

Lavie, Talia and Tractinsky, Noam, Assessing dimensions of perceived visual aesthetics of web sites, *International Journal of Human-Computer Studies* 60, 3 (2004), 269–298.

Lazar, Jonathan, Feng, Jinjuan, and Hochheiser, Harry, *Research Methods in Human-Computer Interaction*, John Wiley & Sons, London, U.K. (2009).

Lewis, James R., IBM computer usability satisfaction questionnaires: Psychometric evaluation and instructions for use, *International Journal of Human-Computer Interaction* 7, 1 (1995), 57–78.

Lingdaard, Gitte and Chattratichart, Jarinee, Usability testing: What have we overlooked?, *Proc. CHI 2007 Conference: Human Factors in Computing Systems*, ACM Press, New York (2007), 1415–1424.

Molich, Rolf, Jeffries, Robin, and Dumas, Joseph S., Making usability recommendations useful and usable, *Journal of Usability Studies* 2, 4 (2007), 162–179.

Molich, Rolf and Dumas, Joseph S., Comparative usability evaluation (CUE-4), *Behaviour & Information Technology* 27, 3 (May/June 2008), 263–281.

National Cancer Institute, *Research-based Web Design and Usability Guidelines*, Dept. of Health & Human Services, National Institutes of Health (updated edition 2006). Available at http://www.usability.gov/pdfs/guidelines.html.

Nielsen, Jakob, *Usability Engineering*, Academic Press, New York (1993).

Nielsen, Jakob and Mack, Robert (Editors), *Usability Inspection Methods*, John Wiley & Sons, New York (1994).

Olsen, Dan R. Jr., Evaluating user interface systems research, *Proc. UIST '07 Conference*, ACM Press, New York (2007), 251–258.

Parush, A., Shwartz, Y., Shtub, A., and Chandra, J., The impact of visual layout factors on performance in web pages: A cross-language study, *Human Factors* 47, 1 (Spring 2005), 141–157.

Petersen, Marianne Graves, Madsen, Kim Halskov, and Kjaer, Arne, The usability of everyday technology—Emerging and fading opportunities, *ACM Transactions on Computer-Human Interaction* 9, 2 (June 2002), 74–105.

Pinelle, David and Gutwin, Carl, Evaluating teamwork support in tabletop groupware applications using collaborative usability analysis, *Personal Ubiquitious Computing* 12 (2008), 237–254.

Pinelle, David, Wong, Nelson, and Stach, Tadeusz, Heuristic evaluation for games: Usability principles for video game design, *Proc. CHI 2008 Conference: Human Factors in Computing Systems*, ACM Press, New York (2008), 1453–1462.

Rahman, M., High velocity human factors: Human factors in mission critical domains in non-equilibrium, *Proc. Human Factors and Ergonomics Society, Fifty-First Annual Meeting*, HFES, Santa Monica, CA (2007), 273–277.

Rubin, Jeffrey and Chisnell, Dana, *Handbook of Usability Testing*, John Wiley & Sons, Indianapolis, IN (2008).

Ryu, Young Sam and Smith-Jackson, Tonya L., Reliability and validity of the mobile phone usability questionnaire (MPUQ), *Journal of Usability Studies* 2, 1 (November 2006), 39–53.

Schultz, David, Usability tips & tricks for testing mobile applications, *ACM interactions* 13, 6 (November/December, 2006), 14–15.

Sharp, Helen, Rogers, Yvonne, and Preece, Jenny, *Interaction Design: Beyond Human-Computer Interaction*, John Wiley & Sons, West Sussex, U.K. (2007).

Sherman, Paul (Editor), *Usability Success Stories*, Gower Publishing, Hampshire, U.K. (2006).

Shneiderman, Ben and Plaisant, Catherine, Strategies for evaluating information visualization tools: Multi-dimensional in-depth long-term case studies, *Proc. 2006 AVI Workshop on Beyond Time and Errors: Novel Evaluation Methods for Information Visualization*, ACM Press, New York (2006), 1–7.

Snyder, Carolyn, *Paper Prototyping*, Morgan Kaufmann, San Francisco, CA (2003).

Spool, Jared, Surviving our success: Three radical recommendations, *Journal of Usability Studies* 2, 4 (August, 2007), 155–161.

Stone, Debbie, Jarrett, Caroline, Woodroffe, Mark, and Minocha, Shialey, *User Interface Design and Evaluation*, Morgan Kaufmann, San Francisco, CA (2005).

Stross, Randall, Can't open your e-mailbox? Good luck, *New York Times*, 4 October 2008, BU4.

Theofanos, Mary and Quesenbery, Whitney, Towards the design of effective formative test reports, *Journal of Usability Studies* 1, 1 (November 2005), 27–45.

Tohidi, Maryam, Buxton, William, Baecker, Ronald, and Sellen, Abigail, User sketches: A quick, inexpensive and effective way to elicit more reflective user feedback, *Proc. CHI 2006 Conference: Human Factors in Computing Systems*, ACM Press, New York (2006a), 105–114.

Tohidi, Maryam, Buxton, William, Baecker, Ronald, and Sellen, Abigail, Getting the right design and the design right: Testing many is better than one, *Proc. CHI 2006 Conference: Human Factors in Computing Systems*, ACM Press, New York (2006b), 1243–1252.

Tullis, Thomas S., A system for evaluating screen formats: Research and application, in Hartson, H. Rex and Hix, D. (Editors), *Advances in Human-Computer Interaction, Volume II*, Ablex, Norwood, NJ (1988), 214–286.

Tullis, Thomas S. and Albert, Bill, *Measuring the User Experience*, Morgan Kaufmann, Burlington, MA (2008).

Tullis, Thomas S. and Stetson, Jacqueline N., A comparison of questionnaires for assessing website usability, *Proc. UPA 2004*, UPA, Bloomingdale, IL (2004).

Wharton, Cathleen, Rieman, John, Lewis, Clayton, and Polson, Peter, The cognitive walkthrough method: A practitioner's guide, in Nielsen, Jakob and Mack, Robert (Editors), *Usability Inspection Methods*, John Wiley & Sons, New York (1994).

PART 3

INTERACTION STYLES

CHAPTER 5

Direct Manipulation and Virtual Environments

> " Leibniz sought to make the form of a symbol reflect its content. "In signs," he wrote, "one sees an advantage for discovery that is greatest when they express the exact nature of a thing briefly and, as it were, picture it; then, indeed, the labor of thought is wonderfully diminished." "

Frederick Kreiling, "Leibniz,"
Scientific American, May 1968

Written in collaboration with Maxine S. Cohen

5.1 Introduction

Certain interactive systems generate a glowing enthusiasm among users that is in marked contrast with the more common reaction of reluctant acceptance or troubled confusion. The enthusiastic users report the following positive feelings:

- Mastery of the interface
- Competence in performing tasks
- Ease in learning originally and in assimilating advanced features
- Confidence in the capacity to retain mastery over time
- Enjoyment in using the interface
- Eagerness to show off the interface to novices
- Desire to explore more powerful aspects

These feelings convey an image of a truly pleased user. The central ideas in such satisfying interfaces, now widely referred to as *direct-manipulation interfaces* (Shneiderman, 1983), are visibility of the objects and actions of interest; rapid, reversible, incremental actions; and replacement of typed commands by a pointing action on the object of interest. Dragging a file to a trash can is a familiar example of direct manipulation, but direct-manipulation ideas are also at the heart of many contemporary and advanced non-desktop interfaces. Game designers continue to lead the way in creating visually compelling three-dimensional (3D) scenes with characters (sometimes designed and user-created) controlled by novel pointing devices. At the same time, interest in teleoperated devices has blossomed, enabling operators to look through distant microscopes or fly reconnaissance drones. As the technology platforms mature, direct manipulation increasingly influences designers of mobile devices and web pages. It also inspires designers of information-visualization systems that present thousands of objects on the screen with dynamic user controls (Chapter 14).

Newer concepts that extend direct manipulation include virtual reality, augmented reality, and other tangible and touchable user interfaces. Virtual reality puts users in an immersive environment in which the normal surroundings are blocked out by a head-mounted display that presents an artificial world; hand gestures in a data glove allow users to point, select, grasp, and navigate. Augmented reality keeps users in the normal surroundings but adds a transparent overlay with information such as the names of buildings or visualizations of hidden objects. Tangible and touchable user interfaces give users physical objects to manipulate so as to operate the interface: for example, putting several plastic blocks near to each other to create an office floorplan. All of these concepts are being applied not only in individual interactions, but also in wider artificial worlds, like *Second Life*, creating collaborative efforts and other types of social-media interactions.

This chapter explores the principles of direct manipulation, reviewing some historically important examples (Section 5.2) and providing psychological justifications while raising some concerns (Section 5.3). Further applications of direct manipulation are covered in sections on 3D interfaces (Section 5.4), teleoperation (Section 5.5), and virtual and augmented reality (Section 5.6).

5.2 Examples of Direct Manipulation

No single interface has every admirable attribute or design feature—such an interface might not be possible. Each of the examples discussed here, however, has sufficient numbers of features to win the enthusiastic support of many users.

A favorite example of direct manipulation is driving an automobile. The scene is directly visible through the front window, and performance of actions such as braking and steering has become common knowledge in our culture. To turn left, for example, the driver simply rotates the steering wheel to the left. The response is immediate and the scene changes, providing feedback to refine the turn. Now imagine how difficult it would be trying to accurately turn a car by typing a command or selecting "turn left 30 degrees" from a menu. The graceful interaction in many applications is due to the increasingly elegant application of direct manipulation.

5.2.1 Word processor history and current status

It may be hard for users of today's word processors to believe, but in the early 1980s, text editing was done with line-oriented command languages. Users might see only one line at a time! Typed commands were needed to move up or down through the file or to make any changes. The enthusiastic users of novel *full-page display editors* were great advocates of their two-dimensional interfaces with cursor controls. A typical comment was, "Once you've used a display editor, you will never go back to a line editor—you'll be spoiled." Similar comments came from users of early personal-computer word processors, such as WordStar™ and display editors such as Emacs on the Unix® system; one beaming advocate called Emacs "the one true editor." In these interfaces, users were able to view a full screen of text and edit by using the backspace key or insert directly by typing. Office-automation evaluations consistently favored full-page display editors, and the clarity of seeing italicized, bolded, underscored, or centered text on the screen enabled users to concentrate on the contents.

By the early 1990s, the display editors—described as *what you see is what you get* (WYSIWYG)—had become standard for word processors. Microsoft Word (Fig . 5.1) is now dominant on the Macintosh and Windows platforms, with most of

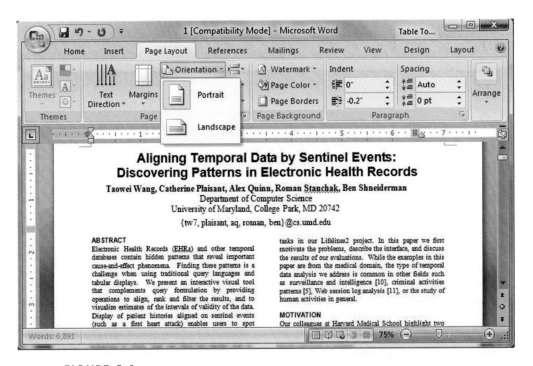

FIGURE 5.1

An example of a WYSIWYG (what you see is what you get) editor: Microsoft Word 2007.

the competing word processors a thing of the past. The advantages of WYSIWYG word processors include the following:

- *Users see a full page of text.* Showing 20 to 60 lines of text simultaneously gives the reader a clearer sense of context for each sentence, while permitting easier reading and scanning of the document. By contrast, working with the one-line view offered by line editors is like seeing the world through a narrow cardboard tube. Modern displays can support two or more full pages of text set side by side.

- *The document is seen as it will appear when printed.* Eliminating the clutter of formatting commands simplifies reading and scanning of the document. Tables, lists, page breaks, skipped lines, section headings, centered text, and figures can be viewed in their final form. The annoyance and delay of debugging the formatting commands are almost eliminated because the errors are usually immediately apparent.

- *Cursor action is visible.* Seeing an arrow, underscore, or blinking box on the screen gives the operator a clear sense of where to focus attention and apply action.

- *Cursor motion is natural.* Arrow keys and devices such as mice, trackpads, or tablets provide natural physical mechanisms for moving the cursor. This is in marked contrast to using cursor-motion commands (such as UP 6) that require the operator to convert the physical action into the correct syntactical form, which may be difficult to learn, hard to recall, and thus, a source of frustrating errors.

- *Labeled icons make frequent actions rapid.* Most word processors have labeled icons in a toolbar for frequent actions. These buttons act as a permanent menu-selection display to remind users of the features and to enable rapid selection.

- *Immediate display of the results of an action.* When users press a button to move the cursor or center text, the results are shown immediately on the screen. Deletions are apparent immediately: The character, word, or line is erased, and the remaining text is rearranged. Similarly, insertions or text movements are shown after each keystroke or function-key press. In contrast, with line editors, users must issue print or display commands to see the results of changes.

- *Rapid response and display.* Most word processors operate at high speed; a full page of text including graphics appears in a fraction of a second. This high display rate, coupled with short response time, produces a satisfying sense of power and speed. Cursors can be moved quickly, large amounts of text can be scanned rapidly, and the results of actions can be shown almost instantaneously. Rapid response also reduces the need for additional commands and thereby simplifies design and learning.

- *Easily reversible actions.* Users can make simple changes by moving the cursor to the problem area and inserting or deleting characters, words, or lines. When entering text, they can repair an incorrect keystroke by merely backspacing and retyping. A useful design strategy is to include natural inverse actions for each action (for example, to increase or decrease type sizes). An alternative offered by many display editors is a simple undo action to return the text to the state that it was in before the previous action. Easy reversibility reduces user anxiety about making a mistake or destroying the file; it also encourages exploration of features.

So many of these issues have been studied empirically that someone once joked that the word processor was the white rat for researchers in human-computer interaction. Switching metaphors, for commercial developers, we might say the word processor is the root for many technological sprouts:

- *Graphics, spreadsheets, and animations* (and the like) are integrated in the body of a document.
- *Desktop-publishing software* produces sophisticated printed formats with multiple columns and allows output to high-resolution printers. Multiple fonts, easy integrations of graphics/pictures, grayscales, and color permit preparation of high-quality documents, newsletters, reports, newspapers, or books. Examples include Adobe InDesign™ and QuarkXPress™.
- *Presentation software* produces color text and graphic layouts for use directly from the computer with a large-screen projector to allow animations. Examples include Microsoft PowerPoint® and Apple Keynote®.
- *Hypermedia environments and the World Wide Web* allow users to jump from one page or article to another with selectable buttons or embedded hot links. Readers can add bookmarks, annotations, and tours.
- *Improved macro facilities* enable users to construct, save, and edit sequences of frequently used actions. A related feature is a style sheet that allows users to specify and save a set of options for spacing, fonts, margins, and so on. Likewise, the saving of templates allows users to take the formatting work of colleagues as a starting point for their own documents. Most word processors come with dozens of standard templates for business letters, newsletters, or brochures.
- *Spell checkers and thesauri* are standard on most full-featured word processors. Spell checking can also be set to function while users are typing and to automatically correct common mistakes, such as changing "teh" to "the."
- *Grammar checkers* offer users comments about potential problems in writing style, such as use of passive voice, excessive use of certain words, or lack of parallel construction. Some writers—both novices and professionals—appreciate these

comments and know that they can decide whether to apply the suggestions. Critics point out, however, that the advice is often inappropriate and therefore wastes time.

- *Document assemblers* allow users to compose complex documents, such as contracts or wills, from standard paragraphs using appropriate language for males or females; citizens or foreigners; high-, medium-, or low-income earners; renters or home owners; and so on.

5.2.2 The VisiCalc spreadsheet and its descendants

The first electronic spreadsheet, VisiCalc™, was the 1979 product of a Harvard Business School student, Dan Bricklin, who became frustrated when trying to carry out repetitious calculations for a graduate course in business. He and a friend, Bob Frankston, built an "instantly calculating electronic worksheet" (as the user manual described it) that permitted computation and immediate display of results across 254 rows and 63 columns.

The spreadsheet can be programmed so that column 4 displays the sum of the values in columns 1 through 3; then, every time a value in one of the first three columns changes, the value in the fourth column changes as well. Complex dependencies between, for example, manufacturing costs, distribution costs, sales revenue, commissions, and profits can be stored for several sales districts and for various months. Spreadsheet users can try out alternate plans or "what if" scenarios and immediately see the effects of changes on profits. This simulation of an accountant's spreadsheet makes it easy for business analysts to comprehend the objects and permissible actions.

Competitors to VisiCalc emerged quickly; they made attractive improvements to the user interface and expanded the tasks that were supported. Lotus 1-2-3™ dominated the market in the 1980s (Fig. 5.2), but the current leader is Microsoft's Excel (Fig. 5.3), which provides numerous features and specialized additions. Excel and other modern spreadsheet programs offer numerous graphics displays, multiple windows, statistical routines, and database access. The huge numbers of features are invoked with menus or toolbars, and extensibility is provided by powerful macro facilities.

5.2.3 Office automation history

Designers of early office-automation systems used direct-manipulation principles. The pioneering Xerox® Star™ (Smith et al., 1982) offered sophisticated text-formatting options, graphics, multiple fonts, and a high-resolution, cursor-based user interface (Fig. 5.4). Users could move (but not drag) a document icon to a printer icon to generate a hardcopy printout. The Apple

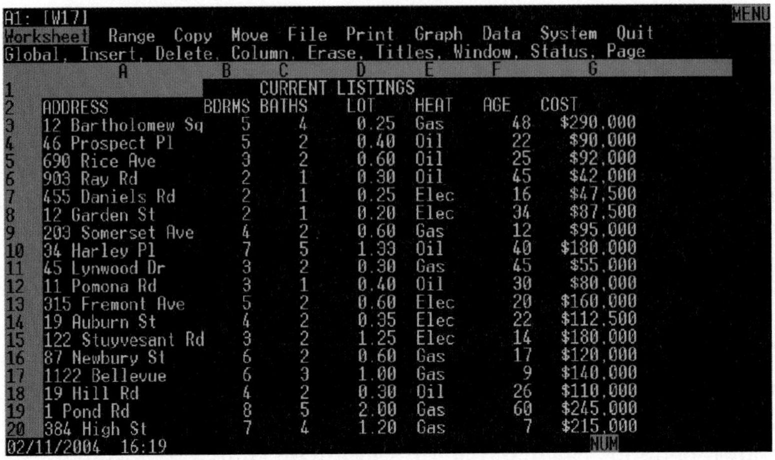

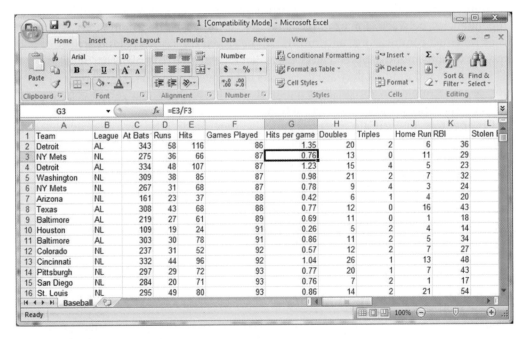

FIGURE 5.2

An early version of Lotus 1-2-3, the spreadsheet program that was dominant through the 1980s.

FIGURE 5.3

A Microsoft Excel 2007 spreadsheet. Notice the improvement in readability and the addition of visible grid lines. More space is dedicated to widgets and other formatting tools.

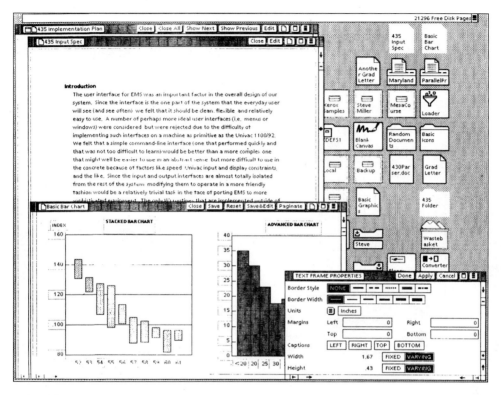

FIGURE 5.4

The Xerox Star 8010 with the ViewPoint™ system enables users to create documents with multiple fonts and graphics. This session shows the Text Frame Properties sheet over sample bar charts, with a document in the background and many desktop icons available for selection.

Lisa™ system also elegantly applied many of the principles of direct manipulation; although it was not a commercial success, it laid the groundwork for the successful Macintosh. The Macintosh designers drew upon the Star and Lisa experiences, making many simplifying decisions while preserving adequate power for users (Fig. 5.5). The hardware and software designs supported rapid and continuous graphical interaction for pull-down menus, window manipulation, editing of graphics and text, and dragging of icons. Variations on the Macintosh appeared soon afterwards for other popular personal computers, and Microsoft now dominates the office-automation market. The Microsoft Windows design is still a close relative of the Macintosh design, and both are candidates for substantial improvements in window management, with simplifications for novices and increased power for sophisticated users.

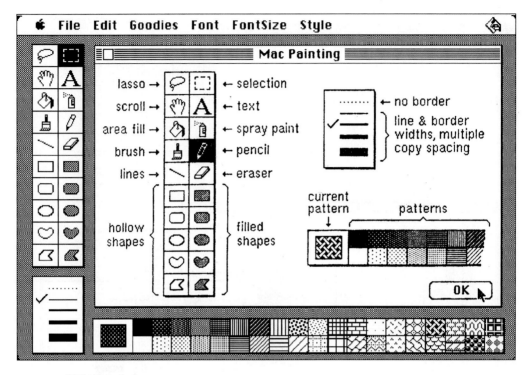

FIGURE 5.5

The original Apple Macintosh MacPaint™. This program offers a command menu on the top, a menu of action icons on the left, a choice of line thicknesses on the lower left, and a palette of textures on the bottom. All actions can be accomplished with only the mouse.

5.2.4 Spatial data management

In geographic applications, it seems natural to give a spatial representation in the form of a map that provides a familiar model of reality. The developers of the prototype Spatial Data Management System (Herot, 1980; 1984) attribute the basic idea to Nicholas Negroponte of MIT. In one early scenario, users were seated before a color-graphics display of the world and could zoom in on the Pacific Ocean to see markers for convoys of military ships. By moving a joystick, users caused the screen to be filled with silhouettes of individual ships; zooming displayed detailed data, such as, ultimately, a full-color picture of the captain.

Later attempts at spatial data management included the Xerox PARC Information Visualizer, which was an ensemble of tools for three-dimensional animated explorations of buildings, cone-shaped file directories, organization charts, a perspective wall that puts featured items up front and centered, and several two- and three-dimensional information layouts (Robertson, et al., 1993).

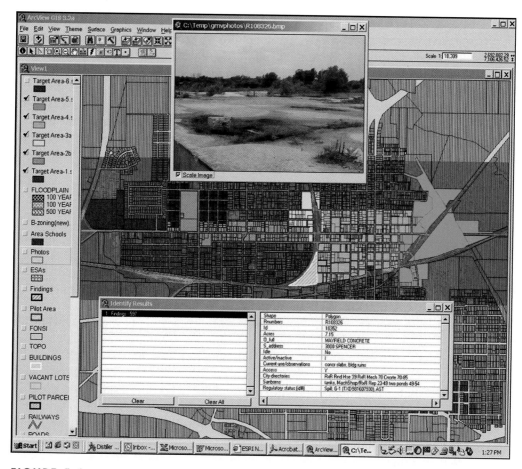

FIGURE 5.6

The ArcGIS (http://www.esri.com/) provides comprehensive mapping functions and management of related data. Users can see geographic data and manipulate various characteristics of the data. A photorealistic view can also be included.

ArcGIS™ by ESRI™ is a widely used geographic-information system (GIS) that offers rich, layered databases of map-related information (Fig. 5.6). Users can zoom in on areas of interest, select the kinds of information they wish to view (roads, population density, topography, rainfall, political boundaries, and much more), and do limited searches. Much simpler but widely popular highway, weather, and economic maps covering whole continents are available on the Web, on CD-ROMs, and for desktop and mobile devices.

Google Maps™ and the more powerful Google Earth™ combines geographic information from aerial photographs, satellite imagery, and other sources to create a database of graphical information that can easily be viewed and displayed. In some areas, the detail can go down to an individual house on a street. It is available for both Mac and PC platforms and is offered as a plug-in for some browsers. A more robust and detailed commercial version is available for a cost, but the free version is used by tens of thousands of users.

The success of a spatial data-management system depends on the skill of the designers in choosing icons, graphical representations, and data layouts that are natural and comprehensible to users. The joy of zooming in and out or of gliding over data entices even anxious users, who quickly demand additional power and data.

5.2.5 Video games

For many people, the most exciting, well-engineered, and commercially successful application of the direct-manipulation concepts lies in the world of video games. The early but simple and popular game *Pong®* required the user to rotate a knob that moved a white rectangle on the screen. A white spot acted as a ping-pong ball that ricocheted off the wall and had to be hit back by the movable white rectangle. Users developed speed and accuracy in placing the "paddle" to keep the increasingly speedy ball from getting past, while the computer speaker emitted a ponging sound when the ball bounced. Watching someone else play for 30 seconds is all the training that a person needs to become a competent novice, but many hours of practice are required to become a skilled expert.

Later games, such as *Missile Command®*, *Donkey Kong®*, *Pacman™*, *Tempest™*, *TRON®*, *Centipede®*, and *Space Invaders®*, were much more sophisticated in their rules, color graphics, and sound effects. More recent games include multi-person competitions (for example, in tennis or karate), three-dimensional graphics, still higher resolution, and stereo sound. The designers of these games provide stimulating entertainment, a challenge for novices and experts, and many intriguing lessons in the human factors of interface design—somehow, they have found a way to get people to put quarters in the sides of computers. Forty million Nintendo game players reside in 70% of those American households that include 8- to 12-year-olds. Brisk sales of games like the *Mario* series testify to their strong attraction, in marked contrast to the anxiety about and resistance to office-automation equipment that many users have shown.

The gaming world is changing rapidly. Last generation's Nintendo Game-Cube™, Sony PlayStation 2, and Microsoft Xbox® have given way to this generation's Nintendo Wii, Sony PlayStation 3, and Microsoft Xbox 360™ in a very short time. These gaming platforms have brought powerful three-dimensional graphics hardware to the home and have created a remarkable international market. Wildly successful games include violent first-person shooters, fast-paced racing games, and more sedate golfing games. Small handheld game devices, such as the Nintendo DS™ (formerly the Game Boy™), provide portable fun for kids on the street as well as executives in their well-appointed offices. These devices also support competitive two-player interactions, such as car racing, tennis, or more violent boxing or shooting games. Multiplayer games on the Internet have also caught on with many users because of the additional opportunity for social encounters and competitions. Gaming magazines and conferences attest to the widespread interest.

The Nintendo Wii, introduced in 2006, has expanded the demographic from 8- to 12-year-olds (especially boys) to a much wider audience, including older adults. One of the unique features of this gaming platform is the Wii wireless remote (Fig. 1.9). The remote can control 3D movement and serve as a pointing device, providing a more immersive gaming experience. When golfing with the Wii, for example, the user makes arm and wrist motions just like on a real golf course. The Wii Fit (a physical activity add-on) provides exercises for users who would typically "play video games" from a seated position. The Wii (and other similar platforms) also has the capability to connect to the Internet.

Electro-mechanical joysticks are increasingly being replaced with wireless controllers of various shapes and sizes. *Guitar Hero* is a music video game for the PlayStation that has a controller in the shape of a guitar (Fig. 5.7). *Rock Band*™, another musical genre type game, has controllers that simulate a guitar, drums, and vocals. The game can be "played" alone or with competitors.

Other games that dominate the virtual type game market include *EverQuest*, *Grand Theft Auto*™, *Halo*™, and *World of Warcraft*™. Both local and virtual gaming communities have emerged to support games such as these. Players can even generate their own characters using tools like Creature Creator™ from Spore™ (Fig. 5.8). The esthetically appealing *Myst®* and its successors *Riven*™ and *Exile*™ have drawn widespread approval even in some literary circles, while the more violent but successful *DOOM®* and *QUAKE®* series have provoked controversy over their psychological effects on teens.

Typical games provide a field of action that is visual and compelling. The physical actions—such as button presses, joystick motions, or knob rotations—produce rapid responses on the screen. There is no syntax to remember, and therefore there are no syntax-error messages. Error messages in general are rare, because the results of actions are obvious and can be reversed easily: If users move their spaceships too far to the left, they merely use the natural inverse action of moving back to the right. These principles, which have been shown to increase user satisfaction, could be applied to office automation, personal computing, or other interactive environments.

Most games continuously display a numeric score so that users can measure their progress and compete with their previous performance, with friends, or with the highest scorers. Typically, the 10 highest scorers get to store their initials

FIGURE 5.7

Two users simultaneously playing *Guitar Hero*. The controller resembles the shape of a guitar and has special controls to simulate the instrumentation. Note the colored controls (fret buttons) on the bridge portion of each instrument.

in the game for public display. This strategy provides one form of positive reinforcement that encourages mastery. Our studies with elementary-school children have shown that continuous display of scores is extremely valuable. Machine-generated feedback—such as "Very good" or "You're doing great!"—is not as effective, since the same score carries different meanings for different people. Most users prefer to make their own subjective judgments and perceive the machine-generated messages as an annoyance and a deception. Providing this combination of behavioral data and attitudinal data adds to the immersion quality of the game (Pagulayan et al., 2008).

Many educational games use direct manipulation effectively. For example, elementary- or high-school students can learn about urban planning by using *SimCity*™ and its variants, which show urban environments visually and let students build roads, airports, housing developments, and so on by direct-manipulation actions. The social simulation game *The Sims* and its online version broke new ground by attracting more women than men.

Studying game design is fun (Lecky-Thompson, 2008), but there are limits to the applicability of the lessons. Game players are engaged in competition with the system or with other players, whereas applications-systems users prefer a strong internal locus of control, which gives them the sense of being in charge. Likewise, whereas game players seek entertainment and focus on the

FIGURE 5.8

Creature Creator from Spore (http://www.spore.com). This is one of several screens available to personalize your own creature. Various body parts and shapes can be selected from the palette on the left. Other controls allow the user to change the creature's characteristics.

challenge, applications users focus on their tasks and may resent too many playful distractions. The random events that occur in most games are meant to challenge the users; in nongame designs, however, predictable system behavior is preferred.

5.2.6 Computer-aided design

Most computer-aided design (CAD) systems for automobiles, electronic circuitry, aircraft, or mechanical engineering use principles of direct manipulation. Building and home architects now have at their disposal powerful tools, such as Autodesk Inventor (Fig 1.14), with components to handle structural engineering, floorplans, interiors, landscaping, plumbing, electrical installation, and much more. With programs like this one, the operator may see a circuit schematic on the screen and, with mouse clicks, be able to move components into or out of the proposed circuit. When the design is complete, the computer can provide information about current, voltage drops, and fabrication costs and warnings about inconsistencies or manufacturing problems. Similarly, newspaper-layout artists or automobile-body designers can easily try multiple designs in minutes and can record promising approaches until they find even better ones. The pleasure of using these systems stems from the capacity to manipulate the object of interest directly and to generate multiple alternatives rapidly.

There are large manufacturing companies using AutoCAD® and similar systems, but there are also other specialized design programs for kitchen and bathroom layouts, landscaping plans, and other homeowner-type situations. These programs allow users to control the angle of the sun during the various seasons to see the impact of the landscaping and shadows on various portions of the house. They allow users to view a kitchen layout and calculate square footage estimates for floors and countertops and even print out materials lists directly from the software. One of the leaders in the field of interior-design software for residential and commercial markets is 20-20 Technologies. Its products are designed to work across all environments, desktop to web; they provide various views (top-down, architectural, front-view) to generate a more realistic overview of the design for the client.

Related applications are for computer-aided manufacturing (CAM) and process control. Honeywell's Experion® Process Knowledge System provides the manager of an oil refinery, paper mill, or power-utility plant with a colored schematic view of the plant. The schematic may be displayed on multiple displays or on a large wall-sized map, with red lines indicating any sensor values that are out of the normal range. With a single click, the operator can get a more detailed view of the troubling component; with a second click, the operator can examine individual sensors or can reset valves and circuits. A basic strategy for this design is to eliminate the need for complex commands that the operator might need to recall only during a once-a-year emergency. The visual overview provided by the schematic facilitates problem solving by analogy, since the linkage between the screen representations and the plant's temperatures or pressures is so close.

5.2.7 The continuing evolution of direct manipulation

A successful direct-manipulation interface must present an appropriate representation or model of reality. With some applications, the jump to visual language may be difficult, but after using visual direct-manipulation interfaces, most users and designers can hardly imagine why anyone would want to use a complex syntactic notation to describe an essentially visual process. It is hard to conceive of learning the commands for the vast number of features in modern word processors, drawing programs, or spreadsheets, but the visual cues, icons, menus, and dialog boxes make it possible for even intermittent users to succeed.

Direct-manipulation interfaces are now being used for a wide range of purposes, including personal finance and travel arrangements. Direct-manipulation checkbook-maintenance and checkbook-searching interfaces, such as Quicken®

(by Intuit®), display a checkbook register with labeled columns for check number, date, payee, and amount. Changes can be made in place, new entries can be made at the first blank line, and a check mark can be added to indicate verification against a monthly report or bank statement; users can search for a particular payee by filling in a blank payee field and then typing a "?". The extension of this functionality into electronic bill paying is a natural progression. Some web-based airline-reservations systems operate graphically as well, showing users a map and prompting for clicks on the departing and arriving cities. Then users can select the date from a calendar and the time from a clock and make their seat selections by clicking on the plane's seating plan.

Another emerging use of direct manipulation involves home automation (Norman, 2002). Since so much of home control involves floorplans, direct-manipulation actions naturally take place on a display of the floorplan with selectable icons for each status indicator (such as a burglar alarm, heat sensor, or smoke detector) and for each activator (such as controls for opening and closing curtains or shades, for air conditioning and heating, or for audio and video speakers or screens). For example, users can route sound from a CD player located in the living room to the bedroom and kitchen by merely dragging the CD icon into those rooms, and they can adjust the volume by moving a marker on a linear scale.

Direct manipulation in video is being expanded by the option of directly dragging the content. With the traditional direct-manipulation widget, users move a slider along a time scale to get to the desired location in the video. A new technique, referred to as *relative flow dragging*, instead allows the user to move through the video by dragging an object of interest along its visual trajectory (Dragicevic et al., 2008). This technique works well with touch-input handheld multimedia devices.

Users are trying to better understand all the data and other visual content that is now available. One way to manage this information is through the use of a *dashboard* (Few, 2006). Being able to see a large volume of information at one time and to directly manipulate it and observe the impact visually is a powerful concept. Businesses and companies are bombarded by volumes of data every day. The ability to organize this user-generated data into a useful graphical format can help them manage resources and spot trends (Fig. 5.9). Companies like Dashboard Spy provide user-generated content and skeleton templates to help users with the design of dashboards (Fig. 5.10).

By the 1990s, direct-manipulation variations had become influential in beyond-the-desktop designs, such as virtual reality, ubiquitous computing, augmented reality, and tangible user interfaces. Virtual reality places users in an immersive environment that blocks out the world. They see an artificial world inside their stereoscopic goggles, which is updated as they turn their heads. Users typically control activity by hand gestures inside a data glove, which

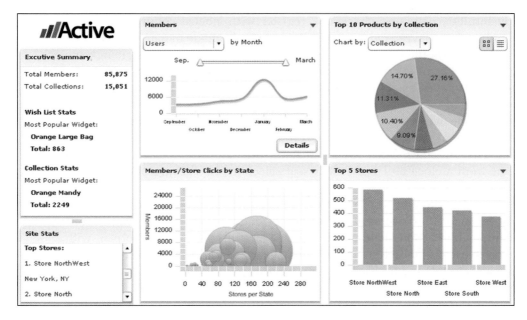

FIGURE 5.9

A dashboard for a retail store (http://www.dashboardspy.com/). Management can view different aspects of the store: the number of members, the types of products, other stores in the system, etc. Different representations of the data are available, ranging from lists to charts and graphs.

allows them to point, select, grasp, and navigate. Handheld controllers allow users to have a six-degrees-of-freedom pointer (three dimensions of position and three dimensions of orientation), to simulate mouse clicks, or to fly in the direction that they point. Virtual worlds allow users to travel through the human body, swim through oceans, ride an electron cloud as it spins around a nucleus, or participate in fantasy worlds with other distant Internet-connected collaborators. This concept has now been extended into Second Life, where users can teleport through space and have social interactions within another whole world. Users can take on the image of various avatars and totally change their characteristics; old can become young, male can become female, long hair can become short.

Weiser's (1991) influential vision of ubiquitous computing described a world where computational devices were everywhere—in your hands, on your body, in your car, built into your home, and pervasively distributed in your environment. The 1993 special issue of *Communications of the ACM* (Wellner et al., 1993) showed provocative prototypes that refined Weiser's vision. It offered multiple visions of beyond-the-desktop designs that used freehand gestures and small mobile devices whose displays changed depending on

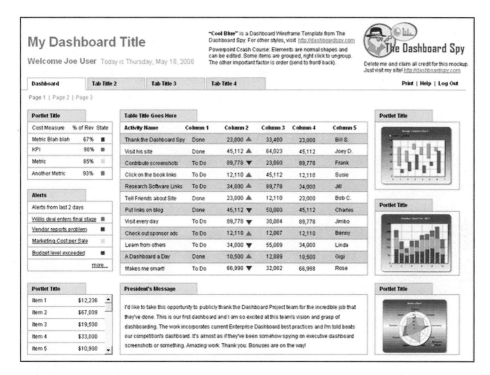

FIGURE 5.10

Another dashboard example, this one showing a skeleton template that can be filled in with user-generated content (http://www.dashboardspy.com).

where users stood and how they pointed the devices. Almost two decades later, Weiser's full vision has not yet been realized, but the social media aspect has blossomed.

Another innovation is augmented reality, in which users see the real world with an overlay of additional information, such as instructions on how to repair a laser printer or information about the location of plumbing behind a wall (Feiner et al., 1993). The notion of tangible user interfaces—in which users grasp physical objects such as bricks, plastic tiles, or marbles to manipulate a graphical display that represents, for example, an urban plan, an optical workbench, or an e-mail interface—was developed at around the same time (Fig. 5.11). Tangible devices use haptic interaction skills to manipulate objects and convert the physical form to a digital form (Ishii, 2008). Ambient devices are also being developed for innovative applications; for example, the Energy Joule monitors energy use in the home and shows the customers if energy prices are rising or falling, so the customers can adjust their discretionary energy use (Fig. 5.12). Virtual, artificial, and augmented reality are discussed further in Section 5.6.

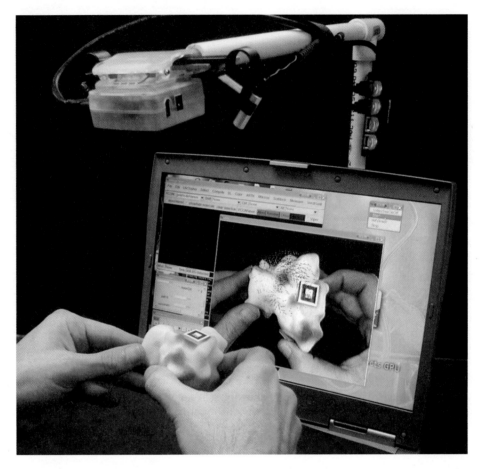

FIGURE 5.11
A tangible user interface for molecular biology, developed in Art Olson's
Laboratory at The Scripps Research Institute, utilizes autofabricated molecular
models tracked with the Augmented Reality Toolkit from the University of
Washington Human Interface Technology Lab. The video camera on the laptop
captures the molecule's position and orientation, enabling the molecular
modeling software to display information such as the attractive/repulsive forces
surrounding the molecule.

Touchable displays such as Microsoft Surface are becoming available as
well; one application of software allows a user to place a camera on the display
surface and have the system automatically download pictures from the camera onto the surface to be viewed, sized, printed, etc. This is all accomplished
without users entering a long string of commands. Another application is virtual maps, which can be manipulated and zoomed by using hand motions as a

FIGURE 5.12

Energy Joule (http://www.ambientdevices.com/) plugs into a conventional electric socket. It displays the current cost of electricity, current energy usage, and the weather forecast. The control changes color to show when energy costs are most expensive and the consumers may want to limit their discretionary energy use. The information on energy costs comes from the utility company and the amount of energy being used comes from a wireless monitor in the home. Its goal is to provide information at a glance. This is not yet available in all areas.

multi-touch interface (Han, 2005). With traditional devices, users place one hand on the mouse, click with one finger, and move the hand back to the keyboard to type when necessary. In contrast, for most everyday operations, people use two hands and some or all of the fingers on each hand. On a touchable display, interactions with both hands seem quite natural (although with small displays, issues of occlusion can be problematic). Two hands perform better than one hand at tasks that require separate control of two points, but when control is for position, orientation, and handspan, control is better using several fingers of one hand (Moscovich and Hughes, 2008).

There will certainly be many future variations of and extensions to direct manipulation, but the basic goals will remain similar: comprehensible interfaces that enable rapid learning, predictable and controllable actions, and appropriate feedback to confirm progress. Direct manipulation has the power to attract users because it is rapid, and even enjoyable. If actions are simple, reversibility is ensured, retention is easy, anxiety recedes, users feel in control, and satisfaction flows in.

5.3 Discussion of Direct Manipulation

Several authors have attempted to describe the component principles of direct manipulation. An imaginative and early interactive system designer, Ted Nelson (1980), perceived user excitement when the interface was constructed by what he calls the *principle of virtuality*—a representation of reality that can be manipulated. Hutchins et al. (1986) reviewed the concepts of direct manipulation and offered a thoughtful decomposition of concerns. They described the "feeling of involvement directly with a world of objects rather than of communicating with an intermediary" and clarified how direct manipulation breaches the *gulf of execution* and the *gulf of evaluation*.

Another perspective on direct manipulation comes from the psychology literature on *problem-solving* and *learning research*. Suitable representations of problems have been clearly shown to be critical to solution finding and to learning. This approach is in harmony with Maria Montessori's (1964) teaching methods for children. She proposed use of physical objects, such as beads or wooden sticks, to convey such mathematical principles as addition, multiplication, or size comparison. The durable abacus is appealing because it gives a direct-manipulation representation of numbers. Physical, spatial, and visual representations also appear to be easier to retain and manipulate than textual or numeric representations (Arnheim, 1972; McKim, 1980).

Papert's (1980) LOGO language created a mathematical microworld in which the principles of geometry are visible. Based on the Swiss psychologist Jean Piaget's theory of child development, LOGO offers students the opportunity to easily create line drawings with an electronic turtle displayed on the screen. In this environment, users derive rapid feedback about their programs, can easily determine what has happened, can spot and repair errors quickly, and can gain satisfaction from creative production of drawings. These features are all characteristic of a direct-manipulation environment.

5.3.1 Problems with direct manipulation

Spatial or visual representations are not necessarily an improvement over text, especially for blind or vision-impaired users who need special software. Graphical user interfaces were a setback for vision-impaired users, who appreciated the simplicity of linear command languages. However, screen readers for desktop interfaces, page readers for Internet browsers, and audio designs for mobile devices enable vision-impaired users to understand some of the spatial relationships necessary to achieve their goals.

A second problem is that direct-manipulation designs may consume valuable screen space and thus force valuable information offscreen, requiring scrolling or multiple actions. Studies of graphical plots versus tabular business data and of flowcharts versus program text demonstrate advantages for compact graphical approaches when pattern-recognition tasks are relevant, but disadvantages when the graphics get too large and the tasks require detailed information. For experienced users, a tabular textual display of 50 document names may be more appropriate than only 10 graphic document icons with the names abbreviated to fit the icon size.

A third problem is that users must learn the meanings of visual representations. A graphic icon may be meaningful to the designer but, for users, may require as much learning time as a word, or more. Some airports that serve multilingual communities use graphic icons extensively, but the meanings of these icons may not be obvious to people from different cultures. Similarly, some computer terminals designed for international use have icons in place of names, but their meanings are not always clear. Titles that appear on icons when the cursor is over them offer only a partial solution.

A fourth problem is that the visual representation may be misleading. Users may grasp the analogical representation rapidly, but then may draw incorrect conclusions about permissible actions, overestimating or underestimating the functions of the computer-based analogy. Ample testing must be carried out to refine the displayed objects and actions and to minimize negative side effects.

A fifth problem is that, for experienced typists, taking a hand off the keyboard to move a mouse or point with a finger may take more time than typing the relevant command. This problem is especially likely to occur if the users are familiar with a compact notation, such as for arithmetic expressions, that is easy to enter from a keyboard but may be more difficult to select with a mouse. While direct manipulation is often defined as replacing typing of commands with pointing with devices, sometimes the keyboard is the most effective direct-manipulation device. Rapid keyboard interaction can be extremely attractive for expert users, but the visual feedback must be equally rapid and comprehensible.

A sixth problem may occur on small mobile devices with limited screen sizes. A finger pointing at a device may partially block the display, rendering a good portion of the device not visible. Also, if the icons are small because of the limited screen size, they may be hard to select or, because of limited resolution and viewing capabilities (especially for older adults), not clearly distinguishable, resulting in their meanings becoming lost or confused.

In addition to these problems, choosing the right objects and actions for a direct-manipulation interface may be difficult. Simple metaphors or analogies with a minimal set of concepts—for example, pencils and paintbrushes in a drawing tool—are a good starting point. Mixing metaphors from two sources may add complexity that contributes to confusion. Also, the emotional tone of the metaphor should be inviting rather than distasteful or inappropriate (Carroll and Thomas, 1982)—sewage-disposal systems are an inappropriate metaphor for electronic-message systems. Since the users are not guaranteed to share the designer's understanding of the metaphor, analogy, or conceptual model used, ample testing is required.

Some direct-manipulation principles can be surprisingly difficult to realize in software. Rapid and incremental actions have two strong implications: a fast perception/action loop (less than 100 ms) and reversibility (the undo action). A standard database query may take a few seconds to perform, so implementing a direct-manipulation interface on top of a database may require special programming techniques. The undo action may be even harder to implement, as it requires that each user action be recorded and that reverse actions be defined. It changes the style of programming, because a nonreversible action is implemented by a simple function call, whereas a reversible action requires recording the inverse action.

Web-based implementers of direct manipulation face further challenges, because the standard markup language (HTML) limits dynamic user interaction, even with the addition of JavaScript™. The newer Dynamic HTML (DHTML) and XML offer greater flexibility (Golub and Shneiderman, 2003), but web-based direct manipulation is more easily accomplished in Java, Flash, or Ajax. As these tools become more widely accepted, web-based direct manipulation will spread, enabling users to move sliders, make selections, and perform drag-and-drop operations with the customized addition of user-generated content.

5.3.2 The three principles of direct manipulation

The attraction of direct manipulation is apparent in the enthusiasm of the users. The designers of the examples in Section 5.2 had an innovative inspiration and an intuitive grasp of what users would want. Each example has problematic features, but they demonstrate the potent advantages of direct manipulation, which can be summarized by three principles:

1. Continuous representations of the objects and actions of interest with meaningful visual metaphors.
2. Physical actions or presses of labeled buttons, instead of complex syntax.
3. Rapid, incremental, reversible actions whose effects on the objects of interest are visible immediately.

Using these three principles, it is possible to design systems that have these beneficial attributes:

- Novices can learn basic functionality quickly, usually through a demonstration by a more experienced user.
- Experts can work rapidly to carry out a wide range of tasks, even defining new functions and features.
- Knowledgeable intermittent users can retain operational concepts.
- Error messages are rarely needed.
- Users can immediately see whether their actions are furthering their goals, and, if the actions are counterproductive, they can simply change the direction of their activity.
- Users experience less anxiety because the interface is comprehensible and because actions can be reversed easily.
- Users gain a sense of confidence and mastery because they are the initiators of action, they feel in control, and they can predict the interface's responses.

In contrast to textual descriptors, dealing with visual representations of objects may be more "natural" and in line with innate human capabilities: Action and visual skills emerged well before language in human evolution.

Psychologists have long known that people grasp spatial relationships and actions more quickly when they are given visual rather than linguistic representations. Furthermore, intuition and discovery are often promoted by suitable visual representations of formal mathematical systems.

The Swiss psychologist Jean Piaget described four *stages of development*: *sensorimotor* (from birth to approximately 2 years), *preoperational* (2 to 7 years), *concrete operational* (7 to 11 years), and *formal operations* (begins at approximately 11 years) (Copeland, 1979). According to this theory, physical actions on an object are comprehensible during the concrete operational stage, when children acquire the concept of *conservation* or *invariance*. At about age 11, children enter the formal-operations stage, in which they use *symbol manipulation* to represent actions on objects. Since mathematics and programming require abstract thinking, they are difficult for children, and designers must link symbolic representations to actual objects. Direct manipulation brings activity to the concrete-operational stage, thus making certain tasks easier for older children and adults.

5.3.3 Visual thinking and icons

The concepts of a *visual language* and of *visual thinking* were promoted by Arnheim (1972) and were embraced by commercial graphic designers (Mullet and Sano, 1995), semiotically oriented academics (*semiotics* is the study of signs and symbols) (de Souza, 2005), and data-visualization gurus. The computer provides a remarkable visual environment for revealing structure, showing relationships, and enabling interactivity that attracts users who have artistic, right-brained, holistic, intuitive personalities. The increasingly visual nature of computer interfaces can sometimes challenge or even threaten the logical, linear, text-oriented, left-brained, compulsive, rational programmers who were the heart of the first generation of hackers. Although these stereotypes—or caricatures—will not stand up to scientific analysis, they do convey the dual paths that computing is following. Traditionalists sometimes scorn the new visual directions as *WIMP* (windows, icons, mouse, and pull-down menu) interfaces, while visual system proponents see the command-line devotees as stubborn and inflexible.

In the computer world, *icons* are usually small (less than 1-inch-square or 64-by 64-pixel) representations of an object or action. Smaller icons are often used to save space or to be integrated within other objects, such as a window border or toolbar. It is not surprising that icons are often used in painting programs to represent tools or actions (for example, lasso or scissors to cut out an image, brush for painting, pencil for drawing, eraser to wipe clean), whereas word processors usually have textual menus for their actions. This difference appears to reflect the differing cognitive styles of visually and textually oriented users, or at least differences in the tasks. Perhaps while users are working on visually oriented tasks it is helpful to "stay visual" by using icons, whereas while working on text documents it is helpful to "stay textual" by using textual menus.

For situations where both a visual icon and a textual item are possible—for example, in a directory listing—designers face two interwoven issues: how to decide between icons and text, and how to design icons. The well-established highway signs are a useful source of experience. Icons are unbeatable for showing ideas such as a road curve, but sometimes a phrase such as ONE WAY! DO NOT ENTER is more comprehensible than an icon. Of course, the smorgasbord approach is to have a little of each (as with, for example, the octagonal STOP sign), and there is evidence that icons plus words are effective in computing situations (Norman, 1991). So the solution to the first problem (deciding between icons and text) depends not only on the users and the tasks, but also on the quality of the icons or words that are proposed. Textual menu choices are covered in Chapter 6; many of the principles discussed there carry over to icon use. In addition, these icon-specific guidelines should be considered:

- Represent the object or action in a familiar and recognizable manner.
- Limit the number of different icons.
- Make the icon stand out from its background.
- Carefully consider three-dimensional icons; they are eye-catching but also can be distracting.
- Ensure that a single selected icon is clearly visible when surrounded by unselected icons.
- Make each icon distinctive from every other icon.
- Ensure the harmoniousness of each icon as a member of a family of icons.
- Design the movement animation: when dragging an icon, the user might move the whole icon, just a frame, possibly a grayed-out or transparent version, or a black box.
- Add detailed information, such as shading to show the size of a file (larger shadow indicates larger file), thickness to show the breadth of a directory folder (thicker means more files inside), color to show the age of a document (older might be yellower or grayer), or animation to show how much of a document has been printed (document folder absorbed progressively into the printer icon).
- Explore the use of combinations of icons to create new objects or actions—for example, dragging a document icon to a folder, trash can, outbox, or printer icon has great utility. Can a document be appended or prepended to another document by pasting of adjacent icons? Can a user set security levels by dragging a document or folder to a guard dog, police car, or vault icon? Can two database icons be intersected by overlapping of the icons?

Icons might include a rich set of gestures with a mouse, touchscreen, or pen. The gestures might indicate copying (up and down arrows), deleting (a cross), editing (a circle), and so on. Icons also might have associated sounds. For example, if each document icon had a tone associated with it (the lower the tone, the bigger the document) when a directory was opened, each tone might be played simultaneously or sequentially. Users might get used to the symphony played by each directory and be able to detect certain features or anomalies, just as we often know telephone numbers by tune and can detect misdialings as discordant tones.

5.3.4 Direct-manipulation programming

Performing tasks by direct manipulation is not the only goal. It should be possible to do programming by direct manipulation as well, at least for certain problems. How about moving a drill press or a surgical tool through a complex series of motions that are then repeated exactly? Automobile seating positions and mirror settings can be set as a group of preferences for a particular driver and then adjusted as the driver settles in place. Likewise, some professional television-camera supports allow the operator to program a sequence of pans or zooms and then to replay it smoothly when required.

Programming of physical devices by direct manipulation seems quite natural, and an adequate visual representation of information may make direct-manipulation programming possible in other domains. Spreadsheet packages, such as Excel, have rich programming languages and allow users to create portions of programs by carrying out standard spreadsheet actions. The result of the actions is stored in another part of the spreadsheet and can be edited, printed, and stored in a textual form. Database programs, such as Access™, allow users to create buttons that when activated will set off a series of actions and commands and generate a report. Similarly, Adobe Photoshop records a history of user actions and then allows users to create programs with action sequences and repetition using direct manipulation.

It would be helpful if the computer could recognize repeated patterns reliably and create useful macros automatically, while the user was engaged in performing a repetitive interface task. Then, with the user's confirmation, the computer could take over and carry out the remainder of the task automatically (Lieberman, 2001). This hope for automatic programming is appealing, but a more effective approach may be to give users the visual tools to specify and record their intentions. Some cell phones have buttons that can be programmed to call home or call the doctor or another emergency number. This allows the user to encounter a simpler interface and be shielded from the details of the tasks. Jitterbug™ designs a simpler cell-phone interface targeted at older adults: the users can dial the phone themselves or contact an operator who will place the call for them (Fig. 5.13).

Direct-manipulation programming offers an alternative to the agent scenarios discussed in Section 2.3.6. Agent promoters believe that the computer can ascertain the users' intentions automatically or can take action based on vague

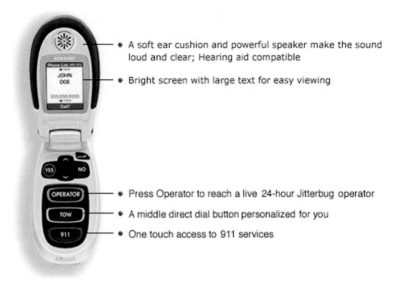

• A soft ear cushion and powerful speaker make the sound loud and clear; Hearing aid compatible

• Bright screen with large text for easy viewing

• Press Operator to reach a live 24-hour Jitterbug operator

• A middle direct dial button personalized for you

• One touch access to 911 services

FIGURE 5.13

Jitterbug phones (http://www.jitterbug.com/) are marketed for older adults who want a cell phone but prefer simple, minimal controls. This particular model is the OneTouch™; it provides the capability with a single button to dial 911 or another preprogrammed number, or call for operator assistance. Jitterbug also provides other phones with additional features. All the phones feature a larger-than-average numerical display and larger backlit buttons for easier viewing.

statements of goals. User intentions are unlikely to be so easily determined, though, and vague statements are not usually too effective. However, if users can specify what they want with comprehensible actions selected from a visual display, they can often rapidly accomplish their goals while preserving their sense of control and accomplishment.

5.4 3D Interfaces

Some designers dream about building interfaces that approach the richness of three-dimensional reality (Bowman et al., 2004). They believe that the closer the interfaces are to the real world, the easier usage will be. This extreme interpretation of direct manipulation is a dubious proposition, since user studies show that disorienting navigation, complex user actions, and annoying occlusions can slow performance in the real world as well as in 3D interfaces (Cockburn and McKenzie, 2002; Risden et al., 2000). Many interfaces (sometimes called 2D interfaces) are designed to be simpler than the real world by constraining movement, limiting interface actions, and ensuring visibility of interface objects. However, the strong utility of "pure" 3D interfaces for medical, architectural, product design, and scientific visualization purposes means that they remain an important challenge for interface designers.

An intriguing possibility is that "enhanced" interfaces may be better than 3D reality. Enhanced features might enable superhuman capabilities, such as faster-than-light teleportation, flying through objects, multiple simultaneous views of objects, and x-ray vision. Playful game designers and creative applications developers have already pushed the technology further than those who seek merely to mimic reality.

For some computer-based tasks—such as medical imagery, architectural drawing, computer-assisted design, chemical-structure modeling, and scientific simulations—pure 3D representations are clearly helpful and have become major industries. However, even in these cases, the successes are often due to design features that make the interface better than reality. Users can magically change colors or shapes, duplicate objects, shrink/expand objects, group/ungroup components, send them by e-mail, and attach floating labels. In these representations, users can also carry out other useful supernatural actions, such as going back in time by undoing recent actions.

Among the many innovations, there have been questionable 3D prototypes, such as for air-traffic control (showing altitude by perspective drawing only adds clutter when compared to an overview from directly above), digital libraries (showing books on shelves may be nice for browsing, but it inhibits searching and linking), and file directories (showing tree structures in three dimensions sometimes leads to designs that increase occlusion and navigation problems). Other questionable applications include ill-considered 3D features for situations in which simple 2D representations would do the job. For example, adding a third dimension to bar charts may slow users and mislead them (Hicks et al., 2003), but they are such an attraction for some users that they are included in most business graphics packages (Cognos, SAS/GRAPH, SPSS/SigmaPlot).

Intriguing, successful applications of 3D representations are game environments. These include first-person action games in which users patrol city streets or race down castle corridors while shooting at opponents, as well as role-playing fantasy games with beautifully illustrated island havens or mountain strongholds (for example, *Myst*, *realMYST®*, or *Riven*). Many games are socially enriched by allowing users to choose 3D avatars to represent themselves. Users can choose avatars that resemble themselves, but often they choose bizarre characters or fantasy images with desirable characteristics such as unusual strength or beauty (White, 2007; Boellstorff, 2008).

Some web-based game environments, such as Second Life (Fig. 5.14), may involve millions of users and thousands of user-constructed "worlds," such as

FIGURE 5.14

An image from a virtual world in Second Life (http://www.secondlife.com/).

schools, shopping malls, or urban neighborhoods. Game devotees may spend dozens of hours per week immersed in their virtual worlds, chatting with collaborators or negotiating with opponents. Sony's *EverQuest* (Fig. 5.15) attracts users with this ambitious description: "Welcome to the world of *EverQuest*, a real 3D massively multiplayer fantasy role-playing game. Prepare to enter an enormous virtual environment—an entire world with its own diverse species, economic systems, alliances, and politics." Another popular role-playing game, *The Sims Online*™ (Fig. 6.6), has 3D characters who live in home environments with rich social behaviors that users control.

These environments may prove to be successful because of the increasingly rich social contexts based on spatial cognition—that is, users may come to appreciate the importance of the setting and value participants who choose to stand close to them. Such environments may come to support effective business meetings (as promoters of There.com, Basecamp®, and Blaxxun® envision), community discussion groups, and even contentious political forums. Imagine taking a virtual tour of the Great Pyramid of Giza, where you explore its internal corridors and view details down to the chisel marks on the stone.

FIGURE 5.15
Sony Online Entertainment's *EverQuest* virtual world. The upper-left picture is
EverQuest, showing a chat box and character controls. The lower-right picture is
EverQuest II, demonstrating real-time multiplayer interaction.

Three-dimensional art and entertainment experiences, often delivered by
web applications, provide another opportunity for innovative applications.
Companies such as 3DNA® create 3D front ends that offer rooms for shopping, games, the Internet, and office applications and are attractive largely for
games, entertainment, and sports enthusiasts. Early web standards like the
Virtual Reality Modeling Language (VRML), which did not generate huge
commercial successes, have given way to richer ones such as X3D®. This standard has major corporate supporters who believe it will lead to viable commercial applications.

A modest use of 3D techniques is to add highlights to 2D interfaces, such as
buttons that appear to be raised or depressed, windows that overlap and leave
shadows, or icons that resemble real-world objects. These may be enjoyable,
recognizable, and memorable because of improved use of spatial memory, but
they can also be visually distracting and confusing because of additional visual
complexity. Attempts to build realistic devices, such as telephones, books, or
CD-players, produce pleasant smiles from first-time users, but these ideas have

not caught on, probably because the design compromises used to produce 3D effects undermine usability.

This enumeration of features for effective 3D interfaces might serve as a checklist for designers, researchers, and educators:

- Use occlusion, shadows, perspective, and other 3D techniques carefully.
- Minimize the number of navigation steps required for users to accomplish their tasks.
- Keep text readable (better rendering, good contrast with background, and no more than 30-degree tilt).
- Avoid unnecessary visual clutter, distraction, contrast shifts, and reflections.
- Simplify user movement (keep movements planar, avoid surprises like going through walls).
- Prevent errors (that is, create surgical tools that cut only where needed and chemistry kits that produce only realistic molecules and safe compounds).
- Simplify object movement (facilitate docking, follow predictable paths, limit rotation).
- Organize groups of items in aligned structures to allow rapid visual search.
- Enable users to construct visual groups to support spatial recall (placing items in corners or tinted areas).

Breakthroughs based on clever ideas seem possible (Bowman et al., 2008). Enriching interfaces with stereo displays, haptic feedback, and 3D sound may yet prove beneficial in more than specialized applications. Bigger payoffs are more likely to come sooner if these guidelines for inclusion of enhanced 3D features are followed:

- Provide overviews so users can see the big picture (plan view display, aggregated views).
- Allow teleportation (rapid context shifts by selecting destination in an overview).
- Offer x-ray vision so users can see into or beyond objects.
- Provide history keeping (recording, undoing, replaying, editing).
- Permit rich user actions on objects (save, copy, annotate, share, send).
- Enable remote collaboration (synchronous, asynchronous).
- Give users control over explanatory text (pop-up, floating, or excentric labels and screen tips) and let them view details on demand.
- Offer tools to select, mark, and measure.
- Implement dynamic queries to rapidly filter out unneeded items.
- Support semantic zooming and movement (simple action brings object front and center and reveals more details).

- Enable landmarks to show themselves even at a distance (Darken and Sibert, 1996).
- Allow multiple coordinated views (users can be in more than one place at a time and see data in more than one arrangement at a time).
- Develop novel 3D icons to represent concepts that are more recognizable and memorable (Irani and Ware, 2003).

Three-dimensional environments are greatly appreciated by some users and are helpful for some tasks (Bowman et al., 2004). They have the potential for novel social, scientific, and commercial applications if designers go beyond the goal of mimicking 3D reality. Enhanced 3D interfaces could be the key to making some kinds of 3D teleconferencing, collaboration, and teleoperation popular. Of course, it will take good design of 3D interfaces (pure, constrained, or enhanced) and more research on finding the payoffs beyond the entertaining features that appeal to first-time users. Success will come to designers who provide compelling content, relevant features, appropriate entertainment, and novel social-media structure support. By studying user performance and measuring satisfaction, those designers will be able to polish their designs and refine guidelines for others to follow.

5.5 Teleoperation

Teleoperation has two parents: direct manipulation in personal computers and process control, where human operators control physical processes in complex environments. Typical tasks are operating power or chemical plants, controlling manufacturing, surgery, flying airplanes, or steering vehicles. If the physical processes take place in a remote location, we talk about *teleoperation* or *remote control*. To perform the control task remotely, the human operator may interact with a computer, which may carry out some of the control tasks without any interference by the human operator. This idea is captured by the notion of *supervisory control* (Sheridan, 1992). Although supervisory control and direct manipulation stem from different problem domains and are usually applied to different system architectures, they carry a strong resemblance.

There are great opportunities for the remote control or teleoperation of devices if acceptable user interfaces can be constructed. When designers can provide adequate feedback in sufficient time to permit effective decision making, attractive applications in manufacturing, medicine, military operations, and computer-supported collaborative work are viable. Home-automation applications extend remote operation of telephone-answering machines to security and access systems, energy control, and operation of appliances. Scientific applications in space, underwater, or in hostile environments enable new research projects to be conducted economically and safely.

In traditional direct-manipulation interfaces, the objects and actions of interest are shown continuously; users generally point, click, or drag rather than type, and feedback indicating change is immediate. However, when the devices being operated are remote, these goals may not be realizable, and designers must expend additional effort to help users to cope with slower responses, incomplete feedback, increased likelihood of breakdowns, and more complex error-recovery procedures. The problems are strongly connected to the hardware, physical environment, network design, and task domain.

A typical remote application is *telemedicine*, or medical care delivered over communication links (Sonnenwald et al., 2006). This allows physicians to examine patients remotely and surgeons to carry out operations across continents. A growing application is telepathology, in which a pathologist examines tissue samples or body fluids under a remotely located microscope (Fig. 5.16). The

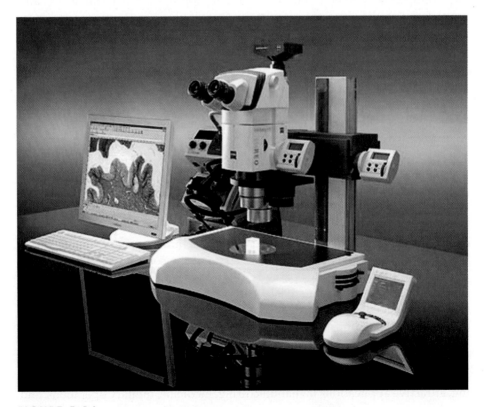

FIGURE 5.16
This telepathology setup enables a pathologist to remotely view and examine the specimen (Courtesy of the Telepathology Lab at the University of Pittsburgh).

transmitting workstation has a high-resolution camera mounted on a motorized light microscope. The pathologist at the receiving workstation can manipulate the microscope using a mouse or keypad and can see a high-resolution image of the magnified sample. The two caregivers talk by telephone to coordinate control, and the remote pathologist can request that slides be placed manually under the microscope. Controls include:

- Magnification (three or six objectives)
- Focus (coarse and fine bidirectional control)
- Illumination (bidirectional adjustment continuous or by step)
- Position (two-dimensional placement of the slide under the microscope objective)

Other medical applications include virtual colonoscopy and robotic surgery. Virtual colonoscopy allows the patient to undergo a CT scan as opposed to a more invasive procedure; the physician can then interactively navigate through a 3D model (Kaufman et al., 2005). Robotic surgery (using the da Vinci® Surgical System, shown in Fig. 5.17) is an alternative to conventional surgery that enables a smaller incision and more accurate and precise surgical movements. The robotic platform expands the surgeon's capabilities and provides a highly magnified 3D image. In addition, the surgeon has control over hand, wrist, and finger movement through robotic instrument arms. The surgeon is comfortably seated across the operating room at a console rather than being over the patient, and the system damps out some involuntary movements that can be problematic. SensAble Technologies, Inc.®, a company with its roots in the development of a system called PHANTOM® at MIT, is now a leader in the field of haptic technology, offering force-feedback systems for many applications, including dentistry.

The architecture of remote environments introduces several complicating factors:

- *Time delays*. The network hardware and software cause delays in sending user actions and receiving feedback: a *transmission delay*, or the time it takes for the command to reach the microscope (in our example, transmitting the command through the modem), and an *operation delay*, or the time until the microscope responds. These delays in the system prevent the operator from knowing the current status of the system. For example, if a positioning command has been issued, it may take several seconds for the slide to start moving.

- *Incomplete feedback*. Devices originally designed for direct control may not have adequate sensors or status indicators. For instance, the microscope can transmit its current position, but it operates so slowly that it does not indicate the *exact* current position.

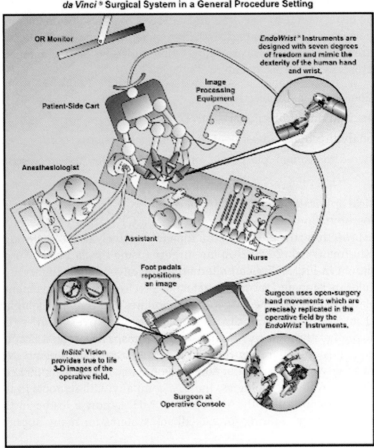

FIGURE 5.17

The da Vinci robotic surgery system controller (http://www.davincisurgery.com/).

- *Unanticipated interferences.* Since the devices operated are remote, unanticipated interferences are more likely to occur than in desktop direct-manipulation environments. For instance, if a local operator accidentally moves the slide under the microscope, the positions indicated might not be correct. A breakdown might also occur during the execution of a remote operation without a good indication of this event being sent to the remote site.

One solution to these problems is to make explicit the network delays and breakdowns as part of the system. The user sees a model of the starting state of the system, the action that has been initiated, and the current state of the system as it carries out the action. It may be preferable for users to specify a destination (rather than a motion) and wait until the action is completed before readjusting the destination if necessary.

Teleoperation is also commonly used by the military and by civilian space projects. Military applications for unmanned aircraft gained visibility during the recent wars in Afghanistan and Iraq. Reconnaissance drones were widely used, and teleoperated missile-firing aircraft were tested. Agile and flexible mobile robots exist for many hazardous duty situations (Goodrich and Schultz, 2007). Military missions and harsh environments, such as undersea and space exploration, are strong drivers for improved designs.

5.6 Virtual and Augmented Reality

Flight-simulator designers work hard to create the most realistic experience for fighter and airline pilots. The cockpit displays and controls are taken from the same production line that creates the real ones. Then, the windows are replaced by high-resolution computer displays, and sounds are choreographed to give the impression of engine start or reverse thrust. Finally, the vibration and tilting during climbing or turning are created by hydraulic jacks and intricate suspension systems. This elaborate technology may cost $100 million, but even so, it is a lot cheaper, safer, and more useful for training than the $400-million jet that it simulates. (And for training actual pilots, the $30 flight simulators that millions of home computer game players have purchased won't quite do the trick!) Flying a plane is a complicated and specialized skill, but simulators are available for more common—and some surprising—tasks under the alluring name of *virtual reality* or the more descriptive *virtual environments*.

High above the office desktop, much beyond multimedia, the gurus of virtuality are promoting immersive experiences (Fig. 5.18). Whether soaring over Seattle, bending around bronchial tubes to find lung cancers, or grasping complex molecules, the

FIGURE 5.18

In the helmet-and-gloves approach to virtual reality, the system tracks the user's hand and head motions and finger gestures to control the scene's movement and manipulation. To enter this virtual environment, you need special gear. Any of several types of stereoscopic devices transform otherwise two-dimensional image data into three-dimensional images.

cyberspace explorers are moving past their initial fantasies to create useful technologies (McMenemy and Ferugson, 2007). The imagery and personalities involved in virtual reality are often colorful (Rheingold, 1991), but many researchers have tried to present a balanced view by conveying enthusiasm while reporting on problems (Stanney, 2002; Stanney and Cohn, 2008).

Architects have been using computers to draw three-dimensional representations of buildings with user-generated content for over three decades. Their design tools show buildings on a standard display, but using a projector to create a wall-sized image gives prospective clients a more realistic impression. Now add animation that allows clients to see what happens if they move left or right or approach the image. Then enable clients to control the animation by walking on a treadmill (faster walking brings the building closer more quickly), and allow them to walk through the doors or up the stairs. Finally, replace the projector with a head-mounted display, and monitor head movement with a head tracker (for example, Polhemus™, Logitech™, or InterTrax2™). Each change takes users a bit farther along the range from "looking at" to "being in." Bumping into walls, falling (gently) down stairs, meeting other people, or having to wait for an elevator could be the next variations.

The architectural application is a persuasive argument for "being in," because we are used to "being in" buildings and moving around them. On the other hand, for many applications "looking at" is actually more effective, which is why air-traffic–control workstations place the viewer above the situation display. The Living Theater of the 1960s created an immersive theatrical experience and "be-ins" were popular for a time, but most theatergoers prefer to take their "suspension of disbelief" experiences from the "looking at" perspective, while seated safely in the audience (Laurel, 1991). Similarly, while it can be fun to watch movies on the large wraparound screens that put viewers "in" racecars or airplanes, these experiences are viewed as special events, and not everyone is comfortable with them. One company that is repeating the "be-in" experience is EveryScape. EveryScape is recording pieces of the actual neighborhoods and streets in several cities. This provides people with the opportunity to explore the cities without traveling, just by using a computer. In some locations, such as Boston, you can even explore inside various buildings.

It remains to be seen whether doctors and surgeons, accustomed to "looking at" a patient, will really want to crawl through the patient's colon or "be in" the patient's brain. Surgeons can benefit by "looking at" video images from inside a patient's heart taken through fiber-optic cameras and from use of remote direct-manipulation devices that minimize invasive surgery, but they don't seem to want the immersive experience of being inside the patient with a head-mounted display. Surgery planning and teleoperation can also be done with three-dimensional "looking at" visualizations shown on desktop displays and guided by handheld props (Hinckley et al., 1994). There are more mundane applications for such video and fiber-optic magic, too—imagine the benefits to household plumbers of being able to see lost wedding rings around the bends of a sink drain or to locate and grasp the child's toy that has fallen down the pipes of a clogged toilet.

Other concepts that were sources for the current excitement include *artificial reality*, pioneered by Myron Krueger (1991). His Videoplace and Videodesk installations with large-screen projectors and video sensors combined full-body movement with projected images of light creatures that walked along a performer's arm or of multicolored patterns and sounds generated by the performer's movement. Similarly, Vincent John Vincent's demonstrations of the Mandala system carried performance art to a new level of sophistication and fantasy. The CAVE™, a room with several walls of high-resolution rear-projected displays with three-dimensional audio, can offer satisfying experiences for several people at a time (Cruz-Neira, et al., 1993; Fig. 5.19). The theatrical possibilities have attracted researchers and media pioneers who are merging reality with virtuality (Benford et al., 2001).

FIGURE 5.19

The CAVE, a multiperson, room-sized, high-resolution, 3D video and audio environment initially developed at the University of Illinois at Chicago. The CAVE is a 10 by 10 by 9-foot theater, made up of three rear-projection screens for walls and a down-projection screen for the floor.

The telepresence aspect of virtual reality breaks the physical limitations of space and allows users to act as though they are somewhere else. Practical thinkers immediately grasp the connection to remote direct manipulation, remote control, and remote vision, but the fantasists see the potential to escape current reality and to visit science-fiction worlds, cartoonlands, previous times in history, galaxies with different laws of physics, or unexplored emotional territories (Whitton, 2003).

There have been medical successes for virtual environments. For example, virtual worlds can be used to treat patients with fear of heights by giving them an immersive experience with control over their viewpoint and movement (Hodges et al., 1995; Hoffman et al., 2003). The safe immersive environment enables phobia sufferers to accommodate themselves to frightening stimuli in preparation for similar experiences in the real world (Fig. 5.20). Another dramatic result is that immersive environments provide distractions for patients so that some forms of pain are controlled (Hoffman et al., 2001; Fig. 5.21).

The direct-manipulation principles outlined in Section 5.3.2 may be helpful to people who are designing and refining virtual environments. When users can select actions rapidly by pointing or gesturing and display feedback occurs immediately, users have a strong sense of causality. Interface objects and actions should be simple, so that users view and manipulate task-domain objects. The surgeon's instruments should be readily available or easily called up. Similarly, an interior designer walking through a house with a client should be able to pick

FIGURE 5.20

Virtual-reality therapy for users who have various phobias. Through the virtual-reality experience, the patient can be "exposed" to the phobic experience with the direction of a trained therapist (http://www.virtuallybetter.com).

FIGURE 5.21

Images shown to children to immerse them in a virtual world while they are receiving painful treatment. The immersive experience seems to lessen the pain experience (http://www.5dt.com/software.html#med).

up a window-stretching tool or pull on a handle to try out a larger window, or to use a room-painting tool to change the wall colors while leaving the windows and furniture untouched. Navigation in large virtual spaces presents further challenges, but overview maps have been demonstrated to provide useful orientation information (Darken and Sibert, 1996).

An important variant, called *augmented reality*, enables users to see the real world with an overlay of additional information; for example, while users are looking at the walls of a building, their semitransparent eyeglasses may show the location of electrical wires and studwork. Medical applications, such as allowing surgeons to look at a patient while they see an overlay of an x-ray or sonogram to help locate a cancer tumor, also seem compelling. Augmented reality could show users how to repair electrical equipment or guide visitors through tourist attractions (Feiner et al., 1993); tourist-guide eyeglasses could allow visitors to view labels about architectural features in an historic town or to find dining halls at a large college campus. Augmented-reality strategies also enable users to manipulate real-world artifacts to see results on graphical models (Ishii, 2008; Poupyrev et al., 2002) with applications such as manipulating protein molecules to understand the attractive/repulsive force fields between them. Strategies and programming examples can provide users with an entry into the world of augmented reality (Cawood and Fiala, 2007).

Alternatives to the immersive environment are appealing because they avoid the problems of simulator sickness, nausea, and discomfort from wearing head-mounted gear. *Desktop* or *fishtank* virtual environments (both references are to standard "looking-at" displays) are becoming more common, because they avoid the physically distressing symptoms and require only standard equipment. Three-dimensional graphics have led to the development of user interfaces that support user-controlled exploration of real places, scientific visualizations, or fantasy worlds. Many applications run on high-performance workstations capable of rapid rendering, but some are appealing even over the Web, using VRML and its successors, such as X3D. Graphics researchers have been perfecting image display to simulate lighting effects, textured surfaces, reflections, and shadows. Data structures and algorithms for zooming in or panning across an object rapidly and smoothly are now practical on common computers.

Successful virtual environments will depend on smooth integration of multiple technologies:

- *Visual display.* The normal-size (12 to 17 inches diagonally) computer display at a normal viewing distance (70 centimeters) subtends an angle of about 5 degrees; large-screen (17- to 30-inch) displays can cover a 20- to 30-degree field, and head-mounted displays cover 100 degrees horizontally and 60 degrees vertically. The head-mounted displays block other images, so the effect is more dramatic, and head motion produces new images, so the users can get the impression of 360-degree coverage. Flight simulators also block extraneous images, but they do so without forcing the users to wear sometimes-cumbersome head-mounted displays. Another approach is a boom-mounted display that senses the users' positions without requiring them to wear heavy goggles (Fig. 5.22).

  As hardware technology improves, it will be possible to provide more rapid and higher-resolution images. Most researchers agree that the displays must approach real time (probably under a 100-millisecond delay) in presenting images to the users. Low-resolution displays are acceptable while users or the objects are moving, but when users stop to stare, higher resolution is necessary to preserve the sense of "being in." Improved hardware and algorithms are needed to display rough shapes rapidly and then to fill in the details when the motion stops. A further requirement is that motion be smooth; both incremental changes and continuous display of the objects of interest are required (Allison et al., 2001).

FIGURE 5.22

A head-coupled stereoscopic display. The Boom Chameleon provides high-quality visual displays and tracking integrated with a counterbalanced articulated arm for full six-degrees-of-freedom motion.

- *Head-position sensing.* Head-mounted displays can provide differing views depending on head position. Look to the right, and you see a forest; look to the left, and the forest gives way to a city. Some head trackers can be cumbersome to wear, but smaller versions embedded in a hat or eyeglasses facilitate mobility. Video recognition of head position is possible. Sensor precision should be high (within 1 degree and within 1 centimeter) and rapid (within 100 milliseconds). Eye tracking to recognize the focus of attention might be useful, but it is difficult to accomplish while the user is moving and is wearing a head-mounted display.

- *Hand-position sensing.* The DataGlove™ is an innovative invention that continues to be refined, with improvements being made to its comfort, accuracy, and sampling rate. Bryson (1996) complains, "the problems with glove devices include inaccuracies in measurement and lack of standard gestural vocabulary." It may turn out that accurate measurement of finger position is required only for one or two fingers or even one or two joints. A six-degrees-of-freedom tracker mounted on the glove or wrist provides hand orientation. Sensors for other body parts, such as knees, arms, or legs, are finding uses in sports training and movement capture. More than one journalist has referred to the potential for sensors and tactile feedback on more erotic body parts.

- *Hand-held manipulatives.* Imaginative approaches have included electronically active surgical tools and small dolls (Pierce and Pausch, 2002). Users can manipulate these objects to produce input, operate devices, create drawings, or make sculptures. A variant, often called "worlds in miniature," is to have a small model of a house or a piece of scientific equipment that users can manipulate to create operations on the larger real-world object, often at a distant location.

- *Force feedback and haptics.* Hand-operated remote-control devices for performing experiments in chemistry laboratories or for handling nuclear materials provide force feedback that gives users a good sense of when they grasp an object or bump into one. Force feedback to car drivers and pilots is carefully configured to provide realistic and useful tactile information. Simulated feedback from software was successful in speeding docking tasks with complex molecules (Brooks, 1988). It might be helpful for surgeons to receive force feedback as they practice difficult operations. A palmtop display mounted on a boom was shown to produce faster and more accurate performance on a remote manipulation task when haptic (touch and force) feedback was added (Noma et al., 1996). Remote handshaking as part of a videoconference has been suggested, but it is not clear that the experience could be as satisfying as the real thing.

- *Sound input and output.* Sound output adds realism to bouncing balls, beating hearts, or dropping vases, as videogame designers found out long ago. Making convincing sounds at the correct moment with full three-dimensional effect is possible, but it too is hard work. The digital-sound hardware is adequate, but the software tools are still inadequate. Music output from virtual instruments is promising; most early work in this area simulates existing instruments (such as a violin or guitar), but novel instruments have also emerged. Speech recognition for initiating actions and making menu selections may be useful, because keyboard and mouse use is restricted.

- *Other sensations.* The tilting and vibration of flight simulators might provide an inspiration for some designers. Tilting and vibrating virtual roller coasters already exist and could become even more popular if users could travel at 60, 600, or 6,000 miles per hour and crash through mountains or go into orbit. Why not include real gusts of air with raindrops, made hot or cold to convey the virtual weather? Finally, the power of smells to evoke strong reactions has been understood by writers from Proust to Gibson. Olfactory computing has been tried, but appropriate and practical applications have yet to be found and developed (Yanagida, 2008).

- *Collaborative and competitive virtual environments.* Collaboration (Chapter 9) is a lively research area, as are collaborative virtual environments or, as one developer called them, "virtuality built for two." Such environments allow two people at remote sites to work together, possibly designing an object, while seeing each other's actions and the object of interest (Benford et al., 2001). Competitive games such as virtual racquetball have been built for two players. Software for training Army tank crews became much more compelling when the designs shifted from playing against the computer to shooting at other tank crews and worrying about their attacks. The realistic sounds created such a sense of engagement that crews experienced elevated heart rates, more rapid breathing, and increased perspiration. By contrast, some virtual environments are designed to bring relaxation and pleasant encounters with other people, enhancing the social media participation aspects.

BOX 5.1
Definition, benefits, and drawbacks of direct manipulation.

Definition
- Visual representation (metaphor) of the "world of action"
- Objects and actions are shown
- Analogical reasoning is tapped
- Rapid, incremental, and reversible actions
- Replacement of typing with pointing and selecting
- Immediate visibility of results of actions

Benefits over commands
- Control/display compatibility
- Less syntax reduces error rates
- Errors are more preventable
- Faster learning and higher retention
- Encourages exploration

Concerns
- Increased system resources, possibly
- Some actions may be cumbersome
- Macro techniques are often weak
- History and other tracing may be difficult
- Visually impaired users may have more difficulty

The opportunities for artistic expression and public-space installations are being explored by performance artists, museum designers, and building architects. Creative installations include projected images, 3D sound, and sculptural components, sometimes combined with video cameras and user control by mobile devices.

Practitioner's Summary

Among interactive systems that provide equivalent functionality and reliability, some systems have emerged to dominate the competition. Often, the most appealing systems have an enjoyable user interface with customized user-generated content that offers a natural representation of the task objects and actions—hence the term *direct manipulation* (Box 5.1). These interfaces are easy to learn, to use, and to retain over time. Novices can acquire a simple subset of the actions and then progress to more elaborate ones. Actions are rapid, incremental, and reversible, and they can be performed with physical movements instead of complex syntactic forms. The results of actions are visible immediately, and error messages are needed less often.

Using direct-manipulation principles in an interface does not ensure its success. A poor design, slow implementation, or inadequate functionality can undermine acceptance. For some applications, menu selection, form fill-in, or command languages may still be more appropriate. However, the potential for direct-manipulation programming, 3D interfaces, and teleoperation is great. Compelling demonstrations of virtual and augmented reality are being applied in a growing set of applications with enhanced social interactions. Iterative design (Chapter 3) is especially important in testing advanced direct-manipulation systems, because the novelty of these approaches may lead to unexpected problems for designers and users.

Researcher's Agenda

We need research to refine our understanding of the contributions of each feature of direct manipulation: analogical representation, incremental action, reversibility, physical action instead of syntax, immediate visibility of results, and graphic displays and icons. Reversibility is easily accomplished by a generic undo action, but designing natural inverses for each action may be more attractive. Complex actions are well represented with direct manipulation, but multilayer design strategies for graceful evolution from novice to expert usage could be a major contribution. For expert users, direct-manipulation programming is still an opportunity, but good methods of history keeping and editing of action sequences are needed, as well as increased attention to user-generated content. Better understanding of touchable interfaces and their uses as well as research on two-handed versus one-handed operations are needed. The allure of 3D interaction is great, but researchers need to provide a better understanding of how and when (and when not) to use features such as occlusion, reduced navigation, and enhanced 3D actions such as teleportation or x-ray vision. The impact of immersion into gaming and virtual worlds using rich social-media interactions across various ages and activities needs to be understood better.

Beyond the desktops and laptops, there is the allure of telepresence, virtual environments, augmented realities, and context-aware devices. The playful aspects will certainly be pursued, but the real challenge is to find the practical designs and a better understanding of being in and looking at three-dimensional worlds, both as individuals and as collaborators and players in the enriched social media participation environments.

WORLD WIDE WEB RESOURCES
http://www.aw.com/DTUI/

Some creative direct-manipulation services and tools are provided, but the majority of sources cover teleoperation and virtual environments, including Second Life. The Web3D Consortium and its specification enables creation of visually appealing web-based three-dimensional environments.

References

Allison, R. S., Harris, L. R., Jenkin, M., Jasiobedzka, J., and Zacher, J. E., Tolerance of temporal delay in virtual environments, *Proc. IEEE Virtual Reality Conference 2001*, IEEE, New Brunswick, NJ (2001).

Arnheim, Rudolf, *Visual Thinking*, University of California Press, Berkeley, CA (1972).

Benford, Steve, Greenhalgh, Chris, Rodden, Tom, and Pycock, James, Collaborative virtual environments, *Communications of the ACM 44*, 7, ACM Press, New York (July 2001), 79–85.

Boellstorff, Tom, *Coming of Age in Second Life: An Anthropologist Explores the Virtually Human*, Princeton University Press, Princeton, NJ (2008).

Bowman, Doug A., Coquillart, Sabine, Froehlich, Bernd, Hirose, Michitaka, Kitamura, Yoshifumi, Kiyokawa, Kiyoshi, and Suerzlinger, Wolfgang, 3D User interfaces: New directions and perspectives, *IEEE Computer Graphics and Applications, 28*, 6 (November/December 2008), 20–36.

Bowman, Doug A., Kruijff, Ernst, Laviola, Joseph J., and Poupyrev, Ivan, *3D User Interfaces: Theory and Practice*, Pearson, New York (2004).

Brooks, Frederick, Grasping reality through illusion: Interactive graphics serving science, *Proc. CHI '88 Conference: Human Factors in Computing Systems*, ACM Press, New York (1988), 1–11.

Bryson, Steve, Virtual reality in scientific visualization, *Communications of the ACM 39*, 5 (May 1996), 62–71.

Carroll, John M. and Thomas, John C., Metaphor and the cognitive representation of computing systems, *IEEE Transactions on Systems, Man, and Cybernetics*, SMC-12, 2 (March–April 1982), 107–116.

Cawood, Stephen and Fiala, Mark, *Augmented Reality: A Practical Guide*, Pragmatic Bookshelf, Raleigh, NC (2007).

Cockburn, Andy and McKenzie, Bruce, Evaluating the effectiveness of spatial memory in 2D and 3D physical and virtual environments, *Proc. CHI 2002 Conference: Human Factors in Computing Systems*, ACM Press, New York (2002), 203–210.

Copeland, Richard W., *How Children Learn Mathematics, Third Edition*, MacMillan, New York (1979).

Cruz-Neira, C., Sandin, D. J., and DeFanti, T., Surround-screen projection-based virtual reality: The design and implementation of the CAVE, *Proc. SIGGRAPH '93 Conference*, ACM Press, New York (1993), 135–142.

Darken, Rudolph, P. and Sibert, John L., Navigating large virtual spaces, *International Journal of Human-Computer Interaction 8*, 1 (1996), 49–71.

Dragicevic, Pierre, Romas, Gonzalo, Bibliowicz, Jacobo, Nowrouzezahrai, Derek, Balakrishnan, Ravin, and Singh, Karan, Video browsing by direct manipulation, *Proc. CHI 2008 Conference: Human Factors in Computing Systems*, ACM Press, New York (2008), 237–246.

de Souza, Clarisse Sieckenius, *Semiotic Engineering of Human-Computer Interaction*, MIT Press, Cambridge, MA (2005).

Feiner, Steven, MacIntyre, Blair, and Seligmann, Doree, Knowledge-based augmented reality, *Communications of the ACM 36*, 7 (1993), 52–62.

Few, Stephen, *Information Dashboard Design*, O'Reilly Media, Sebastopol, CA (2006).

Golub, Evan and Shneiderman, Ben, Dynamic query visualizations on World Wide Web clients: A DHTML solution for maps and scattergrams, *International Journal of Web Engineering and Technology 1*, 1 (2003), 63–78.

Goodrich, Michael A. and Schultz, Alan C., Human-robot interaction: A survey, *Foundations and Trends in Human-Computer Interaction 1*, 3 (2007), 203–275.

Han, Jefferson Y., Low-cost multi-touch sensing through frustrated total internal reflection, *Proc. UIST '05 Conference*, ACM Press, New York (2005), 115–118.

Herot, Christopher F., Spatial management of data, *ACM Transactions on Database Systems 5*, 4 (December 1980), 493–513.

Herot, Christopher, Graphical user interfaces, in Vassiliou, Yannis (Editor), *Human Factors and Interactive Computer Systems*, Ablex, Norwood, NJ (1984), 83–104.

Hicks, Martin, O'Malley, Claire, Nichols, Sarah, and Anderson, Ben, Comparison of 2D and 3D representations for visualising telecommunication usage, *Behaviour & Information Technology* 22, 3 (2003), 185–201.

Hinckley, Ken, Pausch, Randy, Goble, John C., and Kassell, Neal F., Passive real-world props for neurosurgical visualization, *Proc. CHI '94 Conference: Human Factors in Computing Systems*, ACM Press, New York (1994), 452–458.

Hodges, L.F., Rothbaum, B.O., Kooper, R., Opdyke, D., Meyer, T., North, M., de Graaff, J.J., and Williford, J., Virtual environments for treating the fear of heights, *IEEE Computer* 28, 7 (1995), 27–34.

Hoffman, H.G., Patterson, D.R., Carrougher, G.J., Nakamura, D., Moore, M., Garcia-Palacios, A., and Furness, T.A. III, The effectiveness of virtual reality pain control with multiple treatments of longer durations: A case study, *International Journal of Human-Computer Interaction* 13 (2001), 1–12.

Hoffman, H. G., Garcia-Palacios, A., Carlin, C.., Furness, T.A. III, and Botella-Arbona, C., Interfaces that heal: Coupling real and virtual objects to cure spider phobia, *International Journal of Human-Computer Interaction* 15 (2003), 469–486.

Hutchins, Edwin L., Hollan, James D., and Norman, Don A., Direct manipulation interfaces, in Norman, Don A. and Draper, Stephen W. (Editors), *User Centered System Design: New Perspectives on Human-Computer Interaction*, Lawrence Erlbaum Associates, Hillsdale, NJ (1986), 87–124.

Irani, Pourang and Ware, Colin, Diagramming information structures using 3D perceptual primitives, *ACM Transactions on Computer-Human Interaction* 10, 1, (March 2003), 1–19.

Ishii, Hiroshi, Tangible user interfaces, in Sears, Andrew and Jacko, Julie (Eds.), *The Human-Computer Interaction Handbook, Second Edition*, Lawrence Erlbaum Associates, Hillsdale, NJ (2008), 469–487.

Kaufman, Arie E., Lakare, Sarang, Kreeger, Kevin, and Bitter, Ingmar, Virtual colonoscopy, *Communications of the ACM* 48, 2 (February 2005), 37–41.

Krueger, Myron, *Artificial Reality II*, Addison-Wesley, Reading, MA (1991).

Laurel, Brenda, *Computers as Theatre*, Addison-Wesley, Reading, MA (1991).

Lecky-Thompson, Guy W., *Video Game Design Revealed*, Charles River Media, Boston, MA (2008).

Lieberman, Henry, *Your Wish Is My Command: Programming by Example*, Morgan Kaufmann, San Francisco, CA (2001).

McKim, Robert H., *Experiences in Visual Thinking, Second Edition*, Brooks/Cole, Monterey, CA (1980).

McMenemy, Karen and Ferguson, Stuart, *A Hitchhiker's Guide to Virtual Reality*, A.K. Peters, Wellesley, MA (2007).

Montessori, Maria, *The Montessori Method*, Schocken, New York (1964).

Moscovich, Tomer and Hughes, John F., Indirect mappings of multi-touch input using one and two hands, *Proc. CHI 2008 Conference: Human Factors in Computing Systems*, ACM Press, New York (2008), 1275–1283.

Mullet, Kevin and Sano, Darrell, *Designing Visual Interfaces: Communication Oriented Techniques*, Sunsoft Press, Englewood Cliffs, NJ (1995).

Nelson, Ted, Interactive systems and the design of virtuality, *Creative Computing* 6, 11, (November 1980), 56 ff., and 6, 12 (December 1980), 94 ff.

Noma, Haruo, Miyasato, Tsutomu, and Kishino, Fumio, A palmtop display for dexterous manipulation with haptic sensation, *Proc. CHI '96 Conference: Human Factors in Computing Systems*, ACM Press, New York (1996), 126–133.

Norman, Donald A., *The Design of Everyday Things*, Basic Books, New York (2002).

Norman, Kent, *The Psychology of Menu Selection: Designing Cognitive Control at the Human/Computer Interface*, Ablex, Norwood, NJ (1991).

Papert, Seymour, *Mindstorms: Children, Computers, and Powerful Ideas*, Basic Books, New York (1980).

Pagulayan, Randy J., Keeker, Kevin, Fuller, Thomas, Wixon, Dennis, and Romero, Ramon, User-centered design in games, in Sears, Andrew and Jacko, Julie (Editors), *The Human-Computer Interaction Handbook, Second Edition*, Lawrence Erlbaum Associates, Hillsdale, NJ (2008), 731–759.

Pierce, Jeffrey S. and Pausch, Randy, Comparing voodoo dolls and HOMER: Exploring the importance of feedback in virtual environments, *Proc. CHI 2002 Conference: Human Factors in Computing Systems*, ACM Press, New York (2002), 105–112.

Poupyrev, Ivan, Tan, Desney S., Billinghurst, Mark, Kato, Hirokazu, Regenbrecht, Holger, and Tetsutani, Nobuji, Developing a generic augmented-reality interface, *IEEE Computer* 35, 3 (March 2002), 44–50.

Rheingold, Howard, *Virtual Reality*, Simon and Schuster, New York (1991).

Risden, Kirsten, Czerwinski, Mary P., Munzner, Tamara, and Cook, Daniel, An initial examination of ease of use for 2D and 3D information visualizations of web content, *International Journal of Human-Computer Studies* 53, 5 (November 2000), 695–714.

Robertson, George G., Card, Stuart K., and Mackinlay, Jock D., Information visualization using 3-D interactive animation, *Communications of the ACM* 36, 4 (April 1993), 56–71.

Sheridan, T. B., *Telerobotics, Automation, and Human Supervisory Control*, MIT Press, Cambridge, MA (1992).

Shneiderman, Ben, Direct manipulation: A step beyond programming languages, *IEEE Computer* 16, 8 (August 1983), 57–69.

Smith, D. Canfield, Irby, Charles, Kimball, Ralph, Verplank, Bill, and Harslem, Eric, Designing the Star user interface, *Byte* 7, 4 (April 1982), 242–282.

Sonnenwald, D.H., Maurin, H., Cairns, B., Manning, J.E., Freid, E.B., Welch, G., and Fuchs, H., Experimental comparison of 2D and 3D technology mediated paramedic-physician collaboration in remote emergency medical situations, *Proc. 69th Annual Meeting of the American Society of Information Science & Technology (ASIS&T)*, Vol. 43, Austin, TX (2006).

Stanney, Kay (Editor), *Handbook of Virtual Environments Technology: Design, Implementation, and Applications*, Lawrence Erlbaum Associates, Mahwah, NJ (2002).

Stanney, Kay and Cohn, Joseph, Virtual environments, in Sears, Andrew and Jacko, Julie (Editors), *The Human-Computer Interaction Handbook, Second Edition*, Lawrence Erlbaum Associates, Hillsdale, NJ (2008), 621–638.

Weiser, M., The computer for the 21st century, *Scientific American* 265, 3 (1991), 94–104.

Wellner, P., Mackay, W., and Gold, R., Computer augmented environments: Back to the real world, *Communications of the ACM* 36, 7 (July 1993), 24–27.

White, Brian A., *Second Life: A Guide to Your Virtual World*, Que, Indianapolis, IN (2007).

Whitton, Mary C., Making virtual environments compelling, *Communications of the ACM* 46, 7 (July 2003), 40–46.

Yanagida, Yasuyuki, Olfactory interfaces, in Kortum, Philip (Editor), *HCI Beyond the GUI*, Morgan Kaufmann, Burlington, MA (2008), 267–290.

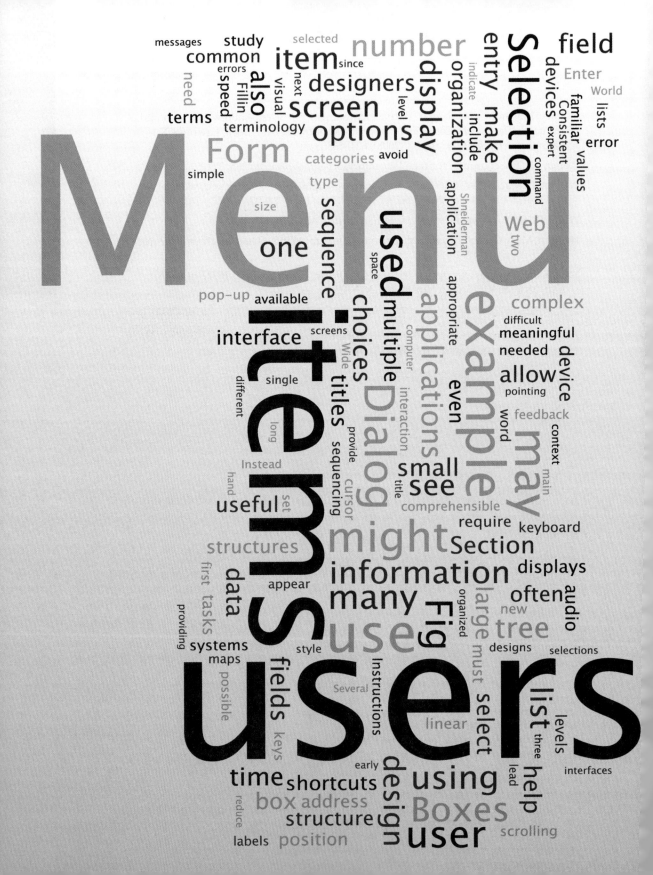

Menu Selection, Form Fill-In, and Dialog Boxes

66 A man is responsible for his choice and must accept the consequences, whatever they may be. 99

W. H. Auden
A Certain World, 1970

6.1 Introduction

When designers cannot create appropriate direct-manipulation strategies, menu selection and form fill-in are attractive alternatives. When the menu items are written with familiar terminology and are organized in a convenient structure and sequence, users can select items easily. Whereas early systems used full-screen menus with lists of numbered items, modern styles include pull-down menus, check boxes, or radio buttons in dialog boxes, and embedded links on World Wide Web pages, all selectable by mouse clicks or a tap of the finger or stylus. Freely available libraries of DHTML and JavaScript programs have opened the door to many variations of those basic menu styles on the Web. Smooth animations, color, and sleek graphic design can turn simple menus into custom widgets that help define the unique look and feel of a web site or application.

Menus are effective because they offer cues to elicit recognition, rather than forcing users to recall the syntax of a command from memory. Users indicate their choices with a pointing device or keystroke and get immediate feedback indicating what they have done. Simple menu selection is especially effective with users who have had little training, use the interface intermittently, are unfamiliar with the terminology, or need help in structuring their decision-making processes. However, with careful design of complex menus and high-speed interaction, menu selection can be made appealing even to expert frequent users.

Of course, just because a designer uses menu selection, form fill-in, and dialog boxes, there is no guarantee that the interface will be appealing and easy to use. Effective interfaces emerge only after careful consideration of and testing for numerous design issues, such as task-related organization, phrasing of items, sequence of items, graphic layout and design, selection mechanisms (keyboard, pointing device, touchscreen, voice, and so on), shortcuts for knowledgeable frequent users, online help, and error correction (Norman, 1991).

After introducing the importance of meaningful organization of menus (Section 6.2), this chapter reviews available menu techniques, from single menus (Section 6.3) to combinations of multiple menus (Section 6.4). Section 6.5 discusses issues related to menu content, and Section 6.6 explores fast movement through menus for expert users. Form fill-in, dialog boxes, and other methods of data entry using menus are covered in Section 6.7. Finally, the special cases of menus for small and audio devices are discussed in Section 6.8.

6.2 Task-Related Menu Organization

The primary goal for menu, form fill-in, and dialog-box designers is to create a sensible, comprehensible, memorable, and convenient organization relevant to the users' tasks. We can learn a few lessons by following the decomposition of a book into chapters, a program into modules, or the animal kingdom into species. Hierarchical decompositions—natural and comprehensible to most people—are appealing because every item belongs to a single category. Unfortunately, in some applications, an item may be difficult to classify as belonging to only one category, and designers are tempted to create duplicate pointers, thus forming a network.

Restaurant menus separate appetizers, main dishes, desserts, and beverages to help customers organize their selections. Menu items should fit logically into categories and have readily understandable meanings. Restaurateurs who list dishes with idiosyncratic names such as "veal Monique," unfamiliar labels such as "wor shu op," or vague terms such as "house dressing" should expect that customers will become puzzled or anxious and that waiters will waste time providing explanations. Similarly, for computer menus, the categories should be comprehensible and distinctive so that users are confident in making their selections and have a clear idea of what the result will be. Computer menus are more difficult to design than restaurant menus, though, because computer displays typically have less space than printed menus. In addition, the number of choices and the level of complexity are greater in many computer applications, and computer users do not have waiters to turn to for help.

An early study by Liebelt et al. (1982) demonstrated the importance of meaningful organization of menu items. Simple menu trees with three levels and a total of 16 items were constructed in both meaningfully organized and disorganized forms. Error rates were nearly halved for the meaningfully organized form, and user think time (time from menu presentation to user's selection of an item) was reduced. In a later study, use of meaningful categories—such as food, animals, minerals, and cities—led to shorter response times than did random or alphabetic organizations (McDonald et al., 1983). The authors concluded that "these results demonstrate the superiority of a categorical menu organization over a pure alphabetical organization, particularly when there is some uncertainty about the terms." With larger menu structures, the effect is even more dramatic. These results suggest that the key to menu-structure design is to carefully consider the task-related objects and actions. For a music-concert ticketing system, the task objects might be locations, performers, cost, dates, and types of music (classical, folk, rock, jazz, and so on), while actions might include browsing lists, searching, and purchasing tickets. The interface objects might be dialog boxes with check boxes for types of music and scrolling menus of concert locations. Performer names might be in a scrolling list or typed in via a form fill-in.

In mobile applications, where simplicity and ease of learning are important, frequency of use often becomes the leading factor in organizing menus. For instance, for a telephone interface adding a phone number is a far more common task than removing a number, so the "add" command should be easily accessible, while "remove" can be pushed to a lower level of the menu (Section 6.8.2).

Menu-selection applications range from trivial choices between two items to complex information systems that can lead through thousands of displays. They can be roughly categorized into four groups. The simplest applications consist of a single menu, but even in these there are many possible variations. The second group of applications uses a linear sequence of menu selections in which the progression of menus is mostly independent of the user's choice; this is typically the case for installation wizards or online surveys. Strict tree structures make up the third and most common group. Acyclic networks (where menus are reachable by more than one path) and cyclic networks (composed of structures with meaningful paths that allow users to repeat menus) constitute the fourth group. The World Wide Web structure is part of this last group.

6.3 Single Menus

Single menus require users to choose between two or more items or may allow multiple selections. The simplest case is a *binary menu* with, for example, yes/no, true/false, or male/female choices. Those simple menus might be used repeatedly (e.g., in a Delete dialog box), so shortcuts and appropriate default behavior should be chosen carefully (Fig. 6.1).

FIGURE 6.1

A binary menu allows users to choose between two options (here, Yes or No). The blue highlighting on Yes indicates that this selection is the default and that pressing Return will select it. Keyboard shortcuts are available as indicated by the underlined letters. Typing the letter N will select No.

When more than two items are present—for example, in a quiz displayed on a touchscreen—users select an item to answer the question:

> Who invented the telephone?
> Thomas Edison
> Alexander Graham Bell
> Lee De Forest
> George Westinghouse

Radio buttons support single-item selection from a multiple-item menu (Fig. 6.2), while *check boxes* allow the selection of one or more items in a menu. A multiple-selection menu is a convenient selection method for handling multiple binary choices, since the user is able to scan the full list of items while deciding (Fig. 6.3).

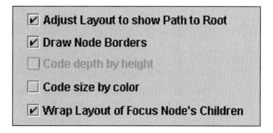

FIGURE 6.3

Users can set their preferences by clicking on one or more check boxes in a menu. Feedback is provided by a check mark. Unavailable items are grayed out.

3. What is your marital status?
○ Single   ○ Married   ○ Widowed/divorced/separated

FIGURE 6.2

An online survey question uses radio buttons to allow users to select a single item in a three-item menu.

FIGURE 6.4

To see updates from friends, photos and feeds, the Zumobi Ziibii interface (http://www.zumobi.com) allows users to choose between two styles of presentation. On the left is a static list of text/image items with a gestural swipe used to control paging, and on the right is a dynamic scrolling ticker (called "River") which horizontally scrolls titles and images across the screen.

Animated *ticker menus* have become popular on dashboards of mobile applications. Primarily an attention-catching display widget, the ticker can act as a menu when display space is limited (e.g., on cell phones; Fig. 6.4). Users don't need to manually scroll or page through the menu items, and with a single click or touch they can stop the scrolling and select an item in view. On the other hand, having to wait for an item to appear or reappear will be frustrating to some users, especially as the number of items grows.

6.3.1 Pull-down, pop-up, toolbar, and ribbon menus

Pull-down menus are menus that the user can always access by making selections on a top menu bar (Fig. 6.5). Introduced by the early Xerox Star, Apple Lisa, and Apple Macintosh interfaces, these menus are used by the majority of desktop applications today. Common items in the menu bar are File, Edit, Format, View, and Help. Clicking on a menu title brings up a list of related items, and users can then make a selection by moving the pointing device over the items (which respond by highlighting), and clicking on the desired choice (or by using the up and down arrow keys to highlight their selection and pressing Enter to select). Since positional constancy is such a strong principle, when an item is not available for selection it is important to gray it out rather than removing it from the list.

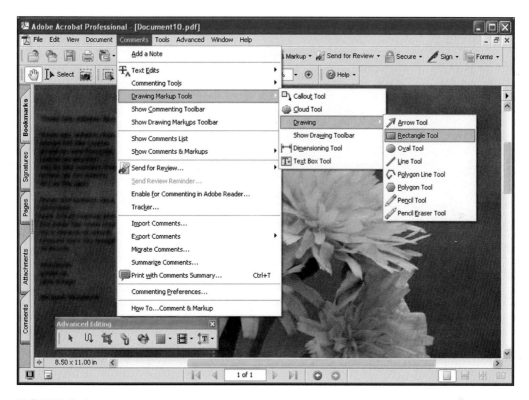

FIGURE 6.5

The cascading pull-down menus of Adobe Acrobat allow users to explore all the functions of the application. To facilitate discovery and learning, icons and keyboard shortcuts are indicated to the left and right of the menu items, respectively (for example, CTRL-T is the keyboard shortcut for Print with Comments Summary, which the user can also select by clicking on the Comment bubble icon). A small black triangle indicates that selection of the menu item will lead to an additional menu. Three dots (. . .) indicate that the selection will lead to a dialog box. Toolbars show groups of menu icons at the periphery of the window. A tool palette (such as the Advanced Editing Palette on the lower left) can also be pulled away in a small separate window placed next to or on top of the document.

The increasing ease of creating custom widgets allows designers to use variants of the basic pull-down design: for example, menus might be placed on the left side of the application window and open sideways. Preserving readability and ensuring that users will be able to identify menus as such are important goals when creating these new designs.

Keyboard shortcuts (such as Ctrl-C for Copy) are essential for expert users, who can memorize the keystrokes for the menu items they use often and thus speed up the interaction considerably. The first letter of the command is often used for the

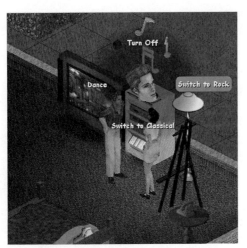
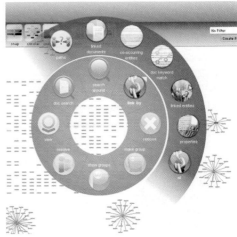

FIGURE 6.6

Two examples of pie menus. On the left, the game The Sims (http://www.maxis.com) allows players to buy and furnish houses, then create characters and make them interact with their environment. For example, clicking on the jukebox pops up a small pie menu of possible actions the character can take. On the right, pie menus are used by Palantir Technologies in a visual analytics tool for financial or intelligence analysis (http://www.palantirtech.com).

shortcut to favor memorability, but caution is required to avoid collisions. If at all possible, shortcuts should be used consistently across applications; for example, Ctrl-S is usually used for Save and Ctrl-P for Print. Keyboard shortcuts should be indicated next to their corresponding menu items. Learning shortcuts (also called *hotkeys*) is extremely useful to reach expert performance, but many users never even attempt to learn them. Grossman et al., (2007) demonstrated that some strategies can improve learning (e.g., using sound or forcing users to use the shortcuts), but finding techniques that are acceptable to all users remains a challenge.

Toolbars, iconic menus, and *palettes* can offer many actions that users can select with a click and apply to a displayed object (Fig. 6.5). Users should be able to customize the toolbars with their choices of items and to control the number and placement of those toolbars. Users who wish to conserve screen space can eliminate most or all of the toolbars.

Pop-up menus appear on the display in response to a click or tap with a pointing device. The contents of the pop-up menu usually depend on the cursor position. Since the pop-up menu covers a portion of the display, there is strong motivation to keep the menu text small (i.e., so that it does not cover the context of the menu). Pop-up menus can also be organized in a circle to form *pie menus* (Callahan et al., 1988; Fig. 6.6), also called *marking menus* (Tapia and Kurtenbach, 1995). Those menus are convenient because selection among a small set of items is more rapid and, with practice, can be done without visual attention. Because pop-up menus can be initiated anywhere on the display, they are particularly adapted to large wall displays: They are unlikely to obscure too much of the screen, and users do not need to travel back to a fixed toolbar to access menus. Innovative designs such as the *FlowMenu* expand the capabilities of pop-up menus by integrating data entry with menu selection (Section 6.7.4).

Ribbons were introduced by Microsoft in Office 2007 (Fig. 5.1). Ribbons attempt to replace menus and toolbars by one-inch tabs grouping commands by task. While this approach might be beneficial for new users, expert users have difficulties adapting to the reorganized menus and finding items they knew existed before, highlighting the challenge of versioning and menu reorganization in professional applications. Ribbons also reduce the screen space for the document, which is a drawback for many users.

6.3.2 Menus for long lists

Sometimes the list of menu items may be longer than the 30 to 40 lines that can reasonably fit on a display. One solution is to create a tree-structured menu (Section 6.4.2), but sometimes the desire to limit the interface to one conceptual menu is strong—for example, when users must select a state from the 50 states in the United States or a country from an extensive list of possibilities. Typical lists are alphabetically ordered to support user typing of leading characters to jump to the appropriate area, but categorical lists may be useful. The principles of menu-list sequencing apply (Section 6.5.2).

Scrolling menus, combo boxes, and fisheye menus *Scrolling menus* display the first portion of the menu and an additional menu item, typically an arrow that leads to the next set of items in the menu sequence. The scrolling (or paging) menu might continue with dozens or thousands of items, using the list-box capabilities found in most graphical user interfaces. Keyboard shortcuts might allow users to type the letter "M" to scroll directly to the first word starting with the letter "M," but this feature is not always discovered. *Combo boxes* make this option more evident by combining a scrolling menu with a text-entry field. Users can type in leading characters to scroll quickly through the list. Another alternative is the *fisheye menu*, which displays all of the menu items on the screen at once but shows only items near the cursor at full size; items further away are displayed at a smaller size. Fisheye menus have been made popular by Apple's Mac OS X (Fig 1.1) and are attractive for menus of 10 to 20 items where the zoom ratio remains small and all items are readable at all times. When the number of items and the zoom ratio are such that smaller items become unreadable, fisheye menus have the potential to improve speed over scrolling menus, but hierarchical menus remain faster (Hornbæk and Hertzum, 2007). Because user preferences vary greatly, fisheye menus can be an eye-catching option but are not recommended as a default menu style for long lists.

Sliders and alphasliders   When items consist of ranges of numerical values, a slider is a natural choice to allow the selection of a value. Ranges of values can also be selected with double-sided (range) sliders. Users select values by using a pointing device to drag the slider thumb (scroll box) along the scale. When greater precision is needed, the slider thumb can be adjusted incrementally by clicking on arrows located at each end of the slider. A similar tool that can be useful for presenting menus with a vast number of options is an *alphaslider*. Because of their compactness, sliders, range sliders, and alphasliders are often used in the control panels of interactive visualization systems (Chapter 14 and Fig. 6.7). When immediate feedback is available, a sweep of the slider thumb allows rapid comparisons between dozens of choices, which would be tedious with other menu styles. Multiple stacked slider thumbs enable multiple levels of granularity and therefore support tens or hundreds of thousands of items (Ahlberg and Shneiderman, 1994).

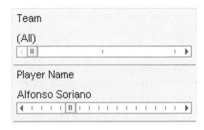

FIGURE 6.7

An alphaslider allows users to select one item from a large number of categorical items. It can also facilitate the rapid comparison of alternatives if the application is immediately updated as the slider thumb moves.

Two-dimensional menus   Alternatively, a multiple-column menu might be used. These "fast and vast" two-dimensional menus give users a good overview of the choices, reduce the number of required actions, and allow rapid selection. Multiple-column menus are especially useful in web-page design, to minimize the scrolling needed to see a long list and to give users a single-screen overview of the full set of choices using icons (Fig. 6.8) or text (Figs. 6.9 and 6.10). Designers have found benefits in using familiar two-dimensional layouts such as calendars for choosing airline departure dates, chromatic spaces for color pickers, and icons or regions on maps. Tag clouds also act as large two-dimensional menus of topics, allowing users to browse user-generated content by topics (Fig. 6.11).

6.3.3 Embedded menus and hotlinks

All the menus discussed thus far might be characterized as *explicit menus*, in that there is an orderly enumeration of the menu items with little extraneous information. In many situations, however, the menu items might be *embedded* in text or graphics and still be selectable. For example, it is natural to allow users reading about people, events, and places to retrieve detailed information by selecting names in context (Koved and Shneiderman, 1986).

FIGURE 6.8

This online grocery-shopping web page (http://www.peapod.com) includes multiple menus using icons and textual labels. Twenty-five labeled icons describe the General Grocery aisles. The icons are attractive and representative of the items. Their locations remain fixed, so users can remember that cereals, for example, are on the top-right corner of the menu. This page also demonstrates an effective tab design to provide access to other services. The order list and the total price tag remain visible at all times.

The highlighted names, places, or phrases are menu items embedded in meaningful text that informs users and help to clarify the meaning of the menu items. Embedded links were popularized in the Hyperties system, which was used for early commercial hypertext projects (e.g., Shneiderman, 1988) and became the inspiration for the *hotlinks* of the World Wide Web (Figs. 1.4 and 1.5).

Embedded links permit items to be viewed in context and eliminate the need for a distracting and screen-space–wasting enumeration of items. Contextual display helps to keep the users focused on their tasks and on the objects of interest. Graphical menus are a particularly attractive way to present many selection options while providing context to help users make their choices. For example,

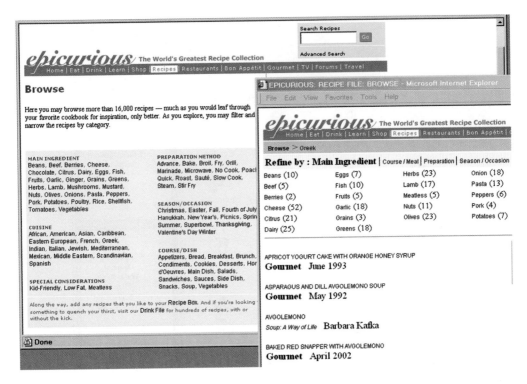

FIGURE 6.9

Epicurious (http://www.epicurious.com/) proposes a menu of a hundred categories of recipes. Once the users have selected a category (here, Greek recipes), they can review the list or narrow it down by selecting from a list of main ingredients. The number of recipes is listed next to each category (for example, there are 10 bean recipes). Other refinement options are course/meal, preparation time, and season/occasion.

maps orient users about the geography of the area before they select a menu item (Fig. 6.12), and calendars can inform users of availability and constraints (Fig. 6.13). Information-abundant compact visualizations can enable the presentation of vast menus (Chapter 14).

6.4 Combinations of Multiple Menus

Menus can be combined in linear series or presented simultaneously. A common strategy is to use a tree structure to organize large menus, but acyclic and cyclic networks are also possible.

craigslist

post to classifieds

my account

help, faq, abuse, legal

search craigslist

[for sale ▼] [>]

event calendar

S	M	T	W	T	F	S
5	6	7	8	9	10	11
12	13	14	15	16	17	18
19	20	21	22	23	24	25
26	27	28	29	30	31	1

avoid scams & fraud

personal safety tips

craigslist blog

craigslist factsheet

best-of-craigslist

register & vote

job boards compared

craigslist movie & dvd

craigslist T-shirts

craigslist foundation

defend net neutrality

system status

terms of use   privacy

about us   help

maryland ᵂ doc nva mld

community
activities   lost+found
artists   musicians
childcare   local news
general   politics
groups   rideshare
pets   volunteers
events   classes

personals
strictly platonic
women seek women
women seeking men
men seeking women
men seeking men
misc romance
casual encounters
missed connections
rants and raves

discussion forums
1099   gifts   pets
apple   haiku   philos
arts   health   politic
atheist   **help**   psych
autos   history   queer
beauty   housing   recover
bikes   jobs   religion
celebs   jokes   rofo
comp   kink   science
crafts   l.t.r.   shop
diet   legal   spirit
divorce   linux   sports
dying   loc pol   t.v.
eco   m4m   tax
educ   money   testing
etiquet   motocy   transg
feedbk   music   travel
film   npo   vegan
fitness   open   w4w
fixit   outdoor   wed
food   over 50   wine
frugal   p.o.c.   women
gaming   parent   words
garden   pefo   writers

housing
apts / housing
rooms / shared
sublets / temporary
housing wanted
housing swap
vacation rentals
parking / storage
office / commercial
real estate for sale

for sale
barter   arts+crafts
bikes   auto parts
boats   baby+kids
books   cars+trucks
business   cds/dvd/vhs
computer   clothes+acc
free   collectibles
furniture   electronics
general   farm+garden
jewelry   games+toys
material   garage sale
rvs   household
sporting   motorcycles
tickets   music instr
tools   photo+video
wanted

services
beauty   automotive
computer   household
creative   labor/move
erotic   skill'd trade
event   real estate
financial   sm biz ads
legal   therapeutic
lessons   travel/vac
write/ed/tr8

jobs
accounting+finance
admin / office
arch / engineering
art / media / design
biotech / science
business / mgmt
customer service
education
food / bev / hosp
general labor
government
human resources
internet engineers
legal / paralegal
manufacturing
marketing / pr / ad
medical / health
nonprofit sector
real estate
retail / wholesale
sales / biz dev
salon / spa / fitness
security
skilled trade / craft
software / qa / dba
systems / network
technical support
transport
tv / film / video
web / info design
writing / editing
[ETC]   [part time]

gigs
computer   event
creative   labor
crew   writing
domestic   talent
adult

resumes

us cities
atlanta
austin
boston
chicago
dallas
denver
houston
las vegas
los angeles
miami
minneapolis
new york
orange co
philadelphia
phoenix
portland
raleigh
sacramento
san diego
seattle
sf bayarea
wash dc
more ...

canada
calgary
edmonton
halifax
montreal
ottawa
toronto
vancouver
victoria
winnipeg
more ...

intl cities
amsterdam
bangalore
bangkok
barcelona
berlin
buenosaires
hongkong
london
manila
mexico
paris
riodejaneiro
rome
shanghai
sydney
tokyo
zurich

us states
alabama
alaska
arizona
arkansas
california
colorado
connecticut
dc
delaware
florida
georgia
guam
hawaii
idaho
illinois
indiana
iowa
kansas
kentucky
louisiana
maine
maryland
mass
michigan
minnesota
mississippi
missouri
montana
n carolina
n hampshire
nebraska
nevada
new jersey
new mexico
new york
north dakota
ohio
oklahoma
oregon
pennsylvania
puerto rico
rhode island
s carolina
south dakota
tennessee
texas
utah
vermont
virginia
washington
west virginia
wisconsin
wyoming

countries
argentina
australia
austria
bangladesh
belgium
brazil
canada
caribbean
chile
china
colombia
costa rica
czech repub
denmark
egypt
finland
france
germany
great britain
greece
hungary
india
indonesia
ireland
israel
italy
japan
korea
lebanon
malaysia
mexico
micronesia
netherlands
new zealand
norway
pakistan
panama
peru
philippines
poland
portugal
russia
singapore
south africa
spain
sweden
switzerland
taiwan
thailand
turkey
UAE
UK
US
venezuela
vietnam

FIGURE 6.10
Craigslist (http://www.craigslist.com/) uses a large two-dimensional menu, allowing users to rapidly browse hundreds of choices.

6.4.1 Linear menu sequences and simultaneous menus

Often, a sequence of interdependent menus can be used to guide users through a series of choices. For example, a pizza-ordering interface might include a linear sequence of menus in which users choose the size (small, medium, or large), thickness (thick, normal, or thin crust), and finally toppings. Other familiar

flickr·

Home   You ▾   Organize ▾   Contacts ▾   Groups ▾   Explore ▾   [   ]   Search ▾

Explore / Tags /

Hot tags

In the last 24 hours
inthecity, day280, lmnb, trimarchi, sanabria, tmdg, heweb08, prolife, rearwindow, week12plants, threesixtyfive, deckthehalls, hpad, bcv08, prettypinktuesday, spx, dnd365, ybike, namethatfilm, macromondays

Over the last week
hardlystrictlybluegrass, lovefest2008, vicepresidentialdebate, aids, atlanticantic, raya2008, tagderdeutscheneinheit, socktoberfest, openhousenewyork, brickcon08, hardlystrictlybluegrassfestival, pittsburgh250, castrostreetfair, dreamfestival, miramarairshow, petitlemans, weekinthelife, nuitblanche, lovefest, veganmofo

Jump to: [   ] GO

All time most popular tags

africa amsterdam animals architecture art august australia baby band barcelona beach berlin bird birthday black blackandwhite blue boston bw california cameraphone camping canada canon car cat chicago china christmas church city clouds color concert cute dance day de dog england europe family festival film florida flower flowers food football france friends fun garden geotagged germany girl girls graffiti green halloween hawaii hiking holiday home house india ireland island italia italy japan july june kids la lake landscape light live london macro may me mexico mountain mountains museum music nature new newyork newyorkcity night nikon nyc ocean paris park party people photo photography photos portrait red river rock rome san sanfrancisco scotland sea seattle show sky snow spain spring street summer sun sunset taiwan texas thailand tokyo toronto tour travel tree trees trip uk urban usa vacation vancouver washington water wedding white winter yellow york zoo

What are tags?
You can give your photos and videos a "tag", which is like a keyword or category label. Tags help you find photos and videos which have something in common. You can assign up to 75 tags to each photo or video.

FIGURE 6.11

Flickr (http://www.flickr.com/) allows users to review the subjects of available photos by selecting tags in a tag cloud. The larger the font size is, the more photos are available.

examples are online examinations that have sequences of multiple-choice test items, each made up as a menu, or "wizards" (a Microsoft term) that steer users through software installation or other procedures by presenting a sequence of cue cards and menu options. Linear sequences guide the user by presenting one decision at a time and are effective for novice users performing simple tasks.

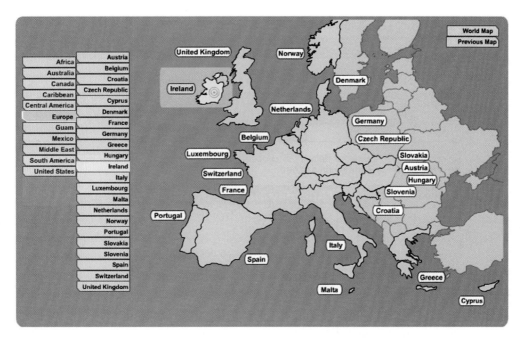

FIGURE 6.12

To search for rental-car office locations, users can select a country by using a cascading menu of regions of the world and countries, or by clicking directly on the area of interest (http://www.alamo.com/). When the user selects a region (here, Europe), the map is updated. Possible choices are shown in yellow, in this case highlighting that the company has no offices in Sweden. The country under the cursor (here, Ireland) is highlighted both on the map and in the menu.

Simultaneous menus present multiple active menus on a screen at the same time and allow users to enter choices in any order (Fig. 6.14). They require more display space, which may render them inappropriate for certain display environments and menu structures; however, a study has shown that experienced users performing complex tasks benefit from simultaneous menus (Hochheiser and Shneiderman, 1999). The faceted metadata search interface of Flamenco (Section 13.4 and Fig. 13.6) is a powerful application of simultaneous menus to browse large image databases (Hearst, 2006).

6.4.2 Tree-structured menus

When a collection of items grows, designers can form categories of similar items, creating a *tree structure*. Some collections can be partitioned easily into mutually exclusive groups with distinctive identifiers. For example, the products in an

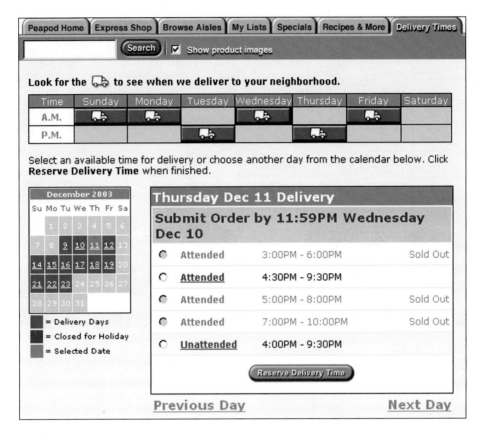

FIGURE 6.13

To select a delivery day, users can pick a day on the current month calendar view (color-coded by availability), or on the week view, which indicates if deliveries are done in the morning or afternoon. The final time selection is made by clicking on the list, where unavailable times are grayed out (http://www.peapod.com/).

online grocery store can be organized into categories such as produce, meat, dairy, cleaning products, and so on. Produce can then be organized into vegetables, fruits, and nuts, while dairy is organized into milk, cheese, yogurt, etc.

Even these groupings may occasionally lead to confusion or disagreement. Classification and indexing are complex tasks, and in many situations there is no single solution that is acceptable to everyone. The initial design can be improved by feedback from users, though, and over time, as the structure is improved and as users gain familiarity with it, success rates will improve.

In spite of the associated problems, tree-structured menu systems have the power to make large collections of data available to novice or intermittent users. If each menu has 30 items, a menu tree with four levels has the capacity to lead

FIGURE 6.14

Shoppers looking for sunglasses can narrow the list of results by selecting any item in three simultaneous menus of brands, features, and frame color in any order (http://www.shopping.com/). Results can be laid out in a row or a grid, and sorting can be done by price or store rating.

an untrained user through a collection of 810,000 destinations. That number would be excessively large for a set of commands in a word processor but would be realistic in a World Wide Web application such as a newspaper, a library (Fig 1.6), or a web portal such as Yahoo! (Fig. 1.11).

If the groupings at each level are natural and comprehensible to users and if users know the target, menu traversal can be accomplished in a few seconds—it is faster than flipping through a book. On the other hand, if the groupings are unfamiliar and users have only vague notions of the items that they're seeking, they may get lost for hours in the tree menus (Norman, 1991). Terminology from the user's task domain can help orient the user: Instead of using a title that is vague and emphasizes the computer domain, such as "Main Menu Options," use terms such as "Friendlibank Services" or simply "Games."

Menus using large indexes, such as library subject headings or comprehensive business classifications, are challenging to navigate. With *expanding menus*, the full context of the choices is preserved while the user browses through the tree structure (as in Windows Explorer). At any point, users have access to the whole set of major and same-level categories. Sequential menus, on the other hand, do not display the full hierarchical context as they drop down to deeper levels in the hierarchy; only elements in the selected category are displayed as options for browsing. A study of expandable menus showed that they were acceptable only for shallow menu hierarchies of a depth of two or three, and should be avoided for deeper hierarchies. It also showed that expandable menus should avoid hard-to-follow indentation schemes and long lists that require excessive scrolling in a browser window (Zaphiris et al., 2002).

The *depth*, or number of levels, of a menu tree depends in part on the *breadth*, or number of items per level. If more items are put into the main menu, the tree spreads out and has fewer levels. This shape may be advantageous, but only if clarity is preserved. Several authors urge using four to eight items per menu, but at the same time, they urge using no more than three to four levels. With large menu applications, one or both of these guidelines must be compromised.

Several empirical studies have dealt with the depth/breadth tradeoff, and the evidence is strong that breadth should be preferred over depth (Norman, 1991). In fact, there is reason to encourage designers to limit menu trees to three levels: when the depth goes to four or five, there is a good chance of users becoming lost or disoriented. Jacko and Salvendy (1996) examined the relationship between task complexity and performance for menus of various breadths and depths. They found that response time and number of errors increased as menu depth increased. Furthermore, users found deeper menus to be more complex. In an interesting variation, another study demonstrated that hierarchical-menu design experiments can be replicated when applied to hierarchies of web links (Larson and Czerwinski, 1998). The navigation problem (getting lost or using an inefficient path) becomes more and more treacherous as the depth of the hierarchy increases.

Even though the semantic structure of the items cannot be ignored, these studies suggest that the fewer levels there are, the greater the ease of decision making is. Of course, screen clutter must be considered in addition to the semantic organization.

FIGURE 6.15

eBay provides a site map that lists all the pages in the site (http://www.ebay.com).

6.4.3 Menu maps

As the depth of a menu tree grows, users find it increasingly difficult to maintain a sense of position in the tree; their sense of disorientation or of "getting lost" increases. Viewing one menu at a time makes it hard to grasp the overall pattern and to see relationships among categories. Evidence from several early studies demonstrated the advantage of offering a spatial map to help users stay oriented. Sometimes menu maps are shown on web-site home pages (Fig. 6.15); sometimes in professional applications they are printed as large posters to give users a visual overview of hundreds of items at several levels.

6.4.4 Acyclic and cyclic menu networks

Although tree structures are appealing, sometimes network structures are more appropriate. For example, in a commercial online service, it might make sense to provide access to banking information from both the financial and consumer parts of a tree structure. A second motivation for using menu networks is that it may be desirable to permit paths between disparate sections of a tree, rather than requiring users to begin a new search from the main menu. Network structures in the form of acyclic or cyclic graphs arise naturally in social relationships, transportation routing, and of course the World Wide Web. As users move from trees to acyclic networks to cyclic networks, however, the potential for getting lost increases. It may be helpful to preserve a notion of "levels," as users may feel more comfortable if they have a sense of how far they are from the main menu, by offering menu maps or site maps.

Many other specialized or hybrid menu structures can also be designed. For example, computerized surveys typically use linear sequences of menus, but conditional branchings alter the sequence of menus and item values might vary according to answers to previous questions. Pursuing new structures and refining existing ones should lead to improved user performance and satisfaction.

6.5 Content Organization

Meaningful grouping and sequencing of menu items, along with careful editing of titles and labels and appropriate layout design, can lead to easier-to-learn menus and increased selection speed. In this section, we review the content-organization issues and provide guidelines for design.

6.5.1 Task-related grouping in tree structures

Grouping menu items in a tree such that they are comprehensible to users and match the task structure is sometimes difficult. The problems are akin to putting kitchen utensils in order; steak knives go together and serving spoons go together, but where do you put butter knives or carving sets? Computer-menu problems include overlapping categories, extraneous items, conflicting classifications in the same menu, unfamiliar jargon, and generic terms. Based on this set of problems, here are several suggested rules for forming menu trees:

- *Create groups of logically similar items.* For example, a comprehensible menu would list countries at level 1, states or provinces at level 2, and cities at level 3.
- *Form groups that cover all possibilities.* For example, a menu with age ranges 0–9, 10–19, 20–29, and > 30 makes it easy for the user to select an item.

- *Make sure that items are nonoverlapping*. Lower-level items should be naturally associated with a single higher-level item. Overlapping categories such as "Entertainment" and "Events" are poor choices compared to "Concerts" and "Sports."
- *Use familiar terminology, but ensure that items are distinct from one another*. Generic terms such as "Day" and "Night" may be too vague; more specific options such as "6 A.M. to 6 P.M." and "6 P.M. to 6 A.M." may be more useful and precise.

There is no perfect menu structure that matches every person's knowledge of the application domain. Designers must use good judgment for the initial implementation but then must be receptive to suggested improvements and empirical data. Users will gradually gain familiarity, even with extremely complex tree structures, and will be increasingly successful in locating required items.

6.5.2 Item presentation sequence

Once the items in a menu have been chosen, the designer is still confronted with the choice of *presentation sequence*. If the items have a natural sequence—such as days of the week, chapters in a book, or sizes of eggs—the decision is trivial. Typical bases for sequencing items include these:

- *Time* (chronological ordering)
- *Numeric ordering* (ascending or descending ordering)
- *Physical properties* (increasing or decreasing length, area, volume, temperature, weight, velocity, and so on)

Many cases have no task-related ordering, though, and the designer must choose from such possibilities as these:

- *Alphabetic sequence of terms*
- *Grouping of related items* (with blank lines or some other demarcation between groups)
- *Most frequently used items first*
- *Most important items first* (importance may be difficult to determine and may be subjective)

A study compared the use of an alphabetical list (645 terms) versus a categorical organization (16 categories) of the same terms in FedStats, a World Wide Web government statistics portal (Ceaparu and Shneiderman, 2004). Users who answered complex questions showed a significant performance improvement

FIGURE 6.16

Adaptive menus in Microsoft Office. A font-selection menu lists the recently used fonts near the top of the menu (as well as in the full list), making it easier to quickly select the popular fonts.

when a categorical organization was used. A further improvement was seen when the categorically organized terms provided links to 215 agency or project home pages, instead of to low-level pages where users may feel lost if they do not find the information they need.

If frequency of use is a potential guide to sequencing menu items, it might make sense to vary the sequence adaptively to reflect the current pattern of use. Unfortunately, adaptations can be disruptive, increasing confusion and undermining the users' learning of menu structures. In addition, users might become anxious that other changes might occur at any moment. Evidence against the utility of such changes was found in a study in which a pull-down list of food items was resequenced to ensure that the most frequently selected items migrated towards the top (Mitchell and Shneiderman, 1989). Users were clearly unsettled by the changing menus, and their performance was better with static menus. In contrast, evidence in favor of adaptation was found in a study of a telephone-book menu tree that had been restructured to make frequently used telephone numbers more easily accessible (Greenberg and Witten, 1985). However, this study did not deal with the issue of potentially disorienting changes to the menu during usage. To avoid disruption and unpredictable behavior, it is probably a wise policy to allow users to specify when they want the menu restructured.

When some menu items are much more frequently selected than others, there is a temptation to organize the menu in order of descending frequency. This organization does speed up selection of the topmost items, but the loss of a meaningful ordering for low-frequency items is disruptive. A sensible compromise is to extract three or four of the most frequently selected items and put them near the top, while preserving the order of the remaining items (Fig. 6.16). In controlled experiments and field studies with a lengthy font menu, the three most popular fonts (Courier, Helvetica, and Times) were put on top, and the remaining list was left in alphabetical order. This split-menu strategy proved appealing and statistically significantly improved performance (Sears and Shneiderman, 1994). An improved theory of menu-selection performance emerged that showed that familiar items were selected in logarithmic time, whereas unfamiliar items were found in linear time, with respect to their position in the menu. The software collected usage frequency data, but the split-menu ordering remained stable until the system administrator decided to make a change.

Microsoft introduced *adaptive menus* in Office 2000. As users work with the programs, the menu items that have not been selected disappear from the menu, making it shorter; items that have recently been selected remain on the short version of the menu. To see the missing items again, users have to click on the arrow at the bottom of the menu or hover over it for a few seconds, causing the menu to show all items. This complex approach is appreciated by some users who have regular patterns of use, but highly disliked by many users who are confused by the constantly changing menus. Office 2007 replaced adaptive menus with a stable ribbon interface that has many more options in spatially stable locations.

Adaptable (user-controlled) menus are an attractive alternative to adaptive menus. One study compared the Microsoft Word version using adaptive menus with a variant providing users with the ability to switch between two modes of operation: the normal full-featured mode, and a personal mode that users could customize by selecting which items were included in the menus (McGrenere et al., 2007). Results showed that participants were better able to learn and navigate through the menus with the personally adaptable version. Preferences varied greatly among users, and the study revealed some users' overall dissatisfaction with adaptive menus but also the reluctance of others to spend significant time customizing the interface.

6.5.3 Menu layout

Little experimental research has been done on menu layout. This section contains many subjective judgments, which are in need of empirical validation (Box 6.1).

Titles   Choosing the title for a book is a delicate matter for an author, editor, or publisher. A particularly descriptive or memorable title can make a big difference in reader responses. Similarly, choosing titles for menus is a complex matter that deserves serious thought.

For single menus, a simple descriptive title that identifies the situation is all that is necessary. With a linear sequence of menus, the titles should accurately represent the stages in the linear sequence. Consistent grammatical style can reduce confusion, and brief but unambiguous noun phrases are often sufficient.

For tree-structured menus, choosing titles is more difficult. Titles such as "Main menu" or topic descriptions such as "Bank transactions" for the root of

BOX 6.1
Menu selection guidelines.

- Use task semantics to organize menus (single, linear sequence, tree structure, acyclic and cyclic networks).
- Prefer broad–shallow to narrow–deep.
- Show position by graphics, numbers, or titles.
- Use items as titles for subtrees.
- Group items meaningfully.
- Sequence items meaningfully.
- Use brief items; begin with the keyword.
- Use consistent grammar, layout, and terminology.
- Allow type ahead, jump ahead, or other shortcuts.
- Enable jumps to previous and main menu.
- Consider online help, novel selection mechanisms, and optimal response time, display rate, and screen size.

the tree clearly indicate that the user is at the beginning of a session. One potentially helpful rule is to use the high-level menu items as the titles for the next-lower-level menus. It is reassuring to users to find that when they select an item such as "Business and financial services" they are shown a screen that is titled "Business and financial services." It might be unsettling to get a screen titled "Managing your money," even though the intent is similar. Imagine looking in the table of contents of a book and seeing a chapter titled "The American Revolution" but then, when you turn to the indicated page, finding instead "Our Early History"—you might wonder if you've made a mistake, and your confidence might be undermined. Similarly, when designing World Wide Web pages, you should ensure that the embedded menu item matches the title on the destination page. Using menu items as titles may encourage the menu author to choose item names more carefully, so that they are descriptive in the context of the other menu items and as the titles of the next menus.

A further concern is consistency in placement of titles and other features in a menu screen. Teitelbaum and Granda (1983) demonstrated that user think time nearly doubled when the position of information such as titles or prompts was varied on menu screens, so efforts should be made to keep the placement constant.

Phrasing and formatting   Just because an interface has English words, phrases, or sentences as menu choices is no guarantee that it is comprehensible.

Individual words may not be familiar to some users (for example, "repaginate"), and often two menu items may appear to satisfy the user's needs, whereas only one actually does (for example, "put away" or "eject"). This enduring problem has no perfect solution, but designers can gather useful feedback from colleagues, users, pilot studies, acceptance tests, and user-performance monitoring. The following guidelines may seem obvious, but we state them because they are so often violated:

- *Use familiar and consistent terminology.* Carefully select terminology that is familiar to the designated user community and keep a list of these terms to facilitate consistent use.
- *Ensure that items are distinct from one another.* Each item should be distinguished clearly from other items. For example, "Slow tours of the countryside," "Journeys with visits to parks," and "Leisurely voyages" are less distinctive than are "Bike tours," "Train tours to national parks," and "Cruise-ship tours."
- *Use consistent and concise phrasing.* Review the collection of items to ensure consistency and conciseness. Users are likely to feel more comfortable and to be more successful with "Animal," "Vegetable," and "Mineral" than with "Information about animals," "Vegetable choices you can make," and "Viewing mineral categories."
- *Bring the keyword to the fore.* Try to write menu items such that the first word aids the user in recognizing and discriminating between items—use "Size of type" instead of "Set the type size." Then, if the first word indicates that this item is not relevant, users can begin scanning the next item.

When applications include multiple screens of menus, using a consistent format helps reduce users' anxiety by offering predictability. Menu designers should establish guidelines for consistency of at least these menu components:

- *Titles.* Some people prefer centered titles, but left justification also may be acceptable.
- *Item placement.* Typically, items are left justified, with the item number or letter preceding the item description. Blank lines may be used to separate meaningful groups of items. If multiple columns are used, a consistent pattern of numbering or lettering should be used (for example, it is easier to scan down columns than across rows). See also Section 11.4 on display design.
- *Instructions.* The instructions should be identical in each menu and should be placed in the same position. This rule includes instructions about traversals, help, or function-key usage.
- *Error messages.* If the users make unacceptable choices, the error messages should appear in a consistent position and should use consistent terminology and syntax. Graying out unacceptable choices will help reduce errors.

Since disorientation is a potential problem, techniques to indicate position in the menu structure can be useful. In books, different fonts and typefaces may indicate chapter, section, and subsection organization. Similarly, in menu trees, as the user goes down the tree structure the titles can be designed to indicate the level or distance from the main menu. Graphics, fonts, typefaces, or highlighting techniques can be used beneficially. For example, this display gives a clear indication of progress down the tree:

Main Menu
HOME SERVICES
NEWSPAPERS
The New York Times

When users want to do a traversal back up the tree or to an adjoining menu at the same level, they will feel confident about what action to take.

With linear sequences of menus, the users can be given a simple visual presentation of position in the sequence: a position marker. For instance, in an application with a series of eight menu screens, a position marker (+) just below the menu items might show progress. In the third frame, the position marker would be

_ _ _ + _ _ _ _

The users can use this marker to gauge their progress and see how much remains to be done. Progress indicators in shopping web sites are examples of useful indicators in mostly linear menu structures (Fig. 11.2).

Given sufficient screen space, it is possible to show a large portion of the menu map and to allow users to point to menu items anywhere in the tree. Graphic designers and layout artists are useful partners in such design projects.

6.6 Fast Movement Through Menus

After optimizing the grouping and sequencing of menu items and considering adaptable menu strategies, there are still techniques available to accelerate the movement through menus, particularly for expert users.

A standard way to permit frequent menu users to speed through the options is to provide keyboard shortcuts. For example, an expert user might memorize that in Microsoft Word the shortcut CTRL-S will save and CTRL-Z undo, or that Alt-I for Insert followed by Alt-S for Symbol will open the dialog box to select a special symbol. Even if the display of the menu items is very fast, such a user will still tend to use the speedy keyboard shortcuts rather than reaching for the mouse, opening the View menu, and selecting the appropriate option. This approach is attractive because it is rapid and allows graceful evolution from novice to expert. Using the mnemonic-letters approach to type ahead requires caution in avoiding collisions and increases the effort of translation to foreign languages, but its clarity and memorability are advantages in many applications. Shortcuts should be indicated next to the menu item labels so that users can progressively learn new shortcuts as needed.

With pie menus, marking menus, and other variations of circular menus, there may be a short delay before the menu items are displayed, allowing users to *mouse ahead* by relying on their muscle memory to reproduce the series of angular displacements necessary for a command selection (for example, in a drawing program a "click-up-left-up" can start dragging an object before the menu appears). When unsure, users can wait until the menu appears.

In web browsers, *bookmarks* provide a way for users to take shortcuts to destinations that they have visited previously. For many users, this menu of destinations can grow quickly and require hierarchical management strategies, becoming a challenge in itself.

Finally, when items of a lower-level menu need to be used multiple times in a row, *tear-off menus* can be useful to keep the list of options visible on the screen.

6.7 Data Entry with Menus: Form Fill-In, Dialog Boxes, and Alternatives

Menu selection is effective for choosing an item from a list, but if data entry of personal names or numeric values is required, keyboard typing becomes more attractive. When many fields of data are necessary, the appropriate interaction style is form fill-in. Few instructions are necessary, since the display resembles familiar paper forms (Fig. 6.17). A combination of form fill-ins, pop-up or scrolling menus, and custom widgets such as calendars or maps can support rapid selection, even for a multistep task such as airline-ticket booking, seat selection, and purchasing.

6.7.1 Form fill-in

There is a paucity of empirical work on form fill-in, but several design guidelines have emerged from practitioners (Galitz, 2007; Brown, 1988). Software tools simplify design, help to ensure consistency, ease maintenance, and speed implementation. But even with excellent tools, the designer must still make many complex decisions (Box 6.2).

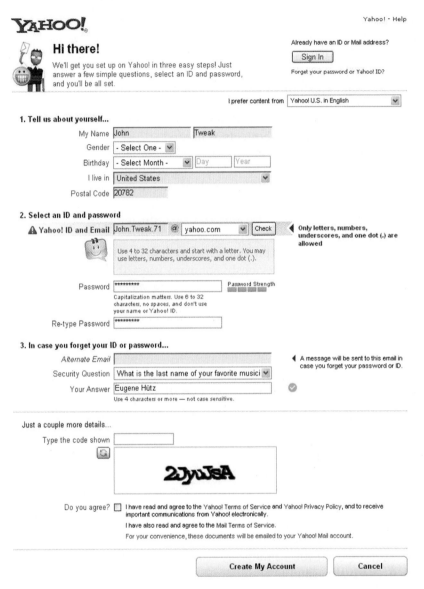

FIGURE 6.17

This form fill-in allows users to enter their personal information when registering on the Yahoo! web site (http://www.yahoo.com/). Fields are grouped meaningfully, and field-specific rules such as password requirements are provided next to the fields or in error messages explaining how to correct any problems. Justifications are provided (for example, why an alternate e-mail address is needed). As users complete each field, the data are checked and a small green check mark appears next to the field for a few seconds confirming that the data have been accepted.

BOX 6.2

Form fill-in design guidelines.

- Meaningful title
- Comprehensible instructions
- Logical grouping and sequencing of fields
- Visually appealing layout of the form
- Familiar field labels
- Consistent terminology and abbreviations
- Visible space and boundaries for data-entry fields
- Convenient cursor movement
- Error correction for individual characters and entire fields
- Error prevention where possible
- Error messages for unacceptable values
- Marking of required fields
- Explanatory messages for fields
- Completion signal to support user control

The elements of form fill-in design include the following:

- *Meaningful title.* Identify the topic and avoid computer terminology.

- *Comprehensible instructions.* Describe the user's tasks in familiar terminology. Be brief; if more information is needed, make a set of help screens available to the novice user. In support of brevity, just describe the necessary action ("Type the address" or simply "Address") and avoid pronouns ("You should type the address") or references to "the user" ("The user of the form should type the address"). Another useful rule is to use the word "type" for entering information and "press" for special keys such as the Tab, Enter, or cursor-movement (arrow) keys. Since "Enter" often refers to the special key with that name, avoid using it in the instructions (for example, do not use "Enter the address"; instead, stick to "Type the address"). Once a grammatical style for instructions is developed, be careful to apply that style consistently.

- *Logical grouping and sequencing of fields.* Related fields should be adjacent and should be aligned with blank spaces for separation between groups. The sequencing should reflect common patterns—for example, city followed by state followed by zip code.

- *Visually appealing layout of the form.* Alignment creates a feeling of order and comprehensibility. For example, the field labels "Name," "Address," and

"City" can be right-justified so that the data-entry fields are vertically aligned. This layout allows the frequent user to concentrate on the entry fields and to ignore the labels.

- *Familiar field labels.* Common terms should be used. If "Home Address" were replaced by "Domicile," many users would be uncertain or anxious about what to enter.

- *Consistent terminology and abbreviations.* Prepare a list of terms and acceptable abbreviations and use the list diligently, making additions only after careful consideration. Instead of varying between such terms as "Address," "Employee Address," "ADDR.," and "Addr.," stick to one term, such as "Address."

- *Visible space and boundaries for data-entry fields.* Users should be able to see the size of the field and to anticipate whether abbreviations or other trimming strategies will be needed. An appropriately sized box can show the maximum field length in a GUI.

- *Convenient cursor movement.* Provide a mechanism for moving the cursor between fields using the keyboard, such as the Tab key or cursor-movement arrows.

- *Error prevention.* Where possible, prevent users from entering incorrect values. For example, in a field requiring a positive whole number, do not allow the user to enter letters, minus signs, or decimal points.

- *Error messages for unacceptable values.* If users enter unacceptable values, the error messages should indicate permissible values for the field; for example, if the zip code is entered as 28K21 or 2380, the message might be "Zip codes should have 5 digits."

- *Immediate feedback.* Immediate feedback about errors is preferable. When feedback can only be provided after the entire form has been submitted, the location of the field needing corrections should be made clearly visible (for example, by displaying the error message in red next to the field, in addition to general instructions at the top of the form).

- *Required fields clearly marked.* For fields that must be filled in, the word "Required" or some other indicator should be visible. Optional fields should follow required fields, whenever possible.

- *Explanatory messages for fields.* If possible, explanatory information about a field or its permissible values should appear in a standard position, such as in a window next to or below the field, whenever the cursor is in the field.

- *Completion signal.* It should be clear to the users what they must do when they are finished filling in the fields. Generally, designers should avoid automatic form submission when the final field is filled in, because users may wish to review or alter previous field entries. When the form is very long, multiple Submit or Save buttons can be provided at different points in the form.

These considerations may seem obvious, but often designers will omit the title or an obvious way to signal completion or will include unnecessary computer file names, strange codes, unintelligible instructions, unintuitive groupings of fields, cluttered layouts, obscure field labels, inconsistent abbreviations or field formats, awkward cursor movement mechanisms, confusing error-correction procedures, or hostile error messages.

6.7.2 Format-specific fields

Columns of information require special treatment for data entry and for display. Alphabetic fields are customarily left-justified on entry and on display. Numeric fields may be left-justified on entry, but then become right-justified on display. When possible, avoid entry and display of leftmost zeros in numeric fields (with zip codes being an exception). Numeric fields with decimal points should line up on the decimal points.

Pay special attention to such common fields as these:

- *Telephone numbers.* Offer a form to indicate the subfields:

```
Telephone: (_ _ _) _ _ _ - _ _ _ _
```

Be alert to special cases, such as the addition of extensions or the need for nonstandard formats for international numbers.

- *Social security numbers.* The pattern for U.S. social security numbers should appear on the screen as

```
Social security number: _ _ _ - _ _ - _ _ _ _
```

When the user has typed the first three digits, the cursor should jump to the leftmost position of the two-digit field.

- *Dates.* How to specify dates is one of the nastiest problems; no good solution exists. Different formats for dates are appropriate for different tasks, and European rules differ from American rules. An acceptable standard may never emerge. Instructions need to show an example of correct entry. For example:

```
Date: _ _/_ _/_ _ _ _  (04/22/2009 indicates April 22, 2009)
```

For many people, examples such as the following are more comprehensible than abstract descriptions:

```
MM/DD/YYYY
```

Providing a pop-up graphical calendar will reduce the number of errors (Fig. 6.13).

- *Times.* Even though the 24-hour clock is convenient, many people in the United States find it confusing and prefer A.M. or P.M. designations. The form might appear as

```
_ _ : _ _  _ _    (09:45 AM or PM)
```

Seconds may or may not be included, adding to the variety of necessary formats.

- *Dollar amounts (or other currency).* The currency sign should appear on the screen, so users enter only the amount. If a large number of whole-dollar amounts are to be entered, users might be presented with a field such as

```
Deposit amount: $_ _ _ _ _._ _
```

with the cursor to the left of the decimal point. As the user types, the numbers should shift left, calculator style. To enter an occasional cents amount, the user can place the cursor on the right field (but again, remember that different countries may have different conventions for entering numbers).

Using custom direct-manipulation graphical widgets will facilitate data entry and reduce errors. Calendars can be used to enter dates, seating maps can help users select airplane seats, and menus using photographs might clarify choices of pizza style.

6.7.3 Dialog boxes

Many tasks are interrupted to request users to select options, perform limited data entry, or review error messages (Section 11.2). The most common solution is to provide a dialog box (Fig. 6.1 and Fig. 6.18).

Dialog-box design combines menu-selection and form fill-in issues with additional concerns about consistency across hundreds of dialog boxes and relationships with other items on the screen (Galitz, 2007). A guidelines document for dialog boxes can help to ensure appropriate consistency (Box 6.3). Dialog

FIGURE 6.18

A dialog box allows users to select style options in Microsoft Word. The preview of a sample bit of text helps users make their selections before they are applied to the text.

boxes should have meaningful titles to identify them, and the titles should have consistent visual properties—for example, centered, mixed uppercase and lowercase, 12-point, black Helvetica font. Dialog boxes are often shaped and sized to fit each situation, but distinctive sizes or aspect ratios may be used to signal errors, confirmations, or components of the application.

Since dialog boxes usually pop up on top of some portion of the screen, there is a danger that they will obscure relevant information. Therefore, dialog boxes should be as small as is reasonable to minimize the overlap and visual disruption. Dialog boxes should appear near, but not on top of, the related screen items: When a user clicks on a city on a map, the dialog box about the city should appear just next to the click point.

BOX 6.3
Dialog box guidelines.

Internal layout: like that of menus and forms
- Meaningful title, consistent style
- Top-left to bottom-right sequencing
- Clustering and emphasis
- Consistent layouts (margins, grid, whitespace, lines, boxes)
- Consistent terminology, fonts, capitalization, and justification
- Standard buttons (OK, Cancel)
- Error prevention by direct manipulation

External relationships
- Smooth appearance and disappearance
- Distinguishable but small boundary
- Size small enough to reduce overlap problems
- Display close to appropriate items
- No overlap of required items
- Easy to make disappear
- Clear how to complete/cancel

The classic annoying example is to have the Find or Spell Check box obscure a relevant part of the text. When multiple displays are used simultaneously, placing the dialog box in multiple locations simultaneously can result in faster interaction (Hutchings and Stasko, 2007).

Dialog boxes should be distinct enough that users can easily distinguish them from the background, but should not be so harsh as to be visually disruptive. Keyboard shortcuts are essential to speed the response to dialog boxes. A common convention is to use Escape to cancel and close the dialog box, and Enter to select the default command when appropriate. Dialog boxes do not always require users to answer or close them (e.g., the Find box in many applications can remain opened after the search is performed). Such non-modal dialog boxes are useful as they allow users to continue their work and return to the dialog box again at a later time.

When tasks are complex, multiple dialog boxes may be needed, leading some designers to choose to use a tabbed dialog box in which two or more protruding tabs in one or several rows indicate the presence of multiple dialog boxes. This technique carries with it the potential problem of too much fragmentation; users may have a hard time finding what they want underneath the tabs. A smaller number of larger dialog boxes may be advantageous, since users usually prefer doing visual searches to having to remember where to find a desired control.

6.7.4 Novel designs combining menus and direct manipulation

Several refinements of circular menus combine menu selection with direct-manipulation data entry (Guimbretière et al., 2005). For example, early pie menus allowed users to specify both the size and style of a typographic font in one gesture (Hopkins, 1991): The direction of movement selects the font style from a set of possible attributes, and the distance moved selects the point size from the range of sizes. An increased distance from the center corresponds to an increase in the point size, and visual feedback is provided by dynamically shrinking and swelling a text sample shown in the center as the user moves the pointer in and out. *Control menus* (Pook et al., 2000) demonstrate a similar technique. When the pointing device reaches a specified threshold, the command is issued and direct manipulation can proceed immediately. *Marking menus* (Tapia and Kurtenbach, 1995) also allow direct manipulation and show that the release of the pointing device can be used as a command-selection mechanism. *Pie cursors* (Fitzmaurice et al., 2008) use a tiny pie menu as a cursor. Instead of being a pop-up menu, it acts as a toolbar, and the tool is selected by the direction of the cursor and activated by clicking in place on the object of interest.

Another novel menu type, called a FlowMenu (Guimbretière and Winograd, 2000), uses the return to the central rest area after the menu selection to trigger the direct manipulation needed to specify a parameter (Fig. 6.19). Multiple

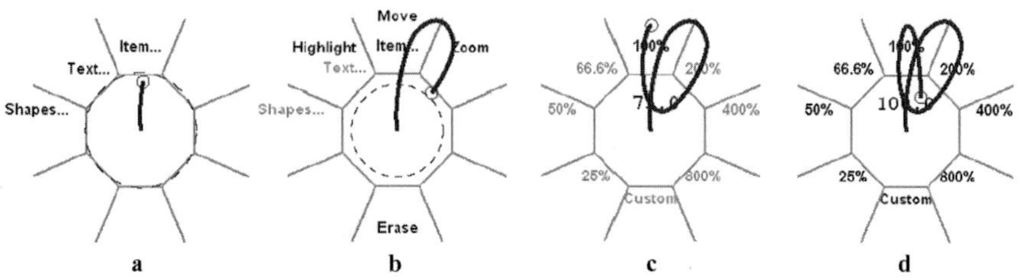

FIGURE 6.19

To zoom in on an object using FlowMenu, users move the cursor or pen from the center to Item . . . (**a**). A second level of menus appears (Highlight, Move, Zoom), and users can select Zoom (**b**). Moving back to the center brings up a third menu of zoom values (**c**). The appropriate zoom value is selected by moving towards 100% and then back to the center (**d**). Note that the figure explicitly shows the pen track. While in normal use, the pen track is not displayed, and the selected object is visible in transparency behind the menu.

selections and direct manipulations can be chained together without lifting the pointing device, allowing complex menu selections and data entry. These techniques are particularly well adapted to wall displays, as they do not require users to return to a faraway menu bar to initiate the interaction.

Another option, Toolglass™ (Bier et al., 1994), uses two-handed operation to combine menu selection and data entry. Users move their nondominant hands to manipulate a translucent tool palette while their dominant hands select commands and perform direct-manipulation tasks. For example, to create a colored line, one hand positions the palette's line tool at the starting point, while the other hand clicks through the transparent tool and drags to draw the line. Toolglass can be useful for medium-sized displays, where all menus remain within arm's reach and users can easily locate them on the display.

6.8 Audio Menus and Menus for Small Displays

Audio menus are useful when hands and eyes are busy, such as when users are driving or testing equipment. Audio menus are also important in telephone interfaces and public-access situations that need to accommodate blind or vision-impaired users, such as information kiosks or voting machines. Mobile devices have small screens that make most desktop screen designs impractical (Section 8.5). They require a radical rethinking of what functionalities should be included and often lead to novel interface and menu designs specifically adapted to the device and the application.

6.8.1 Audio menus

With audio menus, instruction prompts and lists of options are spoken to users, who respond by using the keys of a keyboard, touchtone phone, or by speaking. While visual menus have the distinct advantage of persistence, audio menus have to be memorized. Similarly, visual highlighting can confirm users' selections, while audio menus have to provide audible confirmation. As the list of options is read to them, users must compare each proposed option with their goal and place it on a scale from no match to perfect match. Different designs either request users to accept or reject each option immediately, or allow users to select at any time while the entire list is being read. A way to repeat the list of options and an exit mechanism must be provided (preferably by detecting user inaction).

Complex menu structures should be avoided. A simple guideline is to limit the number of choices to three or four to avoid memorization problems, but this rule should be re-evaluated in light of the application. For example, a theater information system will benefit from using a longer list of all the movie titles rather than breaking them into two smaller, arbitrarily grouped menus. Dial-ahead capabilities allow repeat users to skip through the prompts. For example, users of a drugstore telephone menu might remember that they can dial 1 followed by 0 to be connected to the pharmacy immediately, without having to listen to the store's welcome message and the list of options. Many design variations exist (Marics and Engelbeck, 1997).

Voice recognition enables users of Interactive Voice Systems (Balentine, 2007; Brandt, 2008) to speak their options instead of pressing letter or number keys. An early use of voice activation was to emulate keypresses with voice cues (for example, "To hear your options again, press or say nine"). This is useful when users' hands are busy, such as while driving a car, but it leads to longer prompts and longer task-completion times. Other systems use automatic word recognition to match the spoken words or short phrases to one of the available options.

Advanced systems are exploring the use of natural-language analysis to improve voice recognition. One field study compared traditional touchtone menu selection with the natural-language analysis of users' answers to the prompt "Please tell me, briefly, the reason for your call today." Callers could be routed to one of five types of agent. Results suggested that the number of callers routed to the correct agent increased when natural language was used, and that users preferred it (Suhm et al., 2002). However, effective natural-speech recognition of even modestly complex requests, such as "Reserve two seats on the first flight tomorrow from New York to Washington," is still a challenge and can lead to errors and frustrating dialogs (Section 8.4).

To develop successful audio menus, it is critical to know the users' goals and to make the most common tasks easy to perform rapidly. To speed interaction, interactive voice systems can offer the option to let users speak while the instructional prompt is being read. This *barge-in* technique works well when most users are repeat users who can immediately speak the options they have learned from previous experience. *Out-of-turn interaction* allows users to supply currently unsolicited information that will be needed later in the dialog (Perugini et al., 2007). In all cases, the challenge is to identify novices who attempt to use commands that are not recognized and switch them to a more directed mode that lists options.

6.8.2 Menus for small displays

Distinct application domains dominate the use of devices with small displays: entertainment applications (for example, games played on a Nintendo DS) involve long sessions of informal, content-intensive interactions. On the other hand, the most common use of information and communication applications (for example, calendars, address books, navigation assistants, repair and inventory management systems, or medical devices) consists of repetitive, brief, and highly structured sessions often conducted under time or environmental pressures. Other applications include e-mail, where users read messages and post short answers. Menus and forms often constitute a major part of these interfaces.

Learnability is a key issue, as there is usually no documentation at hand for the growing number of products that are sometimes called *information appliances*. These products need to be learned in a few minutes or risk being abandoned (Bergman, 2000). Successful designs limit the number of functions to the most essential ones (Box 6.4 and Fig. 6.20). They bury other features in less

BOX 6.4

Five design considerations for information appliances (from Michael Mohageg and Annette Wagner in Bergman, 2000).

1. **Account for target domain**
   Entertainment applications versus information access and communication versus assistant devices.
2. **Dedicated devices mean dedicated user interfaces**
3. **Allocate functions appropriately**
   Consider usage frequency and importance.
4. **Simplify**
   Focus on important functions, relegate others to other platforms
5. **Design for responsiveness**
   Plan for interruptions and provide continuous feedback.

FIGURE 6.20

Early and revised designs for entering a new calendar event on Palm devices. The original design is on the left. The new design on the right simplifies the screen and pushes all the recurrent event controls to a secondary screen, greatly simplifying the most common task. (From Rob Haitani in Bergman, 2000)

accessible parts of the interface, relegate them to the counterpart desktop application (if one exists), or even eliminate the features altogether. An often-mentioned rule of thumb for small devices is "less is more." If needed, additional menus might be activated by hardware buttons. For example, on the Palm® handheld devices a permanent button on the device brings up a pull-down menu bar giving access to advanced functions, such as the beaming of address-book entries to other devices. An "Advanced" or "More" button can also be used to add frequently used items to the existing simpler menus that are used most of the time.

The smaller the screen, the more temporal the interface becomes (all the way to entirely linear audio interfaces when no display is available). Small devices can present only part of the information at a time, and therefore particular attention must be given to how users navigate between menu items in a sequence, levels of the hierarchy, and parts of long forms. Many devices have dedicated directional keys or a directional pad (D-pad), providing at least the two keys needed to navigate through sequences, and a Select button. Smaller devices use "soft" keys placed next to or below the screen; their onscreen labels can be changed dynamically depending on the context (Fig. 6.21). Soft keys allow designers to provide direct access to the next-most-logical command at every step (Lindholm and Keinonen, 2003). The D-pad also simplifies the navigation of forms on larger displays with scroll bars, such as Pocket PC devices. The iPod and iPhone have no keys and rely instead on a small set of gestures to scroll through lists or pan across grids of menu icons.

FIGURE 6.21

Telephone menus use soft keys to present context-dependent menu items. The convention used here is to consistently place selections on the left side and back or exit options on the right side. Hard buttons control the connect and disconnect functions. Dedicated buttons facilitate scrolling through lists. The current position in the list is indicated on the right side of the screen.

When designing for responsiveness, ease of launching the most common applications and performing the most common tasks is paramount. This can be achieved by providing hardware buttons. Many personal information devices have dedicated buttons for launching the calendar or the address book; phones have a dedicated button to hang up. On a touchscreen-only device without buttons, like the iPhone, the most commonly used items must fit on the first screen. Temptation is great to include many elements on those larger screens because it is possible, but designers often return to providing designs with fewer items, and a means to expand when needed, at the cost of increased complexity (see, for example, the iPhone Zumobi interface in Fig. 6.22). Small devices without keyboards also present new challenges for data entry (Chapter 8), making it difficult to use form fill-in when this would have been the best interaction method on a larger screen.

Sequencing menu items by frequency of use can be more useful than sequencing by category or alphabetical order, as speed of access to the most commonly used options is critical. Reviewing a list to get a feeling for the natural groupings becomes impractical on smaller screens. Mobile device designers also need to allow users to deal with interruptions and distractions in their environment. Providing an automatic Save function addresses those issues and simplifies the interface. The dismissal of opened dialog boxes may not be necessary either, as they

FIGURE 6.22

The Zumobi interface (http://www.zumobi.com) on a mobile phone starts with four "tiles" using a two-level zoom interaction to see the tile details (left side). The user can specify which tiles are in their "zoomspace". Then, when they become more familiar with the interface, they can add up to a total of 16 tiles using a three-level zoom interaction to smoothly go between overview, "zone" view, and detail view (right side). The application accommodates thumb use on touchscreens, numeric key pads for zone-based zooming, 4-way D-Pads, and even thumb-roller controllers.

can always be superseded by other commands or a tap outside the dialog box. This differs greatly from desktop applications, where they often demand more attention. For example, a word processor will require the Print dialog box(es) to be closed before an emergency Save command can be issued when the phone rings.

Concise writing and careful editing of titles, labels, and instructions will lead to simpler and easier-to-use interfaces. Every word counts on a small screen, and even unnecessary letters or spaces should be eliminated. Consistency remains important, but clear differentiation of menu types helps users remain oriented when no context can be provided. Tiny icons are difficult to design and are rarely used, as they take up space and require labels anyway. On the other hand, large color icons, such as those used in car navigation systems or in the iPhone, can be used successfully because they can be recognized at a glance once they have been learned.

Future applications are likely to use contextual information, such as location or proximity to objects, to present relevant information. These applications can display most likely menu items on soft keys and suggest default values for data entry. Global Positioning System (GPS) or Radio Frequency Identification (RFID) tags might facilitate applications such as tourist guides or medicine-cabinet valets (Fano and Gershman, 2002). Using the back of the device as a touch-sensitive pad might help reach enrich selection mechanisms (Wigdor et al., 2007). Precise position information relative to the user's body might also lead to new modes of interaction with menus. For example, users might be able to move the device in front of them horizontally or vertically to scroll through long lists or pan across maps and diagrams (Yee, 2003).

Finally, audio and visual menus can be combined in surprising ways. Small modern mobile phones often include personal information management services such as calendars, which require users to temporarily stop their conversations to look at the screen. To address this problem, new methods are being devised that allow the device to be operated using the keypad while users receive audio feedback heard only by the person operating the phone, not the person on the other end of the line, therefore allowing hands-free menu selection (Li et al., 2008). Conversely, users with larger screens and headphones might be able to see a visual representation of the audio menus being traversed by an interactive voice-response system (Yin and Zhai, 2006).

Practitioner's Summary

Attention should be focused on organizing the structure and sequence of menus to match the users' tasks, priorities, and environment. Each menu should be a meaningful, task-related unit, and the individual items should be distinctive and comprehensible. Favor broad and shallow hierarchical menus. For users who make frequent use of the system, shortcuts, mouse-ahead options, or dial-ahead options will greatly increase the speed of interaction. Permit simple traversals to the previously displayed menu and to the main menu. Remember that audio menus and menus designed for small devices require careful rethinking of what functions should be included. For such menus, carefully limit the number of items, and consider frequency of use as a criterion for sequencing menu items. Pop-up menus using gestures are useful for large wall displays. Consider direct-manipulation graphical widgets such as calendars or maps to facilitate data entry with form fill-in. Such widgets, along with immediate feedback and dynamic help, will help reduce errors and speed data entry.

Be sure to conduct usability tests and to involve human-factors specialists in the design process. When the interface is implemented, collect usage data, error statistics, and subjective reactions to guide refinement. Consider user-adaptable menu designs.

Researcher's Agenda

Experimental research could help to refine the design guidelines concerning organization and sequencing in menus. How can differing communities of users be satisfied with a common organization when their information needs are markedly different? Should users be allowed to tailor the structure of the menus, or is there greater advantage in compelling everyone to use the same structure and terminology? Should a tree structure be preserved even if some redundancy is introduced? What's the best way to progressively introduce new users to large menu structures? How can users be encouraged to learn keyboard shortcuts? What further improvements will speed menu selection on small and very large displays?

Research opportunities abound, and the quest for better menu-selection strategies for small and large displays continues. Implementers would benefit from advanced software tools to automate creation, management, usage-statistics gathering, and evolutionary refinement. Portability could be enhanced to facilitate transfer across systems, and tools to support redesign for multiple national languages could facilitate internationalization.

```
WORLD WIDE WEB RESOURCES
http://www.aw.com/DTUI/
```

Information on menu, form fill-in, and dialog-box design (including empirical studies and examples of systems) is available online. The most interesting experience is browsing the World Wide Web to see how designers have laid out simultaneous or large menus or form fill-ins in registration or search interfaces.

References

Ahlberg, C. and Shneiderman, B., AlphaSlider: A compact and rapid selector, *Proc. CHI '94 Conference: Human Factors in Computing Systems*, ACM Press, New York (1994), 365–371.

Balentine, Bruce, *It's Better to Be a Good Machine Than a Bad Person: Speech Recognition and Other Exotic User Interfaces at the Twilight of the Jetsonian Age*, International Customer Management Institute, New York (2007).

Bergman, E., *Information Appliances and Beyond*, Morgan Kaufmann, San Francisco, CA (2000).

Bier, E., Stone, M., Fishkin, K., Buxton, W., and Baudel, T., A taxonomy of see-through tools, *Proc. CHI '94 Conference: Human Factors in Computing Systems*, ACM Press, New York (1994), 358–364.

Brandt, J., Interactive voice response interfaces, in Kortum, P. (Editor), *HCI Beyond the GUI: Design for Haptic, Speech, Olfactory and Other Nontraditional Interfaces*, Morgan Kaufmann, Amsterdam (2008).

Brown, C. M., *Human-Computer Interface Design Guidelines*, Ablex, Norwood, NJ (1988).

Callahan, J., Hopkins, D., Weiser, M., and Shneiderman, B., An empirical comparison of pie versus linear menus, *Proc. CHI '88 Conference: Human Factors in Computing Systems*, ACM Press, New York (1988), 95–100.

Ceaparu, I. and Shneiderman, B., Finding governmental statistical data on the web: A study of categorically-organized links for the FedStats topics page, *Journal of the American Society for Information Science and Technology* 55, 11 (2004), 1008–1015.

Fano, A. and Gershman, A., The future of business services in the age of ubiquitous computing, *Communications of the ACM* 45, 12 (2002), 83–87.

Fitzmaurice, G., Matejka, J., Khan, A., Glueck, M., Kurtenbach, G., PieCursor: Merging pointing and command selection for rapid in-place tool switching, *Proc. CHI 2008 Conference: Human Factors in Computing Systems*, ACM Press, New York (2008), 1361–1370.

Galitz, Wilbert O., *The Essential Guide to User Interface Design: An Introduction to GUI Design Principles and Techniques, Third Edition*, John Wiley & Sons, New York (2007).

Greenberg, S. and Witten, I. H., Adaptive personalized interfaces: A question of viability, *Behaviour & Information Technology* 4, 1 (1985), 31–45.

Grossman, T., Dragicevic, P., and Balakrishnan, R., Strategies for accelerating on-line learning of hotkeys, *Proc. CHI 2007 Conference: Human Factors in Computing Systems*, ACM Press, New York (2007), 1591–1600.

Guimbretière, F. and Winograd, T., FlowMenu: Combining command, text, and parameter entry, *Proc. ACM Symposium on User Interface Software and Technology*, ACM Press, New York (2000), 213–216.

Guimbretière, F., Martin, A. and Winograd, T., Benefits of mergings commands and direct manipulation, *ACM Transactions on Computer-Human Interaction* 12, 3 (2005) 460–476.

Hearst, Marti, Clustering versus faceted categories for information exploration, *Communications of the ACM* 49, 4 (2006), 59–61.

Hochheiser, Harry and Shneiderman, Ben, Performance benefits of simultaneous over sequential menus as task complexity increases, *International Journal of Human-Computer Interaction* 12, 2 (1999), 173–192.

Hopkins, Don, The design and implementation of pie menus, *Dr. Dobb's Journal* 16, 12 (1991), 16–26.

Hornbæk, K. and Hertzum, M., Untangling the usability of fisheye menus, *ACM Transactions on Computer-Human Interaction* 14, 2 (2007), #6.

Hutchings, D. R. and Stasko, J., Consistency, multiple monitors, and multiple windows, *Proc. CHI 2007 Conference: Human Factors in Computing Systems*, ACM Press, New York (2007), 211–214.

Jacko, J. and Salvendy, G., Hierarchical menu design: Breadth, depth, and task complexity, *Perceptual and Motor Skills* 82 (1996), 1187–1201.

Koved, L. and Shneiderman, B., Embedded menus: Menu selection in context, *Communications of the ACM* 29 (1986), 312–318.

Larson, K. and Czerwinski, M., Page design: Implications of memory, structure and scent for information retrieval, *Proc. CHI '98 Conference: Human Factors in Computing Systems*, ACM Press, New York (1998), 25–32.

Laverson, A., Norman, K., and Shneiderman, B., An evaluation of jump-ahead techniques for frequent menu users, *Behaviour & Information Technology* 6, 2 (1987), 97–108.

Li, K., Baudisch, P., and Hinckley, K., Blindsight: Eyes-free access to mobile phones, *Proc. CHI 2008 Conference: Human Factors in Computing Systems*, ACM Press, New York (2008), 1389–1398.

Liebelt, L. S., McDonald, J. E., Stone, J. D., and Karat, J., The effect of organization on learning menu access, *Proc. Human Factors Society, Twenty-Sixth Annual Meeting*, Santa Monica, CA (1982), 546–550.

Lindholm, C. and Keinonen, T., *Mobile Usability: How Nokia Changed the Face of the Mobile Phone*, McGraw-Hill, New York (2003).

Marics, M. A. and Engelbeck, G., Designing voice menu applications for telephones, in Helander, M., Landauer, T., and Prabhu P., (Editors), *Handbook of Human-Computer Interaction*, North-Holland, Amsterdam, The Netherlands (1997), 1085–1102.

McDonald, J. E., Stone, J. D., and Liebelt, L. S., Searching for items in menus: The effects of organization and type of target, *Proc. Human Factors Society, Twenty-Seventh Annual Meeting*, Santa Monica, CA (1983), 834–837.

McGrenere, Joanna, Baecker, Ronald M., and Booth, Kellogg S., A field evaluation of an adaptable two-interface design for feature-rich software, *ACM Transactions on Computer-Human Interaction* 14, 1 (2007), #3.

Mitchell, J. and Shneiderman, B., Dynamic versus static menus: An experimental comparison, *ACM SIGCHI Bulletin* 20, 4 (1989), 33–36.

Norman, Kent, *The Psychology of Menu Selection: Designing Cognitive Control at the Human/Computer Interface*, Ablex, Norwood, NJ (1991).

Perugini, S., Anderson, T., and Moroney, W., A study of out-of-turn interaction in menu-based, IVR, voicemail systems, *Proc. CHI 2007 Conference: Human Factors in Computing Systems*, ACM Press, New York (2007), 961–970.

Pook, S., Lecolinet, E., Vaysseix, G., and Barillot, E., Control menus: Execution and control in a single interactor, *CHI 2000 Extended Abstracts*, ACM Press, New York (2000), 263–264.

Sears, Andrew and Shneiderman, Ben, Split menus: Effectively using selection frequency to organize menus, *ACM Transactions on Computer-Human Interaction* 1, 1 (1994), 27–51.

Shneiderman, B. (Editor), *Hypertext on Hypertext*, Hyperties disk with 1 MB of data and graphics incorporating the full issue of *Communications of the ACM*, ACM Press, New York (July 1988).

Somberg, B. and Picardi, M. C., Locus of information familiarity effect in the search of computer menus, *Proc. Human Factors Society, Twenty-Seventh Annual Meeting*, Santa Monica, CA (1983), 826–830.

Suhm, B., Bers, J., McCarthy, D., Freeman, B., Getty, D., Godfrey, K., and Peterson, P., A comparative study of speech in the call center: Natural language call routing vs. touch-tone menus, *Proc. CHI 2002 Conference: Human Factors in Computing Systems*, ACM Press, New York (2002), 283–290

Tapia, M. A. and Kurtenbach, G., Some design refinements and principles on the appearance and behavior of marking menus, *Proc. ACM Symposium on User Interface Software and Technology '95*, ACM Press, New York (1995), 189–195.

Teitelbaum, R. C. and Granda, R., The effects of positional constancy on searching menus for information, *Proc. CHI '83 Conference: Human Factors in Computing Systems*, ACM Press, New York (1983), 150–153.

Wigdor, D., Forlines, C., Baudisch, P., Barnwell, J., and Shen, C., LucidTouch: A See-Through Mobile Device, in *Proc. ACM Symposium on User Interface Software and Technology*, ACM Press, New York (2007), 269–278.

Yee, K.-P., Peephole displays: Pen interaction on spatially aware handheld computers, *Proc. CHI 2003 Conference: Human Factors in Computing Systems*, ACM Press, New York (2003), 1–8.

Yin, M. and Zhai, S., The benefits of augmenting telephone voice menu navigation with visual browsing and search, *Proc. CHI 2006 Conference: Human Factors in Computing Systems*, ACM Press, New York (2006), 319–328.

Zaphiris, P., Shneiderman, B., and Norman, K. L., Expandable indexes versus sequential menus for searching hierarchies on the World Wide Web, *Behaviour & Information Technology* 21, 3 (2002), 201–207.

CHAPTER 7

Command and Natural Languages

> " I soon felt that the forms of ordinary language
> were far too diffuse. . . . I was not long in
> deciding that the most favorable path to pursue
> was to have recourse to the language of signs. It
> then became necessary to contrive a notation
> which ought, if possible, to be at once simple
> and expressive, easily understood at the
> commencement, and capable of being readily
> retained in the memory. "

Charles Babbage
"On a method of expressing by signs the action of machinery," 1826

Written in collaboration with Steven M. Jacobs

7.1 Introduction

The history of written language is rich and varied. Early tally marks and pictographs on cave walls existed for millennia before precise notations for numbers or other concepts appeared. The Egyptian hieroglyphs of 5,000 years ago were a tremendous advance because standard notations facilitated communication across space and time. Eventually, languages with a small alphabet and rules of word and sentence formation dominated because of the relative ease of learning, writing, and reading them. In addition to these natural languages, special languages for mathematics, music, and chemistry emerged because they facilitated communication and problem solving. In the twentieth century, novel notations were created for such diverse domains as dance, knitting, higher forms of mathematics, logic, and DNA molecules.

The basic goals of language design are:

- Precision
- Compactness
- Ease in writing and reading
- Completeness
- Speed in learning
- Simplicity to reduce errors
- Ease of retention over time

Higher-level goals include:

- Close correspondence between reality and the notation
- Convenience in carrying out manipulations relevant to users' tasks
- Compatibility with existing notations

- Flexibility to accommodate novice and expert users
- Expressiveness to encourage creativity
- Visual appeal

Constraints on a language include:

- The capacity for human beings to record the notation
- The match between the recording and the display media (for example, clay tablets, paper, printing presses)
- The convenience in speaking (vocalizing)

Successful languages evolve to serve the goals within the constraints.

The printing press was a remarkable stimulus to language development because it made widespread dissemination of written work possible. The computer has been another remarkable stimulus to language development, not only because widespread dissemination through networks is possible, but also because computers are a tool to manipulate languages and because languages are a tool for manipulating computers.

The computer has had only a modest influence on spoken natural languages, compared to its enormous impact as a stimulus to the development of numerous new formal written languages. Early computers were built to perform mathematical computations, so the first programming languages had a strong mathematical flavor. But computers were quickly found to be effective manipulators of logical expressions, business data, graphics, sound, and text. Increasingly, computers are used to operate on the real world: directing robots, issuing money at bank machines, controlling manufacturing, and guiding spacecraft. These newer applications encourage language designers to find convenient notations to direct the computer while preserving the needs of people to use the languages for communication and problem solving.

Therefore, effective computer languages must not only represent the users' tasks and satisfy human needs for communication, but also be in harmony with mechanisms for recording, manipulating, and displaying these languages on a computer.

Computer programming languages such as FORTRAN, COBOL, ALGOL, PL/I, and Pascal that were developed in the 1960s and early 1970s were designed for use in a noninteractive computer environment. Programmers composed hundreds or thousands of lines of code, carefully checked that code, and then *compiled* or interpreted it with computers to produce a desired result. Incremental programming was one of the design considerations in BASIC and in more advanced languages such as LISP, APL, and PROLOG. Programmers in these languages were expected to build small pieces online and to test the pieces interactively. Still, the common goal was to create a large program that was preserved, studied, extended, and modified. The attraction of rapid compilation and execution led to the widespread success of the compact, but sometimes obscure, notation used in C. The pressures for team programming, organizational standards for sharing, and the increased demands for reusability promoted encapsulation and the development of object-oriented programming concepts in languages such as Ada and C++. The demands of network environments and the pursuit of cross-platform tools led to the emergence of Java and C#.

Scripting languages emphasizing screen presentation and mouse control became popular in the late 1980s, with the appearance of HyperCard™, Super-Card™, ToolBook™, and so on. These languages included novel operators, such as ON MOUSEDOWN, BLINK, and IF FIRST CHARACTER OF THE MESSAGE BOX IS 'A'. Java expanded the possibilities for web-oriented screen management, secure network operations, and portability. Scripting languages such as Perl™ and Python® that enabled richer interactive services also flourished in the web environment.

Database-query languages for relational databases were developed in the middle to late 1970s; they led to the widely used Structured Query Language, or SQL™, which emphasized short segments of code (3 to 20 lines) that could be written at a terminal and executed immediately. The goal of the user was to create a result, rather than a program. A key part of database-query languages and information-retrieval languages was the specification of Boolean operations: AND, OR, and NOT.

Boolean expressions also are key for the experienced web searcher, providing better access to more specific web sites when searching. See Chapter 13 for more on advances regarding searching.

Command languages (a term some authors use to refer to command and control languages), which originated with operating-system commands, are distinguished by their immediacy and by their impact on devices or information. Users issue a command and watch what happens. If the result is correct, the next command is issued; if not, some other strategy is adopted. The commands are brief and their existence is transitory. Command histories are sometimes kept and macros are created in some command languages, but the essence of command languages is that they have an ephemeral nature and that they produce an immediate result on some object of interest.

World Wide Web addresses can be seen as a form of command language. Users come to memorize the structure and favorite site addresses, even though the typical usage is to click on a link to select an address from a web page or a bookmark list. Web addresses begin with a protocol name (*http*, *ftp*, *gopher*, and so on), followed by a colon and two forward slashes, then the server address (which also can include country codes or domain names, such as *gov*, *edu*, *mil*, or *org*), and potentially a directory path and file name. For example:

```
http://www.whitehouse.gov/WH/glimpse/top.html
```

Experienced web surfers become skilled at visually parsing the "command line" of often complex URLs to access files, find server names and locations, and seek specific information.

Command languages are distinguished from menu-selection systems in that their users must recall notation and initiate actions. Menu-selection users view or hear the limited set of menu items; they respond more than initiate. Command-language users, on the other hand, are often called on to accomplish remarkable feats of memorization and typing. For example, this Unix command, used to delete blank lines from a file, is not obvious:

```
grep -v ^$ filea > fileb
```

Even worse, to get a printout on unlined paper on a high-volume laser printer, a user at one installation was instructed to type

```
CP TAG DEV E VTSO LOCAL 2 OPTCD=J F=3871 X=GB12
```

When asking about the command, the puzzled user was met with a shrug of the shoulders and the equally cryptic comment that "Sometimes, logic doesn't come into play; it's just getting the job done." This approach may have been acceptable in the past, but user communities and their expectations are changing. While there are still millions of users of command languages, the development of new command languages has slowed dramatically due to the emergence of direct-manipulation and menu-selection interfaces.

With the advent of increased user-generated content, web and other UI applications require more efficient, better designed command-language tools. Command languages should be designed to suit the operations that users will carry out with them (Section 7.2). They may have simple or complex syntaxes and may have only a few operations or thousands. The commands may have a hierarchical structure or may permit concatenation to form variations. A typical form is a verb followed by a noun object with qualifiers or arguments for the verb or noun—for example, PRINT MYFILE 3 COPIES. Imposing a meaningful structure on the command language can be highly beneficial, and permitting abbreviations may be useful (Section 7.3). Feedback may be generated for acceptable commands, and error messages (Section 11.2) may result from unacceptable forms or typos. Command-language systems may offer the user brief prompts or may be close to menu-selection systems. As discussed in Section 7.4, natural-language interaction can be considered as a complex form of command language.

7.2 Command-Organization Functionality, Strategies, and Structure

People use computers and command-language systems to accomplish a wide range of tasks, such as text editing, operating-system control, bibliographic retrieval, database manipulation, electronic mail, financial management, airline or hotel reservations, inventory monitoring, manufacturing process control, and adventure games.

People will use a computer system if it gives them powers not otherwise available. If the power is attractive enough, people will use a system despite a poor user interface. Therefore, the first step for the designer is to determine the functionality of the system by studying the users' task domain. The outcome is a list of task actions and objects, which is then abstracted into a set of interface actions and objects. These items, in turn, are represented with the low-level interface syntax.

A common design error is to provide excessive numbers of objects and actions, which can overwhelm the user. More objects and actions take more code to maintain, may cause more bugs and slower execution, and require more help screens, error messages, and user documentation (Chapters 11 and 12). For the user, excess functionality slows learning, increases the chance of error, and adds the confusion of longer manuals, more help screens, and less-specific error messages. On the other hand, insufficient objects or actions may leave the user frustrated, because desired functions may not be supported. For instance, users might have to copy a list with a pen and paper because there is no simple print command or to reorder a list by hand because there is no sort command.

Careful task analysis might result in a table of user communities and tasks, with each entry indicating expected frequency of use. The high-volume tasks should be made easy to carry out. The designer must also determine which communities of users are the prime audiences for the system. Users may differ in their position in an organization, their knowledge of computers, or their frequency of system use.

At an early stage, the destructive actions—such as deleting objects or changing formats—should be evaluated carefully to ensure that they are reversible, or at least are protected from accidental invocation. Designers should also identify error conditions and prepare error messages. A transition diagram showing how each command takes the user to another state is a highly beneficial aid to design, as well as to eventual training of users (Fig. 7.1). A diagram that grows too complicated may signal the need for system redesign. Another key feature is the capacity to record histories and review, save, send, search, edit, replay, and annotate them. Finally, help and tutorial features should be provided.

Major considerations for expert users are the possibilities of tailoring the language to suit personal work styles and of creating named macros to permit several

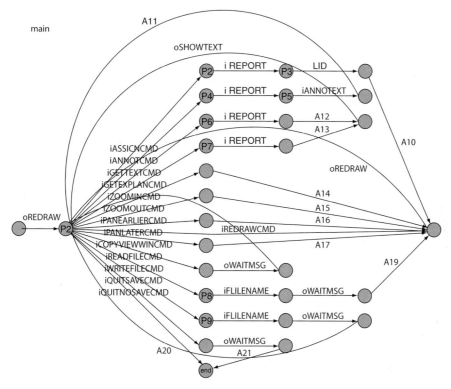

FIGURE 7.1

Transition diagram indicating user inputs with an "i" and computer outputs with an "o." This relatively simple diagram shows only a portion of the system; complete transition diagrams may comprise many pages. (Courtesy of Robert J. K. Jacob, Naval Research Laboratory, Washington, D.C.)

operations to be carried out with a single command. Macro facilities allow extensions that the designers did not foresee or that are beneficial to only a small fragment of the user community. A macro facility can be a full programming language that might include specification of arguments, conditionals, iteration, integers, strings, and screen-manipulation primitives, plus library and editing tools. Well-developed macro facilities are one of the strong attractions of command languages.

7.2.1 Strategies

Several strategies for command organization have emerged. A unifying interface concept or metaphor aids learning, problem solving, and retention. Electronic-mail enthusiasts conduct lively discussions about the metaphoric merits of such task-related objects as file drawers, folders, documents, memos, notes, letters, or messages. They debate the appropriate interface actions (CREATE, EDIT, COPY, MOVE, DELETE) and the choice of action pairs such as LOAD/SAVE (too much in the computer domain), READ/WRITE (acceptable for letters, but awkward for file drawers), or OPEN/CLOSE (acceptable for folders, but awkward for notes).

Designers often err by choosing a metaphor closer to the computer domain than to the users' task domain. Of course, metaphors can mislead the user, but careful design can reap the benefits while reducing the detriments. Having adopted an interface concept or metaphor for actions and objects, the designer must then choose a strategy for the command syntax. Mixed strategies are possible, but learning, problem solving, and retention may be aided by limitation of complexity. This section presents three options for command organization.

In the first and simplest option, *each command is chosen to carry out a single task*, and the number of commands matches the number of tasks. When there are only a small number of tasks, this approach can produce a system that is simple to learn and use. MUD (Multi-User Dungeon) is a multi-player computer game that combines elements of role-playing games, "hack and slash–style" computer games, and social chat rooms. Some MUD commands are simple, such as `look`, `go`, `who`, `rooms`, and `quit`. When there are a large number of commands, however, there is danger of confusion.

The second option is to *follow each command* (COPY, DELETE, PRINT) *by one or more arguments* (FILEA, FILEB, FILEC) that indicate objects to be manipulated:

```
COPY FILEA,FILEB
DELETE FILEA
PRINT FILEA,FILEB,FILEC
```

The commands may be separated from the arguments by a blank space or other delimiter, and the arguments may have blanks or delimiters between them (Schneider et al., 1984). Keyword labels for arguments, such as these, may be helpful to some users:

```
COPY FROM=FILEA TO=FILEB
```

The labels require extra typing and thus increase chances of a typo, but readability is improved and order dependence is eliminated.

Commands may also have *options* (3, HQ, and so on) to indicate special cases. For example, this sequence might produce three copies of FILEA at the printer in the headquarters building:

```
PRINT/3,HQ FILEA
PRINT (3,HQ) FILEA
PRINT FILEA -3,HQ
```

The arguments also may have options, such as version numbers, privacy keys, or disk addresses. As the number of options grows, however, the complexity can become overwhelming and the error messages necessarily less specific.

The number of arguments, options, and permissible syntactic forms can grow rapidly. One airline-reservations system uses the following command to check the seat availability on a flight on August 21, from Washington's Reagan National Airport (DCA) to New York's LaGuardia Airport (LGA) at about 3:00 P.M.:

```
A0821DCALGA0300P
```

Even with substantial training, error rates can be high with this approach, but frequent users seem to manage and even to appreciate the compact form of this type of command. Personnel using more modern airline-reservations systems still require training in the syntax of reservation operations, but task performance is improved by the use of shortcut keys (discussed in Section 7.3), function keys, and web-based user-interface design.

One current airline gate-agent interface solution uses labeled keycaps on the employees' keyboards to enable them to more quickly perform the many repetitive functions available. The use of special keyboard keys in the choice of user-interface dialogue styles can be interpreted as a function-key interface, but they merely serve as shortcut keys in entering command lines. The skilled reservations agent can use these tools much more quickly than a mouse-based, direct-manipulation interface, aiding the hurried traveler with quick responses.

A discussion of command-line interfaces is not complete without a mention of DOS or Unix command lines. DOS commands are still invoked often by system administrators for system maintenance or network connectivity functions, and the Unix command-language system is still widely used in spite of the complexity of its command formats. Here again, users will strive to master complexity to benefit from the rich functionality. One study showed error rates with Unix commands to range from 3 to 53% (Hanson et al., 1984). Even common commands generated high syntactic error rates: 18% for mv and 30% for cp. Still, the complexity has a certain attraction for a portion of the potential user community. Users gain satisfaction in overcoming the difficulties and becoming one of the inner circle ("gurus" or "wizards") who are knowledgeable about system features—command-language machismo.

In the third option, *the set of commands is organized into a tree structure*, like a menu tree. The first level might be the command action, the second might be an object argument, and the third might be a destination argument:

Action	Object	Destination
CREATE	File	File
DISPLAY	Process	Local printer
REMOVE	Directory	Screen
COPY		Networked printer
MOVE		

If a hierarchical structure can be found for a set of tasks, it offers a meaningful structure to a large number of commands. In this case, $5 \times 3 \times 4 = 60$ tasks can be carried out with only five command names and one rule of formation. Another advantage is that a command-menu approach can be developed to aid the novice or intermittent user, as was done in VisiCalc and later in Lotus 1–2–3 and Excel.

7.2.2 Structure

Human learning, problem solving, and memory are greatly facilitated by meaningful structure. If command languages are well designed, users can recognize the structure and can easily encode it in their semantic-knowledge storage. For example, if users can uniformly edit such objects as characters, words, sentences, paragraphs, chapters, and documents, this meaningful pattern is easy for them to learn, apply, and recall. On the other hand, if they must overtype a character, change a word, revise a sentence, replace a paragraph, substitute a chapter, or alter a document, the challenge and potential for error grow substantially, no matter how elegant the syntax is (Scapin, 1982).

Meaningful structure is beneficial for task concepts, computer concepts, and syntactic details of command languages. Yet many systems fail to provide a meaningful structure. Users of one operating system display information with the LIST, QUERY, HELP, or TYPE commands and move objects with the PRINT, TYPE, SPOOL, SEND, COPY, or MOVE commands. Defaults are inconsistent, four different abbreviations for PRINT and LINECOUNT are required, binary choices vary between YES/NO and ON/OFF, and function-key usage is inconsistent. These flaws emerge from multiple uncoordinated design groups and reflect insufficient attention by the managers, especially as features are added over time.

An explicit list of design conventions in a *guidelines document* (Chapter 2) can be an aid to designers and managers. Exceptions may be permitted, but only after thoughtful discussions. Users can learn systems that contain inconsistencies, but they do so slowly and with a high chance of making mistakes.

Several studies have shown that there are benefits associated with using a consistent order for arguments. For example, when presented with commands

with inconsistent and consistent argument ordering, users performed significantly faster with the consistent argument ordering (Barnard et al., 1981):

Inconsistent order of arguments	**Consistent order of arguments**
`SEARCH file no,message id`	`SEARCH message id,file no`
`TRIM message id,segment size`	`TRIM message id,segment size`
`REPLACE message id,code no`	`REPLACE message id,code no`
`INVERT group size,message id`	`INVERT message id,group size`

Evidence that command structure affects performance comes from a comparison of 15 commands in a commercially used symbol-oriented text editor and
revised commands that had a more keyword-oriented style (Ledgard et al.,
1980). Here are three sample commands:

Symbol editor	**Keyword editor**
`FIND:/TOOTH/;-1`	`BACKWARD TO "TOOTH"`
`LIST;10`	`LIST 10 LINES`
`RS:/KO/,/OK/;*`	`CHANGE ALL "KO" TO "OK"`

Single-letter abbreviations (L;10 or L 10 L) were permitted in both editors, so
the number of keystrokes was approximately the same. As discussed in the next
section, a mixture of meaningfulness, mnemonicity, and distinctiveness is helpful.

7.3 Naming and Abbreviations

In discussing command-language names, Schneider et al., (1984) borrow a
delightful quote from Shakespeare's *Romeo and Juliet*: "A rose by any other name
would smell as sweet." As the authors point out, the lively debates in design circles suggest that this concept does not apply to command-language names.
Indeed, the command names are the most visible part of a system and are likely
to provoke complaints from disgruntled users.

Critics such as Norman (1981) tend to focus on the strange names in Unix, such
as `mkdir` (make directory), `cd` (change directory), `ls` (list directory), `rm` (remove
file), and `pwd` (print working directory). Part of their concern is the inconsistent
abbreviation strategies, which may take the first few letters, first few consonants,
first and final letter, or first letter of each word in a phrase. Worse still are abbreviations with no perceivable pattern.

Abbreviations, shortcut and function keys, special characters, and more fill
the lexicon of knowledgeable intermittent to expert users. Advanced searching
methods (discussed in Chapter 13) rely on a command-line array of special characters and Boolean operators to conduct searches of even moderate complexity.

LOL	Laugh out loud
2G2BT	Too good to be true
BBFN	Bye bye for now
CUL8R	See you later
HAGD	Have a great day
IMHO	In my humble opinion
J/K	Just kidding
AATK	Always at the keyboard
OOTO	Out of the office
POV	Point of view
ROTGL	Rolling on the ground laughing
RTSM	Read the silly manual
SWIM	See what I mean?

TABLE 7.1

Sample abbreviations used in online chat, instant messaging, e-mail, blogs, or newsgroup postings (both at work and at home)

Additionally, the advent of text messaging has caused a proliferation of new special acronyms and abbreviations for the speedy, clever text-message generator. Their usage has become pervasive in mobile and cell phone text communication chat rooms, and e-mail. Even communication in the workplace now commonly sports abbreviations such as those listed in Table 7.1. (A good source for a complete list of abbreviations is the NetLingo web site.)

7.3.1 Specificity versus generality

Names are important for learning, problem solving, and retention over time. When it contains only a few names, a command set is relatively easy to master; but when it contains hundreds of names, the choice of meaningful, organized sets of names becomes more important. Similarly, for programming tasks, various name choices have been shown to be less important in small modules with from 10 to 20 names than in larger modules with dozens or hundreds of names.

With larger command sets, names make a difference, especially if they support a meaningful structure. One naming-rule debate revolves around the question of *specificity versus generality* (Rosenberg, 1982). Specific terms can be more descriptive than general ones, and if they are more distinctive, they may be more memorable. General terms, however, may be more familiar and therefore easier to accept. Two weeks after a training session with 12 commands, subjects were more likely to recall and recognize the meanings of specific commands than those of general commands (Barnard et al., 1981).

In a paper-and-pencil test, subjects studied one of seven sets of commands (Black and Moran, 1982). All seven versions of two of the commands—the commands for inserting and deleting text—are shown here:

Infrequent, discriminating words	insert	delete
Frequent, discriminating words	add	remove
Infrequent, nondiscriminating words	amble	perceive
Frequent, nondiscriminating words	walk	view
General words (frequent, nondiscriminating)	alter	correct
Nondiscriminating nonwords (nonsense)	GAC	MIK
Discriminating nonwords (icons)	abc-adbc	abc-ac

The "infrequent, discriminating" command set resulted in faster learning and superior recall than other command sets. The general words were correlated with the lowest performance. The nonsense words did surprisingly well, supporting the possibility that, with small command sets, distinctive names are helpful even if they are not meaningful.

7.3.2 Abbreviation strategies

Command names should be meaningful to facilitate human learning, problem solving, and retention, but they must also satisfy another important criterion: They must be in harmony with the mechanism for expressing the commands to the computer. The traditional and most widely used command-entry mechanism is the keyboard, so commands should use brief and kinesthetically easy codes. Commands requiring Shift or Ctrl keys, special characters, or difficult-to-type sequences are likely to cause higher error rates. For text editing, when many commands are applied and speed is appreciated, single-letter approaches are attractive. Overall, brevity is a worthy goal, since it can speed entry and reduce error rates. Early word-processor designers pursued this approach, even when mnemonicity was sacrificed, thereby making use more difficult for novice and intermittent users.

In less demanding applications, designers have used longer command abbreviations, hoping that the gains in recognizability will be appreciated in spite of the increased keystrokes. Novice users may actually prefer typing the full name of a command to using a shortcut, because they have greater confidence in its success (Landauer et al., 1983).

The phenomenon of preferring to use the full command name also appeared in our study of bibliographic retrieval with the Library of Congress's SCORPIO system: Novices preferred typing the full name, such as BROWSE or SELECT, rather than the traditional four-letter abbreviations BRWS or SLCT, or the single-letter abbreviations B or S. After five to seven uses of the commands, their confidence increased, and they attempted the single-letter abbreviations. A designer of a text adventure game recognized this principle; new users are first instructed to type EAST, WEST, NORTH, or SOUTH to navigate, and then, after five full-length commands have been entered, the system tells the user about the single-letter abbreviations. With experience and frequent use, abbreviations become attractive for and even necessary to satisfy the "power" user.

Efforts have been made to find optimal abbreviation strategies. Several studies support the notion that abbreviation should be accomplished by a consistent strategy (Ehrenreich and Porcu, 1982; Benbasat and Wand, 1984). Here are six potential strategies:

1. *Simple truncation.* Use the first, second, third, and so on letters of each command. This strategy requires that each command be distinguishable by the leading string of characters. Abbreviations can be all of the same length or of different lengths.

2. *Vowel drop with simple truncation.* Eliminate vowels and use some of what remains. If the first letter is a vowel, it may or may not be retained. H, Y, and W may or may not be considered as vowels for this purpose.

3. *First and final letter.* Since the first and final letters are highly visible, use them; for example, use ST for SORT.

4. *First letter of each word in a phrase.* Use the popular acronym technique, for example, with a hierarchical design plan.

5. *Standard abbreviations from other contexts.* Use familiar abbreviations such as QTY for QUANTITY, XTALK for CROSSTALK (a software package), PRT for PRINT, or BAK for BACKUP.

6. *Phonics.* Focus attention on the sound; for example, use XQT for execute.

7.3.3 Guidelines for using abbreviations

Ehrenreich and Porcu (1982) offer this set of guidelines:

1. A *simple* primary rule should be used to generate abbreviations for most items; a *simple* secondary rule should be used for those items where there is a conflict.

2. Abbreviations generated by the secondary rule should have a marker (for example, an asterisk) incorporated in them.

3. The number of words abbreviated by the secondary rule should be kept to a minimum.

4. Users should be familiar with the rules used to generate abbreviations.

5. Truncation should be used because it is an easy rule for users to comprehend and remember. However, when it produces a large number of identical abbreviations for different words, adjustments must be found.

6. Fixed-length abbreviations should be used in preference to variable-length ones.

7. Abbreviations should not be designed to incorporate endings (ING, ED, S).

8. Unless there is a critical space problem, abbreviations should not be used in messages generated by the computer and read by the user.

Abbreviations are an important part of system design, and experienced users appreciate them. Users are more likely to use abbreviations if they are confident in their knowledge of the abbreviations and if the benefit is a savings of more than one to two characters (Benbasat and Wand, 1984).

7.3.4 Command menus and keyboard shortcuts

To relieve the burden of memorization of commands, some designers offer users brief prompts of available commands, in a format called a *command menu*. For example, the text-only web browser called Lynx™ displays this prompt:

```
H)elp O)ptions P)rint G)o M)ain screen Q)uit
      /=search [delete]=history list
```

Experienced users come to know the commands and do not need to read the prompt or the help screens. Intermittent users know the concepts but often refer to the prompt to jog their memories and to help them retain the syntax for future uses. Novice users do not benefit as much from the prompt and may need to take a training course or consult the online help.

Keyboard shortcuts in most graphical user interfaces become a kind of command menu for experienced users. Windows XP indicates the single-letter command shortcut by underscoring a letter in the menu, allowing users to perform all operations with keyboard commands. With a fast display, command menus blur the boundaries between commands and menus.

Command languages, although not as "attractive" a human-computer interface, are still central to computing success. Perform a search for "Windows batch file commands" to easily find an alphabetized index of Windows command lines. Here is an example of a Windows batch file:

```
@ECHO OFF
:BEGIN
CLS
CHOICE /N /C:123 PICK A NUMBER (1, 2, or 3)%1
IF ERRORLEVEL ==1 GOTO ONE
IF ERRORLEVEL ==2 GOTO TWO
IF ERRORLEVEL ==3 GOTO THREE
GOTO END
:ONE
ECHO YOU HAVE PRESSED ONE
GOTO END
:TWO
ECHO YOU HAVE PRESSED TWO
```

(Continued)

```
GOTO END
:THREE
ECHO YOU HAVE PRESSED THREE
:END
```

Mobile devices today are causing a command-line comeback, as users use command grammars, shortcut keys, and abbreviations to send textual data quickly. Command-line interfaces will be the next user-interface breakthrough (Norman, 2007), as command lines are still the norm on many mobile devices.

Scripting languages, mentioned Section 7.1, are a key communications tool in web programming and applications. Here is an example of a Perl script that extracts a subset of documents from a database:

```perl
#!/usr/local/bin/perl

open(C, "$ARGV[0]") || die "can't open candidate doc id list
file:$ARGV[0]\n";

while (<C>) {
    /([^\s]+)/;
    $dict{$1}=1;
}
close(C);

while (<stdin>) {
    if (/<DOC\s+([^\s]+)/) {
        $docID = $1;
    } elsif (/<\/DOC>/) {
        if (defined $dict{$docID}) {
            print "<DOC $docID>\n";
            print "$docText\n";
            print "<\/DOC>\n";
        }
        $docText ="";
        $docID ="";
    } else {
        $docText .= $_;
    }
}
```

7.4 Natural Language in Computing

Even before there were computers, people dreamed about creating machines that would be able to process *natural language*. It is a wonderful fantasy, and the success of word-manipulation devices such as word processors, audio recorders, and telephones may give encouragement to some people. However, language is subtle; there are many special cases, contexts are complex, and emotional relationships have a powerful and pervasive effect in human-human communication.

Although there has been progress in machine translation from one natural language to another (for example, Japanese to English), most effective systems require constrained or preprocessed input, or postprocessing of output. Undoubtedly, improvements will continue and constraints will be reduced, but high-quality, reliable translations of complete documents without human intervention seem difficult to attain. Structured texts such as weather reports are translatable; technical papers are marginally translatable; novels or poems are not easily translatable. Still, machine translation software is helpful, for example, in getting quick translations of web pages to extract information and determine whether the pages are valuable enough to request help from a human translator. Even rough translations may be helpful to language learners, and certainly to tourists. Multilingual search engines, in which users can type query keywords in one language and get appropriate search results in many languages, are another interesting case.

Although full comprehension and generation of language seems an inaccessible goal, there are still many ways that computers can be used in dealing with natural language, such as for interaction, queries, database searching, text generation, and adventure games (Allen, 1995). So much research has been invested in natural-language systems that undoubtedly some successes will emerge, but widespread use may not develop because the alternatives may be more appealing. More rapid progress is made when carefully designed experimental tests are used to discover the users, tasks, and interface designs for which natural-language applications are most beneficial (King, 1996; Oviatt, 2000).

Natural Language Processing (NLP) has made inroads and is the focus of a new online book (Bird et al., 2008). The book describes the Natural Language Toolkit (NLTK), a suite of open-source Python® modules, data, and documentation for research and development in natural-language processing. NLTK contains code supporting dozens of NLP tasks. NLTK has also been proven as a multi-disciplinary teaching tool (Bird et al., 2008).

7.4.1 Natural-language interaction

Researchers hope one day to realize the *Star Trek* scenario in which computers respond to commands users issue by speaking (or typing) in natural language. *Natural-language interaction* (NLI) might be defined as the operation of computers by people using a familiar natural language (such as English) to give instructions and receive responses. With NLI, users do not have to learn command syntax or select from menus. Early attempts at generalized "automatic programming" from natural-language statements have faded, but there are continuing efforts to provide domain-specific assistance.

The problems with NLI lie in not only implementation on the computer, but also desirability for large numbers of users for a wide variety of tasks. Contrary to the common belief, human-human interaction is not necessarily an appropriate model for human operation of computers. Since computers can display information 1,000 times faster than people can enter commands, it seems advantageous to use the computer to display large amounts of information and to allow novice and intermittent users simply to choose among the items. Selection helps to guide the user by making clear what objects and actions are available. For knowledgeable and frequent users who are thoroughly aware of the available functions, a precise, concise command language is usually preferred.

The scenarios of artificial intelligence (smart machines, intelligent agents, and expert systems) are proving to be mind-limiting distractions that inhibit designers from creating more powerful tools. We believe that the next generation of commercially successful interfaces to support collaboration, visualization, simulation, and teleoperated devices are likely to come from user-centered scenarios, rather than from the machine-centered artificial-intelligence scenarios.

The key impediment to NLI is the *habitability* of the user interface—that is how easy it is for users to determine what objects and actions are appropriate. Visual interfaces provide the cues for the semantics of interaction, but NLI interfaces typically depend on assumed user models. Users who are knowledgeable about their tasks—for example, stock-market brokers who know the objects and buy/sell actions—could place orders by voice or by typing in natural language. However, these users prefer compact command languages because they are more rapid and reliable. NLI designs also do not usually convey information about the interface objects and actions (for example, tree structure of information, implications of a deletion, Boolean operations, or query strategies). NLI designs should relieve users from learning new syntactic rules, since they presumably will accept familiar English-language requests. Therefore, NLI can be effective for intermittent users who are knowledgeable about specific tasks and interface concepts but have difficulty retaining the syntactic details of the interface.

By this analysis, NLI might apply well to task domains such as checkbook maintenance (Shneiderman, 1980). In this case, the users recognize that there is an ascending sequence of integer-numbered checks and that each check has a single payee field, amount, and date, and one or more signatures. Checks can be issued, voided, searched, and printed. Following this suggestion, Ford (1981) created and tested a textual NLI system for this purpose. Subjects were paid to maintain their checkbook registers by computer using a program that was refined incrementally to account for unanticipated entries. The final system successfully handled 91% of users' requests, such as these:

```
Pay to Safeway on 3/24 $29.75.
June 10 $33.00 to Madonna.
Show me all the checks paid to George Bush.
Which checks were written on October 29?
```

Users reported satisfaction with the system and were eager to continue to use it after completing several months of experimentation. This study can be seen as a success for NLI, but 25 years later, such systems are still not succeeding in the marketplace. Instead, direct-manipulation alternatives (for example, Quicken from Intuit or Microsoft Money®) have proven to be more attractive. With these programs, showing a full screen of checkbook entries with blank lines for new entries allows many users to accomplish most tasks without any commands and with minimal typing. Users can search by entering partial information (for example, only the payee's name) and then pressing a query key. Direct-manipulation designs guide users, thereby providing a more effective solution to the habitability problem than NLI.

There have been numerous informal tests of NLI systems, but the most famous and controversial is the Loebner Prize, which since 1991 has sponsored an annual contest to choose the system that comes closest to satisfying the Turing Test. The organizers describe the goal as a "computer program whose conversation is indistinguishable from a human's" (http://www.loebner.net/Prizef/loebner-prize.html), and judges rate the performance of the programs in terms of "humanness." In spite of enthusiastic responses from the media, critics complain that the contest "has no clear purpose, that its design prevents any useful outcome."

This controversy reveals the evolution of thinking about and research on natural-language interaction. Early Hollywood imagery, such as HAL in the movie *2001: A Space Odyssey* and research projects such as Weizenbaum's (1996) ELIZA, emphasized dialog-like interaction through a keyboard and display. This 1960s-era goal is still portrayed in some films, but the research and practical outcomes have been modest. A devoted community of linguistically oriented computer scientists still pursues natural-language work, but little of it is devoted to dialog-like interaction. In part, their work has matured because of a positive shift to rigorous evaluations such as the Text Retrieval Conference (TREC), run since 1992 by the U.S. National Institute for Standards and Technology. Workshops on evaluation and scientific journals such as *Natural Language Engineering* have also promoted focused evaluations with appropriate user groups.

As early studies began to reveal the difficulty with and inappropriateness of human-like natural-language interaction, research shifted to more specific goals. Identifying features in documents, such as personal, place, or corporate names, is a realizable and beneficial goal, even when accuracy is less than perfect. Other goals involved linguistic analysis to determine whether a web page contained an answer to a given question and text summarization to extract the key sentences or phrases that would best represent a web page in a result set.

Empirical studies of natural-language interaction for spreadsheets and airline reservations revealed that compact visual interfaces were much faster and preferred by users. Web services grew rapidly by using visual displays with form fill-in and check boxes, while mobile devices flourished with physical buttons and rapid scrolling through meaningful menu choices. An imaginative approach was taken by the Ask Jeeves™ web site (now Ask.com™), which invites natural-language questions but then does keyword extraction to lead to standard web-page result sets. *Chatterbots* may facilitate improvements in research for natural-language interaction. A chatterbot is a program that attempts to simulate typed conversation, with the aim of at least temporarily fooling humans into thinking they are talking to another person.

The START Natural Language System is an interactive software system that attempts to answer questions that are posed to it in natural language (Katz, 2006). START parses incoming questions, matches the queries created from the parse trees against its knowledge base, and presents the appropriate information segments to the user. In this way, START provides untrained users with speedy access to knowledge that in many cases it would take an expert some time to find. The same research team has also presented research dealing with language issues related to cell phones and other mobile devices with their StartMobile system, designed to access information based on written requests in natural language (Katz, 2007).

Some NLI work has turned to automatic speech recognition and speech generation to reduce the barriers to acceptance (Section 8.4). Some users will benefit from NLI, but it may not be as many as promoters believe. Computer users usually seek predictable responses and are discouraged if they must engage in clarification dialogs. By contrast, visually oriented interactions embracing the notions of direct manipulation (Chapter 5) make more effective use of the computer's capacity for rapid display and human capacity for rapid visual recognition. In short, pointing and selecting in context is often more attractive than is typing or even speaking an English sentence.

7.4.2 Natural-language queries and question answering

Since general interaction is difficult to support, some designers have pursued a more limited goal of *natural-language queries* (NLQ) against relational databases. The *relational schema* contains attribute names and the database contains attribute values, both of which are helpful in disambiguating queries. Believers in NLQ may claim that more research and system development is needed before that approach can be excluded, but improvements in menus, command languages, and direct manipulation seem equally likely.

Supporters of NLQ can point with some pride at the modest success of the INTELLECT™ system, which had approximately 400 installations on large mainframe computers during the 1980s. Business executives, sales representatives, and other people used INTELLECT to search databases on a regular basis. Several innovative implementation ideas helped to make INTELLECT appealing. First, the parser used the contents of the database to parse queries; for example, the parser could determine that a query containing "Cleveland" referred to city locations, because Cleveland was an instance in the database. Second, the system administrator could conveniently include guidance for handling domain-specific requests by indicating fields related to who, what, where, when, why, and how queries. Third, INTELLECT rephrased the users' queries and displayed responses, such as PRINT THE CHECK NUMBERS WITH PAYEE = BRITNEY SPEARS. This structured response served as an educational aid, and users gravitated towards using expressions that mimicked the style. Eventually, as users became more knowledgeable, they often used concise, command-like expressions that they believed would be parsed successfully. Even the promoters of INTELLECT recognized that novice users who were unfamiliar with the task domain would have a difficult time, and that the ideal user might be a knowledgeable intermittent user. However, the system's appeal faded as users turned to other approaches.

The first general-purpose, fully automated question-answering system available on the Web to answer questions beyond what search engines can provide was based on a tool called MULDER (Kwok et al., 2001). Later, the work on AskMSR revised this research and a team from Microsoft analyzed its performance (Brill et al., 2002). The latest research on this topic (Banko, 2008) shows that natural-language processors can be adapted to produce better search results.

A more successful product was Q&A™ from Symantec™, which provided rapid, effective query interpretation and execution on IBM PCs. The package made a positive impression during the late 1980s, but few data were reported about actual usage. Later, Q&A was added as a feature of the Sesame Database Manager™ (commercial database) product, still available today. Designers cited many instances of happy users of NLQ and found practical applications in the users' daily work, but the popularity of the package seems to have been more closely tied to its word-processor, database, and form fill-in facilities (Church and Rau, 1995). Microsoft's 1999 SQL Server® product, called English Query, allowed natural-language database queries, provided a restatement to help users interpret the results, and presented a tabular output.

Despite moderate success, INTELLECT, Q&A, English Query, and most other NLQ packages are no longer sold. The dream of NLQ remains alive in some quarters, but commercial applications are rare. There are also extraction systems with a question processor attached that are not true question-and-answer systems. Querying those extraction systems with relationships (e.g., "Who invented . . .?") or proper nouns (e.g., your name) gives a designer a sense of the knowledge base of those systems.

A commercial product called Powerset™ advertises it is "first applying its natural language processing to search, aiming to improve the way we find information by unlocking the meaning encoded in ordinary human language. Powerset's first product is a search and discovery experience for Wikipedia, launched in May 2008."

There are two types of top-performing question-answering systems: consistent, solid, well-established, and multi-faceted systems that do well year after year, and systems that come out of nowhere, employ totally innovative approaches, and out-perform almost everything else (Prager, 2006). In his paper, Prager established what a "typical" question-answering system looks like, aiding designers to build their own question-answering systems.

A variant notion is *natural language question answering* (NLQA), in which users prepare fact questions such as "What is the capital of Zambia?" or "Who was the first Prime Minister of the European Union?" The original challenge was to provide the brief and exact answer, but later systems merely provide a set of web pages in which the users can hunt for the answer. Major difficulties are that user questions often make incorrect assumptions (maybe the European Union has a President, or maybe it should be "European Commission") and that many apparently simple questions need much clarification. Even common words such as "year" can have many interpretations (calendar, fiscal, academic, Martian), and similar terms may be used in diverse situations (wages, earnings, salary, income, pay, take-home pay, paycheck). While evaluations are often done with well-formed questions (Voorhees, 2002), users often have ill-formed questions, and they are notoriously unpredictable. Habitability remains a problem. Therefore, simple key-phrase queries that yield web-page results are an effective and often more informative solution.

The so-called "redundancy-based" approach to question answering represents a successful strategy for mining answers to factoid questions such as "Who shot Abraham Lincoln?" on the World Wide Web. Through contrastive and ablation experiments with Aranea™, a system that has performed well in several TREC question-answering evaluations, one researcher successfully examined underlying assumptions and principles behind redundancy-based techniques (Lin, 2007).

7.4.3 Text-database searching

Text-database searching is a growing application for natural-language enthusiasts who have developed filters and parsers for queries expressed in natural language (Lewis and Jones, 1996). At one end of the spectrum is the full understanding of the meaning of a query and fulfillment of the users' information needs (Lin, 2007). For example, in a legal application ("Find cases of tenants who have sued landlords unsuccessfully for lack of heat"), the system parses the text grammatically, provides synonyms from a thesaurus ("renters" for "tenants"), deals with singulars versus plurals, and handles other problems such as misspellings or foreign terms. Then, the analyzer separates the query into standard components—such as plaintiff, defendant, and cause—and finds all meaningfully related legal citations.

More realistic and typical scenarios are for parsers to eliminate noise words (for example, *the, of,* or *in*), provide stemming (plurals or alternate endings), and produce a relevance-ranked list of documents based on term frequencies.

These systems do not deal with negation, broader or narrower terms, and relationships (such as plaintiff sues defendant), but they can be effective with skilled users. A comparative-evaluation contest among information-retrieval programs that use natural-language strategies to select documents from a large collection continues to be extremely successful in promoting rapid progress (Voorhees, 2002). Many of the popular search tools on the World Wide Web (for example, Google) use natural-language techniques, such as stemming, relevance ranking by word-frequency analysis, latent semantic indexing, and filtering of common words.

Another application with textual databases is *extraction*, in which a natural-language parser analyzes the stored text and creates a more structured format, such as a relational database. The advantage is that the parsing can be done once in advance to structure the entire database and to speed searches when users pose relational queries. Legal (Supreme Court decisions or state laws), medical (scientific journal articles or patient histories), and journalistic (Associated Press news stories or *Wall Street Journal* reports) texts have been used. This application is promising because users appreciate even a modest increase in suitable retrievals, and incorrect retrievals are tolerated better than errors in natural-language interaction. Extraction is somewhat easier than the task of writing a natural-language summary of a long document, as summaries must capture the essence of the content and convey it accurately in a compact manner.

A variant task is to make categories of documents based on contents. For example, it would be useful to have an automated analysis of business news stories to separate out mergers, bankruptcies, and initial public offerings for companies in the electronics, pharmaceutical, or oil industries. The categorization task is appealing because a modest rate of errors would be tolerable (Church and Rau, 1995).

7.4.4 Natural-language text generation

Natural-language text generation (NLTG) includes simple tasks, such as the preparation of structured weather reports ("80% chance of light rain in northern suburbs by late Sunday afternoon"), as well as the generation of complex, full-length stories with rich character development (Church and Rau, 1995). Generated reports from structured databases can be sent out automatically, while timely spoken reports can be made available over the telephone in multiple languages.

Elaborate applications of NLTG include preparation of reports of medical laboratory or psychological tests. The computer generates not only readable reports ("White-blood-cell count is 12,000"), but also warnings ("This value exceeds the normal range of 3,000 to 8,000 by 50%") or recommendations

("Further examination for systemic infection is recommended"). Still more involved scenarios for NLTG involve the creation of legal contracts, wills, or business proposals.

NLTG also has proven successful in choosing words in computer-generated weather forecasting (Reiter et al., 2005). User evaluations of the tool called the SUMTIME-MOUSAM weather-forecast generator have shown a preference for the computer-generated weather forecasting rather than human-generated text due to variations in human-generated responses. Some of the same authors also developed an NLTG system to generate textual summaries of large, time-series (numeric) data sets (Yu et al., 2007). They were able to generate short summaries (a few sentences) of large data sets. In addition, they looked into textual summaries of sensor data from gas turbines.

On the artistic side, computer generation of poems and even novels is a regular discussion point in literary circles. Although computer-generated combinations of randomly selected phrases can be provocative, some hold that they are still ultimately the creative work of the person who chose the set of possible words and decided which of the potential outputs to publish. This position parallels the custom of crediting the human photographer rather than the camera or the subject matter of a photograph.

7.4.5 Adventure games and instructional systems

Natural-language interaction techniques have enjoyed notable and widespread success in a variety of computer-based adventure games. Users may indicate directions of movement, for example, or type commands such as TAKE ALL OF THE KEYS, OPEN THE GATE, or DROP THE CAGE AND PICK UP THE SWORD. Part of the attraction of using natural-language interaction in this situation is that the system is unpredictable, and some exploration is necessary to discover the proper incantation. However, today such games have largely disappeared from the market.

Natural language for instructional tutorials has proven to be successful with some students, especially when the materials and pedagogy have been carefully tested and refined. Providing feedback and guidance in natural language, even in spoken form, can be helpful in encouraging students to stay engaged in the educational process (Di Eugenio et al., 2002). Advanced instructional systems have been developed to teach high-school– and college-level topics in areas such as algebra, physics, electronics, programming, and computer literacy (Fig. 7.2). These systems, often based on rich pedagogical theories, guide students through the learning process by presenting challenges and providing feedback in conversational natural language. Careful design and thorough testing has led to successful tools that have been shown to improve learning over comparable classroom experiences. Some of these systems are used by tens of thousands of students. For example, this

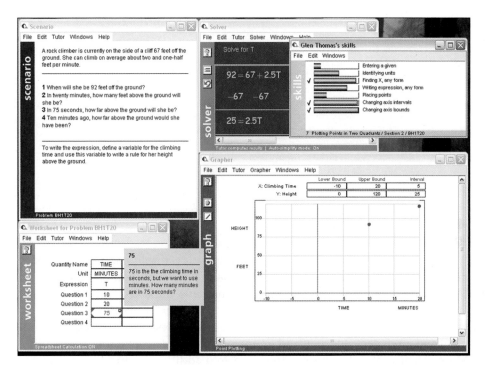

FIGURE 7.2

Cognitive Tutor® software from Carnegie Learning, Inc.® (http://www.carnegielearning. com/product_information.cfm) has been implemented for algebra, geometry, and related areas of mathematics. It traces student progress in mastering skills and concepts, then assigns individually tuned problems. This screen display shows the Scenario, Worksheet, Graph, Solver, and Skills windows.

tutorial dialog in a computer-literacy course was recorded between an onscreen anthropomorphic character and a college student in the AutoTutor system (Graesser et al., 2001):

> TUTOR-1: Alright, let's go on. You want to take photos and send them over the Internet. Consider this problem. What hardware do you need to take photos and send them over the Internet?
> STUDENT-1: First of all you need to have access to the Internet.
> TUTOR-2: What else?
> STUDENT-2: a camera.
> TUTOR-3: Yeah. For what type of connection do you need a network card?
> STUDENT-3: a network card?
> TUTOR-4: Okay. Now, if you have access to the Internet through a network card then your connection is...
>
> *(Continued)*

```
STUDENT-4: I don't know.
TUTOR-5: Is direct. Okay. A network card is needed if you have a
direction connection to the Internet. Okay. How does the user
get hooked up to the Internet?
STUDENT-5: by a plug.
TUTOR-6: Once again, a network card is needed if you have a
direct connection to the Internet. Okay, what does a modem do?
STUDENT-6: connects network card and internet.
TUTOR-7: Okay. Try this. A modem is required when there is ...
STUDENT-5: a connection
TUTOR-6: a dial up connection.
. . .
TUTOR-30: Let's review. To send your photos on the Internet, you
need either a digital camera or a regular camera to take photos.
If you use. . .
```

There have been three excellent workshops on Natural Language Processing in education sponsored as part of Association of Computational Linguistics (ACL) conferences. NLP-based applications have impacted education in the areas of assessment (testing) and instruction. Earlier applications focused on writing for automated essay scoring, short-answer response scoring in assessment and intelligent tutoring, and grammatical error detection for proofreading. More recently, NLP has been introduced into additional educational contexts, including automated scoring of speech and text-based curriculum development for reading support (Tetreault et al., 2008).

NLI for users can also apply to complex products such as home appliances (Vanderheiden et al., 2005), leading designers to assist users with special needs and thereby improving universal accessibility. Another group developed a tool for reading of graphs and graphical data for those needing assistance with that task (Ferres, 2008).

Another research team introduced a framework for learning-situated natural-language interfaces to interactive virtual environments where human users and computer agents interact. Preliminary experimentation in an independently designed interactive application—i.e., the Mission Rehearsal Exercise (MRE)—shows that this situated natural-language interface outperforms a state-of-the-art natural language interface (Fleischman and Hovey, 2006).

NLI has been shown to play a part in interdisciplinary research related to intelligent tutoring and pedagogical experience manipulation (Lane and Johnson, 2008). Combining the disciplines of natural-language processing, emotional modeling, gestural modeling, cultural modeling, and more (Swartout et al., 2006) can aid in intelligent tutoring systems development and enhance the performance of such systems.

Lastly, natural language competency is a key component of technology for robots and androids (Coradeschi et al., 2006). Designers of these robots believe that these applications of NLI can enhance our quality of life.

Practitioner's Summary

Command languages can be attractive when frequent use of a system is anticipated, users are knowledgeable about the task and interface concepts, screen space is at a premium, response times and display rates are slow, and numerous functions can be combined in compact expressions. Users have to learn the semantics and syntax, but they can initiate, rather than just respond, and can rapidly specify actions involving several objects and options. Finally, a complex sequence of commands can easily be specified and stored for future use as a macro.

Designers should begin with a careful task analysis to determine what functions should be provided. Laying out the full set of commands on a single sheet of paper helps to show the structure to the designer and to the learner. Meaningful specific names aid learning and retention. Compact abbreviations constructed according to consistent rules facilitate retention and rapid performance for frequent users.

Command menus can be effective if rapid response to screen actions can be provided. Natural-language interaction and English-language queries have been implemented, but their effectiveness and advantages are limited, mainly because of habitability issues. Natural-language support has shown more success in text searching, text generation, extraction, and instructional systems.

Researcher's Agenda

The benefits of structuring command languages based on hierarchy, consistency, and mnemonicity have been demonstrated in specific cases, but replication in varied situations should lead to a comprehensive cognitive model of command-language learning and use (Box 7.1). Novel input devices and high-speed, high-resolution displays offer new opportunities—such as command and pop-up menus—for breaking free from the traditional syntax of command languages.

Natural-language interaction success stories are still elusive, but natural-language techniques have become an important part of the success of text-database searching (Chapter 13). Natural-language text generation has shown value, so further research is warranted. For those who continue to explore NLI for specific applications, empirical tests and long-term case studies offer successful strategies to identify the appropriate niches and design. Speech-based approaches (Chapter 8) for guided interactions over telephones are also gradually proving to be useful.

BOX 7.1
Command-language guidelines.

- Create an explicit model of objects and actions.
- Choose meaningful, specific, distinctive names.
- Try to achieve a hierarchical structure.
- Provide a consistent structure (hierarchy, argument order, action-object).
- Support consistent abbreviation rules (prefer truncation to one letter).
- Offer frequent users the ability to create macros.
- Consider command menus on high-speed displays.
- Limit the number of commands and ways of accomplishing a task.

WORLD WIDE WEB RESOURCES
http://www.aw.com/DTUI/

Designers will find some information on command languages and lots of activities on natural-language translation, interaction, queries, and extraction. Some sites also possess natural-language services.

The Natural Language Technology Group (NLTG) web site, located at http://www.nltg.brighton.ac.uk/nltg/, explores ways in which computer technology can be applied to tasks that involve the use of natural (human) languages. NLTG is particularly interested in statistical generation, lexical representation, multilingualism, emotional content in text, and natural-language systems and architectures.

References

Allen, James, *Natural Language Understanding, Second Edition*, Addison-Wesley, Reading, MA (1995).

Banko, Michelle and Etzioni, Oren, The tradeoffs between open and traditional relation extraction, *Proc. Association of Computational Linguistics*, ACL, East Stroudsburg, PA (June 2008), 28–36.

Barnard, P. J., Hammond, N. V., Morton, J., Long, J. B., and Clark, I. A., Consistency and compatibility in human-computer dialogue, *International Journal of Man-Machine Studies* 15 (1981), 87–134.

Benbasat, Izak and Wand, Yair, Command abbreviation behavior in human-computer interaction, *Communications of the ACM* 27, 4 (April 1984), 376–383.

Bird, Steven, Klein, Ewan, and Loper, Edward, *Natural Language Toolkit* (2008). Available at http://nltk.org/index.php/Book/.

Bird, Steven, Klein, Ewan, Loper, Edward, and Baldridge, Jason, Multidisciplinary instruction with the Natural Language Toolkit, *Proc. Third Workshop on Issues in Teaching Computational Linguistics*, Columbus, OH (June 2008), 62–70.

Black, J. and Moran, T., Learning and remembering command names, *Proc. CHI'82 Conference: Human Factors in Computing Systems*, ACM Press, New York (1982), 8–11.

Brill, Eric, Dumais, Susan, and Banko, Michelle, An analysis of the AskMSR question-answering system, *Proc. Association of Computational Linguistics*, ACL, East Stroudsburg, PA (2002), 257–264.

Church, Kenneth W. and Rau, Lisa F., Commercial applications of natural language processing, *Communications of the ACM* 38, 11 (November 1995), 71–79.

Coradeshi, Silvia, Ishiguro, Hiroshi, Asada, Minoni, Shapiro, Stuart, Theilscher, Michael, Breazeal, Cynthia, Mataric, Maja, and Ishida, Hiroshi, Human-inspired robots, *IEEE Intelligent Systems* 21, 4 (2006), 74–85.

Di Eugenio, Barbara, Glass, Michael, and Trolio, Michael J., The DIAG experiments: Natural language generation for intelligent tutoring systems, *Proc. International Conference on Natural Language Generation*, ACM Press, New York (2002), 50–57. Available at http://www.cs.uic.edu/~bdieugen/PS-papers/AIED05.pdf.

Ehrenreich, S. L. and Porcu, Theodora, Abbreviations for automated systems: Teaching operators and rules, in Badre, Al and Shneiderman, Ben (Editors), *Directions in Human-Computer Interaction*, Ablex, Norwood, NJ (1982), 111–136.

Fleischman, Michael and Hovey, Eduard, Taking advantage of the situation: Non-linguistic context for natural language interfaces to interactive virtual environments, *Proc. 11th International Conference on Intelligent User Interfaces (IUI)*, ACM Press, New York (2006), 47–54.

Ferres, Leo, A syntactic analysis of accessibility to a corpus of statistical graphs, *Proc. International Cross-Disciplinary Conference on Web Accessibility (W4A) 2008*, ACM Press, New York (2008), 37–44.

Ford, W. Randolph, *Natural Language Processing by Computer—A New Approach*, Ph.D. Dissertation, Department of Psychology, Johns Hopkins University, Baltimore, MD (1981).

Graesser, Arthur C., VanLehn, Kurt, Rose, Carolyn P., Jordan, Pamela W., and Harter, Derek, Intelligent tutoring systems with conversational dialogue, *AI Magazine* 22, 4 (Winter 2001), 39–52.

Hanson, Stephen J., Kraut, Robert E., and Farber, James M., Interface design and multivariate analysis of Unix command use, *ACM Transactions on Office Information Systems* 2, 1 (1984), 42–57.

Hauptmann, Alexander G. and Green, Bert F., A comparison of command, menu-selection and natural language computer programs, *Behaviour & Information Technology* 2, 2 (1983), 163–178.

Katz, Boris, Borchardt, Gary, and Felshin, Sue, Natural language annotations for question answering, *Proc. 19th International FLAIRS Conference*, AAAI Press, Menlo Park, CA (2006), 303–306.

Katz, Boris, Borchardt, Gary, Felshin, Sue, and Mora, Federico, Harnessing language in mobile environments, *Proc. First IEEE International Conference on Semantic Computing (ICSC 2007)*, IEEE Press, Los Alamitos, CA (2007), 421–428.

King, Margaret, Evaluating natural language processing systems, *Communications of the ACM* 39, 1 (January 1996), 73–79.

Kwok, Cody, Etzioni, Oren, and Weld, Daniel S., Scaling question answering to the Web, *Proc. 10th International Conference on the World Wide Web (WWW '01)*, ACM Press, New York (2001), 150–161.

Landauer, T. K., Calotti, K. M., and Hartwell, S., Natural command names and initial learning, *Communications of the ACM* 26, 7 (July 1983), 495–503.

Lane, H. C. and Johnson, W. L., Intelligent tutoring and pedagogical experience manipulation in virtual learning environments, in Schmorrow, D. (Editor), *Intelligent Tutoring in Virtual Environments* (2008), http://www.alelo.com/files/Lane-Johnson ITS Chapter 49.pdf, Chapter 49.

Ledgard, H., Whiteside, J. A., Singer, A., and Seymour, W., The natural language of interactive systems, *Communications of the ACM* 23, 10 (1980), 556–563.

Lewis, David and Jones, Karen Sparck, Natural language processing for information retrieval, *Communications of the ACM* 39, 1 (January 1996), 92–101.

Lin, Jimmy, An exploration of the principles underlying redundancy-based factoid question answering, *ACM Transactions on Information Systems* 27, 2 (2007), 1–55.

Napier, H. Albert, Lane, David, Batsell, Richard R., and Guadango, Norman S., Impact of a restricted natural language interface on ease of learning and productivity, *Communications of the ACM* 32, 10 (October 1989), 1190–1198.

Norman, Donald, The trouble with Unix, *Datamation* 27 (November 1981), 139–150.

Norman, Donald, The next UI breakthrough: Command lines, *ACM interactions* 14, 3 (May/June 2007), 44–45.

Oviatt, Sharon L., Taming speech recognition errors within a multimodal interface, *Communications of the ACM* 43, 9 (September 2000), 45–51.

Prager, John, Open-domain question answering, *Foundations and Trends in Information Retrieval* 1, 2 (January 2006), 91–231.

Reiter, Ehud, Sripada, Somayajulu, Hunter, Jim, Yu, Jin, and Davy, Ian, Choosing words in computer-generated weather forecasts, *Artificial Intelligence* 167, 1–2 (September 2005), 137–169.

Rosenberg, Jarrett, Evaluating the suggestiveness of command names, *Behaviour & Information Technology* 1, 4 (1982), 371–400.

Scapin, Dominique L., Computer commands labeled by users versus imposed commands and the effect of structuring rules on recall, *Proc. CHI '82 Conference: Human Factors in Computing Systems*, ACM Press, New York (1982), 17–19.

Schneider, M. L., Hirsh-Pasek, K., and Nudelman, S., An experimental evaluation of delimiters in a command language syntax, *International Journal of Man-Machine Studies* 20, 6 (June 1984), 521–536.

Shneiderman, Ben, *Software Psychology: Human Factors in Computer and Information Systems*, Little, Brown, Boston, MA (1980).

Swartout, W., Gratch, J., Hill, R., Hovy, E., Marsella, S., and Rickel, J., Toward virtual humans, *AI Magazine* 27, 2 (July 2006), 96–108.

Tetreault, Joel, Burstein, Jill, and De Felice, Rachele (Conference Co-Chairs), *Proc. Third Workshop on Innovative Use of NLP for Building Educational Applications*, Association for Computational Linguistics, Stroudsburg, PA (2008). Available at http://www.cs.rochester.edu/~tetreaul/acl-bea.html#program.

Vanderheiden, Gregg, Zimmerman, Gottfried, Blaedow, Karen, and Trewin, Shari, Hello, what do you do? Natural language interaction with intelligent environments, *Proc. 11th International Conference on Human-Computer Interaction (HCII 2005)*, Lawrence Erlbaum Associates, Mahwah, NJ (2005).

Voorhees, Ellen M., Overview of TREC 2002, *National Institute of Standards and Technology Special Publication SP 500-251: The Eleventh Text Retrieval Conference*, NIST, Gaithersburg, MD (2002). Available at http://trec.nist.gov/pubs/trec11/papers/OVERVIEW.11.pdf.

Weizenbaum, Joseph, ELIZA: A computer program for the study of natural language communication between man and machine, *Communications of the ACM* 9, 1 (January, 1966), 36–45.

Yu, Jim, Reiter, Ehud, Hunter, Jim, and Mellish, Chris, Choosing the content of textual summaries of large time-series data sets, *Natural Language Engineering* 13, 1 (March 2007), 25–49.

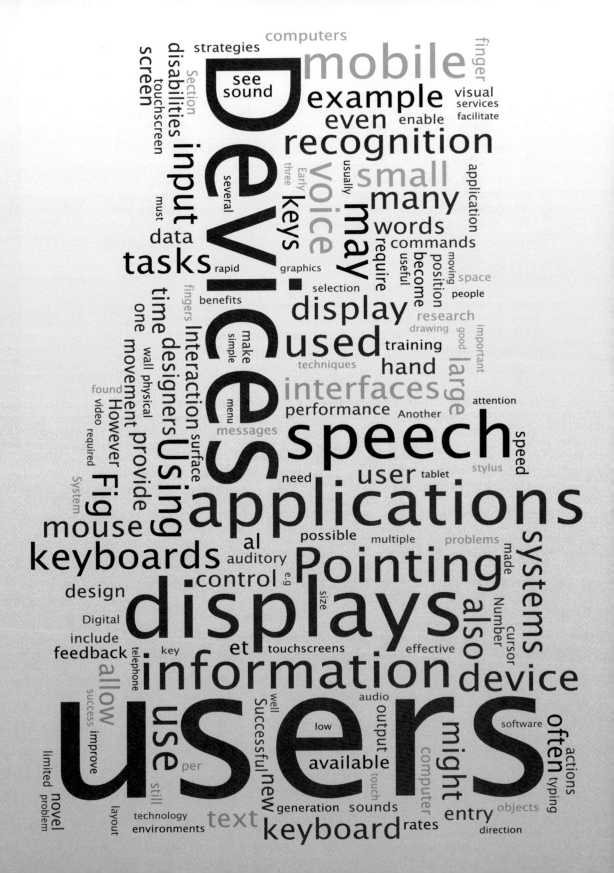

8

Interaction Devices

> The wheel is an extension of the foot,
> the book is an extension of the eye,
> clothing, an extension of the skin,
> electric circuitry an extension
> of the central nervous system.
>
> **Marshall McLuhan and Quentin Fiore**
> *The Medium Is the Message*, 1967

8.1 Introduction

The remarkable progress since 1960 in computer processor speeds and storage capabilities has been matched by improvements in many input/output devices. Ten-character-per-second Teletypes have been replaced by high-speed mega-pixel graphical displays for output. Although the common Sholes or QWERTY keyboard layout is likely to remain the primary device for text input, novel strategies have emerged to meet the needs of mobile device users. Pointing devices, especially the mouse and touchscreen, free users from keyboards for many tasks. The future of computing is likely to include more gestural input, two-handed input, three-dimensional pointing, voice input/output, wearable devices, and whole-body involvement for some input and output tasks.

Pointing devices have undergone hundreds of refinements to accommodate varied users and to squeeze out further performance improvements. More unusual devices, including eye-trackers, DataGloves, and haptic or force-feedback devices, have been applied for specific niche applications such as telemedicine. Experiments with users with severe disabilities are leading the way with brain-controlled mouse movement, while some visionaries have raised still more exotic ideas for implanted devices. Innovative input devices, sensors, and effectors, as well as integration of computers into the physical environment, open the door to a variety of applications (Hinckley, 2008; Abowd and Mynatt, 2000; Jacob et al., 1994).

The still-improving speech recognizers have been joined by more mundane but widely used speech store-and-forward technologies with increased emphasis on telephone-based applications and non-speech auditory interfaces.

Special strategies are needed for large and small displays. Digital cameras with instant viewing on small liquid crystal displays (LCDs) and mobile phones with touchscreens are already a success story, while wall-sized high-resolution displays are opening up new possibilities. Low-cost color printers are widely used, raising further doubts about the idea of the paperless office, while Braille printers open the door to more users and three-dimensional (3D) printers allow the production of custom devices for tangible interfaces.

In addition to the refinement of individual input and output devices, some effort has been devoted to multimodal interfaces, which combine several modes of input and output. Initially, researchers believed that simultaneous use of multiple modes could improve performance, but these methods have had limited applications. Successful examples of simultaneous multimodal interfaces exist, such as combining voice commands with pointing to apply actions to objects. However, the bigger payoff appears to be in giving users the ability to switch between modes depending on their needs—for example, allowing car drivers to operate their navigation systems by touch actions or voice input and to invoke visual or voice output depending on whether they are at a stop or busy attending to traffic (Oviatt et al., 2004). The development of multimodal interfaces will also benefit users with disabilities who may need video captioning, audio transcriptions, or image descriptions. Progress in multimodal interfaces will contribute to the goal of universal usability.

Another lively research direction, encouraged by the widespread use of mobile devices, is context-aware computing. Mobile devices can use location information from Global Positioning System (GPS) satellites, cell-phone sources, wireless connections, or other sensors. Such information allows users to receive information about nearby restaurants or gas stations, enables museum visitors or tourists to access detailed information about their surroundings, or helps users of tablet computers to connect to a printer located in the same room. The provocative applications of context-aware computing may open large markets, although concerns about privacy must be addressed.

This chapter first reviews keyboards and keypads and discusses data-entry techniques for mobile devices (Section 8.2). Section 8.3 describes pointing devices and introduces Fitts' law. The promises and challenges of speech and auditory interfaces are discussed in Section 8.4. Section 8.5 reviews traditional and novel display technologies and design particularities of large and small displays. Examples of possible solutions for users with disabilities are distributed throughout the chapter.

8.2 Keyboards and Keypads

The primary mode of textual data entry is still the keyboard (Fig. 8.1). This much-criticized device is impressive in its success. Hundreds of millions of people use keyboards; although the rate for beginners is generally less than 1 keystroke per second, and the rate for average office workers is 5 keystrokes per second (approximately 50 words per minute), some users achieve speeds of up to 15 keystrokes per second (approximately 150 words per minute). Contemporary

FIGURE 8.1

A laptop with a QWERTY keyboard showing the inverted T movement keys at the bottom right and function keys across the top. Users can choose to use one of the two pointing devices—a trackpoint mounted between the G and H keys or the touchpad below the keyboard—each of which has a corresponding pair of buttons (http://www.ibm.com/).

keyboards generally permit only one keypress at a time, although dual key-presses are used for capitals (Shift plus a letter) and special functions (Ctrl or Alt plus a letter). Alterations to this pattern might allow for higher rates of data entry than are possible with the current computer keyboards. An inspiration might be the piano keyboard, an impressive data-entry device that allows several finger presses at once and is responsive to different pressures and durations.

It has been demonstrated that more rapid data entry can be accomplished if several keys can be pressed simultaneously (i.e., chording). Using chords representing several characters or entire words, courtroom recorders can rapidly enter the full text of spoken arguments, reaching rates of up to 300 words per minute. However, this feat requires months of training and frequent use to retain the complex patterns of chord presses. Chording might allow cell-phone users to reach higher data-entry speeds as well.

Keyboard size and packaging influence user satisfaction and usability. Large keyboards with many keys give an impression of professionalism and complexity, but they may threaten novice users. One-handed keyboards might be useful when users' tasks require simultaneous data entry and manipulation of physical objects. Finally, tiny keyboards and touchscreens on mobile devices are acceptable for limited text entry.

8.2.1 Keyboard layouts

The Smithsonian Institution's National Museum of American History in Washington, D.C. has a remarkable exhibit on the development of the typewriter. During the middle of the nineteenth century, hundreds of attempts were made to build typewriters, with a stunning variety of positions for the paper, mechanisms for producing characters, and layouts for the keys. By the 1870s, Christopher Latham Sholes's design was becoming successful—it had a good mechanical design and a clever placement of the letters that slowed down the users enough that key jamming was infrequent. This *QWERTY layout* put frequently used letter pairs far apart, thereby increasing finger travel distances.

Sholes's success led to such widespread standardization that, more than a century later, almost all keyboards use the QWERTY layout, or one of its variations developed for other languages (Figs. 8.1 and 8.2). The development of electronic keyboards eliminated the mechanical problems of typewriters and led many twentieth-century inventors to propose alternative layouts to reduce finger travel distances. The *Dvorak layout* could increase the typing rate of expert typists from about 150 words per minute to more than 200 words per minute, and even reduced errors. Its failure to gain acceptance is an interesting example of how even documented improvements can be impossible to disseminate because the perceived benefit of change does not outweigh the effort required to learn a new, nonstandard interface.

A third keyboard layout of some interest is the *ABCDE style*, which has the 26 letters of the English alphabet laid out in alphabetical order. The rationale here is that nontypists will find it easier to locate the keys. A few data-entry terminals for numeric and alphabetic codes still use this style, though studies have shown no advantage for the ABCDE style; users with little QWERTY experience are eager to acquire this expertise and often resent having to use the ABCDE layout.

Number pads are a further source of controversy. Telephones have the 1–2–3 keys on the top row, but calculators place the 7–8–9 keys on the top row. Studies have shown a slight advantage for the telephone layout, but most computer keyboards use the calculator layout.

Some researchers have recognized that the wrist and hand placement required for standard keyboards is awkward and have proposed more ergonomic keyboards. Various geometries have been tried with split and tilted keyboards, but empirical verification of benefits in typing speed, accuracy, or reduced repetitive strain injury is elusive.

To address the needs of users with disabilities, designers have reconsidered the typing process entirely. For example, KeyBowl's orbiTouch keyless keyboard

FIGURE 8.2

The popular BlackBerry® smartphone from Research In Motion® (RIM®) (http://www.blackberry.com) shown here on the left demonstrated that many people could use a reduced-size keyboard on a regular basis; users typically type with one finger or with both thumbs. The Nokia device in the middle shows that non-English-speaking countries may use different keyboard layouts (here, a French AZERTY keyboard). On the right, a larger keyboard uses the longer dimension of the device and can be slid back into the device when not needed (http://www.nokia.com).

replaces the keys with two inverted bowls, on top of which users' hands rest comfortably. A combination of small hand movements and small finger presses on the two bowls selects letters or controls the cursor. No finger or wrist movement is needed, which might be helpful to users with carpal tunnel syndrome or arthritis. Another approach is to rely on pointing devices such as mice, touchpads, or eye-trackers for data entry. Early solutions used large menus of fixed choices, but novel techniques are being explored; an example is Dasher (Fig. 8.3), which predicts probable characters and words as users make their selections in a continuous two-dimensional stream of choices (Ward et al., 2000).

8.2.2 Keys

Keyboards keys have been refined carefully and tested thoroughly in research laboratories and the marketplace. The keys have slightly concave surfaces for good contact with fingertips and a matte finish to reduce both reflective glare and the chance of finger slips. The keypresses require a 40- to 125-gram force and a displacement of 1 to 4 millimeters, which enables rapid typing with low error rates while providing suitable feedback to users. An important element in key design is the profile of force displacement. When the key has been depressed far enough to

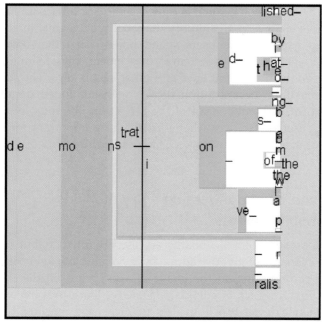

demonstrat

FIGURE 8.3
A user is writing "demonstration" with Dasher. Dasher predicts probable characters or words and allows selection among alternatives by continuous two-dimensional pointing with a mouse, touchpad, or eye-tracker. After the first letters have been selected, possible word choices are "demolished," "demonstrated that," "demonstration," "demonstrative," or "demoralise." The display continuously scrolls to the left, revealing more choices as the cursor is positioned on the chosen character or word (Ward et al., 2000).

send a signal, the key gives way and emits a very light click. This tactile and audible feedback is extremely important in touch typing; hence, membrane keyboards that use a nonmoving surface are unacceptable for extensive touch typing. However, such keyboards are durable and therefore acceptable for challenging environments such as fast-food restaurants, factory floors, or amusement parks.

Certain keys, such as the space bar, Enter key, Shift key, or Ctrl key, should be larger than others to allow easy, reliable access. Other keys, such as Caps Lock and Num Lock, should have a clear indication of their state, such as by physical locking in a lowered position or by an embedded light. Large-print keyboards are available for vision-impaired users. The placement of the *cursor-movement keys* (up, down, left, and right) is important in facilitating rapid and error-free use. The popular and compact inverted-T arrangement (Fig. 8.1) allows users to place their middle three fingers in a way that reduces hand and finger movement. The cross arrangement is a good choice for novice users. Some large keyboards have eight keys to simplify diagonal movements. In some applications, such as games where users spend hours using the movement keys, designers reassign letter keys as cursor-movement keys to minimize finger motion between the movement keys and other action keys. The *auto-repeat feature*, where repetition occurs automatically with continued depression, may improve performance, but control of the repetition rate must be provided to accommodate user preferences (this is particularly important for very young users, older adult users, and users with motor impairments).

8.2.3 Keyboards and other text entry methods for mobile devices

Even on laptop computers, keyboards are usually full size, but many mobile devices use keyboards of greatly reduced size. While cloth keyboards or virtual keyboards (e.g., projecting an the image of a keyboard on the table) seemed promising at first, the lack of adequate tactile feedback prevented widespread acceptance. Mobile device functionalities are increasing considerably, and users who need to type e-mails or enter text often choose devices with small but traditional QWERTY keyboards (for example, the RIM® Blackberry, shown in Fig. 8.2). With practice, users can reach speeds of 60 words per minute when using both thumbs with those mechanical keyboards, or more when the device autocorrects "off-by-one" errors where the user accidentally presses a key adjacent to the one intended (Clawson et al., 2008).

Many devices provide only a numeric keypad. Dynamically labeled soft keys whose functions are dependent on status and context can be useful. Soft keys are usually located immediately below the display (see, for example, the Select and Exit keys in Fig. 6.21). User-interface innovations focus mainly on techniques to enter text. The multi-tap system requires users to hit a number key multiple times to specify a letter and to pause between letters that require using the same key. Predictive techniques, such as T9® by Tegic Communications, use dictionary-based disambiguation and are often preferred for writing text messages. Alternatives include LetterWise, which uses the probabilities of prefixes and facilitates the entry of non-dictionary words, such as a proper nouns, abbreviations, or slang. After training, users could type 20 words per minute with LetterWise compared to 15 words per minute with multi-tap (MacKenzie et al., 2001). New techniques will continue to improve data entry on small keyboards.

Many mobile devices, including Apple's iPhone, have abandoned mechanical keyboards entirely and rely on pointing, drawing, and gesturing on touchscreens for all interactions (Dunlop and Masters, 2008; MacKenzie and Soukoreff, 2002). Users can tap on virtual keyboards if the screen is large enough to display a keyboard (Fig. 8.4). In our studies with touchscreen keyboards that

FIGURE 8.4

The virtual keyboard of the Apple iPhone gains precision by allowing finger repositioning and then activates on lift-off (http://www.apple.com).

were 7 and 25 centimeters wide, users could, with some practice, type from 20 to 30 words per minute, respectively, which is quite acceptable for limited text entry (Sears et al., 1993). A recent study demonstrated that providing tactile feedback using the phone's tactile actuators could improve typing speed (Hoggan et al., 2008).

Another method is to handwrite on a touch-sensitive surface, typically with a stylus, but character recognition remains error-prone. Contextual clues, stroke speed, plus direction can enhance recognition rates, but a successful gestural data-entry methods involve using simplified and more easily recognizable character sets, such as the unistrokes used by Graffiti® on the Palm devices (Fig. 8.5). Recognition is fairly good and most users learn the codes quickly, but the required training can be a hurdle for new and intermittent users. Another promising method is to allow shorthand gesturing on a keyboard instead of tapping on a touchscreen keyboard, using shapes that match the tapping patterns. Long term studies confirm that it is possible to achieve good text entry performance with this technique (Kristensson and Denby, 2009).

For some languages, such as Japanese or Chinese, handwriting recognition has the potential to dramatically increase the number of potential users. On the other hand, users with disabilities, older adults, and young children may not have the necessary fine motor control to use such interfaces on tiny touch-sensitive surfaces. For them, innovations such as EdgeWrite (Wobbrock et al., 2003) might be helpful. EdgeWrite relies on the use of a physical border to frame the drawing area and uses a modified character set that can be recognized by identifying the series of corners being hit instead of the pattern of the pen stroke, resulting in higher accuracy for all users compared to Graffiti. The EdgeWrite character set has also been used successfully with trackballs or eye-trackers to address the needs of users with disabilities (Wobbrock et al., 2008).

8.3 Pointing Devices

With complex information displays such as those found in computer-assisted design tools, drawing tools, or air-traffic–control systems, it is often convenient to point at and select items. This direct-manipulation approach is attractive

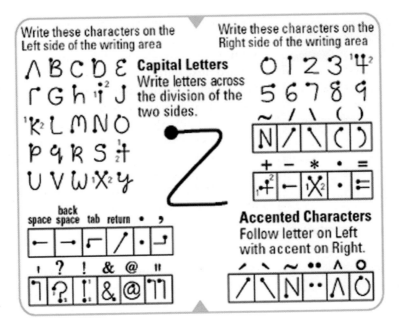

FIGURE 8.5

The Palm Graffiti 2 characters (http://www.polatheschools.com/palm/documents/grafitti2_alphabet.pdf).

because the users can avoid learning commands, reduce the chance of typographic errors on a keyboard, and keep their attention on the display. The results are often faster performance, fewer errors, easier learning, and higher satisfaction. Pointing devices are also important for small devices and large wall displays that make keyboard interaction less practical.

The diversity of tasks, the variety of devices, and the strategies for using them create a rich design space (Hinckley, 2008). Physical device attributes (rotation or linear movement), dimensionality of movement (1, 2, 3 . . .), and positioning (relative or absolute) are useful ways of categorizing devices, but here we focus on tasks and degree of directness as organizing dimensions.

8.3.1 Pointing tasks

Pointing devices are useful for seven types of interaction tasks (expanded from the six tasks of Foley et al., 1984):

1. *Select*. Users choose from a set of items. This technique is used for traditional menu selection, the identification of objects of interest, or marking a part (for example, in an automobile design).

2. *Position.* Users choose a point in a one-, two-, three-, or higher-dimensional space. Positioning may be used to create a drawing, to place a new window, or to drag a block of text in a figure.

3. *Orient.* Users choose a direction in a two-, three-, or higher-dimensional space. The direction may rotate a symbol on the screen, indicate a direction of motion, or control the operation of a device such as a robot arm.

4. *Path.* Users rapidly perform a series of positioning and orientation operations. The path may be realized as a curving line in a drawing program, a character to be recognized, or the instructions for a cloth-cutting or other type of machine.

5. *Quantify.* Users specify a numeric value. The quantify task is usually a one-dimensional selection of integer or real values to set parameters, such as the page number in a document, the velocity of a vehicle, or the volume level of music.

6. *Gesture.* Users indicate an action to perform by executing a simple gesture, such as a swipe motion to the left (or right) to turn a page forward (or backward), or a rapid back and forth motion to erase.

7. *Text.* Users enter, move, and edit text in a two-dimensional space. The pointing device indicates the location of an insertion, deletion, or change. Beyond the simple manipulation of text are more elaborate tasks, such as centering, setting margins and font sizes, highlighting (boldface or underscore), and page layout.

It is possible to perform all these tasks with a keyboard by typing numbers or letters to select, entering integer coordinates to position, typing a number representing an angle to point or a number to quantify, making menu selections to select actions, and entering cursor-control commands to move around in the text. In the past, the keyboard was used for all of these purposes, but now most users employ pointing devices to perform the tasks more rapidly and with fewer errors; expert users can further improve performance by using keyboard shortcuts for tasks that are invoked frequently (e.g., Ctrl-C followed by Ctrl-V to copy and paste).

Pointing devices can be grouped into those that offer *direct control* on the screen surface, such as the touchscreen or stylus, and those that offer *indirect control* away from the screen surface, such as the mouse, trackball, joystick, graphics tablet, or touchpad. Within each category are many variations, and novel designs emerge frequently (Box 8.1).

8.3.2 Direct-control pointing devices

The lightpen was an early device that enabled users to point a tethered pen at a screen and then press a button on the pen to point at objects or draw on the screen. It was fragile, and users were required to pick up the device, so the

BOX 8.1
Pointing devices.

Direct control devices
(easy to learn and use,
but hand may obscure display)

- Lightpen
- Touchscreen
- Stylus

Indirect control devices
(take time to learn)

- Mouse
- Trackball
- Joystick
- Trackpoint
- Touchpad
- Graphics tablet

Non-standard devices and strategies
(for special purposes)

- Multitouch tablets and displays
- Bimanual input
- Eye-trackers
- Sensors
- 3D trackers
- DataGloves
- Boom Chameleon
- Haptic feedback
- Foot controls
- Tangible user interfaces
- Digital paper

Criteria for success

- Speed and accuracy
- Efficacy for task
- Learning time
- Cost and reliability
- Size and weight

lightpen was rapidly replaced by touchscreens that allowed users to interact directly with the material on the screen by touching it with a finger.

The robustness of touchscreens makes them appropriate for public-access kiosks and mobile applications. Touchscreens are often integrated into applications directed at novice users in which the keyboard can be eliminated and touch is the main interface mechanism. Designers of public-access systems value touchscreens because there are no moving parts, and durability in high-use environments is good (the touchscreen is the only input device that has survived at Walt Disney World® theme parks). Strategies have been described to provide access to touchscreen systems, such as for information kiosks or voting systems for people who are vision-impaired or blind, are hard of hearing or deaf, have trouble reading or are unable to read at all, or have physical disabilities (Vanderheiden et al., 2004; Vanderheiden, 1997). For kiosk designs, arm fatigue can be a problem, which can be addressed by tilting the screen and providing a surface on which to rest the arm.

Early touchscreen implementations had problems with imprecise pointing, as the software accepted the touch immediately (the land-on strategy), denying users the opportunity to verify the correctness of the selected spot. These early designs were based on physical pressure, impact, or interruption of a grid of infrared beams. High-precision designs (Sears and Shneiderman, 1991) dramatically improved touchscreens. The resistive, capacitive, or surface-acoustic-wave hardware often provides up to 1600×1600 pixel resolution, and the lift-off strategy enabled users to point at a single pixel. The lift-off strategy has three steps: users touch the surface, and then see a cursor that they can drag to adjust its position; when they are satisfied, they lift their fingers off the display to activate. The availability of high-precision touchscreens has opened the doors to many touchscreen applications, such as in banking, medical, or military systems; more recently, it has transformed mobile applications and multi-touch touchscreens have become available (Section 8.3.6).

With tablet PCs and mobile devices, it is natural to point to spots on the LCD surface, which can be held in the arm or hand, placed on a desk, or rested on the lap. The *stylus* is an attractive device because it is familiar and comfortable for users, and users can guide the stylus tip to the desired location while keeping the whole context in view. These advantages, however, must be balanced against the need to pick up and put down the stylus. Most stylus interfaces (also called "pen-based interfaces"), such as the Palm Pilot, are based on touchscreen technology; users can write with a stylus for more natural handwriting and increased motion control but can also use a finger for quick selection (Vogel and Baudisch, 2007). Like ordinary touchscreens, stylus interfaces misbehave when users touch the screen in two or more locations at once. To avoid this problem, devices with large touchable surfaces, such as tablet PCs, might require the use of an active stylus that can be recognized by the touch-sensitive surface. However, with this approach, users must worry about misplacing or losing the stylus.

Popular mobile devices such as the early Palm Pilot and the iPhone created a huge market for well-designed touch-only services such as address books, calendars, maps, or photo albums. Novel selection methods based on gestures and handwriting recognition are competing with pull-down–menu and direct-manipulation strategies as designers strive to create novel and attractive interfaces for this growing market (Section 8.5.4).

8.3.3 Indirect-control pointing devices

Indirect pointing devices eliminate the hand-fatigue and hand-obscuring-the-screen problems, but they require the hand to locate the device and demand more cognitive processing and hand/eye coordination to bring the onscreen cursor to the desired target.

The *mouse* is appealing because of its low cost and wide availability. The hand rests in a comfortable position, buttons on the mouse are easy to press,

FIGURE 8.6

The Apple wireless mouse on the left has only one button activated by pressing down on the whole mouse. The Microsoft Wireless IntelliMouse® (shown on the right) has two buttons with a tilt wheel between them, which can be used to scroll through documents, and two thumb buttons for backward and forward Internet browsing.

long motions can be done rapidly by moving the forearm, and positioning can be done precisely with small finger movements. However, users must grab the mouse to begin work, desk space is consumed, and the mouse wire can be annoying. Other problems are that pick-up and replace actions are necessary for long motions and some practice is required to develop skills (usually from 5 to 50 minutes, but sometimes much more for older adults or users with disabilities). The variety in terms of mouse technologies (physical, optical, or acoustic), number of buttons, placement of the sensor, weight, and size indicate that designers and users have yet to settle on one preferred design. Personal preferences and the variety of tasks to be done leave room for lively competition. The mouse may be simple or may incorporate a wheel and additional buttons to facilitate scrolling or web browsing (Fig. 8.6). Those additional mouse features can sometimes be programmed to perform common tasks of special-purpose applications, such as adjusting the focus of a microscope and switching its magnification level.

The *trackball* has sometimes been described as an upside-down mouse. It is usually implemented as a rotating ball, 1 to 15 centimeters in diameter, that moves a cursor on the screen as it is moved (Fig. 8.7). The trackball is wear-resistant and can be firmly mounted in a desk to allow users to hit the ball vigorously

FIGURE 8.7

The Logitech Trackman Wheel uses a trackball (http://www.logitech.com/).

and to make it spin. Trackballs have been embedded in control panels for air-traffic–control or museum information systems, and they are commonly used in video-game controllers.

The *joystick*, whose long history began in aircraft-control devices and early computer games, has dozens of versions with varying stick lengths and thicknesses, displacement forces and distances, anchoring strategies for bases, and placement relative to the keyboard and screen. Joysticks are appealing for tracking purposes (to follow or guide an object on a screen), partly because of the relatively small displacements needed to move a cursor, the ease of direction changes, and the opportunity to combine the joystick with additional buttons, wheels, and triggers (Fig. 8.8).

The *directional pad* (or D-pad) originated in game consoles and consists of four directional arrows arranged in a cross with a trigger button in the center. An example is the Wii remote control (Figs. 1.9 and 8.9). This system is also used in mobile devices for navigation in menus.

The *trackpoint* is a small isometric joystick embedded in keyboards between the letters G and H (Fig. 8.1). It is sensitive to pressure and does not move. It has a rubber tip to facilitate finger contact, and with modest practice, users can quickly and accurately use it to control the cursor while keeping their fingers on the keyboard home position. The trackpoint is particularly effective for applications such as word processors that require constant switches between the

FIGURE 8.8

A Saitek™ X45 Flight System used to control the X-Plane™ flight simulator. It combines a throttle and a joystick for two-handed operation (http://www.saitek.com, http://www.x-plane.com).

FIGURE 8.9

The Nintendo Wii remote controller includes a three-axis accelerometer that detects movement in three dimensions. Users can control video games with small and large gestures; for example, here twisting the arm and wrist to steer a car.

keyboard and pointing device. Because of their small size, trackpoints can easily be combined with other devices such as keyboards or even mice to facilitate two-dimensional scrolling.

A *touchpad* (a touchable surface of at least 5×8 centimeters) offers the convenience and precision of a touchscreen while keeping the user's hand off the display surface. Users can make quick movements for long-distance traversals and can gently rock their fingers for precise positioning before lifting off. Often built-in below the keyboard (Fig. 8.1), the touchpad can be used with the thumbs while keeping the hands in typing position. The lack of moving parts and the thin profile make touchpads appealing for portable computers.

The *graphics tablet* is a touch-sensitive surface separate from the screen, usually laid flat on the desk/table or in the user's lap. This separation allows for comfortable hand positioning and keeps the users' hands off the screen. The graphics tablet is appealing when users' hands can remain with the device for long periods without switching to a keyboard. Furthermore, the graphics tablet permits a surface even larger than the screen to be covered with printing to indicate available choices, thereby providing guidance to novice users and preserving valuable screen space. Limited data entry can be done with a graphics tablet. The graphics tablet can be operated by placement of a finger, pencil, puck, or stylus using acoustic, electronic, or contact position sensing. Wireless pens allow a higher freedom that is appreciated by artists using drawing programs (Fig. 8.10).

Among these indirect pointing devices, the mouse has been the greatest success story. Given its rapid, high-precision pointing abilities and comfortable hand position, the modest training period is only a small impediment to its use. Most desktop computer systems offer a mouse, but the battle for the laptop continues, with many vendors offering multiple pointing devices on a single machine.

8.3.4 Comparison of pointing devices

Early studies found that direct pointing devices such as a lightpen or touchscreen were often the fastest but the least accurate devices. Decades of studies have consistently shown the merits of the mouse over alternative devices for speed and accuracy. The trackpoint has been found to be slower than the mouse due to tremors during fine finger movements (Mithal and Douglas, 1996). Trackballs and touchpads fall somewhere inbetween. Users' tasks matter when comparing devices. For example, when browsing the World Wide Web, users are constantly involved in both scrolling and pointing. One study showed that a mouse with a finger wheel did not improve users' performance over a standard mouse. However, performance increased with an isometric joystick mounted on a mouse (Zhai et al., 1997). New accuracy measures for precision pointing tasks (MacKenzie et al., 2001) that capture fine aspects of movement behavior during

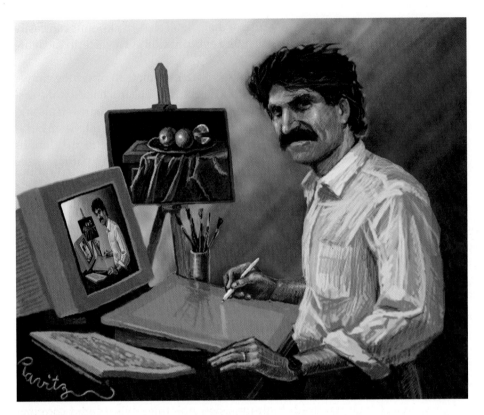

FIGURE 8.10
A digital painting created by Larry Ravitz using Adobe Photoshop and a Wacom®
tablet. The Wacom pressure-sensitive stylus and graphics tablet allow the precise
pointing and accurate control that artists need.

a pointing task such as target re-entry or movement variability might provide a
better understanding of the benefits and limitations of each device.

The usual belief is that for selecting objects pointing devices are faster than
cursor-movement keys, but this assertion depends on the task. When a few
(2 to 10) targets are on the screen and the cursor can be made to jump from one
target to the next, using the cursor jump keys can be faster than using pointing
devices. For short distances and for tasks that mix typing and pointing, cursor
keys have also been shown to be faster than and preferred to the mouse. Many
users never learn keyboard shortcuts (e.g., Ctrl-Z to undo), despite the fact that
menu selections can be performed much faster using those shortcuts than by
using a pointing device.

Users with motor disabilities often prefer joysticks and trackballs over mice,
as their location remains fixed, they have a small footprint (allowing them to be

mounted on wheelchairs), and they can be operated by small residual movements. Touch-sensitive devices are useful when applying force is a difficult—for instance, for users with motor disabilities—but designers should attempt to detect inadvertent or uncontrolled movements and smooth out trajectories. Using active target areas that are larger than the button or icon to be selected is effective to shorten selection time and reduce frustration for every user and, in some cases, might be all that is needed to render an application usable by a much wider audience.

Pointing devices are extremely challenging for users who have vision impairments. Well-designed cursors of adjustable size and shape may help users with limited vision impairments, but indirect-control devices such as the mouse are simply not practical for users with severe vision impairments who have to rely on the keyboard. Alternative keyboard or keypad navigation options should be provided whenever possible. Touchscreen interfaces can more easily be explored and memorized when speech synthesis or sonification is available to describe the display, read menu options, and confirm selections. For example, in a touchscreen voting kiosk, users can use arrow keys to navigate through lists of candidates whose names are read aloud via headphones (Fig. 8.11). Successful examples demonstrate that it is possible to design powerful systems that are truly accessible to the general public, including users with a wide range of disabilities (Vanderheiden et al., 2004). Finally, *tactile graphics* can be produced by using thermal paper expansion machines and placed on top of touchscreens for use by blind users (Fig. 8.12).

In summary, individual differences and the user tasks are critical when selecting a pointing device. The touchscreen and trackball are durable in public-access, shop-floor, and laboratory applications. The mouse, trackball, trackpoint, graphics tablet, and touchpad are effective for pixel-level pointing. Pens are appreciated for drawing and handwriting, and simple gestures can be used to specify actions and quantify their parameters. Tabletop devices are attractive when collaboration between users is important. Cursor jump keys remain attractive when there are a small number of targets. Joysticks are appealing for games or specialized navigation applications.

8.3.5 Fitts' Law

A predictive model of time required to point at an object would be a great help to designers of interfaces and pointing devices. Such a predictive model would help designers decide on the optimal locations and sizes of buttons and other elements when laying out screens and would indicate which pointing devices are best suited to performing common tasks. Fortunately, a model of human hand movement developed by Paul Fitts (1954) has turned out to be well suited to user interfaces. Fitts noticed that the time required to complete hand movements was dependent on the distance users had to move, D, and the target size,

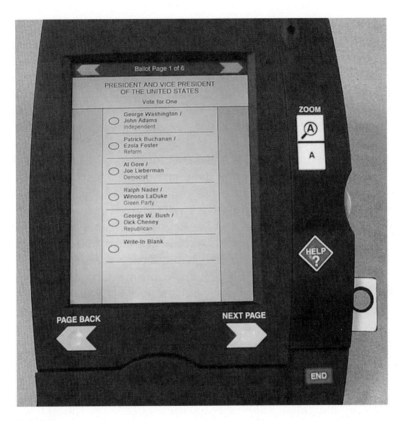

FIGURE 8.11
Users of this touchscreen voting tablet need only touch any text on the screen to have it read aloud, with the sound communicated to them via headphones. Touching the check box marks the vote, with verbal confirmation if headphones are used. Users who are completely blind or have severe physical disabilities that prevent them from using the touchscreen (even with voice) can use a detachable keypad—with or without voice. The keypad also allows connection of custom switches voters bring with them (http://www.trace.wisc.edu/).

W. Doubling the distance (say, from 10 cm to 20 cm) resulted in longer completion times, but not twice as long. Increasing the target's size (e.g., from 1 cm² to 2 cm²) enabled users to point at it more rapidly.

Since the time to start and stop moving is constant, an effective equation for the movement time (*MT*) for a given device, such as a mouse, turns out to be

$$MT = a + b \log_2 (D/W + 1)$$

where *a* approximates the start/stop time in seconds for a given device and *b* measures the inherent speed of the device. Both *a* and *b* need to be determined

FIGURE 8.12

A blind student uses a Touch Graphics tactile map mounted on a touchscreen. Audio descriptions provide information about regions of the map (http://www. touchgraphics.com/).

experimentally for each device. For example, if a were 300 milliseconds, b were 200 msec/bit, D were 14 cm, and W were 2 cm, then the movement time MT would be $300 + 200 \log_2(14/2 + 1)$, which equals 900 milliseconds.

Several versions of Fitts' law are used, but this equation has been demonstrated to provide good predictions in a wide range of situations. The variations are due to differences such as the direction of motion (horizontal or vertical), device weight (heavier devices are harder to move), device grasp, shape of targets, and arm position (on a table or in the air). MacKenzie (1992) lucidly describes what Fitts' law is, how it has been applied, and refinements for cases such as two-dimensional pointing. In our studies of high-precision touchscreens (Sears and Shneiderman, 1991), we found that in addition to the gross arm movement predicted by Fitts there was also a fine-tuning motion of the fingers to move in on small targets such as single pixels. A three-component equation was thus more suited for the precision-pointing movement time (*PPMT*):

$$PPMT = a + b \log_2 (D/W + 1) + c \log_2 (D / W).$$

The third term, time for fine tuning, increases as the target width, *W*, decreases. This extension to Fitts' law is quite understandable; it suggests that the precision-pointing movement time consists of the start/stop time (*a*), a time for gross movement, and a time for fine adjustment. Other studies deal with a greater range of arm motion with pointing in three-dimensional space or with two-thumb text entry.

Fitts' law is well established for adult users, but it may need refinements for special populations such as young children or older adults. In one study, 13 four-year-olds, 13 five-year-olds, and 13 young adults performed point-and-click selection tasks (Hourcade et al., 2004). As expected, age had a significant effect on speed and accuracy (and of course trajectories, as shown in Fig. 8.13). A detailed analysis showed that Fitts' law models children well for the first time they enter the target, but not for the time of final selection.

The open problem remains: How can we design devices that produce smaller constants for the predictive equation? One study has shown that multiscale pointing with zooming works best with two-handed input and a constant zoom speed (Guiard et al., 2001). Another study looked at crossing-based interfaces in which targets are merely crossed instead of pointed at. The target-crossing completion time was found to be shorter than or equal to pointing performance under the same index of difficulty and depended on the type of task performed (Accot and Zhai, 2002). The quest for faster selection times continues.

8.3.6 Nonstandard interaction and devices

The popularity of pointing devices and the quest for new ways to engage diverse users for diverse tasks has led to provocative innovations. Improving the match between the task and the device and refining the input plus feedback strategies are common themes (Kortum, 2008; Jacob et al., 1994).

Multiple-touch touchscreens that allow a single user to use both hands or multiple fingers at once (Han, 2005) or allow multiple users to work together on a shared surface (Hinrichs et al., 2006) have been slow to emerge but are now becoming available (examples include Microsoft Surface and TouchTable). More precise item selection can be achieved by using two fingers: The cursor appears between the two fingers and its position can be adjusted by spreading the fingers apart (Benko et al., 2006). Circle Twelve's DiamondTouch™ display allows the application to tell which user touched the screen, allowing better identification of personal versus collaborative interactions. With horizontal tabletop displays, users can be positioned anywhere around the table, so applications that can be

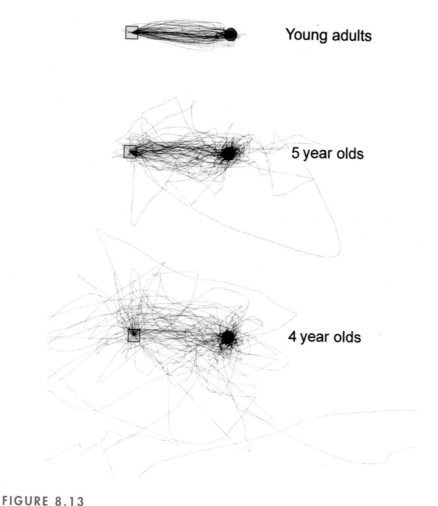

Young adults

5 year olds

4 year olds

FIGURE 8.13

Tracing the trajectory of the pointer during a repeated target-selection task illustrates the dramatic difference between children's and young adults' use of the mouse (Hourcade et al., 2004).

used in any orientation are desirable (Fig. 8.14). Physical objects might also be used to mark positions and facilitate design sessions. Using stereoscopic displays, volumetric displays, or head-mounted displays, it may become possible to design effective 3D tabletop interactions (Grossman and Wigdor, 2007). On a smaller scale, the iPhone's introduction of multitouch displays on mobile devices contributed to the successful use of simple gestures (e.g., users can spread apart two fingers to zoom in on an image).

FIGURE 8.14

On this 6-megapixel SMART tabletop display, users work together to organize photos. A slow-moving stream (called Current) runs on the edge of the display, bringing objects closer to users. Storage bins separate personal and shared space (Hinrichs et al., 2006).

Bimanual input can facilitate multitasking or compound tasks. A theory of bimanual input (Guiard, 1987) suggests that the nondominant hand sets a frame of reference in which the dominant hand operates in a more precise fashion. A natural application of bimanual operation for desktop applications is that the nondominant hand selects actions (for example, the Fill command of a paint program) while the dominant hand precisely selects the objects of the operation (Section 6.7.4 for more on designs combining menus and direct manipulation).

Since users' hands might be busy on the keyboard, designers have explored alternative methods for selection and pointing. *Foot controls* are popular with rock-music performers, organists, dentists, and car drivers, so maybe computer users could benefit from them as well. A foot mouse was tested and was found to take about twice as much time to use as a hand-operated mouse, but benefits in special applications may exist—for example, switches and pedals activated by foot might be effective to specify modes.

Eye-trackers are gaze-detecting controllers that use video-camera image recognition of the pupil position to give 1- or 2-degree accuracy (Fig. 4.3). Fixations of 200 to 600 milliseconds are used to make selections. Unfortunately, the "Midas touch problem" intrudes, since every gaze has the potential to activate an unintended command. Combining eye tracking with manual input is one way to address this problem, but for now, eye tracking remains mostly a research and evaluation tool (Section 4.3.1) and a possible aid for users with motor disabilities (Wobbrock et al., 2008).

Multiple-degree-of-freedom devices can sense multiple dimensions of spatial position and orientation. Control over three-dimensional objects seems a natural application, but comparisons with other strategies reveal low precision and slow responses (Zhai, 1998). Support for virtual reality (Chapter 5) is one motivation, but many design, medical, and other tasks may require three-dimensional input or even six degrees of freedom to indicate a position and an orientation. Commercial tracking devices include the Logitech company's 3Dconnexion®, Ascension®, Intersense®, and Polhemus™.

Ubiquitous computing and *tangible user interfaces* (Abowd and Mynatt, 2000; Ullmer and Ishii, 2000) depend on embedding sensing technologies into the environment. For example, active badges with Radio Frequency Identification (RFID) tags can trigger the preloading of personal files into a room's computer when users enter a room. The positioning of physical objects can specify modes or trigger actions (Figs. 5.11 and 5.12). Ambient light, sound, or airflow can be modified to present a small amount of information to users. Entertainment and artistic applications use video cameras or body sensors to track body positions and create enticing user experiences. Early explorations by performance artist Vincent John Vincent led to three-dimensional environments for theatrical exploration such as Mandala, in which performers or amateur users touch images of harps, bells, drums, or cymbals, and the instruments respond. Myron Krueger's artificial realities contain friendly video-projected cartoon-like creatures that playfully crawl on your arm or approach your outstretched hand. Such environments invite participation, and the serious research aspects fade as joyful exploration takes over and you step inside the computer's world (Section 5.6). StoryRoom is another such application that enables children to actively construct their own interactive environments, using props and magic wands to create stories that other children are invited to experience (Montemayor et al., 2004).

Even *paper* can be used as an input device. Early applications demonstrated the benefits of capturing annotations on large documents such as blueprints or lab notebooks with video cameras (Mackay et al., 2002). Pens such as the Livescribe™ Pulse™ Smartpen (Fig. 8.15) or the Logitech io2™ digital pen with Anoto® functionality facilitate interaction, particularly in mobile situations. The pen has a small camera in its tip, and it records pen strokes drawn on a special paper printed with a unique pattern that identifies the location of each stroke.

FIGURE 8.15

The Livescribe Pulse Smartpen with Anoto technology records the strokes of ink written on digital paper and the data is transferred wirelessly to the computer. The 96 × 18 OLED display can provide feedback to users (here a Spanish translation). A microphone allows users to record audio at the time an annotation is being made to be replayed later via the embedded speaker by tapping on the annotation (http://www.livescribe.com/).

The handwriting can then be transferred to a computer or a mobile phone. The ease of learning might help novice users: Paper Augmented Digital Documents (PADDs) can be edited both in digital and paper form (Liao et al., 2008), or translations can be requested by writing words on paper (Fig. 8.15). We have used digital pens in our research to allow grandparents to share notes and calendar information with distant family members.

Mobile devices can also be used as input devices. For example, Carnegie Mellon University's Pebbles project explored how mobile devices can be used as input devices to communicate with personal computers, other mobile devices, home appliances, automobiles, or factory equipment (Myers, 2005). Mobile devices can act as intelligent universal remote controls, potentially empowering all users by reading aloud product information or menu options, translating instructions written in a foreign language, or offering speech recognition when needed. Finally, the images captured by cameras of mobile phones can be used as input to augmented-reality applications (Rohs and Oulasvirta, 2008).

Sensors added to handheld devices can enrich the interaction with the devices themselves—for example, *accelerometers* allow the Apple iPhone to detect changes in the device's orientation, causing the display to switch dynamically between portait and landscape orientations. As users become familiar with gesture interaction, designers may be able to find additional natural uses of movement information. Users may be able to zoom and pan on a map by adjusting the proximity or lateral position of mobile devices in front of them. Tilting the device could scroll through a list of names, and bringing the device near the ear could answer an incoming call (Hinckley et al., 2000). The remote control of the Nintendo Wii video-game console includes a three-axis accelerometer that can detect movement in three dimensions and respond to gestures. For example, to hit a tennis ball, users swing the controller like a racket with a realistic arm motion. The Wii has inspired many applications that require users to be more active and has successfully attracted more female and older adult users to video games (Fig. 8.9).

Another example of an innovative device is Measurand's ShapeTape, which provides bend and twist information along a one-meter tape, allowing the shape of the tape to be reconstructed in three dimensions for creating or manipulating curves or for tracking angles of arms and legs in motion-capture applications (Grossman et al., 2002).

Devices engineered for particular applications sometimes find unexpected success in other domains. Intel's toy optical microscope, designed for children's exploration, became a huge success as it could help stamp collectors to document their collections and graphic artists to collect abstract patterns (Fig. 8.16). Also, popular game controllers such as the Logitech WingMan Rumblepad™ can be reprogrammed to provide haptic feedback about boundary crossings or color intensity to users with vision impairments.

FIGURE 8.16

The QX5+™ Computer Microscope from Digital Blue™ offers 10x to 200x magnification and takes pictures. It allows children to explore the world around them, and applications for stamp collectors, paleontologists, and watch-repair businesses have also taken advantage of this low-cost unconventional input device (www.digiblue.com).

The VPL *DataGlove* appeared in 1987 and attracted researchers, game developers, cyberspace adventurers, and virtual-reality devotees (Section 5.6). Descendants of the original DataGlove are still often made of sleek black spandex with attached fiber-optic sensors to measure angles of finger joints (Fig. 5.18). The displayed feedback can show the relative placement of each finger; thus, commands such as a closed fist, open hand, index-finger pointing, and thumbs-up gesture can be recognized. Combined with a hand-tracker, complete three-dimensional placement and orientation can be recorded. Devotees claim that the naturalness of gestures will enable use by many keyboard-averse or mouse-phobic users. But while the simple gestures of the Nintendo Wii games are easily learned because their number is small and they mimic the actions being simulated (e.g., the swing of a golf club or the rotation of a wheel), users require substantial training to master more than half a dozen gestures, especially if they do not map to naturally occurring gestures. Still, gestural input with the glove can make special applications possible, such as the recognition of American Sign Language or virtual musical performances.

An alternative to the goggles-and-gloves approach is to allow users to step up to a viewer with handles that can be used to shift vantage points within the range of a mechanical boom. The display updates to create the illusion that the user is moving in three dimensions, and users have an immersive experience without the heavy and confining head-mounted goggles. The Boom Chameleon project combines a boom with a touchscreen and allows voice and gesture interaction to provide a compelling 3D annotation environment (Tsang et al., 2002; Fig. 5.22). Glove-mounted devices and tethered balls are being refined, and other graspable user interfaces are still open for exploration (Fitzmaurice et al., 1995).

Pointing devices with *haptic feedback* are an intriguing research direction (Kortum, 2008). Several technologies have been employed to allow users to push a mouse or other device and to feel resistance (for example, as they cross a window boundary) or a hard wall (e.g., when navigating a maze). Three-dimensional versions, such as SensAble Technology's PHANTOM, are still more intriguing, but commercial applications are slow to emerge. Because sound and vibrations are often a good substitute for haptic feedback, the use of advanced haptic devices remains limited to special-purpose applications (such as training surgeons for heart surgery), while devices using simple vibrations have become mainstream in game controllers.

Finally, custom devices can be created from scratch using an endless variety of sensors. Users with motor disabilities can control wheelchairs, home devices, or computer applications using custom-fitted sensors chosen to best match their remaining motor abilities. Switches can be triggered by small head or shoulder movements, a light blow of air in a tube, the blink of an eye, and even faint myoelectric currents generated when muscles are being tensed.

8.4 Speech and Auditory Interfaces

The dream of speaking to computers and having computers speak has lured many researchers and visionaries. Arthur C. Clarke's 1968 fantasy of the HAL 9000 computer in the book and movie *2001: A Space Odyssey* has set the standard for performance of computers in science fiction and for some advanced developers. The reality is more complex and sometimes more surprising than the dream. Hardware designers have made dramatic progress with speech recognition, generation, and processing, but current successes are sobering compared to the science-fiction fantasy (Gardner-Bonneau and Blanchard, 2007; Balentine, 2007). Even science-fiction writers have shifted their scenarios, as shown by the reduced use of voice interaction in favor of larger visual displays in Star Trek's *Voyager* or movies such as *Minority Report.*

The vision of computers chatting leisurely with users now seems more of an uninformed fantasy than a desirable reality. Practical applications of speech interaction succeed when they serve users' needs to work rapidly with low cognitive load and low error rates. Even as technical problems are being solved and the recognition algorithms are improving, designers are reluctantly recognizing that voice commanding is more demanding of users' working memory than is hand/eye coordination, and thus may be more disruptive to users while they are carrying out tasks. Speech requires use of limited resources, while hand/eye coordination is processed elsewhere in the brain, enabling a higher level of parallel processing. Planning and problem solving can proceed in parallel with hand/eye coordination, but they are more difficult to accomplish while speaking (Ashcraft, 2005).

Unfortunately, background noise and variations in user speech performance make the challenge of *speech recognition* still greater. By contrast, *speech store and forward* and *speech generation* are satisfyingly predictable, low cost, and widely available because of the telephone's ubiquity and the compactness of speech chips. However, every designer must cope with the three obstacles to speech output: the slow pace of speech output when compared to visual displays, the ephemeral nature of speech, and the difficulty in scanning/searching (Box 8.2). Speech store and forward is a success because the emotional content and prosody in human speech is compelling in voice messaging, museum tours, and instructional contexts.

The benefits to people with certain physical disabilities are rewarding to see, but general users of office or personal computers are not rushing to implement speech input and output devices. Speech is the bicycle of user-interface design: It is great fun to use and has an important role, but it can carry only a light load. Sober advocates know that it will be tough to replace the automobile: graphical user interfaces.

Speech enthusiasts can claim success in telephony, where digital circuitry has increased the capacity of networks and improved voice quality. Cellular

BOX 8.2

Speech systems.

Opportunities	Obstacles to speech recognition

Opportunities

- When users have vision impairments
- When the speaker's hands are busy
- When mobility is required
- When the speaker's eyes are occupied
- When harsh or cramped conditions preclude use of a keyboard

Technologies

- Speech store and forward
- Discrete-word recognition
- Continuous-speech recognition
- Voice information systems
- Speech generation

Obstacles to speech recognition

- Increased cognitive load compared to pointing
- Interference from noisy environments
- Unstable recognition across changing users, environments, and time

Obstacles to speech output

- Slow pace of speech output when compared to visual displays
- Ephemeral nature of speech
- Difficulty in scanning/searching

telephones have been a huge success in developed countries and often bring telephone service rapidly to less developed countries. Internet telephony, often called Voice over IP (Internet Protocol), is also becoming increasingly prevalent, providing many users with low-cost long-distance service. The immediacy and emotional impact of a telephone conversation is a compelling component of human-human communication.

For designers of human-computer interaction systems, speech and audio technologies have at least five variations: discrete-word recognition, continuous-speech recognition, voice information systems, speech generation, and non-speech auditory interfaces. These components can be combined in creative ways, ranging from simple systems that merely play back or generate a message to complex interactions that accept speech commands, generate speech feedback, provide sonification of scientific data, and allow annotation and editing of stored speech.

A deeper understanding of neurological processing of sounds would be helpful to designers in this field. Why does listening to Mozart symphonies encourage creative work, whereas listening to radio news reports suspends it? Is the linguistic processing needed to absorb a radio news report disruptive, whereas background Mozart is somehow invigorating? Of course, listening to Mozart with the serious intention of a musicologist would be completely absorbing of mental resources. Are there uses of sound or speech and ways of shifting attention that might be less disruptive or even supportive of symbolic processing, analytic reasoning, or graphic designing? Could sound be a more useful component of drawing software than of word processors?

8.4.1 Discrete-word recognition

Discrete-word–recognition devices recognize individual words spoken by a specific person; they can work with 90 to 98% reliability for 100- to 10,000-word or larger vocabularies. *Speaker-dependent training*, in which users repeat the full vocabulary once or twice, is a part of many systems. Such training yields higher accuracy than in *speaker-independent* systems, but the elimination of training expands the scope of commercial applications. Quiet environments, head-mounted microphones, and careful choice of vocabularies improve recognition rates in both cases.

Applications for users with disabilities have enabled paralyzed, bedridden, or injured people to broaden the horizons of their lives. They can control wheelchairs, operate equipment, or use personal computers for a variety of tasks. Similarly, applications for older adults or cognitively or emotionally challenged individuals might allow them to have a greater level of independence, restore lost skills, and regain confidence in their capabilities. Unfortunately, however, speech impairments are often associated with other disabilities and will greatly limit those benefits.

Telephone-based information services have flourished in recent years, providing weather, sports, stock market, and movie information. Telephone companies offer voice-dialing services, even on cell phones, to allow users simply to say "Call Mom" and be connected. However, difficulties with training for multiple users in a household, user reluctance to use speech commands, and unreliable recognition are apparently slowing acceptance, even in cars, where hands-free operation is a big advantage.

Phone-based recognition of numbers, yes/no answers, and selections from voice menus is successful and increasingly applied. However, full-sentence commands such as "Reserve two seats on the first flight tomorrow from New York to Washington" are just moving from a research challenge into commercial use. Several proposals for structured speech have been made, but even if users learn a limited grammar, such as <action> <object> <qualifier> ("Reserve seats two" "Depart New York tomorrow"), interaction is difficult.

Many advanced development efforts have tested speech recognition in military aircraft, medical operating rooms, training labs, and offices. The results reveal problems with recognition rates even for speaker-dependent training systems when background sounds change, when users are ill or under stress, and when words in the vocabulary are similar (dime/time or Houston/Austin).

Other applications have been successful when at least one of these conditions exist:

- Speaker's hands are busy.
- Mobility is required.
- Speaker's eyes are occupied.
- Harsh or cramped conditions preclude use of a keyboard (for example, in underwater or rescue operations).

Example applications include systems for aircraft-engine inspectors, who wear wireless microphones as they walk around the engine opening coverplates or adjusting components. They can issue orders, read serial numbers, or retrieve previous maintenance records by using a 35-word vocabulary. Implementers of such challenging applications should consider conducting speaker-dependent training in the task environment.

For common computing applications, when a display is used, speech input has marginal benefits. Studies of users controlling cursor movement by voice confirm slower performance for cursor-movement tasks such as button clicking and web browsing (Sears et al., 2002).

On the other hand, a study of drawing program users showed that allowing users to select one of 19 commands by voice instead of by selecting from a palette improved performance times by an average of 21% (Pausch and Leatherby, 1991). The advantage seems to have been gained by avoiding the time-consuming and distracting effort of moving the cursor repeatedly from the diagram to the tool palette and back. Although overall using voice commands was faster than mouse pointing, mainly due to mouse acquisition time, error rates were higher for voice users in tasks that required high short-term–memory load. This unexpected result was explained by psychologists, who pointed out that short-term memory is sometimes referred to as "acoustic memory." Speaking commands is more demanding of working memory than is the hand/eye coordination needed for mouse pointing, which is handled in parallel by other parts of the brain (Ashcraft, 2005).

This phenomenon may explain the slower acceptance of speech interfaces as compared with graphical user interfaces; speaking commands or listening disrupts planning and problem solving more than selecting actions from a menu with a mouse does. This was noted by product evaluators for an IBM dictation package, who wrote that "thought, for many people, is very closely linked to language. In keyboarding, users can continue to hone their words while their fingers output an earlier version. In dictation, users may experience more interference between outputting their initial thought and elaborating on it." (Danis et al., 1994).

An important success story for speech recognition is in toys, where dolls and small robots may speak to users and respond to human voice commands.

Low-cost speech chips and compact microphones and speakers have enabled designers to include playful systems in high-volume products. Errors often add to the fun and charm of such toys and present a challenge in games. Proposals for voice-controlled consumer appliances have been made but are yet to be successful.

Current research projects are devoted to improving recognition rates in difficult conditions, eliminating the need for speaker-dependent training, and increasing the vocabularies handled to 100,000 or more words. Speech-based text entry for mobile devices is also being refined (Price and Sears, 2005), but text-entry rates remain lower using speech than using small keyboards, such as those found in devices like the Blackberry. The newly released Google search application for the iPhone might be a significant step in finding useful applications of voice input on mobile devices. Users can speak search terms such as "movie theater college park" and select among alternatives or correct partial mistakes with the onscreen keyboard instead of typing all the terms. Using extensive search history and location information can improve results; while dialects and noisy environments remain problematic.

Speech recognition for discrete words works well for special-purpose applications, but it does not serve as a general interaction medium. Keyboards, function keys, and pointing devices with direct manipulation are often more rapid, and the actions or commands can be made visible for easy editing. Also, error handling and appropriate feedback with voice input are difficult and slow. However, combinations of voice and direct manipulation may be useful, as indicated by Pausch and Leatherby's study.

8.4.2 Continuous-speech recognition

In Stanley Kubrick's movie "2001: A Space Odyssey", HAL's ability to understand the astronauts' spoken words and even to read their lips was an appealing fantasy, but the reality is more sobering. Many research projects have pursued *continuous-speech recognition*, and widespread hope for commercially successful products flourished during the dot-com boom. Consumers bought the heavily promoted products, but exaggerated promises led to much disappointment. Speech-dictation products work, but error rates and error repair are serious problems (Feng et al., 2006). In addition, the cognitive burdens of dictation interfere with planning and sentence formation, often reducing the quality of documents when compared with typewritten composition.

A major difficulty for software designers is recognizing the boundaries between spoken words, because normal speech patterns blur the boundaries. Other problems are diverse accents, variable speaking rates, disruptive background noise, and changing emotional intonation. The slips produced by speech-recognition programs make for entertaining sections in product reviews in the trade press. Of course, the most difficult problem is matching the semantic interpretation and contextual understanding that humans apply easily to predict and disambiguate words. This problem was nicely highlighted in one of the few humorous titles of IBM Technical Reports: "How to wreck a nice beach" (a play on "How to recognize speech").

To cope with some of these problems, the IBM ViaVoice® speech-dictation system is "trained" by users reading standard passages of text (for example, excerpts from *Treasure Island*) for 15 to 30 minutes. Specialized systems for medical workers (e.g., the Dragon® NaturallySpeaking™ Medical system), lawyers, and certain business professionals have become commercial successes, with systems such as the Philips/Nuance PSRS producing versions in at least 25 languages. Ironically, technical fields with a lot of jargon are good candidates because of the distinctive nature of the terminology.

Continuous-speech–recognition systems enable users to dictate letters and compose reports verbally for automatic transcription. Review, correction, and revision are usually accomplished with keyboards and displays. Users need practice in dictation and seem to do best with speech input when preparing standard reports. Creative writing and thoughtful articles require full use of the scarce cognitive resources of human working memory. These tasks are often done best with keyboard entry, and some users still prefer the familiarity of pen and paper. Writers can improve their dictation skills with practice, however, and developers may improve system accuracy, error-correction strategies, and voice-editing methods.

Continuous-speech–recognition systems also enable automatic scanning and retrieval from radio or television programs, court proceedings, lectures, or telephone calls for specific words or topics (Olsson and Oard, 2007). Summaries of audio conversations can even be generated (Basu et al., 2008). These applications can be highly successful and beneficial even when there are errors. Generation of closed-caption text for television programs is also economically advantageous; errors can be irritating, but they are acceptable for most television viewers. The indexing of audio and video archives can also be facilitated by continuous-speech recognition and do not require real-time performance.

Using voice recognition for identification purposes is a workable feature for security systems, too. Users are asked to speak a novel phrase, and the system ascertains which of the registered users is speaking. However, ensuring robust performance, coping with users with colds, and dealing with noisy environments are still challenges. Voice graphs are accepted in courtrooms, and they may become useful in security systems.

Although many companies and research groups have made progress, the following evaluation (Peacocke and Graf, 1990) still seems valid: "Comfortable and natural communication in a general setting (no constraints on what you can say and how you say it) is beyond us for now, posing a problem too difficult to solve."

8.4.3 Voice information systems

The appeal of the human voice as a source of information and as a basis for communication is strong. Stored speech is commonly used to provide telephone-based information about tourist sites and government services and for after-hours messages from organizations. These voice information systems, often called Inter-active Voice Response (IVR), can provide good customer service at low cost if proper development methods and metrics are used (Suhm and Peterson, 2002). Voice prompts guide users so they can press keys to check on airline flight departure/arrival times, order drug prescription refills, or reserve theater tickets. The use of speech recognition to shortcut through menu trees can be successful when users know the names of what they seek, such as a city, person, or stock name. However, users become frustrated when the menu structures become complex and deep, or when long voice information segments contain irrelevant information (Section 6.8). The slow pace of voice output, the ephemeral nature of speech, and the difficulty in scanning/searching remain great challenges, but voice information systems are widely used because they enable services that would otherwise be too expensive; hiring well-trained customer-service representatives available 24 hours a day is not practical for many organizations.

Voice information technologies are also used in popular personal voicemail systems. These telephone-based speech systems enable storing and forwarding of spoken messages with user commands entered with keypads. Users can receive messages, replay messages, reply to the caller, forward messages to other users, delete messages, or archive messages. The automatic elimination of silences and the increase of replay speed, along with frequency shifting to maintain original frequency ranges, can cut listening time in half. Voicemail technology works reliably, is fairly low cost, and is generally liked by users. Problems arise mainly because of the awkwardness of using the 12-key telephone pad for commands, the need to dial in to check whether messages have been left, and the potential for too many "junk" telephone messages because of the ease of broadcasting a message to many people. Some e-mail developers believe that speech recognition for user commands may enable users to gain telephone-based access to their e-mail messages. However, designers are still struggling to find the right balance between guided instruction and user control (Walker et al., 1998). Even if they find good solutions to command input, the three obstacles of voice output (Box 8.2) raise questions about the utility of this application.

Audio recorders are moving towards digital approaches, with small handheld voice note-takers carving out a successful consumer market. Credit-card–sized devices that cost less than $50 can store and randomly access an hour of voice-quality notes. More ambitious handheld devices, such as Apple's iPod, enable users to manage large audio databases and retrieve selected music segments or recorded lecture segments.

Audio tours in museums and audio books have been successful because they allow users to control the pace, while conveying the curator's enthusiasm or author's emotion. Educational psychologists conjecture that if several senses (sight, touch, hearing) are engaged, learning can be facilitated. Adding a spoken voice to an instructional system or an online help system may improve the learning process. Adding voice annotation to a document may make it easier for teachers to comment on student papers or for business executives to leave detailed responses or instructions. But again, the cognitive burdens for speakers, the difficulty in editing voice annotations, and other obstacles (Box 8.2) may mean that adoption will be limited.

8.4.4 Speech generation

Speech generation is a successful technology with widespread application in consumer products and telephone applications (Pitt and Edwards, 2003). Inexpensive, compact, reliable systems using digitized speech segments (also called "canned speech") have been used in automobile navigation systems ("Turn right onto route M1"), Internet services ("You've got mail"), utility-control rooms ("Danger, temperature rising"), and children's games.

In some cases, the novelty wears off, leading to removal of the speech generation. Talking supermarket checkout machines that read out products and prices were found to violate shoppers' sense of privacy about purchases and to be too noisy. Similarly, annoying warnings from cameras ("Too dark—use flash") and automobiles ("Your door is ajar") were replaced with gentler tones and red-light indicators. Spoken warnings in cockpits and control rooms are still used because they are omnidirectional and elicit rapid responses. However, even in these environments, warnings are sometimes missed or are in competition with human-human communication.

When algorithms are used to generate the sound (synthesis), the intonation may sound robot-like and distracting. The quality of the sound can be improved when phonemes, words, and phrases from digitized human speech can be smoothly integrated into meaningful sentences. However, for some applications, a computer-like sound may be preferred. For example, the robot-like sounds used in the Atlanta airport subway drew more attention than did a tape recording of a human giving directions.

Applications for the blind are an important success story. Text-to-speech utilities like the built-in Microsoft Windows Narrator can be used to read passages of text in web browsers and word processors. Screen readers like Freedom Scientific's JAWS allow users with visual impairments to productively navigate between windows, select applications, browse graphical interfaces, and of course read text. Such tools rely on textual descriptions being made available for visual elements (labels for icons and image descriptions for graphics). Reading speed is adjustable, to speed up interaction when needed.

Book readers are also widely used in libraries. Patrons can place a book on a copierlike device that scans the text and does an acceptable job of reading it. Speech generation for graphical user interfaces and voice browsers for web applications have opened many doors for vision-impaired users. Speech-enabled readers for documents, newspapers, statistical data, and even maps continue to be improved.

Web-based voice applications are also seen as promising by many developers. Standards for voice tagging of web pages (VoiceXML™ and Speech Application Language Tags, or SALT) and improved software could enable several innovative applications. For example, cell-phone users could access web information through combinations of visual displays and speech-generation output.

Speech generation and digitized speech segments are usually preferable when the messages are simple and short, deal with events in time, and require an immediate response (Michaelis and Wiggins, 1982). Speech becomes advantageous to users when their visual channels are overloaded; when they must be free to move around; or when the environment is too brightly lit, too poorly lit, subject to severe vibration, or otherwise unsuitable for visual displays.

Telephone-based voice information systems may mix digitized speech segments and speech generation to allow appropriate emotional tone and current information presentation. Applications based on keypad selections and limited speech recognition include banking applications (Fidelity Automated Service Telephone, or FAST), phone directories (British Telecom), and airline schedules (American Airlines Dial-AA-Flight). The ubiquity of telephones makes these services attractive, but an increasing number of users prefer the speed of web-based visual inquiries.

In summary, speech synthesis is technologically feasible. Now, clever designers must find the situations in which it is superior to pre-recorded and digitized human voice messages. Novel applications by way of the telephone, as a supplement to displays, or through embedding in small consumer products all seem attractive.

8.4.5 Non-speech auditory interfaces

In addition to speech, auditory outputs include individual audio tones and more complex information presented by combinations of sound and music. Research on more sophisticated information presentations often refers to *sonification*, *audiolization*, or *auditory interfaces* (Hermann, 2008). Early teletypes included a bell tone to alert users that a message was coming or that paper had run out. Later computer systems added a range of tones to indicate warnings or to acknowledge the completion of an action. Keyboards and mobile devices such as digital cameras are built with electronically generated sound feedback that provides satisfying confirmation of actions; for visually impaired users, the sounds are vital. On the other hand, after a few hours, the sounds can become a distraction rather than a contribution, especially in a room with several machines and users.

Sound designers are likely to become more regular participants in new product development, especially for mobile and embedded devices. A useful distinction is between familiar sounds, called *auditory icons*, and created abstract sounds whose meanings must be learned, called *earcons*. Auditory icons, such as a door opening, liquid pouring, or a ball bouncing, help reinforce the visual metaphors in a graphical user interface or the product concepts for a toy. Earcons, such as a rising set of tones or a sharp loud sound to draw attention, are effective for mobile devices or in control rooms. Other categories of sound usage include "cartoonified" sounds that exaggerate aspects of familiar sounds or familiar sounds used in novel ways. Game designers know that sounds can add realism, heighten tension, and engage users in powerful ways.

Clever designers have developed a variety of auditory-interface ideas, such as scroll bars that provide feedback about user actions, maps or charts that provide auditory information, and sonification of tabular data or maps presenting statistical information (Zhao et al., 2008). Beyond presentation of static data, sound can be effective in highlighting data changes and supporting animated changes in presentations. Research continues on auditory methods for emphasizing the distributions of data in information visualization or drawing attention to patterns, outliers, and clusters.

Auditory web browsers for blind users or telephonic usage have been developed (Chen et al., 2006; Section 1.4.5), where users can hear text and link labels and then make selections by key entry. Auditory file browsers continue to be refined: Each file might have a sound whose frequency is related to its size and might be assigned an instrument (violin, flute, trumpet). Then, when the directory is opened, each file might play its sound either simultaneously or sequentially. Alternatively, files might have sounds associated with their file types, so that users can hear whether there are spreadsheet, graphic, or other text files.

More ambitious auditory interfaces have been proposed in which data are presented as a series of stereophonic or three-dimensional sounds rather than as images. The technical problems of generating appropriate three-dimensional "spatial audio" include the measurement of the listener's head-related transfer function (HRTF). Each person's unique head and ear shape and density must be measured to enable algorithms to generate sounds that are perceived as having an origin in space: left-right, up-down, front-back, and near-far. Ambitious goals include giving blind or partially sighted users enough auditory feedback to enable them to follow directions along a busy street or steer a wheelchair through a hospital. Other explorations have included sonification of mass-spectrograph output, allowing operators to hear the differences between a standard and a test sample or the generation of appealing musical representations of algorithms running on a computer with parallel processors in order to facilitate debugging.

Adding traditional music to user interfaces seems to be an appropriate idea to heighten drama, to relax users, to draw attention, or to set a mood (patriotic marches, romantic sonatas, or gentle waltzes). These approaches have been used in video games and educational packages; they might also be suitable for public-access systems, home-control applications, sales kiosks, bank machines, and other applications.

The potential for novel musical instruments seems especially attractive. With touch-sensitive and haptic devices, it is possible to offer appropriate feedback to give musicians an experience similar to a piano keyboard, a drum, a woodwind, or a stringed instrument. It is also possible to invent new instruments whose frequencies, amplitudes, and effects are governed by the placement of the touch, as well as by its direction, speed, and acceleration. The composition of music using computers expanded as musical-instrument digital-interface (MIDI) hardware and software became widely available at reasonable prices. Faster hardware and innovative user interfaces are now promoting more novel virtual musical instruments.

8.5 Displays—Small and Large

The display is the primary source of feedback to users from the computer. It has many important characteristics, including:

- Physical dimensions (usually the diagonal dimension and depth)
- Resolution (the number of pixels available)
- Number of available colors and color correctness
- Luminance, contrast, and glare
- Power consumption
- Refresh rates (sufficient to allow animation and video)
- Cost
- Reliability

Usage characteristics also distinguish display devices. Portability, privacy, saliency (need to attract attention), ubiquity (likelihood of being able to locate and use the display), and simultaneity (number of simultaneous users) can be used to describe displays (Raghunath and Narayanaswami, 2003). Mobile phones provide displays for portable and private interaction with the device. Ubiquitous television displays allow social interactions between, for example, multiple users controlling characters in video games. Salient information displays found in malls or museums might offer store location information to a single user or an emotional theatrical experience to dozens of impressed visitors. Whiteboard displays allow collaborators to share information, brainstorm, and make decisions (Fig. 9.13). Immersive displays can transport a user into an imaginary world to learn a new skill (Fig. 5.19).

8.5.1 Display technology

Raster-scan cathode-ray tubes (CRTs) have mostly vanished, replaced by *liquid-crystal displays* (LCDs) with their thin form, light weight, and low electricity consumption. Like LCDs, *plasma displays* have a flat profile, but they consume more electricity. They are very bright and visible even from side locations, making them valuable for mounted wall displays in control rooms, public displays, or conference rooms. *Light-emitting diodes* (LEDs) are now available in many colors and are being used in large public displays. The curved display in New York's famous Times Square uses 19 million LEDs to give stock prices, weather information, or news updates with bright graphics. Matrices of miniature LEDs are also used in some head-mounted displays. Manufacturers are actively developing new displays using organic light-emitting diodes (OLED). These durable organic displays are energy-efficient and can be laid on flexible plastic or metallic foil, leading to new opportunities for wearable or rollable displays.

New products attain paper-like resolution using *electronic ink* technology. They contain tiny capsules in which negatively charged black particles and positively charged white particles can be selectively made visible. Because electronic ink displays use power only when the display content changes, they have an extended battery life over other types of displays and are well suited for eBooks (e.g., Amazon's Kindle™, shown in Fig. 8.17, the Sony Reader, or Bookeen's Cybook). Slow display rates allow some animation but no video displays.

Tiny projectors, such as the Microvision Pico projectors, are becoming available; these may soon be able to project color images on the wall from mobile devices and make collaboration using those devices more practical. *Braille displays* for blind users provide up 80 cells, each displaying a character. A couple of cells can be mounted on a mouse, and small displays can fit above the keyboard. Prototypes of refreshable graphic displays with up to several thousand pins are being developed. Manufacturers and government agencies are addressing health concerns relating to the different types of visual displays, such as visual fatigue, stress, and radiation exposure. Adverse effects seem for the most part attributable to the overall work environment more than the visual display units themselves.

The following sections focus on design issues for large displays and head-mounted displays, followed by displays for mobile devices.

FIGURE 8.17

The Amazon Kindle 2™ book reader (http://www.amazon.com/) is a six-inch diagonal grayscale display that displays 800 × 600 pixels at about 160 pixels per inch. It uses E-Ink® technology (http://www.eink.com/), providing a bright display that uses power only when the display changes and can be read in direct sunlight and at varying angles, which can improve reading comfort (see Section 12.3 for a discussion of reading on paper versus on a display).

8.5.2 Large displays

The ubiquity of computer displays, from desktops to mobile devices, projectors, and large televisions, lets us envision how integrating all those displays could provide more productive work and play environments (Ni et al, 2006). The differentiation might fade in the future, but there are currently three types of large displays. *Informational wall displays* provide shared views to users standing far away from the display, while *interactive wall displays* allow users to walk up to the display and interleave interaction and discussion among participants. Finally, users sitting at their desks can connect *multiple-desktop displays* to their computers to have a larger number of windows and documents visible at the

FIGURE 8.18

Multiple high-resolution plasma screens and CRTs are tiled together to present weather, traffic, message sign status, and road-condition information to the operators in the State of Maryland's Highway Administration control room (http://www.chart.state.md.us/).

same time and within reach of the mouse. Of course, hybrid combinations are possible (see, for example, Guimbretière et al., 2001).

Large informational wall displays are effective in control rooms to provide overviews of the system being monitored (Fig. 8.18); details can be retrieved on individual consoles. Military command and control operations, utility management, and emergency response are common applications, as large displays help to build situation awareness through a common understanding of the information presented and to facilitate coordination. Wall displays also allow teams of collaborating scientists or decision makers to look at applications that may be running on different computers, locally or remotely, but are presented on a single display.

Originally built with matrices of CRTs and made popular in commercial or entertainment settings, wall displays now often use rear-projection techniques. Improved calibration and alignment techniques are leading to seamless tiled displays (Fig. 8.19). When seen from a distance, informational wall displays require bright projectors, but the resolution does not need to be very high—35 dots per inch is sufficient. When users need the close-range interactions of digital whiteboard applications, higher resolution (similar to desktop displays) is required.

FIGURE 8.19

Users discuss and point at details of the NASA Space Station near the Princeton University wall display. Twenty-four projectors are tiled together to create a seamless image of 6000 × 3000 pixels (Wallace et al., 2005) (http://www.cs.princeton.edu/omnimedia/).

For interactive wall displays (Fig. 8.20), the traditional desktop interaction techniques, such as indirect-control pointing devices and pull-down menus, become impractical. New techniques are being devised to maintain fluid interaction with freehand sketching or novel menu techniques (Section 7.7). Even on large interactive group displays, space is limited and designers are exploring new ways to dynamically scale, summarize, and manage the information presented or generated by users on the display.

Simpler digital whiteboard systems, such as the SMART Board® from SMART® Technologies, Inc. (Fig. 9.13), provide a large touch-sensitive screen on which a computer image is projected. Their functionality is identical to that of the desktop machine, using users' fingers as pointing devices. Colored pens and a digital eraser simulate a traditional whiteboard, augmented with annotation recording and a software keyboard.

Facilitating collaboration between local or remote users (Chapter 9), managing the recording and reuse of brainstorming information, providing new creative tools for artists and performers, and designing new interaction methods using mobile devices are examples of challenges and opportunities created by interactive wall displays.

FIGURE 8.20
Users use a wireless pen to interact with the Stanford Interactive Mural, a
6 × 3.5-foot high-resolution (64 dpi) display used for digital brainstorming.
Documents can be brought to the display from different computers or scanners.
When moved to the top portion of the screen, documents are scaled down to free
some space on the display (Guimbretière et al., 2001).

Multiple-desktop displays usually employ traditional flat panels, which
introduce discontinuities in the overall display surface (Fig. 8.21). Those displays can also be of different size or resolution, adding the possibility of mis-
alignments. On the other hand, users can continue interacting with applications
in the familiar way, eliminating training as users simply spread windows
across displays. Another concern is that multiple-desktop displays may
require users to stand, or at least rotate their heads or bodies, to attend to all
displays, and even attentive users might not notice warnings or alarms that
are far from their foci of attention. Organized users might assign displays
to particular functions (for example, the left-hand display may always show
e-mail and calendar applications and the front display always a word processor),
but this strategy can be detrimental when the current task would benefit from
using the entire display space.

Multiple-desktop displays are particularly useful for personal creative applications. For example, creating a Flash application might require a timeline, a
stage, graphic-component editors, a scripting-language editor, a directory
browser, and a preview window, all open at the same time. Multiple-desktop
displays might also facilitate side-by-side comparisons of documents, software
debugging, or reasoning based on a large number of information sources. They

FIGURE 8.21

A multiple-desktop display with eight flat panels. Users are discussing a visual analytics problem that requires them to look at multiple documents and visualizations, gather evidence, take notes, and correspond by e-mail with colleagues (Courtesy of Chris North, Virginia Tech).

are usually greatly appreciated by users, and empirical evidence of their benefits is emerging (Yost et al., 2007). Of course, there is a danger that cluttered displays will become more cluttered and that new strategies will be needed to manage them. Also, direct manipulation on large displays can become a challenge because of the distance between objects. Refinements should be made so that the mouse cursor can easily be found and tracked across displays. Rapid focus switching between windows might be facilitated by clicking on small overviews placed at strategic locations on the display. Strategies for automatic window layout and coordination among windows will become critical, but as the cost of displays continues to drop, it seems clear that multiple-desktop displays or simply larger single displays will become prevalent.

8.5.3 Heads-up and helmet-mounted displays

Personal-display technology involves small portable monitors, often made with LCDs in monochrome or color. A *heads-up display* projects information on the partially silvered windscreen of an airplane or car, for example, so that the pilots or drivers can keep their attention focused on the surroundings while receiving computer-generated information.

An alternative, the *helmet- or head-mounted display* (HMD) used in virtual-reality or augmented-reality applications (Section 5.6 and Fig. 5.18), lets users see information even while turning their heads. In fact, the information that they see may be varied as a function of the direction in which they are looking if the display is equipped with tracking sensors. Different models provide varying levels of visual-field obstruction, audio capabilities, and resolution (for example, the iReality.com CyberEye™ has an 800 × 600 display and fully obstructed vision). Early examples of wearable computers focused attention on small portable devices that people could use while moving or accomplishing other tasks, such as jet-engine repair or inventory control, but current technology still requires hardware to be carried in a backpack or users to remain near the base computer.

Attempts to produce 3D displays include vibrating surfaces, holograms, polarized glasses, red/blue glasses, and synchronized shutter glasses (from companies such as StereoGraphics® and eDimensional™) that give users a strong sense of 3D stereoscopic vision.

8.5.4 Mobile device displays

The use of mobile devices is becoming widespread in personal and business applications and has the potential to improve medical care, facilitate learning in schools, and contribute to more fulfilling sightseeing experiences. Medical monitors can alert doctors when a patient's life signs reach a critical level, school children may gather data or solve problems collaboratively using handheld devices, and emergency rescue personnel can evaluate their situation in dangerous environments by using small devices fixed on their suits. Small displays are also finding ways into our homes, with reprogrammable picture frames and other devices, and even onto our bodies, with ever more powerful wristwatches with GPS capability or customization features to fit the needs of the moment (Fig. 8.22).

Guidelines are emerging from experience with mobile devices (Ballard, 2007; Jones and Marsden, 2006). Industry has been leading the way by providing useful design case studies (Lindholm et al., 2003) and detailed guidelines such as those developed for Palm devices or the iPhone.

FIGURE 8.22

This Seiko™ bracelet watch for women uses E-Ink technology, which allows the wearer to customize the display and choose among different styles for work, where the time is easy to read, or leisure, where the time is expressed in a more imaginative style to reflect the mood of the moment (http://www.seikowatches.com).

Barbara Ballard (2007) sees mobile devices being developed in four classes, depending on their intended usage: (1) general-purpose work (similar to the RIM Blackberry or Pocket PC), (2) general-purpose entertainment (which focus on multimedia features like the Apple iPod), (3) general-purpose communication and control (extensions of today's phones), and (4) targeted devices that do only a few tasks (e.g., the United Parcel Service drivers' DIAD IV). Mobile devices are often used for brief but routine tasks. Therefore, it is critical to optimize the designs for those repetitive tasks, while hiding or eliminating less important functions (Section 6.8 and Fig. 6.20). Whenever possible, data entry should be reduced and complex tasks offloaded to the desktop.

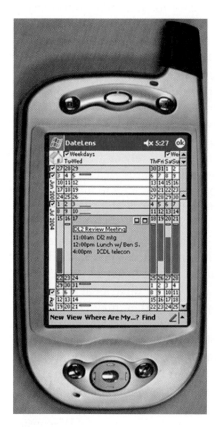

FIGURE 8.23

DateLens is a calendar interface for mobile devices using a fisheye representation of dates coupled with compact overviews, user control over the visible time period, and integrated search capabilities (Bederson et al., 2004).

While researchers and developers are steadily increasing the scope of applications for mobile devices, a framework for thinking about the range of actions may be helpful. Whether the application is financial-, medical-, or travel-related, the following five pairs of actions should be considered: (1) *monitor* dynamic information sources and *alert* when appropriate, (2) *gather* information from many sources and *spread out* information to many destinations, (3) *participate* in a group and *relate* to individuals, (4) *locate* services or items that are not visible (for example, the nearest gas station) and *identify* objects that are seen (for example, the name of a person or flower), and (5) *capture* information from local resources and *share* your information with future users.

Most applications for mobile devices are custom designed to take advantage of every pixel available on a particular platform. Designs might also take advantage of zooming to generate animated displays. The calendar application DateLens (Fig. 8.23) allows compact overviews of available meeting times, feedback on conflicting appointments, and quick zooming on specific weeks or dates on small displays of any size, from handheld devices to desktops. DateLens can be effective because the layout of overviews by week or month is familiar to users and color coding or abbreviations can be learned quickly (Bederson et al., 2004).

Poor readability will be an issue in low light or for users with poor eyesight, and users will appreciate the ability to adjust the font size. Reading on small screens might also be improved with *rapid serial visual presentation* (RSVP), which presents text dynamically at a constant speed or at a speed adapted to the content. Using RSVP, although no differences were found for long texts, a 33% improvement was measured in speed of reading for short texts (Oquist and Goldstein, 2003).

Some applications, such as web searching and browsing, remain very ineffective on small displays (Jones et al., 2003). Custom redesigns are preferable but not always feasible. There are several approaches for migrating information from full-sized to small displays (Lin and Landay, 2008). Direct data migration into long, scrollable displays might be acceptable for linear reading but makes comparisons within the document difficult. Data modification involves summarizing text or creating smaller pictures. It is effective to provide quick access to all parts of the documents and allow users to request more information. Data suppression can be done by eliminating sections of the document, or selectively sampling words. Finally, compact overviews using visualization techniques (Chapter 14) can provide access to all of the original information.

Mobile users often have only one hand available and rely on their thumbs to interact with the devices. Guidelines for mobile interfaces that support one-handed interaction include placing targets close to one another to minimize grip adjustment, allowing users to configure tasks for either left- or right-handed operation, and placing targets towards the center of the device (Karlson et al., 2008). Another challenge facing designers of mobile-device applications is the growing diversity of devices, which may require finding interaction styles that adapt to multiple screen sizes and can be activated by multiple input mechanisms (QWERTY keyboards as well as touchscreens, keypads, or directional pads).

As mobile devices become information appliances, they may contribute to the goal of bridging the digital divide. These low-cost devices, which are easier to master than desktop computers, may enable a wider range of people to benefit from information and communication technologies. Developing countries are seeing a rapid spread of mobile technology, which requires less local infrastructure than providing stable electricity. For users with disabilities, mobile telecommunication devices offer a unique opportunity to design *modality translation services*, as described by a project of the Trace Center at the University of Wisconsin. Remote services can provide instant translation from one presentation mode to another, anywhere and at any time, via mobile devices. This permits text-to-speech, sign language, international language, and language-level translation, as well as print recognition and image/video description services. Modality translation could benefit people with disabilities and people who have no disabilities but experience functional limitations when driving their cars, visiting a foreign country, or touring a museum without reading glasses.

Practitioner's Summary

Choosing hardware always involves making a compromise between the ideal and the practical. The designer's vision of what an input or output device should be must be tempered by the realities of what is commercially available within the project budget. Devices should be tested in the application domain to verify the manufacturer's claims, and testimonials or suggestions from users should be obtained.

New devices and refinements to old devices appear regularly; device-independent architecture and software permit easy integration of novel devices. Avoid being locked into one device, as the hardware is often the softest part of the system. Also, remember that a successful software idea can become even more successful if reimplementation on other devices is easy to achieve and if cross-modality permits users with disabilities to access the system. Remember Fitts' law to optimize speed of performance and consider two-handed operations.

Keyboard entry is here to stay, but consider other forms of input when text entry is limited. Selecting rather than typing has many benefits for both novice and frequent users. Direct-pointing devices are faster and more convenient for novices than are indirect-pointing devices, and accurate pointing is possible, but remember that users on-the-go are likely to use the devices with a single hand. Simple gestures can trigger a few actions and are showing promising applications. Resist the temptation to provide too many features on portable devices, and relegate rarely used features and most data entry to the desktop.

Speech input and output devices are commercially viable and should be applied where appropriate, but take care to ensure that performance is genuinely improved over other interaction strategies. Display technology is moving rapidly, and user expectations are increasing. Higher-resolution and larger displays are becoming prevalent.

Researcher's Agenda

Novel text-entry keyboards to speed input and to reduce error rates will have to provide significant benefits to displace the well-entrenched QWERTY design. For the numerous applications that do require extensive text entry or run on mobile device applications, many opportunities remain to create special-purpose devices or to redesign the tasks to permit direct-manipulation selection instead of keyboarding. Increasingly, input can be accomplished via conversion or extraction of data from online sources. Another input source is optical character recognition of printed text or bar codes (for example, in magazines or bank statements) or RFID tags attached to objects, clothing, or even personalized dolls.

Research on speech systems could be directed at redesigning the applications to make more effective use of the speech input and output technology. Complete and accurate continuous-speech recognition does not seem attainable, but if users will modify their speaking styles in specific applications, more progress is possible. Other worthy directions include improving continuous-speech recognition for tasks such as finding a given phrase in a large body of recorded speech and combining speech and image recognition for video captioning and describing.

The range of display sizes available has widened enormously, and users need applications that can operate on mobile devices, desktops, and large wall or table displays. We need to understand how to design plastic or multimodal interfaces that allow users to adapt their interfaces depending on the environment, their preferences, and their abilities. What are the strategies for increasing productivity with multiple screens? Sensors embedded in the environment and in many mobile devices can provide information about users' locations or activities to enable development of context-aware applications. The benefits may be large, but inconsistent behavior and privacy concerns will have to be addressed before adoption becomes widespread.

WORLD WIDE WEB RESOURCES

http://www.aw.com/DTUI/

Rich resources are available on commercial input devices, especially pointing and handwriting input devices. Commercial packages, software tools, and demonstrations are available for speech generation and recognition. MIDI tools and virtual-reality devices enable serious hobbyists and researchers to create novel experiences for users. Novel strategies and uses for large displays emerge frequently from research and product groups.

References

Abowd, G. and Mynatt, E., Charting past, present, and future research in ubiquitous computing, *ACM Transactions on Computer-Human Interaction* 7, 1 (2000), 29–58.

Accot, J. and Zhai, S., More than dotting the i's: Foundations for crossing-based interfaces, *Proc. CHI '02 Conference: Human Factors in Computing Systems*, ACM Press, New York (2002), 73–80.

Ashcraft, Mark H., *Cognition, Third Edition*, Prentice-Hall, Englewood Cliffs, NJ (2005).

Balentine, Bruce, *It's Better to Be a Good Machine Than a Bad Person: Speech Recognition and Other Exotic User Interfaces at the Twilight of the Jetsonian Age*, ICMI Press, Annapolis, MD (2007).

Ballard, Barbara, *Designing the Mobile User Experience*, John Wiley & Sons, New York (2007).

Basu, Sumit, Gupta, Surabhi, Mahajan, Milind, Nguyen, Patrick, and Platt, John C., Scalable summaries of spoken conversations, *Proc. International Conference on Intelligent User Interfaces*, ACM Press, New York (2008), 267–275.

Bederson, B. B., Clamage, A., Czerwinski, M. P., and Robertson, G. G., DateLens: A fisheye calendar interface for PDAs, *ACM Transactions on Computer-Human Interaction* 11, 1 (2004), 90–119.`

Benko, H., Wilson, A., and Baudisch, P., Precise selection techniques for multi-touch screens, *Proc. CHI 2006 Conference: Human Factors in Computing Systems*, ACM Press, New York (2006), 1263–1272.

Chen, Xiaoyu, Tremaine, Marilyn, Lutz, Robert, Chung, Jae-woo, and Lacsina, Patrick, AudioBrowser: A mobile browsable information access for the visually impaired, *Universal Access in the Information Society* 5, 1 (2006), 4–22.

Clawson, James, Lyons, Kent, Rudnicky, Alex, Iannucci, Jr., Robert A., and Starner, Thad, Automatic whiteout++: Correcting mini-QWERTY typing errors using keypress timing, *Proc. CHI 2008 Conference: Human Factors in Computing Systems*, ACM Press, New York (2008), 573–582.

Danis, C., Comerford, L., Janke, E., Davies, K., DeVries, J., and Bertran, A., StoryWriter: A speech oriented editor, Proc. CHI '94 Conference: *Human Factors in Computing Systems: Conference Companion*, ACM Press, New York (1994), 277–278.

Dunlop, Mark and Masters, Michelle, Pickup usability dominates: A brief history of mobile text entry research and adoption, *International Journal of Mobile Human Computer Interaction* 1, 1 (2008) 42–59.

Feng, Jinjuan, Sears, Andrew, and Karat, Clare-Marie, A longitudinal evaluation of hands-free speech-based navigation during dictation, *International Journal of Human-Computer Studies* 64, 6 (2006), 553–569.

Fitts, P. M., The information capacity of the human motor system in controlling amplitude of movement, *Journal of Experimental Psychology* 47 (1954), 381–391.

Fitzmaurice, G., Ishii, H., and Buxton, W., Laying the foundation for graspable user interfaces, *Proc. CHI '95 Conference: Human Factors in Computing Systems*, ACM Press, New York (1995), 442–449.

Foley, J. D., Wallace, V. L., and Chan, P., The human factors of computer graphics interaction techniques, *IEEE Computer Graphics and Applications* 4, 11 (November 1984), 13–48.

Gardner-Bonneau, Daryle and Blanchard, Harry E. (Editors), *Human Factors and Voice Interactive Systems*, Springer-Verlag, London, U.K. (2007).

Grossman, T., Balakrishnan, R., Kurtenbach, G., Fitzmaurice, G. W., Khan, A., and Buxton, W., Creating principal 3D curves with digital tape drawing, *Proc. CHI 2002 Conference: Human Factors in Computing Systems*, ACM Press, New York (2002), 121–128.

Grossman, Tovi and Wigdor, Daniel, Going deeper: A taxonomy of 3D on the tabletop, *Proc. TableTop 2007: IEEE International Workshop on Horizontal Interactive Human-Computer Systems*, IEEE Press, Los Alamitos, CA (2007), 137–144.

Guiard, Y., Asymmetric division of labor in human skilled bimanual action: The kinematic chain as a model, *Journal of Motor Behavior* 19, 4 (1987), 486–517.

Guiard, Y., Bourgeois, F., Mottet, D., and Beaudouin-Lafon, M., Beyond the 10-bit barrier: Fitts' law in multi-scale electronic worlds, in *People and Computers XV— Interaction Without Frontiers (Joint Proceedings of HCI 2001 and IHM 2001)*, Springer-Verlag, London, U.K. (2001), 573–587.

Guimbretière, F., Stone, M., and Winograd, T., Fluid interaction with high-resolution wall-size displays, *Proc. UIST 2001 Symposium on User Interface Software & Technology*, ACM Press, New York (2001), 21–30.

Han, Jefferson Y., Low-cost multi-touch sensing through frustrated total internal reflection, *Proc. ACM Symposium on User Interface Software and Technology*, ACM Press, New York (2005), 115–118.

Hermann, Thomas, Taxonomy and definitions for sonification and auditory display, *Proc. 14th International Conference on Auditory Display*, ICAD, Paris, France (2008).

Hinckley, K., Input technologies and techniques, in Jacko, Julie and Sears, Andrews (Editors), *The Human-Computer Interaction Handbook*, Laurence Erlbaum Associates, Mahwah, NJ (2008), 161–176.

Hinckley, K., Pierce, J., Sinclair, M., and Horvitz, E., Sensing techniques for mobile interaction, *Proc. ACM Symposium on User Interface Software and Technology*, ACM Press, New York (2000), 91–100.

Hinrichs, Uta, Carpendale, Sheelagh, and Scott, Stacey D., Evaluating the effects of fluid interface components on tabletop collaboration, *Proc. International Working Conference on Advanced Visual Interfaces*, ACM Press, New York (2006), 27–34.

Hoggan, Eve, Brewster, Stephen A., and Johnston, Jody, Investigating the effectiveness of tactile feedback for mobile touchscreens, *Proc. CHI 2008 Conference: Human Factors in Computing Systems*, ACM Press, New York (2008), 1573–1582.

Hourcade, J.-P., Bederson, B., Druin, A., and Guimbretière, F., Differences in pointing task performance between preschool children and adults using mice, *ACM Transactions on Computer-Human Interaction* 11, 4 (December 2004), 357–386.

Jacob, R. J. K., Sibert, L. E., McFarlane, D. C., and Mullen, Jr., M. P., Integrality and separability of input devices, *ACM Transactions on Computer-Human Interaction* 1, 1 (March 1994), 3–26.

Jones, M., Buchanan, G., and Thimbelby, H., Improving web search on small screen devices, *Interacting with Computers (special issue on HCI with Mobile Devices)* 15, 4 (2003), 479–496.

Jones, Matt and Marsden, Gary, *Mobile Interaction Design*, John Wiley & Sons, New York (2006).

Karlson, A., Bederson, B. B., and Contreras-Vidal, J. L., Understanding one handed use of mobile devices, in Lumsden, Johanna (Editor), *Handbook of Research on User Interface Design and Evaluation for Mobile Technology*, Information Science Reference/ IGI Global, Hershey, PA (2008), 86–101.

Kortum, Philip (Editor), *HCI Beyond the GUI: Design for Haptic, Speech, Olfactory and Other Nontraditional Interfaces*, Elsevier/Morgan Kaufmann, Amsterdam, The Netherlands (2008).

Kristensson, P.O. and Denby, L., Text entry performance of state of the art unconstrained handwriting recognition: a longitudinal user study. In *Proc. CHI 2009 Conference: Human Factors in Computing Systems*. ACM Press, New York (2009).

Liao, Chunyuan, Guimbretière, François, Hinckley, Ken, and Hollan, Jim, PapierCraft: A gesture-based command system for interactive paper, *ACM Transactions on Computer-Human Interaction* 14, 4 (2008), #14.

Lin, James and Landay, James, Employing patterns and layers for early-stage design and prototyping of cross-device user interfaces, *Proc. CHI 2008 Conference: Human Factors in Computing Systems*, ACM Press, New York (2008), 1313–1322.

Lindholm, C., Keinonen, T., and Kiljander, H., *Mobile Usability: How Nokia Changed the Face of the Mobile Phone*, McGraw-Hill, New York (2003).

Mackay, W. E., Pothier, G., Letondal, C., Bøegh, K., and Sørensen, H.E., The missing link: Augmenting biology laboratory notebooks, *Proc. ACM Symposium on User Interface Software and Technology*, ACM Press, New York (2002), 41–50.

MacKenzie, S., Fitts' law as a research and design tool in human-computer interaction, *Human-Computer Interaction* 7 (1992), 91–139.

MacKenzie, S., Kober, H., Smith, D., Jones, T., and Skepner, E., LetterWise: Prefix-based disambiguation for mobile text input, *Proc. ACM Symposium on User Interface Software and Technology*, ACM Press, New York (2001), 111–120.

MacKenzie, S. and Soukoreff, R. W., Text entry for mobile computing: Models and methods, theory and practice, *Human-Computer Interaction* 17, 2 (2002), 147–198.

MacKenzie, S., Tauppinen, T., and Silfverberg, M., Accuracy measures for evaluating computer pointing devices, *Proc. CHI '01 Conference: Human Factors in Computing Systems*, ACM Press, New York (2001), 9–16.

Michaelis, P. R. and Wiggins, R. H., A human factors engineer's introduction to speech synthesizers, in Badre, A. and Shneiderman, B. (Editors), *Directions in Human-Computer Interaction*, Ablex, Norwood, NJ (1982), 149–178.

Mithal, A. K. and Douglas, S. A., Differences in movement microstructure of the mouse and the finger-controlled isometric joystick, *Proc. CHI '96 Conference: Human Factors in Computing Systems*, ACM Press, New York (1996), 300–307.

Montemayor, M., Druin, A., Guha, M. L., Farber, A., Chipman, G., Tools for children to create physical interactive storyrooms, *ACM Computers in Entertainment* 1, 2 (2004), 12.

Myers, Brad, Using handhelds for wireless remote control of PCs and appliances, *Interacting with Computers* 17, 3 (2005), 251–264.

Myers, Brad, Using hand-held devices and PCs together, *Communications of the ACM* 44, 11 (November 2001), 34–41.

Ni, T., Schmidt, G., Staadt, O., Livingston, M., Ball, R., and May, R., A survey of large high-resolution display technologies, techniques, and applications, *Proc. IEEE Virtual Reality Conference (VR 2006)*, IEEE Press, Los Alamitos, CA (2006), 223–236.

Olsson, J. Scott and Oard, Douglas W., Improving text classification for oral history archives with temporal domain knowledge, *Proc. ACM SIGIR Conference: Research and Development in Information Retrieval*, ACM Press, New York (2007), 623–630.

Oquist, G. and Goldstein, M., Towards an improved readability on mobile devices: Evaluating adaptive rapid serial visual presentation, *Interacting with Computers* 15, 4 (2003), 539–558.

Oviatt, Sharon, Darrell, Trevor, and Flickner, Myron, Multimodal interfaces that flex, persist, and adapt, *Communications of the ACM* 47, 1 (2004), 30–33.

Pausch, R. and Leatherby, J. H., An empirical study: Adding voice input to a graphical editor, *Journal of the American Voice Input/Output Society* 9, 2 (1991), 55–66.

Peacocke, R. D. and Graf, D. H., An introduction to speech and speaker recognition, *IEEE Computer* 23, 8 (August 1990), 26–33.

Peres, S. C., Best, V., Brock, D., Frauenberger, C., Hermann, T., Neuhof, J. G., Valgerdaeur, V., Shinn-Cunningham, B. G., and Stockman, T., Auditory interfaces, in Kortum, Philip (Editor), *HCI Beyond the GUI*, Morgan Kaufmann, Elsevier/Morgan Kaufmann, Amsterdam, The Netherlands (2008), 147–196.

Pitt, I. and Edwards, A., *Design of Speech-Based Devices: A Practical Guide*, Springer-Verlag, London, U.K. (2003).

Price, Katheen and Sears, Andrews, Speech-based text entry for mobile handheld devices: An analysis of efficacy and error correction techniques for server-based solutions, *International Journal of Human-Computer Interaction* 19, 3 (2005), 279–304.

Raghunath, M. and Narayanaswami, C., Fostering a symbiotic handheld environment, *IEEE Computer* 36, 9 (2003), 57–65.

Rohs, Michael and Oulasvirta, Antti, Target acquisition with camera phones when used as magic lenses, *Proc. CHI 2008 Conference: Human Factors in Computing Systems*, ACM Press, New York (2008), 1409–1418.

Sears, A., Lin, M., and Karimullah, A. S., Speech-based cursor control: Understanding the effects of target size, cursor speed, and command selection, *Universal Access in the Information Society* 2, 1 (November 2002), 30–43.

Sears, A., Revis, D., Swatski, J., Crittenden, R., and Shneiderman, B., Investigating touchscreen typing: The effect of keyboard size on typing speed, *Behaviour & Information Technology* 12, 1 (January/February 1993), 17–22.

Sears, A. and Shneiderman, B., High precision touchscreens: Design strategies and comparison with a mouse, *International Journal of Man-Machine Studies* 34, 4 (April 1991), 593–613.

Suhm, B. and Peterson, P., A data-driven methodology for evaluating and optimizing call center IVRs, *International Journal of Speech Technology* 5, 1 (2002), 23–38.

Tsang, M., Fitzmaurice, G. W., Kurtenbach, G., Khan, A., and Buxton, W. A. S., Boom Chameleon: Simultaneous capture of 3D viewpoint, voice and gesture annotations on a spatially-aware display, *Proc. ACM Symposium on User Interface Software and Technology*, ACM Press, New York (2002), 111–120.

Ullmer, B. and Ishii, H., Emerging frameworks for tangible user interfaces, *IBM Systems Journal* 39, 3–4 (2000), 915–931.

Vanderheiden, G., Cross-disability access to touch screen kiosks and ATMs, *Advances in Human Factors/Ergonomics, 21A, International Conference on Human-Computer Interaction*, Elsevier, Amsterdam, The Netherlands (1997), 417–420.

Vanderheiden, G., Kelso, D., and Krueger, M., Extended usability versus accessibility in voting systems, *Proc. RESNA 27th Annual Conference*, RESNA Press, Arlington, VA (2004).

Vogel, Daniel and Baudisch, Patrick, Shift: A technique for operating pen-based interfaces using touch, *Proc. CHI 2007 Conference: Human Factors in Computing Systems*, ACM Press, New York (2007), 657–666.

Walker, M. A., Fromer, J., Di Fabbrizio, G., Mestel, C., and Hindle, D., What can I say? Evaluating a spoken language interface to email, *Proc. CHI '98 Conference: Human Factors in Computing Systems*, ACM Press, New York (1998), 582–589.

Wallace, Grant, Anshus, Otto J., Bi, Peng, Chen, Han, Chen, Yuqun, Clark, Douglas Cook, Perry, Finkelstein, Adam, Funkhouser, Thomas, Gupta, Anoop, Hibbs, Matthew, Li, Kai, Liu, Zhiyan, Samanta, Rudrajit, Sukthankar, Rahul and Troyanskaya, Olga, Tools and Applications for Large-Scale Display Walls, *IEEE Computer Graphics and Applications* 25, 4 (2005), 24–33.

Ward, D., Blackwell, A., and MacKay, D., Dasher: A data entry interface using continuous gestures and language models, *Proc. ACM Symposium on User Interface Software and Technology*, ACM Press, New York (2000), 129–137.

Wobbrock, J., Myers, B., and Kembel, J., EdgeWrite: A stylus-based text entry method designed for high accuracy and stability of motion, *Proc. ACM Symposium on User Interface Software and Technology*, ACM Press, New York (2003), 61–70.

Wobbrock, J. O., Rubinstein, J., Sawyer, M. W., and Duchowski, A. T., Longitudinal evaluation of discrete consecutive gaze gestures for text entry, *Proc. ACM Symposium on Eye Tracking Research and Applications (ETRA '08)*, ACM Press, New York (2008), 11–18.

Yost, B., Haciahmetoglu, Y., and North, C., Beyond visual acuity: The perceptual scalability of information visualizations for large displays, *Proc. CHI 2007 Conference: Human Factors in Computing Systems*, ACM Press, New York (2007), 101–110.

Zhai, S., User performance in relation to 3D input device design, *Computer Graphics* 32, 4 (November 1998), 50–54.

Zhai, S., Smith, B., and Selker, T., Improving browsing performance: A study of four input devices for scrolling and pointing tasks, *Proc. INTERACT '97*, Elsevier, Amsterdam, The Netherlands (1997), 286–292.

Zhao, Haixia, Shneiderman, Ben, Plaisant, Catherine and Lazar, Jonathan, Data sonification for users with visual impairments: A case study with geo-referenced data, *ACM Transactions on Computer-Human Interaction* 15, 1 (2008), #4.

CHAPTER 9

Collaboration and Social Media Participation

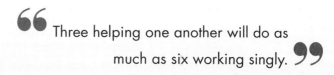

Three helping one another will do as much as six working singly.

Spanish Proverb

Written in collaboration with Maxine S. Cohen

9.1 Introduction

The introversion and isolation of early computer users has given way to extremely lively online communities of busily interacting teams and bustling crowds of chatty diverse users that span the gamut in terms of age, computer expertise, and geographic locations. The pursuit of human connections has prompted millions of users to join listservers, visit chat rooms, and fill online communities with useful information and supportive responses, peppered with outrageous humor. But, as in most human communities, there is also controversy, anger, slander, and pornography. The World Wide Web has dramatically enriched textual communications with colorful graphics and sometimes too-dazzling Java or Flash animations. The Web is sometimes derided as a playground, but serious work and creative endeavors are enormously facilitated by the easy flow of information it provides. Cell phones and mobile devices have also expanded the possibilities for communication by voice, text messages, digital photos, videos, and other forms of user-generated content.

The expanding options for collaboration and social media participation have benefits for everyone. Goal-directed individuals quickly recognize the benefits of electronic collaboration and the potentials for business in the networked global village. Playful and social personalities enjoy laughing with siblings and surprising their friends halfway around the world. The distance to colleagues is no longer measured in miles or kilometers, but rather in intellectual compatibility and responsiveness; a close friend is someone who responds from across an ocean within three minutes at 3:00 A.M. with the rare music file that you long to hear.

The good news is that computing, once seen as alienating and antihuman, is becoming a socially respectable and interpersonally positive force. Enthusiasts hail collaborative interfaces, such as *groupware* for team processes, health support groups, scientific collaboratories, and shared documents as productivity and creativity support tools. They also cheer for the successes of virtual environments like Second Life, communal creations such as Wikipedia, and social networking sites such as Facebook. Even lightweight participation in social media, such as tagging a photo in Flickr, rating a movie in Netflix, or marking a new story in Digg™, can have a transformative effect through the cumulative efforts of millions of people.

However, these interfaces for collaboration and social media participation have limitations, and there may be a dark side to the force. Will the speedup in work rates reduce quality, increase burnout, or undermine loyalty? Can collaborative interfaces be turned into oppressive tools or confrontive environments? Does intimacy survive when participants are remote in time and physical space? Can laughter, hugs, and tears mean the same thing for electronic-dialog partners as for face-to-face partners? For participants immersed in this online connected world, the cell-phone number, e-mail address, or other electronic "handle" is part of the infrastructure for social relationships. Giving out your electronic contact information or accepting an invitation from someone else (e.g., in Facebook or LinkedIn) is a step in the direction of personal intimacy and business trust.

The first steps in understanding the social dimension of collaboration and social media participation are coming to grips with its terminology and scope. Although the conferences on *computer-supported cooperative work* have established *CSCW* as an acronym, the organizers still debate whether that acronym covers *cooperative*, *collaborative*, and *competitive* work and whether it includes play, family activities, and educational experiences. CSCW researchers focus on designing and evaluating new technologies to support work processes, but some researchers also study social exchanges, learning, games, and entertainment. In 2006, the CSCW conference celebrated its 20th birthday. The structure of the conference core and clusters were analyzed automatically using a citation graph methodology (Jacovi et al., 2006). Several new clusters emerged in 2002 and continued to grow in 2004 (the last year of the analysis). These clusters included social media participation activities such as meetings, media spaces, and conferencing; instant messaging (IM), social spaces, and presence; and video-mediated communication, shared visual space, and workspace awareness, which itself emerged in 2004. This burgeoning of new clusters shows the impact of social media participation in CSCW.

It is important to distinguish between collaboration and social media participation (Table 9.1). Collaborations can be seen as activities carried out by small teams of 2 to 20 people—or perhaps more, as in collaboratories (Bos et al., 2007). Collaborations emphasize work-related projects and they are well represented at CSCW and SIGGROUP conferences. The work is typically goal-directed and has a time frame for completion. Collaboration is purposeful and often business-related (as opposed to social media participation, which is more discretionary

Collaboration	Crossover	Social Media Participation
E-mail, phone calls, audio- and videoconferences, shared documents, collaboratories	Wikis, blogs, chat rooms, instant messages, short messages, listservers, Yahoo!/Google groups	Chat rooms, blogs, user-generated content sites, tagging, rating, reviewing
GoToMeeting®, LiveMeeting®, WebEx®, Skype®, Google Docs™, GeneBank™	Wikipedia, Wikia™, LinkedIn, Second Life, Blogger®	YouTube, Flickr, Picasa, Netflix, Technorati™, MySpace, Facebook, Digg, del.icio.us™
Want recognition for contributions May Aspire to Leadership		
Typically 2 to 2000 people		Typically 20 to 200,000,000 people
Work-related, goal-directed		Playful, process-oriented
Time-limited, milestones		Open-ended
Selected identified partners		Open unknown partners
Assign tasks and review each other's work		Act independently

TABLE 9.1

Characteristics and examples of collaboration and social media participation, including crossover characteristics

and oriented towards enjoyment). Participants know whom they are collaborating with, and the purposeful relationship may endure for days or years. E-mail, listservers, Skype (and other Voice over IP systems), teleconferencing, and videoconferencing are the tools used primarily for collaboration.

Social media participation can involve 10 people in a chat room or hundreds of millions of discretionary users in an environment such as Facebook or MySpace. The participation may support existing relationships or help users establish new ones, but often these relationships persist only in the online world. Sometimes there are no personal relationships, but only lightweight intersections, as when someone tags someone else's photo in Flickr or rates someone else's YouTube video. Amazon.com reviews, Netflix ratings/recommendations, restaurant reviews, Craigslist, Angie's List, and eBay are all social media, even though there may be little direct contact between participants. Many users remain in lightweight contact as occasional or even frequent lurkers. However, some users develop stronger relationships as they repeatedly make minor contributions, then become more active and substantial contributors, and eventually participate in governance, increasingly taking leadership positions (Li and Bernoff, 2008).

Some tools, such as blogs and wikis, can be used for team collaboration and social media participation. For example, Wikipedia, which is managed by a well-organized team who are familiar with each other, also has tens of thousands of minor contributors who have little contact with others, as well as millions of users who benefit but don't contribute. Online communities such as healthcare discussion groups are social media with many unidentified participants and lurkers, but these tools may be part of a larger effort to collaborate purposefully.

Leading designers already support users' needs to learn from colleagues, consult with partners, annotate documents received from associates, and present results to managers. These designers also have started to design software that accommodates interruptions from coworkers, deals with privacy, establishes responsibility, and can be used by large numbers of users, if appropriate. It may be useful to think of collaboration and social media participation as the motivating force for using computers. This expansion of scope for interaction designers is why Part II of this book includes collaboration and social media participation—they are design requirements for most interfaces.

This chapter begins with an analysis of why people collaborate, then presents the traditional 2×2 matrix of collaborative interfaces to support the needs people have. The next three sections cover asynchronous distributed, synchronous distributed, and face-to-face interfaces. Section 9.3 focuses on e-mail; collaborative interfaces such as listservers, Yahoo! Groups, and Google Groups; and the more ambitious online and networked communities. Section 9.4 covers synchronous distributed tools such as chat, instant messaging, texting, and videoconferencing. Section 9.5 addresses the growing array of face-to-face software for electronic meetings and shared displays.

9.2 Goals of Collaboration and Participation

People collaborate because doing so is satisfying or productive. Collaboration can have purely emotionally rewarding purposes or specific task-related goals. It can be sought personally or imposed managerially. It can be a one-time encounter or an enduring partnership. Understanding the processes and strategies of the participants facilitates analysis of these varied situations for collaborative interfaces:

- *Focused partnerships* are collaborations between two or three people who need each other to complete a task, such as joint authors of a technical report, two pathologists consulting about a cancer patient's biopsy, programmers debugging a program together, or an astronaut and a ground controller repairing a faulty satellite. The growing set of partnerships also involves consumers who may negotiate with a travel agent, stockbroker, or customer-support staffer. Often, there are electronic documents or images to "conference over." Partners can use e-mail, chat, instant messaging, telephone, voice mail, videoconferencing, or a combination of these technologies. Newer strategies enable partnering through mobile devices, such as text messaging (texting) or photo exchanging via cell phones or discussions over a shared electronic tabletop.

- *Lecture or demo* formats involve one person sharing information with many users at remote sites. The start time and duration are the same for all, and the recipients may ask questions. No history keeping is required, but a replay capability is helpful for later review and for those who could not attend.

- *Conferences* allow groups whose participants are distributed to communicate at the same time (synchronous) or spread out over time (asynchronous). Many-to-many messaging may be used, and there is typically a record of conversations. Examples include a program committee making plans for an upcoming event or a group of students discussing a set of homework problems. In more directed conferences, a leader or moderator supervises the online discussion to achieve goals within deadlines. Blogs (postings that invite outside commenting) and wikis (group editing spaces) are often used for conferences.

- *Structured work processes* let people with distinct organizational roles collaborate on some task: a scientific-journal editor arranges online submission, reviewing, revisions, and publication; a health-insurance agency receives, reviews, and reimburses or rejects medical bills; or a university admissions committee registers, reviews, chooses, and informs applicants.

- *Meeting and decision support* can be done in a face-to-face meeting, with each user working at a computer and making simultaneous contributions. Shared and private windows plus large-screen projectors enable simultaneous shared comments that may be anonymous. Anonymity not only encourages shy participants to speak up, but also allows forceful leaders to accept novel suggestions without ego conflicts. Voting and polling can also play a significant role.

- *Electronic commerce* includes customers browsing and comparing prices online, possibly followed by short-term collaborations to inquire about a product before ordering it. Several e-commerce sites offer a live help link to allow synchronous communication. Electronic commerce also includes business-to-business negotiations to formulate major sales or contracts. Electronic negotiations can be distributed in time and space, while producing an accurate record and rapid dissemination of results.

- *Teledemocracy* allows small organizations, professional groups, and city, state, or national governments to conduct online town-hall meetings, to expose officials to comments from constituents, or to produce consensus through online conferences, debates, and votes.

- *Online communities* are groups of people who may be widely distributed geographically and across time zones. These people come online to discuss, share information or support, socialize, or play games. Communities that focus on shared interests, such as health concerns or a hobby, are often referred to as *communities of interest* (CoIs). Communities whose focus is professional are known as *communities of practice* (CoPs). Communities whose members are located in the same geographical region are known as *networked communities*; these people usually meet face-to-face as well as virtually.

- *Collaboratories* are novel organizational forms for groups of scientists or other professionals to work together across time and space, possibly sharing expensive equipment such as telescopes or orbiting sensor platforms. These groups share interests, but may compete for resources. There is sufficient variety in the types of collaboration that a seven-category taxonomy (distributed research centers, shared instruments, community data systems, open community contribution systems, virtual communities of practice, virtual learning communities, and community infrastructure projects) of collaboratories has been developed (Bos et al., 2007).

- *Telepresence* enables remote participants to have experiences that are almost as good as being physically co-present. Telepresence is supported by immersive 3D virtual environments, which often involve users donning electronic devices (DataGloves, goggles), wearing special clothing, or entering an environment containing electronic sensors so that they can manipulate objects and communicate with each other in 3D space (Section 5.6). These virtual environments also include games and virtual worlds like Second Life.

This list is just a starting point—there are undoubtedly other collaborative processes and strategies, such as for entertainment, multiperson games, challenging contests, theatrical experiences, or playful social encounters. The potential market for innovative software tools is large; however, designing for collaboration is a challenge because of the numerous and subtle questions of etiquette, trust, and responsibility. The challenge is increased by the need to account for anxiety, deceit, desire for dominance, and abusive behavior.

Collaboration is critical in today's global industries and markets. People often work in distributed development teams, where collaborators may be located across the hall or across the country (or even at home, telecommuting) while working on the same product. They are forced to efficiently use various social interaction tools (such as teleconferencing, calendaring, e-mail, chat, blogs, wikis, and IM) to collaborate on designs. In addition, they are forced to use development environments and tools that enforce the application of version control and other essential development processes/standards. Typically, multiple identically configured and networked development and test environments are set up and tests are run to be sure that everything works the same wherever it is installed. Then the social interaction tools are used once again to be sure everyone understands what they are supposed to do. Collaboration is what makes industry run.

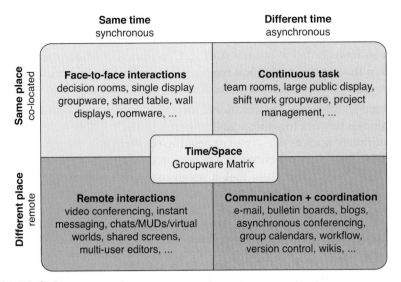

FIGURE 9.1

Time/space four-quadrant matrix model of group-supported work.

This variety of collaborative processes and strategies begs the question, how can we make sense of such a mix? The traditional way to decompose collaborative interfaces is by a time/space matrix generating four quadrants: same time, same place; same time, different place; different time, same place; and different time, different place. The common activities performed in each cell are listed in Figure 9.1. This descriptive model focuses on two critical dimensions and guides designers and users. However, as collaboration and participation strategies become more sophisticated, many designers combine interfaces from two or more cells in this matrix. For example, many social networking environments offer combinations of personal profiles, public postings, personal e-mail, and chat for flexibility in discussions; some also have voting and group-decision-support tools for structured decision making. Choosing which software to include depends on the users' needs and budgets.

Research in collaborative interfaces is often more complicated than in single-user interfaces. The multiplicity of users makes it difficult to conduct controlled experiments, and the flood of data from multiple users defies orderly analysis. Studies of small-group psychology, industrial and organizational behavior, sociology, and anthropology provide useful research paradigms, but many researchers must invent their own methodologies. Designers need to understand online communities. One step in that direction is the development of a theoretically-based online community framework (de Souza and Preece, 2004). Participant reports and ethnographic observations are appealing because they emphasize the colorful raw data from human discourse. Reflective case studies of groupware tools provide well-reasoned analyses to guide improvement and adoption, but the most compelling indicator of success for many organizations is the willingness of users to continue using a software tool. Social networking analysis has become a growth industry with increasingly effective visualization tools to show the evolution of communities or their decay as well as to better understand the social roles of users communicating (Balakrishnan et al., 2008; Welser et al., 2007).

Collaborative interfaces and social media web sites are maturing, but the determinants of success are still not clear. Advocates of rich media aspire to match face-to-face encounters, but proponents of lean media see benefits in lightweight text-only tools. Researchers and entrepreneurs are trying to find answers to numerous questions. Why is e-mail so widely used, while videoconferencing is limited mostly to corporate meetings? Why are cellphones intensely popular worldwide, while immersive environments remain a research topic? Understanding the causes of failures in work-oriented groupware, such as disparities between who does the work and who gets the benefit, could lead to refinements. How is the informal communication captured when groups are located remotely (Gutwin et al., 2008)? Other potential problems that must be overcome are threats to existing political power structures and insufficient critical mass of users who have convenient access. More subtle problems involve violation of social taboos and resistance to change. Successful designers will be those who find ways to accommodate strongly held community values and create acceptable social norms.

Arguments over measures of success complicate any evaluation. Whereas some people cite the high utilization of e-mail, others question whether e-mail aids or hinders job-related productivity (Jackson et al., 2003). The number of participants registered in a discussion board, the number of messages posted, and the regularity of return visits are automatable metrics that can be viewed as indicators of success. Subjective measures obtained by surveys and ethnographic observation include how satisfied participants are with the discussions and whether they feel a sense of belonging to the community. These individual measures need to be supplemented by community measures of the ambience (empathic or hostile), thread depth, and goal achievement (Smith, 2002). For business managers, cost/benefit analyses are also important (Millen et al., 2002). Videoconferencing may initially reduce travel expenses, but it can encourage collaboration and familiarity with more distant partners. However, eventually these relationships may lead to increasing costs and possibly more travel as a desire for face-to-face meetings grows. In educational environments, improved outcomes can be measured by comparison of scores on final exams, but when students work collaboratively in networked environments, they are often learning new skills that cannot be measured quantitatively. Too many educators ignore these collaboration skills, which are needed in the workplace, where teamwork and effective communication are essential.

For all the talk about how communication technologies are once again bringing about the "death of distance," distance really does matter for many activities and relationships (Olson and Olson, 2000). Physically close partnerships have the advantage of serendipitous encounters for informal exchanges, plus the facile capacity to confer easily over documents, maps, diagrams, or objects. Co-location also facilitates awareness of a partner's gaze and body language and enhances trust-building eye contact; for more personal encounters, electronic hugs are still no match for the real thing. Wide-angle, high-resolution, and low-latency video technologies can't yet match the richness of being there. Another often-overlooked factor is that there is something profound about the shared risk accepted by those who participate in face-to-face encounters. The willingness to separate oneself from familiar surroundings and possibly even expose oneself to physical harm, especially if arduous travel is required, raises the status of a meeting among all partners and can increase the commitment to making a constructive outcome.

Collaboration and social media participation take time, effort, and motivation. Researchers are starting to understand the reasons people participate in these activities and how to motivate higher levels of participation. One approach is to divide motivation into four categories: egoism (you will personally benefit from the activity), altruism (you genuinely want to help others), collectivism (you believe in supporting the community), and principlism (you've been taught principles such as "do unto others, as you would have them do unto you") (Batson et al., 2002). Another similar four-way division deals with value: value to self, value to a small group the user is involved with, value to a small group where there is no real involvement, and value to the entire user community (Rashid et al., 2006). Assigning points and status levels is yet another way to keep users involved and participating (Farzan et al., 2008). Designers are coming to understand that they must make contributions visible, enable participants to gain recognition or build their reputation, and reward exceptional contributions (Preece and Shneiderman, 2009).

9.3 Asynchronous Distributed Interfaces: Different Place, Different Time

Close collaboration across time and space is one of the gifts of technology. Durable messages transmitted electronically enable collaboration. For many users, electronic communication in various forms has become as much a way of life as the telephone. This communication can range from distributed loosely structured online communities to more formal e-mail. E-mail is widely appreciated because of its simple, personal, and prompt service, enabling communication between business partners or family members and friends across the street as well as across the world. It is excellent for clearly conveying facts (since there is a record of the communication) and convenient because cutting and pasting from/to other documents is easy. On the other hand, for complex negotiations or extended discussions, it can be too loosely structured (endless chatting with no leader, chaotic processes that don't lead to a decision), overwhelming (hundreds of messages per day can be difficult to absorb), and frustrating when it comes to locating relevant messages. In addition, late joiners to an e-mail discussion will find it hard to catch up on earlier comments. To remedy these problems, structured methods for electronic conferencing and various discussion-group methods have emerged (Olson and Olson, 2008).

9.3.1 E-mail

The atomic unit of collaboration for e-mail users is the *message*; the FROM party sends a message to the TO party. E-mail systems (Fig. 9.2) share the notion that one person can send a message to another person or a list of people. Messages usually are delivered in seconds or minutes; replying is easy and rapid, but recipients retain control of the pace of interaction by deciding how long to wait before replying.

E-mail messages typically contain text, but carefully formatted document, photo, music, or video files can be attached. Downloading long messages and large attachments can be a problem on mobile devices, but some images contain essential information such as diagrams or maps, so users may be willing to wait for and pay for these.

Most e-mail systems provide fields for FROM (sender), TO (list of recipients), CC (list of copy recipients), DATE, and SUBJECT. Users can specify that copies be sent to colleagues or assistants, and filters allow users to specify that they do not want to receive notices from a given sender or about a certain subject. Additional tools for filtering, searching, and archiving in commercial e-mail packages (for example, Microsoft Outlook®, Lotus Notes®, and Eudora®) enable users to manage incoming and previously received e-mail. However, better tools are still needed for high-volume users who receive hundreds of messages each day. Spam—unwanted, unsolicited advertisements, personal solicitations, and pornographic invitations—seriously annoys and frustrates many users. Most Internet services provide steadily improving filtering tools, but for many users spam dramatically undermines their satisfaction in using e-mail and impacts productivity.

Many web services offer their own e-mail programs, sometimes for free; examples include Microsoft's Hotmail® (now Windows Live Hotmail®), Yahoo!

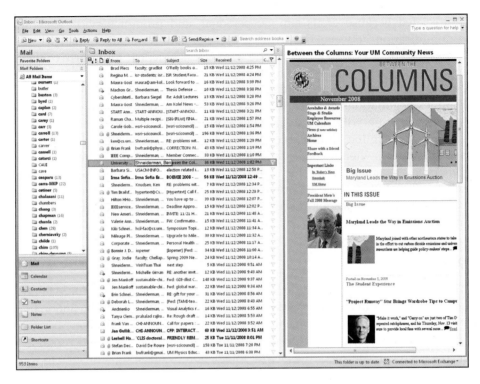

FIGURE 9.2

Interface for Microsoft Outlook 2007, showing the content of a folder selected in a hierarchy of folders and the content of an e-mail message. This is also a good example of coordinated windows and effective use of display space.

Mail®, and Google's Gmail™ (Fig. 9.3). Web-based e-mail services have become increasingly popular because they provide easy access from anywhere in the world via any computer equipped with a web browser. E-mail is also available on mobile devices, such as the RIM Blackberry or iPhone (Fig. 9.4), and is offered by most cell-phone service providers. These services have exploded in scope and range, and many people are now staying connected via e-mail through mobile devices as well as conventional computers.

In the U.S., more than three-fourths of the population use e-mail at work, at home, or via public-access terminals. Internet cafes are springing up all over the world, sometimes in the most unlikely places. A traveler from Tibet recently reported that getting access to e-mail was easier and cheaper than getting a shower. She paid $0.50 for one hour of fast e-mail access, while a shower cost $1.00 for a few minutes. Free e-mail is often available in airline terminals, Wi-Fi hot spots, and communal places like Starbucks and hotel lobbies.

Online directories and the ease with which e-mail addresses can be found on the Web are good facilitators, since it is necessary to know a person's e-mail

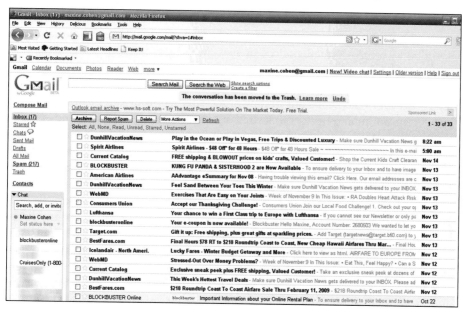

FIGURE 9.3

Web-based e-mail through Gmail showing the user's Inbox (http://www.gmail.com).

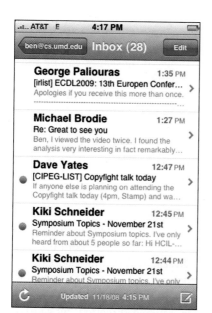

FIGURE 9.4

E-mail message on an iPhone.

address before sending a message. Such online directories often include the capacity to create new group lists, so that large groups can be reached easily. The dangers and frustrations of spam remain, though, and even noble ideas of collaboration can be undermined by users who fail to be polite, nuisances who persistently disrupt, electronic snoopers who do not respect privacy, or calculating opportunists who abuse their privileges. E-mail easily can become overwhelming (Bellotti et al., 2005).

9.3.2 Listservers and Yahoo!/ Google groups

E-mail is a great way to get started in electronic communication, but its basic features need extension to serve the needs of groups. When groups want more structured discussions, they need tools to organize, archive, and search the discussion history. A popular community structure is the *listserver*, to which individuals must subscribe to receive e-mail notices of new messages. LISTSERV® is a popular example of listserver software that uses *push technology*: Users subscribe to a list, and new messages are pushed into their e-mail inboxes. Listservers can be moderated by a leader who keeps out irrelevant messages, or they can be unmoderated, simply acting as mail reflectors that send out copies of received e-mail messages to all subscribers. Users can opt to receive these messages as they trickle through one by one, or choose to have them collected into long messages known as *digests*. Receiving messages individually makes replying to a single user straightforward, whereas it is cumbersome to extract a message from a digest of dozens of messages. Either way, keeping track of how messages relate to each other can be a problem, particularly when they get mixed in with regular e-mail. Many high-volume users try to get around the problem by setting filters to catch messages from different sources. Getting flooded with listserver-related e-mail can be a burden, so the decision to subscribe is sometimes a serious commitment. Listservers keep lists of subscribers and searchable archives of notes. L-Soft™, a major supplier of free and professional versions of listserver software, claims to support more than 30 million messages a day and 130 million list subscribers.

A second popular form of community structure is the web-based *Yahoo!* or *Google groups*, which evolved from the older *bulletin boards*. Each message has a short one-line heading and an arbitrarily long body. Messages may contain a question or an answer, an offer to buy or sell, an offer of support, interesting news, a joke, or a *flame* (abusive criticism). Topic *threads* starting with the initial question and then listing all the responses make it easier to follow the progress of a discussion (Fig. 12.14). Two basic types of messages can be sent: those that launch a new discussion topic, and those that reply to an existing message. To send a reply, users simply click a reply button on the existing message and complete the template that is presented. To initiate a new topic, users specify a subject heading that clearly describes the contents of the message. The date of posting is usually shown with the user's username.

Many web-based discussion groups now support graphical attachments, links to web sites, private discussion areas, improved message archiving and searching, and e-mail notification about new messages. Aesthetic features that may enhance the experience include colorful backgrounds that complement the graphic design of the site, graphics, emoticons to signal mood, topic icons to indicate the type of topic, and personal pictures. Robust software on powerful servers supports service to large numbers of participants, provides archival backup, and ensures security, privacy, and protection against viruses and hackers.

Enabling users to search message archives by subject, date, and sender and to view archives in various ways (threaded by date, reverse threaded, by sender) extends the usability of the discussion groups. Allowing users to represent themselves with pictures or icons or to link to their home pages increases a sense of presence (the impression that one is actually talking to another human being) and helps users to identify each other. *Emoticons*, also known as *smilies* (for example, ☺ and ☹), can ease tension by signaling the sender's emotional state in an otherwise textual environment devoid of smiles, laughing, and other body language.

Access to discussion groups may be open or restricted to members who must register and be approved. Restricting membership helps to deter people who are not interested in the topic and troublemakers. It also helps to ensure that discussions stay on topic. For example, to join an online discussion group for anesthesiologists, a prospective member had to present certification paperwork. This is to prevent unqualified people taking part in the discussions. Membership-only discussion groups may have only tens or hundreds of participants, whereas open boards may be visited by thousands of people each day.

In large discussion groups, most users read and do not post; they are silent members who are known as *lurkers*. Some researchers estimate that lurkers outnumber posters by as much as 100 to 1, but in some discussion boards—particularly in patient-support communities—the ratios are much lower (Nonnecke and Preece, 2000). Whether lurking is a problem depends on the goals of the discussion and the number of people who participate. In a small discussion board where most of the members lurk, the feeling of lively discussion dissipates. In a large discussion board, large numbers of lurkers may be attractive to those who wish to stand out and influence the group. Some participants and moderators like to spark discussion by asking provocative questions or making bold statements. At other times, they may ask active posters to take their discussions offline or to start a separate group, so as to keep the volume of messages low and of interest to the entire group.

Thousands of Yahoo!/Google and listserver groups have emerged around the world, administered by devoted moderators. These Gertrude Steins of electronic salons keep the discussion moving and on-topic, while filtering out malicious or unsavory messages. Indeed, groups without such dedicated moderators usually do not survive; nurturing the group through all stages of its growth is usually a requirement for success. Social roles of these participants (Welser et al., 2007) are evolving. Visualization methods can clearly demonstrate the communication patterns. The pattern for an "answer person" is quite different from the pattern for a "discussion person" (Fig. 9.5).

A typical business use of discussion groups is for an online conference that might support a product-planning group in which members propose possible products to develop in time for an annual industry exposition and then vote to stipulate their choices. Thoughtful discussions within a conference are facilitated because asynchronous communications systems allow time for participants to consider their positions judiciously, consult other materials such as market surveys, discuss issues with colleagues, and review competitors' offerings. Then participants can phrase their contributions carefully, without the pressure to make an immediate comment that is inherent in a telephone call, in a face-to-face meeting, or when using synchronous communications software

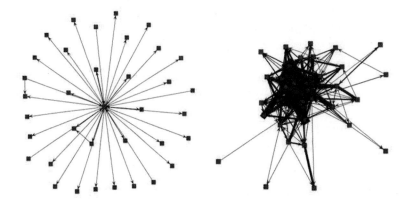

FIGURE 9.5

Visualization of the communication pattern of an "answer person" on the left, and a "discussion person" on the right (Welser et al., 2007).

(Section 9.4). There is a powerful advantage of 24-hour availability, so users can participate when it is convenient for them. Skeptics who argue for immediacy and high-bandwidth videoconferencing should consider the advantages of a slower pace for many personalities and for those for whom writing a well-formed sentence is a challenge. This approach also provides advantages for teams that are distributed across the world, for whom finding a convenient synchronous time is nearly impossible.

9.3.3 Blogs and wikis

Web-logs or *blogs* and *wikis* are new forms of social software that started to become popular around 2001. Both types of software support the democratic philosophy that underpins the Web—namely, that all people should be able to make their opinions widely available to others without having to cross the hurdles of editorial boards and censorship that govern traditional media such as print, TV, and radio. Blogs are open electronic documents or diaries that are "owned" by their creators, but readers can contribute comments. Blogs can focus on any topic; popular themes include politics, music, popular literature, travels, film critiques, and personal diaries. Blog software, provided by Blogger.com and others, makes it easy for the blog owners to tell their stories and allows readers to add comments (Fig. 9.6). The software provides templates for readers to add pictures and provide links. The success of one's blog is judged according to how many people visit it, link to it, and discuss it—in other words, by the attention that it gets from other bloggers. Some companies pay people to blog and profess their expert opinions and viewpoints. Some of the reasons for blogging

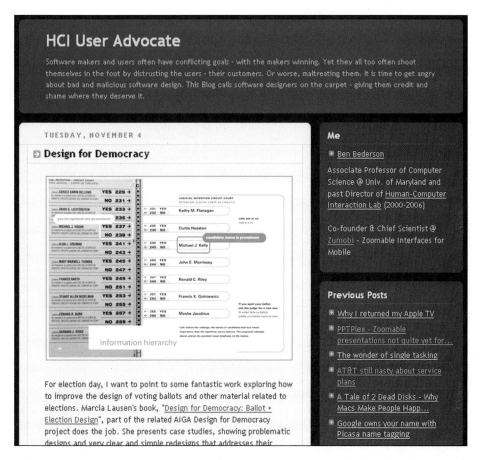

FIGURE 9.6

Sample blog posting using the Blogger tool (www.blogger.com). Graphics as well as text appear on the blog page, and the entries are listed with the newest at the top (Courtesy of Ben Bederson).

include documenting one's life, providing comments and opinions, expressing emotions, articulating ideas through writing, and forming and maintaining community forums (Nardi et al., 2004).

Wikis are collaborative web pages that are open for anyone to add or revise content, unless they are limited to members who must supply a password. "Wiki" is a Hawaiian word meaning fast. Wikis are used for discussing a variety of topics, but they are particularly popular with project teams, who like to discuss and record innovative ideas, plan meetings, and develop agendas on the team wiki. *Wikipedia* is a collaborative encyclopedia developed by people from over 40 countries and in over 250 different languages (Fig. 9.7). This amazing venture demonstrates the power of collaboration. Anyone can add to

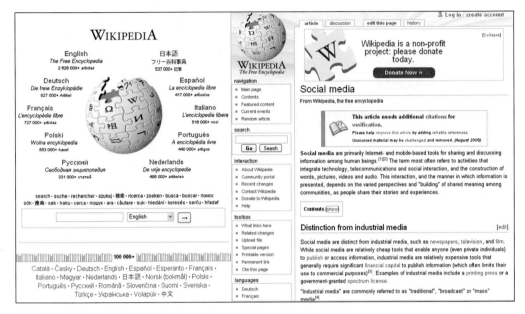

FIGURE 9.7

The home page of Wikipedia and a sample page on social media.

an existing topic or start a new one. Contributors are asked to be respectful to others when editing or adding to their work. An archive of previous pages also helps to ensure that valuable work can be recovered. In spite of the high levels of controversy and vandalism, Wikipedia devotees are quick to resolve differences and repair attacks. Wikipedia (and other forms of social media participation) are often perceived as the "wild west" with few rules and running rampant, but there are 44 wiki pages in the Wikipedia Official Policy that guide behavior (Butler et al., 2008). There is also a well-organized infrastructure of admins, bureaucrats, and stewards, plus an active Board of Directors to resolve differences and set policy. Interestingly enough, Wikipedia provides an example of supporting a wide range of activities, contributors, and structures and still producing an excellent collaborative product. It is a primary example of how the "wisdom of the crowds" phenomenon works (Kittur et al., 2007; Surowiecki, 2004).

Initially, Wikipedia was scorned by academics as an unreliable source of information. That opinion is now changing, and studies have shown Wikipedia to be appropriately researched and well written. Incorrect information seems to be monitored and removed. It is updated by millions of people daily and is very current. When a major news reporter (Tim Russert) died, his Wikipedia site was updated within minutes of the reporting of his death. One of the interesting points of Wikipedia is how naturally it supports a wide range of users, from the novice to the expert. Novices find Wikipedia easy to use and see it as an information-gathering tool. They may even feel they have some limited expertise and participate in the editing part of Wikipedia. Experts look at Wikipedia from more of a community perspective and become more like peer reviewers as they transition to "Wikipedians" (Bryant et al., 2005).

The phenomenon of Wikipedia was rather unexpected: It was a grass-roots effort that has changed the way we find and use information. This form of social media participation has created a new field called *Wikinomics* (Tapscott and Williams, 2006). Three conditions feed this development. First, the cost for contribution is low; editing a wiki is rather straightforward. Second, tasks are easily broken down into manageable pieces, and minor editing can easily be done on small contributions to the wiki. Finally, the cost of integration and quality control is low, as wikis are based on volunteer contributions. The number of users of Wikipedia is huge and growing constantly; the contributors constitute only a small percentage of the users (Rafaeli and Ariel, 2008).

Microblogging or *mini-blogging* is yet another new collaborative type of social media participation. People use this to talk about their life as it happens, in short bursts (usually less than 200 characters). These entries can be shared via text messages, instant messages, e-mail, or the Web. The current services include Twitter™, Jaiku™, Tumblr, and Pownce™. Since people seem to be so rushed and time is of the essence, these communications have become more common. Twitter, launched in 2006, seems to be the most popular microblogging service (Fig. 9.8). Communications, which are limited to 140 characters, are called *tweets*. Users can "follow" other users, who are added as "friends." Users who are not friends can still monitor the communication and be "followers"; that is, friendships can be one way (followers) or two way (friends). This model maps nicely into directed graphs (Java et al., 2007). One software developer has created a web site that superimposes a public timeline onto a Google map (http://twittervision.com/) and tracks twitters all over the world.

The creation of all this user-generated content has spawned a need to be able to

FIGURE 9.8

An example of Twitter on an iPhone (from http://daringfireball. net/2008/04).

search this material as well. Sites like Technorati provide real-time search engines that look at blogs and other user-generated content. Other sites, such as del.icio.us and Digg, provide facilities to share bookmarks and other shared content. Digg functions by users voting and commenting on stories; these activities can either raise a story to the top or bury it. Users are creating their own taxonomies to better manage the social tagging activity. For example, a bottom-up classification system called a *folksonomy* has emerged.

9.3.4 Online and networked communities

Online and *networked communities* have become talk-show topics, with social commentators celebrating or warning about their transformational power. Online communities are topically focused and geographically dispersed; they exist for AIDS patients, archaeologists, and agronomists (Maloney-Krichmar and Preece, 2005; Kim, 2000). Some networked communities are geographically bounded, such as the ones in Seattle, WA; Blacksburg, VA; Milan, Italy; and Singapore (Cohill and Kavanaugh, 2000; Schuler, 1996). The frequency of contact may vary from often to on certain occasions. Some may even display a hybrid capability and have a physical face-to-face component; for example getting together for an annual car show. Online and networked community members may use all the software discussed earlier and then add other features, such as information resources, community histories, bibliographies, and photo archives.

Howard Rheingold's (1993) popular book tells charming and touching stories of collaboration and support in the San Francisco–based WELL online community. The positive side is the facilitation of communication among like-minded people who have shared interests. Patient-support communities have been particularly successful for bringing together those with similar medical problems; patients with rare diseases and those who are house-bound or who live in isolated rural areas are pleased to be able to share their stories and problems and get support. Similarly, online communities are bringing together people from across the world whose access to high-bandwidth communication is limited. As low-cost mobile devices become more pervasive, this trend will continue. The negative side is that online community participants may have lower levels of commitment than people who attend face-to-face meetings of hobby clubs, neighborhood groups, and parent/teacher associations. Furthermore, there are problems with false identities, malicious users, and deceptive invitations (Donath, 2007). Some early studies suggested that active participants on the Internet withdrew from other social contacts and felt more alienated, but later studies have shown more positive outcomes (Kraut et al., 2002; Robinson and Nie, 2002).

Community members typically have a shared goal, identity, or common interest and participate electronically on a continuing basis. Some communities have strict rules on membership, and some members have an intense devotion to their online communities. This generates a sometimes remarkable willingness to trust and assist other community members, leading to what sociologists call "generalized reciprocity"—helping others in the belief that someday someone will help you. In health-support communities, the help is often in the form of information about treatments or physicians, but a striking aspect to any reader of these discussions is the high level of empathic support conveyed among participants (Preece, 1999). Postings can reveal personal fears about surgery and generate supportive comments such as "Don't worry, I've been through it and you'll do fine" or "Just hang in there—you are not alone" and requests to "Let the group know how your surgery turns out—we're cheering for you."

Developing successful online and networked communities is not easy, as revealed by the thousands of electronic ghost towns without any participants. Good interfaces are just one factor in determining success. Attention to and support for social interaction as the community grows are equally important. The skill, energy, and nurturing attention of community leaders and moderators are often the determining factors in a thriving community. These leaders may take on various roles in the life of these communities, including social roles such as community-seeker, community-builder, evangelist, publisher, or small team leader (Thom-Santelli et al., 2008). Successful communities tend to have clearly stated purposes, well-defined memberships, and explicit policies to guide behavior (Maloney-Krichmar and Preece, 2005). For example, Bob's ACL Kneeboard (Fig. 9.9) is for people who have suffered tears of the anterior cruciate ligaments (ACL) in their knees and are facing decisions about surgical methods. Bob started this online community in 1996, and his medical history, with explicit pictures of surgery on both his knees, tells his story. Members return year after year to help recent sufferers with their decisions, provide information about new surgical practices, and offer emotional support for their pain and difficult choices.

Community policies must deal with rude behavior, off-topic comments, and commercial notices. Some communities have written policy documents enforced by moderators, while others establish norms of behavior that are upheld by members. Principles of freedom of speech should be extended into the online world, but there are novel dangers of disruptive behaviors, illegal activities, and invasion of privacy. Some online communities have been criticized for spreading racist or otherwise harmful material, so the challenge is to preserve valued freedoms and rights while minimizing harm. Each online community has to decide how to interpret such policies, just as each town and state must decide on local rules.

The user interfaces for online communities tend to be simple in order to accommodate the large number of users, some still with low-speed dial-in access. The intrigue lies in the complexity of the conversations, especially in spirited replies and debates. As usage increases, the moderator must decide whether to split the community into more focused groups to avoid overwhelming participants with thousands of new messages. Ensuring that the communities remain interesting and consistent is a challenge; if a group of physics researchers who are discussing current theories is visited by students asking beginner-level questions,

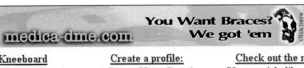

The Kneeboard
Community is here!

Create a profile:
tell your Knee Story!

Check out the new
Knee article library!

[Post New Message] [Search] [Set Preferences] [Mark All Messages Read]
[View User Profiles] [Create Profile] [Knee Library] [Who's Bob?]

Bob's ACL WWWBoard
Message Index
Welcome!

Messages Posted
Within the Last 7 Day(s)

32 of 6,970 Messages Displayed
(Reversed Threaded Listing)

- girls flash -- girls flash -- Friday, 31 October 2008, at 8:46 p.m.
- eminent domain property right -- eminent domain property right -- Friday, 31 October 2008, at 7:28 p.m.
- symantec corp -- symantec corp -- Friday, 31 October 2008, at 7:28 p.m.
- Post op weight bearing (views: 35) -- karatechic -- Thursday, 30 October 2008, at 1:56 p.m.
  - Re: Post op weight bearing (views: 24) -- OLarryR -- Thursday, 30 October 2008, at 7:07 p.m.
    - Re: Post op weight bearing (views: 26) -- OLarryR -- Thursday, 30 October 2008, at 7:12 p.m.
  - Re: Post op weight bearing (views: 41) -- SueBW -- Thursday, 30 October 2008, at 2:27 p.m.
- Brace Separation Anxiety (views: 62) -- Joel -- Thursday, 30 October 2008, at 8:57 a.m.
  - Re: Brace Separation Anxiety (views: 27) -- OLarryR -- Thursday, 30 October 2008, at 7:05 p.m.

FIGURE 9.9

Bob's ACL Kneeboard, a threaded discussion board for people who have suffered tears of the anterior cruciate ligaments in their knees (http://factotem.org/cgi-bin/kneebbs.pl).

the experts will want the moderator to steer the students to other discussion boards or communities. An alternative is for the researchers to move their discussion to a new online community web site.

Within corporations, universities, or government agencies, communities may be established for topics such as corporate direction, new technologies, or product development. These specialist groups are often referred to as communities of practice, to acknowledge their professional orientation (Wenger, 1998). Understanding how to make CoPs thriving places for discussion can be a challenge. How can management motivate employees to spend time on helping colleagues, when they may be in competition for a promotion? One school of thought is that automated tools can be used to mine the content of old discussions for nuggets of knowledge that are relevant to a current problem—a hot topic among knowledge-management professionals. However, skeptics suggest that it may be more effective to designate individuals and develop processes for compiling, summarizing, and classifying organizational knowledge so as to facilitate future retrieval. Communities of inquiry are promoted in educational circles as web-based conferences to promote discussions using these stages of action: (1) ask, (2) investigate, (3) create, (4) discuss, and (5) reflect (Bruce and Easley, 2000).

Online communities have become common for distance education courses and as supplements to face-to-face classes, because they can stimulate lively educational experiences. Widespread adoption of educational course-management systems such as Blackboard®, Moodle™, Sakai™, Angel™, and FirstClass® demonstrate the efficacy of an online format for college courses, complete with homework assignments, projects, tests, and final examinations. Instructors find the constant flow of messages to be a rewarding challenge, and students are generally satisfied with the experience. The essence of the virtual classroom is an environment to facilitate collaborative learning, often with team projects (Fig. 9.10). For distance-seperated education students, the increased ability to be in constant communication with other learners is an obvious benefit. But even for campus-based courses, the technology provides a means for a rich, collaborative learning environment that exceeds the traditional classroom in its ability to connect students and make course materials available on an around-the-clock basis (Hiltz and Goldman, 2005; Hazemi and Hailes, 2001). The University of Phoenix and the British Open University are impressive examples of how interactive technologies are being employed to serve educational needs.

Some online communities support thousands of contributors to important projects such as the Linux operating system. The phenomenal growth of this open-source movement and its remarkable impact demonstrate how effective geographically dispersed online communities can be. Hundreds of thousands of programmers also feel devotion to the Slashdot community, whose lively discussions of technical topics often receive hundreds of comments per hour. Millions of people participate in eBay to buy or sell products, generating feelings of shared experiences that are the hallmark of a community. Sellers strongly identify with their colleagues and collaborate to pressure eBay management for new policies. The reputation manager (Feedback Forum) enables purchasers to record comments on sellers, such as these typically complimentary notes: "Everything works," "Quick shipment," "thank you," "Peace," "A+ seller," "Item exactly as described, fast shipping, smooth transaction," "A++++++++++," "I'm very satisfied A++++." And these are just the first steps. Creative entrepreneurs and visionary political organizers are still exploring novel networked approaches for business development and consensus seeking.

For scientists who need to collaborate at a distance, discussing ideas, viewing objects, and sharing data and other resources, *collaboratories*—laboratories

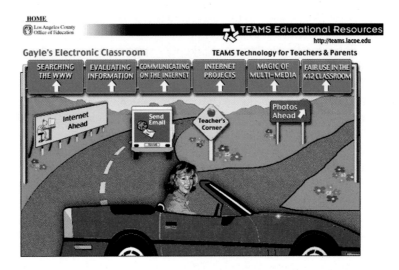

FIGURE 9.10

Starting screen for a virtual classroom example from the Los Angles County Office of Education. There are many clickable links that open various windows and applications, including a link to send e-mail directly to the teacher. There is a picture of Gayle (the teacher) to personalize the site (http://teams.lacoe.edu/documentation/classrooms/classrooms.html).

without walls—provide new opportunities (Bos et al., 2007). Geographically dispersed teams, for example, can benefit from sharing costs for and being able to access remote instruments for space or environmental research. Collaboratories can employ all forms of collaborative interfaces, but the asynchronous technologies seem to be most valuable. Collaboratories are also social structures that promote collaboration among groups with complementary skills, accelerate dissemination of novel results, and facilitate learning by students or new researchers. Standard data formats facilitate sharing that leads to multiple analyses, and well-maintained archives reduce redundant experimentation.

Social media web-site designers are also trying to create communities around their users. For example, Flickr users can invite friends to view, tag, and comment on their photos and can sign up for notifications when new photos are posted. Whole families can sign up to see marriage ceremony photos or keep up with traveling cousins, thereby strengthening family bonds. Similarly, book-, restaurant-, or movie-reviewing web sites encourage discussions among reviewers. Political, sports, religious, or financial blogs can easily trigger hundreds of postings to discuss controversial positions. Here again, the lively discussions are highly visible, but most invitations to participate fail to generate any comments, so more research is needed to understand the determinants of success (Preece and Shneiderman, 2009).

9.4 Synchronous Distributed Interfaces: Different Place, Same Time

Collaborative interfaces are increasingly flexible, allowing distributed groups to work together at the same time by using chat, instant messaging, or text messaging via cell phones. Shared screens allow teachers and trainers to present web seminars (*webinars* or *webcasts*) from their homes with audio accompaniment and video windows, while thousands watch their slides and demonstrations from anywhere that they can find an Internet connection. Physicians in hospitals hundreds of miles apart can share X-rays, MRIs, and body scans so that they can discuss treatments for rare cancers and other ailments. Voice over Internet (VoIP) services, such as Skype, offer free or low-cost phone calls and audio- or videoconferences.

Social media participation also enables discretionary and playful collaborations for connecting with friends, meeting new people, or playing games. Active voting by text messaging and phone for *American Idol* performers has become a cultural phenomenon. Lightweight awareness technologies like Twitter allow friends to keep up with one another all day long, while richer, immersive 3D experiences engage thousands of participants in Second Life. Some of the most innovative commercial developments are interactive games that permit two or more people to participate simultaneously in poker, chess, or complex fantasy games such as *EverQuest* or *World of Warcraft*. These games offer 3D graphics and animations that engage players as they try to outwit each other; enthusiastic users eagerly acquire high-speed Internet connections, powerful game-playing machines, and special input devices such as paddles with numerous buttons.

9.4.1 Chat, instant messaging, and texting

Even simple synchronous exchanges of text messages among groups of 2 to 20 participants can be exciting. Internet Relay Chat (IRC) programs and software such as Second Life and Microsoft's LiveMeeting® have *chat* windows as well as graphical interfaces. Brief greetings and short comments are typical of fast-moving chat environments, where participants must type quickly and hope that their comments appear on the screen near to the ones that they answer. There is little time to reflect.

In Second Life, users can explore 3D worlds by teleporting their avatars (graphic characters that represent users instead of mere login names) around the screen using a touchpad, cursor keys, or a joystick. They can move close to other characters and interact with them, or simply tour the environment. The menu of viewing options also allows users to look up or down, turn around, and jump or wave to express their emotions. Participation in Second Life varies from game-playing teenagers to the more staid corporate presences: Some corporations and educational institutions have established their own islands in Second Life.

Users can tire of navigating through the graphical worlds, however, so they often spend more time on the textual chat. This begs the question, what is the added value that avatars and 3D graphics bring to such environments? If avatars are moving around, social proximity can facilitate discussion, since users will know who else is participating. Avatars are an essential feature for many games, but they may be less important for other topics or groups with a stable set of participants. Once past the initial rapid exchange during greetings, text users can conduct useful business meetings, support lively social club-houses, and offer sincere care for those in need.

Another aspect of chat environments is that they allow participants to take on new personalities, underscored by engaging and imaginative names such as Gypsy, Larry Lightning, or Really Rosie. The social chatter can be light, provocative, or intimidating. Unfortunately, some chat participants turn into wisecrack-ing *flamers* more intent on a putdown than a conversation, and with a tendency to violent or obscene language. Even worse, chat rooms, like the real world, can be environments for deception, illicit invitations, and various forms of entrap-ment. Children and parents, as well as unsuspecting business people, need to take precautions.

Instant messaging is a popular alternative to open chat rooms, in part because membership can be tightly controlled. IM is ideal for quick exchanges between close friends, family members, or small groups who are readily available at their desktop or laptop computers. Facebook, Microsoft, and Yahoo! have created IM systems that have hundreds of millions of subscribers.

On some systems, users launch IM programs by clicking on a small icon on the desktop, in a toolbar, or in an applications list. Other systems automatically show users which of their friends are also logged on when they log on. Either way, there is a window that shows the buddy or friends lists that the users have cre-ated. Each list contains the names of the participants in that community. A chat window similar to that found in chat systems contains the conversation, and new messages can be typed in the lower pane. Conversations can involve two or more people. Typically, IM communities contain fewer than 20 people, but they may be larger. Membership is usually restricted to groups whose members know each other and want to be in regular contact. For example, students from Thailand studying in the United States may share one IM community, as well as another with Thai friends across the United States and friends back home. Much of the motivation is to enable users to track each other's movements and to chat. It's comforting to know when friends come online, how their work is progressing, whether they are sick or well, and so on. IM is used in a similar way to text messaging. It's all about knowing which friends are where and when; it can also be an inexpensive way to have long-distance conversations.

Most IM systems include features such as emoticons, the ability to send photographs and other files, and a wide variety of sounds and backgrounds. Research into novel ways for users to identify each other indicates that sound may have a role (Isaacs et al., 2002); an office manager might be represented by a high-pitched "ping," peers by the "doh, rei, me" musical scale, and a partner or spouse by the first three bars of his or her favorite tune. Comments, like those typical of chats, are short and concise. Groups in which members know each other delight in developing standard phrases (see Table 7.1; for example, LOL for "laughing out loud" or IMHO for "in my humble opinion") and cryptic shorthand ways to communicate using symbols and characters (for example, "me4u", "cu@1", or "☺2cu"). Teenagers are particularly adept and creative users of such shorthand, especially when texting on their cellphones. Researchers report that teenagers (Grinter and Palen, 2002) and office workers (George, 2002; Herbsleb et al., 2002) are the largest user groups of IM. This finding has generated concern for parents who want to monitor their children's online activities (Fig. 9.11).

Security and privacy are essential for all IM users, although needs may differ. For example, office workers may not want their colleagues and bosses to read their communications. However, the popular assumption that workplace instant messaging is only for idle chatter has been shown to be wrong. According to one study (Isaacs et al., 2002), productive work was carried out by the frequent IM users, who used it to discuss a broad range of topics with colleagues via many fast-paced interactions per day, each with many short turns and much threading and multitasking. Users rarely switched from IM to another medium when the conversations got complex. Only 28% of conversations were simple interactions, and only 31% were about scheduling or coordination. Still, evidence that serious work can be accomplished via this means of interaction does not take away from the capacity for IM's informal, flexible style to also support the lightweight exchanges that contribute to awareness of what colleagues, family, or friends are doing and where they are (Nardi et al., 2000).

Texting via cell phones (using the *Short Message Service*, or SMS) has also become an extremely popular means of communication. The mobile nature of cellphone texting allows for lively but private exchanges, but texting is also used to send messages to be read later or simple alerts. Worldwide acceptance is high, in part because texting costs are low. Some organizations use text-messaging capabilities to inform their constituents of activities, such as traffic alerts or weather-related emergencies, or to provide disaster-response instructions. Fishermen in India use their cellphones to check out the best prices before deciding where to come ashore (Rheingold, 2002).

People can now easily check in with each other to report where they are, what they are doing, and what they intend to do next. A typical text on the D.C. Metro

FIGURE 9.11

Parental control system to oversee children's online activities (http://www.
sentryparentalcontrols.com/). This is a sample activity log: It shows the history
of online activities, violations, and time spent on various activities.

goes like this: "I'm at VanNess, eta 10 min" (meaning estimated time of arrival in 10
minutes). Political groups at rallies or partying teenagers can organize and coordinate smoothly because of the ease and speed of communication. Similarly, text
messages relaying emergency information can reach people wherever they are.

Teenagers are large users of these forms of communication. Both texting and
IM are used for different types of activities. IM is better when trying to set up a
plan to get together, as several teenagers can converse all at once. The convenience of being at home also provides accessibility to parents to arrange transportation and inform them of the planned activity. Being online additionally
provides the opportunity to check out web sites (Grinter et al., 2006). Text messages, on the other hand, are better for a shorter confirmatory communication.
Needless to say, however, this distinction is blurring as web sites and conferencing capabilities become more widely available on phones.

9.4.2 Audio- and videoconferencing

Audio- and videoconferencing are steadily growing commercial successes for when synchronous communication is needed to organize a special event, deal with tense negotiations, or build trust among new contacts. Standard telephones or cell phones anywhere in the world can be used to dial into an audioconferencing system, and the convenience of *desktop videoconferencing* from offices or homes enables architects to show their models or grandparents to keep in contact with grandchildren. At the other end of the spectrum, specialized videoconferencing rooms with high-resolution multi-camera setups that must be reserved by appointment give these events greater significance. The hardware, network, and software architectures that support synchronous videoconferencing have dramatically improved. However, users must still deal with the problems of delays, sharing, synchronization of actions, narrow field of view, and poorly transmitted social cues such as gaze and changes in body language, which are essential for effective turn taking and reading the moods of remote participants (Olson and Olson, 2008).

Today, Microsoft's meeting software has improved the video-conferencing capabilities. There can be multiple conferencing windows, so more can be captured and the conference can be more realistic. For example, one window can display a device being discussed, another window can show a video and another window can capture the faces of the participants. As the resolution becomes more robust, expressions and images become clearer, adding fidelity to the experience. Similar services are also available from Yahoo!, Cisco®, Citrix®, and WebEx.

The Polycom®, Sony, TANDBERG®, and HP Halo videoconferencing platforms provide increasingly high-quality images and sound (Fig. 9.12). Some meetings are simple discussions that replace face-to-face visits; the improvement over the telephone is the capacity to assess facial expressions and body-language cues for enthusiasm, disinterest, or anger. Many professional meetings include conferencing over some object of interest, such as a document, map, or photo. Developers emphasize the need for convenient turn taking and document sharing by using terms such as *smooth*, *lightweight*, or *seamless integration*. These same requirements are needed for the growing family market. Grandparents love interacting with grandchildren via videoconferencing—they speak about their experiences in glowing terms and schedule regular meetings. Likewise, some parents who must travel make a ritual of after-dinner or bedtime videoconferences with their kids to keep in touch. Videoconferencing capabilities in hospital settings allow patients and families to visit, diminishing some of the stress caused by a hospital confinement for both parties.

Controlled experimentation on performance with different media reinforces the importance of having a clear voice channel for coordination while users are looking at the objects of interest, while adding video of the person speaking can distract participants from focusing on the objects of interest.

FIGURE 9.12

An example of high-quality videoconferencing from HP Halo. Some of the participants are local; others are remote (http://www.hp.com/).

Instead of a scheduled videoconference, some researchers believe that continuously available video windows, tunnels, or spaces would enable an enriched form of communication that supports opportunistic collaborations and informal awareness. These continuous video connections from public spaces such as kitchens or hallways could enable colleagues to see who is at work and ask the casual questions that might lead to closer ties. Some test subjects appreciated these opportunities, but others found them intrusive, distracting, or violating of their privacy (Jancke et al., 2001). Video connections from individual offices might enable participants to access the resources of their office environments while affording a chance for communication and emotional contact, but again, the intrusion of such systems is often seen as an annoyance (Olson and Olson, 2000).

Researchers are still trying to understand the conditions under which the richer media of audio- or videoconferencing are more effective and appealing than the lean media of chat, IM, and texting. Similarly, there are times when these synchronous media are less effective and appealing than asynchronous textual discussions. First-time meetings may be improved by a videoconference if a face-to-face meeting is not possible, whereas reflective discussion may be better supported by a listservers, a wiki, or e-mail.

Electronic classrooms balance the inclusion of new technologies with the exploration of new teaching and learning styles. At the University of Toronto, the ePresence project gives distant learners increased opportunities for participation during the lectures and the capacity to review later. Webcasting allows remote viewers to see and hear the lecturer, and students can have private chats during and after the lectures (Baecker et al., 2007). The Georgia Tech eClass project emphasized capturing videos of lecturers and their presentations so students could review them or make up missed classes (Pimentel et al., 2001). Nova Southeastern University was an early pioneer in distance learning and electronic classrooms. Its early electronic classrooms, starting in the 1980s, ran on a Unix platform using dial-up connections. The communication was all text-based, but it did permit students and an instructor to hold online classes. Later versions included microphones and faster connections. Today this technology has been replaced by more modern course management systems (CMSs) like Blackboard (formerly WebCT®), Sakai, and Moodle that provide electronic classrooms in addition to discussion-posting features, electronic grading and gradebooks, electronic testing, and syllabus-creation features.

9.5 Face-to-Face Interfaces: Same Place, Same Time

Teams of people often work together in the same room and use complex shared technology. Pilot and copilot collaboration in airplanes has been designed carefully with shared instruments and displays, and coordination among air-traffic controllers has a long history that has been studied thoroughly (Wiener and Nagel, 1988). Stock-market traders and commodity-market brokers view complex displays, receive orders from customers, and engage in rapid face-to-face collaboration or negotiations to achieve deals. Brainstorming and design teams often work closely together and have special needs because of the rapid exchanges, frequent updates, and the necessity for accurate recordings of events and outcomes. Even the familiar classroom lecture has changed, as some professors give up chalk and present their notes as slide shows via projectors. Classroom lectures can also be made interactive, with electronic polling devices at each student station and the capability to project a student's desktop for the entire class to view.

9.5.1 Electronic meeting rooms, control rooms, and public spaces

Ordinary business meetings are rapidly integrating computer technology, because so many participants arrive with relevant information already on their laptops or networks. However, computer presentations in business meetings can interfere with communication by reducing eye contact and turning a lively dialog into a boring monologue in a darkened room. The first challenge is to understand the role of technology in supporting information transfer, while preserving the trust-building and motivational aspects of face-to-face encounters. The second challenge is to recognize the appropriate role of shared control of computing and presentation tools so that participants can be more active, while preserving the leadership role of the meeting organizer.

In business meetings, structured social processes for brainstorming, voting, and ranking can produce highly productive outcomes. The University of Arizona was a pioneer in developing the social process, the physical environment, and the software tools that continue to be marketed by GroupSystems®. This environment promises to "reduce or eliminate the dysfunctions of the group interaction so that a group reaches or exceeds its task potential" (Valacich et al., 1991). By allowing anonymous submission of suggestions and ranking of proposals, the authors introduced a wider range of possibilities; the approach also ensured that ideas were valued on their merits, independently of their "originators." Because ego investments and conflicts were reduced, groups seemed to be more open to novel suggestions. With this approach, well-trained facilitators with backgrounds in social dynamics consult with the team leader to plan the decision session and to write the problem statement. In a typical task, 45 minutes of brainstorming by 15 to 20 people can produce hundreds of lines of suggestions for questions such as "How can we increase sales?" or "What are the key issues in technological support for group work?" Then, items can be filtered, clustered into similar groups, and presented to participants for refinement and ranking. Afterwards, a printout and electronic-file version of the entire session is immediately available.

Even informal processes can be facilitated by shared workspaces in which multiple participants can add their contributions by projecting their displays for the group to see or by cutting and pasting from their materials to the group display. For example, three architects' proposals or three business plans might be shown on a common display to facilitate comparison. Another approach is for managers to arrive at a meeting and offer copies of slides for all to annotate and take home.

Several shared-workspace designs have found a growing audience. Newer devices, such as the simple, cheap sensors tied to special pen holders available from mimio®, allow participants to get electronic copies of what is written on the large whiteboard in front of the group. SMART Technologies, Inc. produces a SMART Board that allows interaction with fingers or pens, locally or remotely (Fig. 9.13); it also offers the SMART Table™ (Fig. 8.14), which serves a similar purpose to Microsoft Surface. Another leader in interactive whiteboard technology is Numonics.

Expensive control rooms for electric utilities, chemical plants, and transportation networks often have large wall displays so all participants have a shared situation awareness. Similarly, military war rooms and NASA space-flight operations centers enable rapid collaboration among participants, often in stressful

FIGURE 9.13

Children using the SMART Board electronic whiteboard from Smart Technologies Inc. to annotate a diagram in the classroom (left) and compose a story across distributed locations (right) (www.smarttech.com).

conditions. Researchers are developing high-resolution interactive wall displays for smaller groups to conduct brainstorming or design sessions (Guimbretière et al., 2001; Section 8.5).

Interaction in *public spaces* with wall displays may be through personal computers, mobile devices, or special input devices (Vogel and Balakrishnan, 2004; Streitz et al., 2007). The advantage of a shared public space is that everyone sees the same display and can work communally to produce a joint product, but privacy concerns and distractions trouble some users. Some technologies support fewer goal-directed activities, such as keeping colleagues informed about your whereabouts or a project's status or just presenting public notices in stores or offices.

Sharing photos is a growing topic for collaborative interfaces. Personal collections made public on the Web or sent as e-mail attachments are the most common approaches, but some innovative methods of sharing are appearing. Projections on living-room walls emulate the traditional slide shows of family pictures, but newer approaches include projections on tables with shared capabilities for manipulating the layout of the photos. Another idea is to mount a computer display in an elegant photo frame connected to the Internet. Then parents can upload a changing set of photos of children for grandparents to view on a rotating basis.

Other forms of notification or ambient awareness include reports and alerts about the weather, stock prices, production processes, or equipment status. This can be accomplished by small computer windows that display current information or by audio tones that draw attention to changes. Innovative products from Ambient Devices, Inc. include softly glowing colored lights to gently signal changes. Various forms of sculpture, mobiles, light shows, or even changing odors have been suggested to provide minimally intrusive awareness information to users of public spaces. Public spaces are also becoming the objects of creative explorations. Hallways of buildings, foyers of hotels, and museum galleries are beginning to glow with more than advertising signs and hanging pictures. Projected images, large displays, and spatial sound installations can reflect the work tempo or changes in the weather. The goal may be to calm users or make them aware of outside conditions. Lobbies may offer multimedia presentations about the organizations in the building, celebrate historic figures, or make artistic statements in sound and light. Designers may strive to create emotional responses that calm or excite, intrigue or offend—public art pieces are hard to categorize, but they can serve as innovative uses of technology or provocative commentaries on modern life (Halkia and Local, 2003; Fig. 9.14).

9.5.2 Electronic classrooms

The potential for a groupware-mediated paradigm shift in education evokes passion from devotees, but there is ample reason for skepticism and resistance. By giving each student a keyboard and simple software, it is possible to create an inviting environment for conversation, comparison, or brainstorming. For example, each student can respond to a professor's question by typing a line of text that is shown immediately, with the author's name, on every student's display. With 10 to 50 people typing, new comments may appear a few times per second, and lively (if sometimes confusing) conversations ensue. The academic developers note that

> It seems slightly ironic that the computer, which for twenty-five years has been perceived as anti-human, a tool of control and suppression of human instinct and intuition, has really humanized my job . . . . Freed of having to be the cardboard figure at the front of the classroom, I became a person again, with foibles, feelings and fantasies. As a group, we were more democratic and open with each other than any other writing class I'd had, (Bruce et al., 1992)

At the University of Maryland, teaching/learning theaters were built with 40 seats and 20 personal computers to explore face-to-face collaboration methods. Hundreds of faculty members who use the electronic classrooms for semester-long

FIGURE 9.14

Modulor II is a time-dependent architectural work of art in which participants create new patterns daily by collaboratively weaving colored strings through an interactive labyrinth of luminous poles (Halkia and Local, 2003).

courses explored novel teaching and learning styles to create more engaging experiences for students. While traditional lectures with or without discussion remain common, electronic-classroom technologies can enliven lectures while enabling active individual learning, small-group collaborative learning, and entire-class collaborative learning. Most faculty members acknowledged spending more preparation time to use the electronic classrooms, especially in their first semesters, but one wrote that it was "well worthwhile in terms of greater learning efficiency" (Shneiderman et al., 1998).

The assumption that improved lectures was the main goal changed as more faculty tried out the teaching/learning theaters. Faculty who had used paper-based collaborations appreciated the smoothness of showing student work—paragraphs from essays, poems, computer programs, statistical results, web pages, and so on— to the whole class. Faculty who had not used these methods still appreciated the ease and liveliness of an anonymous electronic brainstorming session. The transformational breakthrough was in opening the learning process by rapidly showing many students' work to the entire class. Doing so at first generates student and faculty anxiety, but quickly becomes normal. Seeing and critiquing exemplary and ordinary work by fellow students provides feedback that inspires better work on subsequent tasks. As the technology is becoming more ubiquitous and easier to use, more adopters are becoming devotees. Still, there is room for improvement. Although classroom teaching has been around for over a century, full understanding of pedagogy has not yet been achieved. When an instructor is splitting cognitive resources between managing the class and running the technology, it is hard to pay attention to everything and still be effective. Better understanding of the "pulse of the classroom" would help (Chen, 2003; Fig. 9.15).

Small-group collaborative-learning experiences include having pairs of students work together at a machine on a time-limited task. Pairs often learn better than individuals, because they can discuss their problems, learn from each other, and split their roles into problem solver and computer operator. With paired teams, the variance of completion time for tasks is reduced compared to

speech activity
hand motion
body motion

FIGURE 9.15

Students in an online classroom. Activity is monitored by color: speech in yellow, hand motion in red, body motion in green. Under each student is a timeline of their individual activity and at the bottom is an activity picture (using the colors) of the class (Chen, 2003).

individual use, and fewer students get stuck in completing a task. Furthermore, verbalization of problems has often been demonstrated to be advantageous during learning and is an important job skill to acquire for modern team-oriented organizations. Displaying and sharing a learning experience with technology can be accomplished with relatively young students (Fig. 9.16).

Innovative approaches with larger teams include simulated hostage negotiations with terrorist airplane hijackers in a course on conflict resolution, and business trade negotiations in a United Nations format for a course on commercial Spanish. Teams work to analyze situations, to develop position statements online, and to communicate their positions to their adversaries over the network. In an introductory programming course, 10 teams wrote components and sent them through the network to the lead team, who combined the pieces into a 173-line program, all in 25 minutes. The class performed a walkthrough of the code using the large-screen display and quickly identified bugs.

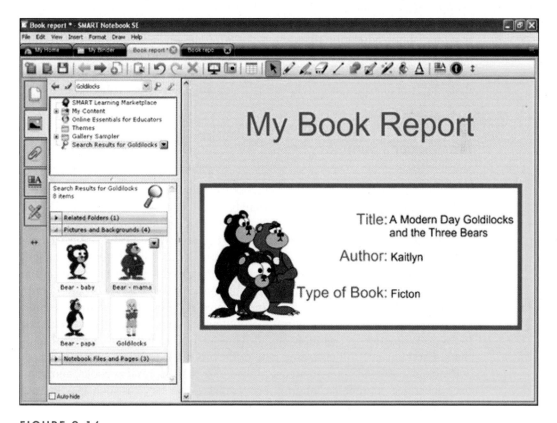

FIGURE 9.16

A sample application created with the SMART Board electronic whiteboard from SMART Technologies, Inc. (http://www.smarttech.com/).

Some faculty find that adapting to the electronic-classroom environment impacts their style so much that they teach differently even in traditional classrooms. Other faculty vow that they will never teach in a traditional classroom again. Most faculty users want to continue teaching in these electronic classrooms and discover that more than their teaching styles change—their attitudes about the goals of teaching and about the content of the courses often shift as well. Many faculty develop higher expectations for student projects. Some become evangelists within their disciplines for the importance of teamwork and its accompanying communication skills.

On the negative side, a math professor who used the computers only to do occasional demonstrations returned to teaching in a traditional classroom, where he had much more blackboard space. Some reluctant instructors express resistance to changing their teaching styles and anticipate having to make a large effort to use the electronic classrooms. Students, however, are generally positive and often enthusiastic: "Everyone should have a chance to be in here at least once . . . Great tech. Great education technique . . . Even though there were a few humps to get over at the beginning—it was well worth the effort (and money)."

The business case for technology-rich classrooms is more difficult to make than that for distance education (Baecker et al., 2007). However, as computer projectors in classrooms become as common as chalkboards, faculty notes migrate to slide presentations, and most students carry laptops and mobile devices, it seems likely that educational experiences will become more interactive and collaborative.

Practitioner's Summary

Collaboration tools have restructured work teams by allowing greater freedom in terms of when and where to work. E-mail has made it easy to reach out and touch someone, or thousands of someones. Listservers, online communities, instant messaging, and texting have enabled users to be in closer communication. Coordination within projects and between organizations is facilitated by easy exchanges of text, graphic, audio, and video files, and even face-to-face meetings are getting a facelift with new tools for electronic meetings and with the advents of teaching/learning theaters. The introspective and isolated style of past computer use has given way to a lively social environment where training has to include *netiquette* (network etiquette) and cautions about flame wars. Social media participation is the remarkable and still emerging new opportunity for users and entrepreneurs. Technology that enables users to tag photos, rate movies, review books, and view user-generated content is changing society; innovative services such as wikis and blogs give users new sources of information and forms of expression. As with all new technologies, there will be failures and surprising discoveries that will guide the next generation of designers (Box 9.1). Thorough testing of new applications is necessary before widespread dissemination.

BOX 9.1

Questions for consideration. The novelty and diversity of computer-supported cooperative work means that clear guidelines have not emerged, but these sobering questions might help designers and managers.

Computer-supported cooperative work questions

- How would facilitating communication improve or harm teamwork?
- Where does the community of users stand on centralization versus decentralization?
- What pressures exist for conformity versus individuality?
- How is privacy compromised or protected?
- What are the sources of friction among participants?
- Is there protection from hostile, aggressive, or malicious behavior?
- Will there be sufficient equipment to support convenient access for all participants?
- What network delays are expected and tolerable?
- What is the user's level of technological sophistication or resistance?
- Who is most likely to be threatened by computer-supported cooperative work?
- How will high-level management participate?
- Which jobs may have to be redefined?
- Whose status will rise or fall?
- What are the additional costs or projected savings?
- Is there an adequate phase-in plan with sufficient training?
- Will there be consultants and adequate assistance in the early phases?
- Is there enough flexibility to handle exceptional cases and special needs (users with disabilities)?
- What international, national, and organizational standards must be considered?
- How will success be evaluated?

Researcher's Agenda

Understanding the motivations for collaboration and social media participation remains a dominant task. For all the much-debated successes, predicting the trajectory for new designs is difficult. Even basic products, such as for e-mail clients, could be improved dramatically by inclusion of advanced features such as online directories, improved filtering, and sophisticated archiving tools that enable easy finding of key documents. As users grow more numerous internationally, universal-usability features such as improved tutorials, translations, and assistance for users with special needs (including disabilities) will be needed.

There are multiple opportunities for research on user-interface designs for collaborative and social media interfaces, but the larger and more difficult research problems lie in studying their organizational and societal impacts. Research evidence shows that collaborative and social media interfaces increase the breadth of participation, allowing marginalized individuals greater influence. However, critics complain that time devoted to forming and maintaining relationships could reduce productivity or undermine organizational loyalty. How will home life and work be changed? Can Internet technologies restore community social capital, or will time online increase distance from neighbors and colleagues? Will trust and responsibility increase because of electronic archives or decrease because of the disembodied nature of electronic communications? Will patients, consumers, and students be more informed, more misinformed, or more argumentative? What are the taxonomies of social roles and author types in online discussions and Yahoo!/Google groups? How can visualization techniques be used to better understand the social roles? The existing tools are primarily for information sharing, cooperation, and coordination. Additional work is needed to better understand collaboration and to create tools to support it (Denning and Yaholkovsky, 2008). Some of the attraction for researchers in computer-supported collaborative work stems from the vast uncharted territory: theories lack validation, controlled studies are difficult to arrange, data analysis is daunting, and predictive models are rare. In short, this is a grand opportunity for researchers to influence a potent, yet still emerging, technology.

WORLD WIDE WEB RESOURCES

http://www.aw.com/DTUI/

Computer-supported cooperative work is naturally a part of the World Wide Web, and novel tools are springing up on many web sites. You can try various chat services, download special-purpose software, or shop for conferencing tools (video-, audio-, or text-based).

References

Anson, Rob and Munkvold, Bjorn Erik, Beyond face-to-face: A field study of electronic meetings in different time and place modes, *Journal of Organizational Computing and Electronic Commerce* 14, 2 (2004), 127–152.

Baecker, R. M., Birnholtz, J. M., Causey, R., and Laughton, S., Webcasting made interactive: Integrating real-time videoconferencing in distributed learning spaces, *Proc. HCI International 2007: Human Interface and the Management of Information – Part II*, Beijing, China, Springer (2007), 269–278.

Balakrishnan, Aruna, Fussell, Susan R., and Kiesler, Sara, Do visualizations improve synchronous remote collaboration? *Proc. CHI 2008 Conference: Human Factors in Computing Systems*, ACM Press, New York (2008), 1227–1236.

Batson, C. D., Ahmad, N., and Tsang, J., Four motives for community involvement, *Journal of Social Issues* 58 (2002), 429–445.

Bellotti, Victoria, Ducheneaut, Nicolas, Howard, Mark, Smith, Ian, and Grinter, Rebecca E., Quality versus quantity: E-mail-centric task management and its relation with overload, *Human-Computer Interaction* 20 (2005), 89–138.

Bos, N., Zimmerman, A., Olson, J., Yes, J., Yerkie, J., Dahl, E., and Olson, D., From shared databases to communities of practice: A taxonomy of collaboratories, *Journal of Computer-Mediated Communication* 12, 2 (2007), #16. Available at http://jcmc.indiana.edu/vol12/issue2/bos.html.

Bruce, B. C. and Easley, J. A., Jr., Emerging communities of practice: Collaboration and communication in action research, *Educational Action Research* 8 (2000), 243–259.

Bruce, Bertram, Peyton, Joy, and Batson, Trent, *Network-Based Classrooms*, Cambridge University Press, Cambridge, U.K. (1992).

Bruckman, Amy, The future of e-learning communities, *Communications of the ACM* 45, 4 (April 2002), 60–63.

Bryant, Susan, Forte, Andrea, and Bruckman, Amy, Becoming Wikipedian: Transformation of participation in a collaborative online encyclopedia, *Proc. ACM SIGGROUP International Conference on Supporting Group Work*, ACM Press, New York (2005), 1–10.

Butler, Brian, Joyce, Elisabeth, and Pike, Jacqueline, Don't look now, but we've created a bureaucracy: The nature and roles of policies and rules in Wikipedia, *Proc. CHI 2008 Conference: Human Factors in Computing Systems*, ACM Press, New York (2008), 1101–1110.

Chen, Milton, Visualizing the pulse of a classroom, *Proc. ACM Multimedia Conference (MM '03)*, ACM Press, New York (2003), 555–561.

Cohill, A. M. and Kavanaugh, A. L., *Community Networks: Lessons from Blacksburg, Virginia, Second Edition*, Artech House, Cambridge, MA (2000).

de Souza, Clarisse Sieckenius, and Preece, Jenny, A framework for analyzing and understanding online communities, *Interacting with Computers* 16, 3 (2004), 579–610.

Denning, Peter J. and Yaholkovsky, Peter, Getting to we, *Communications of the ACM* 51, 4 (April 2008), 19–24.

Donath, Judith, Signals in social supernets, *Journal of Computer-Mediated Communication* 13, 1 (2007), #12. Available at http://jcmc.indiana.edu/vol13/issue1/donath.html.

Farzan, Rosta, DiMicco, Joan M., Millen, David R., Brownholtz, Beth, Geyer, Werner, and Dugan, Casey, Results from deploying a participation incentive mechanism within the enterprise, *Proc. CHI 2008 Conference: Human Factors in Computing Systems*, ACM Press, New York (2008), 563–572.

George, T., Communication gap: Tech-savvy young people bring their own ways of communicating to the workplace, and employees old and young need to adapt, *Information Week* (21 October 2002), 81–82.

Grinter, R. and Palen, L., Instant messaging in teen life, *Proc. CSCW 2002 Conference: Computer-Supported Cooperative Work*, ACM Press, New York (2002), 21–30.

Grinter, Rebecca, Palen, Leysia, and Eldridge, Margery, Chatting with teenagers: Considering the place of chat technologies in teen life, *ACM Transactions on Computer-Human Interaction* 13, 4 (December 2006), 423–447.

Guimbretière, Francois, Stone, Maureen, and Winograd, Terry, Fluid interaction with high-resolution wall-size displays, *Proc. ACM Symposium on User Interface Software and Technology*, ACM Press, New York (2001), 21–30.

Gutwin, Carl, Greenberg, Saul, Blum, Roger, Dyck, Jeff, Tee, Kimberly, and McEwan, Gregor, Supporting informal collaboration in shared-workspace groupware, *Journal of Universal Computer Science* 14, 9 (2008), 1411–1434.

Halkia, Matina and Local, Gary, Building the brief: Action and audience in augmented reality, *Proc. Human-Computer Interaction International 2003: Volume 4, Universal Access in HCI*, Lawrence Erlbaum Associates, Mahwah, NJ (2003), 389–393.

Hazemi, Reza and Hailes, Stephen, *The Digital University: Building a Learning Community*, Springer-Verlag, London, U.K. (2001).

Herbsleb, J., Atkins, D., Boyer, D., Handel, M., and Finholt, T., Introducing instant messaging and chat in the workplace, *Proc. CHI 2002 Conference: Human Factors in Computing Systems*, ACM Press, New York (2002), 171–178.

Hiltz, Starr Roxanne and Goldman, Ricki (Editors), *Learning Together Online: Research on Asynchronous Learning Networks*, Lawrence Erlbaum Associates, Mahwah, NJ (2005).

Isaacs, E., Walendowski, A., Whittaker, S., Schiano, D. J., and Kamm, C., The character, functions, and styles of instant messaging in the workplace, *Proc. CSCW 2002 Conference: Computer-Supported Cooperative Work*, ACM Press, New York (2002), 11–20.

Isaacs, E., Walendowski, A., and Ranganathan, D., Hubbub: A sound-enhanced mobile instant messenger that supports awareness and opportunistic interactions, *Proc. CHI 2002 Conference: Human Factors in Computing Systems*, ACM Press, New York (2002), 179–186.

Jackson, W. J., Dawson, R., and Wilson, D., Understanding email interaction increases organizational productivity, *Communications of the ACM* 46, 8 (2003), 80–84.

Jacovi, Michael, Soroka, Vladmir, Gilboa-Freedman, Gail, Ur, Sigalit, Shahar, Elad, and Marmasse, Natalia, The chasms of CSCW: A citation graph analysis of the CSCW conference, *Proc. CSCW '06*, ACM Press, New York (2006), 289–298.

Jancke, G., Venolia, G., Grudin, J., Cadiz, J., and Gupta, A., Linking public spaces: Technical and social issues, *Proc. CHI 2001 Conference: Human Factors in Computing Systems*, ACM Press, New York (2001), 530–537.

Java, Akshay, Finin, Tim, Song, Xiaodan, and Tseng, Belle, Why we twitter: Understanding microblogging usage and communities, *Proc. Joint 9ᵗʰ WEBKDD and 1ˢᵗ SNA-KDD Workshop '07*, ACM Press, New York (2007), 56–65.

Kim, Amy Jo, *Community Building on the Web*, Peachpit Press, Berkeley, CA (2000).

Kittur, Aniket, Chi, Ed, Pendleton, Bryan A., Suh, Bongwon, and Mytkowica, Todd, Power of the few vs. wisdom of the crowd: Wikipedia and the rise of the bourgeoisie, *Proc. CHI 2007 Conference: Human Factors in Computing Systems*, ACM Press, New York (2007).

Kraut, R., Kiesler, S., Boneva, B., Cummings, J., Helgeson, V., and Crawford, A., Internet paradox revisited, *Journal of Social Issues* 58, 1 (2002), 49–74.

Li, Charlene and Bernoff, Josh, *Groundswell: Winning in a World Transformed by Social Technologies*, Harvard Business School Press, Cambridge, MA (2008).

Maloney-Krichmar, Diane and Preece, Jennifer, A multilevel analysis of sociability, usability and community dynamics in an online health community, *ACM Transactions on Computer Human Interaction* 12, 2 (2005), 1–32.

Mantei, M., Capturing the capture lab concepts: A case study in the design of computer supported meeting environments, *Proc. CSCW '88 Conference: Computer-Supported Cooperative Work*, ACM Press, New York (1988), 257–270.

Millen, D. R., Fontaine, M. A., and Muller, M. J., Understanding the benefit and costs of communities of practice, *Communications of the ACM* 45, 4 (April 2002), 69–75.

Nardi, B., Whittaker, S., and Bradner, E., Interaction and outeraction: Instant messaging in action, *Proc. CSCW 2000 Conference: Computer-Supported Cooperative Work*, ACM Press, New York (2000), 79–88.

Nardi, Bonnie A., Schiano, Diane J., Gumbrecht, Michelle, and Swartz, Luke, Why we blog, *Communications of the ACM* 47, 12 (December 2004), 41–46.

Nonnecke, B. and Preece, J., Lurker demographics: Counting the silent, *Proc. CHI 2000 Conference: Human Factors in Computing Systems*, ACM Press, New York (2000), 73–80.

Nunamaker, J. F., Dennis, Alan R., Valacich, Joseph S., Vogel, Douglas R., and George, Joey F., Electronic meeting systems to support group work, *Communications of the ACM* 34, 7 (July 1991), 40–61.

Olson, Gary M. and Olson, Judith S., Groupware and computer-supported cooperative work, in Jacko, J. and Sears, A. (Editors), *The Human-Computer Interaction Handbook, Second Edition*, Lawrence Erlbaum Associates, Mahwah, NJ (2008), 545–558.

Olson, J. S. and Olson, G. M., Distance matters, *Human-Computer Interaction* 15, 2/3 (2000), 139–178.

Pimentel, Maria Da Graca, Ishiguro, Yoshihide, Abowd, Gregory D., Kerimbaev, Bolot, and Guzdial, Mark, Supporting educational activities through dynamic web interfaces, *Interacting with Computers* 13, 3 (February 2001), 353–374.

Prante, Thorsten, Magerkurth, Carsten, and Streitz, Norbert, Developing CSCW tools for ideas finding: Empirical results and implications for design, *Proc. CSCW 2002 Conference: Computer-Supported Cooperative Work*, ACM Press, New York (2002), 106–115.

Preece, Jennifer and Shneiderman, Ben, The Reader-to-Leader Framework: Motivating technology-mediated social participation., *AIS Transactions on Human-Computer Interaction* 1, 1 (July 2009).

Preece, Jenny, Empathic communities: Balancing emotional and factual communications, *Interacting with Computers* 12, 1 (1999), 63–77.

Rafaeli, Sheizaf and Ariel, Yaron, Online motivational factors: Incentives for participation and contribution in Wikipedia, in Barak, A. (Editor), *Psychological Aspects of Cyberspace: Theory, Research, Applications,* Cambridge University Press, Cambridge, U.K. (2008), 243–267.

Rashid, A. M., Ling, K., Tassone, R. D., Resnick, P., Kraut, R., and Riedl, J., Motivating participation by displaying the value of contribution, *Proc. CHI 2006 Conference: Human Factors in Computing Systems,* ACM Press, New York (2006), 955–958.

Rheingold, Howard, *The Virtual Community: Homesteading on the Electronic Frontier,* Addison-Wesley, Reading, MA (1993).

Rheingold, Howard, *Smart Mobs: The Next Social Revolution,* Perseus Publishing, New York (2002).

Robinson, John and Nie, Norman, Introduction to IT & Society, Issue 1: Sociability, *IT & Society: A Web Journal Studying How Technology Affects Society* 1, 1 (Summer 2002), i–xi. Available at http://www.stanford.edu/group/siqss/itandsociety/v01i01.html.

Schuler, Doug, *New Community Networks: Wired for Change,* Addison-Wesley, Reading, MA (1996).

Shneiderman, B., Borkowski, E., Alavi, M., and Norman, K., Emergent patterns of teaching/learning in electronic classrooms, *Educational Technology Research & Development* 46, 4 (1998), 23–42.

Smith, M., Tools for navigating large social cyberspaces, *Communications of the ACM* 45, 4 (April 2002), 51–55.

Streitz, Norbert, Kameas, Achilles, and Mavrommati, Irene (Editors), *The Disappearing Computer: Interaction Design, System Infrastructures and Applications for Smart Environments,* Lecture Notes in Computer Science 4500, Springer, Heidelberg, Germany (2007).

Surowiecki, James, *The Wisdom of Crowds,* Doubleday, New York (2004).

Tapscott, Don and Williams, Anthony, *Wikinomics: How Mass Collaboration Changes Everything,* Portfolio, New York (2006).

Thom-Santelli, Jennifer, Muller, Michael J., and Millen, David R., Social tagging roles: Publishers, evangelists, leaders, *Proc. CHI 2008 Conference: Human Factors in Computing Systems,* ACM Press, New York (2008), 1041–1044.

Valacich, J. S., Dennis, A. R., and Nunamaker, Jr., J. F., Electronic meeting support: The GroupSystems concept, *International Journal of Man-Machine Studies* 34, 2 (1991), 261–282.

Vogel, Daniel and Balakrishnan, Ravin, Interactive public ambient displays: Transitioning from implicit to explicit, public to personal, interaction with multiple users, *Proc. ACM Symposium on User Interface Software and Technology,* ACM Press, New York (2004), 137–146.

Welser, H. T., Gleave, E., Fisher, D., and Smith, M. A., Visualizing the signatures of social roles in online discussion groups, *Journal of Social Structure* 8, 2 (2007). Available at http://www.cmu.edu/joss/content/articles/volume8/Welser/.

Wenger, E., *Communities of Practice: Learning, Meaning and Identity,* Cambridge University Press, Cambridge, U.K. (1998).

Wiener, Earl L. and Nagel, David C. (Editors), *Human Factors in Aviation,* Academic Press, New York (1988).

PART 4

DESIGN ISSUES

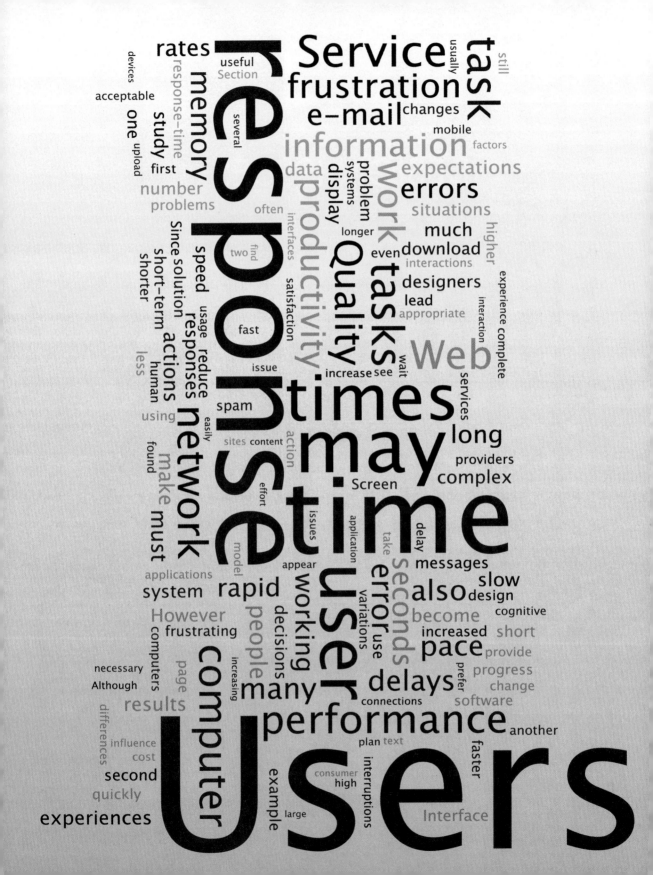

Quality of Service

Written in collaboration with Steven M. Jacobs

10.1 Introduction

In the 1960s, user perception of computer speed was determined by response time for mathematical computations, program compilations, or database searches. Then, as time-shared systems emerged, contention for the scarce computational resources led to more complex reasons for delays. With the emergence of the World Wide Web, user expectations for expanded services grew, along with still more complex explanations of delays. Users now have to understand the size differences between text and graphics pages to appreciate the huge variations in server loads and to tolerate network congestion. They also have to understand the multiple sources of problems, such as dropped connections, unavailable web sites, and network outages. This complex set of concerns is usually discussed under the umbrella term *Quality of Service* (QoS). This term was originally derived from the telecommunications industry, where Quality of Service can be measured in terms of telephone call quality, lost connections, customer satisfaction, connection time, cost, and other factors.

Concern over Quality of Service stems from a basic human value: Time is precious. When externally imposed delays impede progress on a task, many people become frustrated, annoyed, and eventually angry. Lengthy or unexpected system responses resulting in long times to display or refresh screens produce these reactions in computer users, leading to frequent errors and low satisfaction. Some users accept the situation with a shrug of their shoulders, but most users prefer to work more quickly than the computer allows.

Discussions of Quality of Service must also take into account a second basic human value: Harmful mistakes should be avoided. However, balancing rapid performance with low error rates sometimes means that the pace of work must slow. If users work too quickly, they may learn less, read with lower comprehension, commit more data-entry errors, and make more incorrect decisions. Stress can build in these situations, especially if it is hard to recover from errors, or if the errors destroy data, damage equipment, or imperil human life, as they may in air-traffic–control or medical systems (Kohlisch and Kuhmann, 1997).

A third aspect of Quality of Service is reducing user frustration. With long delays, users may become frustrated enough to make mistakes or give up working. Delays are often a cause of frustration, but there are others, such as crashes that destroy data, software bugs that produce incorrect results, and poor designs that lead to user confusion. Networked environments generate further frustrations: unreliable service providers, dropped lines, e-mail spam, and malicious viruses.

Quality of Service discussions usually focus on the decisions to be made by network designers and operators. This is appropriate, because their decisions have a profound influence on many users. They also have the tools and knowledge to be helpful, and increasingly, they must adhere to legal and regulatory controls. Interface designers and builders must also make design decisions that dramatically influence the user experience. For example, they can optimize web pages to reduce byte counts and numbers of files or provide previews of materials available in digital libraries or archives to help reduce the number of queries and accesses to the network (Fig. 10.1 and Section 13.2). In addition, users may have the opportunity to choose from fast or slow services and from viewing low-resolution versus high-resolution images. Users need guidance to understand the implications of their choices and help them to accommodate varying levels of Quality of Service. For users, the main experience of Quality of Service is the computer system's *response time*, so we'll deal with those issues first, before addressing application crashes, unreliable network service, and malicious threats.

Section 10.2 begins by discussing a model of response-time impacts, then looks at response-time issues, reviews short-term human memory, and identifies the sources of human error. Section 10.3 focuses on the role of users' expectations and attitudes in shaping their subjective reactions to the Quality of Service. Section 10.4 deals with productivity as a function of response time, and Section 10.5 reviews the research on the influence of variable response times. Section 10.6 examines the severity of frustrating experiences, including spam and viruses.

10.2 Models of Response-Time Impacts

Response time is defined as the number of seconds it takes from the moment a user initiates an action, usually by pressing the Enter key or a mouse button, until the computer begins to present results (whether on the display, via a printer, through a speaker, or on a mobile device). When the response is completed, the user begins formulating the next action. The *user think time* is the

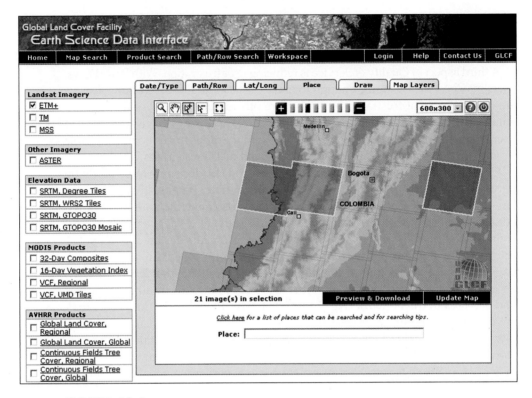

FIGURE 10.1

The University of Maryland's Global Land Cover Facility's online search page (http://glcf.umiacs.umd.edu/) indicates where data is available in red on a zoomable map. Users looking for data in Africa can thus tell where to focus their searches, allowing them to find what they need with fewer queries and network accesses.

number of seconds that elapse between the computer's response and the user's initiation of the next action. In this simple stages-of-action model, users (1) initiate, (2) wait for the computer to respond, (3) watch while the results appear, (4) think for a while, and then initiate again (Fig. 10.2).

In a more realistic model (Fig. 10.3), users plan while interpreting results, while typing/clicking, and while the computer is generating results or retrieving information across the network. Most people will use whatever time they have to plan ahead; thus, precise measurements of user think time are difficult to obtain. The computer's response is usually more precisely defined and measurable, but there are problems here as well. Some interfaces respond with distracting messages, informative feedback, or a simple prompt immediately after an action is initiated, but actual results may not appear for a few seconds. For example, the user may drag a file to a network printer icon using direct manipulation, but it may take many seconds for confirmation that the printer has been

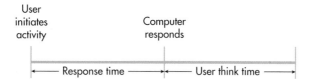

FIGURE 10.2

Simple stages of action model of system response time and user think time.

activated or for a dialog box reporting that the printer is offline to appear. Delays of more than 160 milliseconds while dragging the icon are noticed and become annoying, but users have come to accept delays for responses from net-worked devices.

Designers who specify response times and network managers who seek to provide high Quality of Service have to consider the complex interaction of technical feasibility, costs, task complexity, user expectations, speed of task performance, error rates, and error-handling procedures. Decisions about these variables are further complicated by the influence of users' personality differences, fatigue, familiarity with computers, experience with the task, and motivation (King, 2008; Guastello, 2006; Wickens et al., 2004; Bouch et al., 2000).

Although some people are content with slower responses for some tasks, the overwhelming majority prefer rapid interactions. Overall productivity depends not only on the speed of the interface, but also on the rate of human error and the ease of recovery from those errors. Lengthy (longer than 15 seconds) response times are generally detrimental to productivity, increasing error rates and decreasing satisfaction. More rapid (less than 1 second) interactions are generally preferred and can increase productivity, but they may also increase error rates for complex tasks. The high cost of providing rapid response times and the loss from increased errors must be evaluated in the choice of an optimum pace.

Web-site display performance was studied by evaluating delay plus two web-site design variables (site breadth and content familiarity) to examine interaction effects on user performance, attitudes, stress, and behavioral intentions.

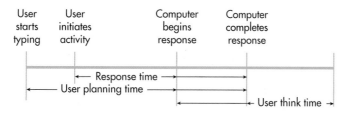

FIGURE 10.3

Model of system response time, user planning time, and user think time. This model is more realistic than the one in Fig. 10.2.

The three experimental factors (delay, familiarity, and breadth) were demonstrated to collectively impact the cognitive costs and penalties that users incur when making choices in their search for target information (Galletta, 2006; Galletta et al., 2006). Laboratory experiments were also conducted (though not all of the results have yet been published) to examine "acceptable" perceived delay, whether this perception holds across two cultures (U.S. and Mexico), and combinations of a number of variables, including acceptable perceived delay, information sent (in the right direction), site depth, feedback, stress, and time constraints. Preliminary conclusions are that user impatience is high, especially in the U.S. as compared with Mexico, and that the effects of delay and poor information sent explain significant variance in a number of outcomes, especially when considering other interacting antecedents.

Screen refresh rates for web-based applications and mobile communications (text messaging, accessing the Internet via web-enabled mobile devices, etc.) can lead to frustration when slow and can sooth the soul when working speedily. In demanding web applications on desktop machines, screen refresh rates are usually limited by network transmission speed or server performance. Portions of images or fragments of a page may appear with interspersed delays of several seconds.

A home user with only a dial-up modem that has a 56-kilobits-per-second (Kbps) data throughput rate may find that it takes 30 seconds or more to display a page of text or a small image. Home or business users with digital subscriber lines (DSL) connections, Fiber Optic Service (FiOS™), or cable modems can perform tasks at much higher rates (thousands or even millions of bps); however, those rates vary by location, service provider, and subscribed options.

Broadband service providers typically do not offer the same upload and download speeds: Since the majority of users download much more information to their computers (text, photos, audio, video, software, etc.) than they upload, most service providers have opted for much higher download speeds at the expense of fast upload capability. Those who require faster upload times—for example, webmasters, software developers working on collaborative projects, or users who regularly transfer large files—might find that their broadband service providers have left much to be desired in terms of upload times. In an era of user-generated content, for an increasing number of users, it is important for upload speeds to keep pace with download capability.

There are web tools that can permit computer users to assess their download and upload speeds (to find them, run a search on "download upload speed test"). Running this test gives users a better idea of the Quality of Service and provides them with useful information to present to their broadband service providers when asking for better service or an upgrade to meet their network response-time needs.

Users working on a company or university intranet with firewall protection will often notice changes in network performance based on traffic, infrastructure tools and services running on the network, and occasional virus or other attacks on the network infrastructure. Those individuals benefit from the best communications capability with advanced, direct network connections (such as Asynchronous Transfer Mode, or ATM); T1 lines and/or satellite connections can also reduce transfer delays and provide faster screen refresh rates. Wireless network devices are not always in service and often cannot match the speeds of their wired counterparts; however, that too is improving as entire communities embrace wireless networking (which can aid in universal accessibility).

Cell-phone users express frustration if a contact cannot be dialed quickly, if "roaming" takes too long to find a signal in an out-of-the-way place, or if a call is dropped. Just as there are web-based tools that can measure network performance, there are also web forums that focus on testing cell-phone speed (both in-person testing by consumer groups and test results posted to user communities).

While improvements are being made in the technology of computer-to-computer communication, user task performance times will not automatically improve at the same rate. As this section will illustrate, improved throughput does not necessarily imply improved productivity. Computing systems still need to be user-centered, promoting universal usability (Shneiderman, 2003; Raskin, 2000).

Reading textual information from a screen is more difficult than reading from a book (Section 12.3). If the screen display appears to fill instantly (beyond the speed at which someone might feel compelled to keep up), users seem to relax, to pace themselves, and to work productively. Since users often scan a web page looking for highlights or links, rather than reading the full text, it is useful to display text first, leaving space for the graphical elements that are slower to display. Since a graphics file can easily be more than a megabyte in size, user control over image quality and size should be possible.

The relative merits of reading online versus printed copy have long been the subject of heated discussion, although admittedly much of the debate is based on personal preference and experience. With computer-display technology improving, a renewed emphasis on a more paperless "green" environment, and the increased availability and depth of online books and newspapers, it does seem inevitable that we are moving in a direction of increased demand for rapid display of textual and graphical data. High-end performance needs such as photo, movie, simulation, and gaming applications add to the mix, increasing user expectations and demand.

Consumer demand is a key factor in promoting rapid performance. Many desktop and laptop computers still start up slowly, but cell phones, mobile devices, and games are designed to start in seconds. If market competition is insufficient to produce change, consumer pressure on software and hardware makers will be needed to force changes that result in more rapid computer start-ups. Web sites often distinguish themselves with rapid performance—an attribute that surfers expect from Google or Yahoo! and buyers demand at

Amazon.com or eBay (King, 2008; Morris and Turner, 2001)—and manufacturers may soon start making similar claims about their products to attract customers.

A cognitive model of human performance that accounts for the experimental results in response time would be useful in making predictions, designing interfaces, and formulating management policies. A complete predictive model that accounts for all the variables may never be realized, but even fragments of such a model are useful to designers.

Robert B. Miller's review (1968) presented a lucid analysis of response-time issues and a list of 17 situations in which preferred response times might differ. Much has changed since his paper was written, but the principles of *closure, short-term memory* limitations, and *chunking* still apply. Any cognitive model must emerge from an understanding of these human problem-solving abilities and information-processing capabilities. A central issue is the limitation of short-term memory capacity, as outlined in George Miller's (1956) classic paper, "The magical number seven, plus or minus two." Miller identified the limited capacities people have for absorbing information: People can rapidly recognize approximately seven (this value was contested by later researchers, but it serves as a good estimate) "chunks" of information at a time and can hold those chunks in short-term memory for 15 to 30 seconds. The size of a chunk of information depends on the person's familiarity with the material.

For example, most people can look at seven binary digits for a few seconds and then recall the digits correctly from memory within 15 seconds. However, performing a distracting task during those 15 seconds, such as reciting a poem, erases the binary digits. Of course, if people concentrate on remembering the binary digits and succeed in transferring them to long-term memory, they can retain the binary digits for much longer periods. Most Americans can also probably remember seven decimal digits, seven alphabetic characters, seven English words, or even seven familiar advertising slogans. Although these items have increasing complexity, they are still treated as single chunks. However, Americans might not succeed in remembering seven Russian letters, Chinese pictograms, or Polish sayings. Knowledge and experience govern the size of a chunk and the ease of remembering for each individual.

People use short-term memory in conjunction with *working memory* for processing information and for problem solving. Short-term memory processes perceptual input, whereas working memory is used to generate and implement solutions. If many facts and decisions are necessary to solve a problem, short-term and working memory may become overloaded. People learn to cope with complex problems by developing higher-level concepts that bring together several lower-level concepts into a single chunk. Novices at any task tend to work with smaller chunks until they can cluster concepts into larger chunks. Experts rapidly decompose a complex task into a sequence of smaller tasks that they are confident about accomplishing.

Short-term and working memory are highly volatile; disruptions cause loss of information, and delays can require that the memory be refreshed. Visual distractions or noisy environments also interfere with cognitive processing. Furthermore, anxiety apparently reduces the size of the available memory, since the person's attention is partially absorbed in concerns that are beyond the realm of the problem-solving task.

If people are able to construct a solution to a problem in spite of interference, they must still record or implement that solution. If they can implement the solution immediately, they can proceed quickly through their work. On the other hand, if they must record the solution in long-term memory, on paper, or on a complex device, the chances for error increase and the pace of work slows.

Multiplying two four-digit numbers in your head is difficult because the intermediate results cannot be maintained in working memory and must be transferred to long-term memory. Controlling nuclear reactors or air traffic is a challenge in part because these tasks often require integration of information (in short-term and working memory) from several sources, as well as maintenance of awareness of the complete situation. In attending to newly arriving information, operators may be distracted and may lose the contents of their short-term or working memory.

When using an interactive computer system, users may formulate plans and then have to wait while they execute each step in the plan. If a step produces an unexpected result or if the delays are long, the users may forget part of the plan or be forced to review the plan continually. This model leads to the conjecture that, for a given user and task, there is a preferred response time. Long response times lead to wasted effort and more errors, because the solution plan must be reviewed repeatedly. On the other hand, short response times may generate a faster pace in which solution plans are prepared hastily and incompletely. More data from a variety of situations and users would clarify these conjectures.

As response times grow longer, users may become more anxious because the penalty for an error increases. As the difficulty in handling an error increases, users' anxiety levels intensify, further slowing performance and increasing errors. However, as response times grow shorter and screens refresh more quickly, users tend to pick up the pace of the interface and may fail to fully comprehend the presented material, may generate incorrect solution plans, and may make more execution errors. The term "screen refresh" used here can apply both to updates of displayed data (e.g., animated weather maps) and to the initial presentation of data on the screen (e.g., when first loading a web page that contains several graphics or animations, potentially invoking plug-ins to fully display its contents on the screen).

The speed/accuracy tradeoff that is a harsh reality in so many domains is also apparent in interface usage. A related factor is performance in paced versus unpaced tasks. In paced tasks, the computer forces decisions within a fixed time period, thereby adding pressure. Such high-stress interfaces may be appropriate with trained users in life-critical situations or in manufacturing, where high productivity is a requirement. However, errors, poor-quality work, and operator burnout are serious concerns. In unpaced tasks, users decide when to respond and can work at a more relaxed pace, taking their time to make careful decisions.

Car driving may offer a useful analogy. Although higher speed limits are attractive to many drivers because they lead to faster completion of trips, they also lead to higher accident rates. Since automobile accidents can have dreadful consequences, we accept speed limits. When incorrect use of computer systems can lead to damage to life, property, or data, should not speed limits be provided?

Distracted car driving offers another analogy to Quality of Service issues. For example, driving while speaking on a cell phone has been shown to result in higher accident rates. Similarly, computer users who pride themselves on multitasking can easily make mistakes. There are computer systems that can help drivers make fewer mistakes, such as GPS systems that aid drivers in getting from one destination to another. Will it be that far in the future when there are agents and wizards guiding novice computer users to successful conclusions?

Another lesson from driving is the importance of progress indicators. Drivers like to know how far it is to their destination and what progress they are making, and they get feedback by seeing the declining number of miles on road signs. Similarly, computer users may want to know how long it will take for a web page to load or a file directory scan to be completed (Fig. 10.4). Users given graphical dynamic progress indicators rather than static ("Please wait"), blinking, or numeric (number of seconds left) messages report higher satisfaction and shorter perceived elapsed times to completion (Meyer et al., 1996). It is important, however, that the progress indicators be truthful representations of the state of affairs. How often have computer users been lulled into an increasingly frustrating state of anticipation, for example, watching a web-page download-indicator status bar show that the page is loading, only to find that the Internet connection has been lost or the server is down?

Users may achieve rapid task performance, low error rates, and high satisfaction if the following criteria are met:

- Users have adequate knowledge of the objects and actions necessary for the problem-solving task.

FIGURE 10.4

Dynamic progress indicators reassure users that the process is underway. Providing time estimates is best, but when that information is difficult to calculate other progress indicators— such as the name of the file or the file count—can be updated at regular intervals.

- The solution plan can be carried out without delays.
- Distractions are eliminated.
- User anxiety is low.
- There is feedback about progress towards the solution.
- Errors can be avoided or, if they occur, can be handled easily.

These conditions for optimum problem solving, with acceptable cost and technical feasibility, are the basic constraints on design. However, other conjectures may play a role in choosing the optimum interaction speed:

- Novices may exhibit better performance with somewhat slower response times.
- Novices prefer to work at speeds slower than those chosen by knowledgeable, frequent users.
- When there is little penalty for an error, users prefer to work more quickly.
- When the task is familiar and easily comprehended, users prefer more rapid action.
- If users have experienced rapid performance previously, they will expect and demand it in future situations.

These informal conjectures need to be qualified and verified. Then, a more rigorous cognitive model needs to be developed to accommodate the great diversity in human work styles and in computer-use situations. Practitioners can conduct field tests to measure productivity, error rates, and satisfaction as a function of response times in their application areas.

Researchers are extending models of productivity to accommodate the realities of work and home environments. These situated action models now include tempting distractions and unavoidable interruptions, such as arriving e-mail messages, pop-up instant messages, phone calls, and requests from fellow workers or family members. Enabling users to easily limit or block interruptions is becoming necessary. Another useful functionality is to provide users with feedback about the amount of time spent on various tasks and a log of how they handled interruptions. Personal, organizational, and cultural differences will have to be accommodated, as well as variations in the necessity to accept interruptions from managers or family members.

The research and experiments described in the following sections are tiles in the mosaic of human performance with computers, but many more tiles are necessary before the fragments can form a complete image. Some guidelines have emerged for designers and information-system managers, but local testing and continuous monitoring of performance and satisfaction are still necessary.

The remarkable adaptability of computer users means that researchers and practitioners will have to be alert to novel conditions that require revisions of these guidelines.

10.3 Expectations and Attitudes

How long will users wait for the computer to respond before they become annoyed? This simple question has provoked much discussion and several experiments. There is no simple answer, though, and more importantly, it may be the wrong question to ask. More refined questions focus on users' needs: Will users more happily wait for a valued document than an undesired advertisement?

Related design issues may clarify the question of what an acceptable response time is. For example, how long should users have to wait before they hear a dial tone on a telephone or see a picture on a television? If the cost is not excessive, the frequently mentioned two-second limit (Miller, 1968) seems appropriate for many tasks. In some situations, however, users expect responses within 0.1 second (for example, when turning the wheel of a car; pressing a key on a keyboard, piano, or telephone; dragging an icon; or scrolling through a list on a cell phone). Two-second delays in these cases might be unsettling, because users have adapted a working style and expectations based on responses within a fraction of a second. In other situations, users are accustomed to longer response times, such as waiting 30 seconds for a red traffic light to turn green, two days for a letter to arrive, or a month for flowers to grow.

The first factor influencing acceptable response time is that people have established expectations based on their past experiences of the time required to complete a given task. If a task is completed more quickly than expected, people will be pleased; but if the task is completed much more quickly than expected, they may become concerned that something is wrong. Similarly, if a task is completed much more slowly than expected, users are likely to become concerned or frustrated. Even though people can detect 8% changes in a 2- or 4-second response time (Miller, 1968), users apparently do not become concerned until the change is much greater.

Two installers of networked computer systems have reported a problem concerning user expectations with new systems. The first users are delighted, because the response time is short when the load is light. As the load builds, however, these first users become unhappy because the response time deteriorates. Users who join later, on the other hand, may be satisfied with what they perceive as normal response times. In response to this problem, both installers devised a *response-time choke* by which they could slow down the system when the load was light. This surprising policy makes the response time uniform over time and across users, thus reducing complaints.

Network managers have similar problems with varying response times as new equipment is added or as large projects begin or complete their work. The variation in response time can be disruptive to users who have developed expectations and working styles based on a certain level of responsiveness. There are also periods within each day when the response time tends to be shorter, such as at lunchtime, or longer, such as midmorning or late afternoon. Both extremes can be problematic: Some users rush to complete tasks when response times are short, and as a result, they may make more errors; on the other hand, some workers refuse to work when the response time is slow relative to their expectations. One subject in a study of web shopping commented, "You get a bit spoiled . . . once you are used to the quickness, then you want it all the time" (Bouch et al., 2000).

An important design issue is that of rapid start-up. Users are annoyed if they have to wait for a laptop or a digital camera to be ready for usage, and consequently, fast starts are a strong distinguishing feature in consumer electronics. A related issue is the tradeoff between rapid start-up and rapid usage. For example, it may take several minutes to download a Java or other web application, but then performance is rapid for most actions. An alternative design might speed the start-up, but the cost could be occasional delays during usage.

A second factor influencing response-time expectations is the individual's tolerance for delays. Novice computer users may be willing to wait much longer than experienced users. In short, there are large variations in what individuals consider acceptable waiting time. These variations are influenced by many factors, such as personality, cost, age, mood, cultural context, time of day, noise, and perceived pressure to complete work. The laid-back web surfer may enjoy chatting with friends while pages load, but the anxious deadline-fighting journalist may start banging on desks or keys in a vain attempt to push the computer along.

Other factors influencing response-time expectations are the task complexity and the users' familiarity with the task. For simple, repetitive tasks that require little problem solving, users want to perform rapidly and are annoyed by delays of more than a few tenths of a second. For complex problems, users will typically perform well even as response time grows, as they can use the delays to plan ahead. Users are highly adaptive and can change their working styles to accommodate different response times. This factor was found in early studies of batch-programming environments and in recent studies of interactive-system usage. If delays are long, users will seek alternate strategies that reduce the number of interactions whenever possible. They will fill in the long delays by performing other tasks, daydreaming, or planning ahead in their work. But even if diversions are available, dissatisfaction grows with excessively long response times.

An increasing number of tasks place high demands on rapid system performance; examples are user-controlled three-dimensional animations, flight simulations, graphic design, and dynamic queries for information visualization. In these applications, users are continuously adjusting the input controls, and they expect changes to appear with no perceived delay—that is, within less than 100 milliseconds. Similarly, some tasks (for example, video-conferencing, Voice over IP telephony, and streaming multimedia) require rapid performance to ensure high Quality of Service, because intermittent delays cause jumpy images and broken sound patterns that seriously disrupt users. Promoters of these services see the need for ever faster and higher-capacity networks.

The expanded audiences and novel tasks on the World Wide Web have brought new considerations into the sphere of Quality of Service. Since e-commerce shoppers are deeply concerned with trust, credibility, and privacy, researchers have begun to study interactions with time delay. The range of response times is highly varied across web sites (Huberman, 2001; Fig. 10.5), and site managers are regularly compelled to decide what level of resource expenditure is appropriate to reduce response times for users. Studies have found that as the response times increase, users find web page content less interesting (Ramsay et al., 1998) and lower in quality (Jacko et al., 2000). Long response times may even have a negative influence on user perceptions of the companies who provide the web sites (Bouch et al., 2000). One web-shopping study participant who believed that successful companies have the resources to build high-performance web sites remarked, "This is the way the consumer sees the company . . . it should look good, it should be fast." Increased use of Ajax (Asynchronous JavaScript and XML) and dynamic techniques increase both responsiveness and user expectations.

In summary, three primary factors influence users' expectations and attitudes regarding response time:

1. Previous experiences
2. Individual personality differences
3. Task differences

Experimental results show interesting patterns of behavior for specific backgrounds, individuals, and tasks, but it is difficult to distill a simple set of conclusions. Several experiments attempted to identify acceptable waiting times by allowing participants to press a key if they thought that the waiting time was too long. Participants who could shorten the response time in future interactions took advantage of that feature as they became more experienced, forcing response times for frequent actions down to well below one second. It seems appealing to offer users a choice for the pace of the interaction. Video-game designers recognize the role of user-controlled pace setting and the increased challenge from fast pacing, which expert users crave. On the other hand, older

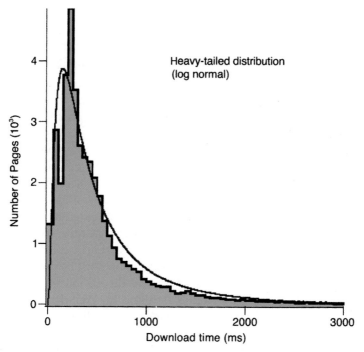

FIGURE 10.5

Distribution of response times for 40,000 randomly selected web pages, showing a log normal distribution. Half the pages were delivered in under half a second, but the long tail shows the variability (Huberman, 2001).

adults and users with disabilities may appreciate being able to slow the pace of interaction. Differing desires also open opportunities to charge premiums for faster service; for example, many World Wide Web users are willing to pay extra for faster network performance.

In summary, three conjectures emerge:

1. Individual differences are large and users are adaptive. They will work faster as they gain experience and will change their working strategies as response times change. It may be useful to allow people to set their own pace of interaction.

2. For repetitive tasks, users prefer and will work more rapidly with short response times.

3. For complex tasks, users can adapt to working with slow response times with no loss of productivity, but their dissatisfaction increases as response times lengthen.

10.4 User Productivity

Shorter system response times usually lead to higher productivity, but in some situations, users who encounter long system response times can find clever shortcuts or ways to do concurrent processing to reduce the effort and time required to accomplish a task. Working too quickly, though, may lead to errors that reduce productivity.

In computing, just as in driving, there is no general rule about whether the high-speed highway or the slower, clever shortcut is better. The designer must survey each situation carefully to make the optimal choice. The choice is not critical for occasional usage, but it becomes worthy of investigation when the frequency is great. When computers are used in high-volume situations, more effort can be expended in discovering the proper response time for a given task and set of users. It should not be surprising that a new study must be conducted when the tasks and users change, just as a new route evaluation must be done for each trip.

An alternative solution is masking delay, by displaying important, crucial information first while the background is filling in. Well-designed web sites often download critical information first; likewise, web designers may choose to download the intriguing information first, so the user is motivated and encouraged to wait during any download delay to see the end result. Some news web sites download the textual headlines first to motivate the news reader to remain patient while the remainder of the articles is downloaded. The user can then start reading an article while additional animations, advertisements, etc. download, until eventually the screen is fully painted with its intended information.

The nature of the task has a strong influence on whether changes in response time alter user productivity. A *repetitive control task* involves monitoring a display and issuing actions in response to changes in the display. Although the operator may be trying to understand the underlying process, the basic activities are to respond to a change in the display, to issue commands, and then to see whether the commands produce the desired effect. When there is a choice among actions, the problem becomes more interesting, and the operator tries to pick the optimal action in each situation. With shorter system response times, the operator picks up the pace of the system and works more quickly, but decisions on actions may be less than optimal. On the other hand, with short response times, the penalty for a poor choice may be small because it may be easy to try another action. In fact, operators may learn to use the interface more quickly with short system response times because they can explore alternatives more easily.

In a study of a data-entry task, users adopted one of three strategies, depending on the response time (Teal and Rudnicky, 1992). With response times under one second, users worked automatically without checking whether the system was ready for the next data value. This behavior resulted in numerous anticipation errors, in which the users typed data values before the system could accept those values. With response times above two seconds, users monitored the display carefully to make sure that the prompt appeared before they typed. In the middle ground of one to two seconds, users paced themselves and waited an appropriate amount of time before attempting to enter data values.

When complex problem solving is required and many approaches to the solution are possible, users will adapt their work styles to the response time. Productivity with statistical problem-solving tasks was also found to be constant despite response-time changes over the range of 0.1 to 5.0 seconds (Martin and Corl, 1986). The same study with regular users found linear productivity gains for simple data-entry tasks. The simpler and more habitual the task was, the greater the productivity benefit of a short response time was.

Barber and Lucas (1983) studied professional circuit-layout clerks who assigned telephone equipment in response to service requests. For this complex task, the lowest error rate occurred with a 12-second response time (Fig. 10.6). With shorter response times, the workers made hasty decisions; with longer response times, the frustration of waiting burdened short-term memory. The number of productive transactions (total minus errors) increased almost linearly with reductions in response time, and subjective preference was consistently in favor of the shorter response time.

In summary, users pick up the pace of the interface, and they consistently prefer a faster pace. Error rates at shorter response times increase with the cognitive complexity of the tasks. Each task appears to have an optimal pace—response times that are shorter or longer than this pace lead to increased errors. If error damage can be large and recovery is difficult, users should slow themselves down and make careful decisions.

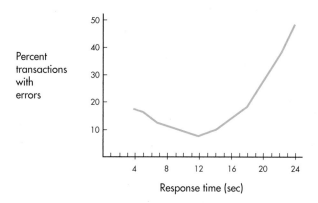

FIGURE 10.6

Error rates as a function of response time for a complex telephone-circuit–layout task by Barber and Lucas (1983). Although error rates were lowest with long response times (12 seconds), productivity increased with shorter times because the system could detect errors and users could rapidly correct them.

10.5 Variability in Response Time

People are willing to pay substantial amounts of money to reduce the variability in their lives. The entire insurance industry is based on the reduction of present pleasures, through the payment of premiums, to reduce the severity of potential future losses. Most people appreciate predictable behavior that lessens the anxiety of contemplating unpleasant surprises.

When using computers, users cannot see into the machines to gain reassurance that their actions are being executed properly, but the response time can provide a clue. If users come to expect a response time of 3 seconds for a common action, they may become apprehensive if this action takes 0.5 or 15 seconds. Such extreme variation is unsettling and should be prevented or acknowledged by the interface, with some indicator for an unusually fast response or a progress report for an unusually slow response.

The more difficult issue is the effect of modest variations in response time. As discussed earlier, Miller (1968) raised this issue and reported that 75% of participants tested could perceive 8% variations in time for periods in the interval of 2 to 4 seconds. These results prompted some designers to suggest restrictive rules for variability of response time. Since it may not be technically feasible to provide a fixed short response time (such as 1 second) for all actions, several researchers have suggested that the time be fixed for classes of actions. Many actions could have a fixed response time of less than 1 second, other actions could take 4 seconds, and still other actions could take 12 seconds.

Experimental results suggest that modest variations in response time do not severely affect performance. Users are apparently capable of adapting to varying situations, although some of them may become frustrated when performing certain tasks. Goodman and Spence (1982) measured performance changes as a result of response-time variation in a problem-solving situation (a similar situation was used in their earlier experiment, described in Section 10.4). They found no significant performance changes as the variability was increased. The time to solution and the profile of command use were unchanged. As the variability increased, participants took advantage of fast responses by entering subsequent commands immediately, balancing the time lost in waiting for slower responses. Other researchers found similar results.

The physiological effect of response time is an important issue for stressful, long-duration tasks such as air-traffic control, but it is also a concern for office workers and sales personnel. While no dramatic differences have been found between constant and variable response-time treatments statistically, significantly higher error rates, higher systolic blood pressure, and more pronounced pain symptoms were found repeatedly with shorter response times (Kohlisch and Kuhmann, 1997). Although diastolic blood pressure and masseter (jaw-muscle) tension did increase when compared to resting baseline values, there were no significant differences in these physiological measures between constant and variable treatments.

In summary, modest variations in response time (plus or minus 50% of the mean) appear to be tolerable and to have little effect on performance. Frustration emerges only if delays are unusually long (at least twice the anticipated time). Similarly, anxiety about an erroneous command may emerge only if the response time is unusually short—say, less than one-quarter of the anticipated time. But even with extreme changes, users appear to be adaptable enough to complete their tasks.

It may be useful to slow down unexpected fast responses to avoid surprising users. This proposal is controversial, but it would affect only a small fraction of user interactions. Certainly, designers should also make a serious effort to avoid extremely slow responses or, if responses must be slow, should give users information to indicate progress towards the goal. One graphics interface displays a large clock ticking backwards; the output appears only when the clock has ticked down to zero. Likewise, many printing and downloading programs display the page numbers to indicate progress and to confirm that the computer is at work productively on the appropriate document.

10.6 Frustrating Experiences

Quality of Service is usually defined in terms of network performance, but another perspective is to think about the quality of user experiences. Many technology promoters argue that the quality of user experiences with computers has been improving over the past four decades, pointing to the steadily increasing chip and network speeds and harddrive capacities. However, critics believe frustration from interface complexity, network disruptions, and malicious interference has grown. Recent research has begun to document and help us understand the sources of user frustration with contemporary user interfaces.

When hard-to-use computers cause users to become frustrated, it can affect workplace productivity, users' moods, and interactions with other coworkers (Lazar et al., 2006). Analysis was accomplished by collecting modified time diaries from 50 workplace users, who spent an average of 5.1 hours on the computer. Users reported wasting, on average, 42 to 43% of their time on the computer due to frustrating experiences. The largest number of frustrating experiences occurred while using word processors, e-mail, and web browsers. The causes, time lost, and effects on the mood of the users were analyzed in this research, along with implications for designers, managers, users, information technology staff, and policymakers.

Another study of 107 student computer users and 50 workplace computer users showed high levels of frustration and loss of 1/3 to 1/2 of time spent (Lazar et al., 2006). This research reported incident-specific and user-specific factors that caused frustration, how those factors impacted the severity of the users' frustration, and explored how frustration impacted the daily interactions of the users. For both student and workplace users, frustration levels were strongly correlated with the amount of time lost/time required to fix the problem and with the importance of the task.

Interruptions appear to be troubling to users regardless of whether they originate from the current task or an unrelated task, but surprisingly, people have been shown to complete interrupted tasks in less time than uninterrupted tasks and with no difference in quality (Mark et al., 2008). The authors of this study conjectured that people compensate for interruptions by working faster; however, this comes at the price of more stress and higher frustration, time pressure, and effort. An appropriate interface design change would allow users to limit interruptions, reducing their negative effects.

One study used memory as an indication of where frustration occurs while using technologies such as operating systems, web browsers, text editors, e-mail clients, mobile devices, digital video recorders (TiVo), and others (Mentis, 2007). The majority of users remembered frustrating incidents such as incorrect autoformatting, computer errors or bugs, slow or dropped Internet connections, and unwanted pop-ups. These incidents all seem to have two things in common: They are external to the user's cognitive processing, and they interrupt the user's task and take control away from the user. The users' memories of their experiences, usability incidents, and the users' emotional reactions can lead designers to create a better overall user experience by avoiding interrupting the user's cognitive flow. This principle also would apply to interfaces outside of desktop environments.

Another study examining user frustration with mobile devices evaluated users' experiences with using location-sensitive mobile services in an urban environment, collected through a diary study and user interviews (Häkkilä and Isomursu, 2005). User-perceived problems and the resulting frustration and difficulties in use were mainly caused by slow or unreliable data connections and lack of content in the mobile services.

User surveys elicit strong responses that convey unsatisfactory experiences amongst the general population. A British study of 1,255 office workers by a major computer manufacturer found that nearly half of the respondents felt frustrated or stressed by the amount of time it takes to solve problems. In an American survey of 6,000 computer users, the average amount of wasted time was estimated at 5.1 hours per week.

Replacing these possibly exaggerated impressions with more reliable data is a serious challenge. Self-reports and observations from more than 100 users doing their own work for an average of 2.5 hours each produced disturbing results: 46 to 53% of the users' time was seen as being wasted (Ceaparu et al., 2004). Frequent complaints included dropped network connections, application crashes, long system response times, and confusing error messages, but no individual cause contributed more than 9%. The major sources of problems were the popular applications for web browsing, e-mail, and word processing. Recommendations for reducing frustration include interface redesign, software quality improvement, and network reliability increases. Other recommendations focus on what users can do through increased learning, careful use of services, and self-control of their attitudes.

Infrastructure improvements to server capacity and network speed and reliability will improve user experiences, but the continuing growth of Internet usage means there will be problems for many years to come. Improved network performance and reliability promotes trust in users, easing their concerns and ultimately improving work performance and output. Consequently, poor Quality of Service is a still greater difficulty in emerging markets and developing nations, where infrastructure reliability remains a problem.

Since user training can have a profound influence on reducing frustrating experiences, efforts to improve education through schools and workplaces could improve user experiences. Improved educational programs and refined user interfaces are likely to have the largest effect on poorly educated users, whose difficulties in using Internet services undermine efforts to provide e-learning, e-commerce, and e-government services.

Networked services, especially e-mail, are among the most valued benefits of information and communications technologies. There are numerous sources of information on "netiquette," proper usage, and productivity to guide users in the proper use of e-mail. Many corporations publish e-mail guidelines, not only to coach their employees on the proper use of e-mail in the workplace, but also to address best practices for reducing e-mail information overload, thus enhancing workplace productivity.

E-mail has become the source of frustrating "spam" (the pejorative term given to unwanted, unsolicited e-mail, including advertisements, personal solicitations, and pornographic invitations). Some of these messages come from major corporations who make an effort to focus their e-mail on current customers, but much spam comes from small companies and individuals who take advantage of the low cost of e-mail to send blanket notices to huge lists of unfiltered e-mail addresses. Anti-spam legislation is being passed in many nations, but the Internet's international reach and open policies limit the success of legal controls. Many network providers intercept e-mail from known spam sources, which account for 80% of all e-mails, but users still complain of too much spam. User-controlled spam filters also help, but the complexity of installation and user controls undermines many users' willingness to use these tools. Furthermore, the increasingly clever spam senders rapidly change their messages to bypass existing filters. Similarly, distributors of pop-up advertisements refine their schemes to account for changing technology and to bypass user-protection strategies. A consumer uprising could pressure software developers, network providers, and government agencies to deal more directly with these annoying problems. Some spam senders and advertisers claim freedom of speech in their right to send spam or ads, but most users wish to see some limitation on the right to send bulk e-mails or unsolicited pop-up ads.

Another frustrating problem for users is the prevalence of malicious viruses that, once installed on a machine, can destroy data, disrupt usage, or produce a cancerous spread of the virus to everyone on the user's e-mail contact list. Viruses are created by malevolent programmers who want to spread havoc, usually via e-mail attachments. Unsuspecting recipients may get an infected e-mail from a known correspondent, but the absence of a meaningful subject line or message is often a clue that the e-mail contains a virus. Deceptive messages that mention previous e-mails or make appealing invitations complicate user decisions, but safety-conscious users will not open attachments unless they expect a document or photo and get an appropriate message from the sender. In 2000, before anti-virus software became effective, the famed ILOVEYOU virus contaminated millions of personal computers worldwide by tricking users to open e-mail messages by placing the words "I Love You" in the subject line; recovering from the damage cost an estimated $10.2 billion. Most network service providers offer virus filters that stop known viruses, but professional programmers must make weekly or even daily revisions to anti-virus software (suppliers include McAfee™ and Symantec™) to keep up with the increasingly sophisticated virus developers. Since e-mail is the source of so many threats, developers of e-mail software must take more initiatives to protect users.

Universal usability presents its own set of challenges in terms of user frustration. In one research project, 100 blind users, using time diaries, recorded their frustrations using the Web (Lazar et al., 2007). The top causes of frustration reported were: (1) page layout causing confusing screen-reader feedback; (2) conflict between the screen reader and the application; (3) poorly designed/unlabeled forms; (4) no alternative text for pictures; and (5) a three-way tie between misleading links, inaccessible PDFs, and screen-reader crashes. In this study, the blind users reported losing, on average, 30.4% of their time due to these frustrating situations. Web designers concerned with universal usability can improve matters by using more appropriate form and graphic labels and avoiding confusing page layouts.

Since frustration, distractions, and interruptions can impede smooth progress, design strategies should enable users to maintain concentration. Three initial strategies can reduce user frustration: reduce short-term and working memory load, provide information-abundant interfaces, and increase automaticity (Shneiderman, 2005). Automaticity in this context is the processing of information (in response to stimuli) in a way that is automatic and involuntary, occurring without conscious control. An example is when a user performs a complex sequence of actions with only a light cognitive load, like a driver following a familiar route to work with little apparent effort.

Practitioner's Summary

Quality of Service is a growing concern for users and providers on networks, computers, and mobile devices. Rapid system response times with fast screen refreshes are necessary, because these factors are determinants of user productivity, error rates, working style, and satisfaction (Box 10.1). In most situations, shorter response times (less than one second) lead to higher productivity. For mouse actions, multimedia performances, and interactive animations, even faster performance is necessary (less than 0.1 second). Satisfaction generally increases as the response time decreases, but there may be a danger from stress induced by a rapid pace. As users pick up the pace of the system, they may make more errors. If these errors are detected and corrected easily, productivity will generally increase. However, if errors are hard to detect or are excessively costly, a moderate pace may be most beneficial.

Designers can determine the optimal response time for a specific application and user community by measuring productivity, errors, and the cost of providing

BOX 10.1

Response-time guidelines.

- Users prefer shorter response times.
- Longer response times (> 15 seconds) are disruptive.
- Users' usage profiles change as a function of response time.
- Shorter response time leads to shorter user think time.
- A faster pace may increase productivity, but it may also increase error rates.
- Error-recovery ease and time influence optimal response time.
- Response time should be appropriate to the task:
  - Typing, cursor motion, mouse selection: 50–150 milliseconds
  - Simple, frequent tasks: 1 second
  - Common tasks: 2–4 seconds
  - Complex tasks: 8–12 seconds
- Users should be advised of long delays.
- Strive to have rapid start-ups.
- Modest variability in response time is acceptable.
- Unexpected delays may be disruptive.
- Offer users a choice in the pace of interaction.
- Empirical tests can help to set suitable response times.

BOX 10.2
Reducing user frustration.

- Increase server capacity, network speed, and network reliability.
- Improve user training, online help, and online tutorials.
- Redesign instructions and error messages.
- Protect against spam, viruses, and pop-up advertisements.
- Organize consumer-protection groups.
- Increase research on user frustration.
- Catalyze public discussion to raise awareness.

short response times. Managers must be alert to changes in work style as the pace quickens; productivity is measured by correctly completed tasks rather than by interactions per hour. Novices may prefer a slower pace of interaction. Modest variations around the mean response time are acceptable, but large variations (less than one-quarter of the mean or more than twice the mean) should be accompanied by informative messages. An alternative approach for overly rapid responses is to slow them down and thus to avoid the need for explanatory messages.

A continuing concern is the frustration level of the increasingly diverse set of computer users (Box 10.2). In an era of user-generated content and social media participation, a satisfying user experience is determined by a preferred or, at least, an acceptable level of Quality of Service. Malicious spreaders of spam and viruses are a serious threat to the expanding community of Internet users. Application crashes, confusing error messages, and network disruptions are problems that could be addressed by improved interface and software design.

Researcher's Agenda

The increased understanding of Quality of Service issues today is balanced by the richness of new technologies and applications. The taxonomy of issues provides a framework for research, but a finer taxonomy of tasks, of relevant cognitive-style differences, and of applications is needed. Next, a refined theory of problem-solving and consumer behavior is necessary if we are to generate useful design hypotheses.

The interesting result of a U-shaped error curve for a complex task, with the lowest error rate at a 12-second response time (Barber and Lucas, 1983), invites further work. It would be productive to study error rates as a function of response time for a range of tasks and users. Another goal is to accommodate the real-world interruptions that disrupt planning, interfere with decision making, and reduce productivity.

It is understandable that error rates vary with response times, but how else are users' work styles or consumers' expectations affected? Is the modern era of employee multitasking between numerous applications coupled with routine office distractions spreading us too thin, adding stress, and drastically reducing productivity, ultimately affecting corporate profits? Can we train modern users to better manage their time among diverse applications and tasks, yet provide tools for improved communication, collaboration, user-generated content, and networking? Can users be encouraged to be more careful in their decisions by merely lengthening response times and degrading Quality of Service? Does the profile of actions shift to a smaller set of more familiar actions as the response time shortens?

Many other questions are also worthy of investigation. When technical feasibility prevents short responses, can users be satisfied by diversionary tasks, or are progress reports sufficient? Do warnings of long responses or apologies relieve anxiety or simply further frustrate users?

Methods for assessing user frustration levels are controversial. Time diaries may be more reliable than retrospective surveys, but how could automated logging and observational techniques be made more effective? More importantly, how could software developers and network providers construct reliable monthly reports to gauge improvements in Quality of Service and reductions in user frustration?

WORLD WIDE WEB RESOURCES

http://www.aw.com/DTUI/

Response-time issues have a modest presence on the Internet, although the issue of long network delays gets discussed frequently. User frustration is a lively topic, and many web sites point out flawed interfaces and related frustrating experiences. The New Computing movement's web site (http://www.cs.umd.edu/hcil/newcomputing/) suggests ways to help bring about change.

References

Barber, R. E. and Lucas, H. C., System response time, operator productivity and job satisfaction, *Communications of the ACM* 26, 11 (November 1983), 972–986.

Bouch, Anna, Kuchinsky, Allen, and Bhatti, Nina, Quality is in the eye of the beholder: Meeting user requirements for Internet quality of service, *Proc. CHI 2000 Conference: Human Factors in Computing Systems*, ACM Press, New York (2000), 297–304.

Ceaparu, I., Lazar, J., Bessiere, K., Robinson, J., and Shneiderman, B., Determining causes and severity of end-user frustration, *International Journal of Human-Computer Interaction* 17, 3 (September 2004), 333–356.

Galletta, Dennis F., Understanding the direct and interaction effects of web delay and related factors, in Galletta, Dennis F. and Zhang, Ping (Editors), *Human-Computer Interaction and Management Information Systems: Applications (Advances in Management Information Systems)*, M. E. Sharpe, Armonk, New York (2006), 29–69.

Galletta, Dennis F., Henry, Raymond, McCoy, Scott, and Polak, Peter, When the wait isn't so bad, *Information Systems Research* 17, 1 (March 2006), 20–37.

Goodman, Tom and Spence, Robert, The effects of potentiometer dimensionality, system response time, and time of day on interactive graphical problem solving, *Human Factors* 24, 4 (1982), 437–456.

Guastello, Stephen J., *Human Factors Engineering and Ergonomics: A Systems Approach*, Lawrence Erlbaum Associates, Mahwah, NJ (2006).

Häkkilä, Jonna and Isomursu, Minna, User experiences on location-aware mobile services, *Proc. OZCHI 2005*, ACM Press, New York (2005), 1–4.

Huberman, Bernardo A., *The Laws of the Web: Patterns in the Ecology of Information*, MIT Press, Cambridge, MA (2001).

Jacko, J., Sears, A., and Borella, M., The effect of network delay and media on user perceptions of web resources, *Behaviour & Information Technology* 19, 6 (2000), 427–439.

King, Andrew B., *Website Optimization: Speed, Search Engine & Conversion Rate Secrets*, O'Reilly Media, Sebastopol, CA (2008).

Kohlisch, Olaf and Kuhmann, Werner, System response time and readiness for task execution: The optimum duration of inter-task delays, *Ergonomics* 40, 3 (1997), 265–280.

Lazar, J., Allen, A., Kleinman, J., and Malarkey, C., What frustrates screen reader users on the Web: A study of 100 blind users, *International Journal of Human-Computer Interaction* 22, 3 (May 2007), 247–269.

Lazar, J., Jones, A., Hackley, M., and Shneiderman, B., Severity and impact of computer user frustration: A comparison of student and workplace users, *Interacting with Computers* 18, 2 (2006), 187–207.

Lazar, J., Jones, A., and Shneiderman, B., Workplace user frustration with computers: An exploratory investigation of the causes and severity, *Behaviour & Information Technology* 25, 3 (May/June 2006), 239–251.

Mark, Gloria, Gudith, Daniela, and Klocke, Ulrich, The cost of interrupted work: More speed and stress—Don't interrupt me, *Proc. CHI 2008 Conference: Human Factors in Computing Systems*, ACM Press, New York (2008), 107–110.

Martin, G. L. and Corl, K. G., System response time effects on user productivity, *Behaviour & Information Technology* 5, 1 (1986), 3–13.

Mentis, Helena, Memory of frustrating experiences, in Nahl. D. and Bilal, D. (Editors), *Information and Emotion*, Information Today, Medford, NJ (2007).

Meyer, Joachim, Shinar, David, Bitan, Yuval, and Leiser, David, Duration estimates and users' preferences in human-computer interaction, *Ergonomics* 39, 1 (1996), 46–60.

Miller, George A., The magical number seven, plus or minus two: Some limits on our capacity for processing information, *Psychological Science* 63 (1956), 81–97.

Miller, Robert B., Response time in man-computer conversational transactions, *Proc. AFIPS Spring Joint Computer Conference* 33, AFIPS Press, Montvale, NJ (1968), 267–277.

Morris, Michael G. and Turner, Jason M., Assessing users' subjective quality of experience with the World Wide Web: An exploratory examination of temporal changes in technology acceptance, *International Journal of Human-Computer Studies* 54 (2001), 877–901.

Ramsay, Judith, Barbesi, Alessandro, and Preece, Jenny, A psychological investigation of long retrieval times on the World Wide Web, *Interacting with Computers* 10 (1998), 77–86.

Raskin, Jef, *The Humane Interface: New Directions for Desgining Interactive Systems*, Addison-Wesley, Reading, MA (2000).

Shneiderman, Ben, *Leonardo's Laptop: Human Needs and the New Computing Technologies*, MIT Press, Cambridge, MA (2003).

Shneiderman, Ben and Bederson, Ben, Maintaining concentration to achieve task completion, *Proc. Conference on Designing for User Experiences* 135, ACM Press, New York (November 2005), 2–7.

Teal, Steven L. and Rudnicky, Alexander I., A performance model of system delay and user strategy selection, *Proc. CHI '92 Conference: Human Factors in Computing Systems*, ACM Press, New York (1992), 295–305.

Wickens, Christopher D., Lee, John D., Liu,Yili, and Becker, Sallie E. Gordon, *An Introduction to Human Factors Engineering, Second Edition*, Pearson Prentice-Hall, Upper Saddle River, NJ (2004).

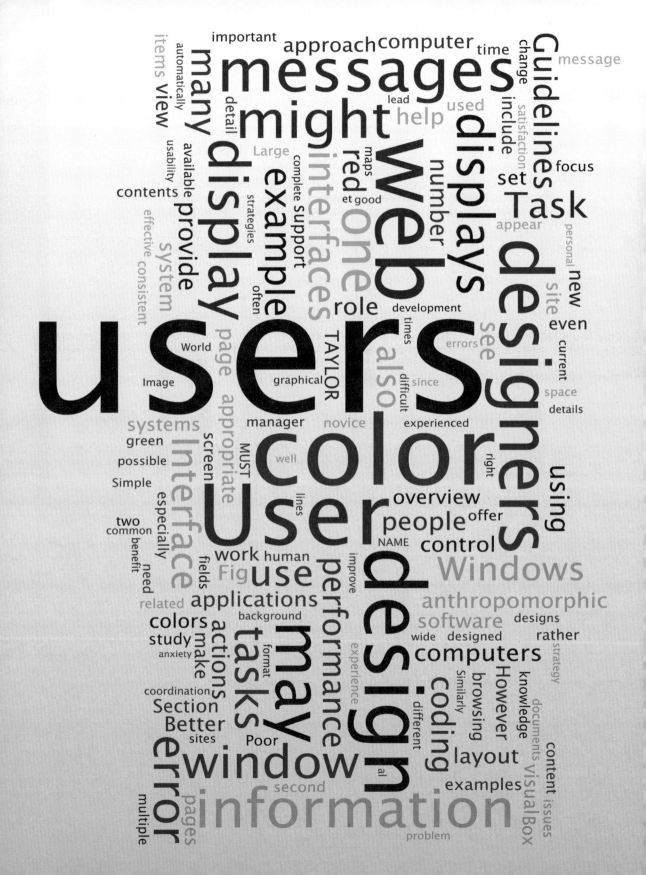

11

Balancing Function and Fashion

> " Words are sometimes sensitive instruments
> of precision with which delicate operations
> may be performed and swift, elusive
> truths may be touched. "

Helen Merrell Lynd
On Shame and the Search for Identity

Written in collaboration with Steven M. Jacobs

11.1 Introduction

Interface design has yet to match the high art of architecture or trendiness of clothing design. However, we can anticipate that, as the audience for computers expands, competition over design will heighten. Early automobiles were purely functional, and Henry Ford could joke about customers getting any color as long as it was black, but modern car designers have learned to balance function and fashion. This chapter deals with six design matters that are functional issues with many human-factors criteria, but also leave room for varying styles to suit a variety of customers: error messages, nonanthropomorphic design, display design, web page design, window design, and color.

User experiences with computer-system prompts, explanations, error diagnostics, and warnings play a critical role in influencing acceptance of software systems. The wording of messages is especially important in systems designed for novice users, but experts also benefit from improved messages (Section 11.2). Messages are sometimes meant to be conversational, as modeled by human-human communication, but this strategy has limits because people are different from computers. This fact may be obvious, but a section on nonanthropomorphic design (Section 11.3) seems necessary to steer designers towards comprehensible, predictable, and controllable interfaces.

Another opportunity for design improvements lies in the layout of information on a display (Section 11.4). Cluttered displays may overwhelm even knowledgeable users, but with only modest effort we can create well-organized, information-abundant layouts that reduce search time and increase subjective satisfaction. Issues related to universal usability, user-generated content, and the proliferation of web design and development techniques are also addressed.

Web page designs are improving as standards and tools emerge to address web page design and development, user-generated content, and universal usability (Section 11.5). Window management has become standardized, but an understanding of the motivations for multiple-window coordination could lead to improvements and to novel proposals, such as the personal role manager (Section 11.6).

Large, fast, high-resolution color displays offer many possibilities and challenges for designers. Guidelines for color design are useful, but experienced designers know that repeated testing is needed to ensure success (Section 11.7).

Recognition of the creative challenge of balancing function and fashion might be furthered by having designers put their names and photos on a title or credits page, just as authors do in a book. Such acknowledgment is common in games and in some educational software, and it seems appropriate for all software. Credits provide recognition for good work and identify the people responsible. Having their names in lights may also encourage designers to work even harder, since their identities will be public.

11.2 Error Messages

Error messages are a key part of an overall interface design strategy of guidance for the user. The strategy should ensure integrated, coordinated error messages that are consistent across one or multiple applications.

Design disasters have appeared in systems and web sites where error messages written by multiple authors read quite obviously as though they were written by multiple authors. There are several "hall of shame" error-message web sites where communities of users and developers share bizarre and misleading error-message experiences. Some are critical and humorous, while others are informative, providing lessons learned and suggestions for improvement; an example is the error-message discussion on the Microsoft Developers Network (Microsoft, 2008).

Solutions for avoiding error-message design disasters include discussing help and error handling in a style guide for all designers to review and follow, and ensuring that error messages are designed into a computing system or web site rather than being added as a final step or afterthought.

One problem that is sometimes seen is when error messages do not clearly correspond with the help provided, illustrating an obvious information gap in transitioning from the error message to assisting the user in performing the corrective action. With respect to international user interfaces, designers can run into trouble when having third-party language experts translate error messages, help text, prompts, and other guidance features. Experienced designers isolate the error messages and help text information into separate files (not hard-coded) for ease of translation during the development phase and later maintenance updates. This also permits on-site, local language selection when a system is installed in a country other than the one where the software was originally created.

Normal prompts, advisory messages, and system responses to user actions may influence user perceptions, but the phrasing of error messages and diagnostic warnings is critical. Since errors occur because of lack of knowledge, incorrect understanding, or inadvertent slips, users are likely to be confused, to feel inadequate, and to be anxious when they encounter these messages. Error messages with an imperious tone that condemn users can heighten anxiety, making it more difficult to correct the problems and increasing the chances of further errors. Messages that are too generic, such as WHAT? or SYNTAXERROR, or that are too obscure, such as FACRJCT 004004400400 or 0C7, offer little assistance to most users.

These concerns are especially important with respect to novices, whose lack of knowledge and confidence amplifies the stress that can lead to a frustrating sequence of failures. The discouraging effects of a bad experience in using a computer are not easily overcome by a few good experiences. In some cases, interfaces are remembered more for what happens when things go wrong than for when things go right. Although these concerns apply most forcefully to novice computer users, experienced users also suffer. Experts in one interface or part of an interface are still novices in many situations.

Improving error messages is one of the easiest and most effective ways to improve an existing interface. If the software can capture the frequency of errors, designers can focus on optimizing the most important messages. Error-frequency distributions also enable interface designers and maintainers to revise error-handling procedures, to improve documentation and tutorials, to alter online help, or even to change the permissible actions. The complete set of messages should be reviewed by peers and managers, tested empirically, and included in user documentation.

Specificity, constructive guidance, a positive tone, a user-centered style, and an appropriate physical format are recommended as the bases for preparing error messages (Box 11.1). These guidelines are especially important when the users are novices, but they can benefit experts as well. The phrasing and contents of error messages can significantly affect user performance and satisfaction.

11.2.1 Specificity

Messages that are too general make it difficult for the novice to determine what has gone wrong. Simple and condemning messages are frustrating because they provide neither enough information about what has gone wrong nor the knowledge to

BOX 11.1
Error-message guidelines for the end product and for the development process.
These guidelines are derived from practical experience and empirical data.

Product
- Be as specific and precise as possible. Determine necessary, relevant error messages.
- Be constructive. Indicate what the user needs to do.
- Use a positive tone. Avoid condemnation. Be courteous.
- Choose user-centered phrasing. State problem, cause, solution.
- Consider multiple levels of messages. State brief, sufficient information to assist with the corrective action.
- Maintain consistent grammatical forms, terminology, and abbreviations.
- Maintain consistent visual format and placement.

Process
- Increase attention to message design.
- Establish quality control.
- Develop guidelines.
- Carry out usability tests.
- Record the frequency of occurrence for each message.

set things right. The right amount of specificity therefore is important. Here are some examples:

> **Poor:** SYNTAX ERROR
> **Better:** Unmatched left parenthesis

> **Poor:** ILLEGAL ENTRY
> **Better:** Type first letter: Send, Read, or Drop

> **Poor:** INVALID DATA
> **Better:** Days range from 1 to 31

> **Poor:** BAD FILE NAME
> **Better:** The file C:\demo\data.txt.txt was not found

Here is another recent example that can add to user frustration, particularly with novice users:

```
Task 'Microsoft Exchange Server' reported error (0x80040600) :
'Unknown Error 0x80040600'
```

One interface for hotel check-in required the desk clerk to enter a 40- to 45-character string containing the name, room number, credit-card information, and so on. If the clerk made a data-entry error, the only message was INVALID INPUT. YOU MUST RETYPE THE ENTIRE RECORD. This led to frustration for users and delays for irritated guests. Interactive systems should be designed to minimize input errors by use of proper form fill-in strategies (Chapter 6); when an error occurs, the users should have to repair only the incorrect part.

Interfaces that offer an error-code number leading to a paragraph-long explanation in user documentation are also annoying, because the user documentation may not be available or consulting it may be disruptive and time-consuming. In most cases, interface developers can no longer hide behind the claim that printing meaningful messages consumes too many system resources.

11.2.2 Constructive guidance and positive tone

Rather than condemning users for what they have done wrong, messages should, where possible, indicate what users need to do to set things right:

> **Poor:** Run-Time error '-2147469 (800405)': Method 'Private Profile
>   String' of object 'System' failed.
> **Better:** Virtual memory space consumed. Close some programs and retry.

> **Poor:** Resource Conflict Bus: 00 Device: 03 Function: 01
> **Better:** Remove your compact flash card and restart.

> **Poor:** Network connection refused.
> **Better:** Your password was not recognized. Please retype.

> **Poor:** Invalid date.
> **Better:** Drop-off date must come after pickup date.

Unnecessarily hostile messages using violent terminology can disturb nontechnical users. An interactive legal-citation–searching system uses this message: FATAL ERROR, RUN ABORTED. Similarly, an early operating system threatened many users with CATASTROPHIC ERROR; LOGGED WITH OPERATOR. There is no excuse for these hostile messages; they can easily be rewritten to provide more information about what has happened and what must be done to set things right. Where possible, be constructive and positive. Such negative words as ILLEGAL, ERROR, INVALID, or BAD should be eliminated or used infrequently.

It may be difficult for the software writer to create a program that accurately determines the user's intention, so the advice to "be constructive" is often difficult to apply. Some designers argue for automatic error correction, but the disadvantage is that users may fail to learn proper syntax and may become dependent on alterations that the system makes. Envision the elementary-school language teacher trying to train school children in spelling when the papers students hand in are spell-checked, grammar-checked, and even autocorrected as they are typed; the students will have no incentive to self-correct and the teacher will not be able to see what mistakes they are making. Another approach is to inform users of the possible alternatives and to let them decide. A preferred strategy is, where possible, to prevent errors from being made (Section 2.3.5).

11.2.3 User-centered phrasing

The term *user-centered* suggests that the user controls the interface—initiating more than responding. Designers partially convey this feel by avoiding a negative and condemning tone in messages and by being courteous to the user.

Brevity is a virtue, but users should be allowed to control the kind of information provided. For example, if the standard message is just one line, by keying a ? in a command-language interface, users should be able to obtain a few lines of explanation. ?? might yield a set of examples, and ??? might produce explanations of the examples and a complete description. A graphical user interface can provide a progression of ScreenTips, a special Help button to provide context-sensitive explanations, and thorough, hyperlinked online user documentation.

Some telephone companies, long used to dealing with nontechnical users, offer this tolerant message: "We're sorry, but we were unable to complete your call as dialed. Please hang up, check your number, and dial again, or consult the operator for assistance." They take the blame and offer constructive guidance for what to do. A thoughtless programmer might have generated a harsher message: "Illegal telephone number. Call aborted. Error number 583-2R6.9. Application will be terminated. Consult your user documentation for further information."

11.2.4 Appropriate physical format

Most users prefer and find it easier to read mixed uppercase and lowercase messages. Uppercase-only messages should be reserved for brief, serious warnings. Messages that begin with a lengthy and mysterious code number serve only to remind the user that the designers were insensitive to the users' real needs. If code numbers are needed at all, they might be enclosed in parentheses at the end of a message, or as a "provide more details" function.

There is disagreement about the optimal placement of messages in a display. One school of thought argues that the messages should be placed on the display near where the problem has arisen. A second opinion is that the messages clutter the display and should be placed in a consistent position on the bottom of the display. The third approach is to display a dialog box near to, but not obscuring the relevant problem.

Some applications ring a bell or sound a tone when an error has occurred. This alarm can be useful if the operator might otherwise miss the error, but it can be embarrassing if other people are in the room and is potentially annoying even if the operator is alone.

Designers must walk a narrow path between calling attention to a problem and avoiding embarrassment to users. Considering the wide range of experience and temperament in users, maybe the best solution is to offer users control over the alternatives—this approach coordinates well with the user-centered principle.

Improved messages will be of the greatest benefit to novice users, but regular users and experienced professionals will also benefit; the error messages presented by Google's Chrome browser are a good example (Fig. 4.7). As examples of excellence proliferate, complex, obscure, and harsh interfaces will seem increasingly out of place. The crude environments of the past will be replaced gradually by interfaces designed with the users in mind. Resistance to such a transition should not be allowed to impede progress towards the goal of serving the growing user community.

11.3 Nonanthropomorphic Design

There is a great temptation to have computers "talk" as though they were people. Children accept human-like references and qualities for almost any object, from Humpty Dumpty to Tootle the Train. Some adults still reserve *anthropomorphic* references for objects of special attraction, such as cars, ships, computers, and even cell phones.

The words and graphics in user interfaces can make important differences in people's perceptions, emotional reactions, and motivations. Attributions of intelligence, autonomy, free will, or knowledge to computers are appealing to some people, but to others such characterizations may be seen as deceptive, confusing, and misleading. The suggestion that computers can think, know, or understand may give users an erroneous model of how computers work and what the machines' capacities are. Ultimately, the deception becomes apparent, and users may feel poorly treated. Martin (1995/96) carefully traces the media impact of the 1946 ENIAC announcements: "Readers were given hyperbole designed to raise their expectations about the use of the new electronic brains. . . . This engendered premature enthusiasm, which then led to disillusionment and distrust of computers on the part of the public when the new technology did not live up to these expectations."

A second reason for using nonanthropomorphic phrasing is to clarify the differences between people and computers. Relationships with people are different from relationships with computers. Users operate and control computers, but they respect the unique identities and autonomy of individuals. Furthermore, users and designers must accept responsibility for misuse of computers, rather than blaming the machines for errors. It is worrisome that, in one study, 24 of 29 computer-science students believed that computers can have intentions or be independent decision makers, and 6 consistently held computers morally responsible for errors (Friedman, 1995).

A third motivation is that, although an anthropomorphic interface may be attractive to some people, it can be distracting or produce anxiety for others. Some people express anxiety about using computers and believe that computers "make you feel dumb." Presenting the computer through the specific functions it offers may be a stronger stimulus to user acceptance than promoting the fantasy that the computer is a friend, parent, or partner. As users become engaged, the computer becomes transparent, and they can concentrate on their writing, problem solving, or exploration. At the end, they have the experience of accomplishment and mastery, rather than the feeling that some magical machine has done their job for them. Anthropomorphic interfaces may distract users from their tasks and waste their time as they consider how to please or be socially appropriate to the onscreen characters.

Experts in consumer product interface design often speak of *making technology invisible* (Bergman, 2000). Designers have fielded interfaces on such items as mall kiosks, postage dispensers, and interactive voice response (IVR) systems that anthropomorphize, giving an impression to the novice user that the computer systems are doing some intelligent reasoning while adding stress on and disempowering the user. IVR systems are notorious for anthropomorphizing interfaces. Here are some current examples: one airline reservation system says "OK, I can help with that . . ." after you request to initiate a domestic reservation; an automated banking system says "Please hold, while I check your account balance . . ."; a mail-order pharmacy says "Would you like me to send your prescription to the address on record?" Of course, the speech-recognition technology for many of these systems is not quite mature, adding to user frustration.

Individual differences in the desire for internal locus of control are important, but there may be an overall advantage to clearly distinguishing human abilities from computer powers for most tasks and users (Shneiderman, 1995). On the other hand, there are persistent advocates of creating anthropomorphic interfaces, often called virtual humans, lifelike autonomous agents, or embodied conversational agents (D'Mello et al., 2007; Gratch et al., 2002; Cassell et al., 2000).

Advocates of anthropomorphic interfaces assume that human-human communication is an appropriate model for human operation of computers. It may be a useful starting point, but some designers pursue the human-imitation approach long after it becomes counterproductive. Mature technology has managed to overcome the *obstacle of animism*, which has been a trap for technologists for centuries (Mumford, 1934); a visit to the Museum of Automata in York, England reveals the ancient sources and persistent fantasies of animated dolls and robotic toys.

Historical precedents of failed anthropomorphic bank tellers, such as Tillie the Teller, Harvey Wallbanker, and BOB (Bank of Baltimore), and of abandoned talking automobiles and soda machines do not seem to register on some designers. The bigger-than-life-sized Postal Buddy was supposed to be cute and friendly while providing several useful automated services, but users rejected this pseudo–postal clerk after the project had incurred costs of over

$1 billion. The web-based newsreader Ananova was heralded as the future of computing, but it has fallen into disuse. Advocates of anthropomorphic interfaces suggest that they may be most useful as teachers, salespeople, therapists, or entertainment figures.

In early studies with a text-based computer-assisted instruction task, participants felt less responsible for their performance when interacting with an anthropomorphic interface. Animated characters that range from cartoon-like to realistic have been embedded in many interfaces, but evidence is growing that they increase anxiety and reduce performance, especially for users with an external locus of control. Many people are more anxious when someone is observing their work, so it is understandable that animated characters that monitor their performance might trouble computer users. This effect was found in a study with an animated character that appeared to be taking notes on users' work and making screen copies: Participants with an external locus of control had elevated anxiety levels and were less accurate in their tasks (Reeves and Rickenberg, 2000).

One specific design controversy is over the use of first-person pronouns in an interface. Advocates believe it makes the interaction friendly, but such interfaces may be counterproductive because they can deceive, mislead, and confuse users. It may seem cute on the first encounter to be greeted by "I am SOPHIE, the sophisticated teacher, and I will teach you to spell correctly." By the second session, however, this approach strikes many people as silly; by the third session, it can be an annoying distraction from the task. The alternative for the interface designer is to focus on the user and to use third-person singular pronouns or to avoid pronouns altogether. Improved messages may also suggest a higher level of user control. For example:

> **Poor:** I will begin the lesson when you press RETURN.
> **Better:** You can begin the lesson by pressing RETURN.
> **Better:** To begin the lesson, press RETURN.

The *you* form seems preferable for introductions; however, once the session is underway, reducing the number of pronouns and words avoids distractions from the task. In one study, student participants carried out a travel-reservation task with a simulated natural-language interface using the *I*, *you*, or *neutral* styles, called *anthropomorphic*, *fluent*, and *telegraphic* by the authors (Brennan and Ohaeri, 1994). Users' messages mimicked the style of the messages they received, leading to lengthier user inputs and longer task-completion times in the anthropomorphic treatment. Users did not attribute greater intelligence to the anthropomorphic computer.

The issue of pronoun usage reappears in the design of interactive voice-response telephone interfaces, especially if speech recognition is employed. Advocates argue that greetings from a rental-car reservation service, for example, might be more appealing if they simulate a human operator: "Welcome to

Thrifty Car Rentals. I'm Emily, let me help you reserve your car. In what city will you need a car?" While most users won't care about the phrasing, opponents claim that this deception does annoy and worry some users, and that the expedient solution of deleting the chatty second sentence produces higher customer satisfaction.

Some designers of children's educational software believe that it is appropriate and acceptable to have a fantasy character, such as a teddy bear or busy beaver, serve as a guide through a lesson. A cartoon character can be drawn on the screen and possibly animated, adding visual appeal, speaking to users in an encouraging style, and pointing to relevant items on the display. Successful educational software packages such as Reader Rabbit® and some empirical research (Mayer, 2009) provide support for this position.

Unfortunately, cartoon characters were not successful in BOB, a heavily promoted but short-lived home-computing product from Microsoft. Users could choose from a variety of onscreen characters that spoke in cartoon bubbles with phrases such as: "What a team we are," "Good job so far, Ben," and "What shall we do next, Ben?" This style might be acceptable in children's games and educational software, but it is probably not acceptable for adults in the workplace. Interfaces should neither compliment nor condemn users, just provide comprehensible feedback so users can move forward in achieving their goals. However, anthropomorphic characters will not necessarily succeed here either. Microsoft's ill-fated Clippit character (a lively paper-clip cartoon character, shown in Fig. 12.9) was designed to provide helpful suggestions for users. It amused some but annoyed many, and it was soon demoted to an optional extra. Defenders of anthropomorphic interfaces found many reasons to explain Clippit's rejection (primarily its disruptive interference with users). Others believe that successful anthropomorphic interfaces require socially appropriate emotional expressions, as well as well-timed head movements, nods, blinks, and eye contact.

An alternative instructional design approach that seems acceptable to many users is to present the human author of a lesson or software package. Through an audio or video clip, the author can speak to users, much as television news announcers speak to viewers. Instead of making the computer into a person, designers can show identifiable and appropriate human guides. For example, the Secretary-General might record a video welcome for visitors to a web site about the United Nations, or Bill Gates might provide greetings for new users of Windows.

Once past these introductions, several styles are possible. One is a continuation of the guided-tour metaphor, in which the respected personality introduces segments but allows users to control the pace, to repeat segments, and to decide when they are ready to move on. A variant of this approach creates an interview-like experience in which users read from a set of three prompts and issue spoken commands to get pre-recorded video segments by noted figures such as

Senator John Glenn or biologist Joshua Lederberg (Harless et al., 2003). This approach works for museum tours, tutorials on software, and certain educational lectures.

Another strategy is to support user control by showing an overview of the modules from which users can choose. Users decide how much time to spend visiting parts of museums, browsing a timeline with details of events, or jumping between articles in a hyperlinked encyclopedia. These overviews give users a sense of the magnitude of information available and allow them to see their progress in covering the topics. Overviews also support users' needs for closure, give them the satisfaction of completely touring the contents, and offer a comprehensible environment with predictable actions that foster a comforting sense of control. Furthermore, they support the need for replicability of actions (to revisit an appealing or confusing module, or to show it to a colleague) and reversibility (to back up or return to a known landmark). While in games users may enjoy the challenge of confusion, hidden controls, and unpredictability, this is not the case in most applications; rather, designers must strive to make their products comprehensible and predictable. A summary of nonanthropomorphic guidelines appears in Box 11.2.

Japanese nursing homes have begun experimenting with using robots to help care for the elderly (Brooke, 2004). Sensors in a teddy bear can talk to the patients and ascertain whether human assistance is needed. Bathing can be assisted with robot bathtubs that can perform an automatic wash and rinse cycle, due to limited people resources to fulfill that function. The Japan Robot Association expects the demand for elder-care robots to help the personal-robot industry grow to $40 billion by 2025.

BOX 11.2
Guidelines for avoiding anthropomorphism and building appealing interfaces.

Nonanthropomorphic guidelines
- Be cautious in presenting computers as people, either with synthesized or cartoon characters.
- Design comprehensible, predictable, and user-controlled interfaces.
- Use appropriate humans for audio or video introductions or guides.
- Use cartoon characters in games or children's software, but avoid them elsewhere.
- Provide user-centered overviews for orientation and closure.
- Do not use "I" when the computer responds to human actions.
- Use "you" to guide users, or just state facts.

11.4 Display Design

For most interactive systems, the displays are a key component of successful designs, and are the source of many lively arguments. Dense or cluttered displays can provoke anger, and inconsistent formats can inhibit performance. The complexity of this issue is suggested by the 162 guidelines for data display offered by Smith and Mosier (1986). This diligent effort (see Box 11.3 for examples) represents progress over the vague guidelines given in earlier reviews. Display design will always have elements of art and require invention, but perceptual principles are becoming clearer and theoretical foundations are emerging (Galitz, 2007; Tullis, 1997). Innovative information visualizations with user interfaces to support dynamic control are a rapidly emerging theme (Chapter 14).

Research suggests that the visual aesthetics of computer interfaces are a strong determinant of users' satisfaction and pleasure. However, there is a lack of appropriate concepts and measures of aesthetics. One study looked at website aesthetics using exploratory and confirmatory factor analyses to obtain user perceptions of "classical aesthetics" and "expressive aesthetics" (Lavie and Tractinsky, 2004).

Designers should begin, as always, with a thorough knowledge of the users' tasks, free from the constraints of display size or available fonts. Effective display designs must provide all the necessary data in the proper sequence to carry out the task. Meaningful groupings of items (with labels suitable to the users' knowledge), consistent sequences of groups, and orderly formats all support task performance. Groups can be surrounded by blank spaces or boxes. Alternatively, related items can be indicated by highlighting, background shading, color, or special fonts. Within a group, orderly formats can be accomplished by left or right justification, alignment on decimal points for numbers, or markers to decompose lengthy fields.

Graphic designers have produced principles suited to print formats, and they are now adapting these principles for display design. Mullet and Sano (1995) offer thoughtful advice with examples of good and bad design in commercial systems. They propose six categories of principles that reveal the complexity of the designer's task:

1. *Elegance and simplicity:* Unity, refinement, and fitness
2. *Scale, contrast, and proportion:* Clarity, harmony, activity, and restraint
3. *Organization and visual structure:* Grouping, hierarchy, relationship, and balance
4. *Module and program:* Focus, flexibility, and consistent application
5. *Image and representation:* Immediacy, generality, cohesiveness, and characterization
6. *Style:* Distinctiveness, integrity, comprehensiveness, and appropriateness

BOX 11.3

Samples of the 162 data-display guidelines from Smith and Mosier (1986).
(Courtesy MITRE Corporate Archives: Bedford, MA.)

- Ensure that any data that a user needs, at any step in a transaction sequence, are available for display.
- Display data to users in directly usable forms; do not require that users convert displayed data.
- Maintain a consistent format for any particular type of data display from one display to another.
- Use short, simple sentences.
- Use affirmative statements, rather than negative statements.
- Adopt a logical principle by which to order lists; where no other principle applies, order lists alphabetically.
- Ensure that labels are sufficiently close to their data fields to indicate association yet are separated from their data fields by at least one space.
- Left-justify columns of alphabetic data to permit rapid scanning.
- Label each page in multipaged displays to show its relation to the others.
- Begin every display with a title or header, describing briefly the contents or purpose of the display; leave at least one blank line between the title and the body of the display.
- For size coding, make larger symbols be at least 1.5 times the height of the next-smaller symbol.
- Consider color coding for applications in which users must distinguish rapidly among several categories of data, particularly when the data items are dispersed on the display.
- When you use blink coding, make the blink rate 2 to 5 Hz, with a minimum duty cycle (ON interval) of 50%.
- For a large table that exceeds the capacity of one display frame, ensure that users can see column headings and row labels in all displayed sections of the table.
- Provide a means for users (or a system administrator) to make necessary changes to display functions, as data-display requirements may change (as is often the case).

This section deals with some of these issues, offering empirical support for concepts where available.

11.4.1 Field layout

Exploration with a variety of layouts can be a helpful process. These design alternatives should be developed directly on a display screen. An employee record with information about a spouse and children could be displayed crudely as follows:

> **Poor:** `TAYLOR,SUSAN34787331WILLIAM TAYLOR`
>
> `THOMAS10291974ANN08211977ALEXANDRA09081972`

This record may contain the necessary information for a task, but extracting the information will be slow and error-prone. As a first step at improving the format, blanks and separate lines can distinguish fields:

> **Better:** `TAYLOR,` `SUSAN 34787331` `WILLIAM TAYLOR`
>
> `THOMAS` `10291974`
>
> `ANN` `08211977`
>
> `ALEXANDRA` `09081972`

The children's names can be listed in chronological order, with the dates aligned. Familiar separators for the dates also aid recognition:

> **Better:** `TAYLOR,` `SUSAN 34787331` `WILLIAM TAYLOR`
>
> `ALEXANDRA` `09-08-1972`
>
> `THOMAS` `10-29-1974`
>
> `ANN` `08-21-1977`

The reversed order of "last name, first name" for the employee may be desired to highlight the lexicographic ordering in a long file, but the "first name, last name" order for the spouse is more readable. Consistency is important, however, so a compromise might be made:

> **Better:** `SUSAN` `TAYLOR 34787331` `WILLIAM TAYLOR`
>
> `ALEXANDRA` `09-08-1972`
>
> `THOMAS` `10-29-1974`
>
> `ANN` `08-21-1977`

For frequent users, this format may be acceptable, since labels have a cluttering effect. For most users, however, labels will be helpful. Indenting the information about children will also help to convey the grouping of these repeating fields:

> **Better:** `Employee:` `SUSAN TAYLOR ID Number: 34787331`
>
> `Spouse:` `WILLIAM TAYLOR`
>
> `Children:` `Names` `Birthdates`
>
> `ALEXANDRA` `09-08-1972`
>
> `THOMAS` `10-29-1974`
>
> `ANN` `08-21-1977`

Mixed upper- and lowercase letters have been used for the labels to distinguish them from the record information, but the coding might be switched to use boldface and mixed upper- and lowercase for the contents. The employee name and ID number can also be placed on the same line to tighten up the display:

Better: Employee: **Susan Taylor** ID Number: **34787331**
         Spouse: **William Taylor**

         Children: Names   Birthdates
                      Alexandra   **09-08-1972**
                      Thomas   **10-29-1974**
                      Ann   **08-21-1977**

Finally, if boxes are available, an orderly pattern is sometimes more appealing (although it may consume more screen space):

Better:
Employee:	**Susan Taylor** ID Number: **34787331**
Spouse:	**William Taylor**

Children:	Names	Birthdates
	Alexandra	**09-08-1972**
	Thomas	**10-29-1974**
	Ann	**08-21-1977**

For an international audience, the date format might need to be clarified (month-day-year). Even in this simple example, the possibilities are numerous. Further improvements could be made with other coding strategies, such as the use of background shading, color, or graphic icons. In any situation, a variety of designs should be explored. An experienced graphic designer can be a great benefit to the design team. Pilot testing with prospective users can yield subjective satisfaction scores, objective times to complete tasks, and error rates for a variety of proposed formats.

11.4.2 Empirical results

Guidelines for display design were an early topic in human-computer interaction research because of the importance of displays in control-room and life-critical applications (Section 2.3). As technology evolved and high-resolution graphical color displays became available, new empirically validated guidelines became necessary. Then, web-based markup languages, user-generated content, and the need to accommodate older adults and provide universal usability presented further design challenges. User control of font size, window size, and brightness meant designers had to ensure that the information architecture could be understood, even as some display elements changed. Now, as small-, wall-, and mall-sized displays have opened further possibilities, there is again renewed interest in display design.

Early studies with alphanumeric displays laid the foundation for design guidelines and predictive metrics. These studies clearly demonstrated the benefits of eliminating unnecessary information, grouping related information, and emphasizing information relevant to required tasks. Simple changes could cut task performance times almost in half.

Expert users can deal with dense displays and may in fact prefer these displays because they are familiar with the format and they must initiate fewer actions. Performance times are likely to be shorter with fewer but denser displays than with more numerous but sparse displays. This improvement will be especially marked if tasks require comparison of information across displays. Systems for stock-market data, air-traffic control, and airline reservations are examples of successful applications that have dense packing, multiple displays, limited labels, and highly coded fields.

In a study of nurses, laboratory reports of blood tests were shown in the standard commercial format of three screens, in a compressed two-screen version, and in a densely packed one-screen version (Staggers, 1993). Search times dropped by half (approximately) over the five trial blocks for novice and experienced nurses, demonstrating a strong learning effect. The dramatic performance result (Fig. 11.1) was that search times were longest with the three-screen version (9.4 seconds per task) and shortest with the densely packed one-screen version (5.3 seconds per task). The high cost of switching windows and of reorienting to the new material appears to be far more destructive of concentration than scanning dense displays. Accuracy and subjective satisfaction were not significantly different across the three versions.

Increased understanding of human visual scanning based on eye-tracking studies has led to a growing understanding of basic perceptual and cognitive principles. One set of web-oriented guidelines encourages designers to "Visually chunk related elements through the use of space, graphical boundaries, or similarities in lightness, color, or orientation. Ensure that the graphical treatment of elements in a display is consistent and predictable" (Williams, 2000).

Every guidelines document implores designers to preserve consistent locations, structure, and terminology across displays. Supportive evidence for use of consistent locations comes from an early study of inexperienced computer users of a menu interface (Teitelbaum and Granda, 1983). The positions of the title, page number, topic heading, instruction line, and entry area were varied across displays for half of the participants, whereas the other half saw constant positions. Mean response time to questions about these items for participants in the varying condition was 2.54 seconds, but it was only 1.47 seconds for those seeing constant positions. A student project with experienced computer users showed similar benefits from consistent placement, size, and color of buttons in graphical user interfaces. Even stronger benefits came from consistent button labels. Consistency and quality in web-page contents were also demonstrated to be beneficial in information-gathering tasks (Ozok and Salvendy, 2003).

Low Density Screen

```
Patient Laboratory Inquiry    Large University Medical Center    Pg 1 of 3

Robinson, Christopher  #XXX-XX-4627  Unit: 5E, 5133D  M/13  Ph:301-XXX-5885

        <CBC>      Result    Normal    Range         Units
        --------------------------------------------------------
11/20   Wbc        115.01    114.8  -  110.8         th/cumm
22:55   Rbc        114.78    114.7  -  116.1         m/cumm
        Hgb        112.81    114.0  -  118.0         g/dL
        Hct        137.91    142.0  -  152.0         %
        Plt        163.0     130.0  -  400.0         th/cumm
        Mcv        188.51    182.0  -  101.0         fL
        Mch        130.61    127.0  -  134.0         picogms
        Mchc       134.61    132.0  -  136.0         g/dL
        Rdw        114.51    111.5  -  114.5         %
        Mpv        119.31    117.4  -  110.4         fL
        Key:   * = abnormal
             PgDn for more
```

```
Patient Laboratory Inquiry    Large University Medical Center    Pg 2 of 3

Robinson, Christopher  #XXX-XX-4627  Unit: 5E, 5133D  M/13  Ph:301-XXX-5885

        <DIFF>      Result    Normal    Range         Unit
        --------------------------------------------------------
11/20   Segs       35        34  -  75               %
22:55   Bands       5         0  -   9               %
        Lymphs     33        10  -  49               %
        Monos      33         2  -  14               %
        Eosino      5         0  -   8               %

        Baso        2         0  -   2               %
        Atyplymph  20         0  -   0               %
        Meta        0         0  -   0               %
        Myleo       0         0  -   0               %
        Platelets(estimated)                        adeq
        Key:   * = Abnormal
             PgDn for more
```

```
Patient Laboratory Inquiry    Large University Medical Center    Pg 3 of 3

Robinson, Christopher  #XXX-XX-4627  Unit: 5E, 5133D  M/13  Ph:301-XXX-5885

11/20    22:55

<MORPHOLOGY    Macrocytosis 1+   Basophilic Stippling 1+   Toxic Gran Occ

Hypochromia 1+  Polychromasia 1+   Target Cells      3+    Normocytic  No

Key: * = Abnormal    Priority:  Routine              Acc#: 122045-015212
Ordered by: Holland, Daniel on 10/22/91, 10:00      Ord#: 900928-HH1131
     (PL  93-579)
     End of report
```

FIGURE 11.1

In a study with 110 nurses, results showed an average task time of 9.4 seconds with the low-density version and 5.3 seconds with the high-density version (Staggers, 1993).

High Density Screen

```
Patient Laboratory Inquiry        Large University Medical Center      Pg 1 of 1

Robinson, Christopher  #XXX-XX-4627  Unit: 5E, 5133D  M/13  Ph:301-XXX-5885

         <CBC>   Result    Normal Range      Units     <DIFF>    Result Norm Range  Unit
         -------------------------------------------------     --------------------------------
10/23    Wbc      15.0    114.8 - 110.8    th/cumm    Segs       40    34 - 74     %
 0600    Rbc       4.78   114.7 - 116.1    m/cumm     Bands       5     0 -  9     %
         Hgb      15.1    114.0 - 118.0    g/dL       Lymphs     33    10 - 49     %
         Hct      47.9    142.0 - 152.0      %        Monos      10     2 - 14     %
         Plt     163.0    130.0 - 400.0    th/cumm    Eosino      5     0 -  8     %
         Mcv      88.5    182.0 - 101.0      fL       Baso        2     2 -  2     %
         Mch      30.6    127.0 - 134.0    picogms    Atyplymph   0     0 -  0     %
         Mchc     34.6    132.0 - 136.0    g/dL       Meta        0     0 -  0     %
         Rdw      14.5    111.5 - 114.5      %        Myelo       0     0 -  0     %
         Mpv       8.3    117.4 - 110.4      fL                  Plt   (estm)     adeq
<MORPHOLOGY          Macrocytosis  1+   Basophilic Stippling  1+   Toxic Gran  Occ
Hypochromia 1+   Polychromasia 1+   Target Cells          3+   Normocytic  No

Key: * = Abnormal Priority:  Routine      Acc#: 122045-015212
  Ordered by:  Holland, Daniel on 10/22/91, 10:00    Ord#: 900928-HH1131
     (PL  93-579)
```

FIGURE 11.1 (*Continued*)

Sequences of displays should be similar throughout the system for similar tasks, but exceptions will certainly occur. Within a sequence, users should be offered some sense of how far they have come and how far they have to go to reach the end (Fig. 11.2). It should be possible to go backwards in a sequence to correct errors, to review decisions, or to try alternatives.

11.5 Web Page Design

Web page designers have dramatically improved their output in recent years. Numerous guidelines and Internet sources contribute to maturity in this discipline. Visual layout has a strong impact on (human) performance and is a critical factor in web page design. Newer studies illustrate more specific patterns of

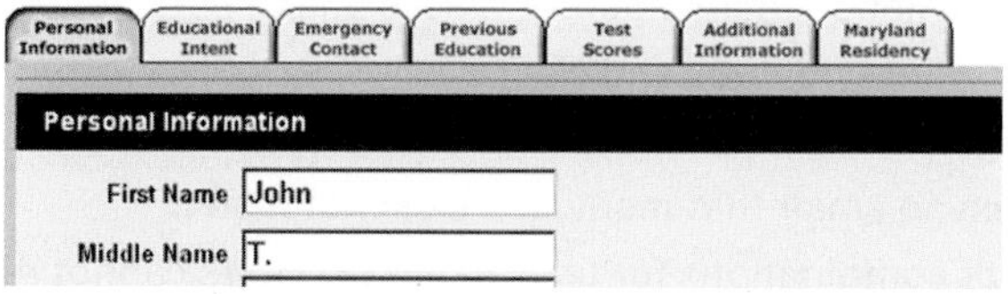

FIGURE 11.2

Users should be given a sense of how far they have gone within a sequence of displays and of what remains to be done.

performance with web pages that may reflect some differences between web page and traditional GUI design.

Interactions among four visual layout factors in web page design (quantity of links, alignment, grouping indications, and density) were investigated in one study using languages as a basis of comparison (Parush et al., 2005). The experiment was conducted with two approaches: one with pages in Hebrew, entailing right-to-left reading, and the other with English pages, entailing left-to-right reading. Results indicated that some performance patterns (measured by search times and eye movements) were similar between languages. Performance was particularly poor in pages with many links and variable densities, but it improved with the presence of uniform density. Alignment was not shown to be a performance-enhancing factor.

Web page designers can easily make mistakes that may not be immediately apparent but can result in distracting or misleading the user. Tullis (2005) has compiled a top-ten list of common design mistakes made in presenting information on the Web (Box 11.4), based on why the human-factors literature shows that these are indeed mistakes.

Universal usability again is a key factor in web page design. Web usability for low-vision users was explored in a study that looked at financial web pages to ascertain whether designers could build an interface that would specifically address the needs of these users and improve both their performance and the overall user experience (Bergel et al., 2005). The solution involved both visual and audio help, the ability to increase text size, and the ability to view the site in reverse contrast. Users rated the new (prototype) site

BOX 11.4
The top ten mistakes of web-based presentation of information (from Tullis, 2005).

Top Ten Mistakes
1. Burying information too deep in a web site
2. Overloading pages with too much material
3. Providing awkward or confusing navigation
4. Putting information in unexpected places on the page
5. Not making links obvious and clear
6. Presenting information in bad tables
7. Making text so small that many users cannot read it
8. Using color combinations for text that many users cannot read
9. Using bad forms
10. Hiding (or not providing) features that could help users

significantly more positively than the live site and appeared more skilled in navigating the prototype site.

Web content presentation issues can be broken up into site-level issues, page-level issues, and "special" types of information (Tullis, 2004). Site-level issues are, obviously, apparent throughout the entire web site rather than only on individual pages; they include the depth versus breadth of the site, the use of frames, and the presentation of navigation options. Page-level issues are observed at the individual page level; they include components of pages, such as tables, graphs, forms, and controls, as well as issues such as page layout and presentation of links. "Special" web content can include site maps, search functions, user assistance, and feedback. This particular study addresses human-factors issues related to these facets of web site and page design.

Web-based designs were dramatically different, because the broader consumer-oriented audience appreciated colorful graphics and many site designers employed eye-catching photos. The race was on to create cool designs, hot images, and attention-grabbing layouts. User preferences became crucial, especially if market researchers could demonstrate that site visitors stayed longer and bought more products at visually compelling web sites. The downside of the increased use of graphics was the download times, which were significantly slower, especially for dial-up users with slow modems.

In an attempt to quantify design-feature impacts on preference, researchers correlated Webby Award winning pages with 141 layout metrics (Ivory and Hearst, 2002). The results were complex, showing interactions among types and sizes of web pages. Some of the easily applicable results were that high preferences could be expected if large pages had a columnar organization, animated graphical ads were limited, average link text was kept to two to three words, sans-serif fonts were used, and varied colors were used to highlight text as well as headings. These results could also lead to conjectures about the design goals that support high preference—for example, comprehensibility, predictability, familiarity, visual appeal, and relevant content.

A more accurate prediction of user performance is likely to come with metrics that integrate task frequencies and sequences. Sears (1993) developed a task-dependent metric called *layout appropriateness* to assess whether the display's spatial layout is in harmony with the users' tasks (Fig. 11.3). If users can accomplish frequent tasks by moving through a display in a top-to-bottom pattern, faster performance is likely compared to that with a layout that requires numerous jumps between widely separated parts of the display. Layout appropriateness is a widget-level metric that deals with buttons, boxes, and lists. Designers specify the sequences of selections that users make and the frequencies for each sequence. Then, the given layout of widgets is evaluated by how well it matches the tasks. An optimal layout that minimizes visual scanning can be produced, but since it may violate user expectations about positions of fields, the designers must make the final layout decisions.

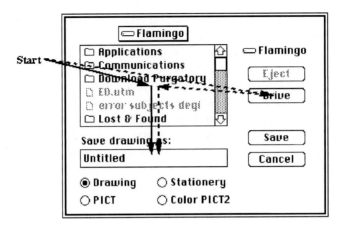

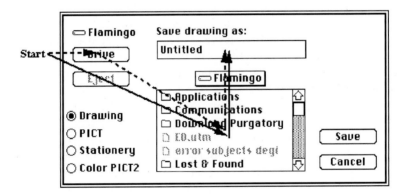

FIGURE 11.3

Layout appropriateness can help designers to analyze and redesign dialog boxes. Here, the existing dialog box (top) was redesigned based on frequencies of action sequences (bottom). The solid line represents the most frequent sequence of actions; the dashed line represents the second most frequent sequence of actions (Sears, 1993).

Numerous guidelines for web designers are available on the Web and can be incorporated into your design process to ensure consistency and adherence to emerging standards. Examples include, but are not limited to:

- *The Java Look and Feel Design Guidelines,* Second Edition (Sun, 2001)
- *Sun's Web Design Guide* (Sun, 2008)
- *The National Cancer Institute's Research-Based Web Design & Usability Guidelines* (NCI, 2008)

- *The World Wide Web Consortium's Web Accessibility Initiative* (WAI, 2008)
- *The Web Style Guide* (Lynch and Horton, 2008)

There are numerous web sites that address web design, some of which were created as companions to relevant books. :

- *Web 2.0 How-To Design Guide* (Hunt, 2008)
- *Web Bloopers* (Johnson, 2003)
- *KillerSites.com* (Siegel, 1997)

Mash-ups are web pages or applications that integrate complementary elements from two or more sources (for example, Craigslist and Google Maps™; see Fig. 11.4). They often combine data and services from across the Web. Examples of mash-ups include integrated maps and geopositioned photographs, maps of real-estate or rental properties, book web sites and hiking information resources, and many more. Popular web sites that take advantage of this technology include Flash Earth, where there exists a

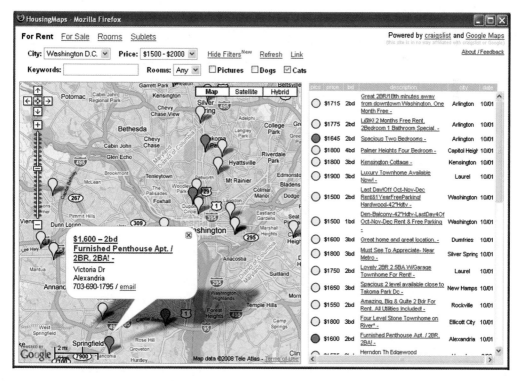

FIGURE 11.4

Example of a mash-up (combination of Craigslist and Google Maps).

zoomable mash-up of Google Maps and Microsoft's Virtual Earth™. Mash-ups are part of an ongoing shift towards a more interactive and participatory World Wide Web aimed at enhancing creativity, collaboration, and functionality. The Web offers an ever-increasing selection of user-generated content and services.

Mash-ups are often created using Ajax, a group of interrelated web-development techniques used for creating interactive web applications or rich Internet applications. With Ajax, web applications can retrieve data from the server asynchronously in the background without interfering with the display and behavior of the existing page.

The recent emergence of web mash-ups and open-source software is driving the development of new practices in software and systems development (Jones et al., 2007). In the area of user-generated content, designers can rapidly create web site applications by combining pre-existing software components. Current World Wide Web technologies such as these permit rapid user interface prototyping and application development, reduce the development risk, and reduce the time-to-market for new web sites.

11.6 Window Design

Computer users frequently have to consult documents, forms, e-mail messages, web pages, and more to complete their tasks. For example, a travel agent may jump from reviewing a client's e-mail request to viewing the proposed itinerary to reviewing calendars and flight schedules to choosing seat assignments and selecting hotels. Even with large desktop displays, there is a limit to how many documents can be displayed simultaneously. An increasing number of users are adopting large, multi-monitor displays, but without sufficient visual cues on such display workstations, they can they miss details (Hoffman et al., 2008).

Designers have long struggled with strategies to offer users sufficient information and flexibility to accomplish their tasks while reducing window-housekeeping actions and minimizing distracting clutter. If users' tasks are well understood and regular, there is a good chance that an effective *multiple-window display* strategy can be developed. The travel agent, for example, might start a client-itinerary window, review flight segments in a schedule window, and drag selected flight segments to the itinerary window. Windows labeled "Calendar," "Seat Selection," "Food Preferences," and "Hotels" might appear as needed, with a charge-card information window appearing at the end to complete the transaction.

If window-housekeeping actions can be reduced, users can complete their tasks more rapidly, and probably with fewer mistakes. The visual nature of window use has led many designers to apply direct-manipulation strategies (Chapter 5) to window actions. To stretch, move, and scroll a window, users can point at appropriate icons on the window border and simply click on the mouse button and drag. Since the dynamics of windows have a strong effect on user perceptions, the animations for transitions (zooming boxes, repainting when a window is opened or closed, blinking outlines, or highlighting during dragging) must be designed carefully.

Window design evolved rapidly in the 1980s from influential designs at Xerox PARC to innovative syntheses by Apple for the Macintosh (Fig. 1.1) and finally Microsoft's modest refinements, which led to the highly successful Windows series (1.0, 2.0, 3.1, 95, 98, 2000, NT, ME, XP, and Vista; Fig. 1.2). Overlapping, draggable, resizable windows on a broad desktop have become the standard for most users. Advanced users who work on multiple tasks can switch among collections of windows called "workspaces" or "rooms"; each workspace holds several windows whose states are saved, allowing easy resumption of activity. Much progress has been made, but there is still an opportunity to reduce dramatically the housekeeping chores tied to individual windows and to provide task-related multiple-window coordination.

11.6.1 Coordinating multiple windows

Designers may break through to the next generation of window managers by developing *coordinated windows*: windows that appear, change contents, and close as a direct result of user actions in the task domain. For example, in a medical insurance claims-processing application, when the agent retrieves information about a client, such fields as the client's address, telephone number, and membership number should be automatically filled in on the display. Simultaneously, and with no additional commands, the client's medical history might appear in a second window, and the record of previous claims might appear in a third window. A fourth window might contain a form for the agent to complete to indicate payment or exceptions. Scrolling the medical-history window might produce a synchronized scroll of the previous-claims window to show related information. When the claim is completed, all window contents should be saved and all the windows should be closed with one action. Such sequences of actions can be established by designers or by users with end-user programming tools.

Similarly, for web browsing, job-hunting users should be able to select the five most interesting position-description links and open them all with a single click. Then, it should be possible to explore all of them synchronously to compare the job details (description, location, salary, etc.) using one scrolling action. When one position is selected, it should fill the screen, and the other four should close automatically.

Coordination is a task concept that describes how information objects change based on user actions. A careful study of user tasks can lead to the development of task-specific coordinations based on sequences of actions. The especially interesting case of work with large images such as maps, circuit diagrams, or magazine layouts is covered in the next section. Other important coordinations that might be supported by interface developers include:

- *Synchronized scrolling.* A simple coordination is synchronized scrolling, in which the scroll bar of one window is coupled to another scroll bar, and action on one scroll bar causes the other window's contents to scroll in parallel. This technique is useful for comparing two versions of a program or document. Synchronization might be on a line-for-line basis, on a proportional basis, or keyed to matching tokens in the two windows.

- *Hierarchical browsing.* Coordinated windows can be used to support hierarchical browsing. For example, if one window contains a book's table of contents, selection of a chapter title by a pointing device should lead to the display, in an adjoining window, of that chapter's contents. Hierarchical browsing has been integrated into Windows Explorer to allow users to browse hierarchical directories, into Outlook to enable browsing of folders of e-mails (Fig. 9.2), and into many other applications (Fig. 11.5).

- *Opening/closing of dependent windows.* One option on opening a window is to simultaneously open dependent windows in a nearby and convenient location. For example, when a user browsing a program opens a main procedure, the dependent set of procedures could open up automatically (Fig. 11.6). Sim-

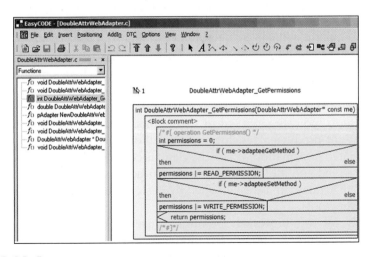

FIGURE 11.5

Hierarchical browsing in the XperCASE tool (now called EasyCASE with EasyCODE). The specification is on the left. As users click on components (DoubleAttrWebAdapter), the detail view appears on the right in a Nassi-Shneiderman chart.

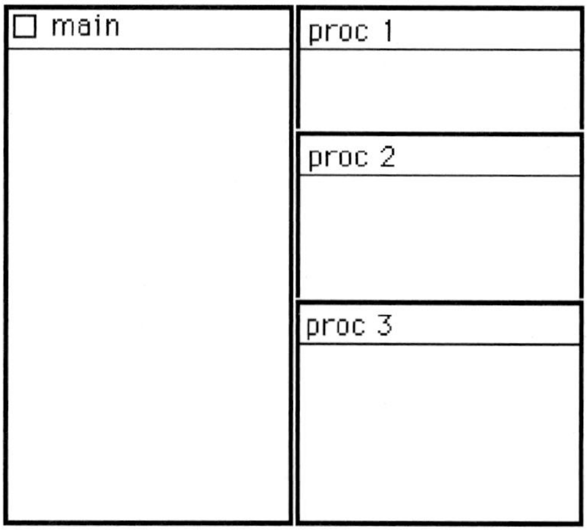

FIGURE 11.6

Dependent windows. When such windows open, several other windows may open automatically. In this example, the main procedure of a program has been opened, and the dependent procedures 1, 2, and 3 have also been opened and placed at convenient locations. Connecting lines, shading, or decoration on the frame might indicate the parent and child relationships.

ilarly, when filling in a form, a user might automatically be presented with a dialog box listing a choice of preferences. That dialog box might lead the user to activate a pop-up or error-message window, which in turn might lead to an invocation of the help window. After the user indicates the desired choice in the dialog box, it would be convenient to have automatic closing of all the windows (Fig 11.7).

- *Saving/opening of window state.* A natural extension of saving a document or a set of preferences is to save the current state of the display with all the windows and their contents. This feature might be implemented by the simple addition of a "Save screen as . . ." menu item to the "File" menu of actions. This action would create a new icon representing the current state; clicking on the icon would reproduce that state. This feature is a simple version of the rooms approach (Henderson and Card, 1986).

- *Tabbed browsing.* Browser tabs allow you to view multiple web pages in the same browser without the need to open a new browser session.

- *Tiled windows.* Windows can automatically be resized and arranged so that they do not overlap each other. Overlapping windows are sometimes referred to as *overlaid* or *cascading windows.*

- *Ribbon interface.* The Microsoft Office 2007 interface is designed to make it easier for users to find the features they need to get their work done (Fig. 6.5). Microsoft calls this its "Fluent" user interface.

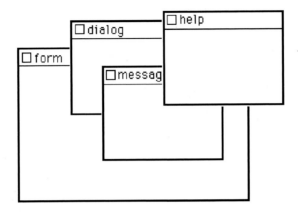

FIGURE 11.7

Dependent windows. When such windows close, other windows may close too. Here, all four windows will be closed automatically when the parent window, "form," is closed. Lines, shading, or border decorations may indicate families of windows, with special marks to indicate parents and children.

There are many interface schemes that allow users to work in and move between focused and contextual views of screens. These interface schemes have been studied and categorized according to the interface mechanisms used to separate and blend views (Cockburn et al., 2009). The four approaches are: spatial separation, typified by overview+detail interfaces; temporal separation, typified by zoomable interfaces; seamless focus+context, typified by fisheye views; and cue-based techniques that selectively highlight or suppress items within the information space.

11.6.2 Image browsing

A two-dimensional cousin of hierarchical browsing is image browsing, which enables users to work with large maps, circuit diagrams, magazine layouts, photos, or artwork. Users see an overview in one window and the details in a second window. They can move a field-of-view box in the overview to adjust the detail-view content. Similarly, if users pan in the detail view, the field-of-view box should move in the overview. Well-designed coordinated windows have matching aspect ratios in the field-of-view box and the detail view, and a change to the shape of either produces a corresponding change in the other.

The magnification from the overview to the detail view is called the *zoom factor*. When the zoom factors are between 5 and 30, the coordinated overview and detail view pair are effective; for larger zoom factors, however, an additional intermediate view is needed. For example, if an overview shows a map of France, a detail view showing the Paris region is effective. However, if the overview were of the entire world, intermediate views of Europe and France would preserve orientation (Fig. 11.8).

Side-by-side placement of the overview and detail views is the most common layout, since it allows users to see the big picture and the details at the same time. However, some systems provide a single view, either zooming smoothly to move in on a selected point (Bederson and Hollan, 1994) or simply replacing the overview with the detail view. This zoom-and-replace approach is simple to implement and gives the maximal screen space for each view, but it denies the users the chance to see the overview and detail view at the same time. A variation is to have the detail view overlap the overview, but it may obscure key items. Semantic zooming, in which the way objects are represented changes depending on their magnification, might help users see an overview by rapidly zooming in and out (Hornbaeck et al., 2002).

Attempts to provide detail views (focus) and overviews (context) without obscuring anything have motivated interest in *fisheye views* (Baudisch et al., 2004; Bartram et al., 1995; Sarkar and Brown 1994). The focus area (or areas) is magnified to show detail, while preserving the context, all in a single display (Fig. 11.9). This distortion-based approach is visually appealing, even compelling, but the continually changing magnified area may be disorienting, and the zoom factor in published examples rarely exceeds 5.

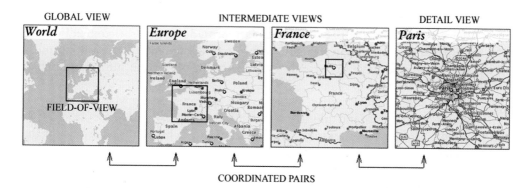

FIGURE 11.8

Global and intermediate views, which provide overviews for the detail view of Paris. Movements of the field-of-view boxes change the content in the detail view (Plaisant et al., 1995).

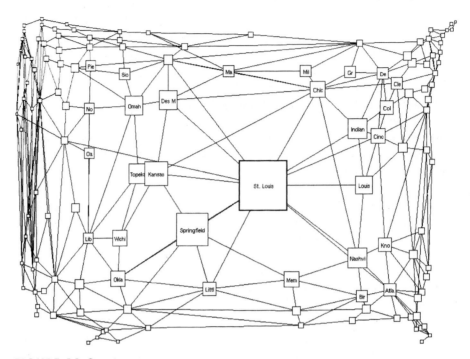

FIGURE 11.9

Fisheye view of U.S. cities, with the focus on St. Louis. The context is preserved, although the distortions can be disorienting (Sarkar and Brown, 1994).

The bifocal display (similar to the fisheye approach) was arguably the first demonstration of the use of distortion to provide a "focus + context" view of information. A user can focus on one or two documents, for example, and at the same time have an overall view of the whole of the information space (Spence, 2001).

One success story with a fisheye view approach is the Mac OS X Dock, a menu of program and file icons that appears typically at the bottom of the screen. Scrolling over an icon magnifies the item to highlight readiness for that icon (application/file) to be selected (Fig. 1.1). The distortion is still present, but the highlighting is visually apparent.

The design for image browsers should be governed by the users' tasks, which can be classified as follows (Plaisant et al., 1995):

- *Image generation.* Paint or construct a large image or diagram.
- *Open-ended exploration.* Browse to gain an understanding of the map or image.

- *Diagnostics.* Scan for flaws in an entire circuit diagram, medical image, or newspaper layout.
- *Navigation.* Have knowledge of the overview, but need to pursue details along a highway or vein.
- *Monitoring.* Watch the overview and, when a problem occurs, zoom in on details.

Within these high-level tasks, users carry out many low-level actions, such as moving the focus (jumping from city to city on a map), comparing (viewing two harbors at the same time to compare their facilities, or viewing matching regions in X-ray images of left and right lungs), traversing (following a vein to look for blockages), or marking locations to return to them at a later time.

11.6.3 Personal role management

Window coordination facilitates handling of larger images and tasks that have been too complex to deal with in the past. However, there are other potent opportunities to improve window management. The current graphical user interfaces offer a desktop with applications represented as icons and documents organized into folders, but refinements to this approach are possible.

A natural progression is towards a *role-centered* design, which emphasizes the users' tasks rather than the applications and documents. While computer-supported cooperative work (Chapter 9) is aimed at coordination of several people performing a common task, by contrast, a role-centered design could substantially improve support for individuals in managing their multiple roles. Each role brings individuals into contact with different people as they carry out a hierarchy of tasks following an independent schedule. A *personal role manager*, instead of a window manager, could improve performance and reduce distraction while the user is working in a given role and could facilitate shifting of attention from one role to another. For example, one research study evaluated whether e-mail user interfaces could be improved to serve a specific target population: college students. It found that e-mail overload and feature intimidation hindered e-mail communication on campus. Integrating role management into the e-mail software helped the college students manage their e-mail more effectively (Plaisant and Shneiderman, 2007).

In a personal role manager, each role has a *vision statement* (a document that describes responsibilities and goals) that is established by the user or manager. The explicitness of the vision can simplify the training and integration into the organization of new personnel and can facilitate the temporary covering of employees' responsibilities (during vacations or parental leave, for example). Each role also has a *set of people*, a *task hierarchy*, a *schedule*, and a *set of documents*. In addition, web bookmarks and recent documents can be maintained for each role.

Screen management is one of the key functions of the personal role manager. All roles should be visible, but the current focus of attention may occupy most of the screen. As users shift attention to a second role, the current one shrinks and the second one grows to fill the screen. Users can simultaneously enlarge two roles if there are interactions between them.

For example, a professor may have roles such as teacher of courses, advisor to graduate students, member of the recruiting committee, principal investigator of grants, author of technical reports, and liaison to industry. In the teacher role, the professor's vision statement might include the intention to make lectures and assignments available via the Web to facilitate a large undergraduate course. Files might include homework assignments, a bibliography, a course outline, and so on. The task hierarchy might begin with tasks such as choosing a textbook and end with administering the final exam. The subtasks for administering the final exam might include preparing the exam, reserving a room, proctoring the exam, and grading the exam. The set of people includes the students, teaching assistants, bookstore manager, registrar, and colleagues teaching other sections of the course. The schedule would begin with deadlines for submitting the book order to the bookstore manager and end with turning in the final grades to the registrar.

The personal role manager could simplify and accelerate the performance of common coordination tasks, in the same way that graphical user interfaces simplify file-management tasks. The requirements for a personal role manager include these:

- Support a *unified framework* for information organization according to users' roles.

- Provide a *visual, spatial layout* that matches tasks.

- Support *multiwindow actions* for fast arrangement of information.

- Support *information access* with partial knowledge of an information item's nominal, spatial, temporal, and visual attributes and its relationships to other pieces of information.

- Allow *fast switching* and *resumption* of roles.

- Free users' *cognitive resources* to work on *task-domain actions*, rather than making users concentrate on interface-domain actions.

- Use *screen space* efficiently and productively for tasks.

11.7 Color

Color displays are attractive to users and can often improve task performance, but the danger of misuse is high. Color can do all of the following:

- Soothe or strike the eye.
- Add accents to an uninteresting display.
- Facilitate subtle discriminations in complex displays.
- Emphasize the logical organization of information.
- Draw attention to warnings.
- Evoke strong emotional reactions of joy, excitement, fear, or anger.

The principles developed by graphic artists for using color in books, magazines, highway signs, and other print media have been adapted for user interfaces (Stone, 2003; MacDonald, 1999; Marcus, 1992). Programmers and interactive-systems designers are learning how to create effective computer displays and to avoid pitfalls (Galitz, 2007; Brewer et al., 2003).

There is no doubt that color makes video games more attractive to users, conveys more information on power-plant or process-control diagrams, and is necessary for realistic images of people, scenery, or three-dimensional objects (Foley et al., 2002; Weinman, 2002). These applications require color. However, greater controversy exists about the benefits of color for alphanumeric displays, spreadsheets, graphs, and user-interface components.

No simple set of rules governs use of color, but these guidelines are a starting point for designers:

- *Use color conservatively.* Many programmers and novice designers are eager to use color to brighten up their displays, but the results are often counterproductive. One home-information system displayed the seven letters of its name in a large font, each in a different color. At a distance, the display appeared inviting and eye-catching; up close, however, it was difficult to read.

  When the colors do not show meaningful relationships, they may mislead users into searching for relationships that do not exist. Using a different color for each of 12 unrelated items in a menu produces an overwhelming effect. However, using four colors (such as red, blue, green, and yellow) for the 12 items will mislead users into thinking that all the similarly colored items are related. An appropriate strategy might be to show all the menu items in one color, the title in a second color, the instructions in a third color, and error messages in a fourth color, but even this strategy can be overwhelming if the colors are too visually striking. A safe approach is to always use black letters on a white background, with italics or bold for emphasis and to reserve color for special highlighting.

- *Limit the number of colors.* Many design guides suggest limiting the number of colors in a single display to four, with a limit of seven colors in the entire sequence of displays. Experienced users may be able to benefit from a larger number of color codes, but for novice users, too many color codes can cause confusion.

- *Recognize the power of color as a coding technique.* Color speeds recognition for many tasks. For example, in an accounting application, if data lines with accounts overdue more than 30 days are coded in red, they will be readily visible among the nonoverdue accounts coded in green. In an air-traffic–control system, high-flying planes might be coded differently from low-flying planes to facilitate recognition. In programming workstations, keywords are color coded differently from variables.

- *Ensure that color coding supports the task.* Be aware that using color as a coding technique can inhibit performance of tasks that go against the grain of the coding scheme. If, in the above accounting application with color coding by days overdue, the task is to locate accounts with balances of more than $55, the existing coding scheme may inhibit performance on the second task. Designers should attempt to make a close linkage between the users' tasks and the color coding and offer users control where possible.

- *Have color coding appear with minimal user effort.* In general, users should not have to activate color coding each time they perform a task; rather, the color coding should appear automatically. For example, when the users start the task of checking for overdue accounts, the color coding should be set automatically; when they click on the task of locating accounts with balances of more than $55, the new color-coding scheme should also take effect automatically.

- *Place color coding under user control.* When appropriate, the users should be able to turn off color coding. For example, if a spelling checker highlights possibly misspelled words in red, the user should be able to accept or change the spelling and to turn off the coding. The presence of the highly visible red coding is a distraction from reading the text for comprehension.

- *Design for monochrome first.* The primary goal of a display designer should be to lay out the contents in a logical pattern. Related fields can be shown by contiguity or by similar structural patterns; for example, successive employee records may have the same indentation pattern. Related fields can also be grouped by a box drawn around the group. Unrelated fields can be kept separate by inserting blank space (at least one blank line vertically or three blank characters horizontally). It may also be advantageous to design for monochrome rather than relying on color, because color displays may not be universally available.

- *Consider the needs of color-deficient users.* One important aspect to consider is readability of colors by users with color-vision impairments (either red/green confusion, the most common case, or total color blindness). Color impairment is a very common condition that should not be overlooked (Rosenthal and Phillips, 1997; Olson and Brewer, 1997). Approximately eight percent of males and less than one percent of females in North America and Europe have some permanent color deficiency in their vision. Many others have temporary deficiencies due to illness or medications. They may, for example, confuse some shades of orange or red with green, or not see a red dot on a black background. Designers can easily address this problem by limiting the use of color, using double encoding when appropriate (that is, using symbols that vary in both shape and color or location and color), providing alternative color palettes to choose from, or allowing users to customize the colors themselves. For example, the SmartMoney® Map of the Market provides two choices of color schemes: red/green and blue/yellow. Various tools, such as Vischeck, are available to both simulate color-vision impairments and optimize graphics for some of the various forms of color impairment that exist. Black on white or white on black will work well for most users. ColorBrewer, an online tool designed to help people select good color schemes for maps and other graphics, offers guidelines on color schemes that work for those with color-vision impairments (Brewer and Harrower, 2008).

- *Use color to help in formatting.* In densely packed displays where space is at a premium, similar colors can be used to group related items. For example, in a police dispatcher's tabular display of assignments, the police cars on emergency calls might be coded in red, and the police cars on routine calls might be coded in green. Then, when a new emergency arises, it will be relatively easy to identify the cars on routine calls and to assign one to the emergency. Dissimilar colors can be used to distinguish physically close but logically distinct fields. In a block-structured programming language, designers could show the nesting levels by coding the statements in a progression of colors—for example, dark green, light green, yellow, light orange, dark orange, red, and so on.

- *Be consistent in color coding.* Use the same color-coding rules throughout the system. If some error messages are displayed in red, make sure that every error message appears in red; a change to yellow may be interpreted as a change in the importance of the message. If the various system designers use colors differently, users will hesitate as they attempt to assign meaning to the color changes.

- *Be alert to common expectations about color codes.* Designers need to speak to users to determine what color codes are applied in the task domain. From automobile-driving experience, red is commonly considered to indicate stop or danger, yellow is a warning, and green is all clear or go. In investment circles, red is a financial loss and black is a gain. For chemical engineers, red is hot and blue is cold. For mapmakers, blue means water, green means forests, and yellow means deserts. These differing conventions can cause problems for designers. Designers might consider using red to signal that an engine is warmed up and ready, but users might understand the red coding as an indication of danger. A red light is often used to indicate that power is on for electrical equipment, but some users are made anxious by this decision since red has a strong association with danger or stopping. When appropriate, indicate the color-code interpretations on the display or in a help panel.

- *Be alert to problems with color pairings.* If saturated (pure) red and blue appear on a display at the same time, it may be difficult for users to absorb the information. Red and blue are on the opposite ends of the spectrum, and the muscles surrounding the human eye will be strained by attempts to produce a sharp focus for both colors simultaneously: The blue will appear to recede and the red will appear to come forward. Blue text on a red background would present an especially difficult challenge for users to read. Other combinations (yellow on purple, magenta on green) will similarly appear garish and be difficult to read. Too little contrast also is a problem: Imagine yellow letters on a white background or brown letters on a black background.

- *Use color changes to indicate status changes.* For automobile speedometers with digital readouts and a wireless receiver of the driving speed limits, it might be helpful to change from green numbers below the speed limit to red above the speed limit to act as a warning. Similarly, in an oil refinery, pressure indicators might change color as the value goes above or below acceptable limits. In this way, color acts as an attention-getting method. This technique is potentially valuable when there are hundreds of values displayed continuously.

- *Use color in graphic displays for greater information density.* In graphs with multiple plots, color can be helpful in showing which line segments form the full graph. The usual strategies for differentiating lines in black-on-white graphs—such as dotted lines, thicker lines, and dashed lines—are not as effective as using separate colors for each line. Architectural plans benefit from color coding of electrical, telephone, hot-water, cold-water, and natural-gas lines. Similarly, maps can have greater information density when color coding is used.

Color displays are becoming nearly universal, even in mobile devices, and designers usually make heavy use of color in interface designs. There are undoubtedly benefits in terms of increased user satisfaction and often enhanced performance, but there are also real dangers in misusing color. Care should be taken to make appropriate design choices and to conduct thorough evaluations (Box 11.5).

BOX 11.5

Guidelines that highlight the complex potential benefits and dangers of using color coding.

Guidelines for using color

- Use color conservatively: Limit the number and amount of colors.
- Recognize the power of color to speed or slow tasks.
- Ensure that color coding supports the task.
- Make color coding appear with minimal user effort.
- Keep color coding under user control.
- Design for monochrome first.
- Consider the needs of color-deficient users.
- Use color to help in formatting.
- Be consistent in color coding.
- Be alert to common expectations about color codes.
- Be alert to problems with color pairings.
- Use color changes to indicate status changes.
- Use color in graphic displays for greater information density.

Benefits of using color

- Various colors are soothing or striking to the eye.
- Color can improve an uninteresting display.
- Color facilitates subtle discriminations in complex displays.
- A color code can emphasize the logical organization of information.
- Certain colors can draw attention to warnings.
- Color coding can evoke more emotional reactions of joy, excitement, fear, or anger.

Dangers of using color

- Color pairings may cause problems.
- Color fidelity may degrade on other hardware.
- Printing or conversion to other media may be a problem.

Practitioner's Summary

The wording of system messages may have an effect on users' performance and attitudes, especially for novices, whose anxiety and lack of knowledge put them at a disadvantage. Designers might make improvements by merely using more specific diagnostic messages, offering constructive guidance rather than focusing on failures, employing user-centered phrasing, choosing a suitable physical format, and avoiding vague terminology or numeric codes.

When giving instructions, focus on the user and the user's tasks. In most applications, avoid anthropomorphic phrasing. Use the *you* form to guide the novice user. Avoid judging the user. Simple statements of status are more succinct and usually are more effective.

Pay careful attention to display design, and develop a local set of guidelines for all designers. Use spacing, indentation, columnar formats, and field labels to organize the display for users. Denser displays, but fewer of them, may be advantageous. Organizations can benefit from careful study of display-design guidelines documents and from the creation of their own sets of guidelines tailored to local needs (Section 3.2). These documents should also include lists of local terminology and abbreviations. Consistency and thorough testing are critical.

Current World Wide Web technologies and supporting new web design guidelines provide new tools and emerging methods for user-generated content to be easily and rapidly inserted into web sites. Universal usability is also addressed by current web design guidelines. Good window design methods can enhance the user experience. Color can improve some displays and can lead to more rapid task performance with higher satisfaction, but improper use of color can mislead and slow users.

Researcher's Agenda

Experimental testing could refine the error-message guidelines proposed here and could identify the sources of user anxiety and confusion. Message placement, highlighting techniques, and multiple-level message strategies are candidates for exploration. Improved analysis of sequences of user actions to provide more effective messages automatically would be useful. Since anthropomorphic designs are rarely successful, believers in human-like agents should conduct empirical studies to test their efficacy.

There is a great need for testing to validate data-display and color-design guidelines. Basic understanding and cognitive models of visual perception of displays would be a dramatic contribution. Do users follow a scanning pattern from the top left? Would research using eye-tracking systems clarify reading and focus of attention patterns? Do users whose natural language reads from right to left or users from different cultures scan displays differently? Does use of whitespace around or boxing of items facilitate comprehension and speed interpretation? When is a single dense display preferable to two sparse displays? How does color coding reorganize the pattern of scanning?

Increase designer knowledge utilizing World Wide Web tools and methods as they apply to web site design to enhance the user experience, facilitate user-generated content and promote universal usability.

Window-management strategies have become standardized, but there are opportunities for innovation with large and multiple displays, novel applications that require multiple-window coordination, and innovative work-management strategies, such as using personal role managers.

WORLD WIDE WEB RESOURCES

http://www.aw.com/DTUI/

Guidelines for display design, web pages, and window management exists on the World Wide Web with some empirical results, but the most informative and enjoyable experience is simply browsing through the lively and colorful web sites. Web and other interface styles and fashions come and go quickly. Save the examples you like best.

References

Bartram, Lyn, Ho, Albert, Dill, John, and Henigman, Frank, The continuous zoom: A constrained fisheye technique for viewing and navigating large information spaces, *Proc. ACM Symposium on User Interface Software and Technology*, ACM Press, New York (1995), 207–215.

Baudisch, P., Lee, B., and Hanna, L., Fishnet, a fisheye web browser with search term popouts: A comparative evaluation with overview and linear view, *Proc. Working Conference on Advanced Visual Interfaces*, ACM Press, New York (May 2004), 133–140.

Bederson, B. and Hollan, J. D., Pad++: A zooming graphical interface for exploring alternate interface physics, *Proc. ACM Symposium on User Interface Software and Technology*, ACM Press, New York (1994), 17–26.

Bergel, M., Chadwick-Dias, A., Le-Doux, L., and Tullis, T., Web accessibility for the low vision user, *Usability Professionals Association (UPA) 2005 Presentation*, Montreal, Canada (2005).

Bergman, Eric, *Information Appliances and Beyond: Interaction Design for Consumer Products*, Morgan Kaufmann, San Francisco, CA (2000).

Brennan, Susan E. and Ohaeri, Justina O., Effects of message style on users' attributions towards agents, *Proc. CHI '94 Conference: Human Factors in Computing Systems*, ACM Press, New York (1994), 281–282.

Brewer, C. and Harrower, M., at http://www.ColorBrewer.org/ (2008).

Brewer, Cynthia A., Hatchard, Geoffrey W., and Harrower, Mark A., ColorBrewer in print: A catalog of color schemes for maps, *Cartography and Geographic Information Science* 30, 1 (2003), 5–32.

Brooke, J., Japan seeks robotic help in caring for the aged, *New York Times* (5 March 2004).

Cassell, Justine, Sullivan, Joseph, Prevost, Scott, and Churchill, Elizabeth, *Embodied Conversational Agents*, MIT Press, Cambridge, MA (2000).

Cockburn, A., Karlson, A., and Bederson, B., A review of overview+detail, zooming, and focus+context interfaces, to appear in *ACM Computing Surveys*, ACM Press, New York (March 2009).

D'Mello, S. K., Picard, R., and Graesser, A. C., Toward an affect-sensitive AutoTutor, *IEEE Intelligent Systems* 22, 4 (July/August 2007), 53–61.

Foley, James D., van Dam, Andries, Feiner, Steven K., and Hughes, John F., *Computer Graphics: Principles and Practice, Second Edition in C*, Addison-Wesley, Reading, MA (2002).

Friedman, Batya, "It's the computer's fault"—Reasoning about computers as moral agents, *Proc. CHI '95 Conference: Human Factors in Computing Systems*, ACM Press, New York (1995), 226–227.

Galitz, Wilbert O., *The Essential Guide to User Interface Design: An Introduction to GUI Design Principles and Techniques, Third Edition*, John Wiley & Sons, New York (2007).

Gratch, J., Rickel, J., Andre, E., Badler, N., Cassell, J., and Petajan, E., Creating interactive virtual humans: Some assembly required, *IEEE Intelligent Systems* 17, 4 (2002), 54–63.

Harless, William G., Zier, Marcia A., Harless, Michael G., and Duncan, Robert C., Virtual conversations: An interface to knowledge, *IEEE Computer Graphics and Applications* 23, 5 (September/October 2003), 46–53.

Henderson, Austin and Card, Stuart K., Rooms: The use of multiple virtual workspaces to reduce space contention in a window-based graphical user interface, *ACM Transactions on Graphics* 5, 3 (1986), 211–243.

Hoffman, R., Baudisch, P., and Weld, D., Evaluating visual cues for window switching on large screens, *Proc. CHI 2008 Conference: Human Factors in Computing Systems*, ACM Press, New York (April 2008), 929–938.

Hornbaek, K., Bederson, B. B., and Plaisant, C., Navigation patterns and usability of zoomable user interfaces with and without an overview, *ACM Transactions on Computer-Human Interaction* 9, 4 (December 2002), 362–389.

Hunt, Ben, Web 2.0 How-To Design Guide, http://www.webdesignfromscratch.com/web-2.0-design-style-guide.cfm (2008).

Ivory, M. Y. and Hearst, M. A., Statistical profiles of highly-rated web site interfaces, *Proc. CHI 2002 Conference: Human Factors in Computing Systems*, ACM Press, New York (2002), 367–374.

Johnson, Jeff, *Web Bloopers*, Morgan Kaufmann, San Franciso, CA, (2003). Updates available at http://www.web-bloopers.com/ (2008).

Jones, M. C., Floyd, I. R., Rathi, D., and Twidale, M. B., Web mash-ups and patchwork prototyping: User-driven technological innovation with Web 2.0 and open source software, *Proc. 40th Annual Hawaii International Conference on System Sciences (HICSS '07)*, IEEE Press, Los Alamitos, CA (2007).

Lavie, T. and Tractinsky, N., Assessing dimensions of perceived visual aesthetics of web sites, *International Journal of Human-Computer Studies* 60, 3 (2004), 269–298.

Lynch, Patrick J. and Horton, Sarah, *Web Style Guide: Basic Design Principles for Creating Web Sites, Third Edition*, Yale University Press, New Haven, CT (2008). Second edition available online at http://webstyleguide.com/.

MacDonald, L., Using color effectively in computer graphics, *IEEE Computer Graphics & Applications* 19, 4 (July/Aug 1999), 20–35.

Mahajan, R. and Shneiderman, B., Visual and textual consistency checking tools for graphical user interfaces, *IEEE Transactions on Software Engineering* 23, 11 (1997), 722–735.

Marcus, Aaron, *Graphic Design for Electronic Documents and User Interfaces*, ACM Press, New York (1992).

Martin, Dianne, ENIAC: Press conference that shook the world, *IEEE Technology and Society Magazine*, 14, 4 (Winter 1995/96), 3–10.

Mayer, Richard E., *Multimedia Learning, Second Edition*, Cambridge University Press, New York (2009).

Microsoft Developers Network, Error messages, http://msdn.microsoft.com/en-us/library/aa511267.aspx (2008).

Mullet, Kevin and Sano, Darrell, *Designing Visual Interfaces: Communication Oriented Techniques*, Sunsoft Press, Englewood Cliffs, NJ (1995).

Mumford, Lewis, *Technics and Civilization*, Harcourt Brace and World, New York (1934), 31–36.

National Cancer Institute, U.S. Department of Health and Human Services, Research-Based Web Design & Usability Guidelines, http://www.usability.gov/pdfs/guidelines.html (2008).

Olson, J. and Brewer, C. A., An evaluation of color selections to accommodate map users with color-vision impairments, *Annals of the Association of American Geographers* 87, 1 (1997), 103–134.

Ozok, A. Ant and Salvendy, Gavriel, The effect of language inconsistency on performance and satisfaction in using the Web: Results from four experiments, *Behaviour & Information Technology* 22, 3 (2003), 155–163.

Parush, A., Nadir, R., and Shtub, A., Evaluating the layout of graphical user interface screens: Validation of a numerical computerized model, *International Journal of Human-Computer Interaction* 10, 4 (1998), 343–360.

Parush, A., Shwartz, Y., Shtub, A., and Chandra, J., The impact of visual layout factors on performance in web pages: A cross-language study, *Human Factors* 47, 1 (Spring 2005), 141–157.

Plaisant, C. and Shneiderman, B., Personal role management: Overview and a design study of email for university students, in Czerwinski, M. and Kaptelinin, V. (Editors), *Designing Integrated Digital Work Environments: Beyond the Desktop*, MIT Press, Cambridge, MA (2007), 143–170.

Plaisant, Catherine, Carr, David, and Shneiderman, Ben, Image browsers: Taxonomy and design guidelines, *IEEE Software* 12, 2 (March 1995), 21–32.

Reeves, B. and Rickenberg, R., The effects of animated characters on anxiety, task performance, and evaluations of user interfaces, *Proc. CHI 2000 Conference: Human Factors in Computing Systems*, ACM Press, New York (2000), 49–56.

Rosenthal, O. and Phillips, R., *Coping with Color-Blindness*, Avery Publishing Group, New York (1997).

Sarkar, Manojit and Brown, Marc H., Graphical fisheye views, *Communications of the ACM* 37, 12 (July 1994), 73–84.

Sears, Andrew, Layout appropriateness: Guiding user interface design with simple task descriptions, *IEEE Transactions on Software Engineering* 19, 7 (1993), 707–719.

Shneiderman, Ben, Looking for the bright side of agents, *ACM Interactions* 2, 1 (January 1995), 13–15.

Siegel, David, *Creating Killer Web Sites*, Hayden Books, Indianapolis, IN (1997). Updates can be found at http://www.killersites.com/ (2008).

Smith, Sid L. and Mosier, Jane N., *Guidelines for Designing User Interface Software*, Report ESD-TR–86–278, Electronic Systems Division, MITRE Corporation, Bedford, MA (1986). Available from the National Technical Information Service, Springfield, VA.

Spence, Robert, *Information Visualization*, Addison-Wesley, Reading, MA (2001).

Staggers, Nancy, Impact of screen density on clinical nurses' computer task performance and subjective screen satisfaction, *International Journal of Man-Machine Studies* 39, 5 (November 1993), 775–792.

Stone, Maureen, *A Field Guide to Digital Color*, A. K. Peters, Wellesley, MA (2003).

Sun Microsystems, Inc., Java Look and Feel Design Guidelines, Second Edition, http://java.sun.com/products/jlf/ed2/book/index.html (2001).

Sun Microsystems, Inc., Web Design Standards, http://www.sun.com/webdesign/ (2008).

Teitelbaum, Richard C. and Granda, Richard F., The effects of positional constancy on searching menus for information, *Proc. CHI '83 Conference: Human Factors in Computing Systems*, ACM Press, New York (1983), 150–153.

Tullis, T. S., Information presentation, in Proctor, R. and Vu, K. (Editors), *Handbook of Human Factors in Web Design*, Routledge, New York (2004).

Tullis, T. S., Screen design, in Helander, M., Landauer, T. K., and Prabhu, P. (Editors), *Handbook of Human-Computer Interaction, Second Edition*, Elsevier, Amsterdam, The Netherlands (1997), 377–411.

Tullis, T. S., Web-based presentation of information: The top ten mistakes and why they are mistakes, *Proc. HCI International 2005*, Las Vegas, NV, Lawrence Erlbaum Associates (July 2005).

Walker, Janet H., Sproull, Lee, and Subramani, R., Using a human face in an interface, *Proc. CHI '94 Conference: Human Factors in Computing Systems*, ACM Press, New York (1994), 85–91.

Web Accessibility Initiative, World Wide Web Consortium,   http://www.w3.org/WAI/ (2008).

Weinman, Lynda, *Designing Web Graphics, Fourth Edition*, New Riders, Indianapolis, IN (2002).

Williams, T. R., Guidelines for the display of information on the Web, *Technical Communication* 47, 3 (2000), 383–396.

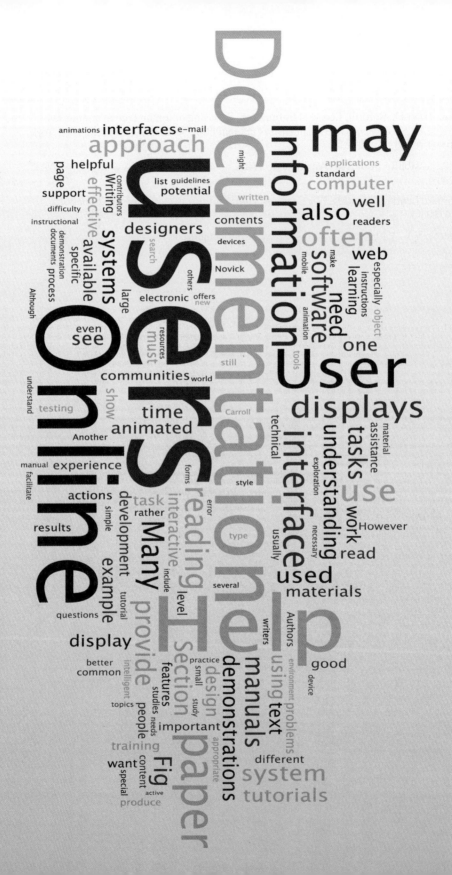

CHAPTER 12

User Documentation and Online Help

> " What is really important in education is . . . that the mind is matured, that energy is aroused. "

Soren Kierkegaard
Either/Or, Volume II

Written in collaboration with Maxine S. Cohen

CHAPTER OUTLINE

12.1 Introduction

12.2 Online Versus Paper Documentation

12.3 Reading from Paper Versus from Displays

12.4 Shaping the Content of the Documentation

12.5 Accessing the Documentation

12.6 Online Tutorials and Animated Demonstrations

12.7 Online Communities for User Assistance

12.8 The Development Process

12.1 Introduction

Standardization and improvements in user interfaces have made computer applications easier to use, but using new interfaces is still a challenge. First-time computer users struggle to understand basic interface objects and actions, as well as their tasks. For experienced users, learning advanced features and understanding novel task domains takes commitment and concentration. Many users learn from someone else who knows the interface; others learn by trial and error, while others use the supplied (typically online) documentation. User manuals, online help and documentation, and tutorials are often ignored or minimally used, but when users get stuck in trying to complete their tasks under certain conditions, these resources are invaluable.

Learning anything new is a challenge. Challenges can be joyous and satisfying, but when it comes to learning about computer systems, many people experience anxiety, frustration, and disappointment. Much of the difficulty stems directly from the poor design of the menus, displays, or instructions—which leads to errors and confusion—or simply from users' inability to easily determine what to do next. As the goal of providing universal usability becomes more prominent, online help services are increasingly necessary to bridge the gap between what users know and what they need to know.

Older empirical studies show that well-written and well-designed user manuals, on paper or online, can be effective (Carroll, 1998; Hackos and Stevens, 1997; Horton, 1994). Today's modern interactive systems are expected to provide online help, online manuals, online documentation, quick-start guides, and interactive tutorials to serve user needs for training and reference. In fact, as displays appear in cars, phones, cameras, public kiosks, small personal mobile devices, and elsewhere, ubiquitous and customizable online help should be the norm. Increasing attention is being paid to improving user-interface design, but the complexity and diversity of interactive applications are also growing. Evidence suggests that there will always be a need for supplemental materials that aid users, in both paper and online forms (though the use of printed manuals seems to be fading).

There are diverse ways of providing guidance to users online (Box 12.1). Many paper manuals have been transferred into online formats; software manufacturers

BOX 12.1
Taxonomy of user documentation, online help, and tutorials.

Domain covered by help system

- Description of interface objects and actions (syntactic)
- Sequences of actions to accomplish tasks (semantic)
- Task-domain–specific knowledge (pragmatic)

Degree of integration in the interface (from less to more integrated)

- Online documentation and tutorial: independent interface, even possibly developed by a different company
- Online help: integrated into the interface, separate window usually invoked from a "help" button
- Context-sensitive help: a) user-controlled—depends on where the user points (pop-up box, balloon, tool tip, or ScreenTip), or b) system initiated—the system makes suggestions and sometimes takes action
- Animated demonstrations: usually integrated into the interface

Time of intervention

- Before starting (quick guide, manual, and tutorial)

- At the beginning of the interaction (getting started, animated demonstration)
- During the task (context sensitive, either user- or system-initiated help)
- After failure (help button, FAQs)
- When the user returns the next time (start-up tips)

Media

- Text (paragraphs, with a list of steps)
- Graphics (screen prints can illustrate explanations)
- Voice recording
- Video recording of someone using the interface
- Animation
- Recording of the interface itself in action, with or without annotations
- Simulation environments for computer-based training

Extensibility

- Closed system
- Users can add more information (annotations, synonyms, or translations)

often provide online manuals, online help systems, online tutorials, or animated demonstrations. Context-sensitive help is often also available, ranging from a simple pop-up box (often called a *tool tip*, *ScreenTip*, or *balloon help*) to more advanced assistants and wizards. Most manufacturers have web sites, which may feature compilations of frequently asked questions (FAQs). In addition, there are lively user communities that provide a more "grass roots" type of help and support. This help may be available through formal online and structured user communities and newsgroups, or more informal e-mail, chat, and instant messaging modalities. A broad variety of formats and styles are used to meet the ever-present need for documentation.

Other forms of instruction include classroom instruction (traditional, web-based, or online), personal training and assistance, telephone consultation, video and audio recordings, and Flash demos. These forms are not discussed here, but many of the same instructional-design principles apply. Another important approach is personal, human help from a telephone-accessible help desk. This can be a valuable asset for users, but it is an expensive one for providers. To minimize the cost, some providers utilize a hybrid system that is staffed by a small cadre of real users, supplemented by computerized agents and intelligent help systems.

This chapter starts by reviewing the benefits of online versus paper documentation (Section 12.2), then summarizes the results of user studies that have compared reading on paper and on computer displays (Section 12.3). Section 12.4 discusses the shaping of the contents of documentation, and Section 12.5 explores specific approaches for accessing the documentation and help systems, including access by special populations. Next, tutorials and demonstrations (Section 12.6) and online communities for user assistance (Section 12.7) are reviewed. The chapter closes with a brief section on the development process for user documentation (Section 12.8).

12.2 Online Versus Paper Documentation

There are many reasons to have online documentation. The positive reasons for doing so include:

- *Physical advantages*
    - Information is available whenever the electronic device or computer is available. There is no need to locate the correct documentation (an activity that could cause a minor disruption if the proper material is close by, or a major disruption if the material must be retrieved from another building or person). The harsh reality is that many users lose their paper documentation or do not keep it current with new versions of the software.
    - Users do not need to allocate physical workspace to opening up the documentation. Paper documentation can be clumsy to use and can clutter a

workspace; in a mobile environment, there may not be an available location to physically place the paper documentation.

- Information can be electronically updated rapidly and at low cost. Electronic dissemination of revisions ensures that out-of-date material cannot be retrieved inadvertently.

- *Navigation features*
  - Specific information necessary for a task can be located rapidly if the online documentation offers indexes, tables of contents, lists of figures, glossaries, and lists of keyboard shortcuts.
  - Searching for one page in hundreds can usually be done much more quickly on a computer than with paper documentation.
  - Linking within texts can guide readers to related materials; linking to external materials such as dictionaries, encyclopedias, translations, and web resources can facilitate understanding.

- *Interactive services*
  - Readers can bookmark and annotate or tag the text (Fig. 12.1) and send text and annotations by e-mail.
  - Authors can use graphics, sound, color, and animations that may be helpful in explaining complex actions and creating an engaging experience for users (Fig. 12.2).
  - Readers can turn to newsgroups, listservers, online communities, e-mail, chat, and instant messaging for further help from other users (Section 12.7).
  - Visually impaired users (or users needing a hands-free mode) can use screen readers and listen to instructions.

- *Economic advantages*
  - Online documentation is cheaper to duplicate and distribute than paper documentation.

Although there are advantages to online documentation, some of these advantages can be compromised by some potentially negative side effects. These include:

- Displays may not be as readable as reading from paper (Section 12.3).

- Each display may contain substantially less information than a sheet of paper. The display resolution is also lower than that for paper, which is especially important when pictures or graphics are used.

- The user interfaces of online help systems may be novel and especially confusing to novices. By contrast, most people are thoroughly familiar with the "user interface" of paper documentation or paper manuals.

- The extra mental effort required for navigating and scrolling through many screens may interfere with concentration and learning, and annotation can be difficult.

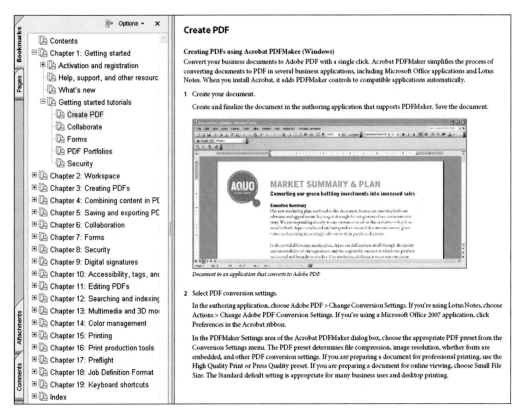

Create PDF

Creating PDFs using Acrobat PDFMaker (Windows)

Convert your business documents to Adobe PDF with a single click. Acrobat PDFMaker simplifies the process of converting documents to PDF in several business applications, including Microsoft Office applications and Lotus Notes. When you install Acrobat, it adds PDFMaker controls to compatible applications automatically.

1   Create your document.

Create and finalize the document in the authoring application that supports PDFMaker. Save the document.

Document in an application that converts to Adobe PDF

2   Select PDF conversion settings.

In the authoring application, choose Adobe PDF > Change Conversion Settings. If you're using Lotus Notes, choose Actions > Change Adobe PDF Conversion Settings. If you're using a Microsoft Office 2007 application, click Preferences in the Acrobat ribbon.

In the PDFMaker Settings area of the Acrobat PDFMaker dialog box, choose the appropriate PDF preset from the Conversion Settings menu. The PDF preset determines file compression, image resolution, whether fonts are embedded, and other PDF conversion settings. If you are preparing a document for professional printing, use the High Quality Print or Press Quality preset. If you are preparing a document for online viewing, choose Small File Size. The Standard default setting is appropriate for many business uses and desktop printing.

FIGURE 12.1

The user manual for Adobe Reader® 9.0 (http://www.adobe.com/) is a linear PDF document that can be printed or read online. Tabs provide access to an expandable table of contents, page thumbnails, or bookmarks. Users can click on links to related sections, zoom, add comments, search, and more.

- Splitting the display between work and help or tutorial windows reduces the space for work displays. If users must switch to a separate help or tutorial application, the burden on short-term memory can be large; users may lose the context of their work and have difficulty remembering what they read in the online documentation. (Large displays provide a potential resolution for this problem for desktop applications; Section 8.5.)

- Small devices such as cell phones do not have enough display space to provide online help. They usually have to rely on paper documentation, including quick-start guides or separate web-based online documentation and tutorials.

The current trend is to provide most documentation online. The increased cost of printing, shipping, and updating makes the market for printed manufacturer-supplied documentation rather limited. However, the lively market for training

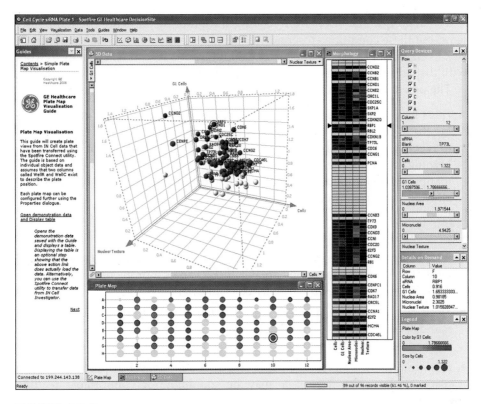

FIGURE 12.2

The discovery tool Spotfire™ (http://www.spotfire.com/) provides examples that guide users while they learn to use the interface. Here, a sample dataset about cancer cells was loaded in the tool; users follow step-by-step instructions and alter the view based on the various sliders and other adjustment tools.

books testifies to the appeal of high-quality instructional materials supplied in hard-copy format (often with interactive CDs/DVDs included). Researchers caution that words should be treated as valuable commodities and used sparingly in documentation, whether in printed form or online.

12.3 Reading from Paper Versus from Displays

The technology of printing text on paper has been evolving for more than 500 years. The paper surface and color, the typeface, character width, letter sharpness, text contrast with the paper, width of the text column, size of margins, spacing between lines, and even room lighting all have been experimented with in efforts to produce the most appealing and readable format.

Visual fatigue and stress from reading computer displays are common problems, but these conditions respond well to rest, frequent breaks, and task diversity. Even if users are not aware of visual fatigue or stress, their capacity to work with displays may be below their capacity to work with paper documentation. The potential disadvantages of reading from displays include these:

- *Fonts* may be poor, especially on low-resolution displays. The dots composing the letters may be so large that each is visible, making users expend effort to recognize characters. Monospace (fixed-width) fonts, lack of appropriate kerning (for example, adjustments to bring "V" and "A" closer together), inappropriate interletter and interline spacing, and inappropriate colors may all complicate recognition.

- *Low contrast* between the characters and the background and *fuzzy character boundaries* also can cause trouble.

- *Emitted light* from displays may be more difficult to read by than reflected light from paper; *glare* may be greater, *flicker* can be a problem, and the *curved display surface* of some screens may be troubling.

- *Small displays* require frequent *page turning*; issuing the page-turning commands is disruptive, and the page turns are unsettling, especially if they are slow and visually distracting.

- *Reading distance* is easily adjustable for paper, while most displays are *fixed* in place, and display *placement* may be too high for comfortable reading (optometrists suggest reading be done with the eyes in a downward-looking direction). The "near quintad" (Grant, 1990) are the five ways eyes adjust to seeing close items: *accommodation* (lens-shape change), *convergence* (looking towards the center), *meiosis* (pupillary contraction), *excyclotorsion* (rotation), and *depression of gaze* (looking down). Users of tablet computers and mobile devices often hold their displays in a lower position than desktop displays to facilitate reading.

- *Layout and formatting* can be problems—for example, improper margins, inappropriate line widths (35 to 55 characters is recommended), or awkward justification (left justification and ragged right are recommended). Multicolumn layouts may require constant scrolling up and down. Page breaks may be distracting and waste space.

- *Reduced hand and body motion* with fixed-position displays, as compared to paper, may be more fatiguing.

- *Unfamiliarity of displays* and the *anxiety* of navigating the text can increase stress.

The interest in reading from displays has increased as mobile devices, iPhones (Fig. 1.8), specialized electronic book platforms (Fig. 8.20), and web-based libraries have grown more common. Being able to download the morning newspaper onto a pocket-sized electronic device or cellphone to read while standing in a crowded subway or to carry a full city guide on such a device while touring are strong attractions. If users are to read large amounts of material online, high-resolution and larger displays are recommended. Other studies recommend that quick response times, fast display rates, black text on a white background, and page-sized displays are important considerations if displayed text is meant to replace paper documents. Some applications, such as Microsoft Word, provide a dedicated reading layout view that limits the number of controls and increases the space available for the text. Dynamic pagination can take into account the display size to facilitate paging through the document instead of scrolling. Sans-serif fonts (Fig. 12.3) should be used, as they are crisper and produce a less cluttered appearance. Sans-serif fonts are also preferred for low-vision readers.

Large online libraries of books—whether they are made available for free, as by the Gutenberg archives or the Library of Congress (Fig. 1.6), or for pay, a service offered by numerous publishers—promote efforts to improve the reading experience. Publishers of newspapers and scientific journals are evolving to satisfy the intense demand for online access to articles, while struggling to ensure a way to recover their costs. Plasticity of documents is becoming a requirement. The ability to automatically sense the correct orientation for reading a document is becoming a standard feature. Documentation designers have to structure their materials so that they can be read on small, medium, and large displays and at different font sizes to accommodate vision-impaired users.

Gaining a better understanding of users' reading patterns in online environments is important. A reading study offering three different interfaces—overview + detail, fisheye, and linear—showed some interesting results: the poorest performance was with the traditional linear interface (Hornbaek and Frokjaer, 2003). Another study using eyetracking and displaying where and how users viewed a web page clearly shows an F-shaped pattern (Fig. 12.4). This indicates that users do not read online text word by word. The beginning paragraphs should contain the most important information; after reading them users tend to scan down the left side of the page, so the words they see there should also carry the important information content (Nielsen, 2006).

Markups of the text (for example, XML or XHTML markups) can support the automatic generation of paper and online versions, tables of contents,

> This is an example of a serif font, specifically Times New Roman.
>
> This is an example of a sans-serif font, specifically Tahoma.

FIGURE 12.3

A simple example using Times New Roman, a serif font, and Tahoma, a sans-serif font. See how much cleaner and crisper the sans-serif font looks.

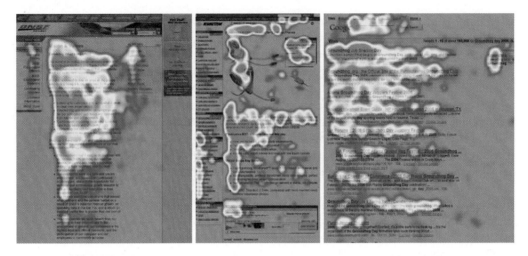

FIGURE 12.4

The heatmaps from the eyetracking study. Red indicates the area where the user looked most, yellow indicates fewer views, and blue indicates the fewest views. Gray is used for areas that were not viewed. The image on the left is from an article in the "About us" section of a corporate web site, the center image is a product page on an e-commerce web site, and the image on the right is from a search engine results page (http://www.useit.com/alertbox/reading_pattern.html and Jakob Nielsen).

diverse indexes, enhanced search capabilities, shortened versions for quick scanning, and links for further details. Advanced features could include automatic conversion to foreign languages, tools for annotation, bookmarks, tagging, capacity to have the text read out loud, and highlights for different classes of readers.

12.4 Shaping the Content of the Documentation

Traditionally, training and reference materials for computer systems were paper manuals. Writing these manuals was frequently left to the most junior member of the development team as a low-effort task to be completed at the end of the project. As a result, the manuals often were poorly written, were not suited to the users' backgrounds, were delayed or incomplete, and were tested inadequately, if at all. Today, managers recognize that designers may not fully understand the users' needs, that system developers might not be good writers, and that it takes time and skill to write effective documentation. They have also learned that testing and revision must be done before widespread dissemination and that system success is closely coupled to documentation quality. Users show little interest in reading manuals or documentation from cover to cover; their interest is focused on gathering information or completing a task (Redish, 2007). Users also like to have choices and prefer different types of documentation for different tasks (Smart et al., 2001). Horton (1994) concluded that "good online documentation is better than poor paper documentation and good paper documentation is better than poor online documentation," and that maxim still holds true today.

12.4.1 Towards minimal manuals

Thinking-aloud studies (Section 4.3.3) of subjects who were learning word processors have revealed the enormous difficulties that most novices have and the strategies that they adopt to overcome those difficulties (Carroll and Mack, 1984). Learners actively try to make the system work, to read portions of the manual, to understand the displays, to explore the functions of keys, and to overcome the many problems that they encounter. Learners apparently prefer trying out actions on the computer rather than reading lengthy manuals. They want to perform meaningful, familiar tasks immediately and to see the results for themselves. They apply real-world knowledge, experience with other interfaces, and frequent guesswork. The image of the new user patiently reading sequentially through and absorbing the contents of a manual is rare in reality.

These observations led to the design of *minimal manuals* that anchor the tool in the task domain, encourage active involvement with hands-on experience as soon as possible, promote *guided exploration* of system features, and support error recognition and recovery. The key principles of user manual and documentation design (Box 12.2) have been refined over time, described in detail, and validated in practice (van der Meij and Carroll, 1995; Carroll, 1998). Of course, every good manual should have a *table of contents* and an *index*. *Glossaries* can be helpful for clarifying technical terms. *Appendices* with error messages are recommended.

Visual aspects are helpful to readers, especially with highly visual direct-manipulation interfaces and graphical user interfaces. Viewing numerous well-chosen screen prints that demonstrate typical uses enables users to develop an understanding and a *predictive model* of the interface. Often, users will mimic the examples in the documentation during their first trials of the software. Figures containing complex data structures, transition diagrams, and menus can improve performance dramatically by giving users access to systems models created by designers.

In today's interactive world, many users are technologically sophisticated. There is no appeal to reading or browsing through many pages of documentation; users want to get going quickly with their technology products. Only

BOX 12.2

User manual guidelines based on practice and empirical studies (mostly based on Carroll, 1998).

Choose an action-oriented approach

- Provide an immediate opportunity to act.
- Encourage and support exploration and innovation.
- Respect the integrity of the user's activity.
- Show numerous examples.

Let users' tasks guide organization

- Select or design instructional activities that are real tasks.
- Present task concepts before interface objects and actions.
- Create components of instructions that reflect the task structure.

Support error recognition and recovery

- Prevent mistakes whenever possible.

- Provide error information when actions are error-prone or correction is difficult.
- Provide error information that supports detection, diagnosis, and correction.
- Provide on-the-spot error information.

Support reading to do, study, and locate

- Be brief; don't spell out everything.
- Provide a table of contents, index, and glossary.
- Keep the writing style clean and simple.
- Provide closure for chapters.

with the most sophisticated electronic systems is there a need or desire for extensive training and long start-up times. Users want quick-start guides (Fig. 12.5), easy-to-navigate material, and lots of examples (Novick and Ward, 2006a); they also want information that is complete, accurate, and well organized, and at the right level of technical detail (Smart et al., 2001). Some of these attributes are difficult to produce in general documentation for a wide-ranging audience.

Whether to give *credit* to authors and designers is the subject of lively and frequent debate. Advocates encourage giving credit in the documentation to honor good work, to encourage contributors to strive to do an excellent job, and to build the users' trust. Having the writers' and designers' names in the documentation also makes software fit in with other creative human endeavors (such as books, films, and music) in which contributors are acknowledged, even if there are dozens of them. Opponents say that it is sometimes difficult to identify who contributed what, detracting from the desired goal of increasing contributors' sense of responsibility for the work they produce, and that contributors might receive unwelcome telephone calls or e-mail.

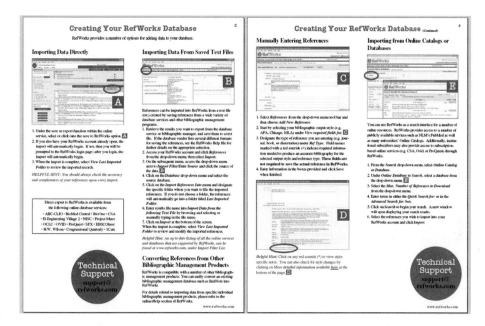

FIGURE 12.5

Two pages from the Quick Start guide from RefWorks.com, an online research management, writing, and collaboration tool. Different-sized fonts and different colors are used to help the user scan the material, and large letters (A, B, C, etc.) are used to guide the user through the material. Helpful hints are also indicated (http://www.refworks.com).

12.4.2 Organization and writing style

Designing instructional materials is a challenging endeavor. The author must be knowledgeable about the technical content; sensitive to the background, reading level, and intellectual ability of the reader; and skilled in writing lucid prose. Assuming that the author has acquired the technical content, the primary job in creating documentation is to understand the readers and the tasks that they must perform.

A precise statement of the *instructional objectives* (Mager, 1997) is an invaluable guide to the author and the reader. The sequencing of the instructional content should be governed by the reader's current knowledge and ultimate objectives. Precise rules are hard to identify, but the author should attempt to present concepts in a logical sequence in increasing order of difficulty, to ensure that each concept is explained before being used in subsequent sections, to avoid forward references, and to construct sections that contain approximately equal amounts of new material. In addition to these structural requirements, the documentation should have sufficient examples and complete sample sessions. These guidelines are valid for manuals and other documentation that is typically read sequentially.

Before starting to write any documentation, it's important to thoroughly investigate who the intended users are and how the documentation will be used (Smart et al., 2001). Frampton (2008) suggests numerous questions that should be considered. Who is the intended audience for the documentation? What are the market expectations for the documentation? What amount of the budget has been allocated for it? Are some components of the documentation considered essential or required and others supplemental or nice to have? How will the documentation be used? Will it be used once and thrown away, or used repeatedly over a long period of time? What is the reading level of the potential users? Is the documentation written in their native language? What is the intended user's level of comfort with technology? Following the user-centered design process is a good way for the documentation authors to communicate and discuss requirements with the users, and this approach will yield better-designed documentation.

Redish (2007) encourages authors to divide documentation into topics and subtopics. Topics can be organized according to time or sequence, tasks, people, type of information presented, or questions people ask. Today's online world is one of agile information development (Hackos, 2006). Development cycles are short and competition is fierce.

Users interact with the documentation on several different cognitive levels. They go to the documentation to find information that is relevant to accomplishing a task. They need to understand what the documentation is explaining, and they then need to apply that understanding to the task that caused them to consult the documentation in the first place (Galitz, 2007). In this process, there are lots of places for misunderstandings and increased cognitive load. Additionally, users may already be in a stressful situation and frustrated because the interface is not letting them accomplish their task.

The choice of words and their phrasing is as important as the overall structure. A poorly written sentence mars a well-designed manual, just as an incorrect note mars a beautifully composed sonata. *The Elements of Style* (Strunk et al., 2000) and *On Writing Well* (Zinsser, 2006)—two classic and recently updated books on writing—are valuable resources. Style guides for organizations represent worthy attempts at ensuring consistency and high quality (Mandel, 2002). But of course, no set of guidelines can turn a mediocre writer into a great writer. Writing is a highly creative act; effective writers are national treasures.

There are numerous resources available for professional communicators, with an emphasis on technical communication. Formal courses and degree programs exist as well as specialized institutes and workshops. Books (Robinson and Etter, 2000; Hackos, 2006; Lannon, 2007; Redish, 2007) exist to explain techniques for writing documentation (and specifically web content), as well as formal pedagogy. Both the IEEE (through their Professional Communication Society) and the Society for Technical Communication (STC) provide theoretical publications as well as information of a more practical nature.

12.5 Accessing the Documentation

Studies in the past have confirmed that well-designed documentation can be very effective (Cohill and Williges, 1982; Magers, 1983). In spite of improvements, however, most users avoid user manuals and prefer to learn interface features by exploration (Rieman, 1996) and other means (Novick and Ward, 2006b; Novick et al., 2007). If users read the documentation, they read at a high level; they "satisfice," skip, scan, and skim (Mehlenbacher, 2003). Users typically do not want to sift through voluminous user manuals that can be difficult to navigate. Instead, they want quick and easy access to instructions for the specific tasks they are trying to carry out (Redish, 2007). Even when problems arise, many users are reluctant to consult written documentation and may do so only as a last resort. Although guidelines have been applied to improve the design of online components to take advantage of their unique media, studies still show low use of documentation (Novick et al., 2007).

Standard formats such as WinHelp and Windows HTML Help have stimulated development of a growing number of software tools, such as Adobe RoboHelp™ and helpMATIC Pro. These tools facilitate coordination among teams of authors in creating interactive online help in multiple formats for multiple platforms.

Documentation is often placed online and with good reasons. The issue becomes one of making the best use of the online environment when accessing the documentation. Multiple ways are available to search and traverse the online information that is different from paper documentation. Being able to offer context-sensitive help is another asset of online documentation. Documentation can be customized for various user populations, such as users with disabilities, international users, and varying age ranges.

12.5.1 Online documentation

The low production and shipping costs of CD-ROMs first encouraged hardware suppliers to produce online documentation that was an exact duplicate of the paper documentation and/or manuals. Most manufacturers now put their user documentation online. Modern designs assume that online documentation or web-based documentation will be available, usually with standard browsing interfaces to reduce learning effort. For mobile devices, small displays limit the possibilities, but providing helpful instructions on the device to complement printed user documentation should still be a priority. To keep this information up-to-date, users are often referred to the manufacturer's web site, where downloadable manuals and other forms of documentation are readily available.

Although they are frequently generated from the same source document (usually an XML or XHTML document), online documentation now tends to differ from paper documentation in many ways. Online documents can benefit from all the physical advantages, navigation features, and interactive services mentioned in Section 12.2. On the other hand, paper documents have traditionally housed supplementary local information that is often written in margins or included on slips of paper stuck in at the appropriate pages. Some printed documentation remains pristine, neatly encased in its original shrink-wrapped packaging, but dog-eared, stained, and worn pages are often seen on well-used documentation. Online documentation that allows for local annotations, synonyms, alternate phrasing, or translations has enhanced value. Additional desirable services include support for bookmarking and automatic history keeping, which allows backtracking. Designers will be most effective when they design online documentation to fit the electronic medium and take advantage of text highlighting, color, sound, animation, and string search with relevance feedback.

A vital feature for online documentation—especially manuals—is a properly designed table of contents that can remain visible to the side of the displayed page of text. Selection of a chapter or other entry in the table of contents should immediately result in the appropriate page being displayed (Fig. 12.1). Use of expanding or contracting tables of contents (the common use of the plus and minus signs) or multiple panes to show several levels at once can be beneficial (Chimera and Shneiderman, 1994). Being able to conveniently and easily navigate through large volumes of online documentation is vital for the user.

12.5.2 Online help

Users typically seek out help in solving specific problems, and rather than sequentially reading through a full set of online documentation, they will want to go directly to the information that is needed. The traditional approach with online documentation is to have users type in or select a help-menu item and the system displays a list of alphabetically arranged topics that they can click on to read a paragraph or more of helpful information. This method can work, but it is often frustrating for those users who are not sure of the correct terms to use to find information on the tasks they wish to accomplish. They may see several familiar terms (search, query, select, browse, find, reveal, display, info, or view) but not know which one to select. Worse still, there may not be a single command that accomplishes the task, and there is usually little information about how to assemble actions to perform tasks (such as converting graphics into a different format). Online help that offers concise descriptions of the interface objects and actions is probably most effective for intermittent knowledgeable users; it is likely to be less useful for novices, who have more need for tutorial training.

Sometimes simple lists—for example, of *keyboard shortcuts*, *menu items*, or *mouse shortcuts*—can provide the necessary information. Each item in the list might have an accompanying feature description. However, many designers recognize that such lists can be overwhelming and that users usually want guidance for accomplishing their specific intended tasks (for example, printing on envelopes).

Some of the complaints about using online help include the following (Smart et al., 2001):

Trouble navigating the help menu
Finding the terminology too technical
Difficulty with search strategies
Incomplete information provided
Too many choices or paths
Difficulty with having multiple windows open
Too much information

The online help and support center found with most Microsoft products offers many ways of finding relevant articles, called *topics*. Users can browse an organized table of contents that lists the topics hierarchically, or search the text of the articles (Fig. 12.6). Finally, Microsoft's Answer Wizard approach allows users to type requests using natural-language statements; the program then selects the relevant keywords and offers a list of topics organized into categories. For example, typing "Tell me how to print addresses on envelopes" produces:

What do you want to do?
Create and print an envelope
Print envelopes by merging an address list

This example shows a successful response from the natural-language system, but the quality of the responses varies greatly in typical usage situations. Users may not type in appropriate terms, and they often have difficulty understanding the instructions.

12.5.3 Context-sensitive help

The ability to provide context-sensitive information is a powerful advantage when using online help systems. The simplest way to take context into account is to monitor the cursor location and provide helpful information about the object under the cursor. This form of user-controlled interactive object help is readily understandable to users and even fun to use. Another approach is to provide system-initiated help, often called "intelligent help," that tries to make use of the interaction history, a model of the user population, and a representation of their tasks to make assumptions about what users need.

User-controlled, interactive object help   A simple approach to context-sensitive help is based on the interactive widgets in the interface. Users position the cursor on a widget (or other visible interface object) and then press a help key or hover the mouse over the object for a couple of seconds to produce information about the object on which the cursor is resting. In a common version of this technique, users simply move the cursor to the desired location and hover over the

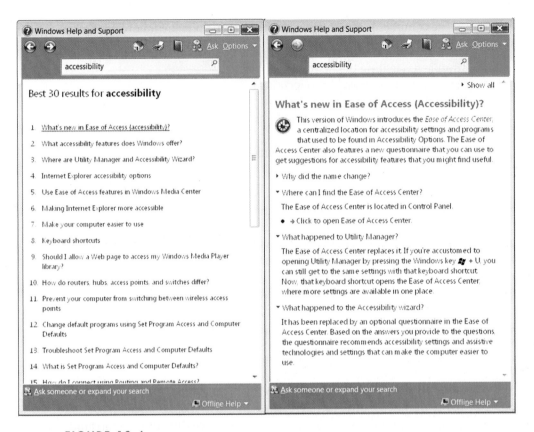

FIGURE 12.6

The Microsoft Windows Vista Help and Support Center provides multiple ways to navigate to the pages of information. Here, a search for "accessibility" returns the Best Results and What's New. In addition, there are other links to offline help. Commands (such as the opening of the Magnifier) can be activated within the help pages.

object, causing a small pop-up box (often called a tool tip, ScreenTip, or balloon help) to appear with an explanation of that object (Fig. 12.7). Alternatively, all of the balloons may be displayed at once, so that users can see all of the explanations simultaneously. Another approach is to dedicate a portion of the display to help, which is updated automatically as users hover over or select interface widgets (Fig. 12.8). User-controlled help can also be used for objects more complex than widgets, such as control panels or forms. These features provide a narrower window into the extensive volume of help that is available to the user.

System-initiated help   By keeping track of user actions, some researchers believe that they can provide effective system guidance, such as suggesting that users should redefine their margins since they are indenting every line. Research in computer-based intelligent user interfaces has seen mixed results

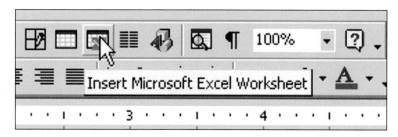

FIGURE 12.7

In Microsoft Office, when users hover over an icon a ScreenTip appears that explains the command represented by the icon, providing help at the widget level.

(Hook, 2000). Early on, a simulated "intelligent help" system was tested with eight users doing business tasks, such as printing a mailing list (Carroll and Aaronson, 1988). The researchers prepared messages for expected error conditions, but they found that "people are incredibly creative in generating errors and misconceptions, and incredibly fast." The results, even with a simulated system, were mixed; the authors concluded "Development of intelligent help systems faces serious usability challenges." Intelligent help systems that provide system-initiated support have generally failed. The most infamous example illustrating the problems of this approach is Microsoft's Office Assistant (or "Clippit"), which has created much controversy (Shroyer, 2000). One of its functions was that as soon as users typed "Dear . . .", Clippit popped up and offered assistance in formatting a letter. Many users considered the paper clip so intrusive that they immediately turned it off. Today, the Office Assistant (Fig. 12.9) still exists in the Microsoft suite of products, but it is an option that is user-controlled, and the default status is not to display it (it is hidden).

A system-initiated help system has also been implemented in the Smalltalk™ programming environment, where cartoon-like gurus appear on the display and offer audio commentaries with animated demonstrations of the graphical user interface (Alpert et al., 1995). Smalltalk's designers considered many of the problems of anthropomorphic help, such as user initiation, pacing, and user control of remediation; unfortunately, however, no empirical evidence as to the efficacy of the help system is available.

Hybrid approaches   Intelligent help advocates have promoted as alternatives a mixed-initiative approach, in which initiative is shared between the user and the system (Horvitz, 1999), and an advice-giving approach (Lieberman, 2001). For example, Letizia (Lieberman, 1997) gives advice and suggestions to users browsing the Web, but its focus is on web-site suggestions rather than interface training. A Telephone Triage Assistant for junior nurses received good feedback during usability testing (Mao and Leung, 2003); the content of the advice window was unpredictable but rather unobtrusive, and it did not interfere

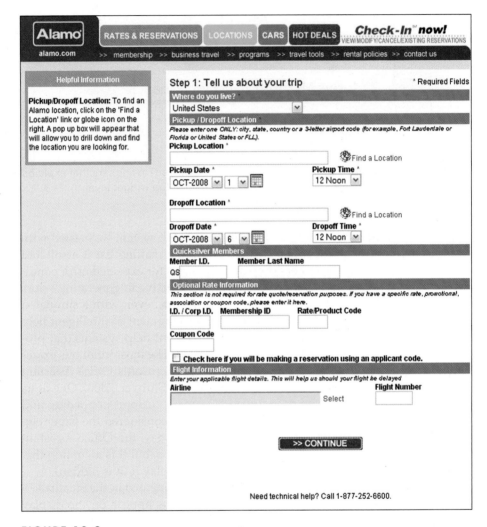

FIGURE 12.8

To rent a car from Alamo (http://www.alamo.com), users fill in a form with information about their trips. As they click on a field (here, the "pick up location" menu), context-sensitive, detailed help information appears on the left part of the screen. Notes in italics give brief directions and explain why the data is needed.

with users' tasks. This approach requires dedicating a large portion of the display to the help information, but it keeps users in control of the amount and timing of the advice they receive, making this technique an effective hybrid of online help and tutorial approaches.

Although many of the earlier attempts have had mixed results, a concerted effort for personalization of interfaces is being made. Research by Russell

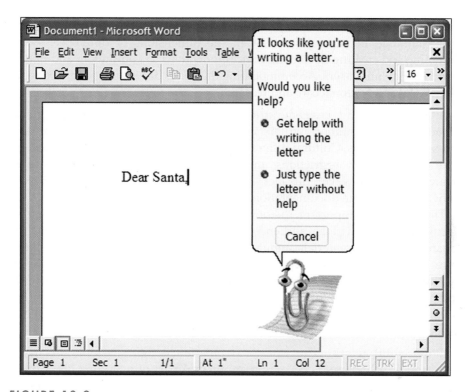

FIGURE 12.9

Clippit the Office Assistant guesses that a letter is being written and offers help to prepare a standard letter in Word 2000.

(2003) has shown that clearly defined operations coupled with extensive data-mining techniques can yield acceptable results. His study investigated a heterogeneous audience with varying levels of experience interfacing with a large documentation library at Oracle® Corporation. Usage data was analyzed over a 90-day period and consisted of several hundred thousand searches. Russell observed a difference between *persistent choice* and *single-use choice*, and he warns against inconsistency in user choices, which is often based on the lack of a full understanding of the system. He distinguishes between *customization* (where the user makes explicit choices) and *personalization* (where the system observes and adapts) and recommends a hybrid approach that balances the two.

12.5.4 Special populations

Computer systems and their accompanying documentation are used by a diverse population interacting with a range of applications of differing complexities. These users vary in age, computer experience, and language understanding, to name just a few of the dimensions of difference. When designing and creating documentation, authors need to know about and understand the potential users. Accommodating the needs of certain special user populations takes additional care and research.

International and cross-cultural issues   When dealing with the global economy, documentation writers need to be aware of international and cross-cultural issues. Cultural differences are often ignored, perhaps because of time and budgetary restrictions, and the documentation is simply translated (Warren, 2006). However, this lack of sensitivity can create problems with the understanding of the documentation.

There are five important rhetorical elements to consider when designing documentation for a global audience: the purpose, the audience, the content, the organization of the materials, and the style (Dong, 2007). Deeper cultural differences, including differing vocabularies, must be taken into account. Even eye-movement and scanning patterns can vary across cultures. A full sociological comparison of various cultures is beyond the scope of this book, but an author writing global documentation needs to be aware of the differences. Again, a user-centered design approach can be quite helpful.

Older adult users   The world's population is aging, people are living longer, and technology is becoming an integral part of everyday life. Consequently, special attention should be given to older adult users (Section 1.4.6). Most computer documentation is written with many assumptions about the users' experiences and vocabulary that may not hold true with this subset of the population (Tilley, 2003). Using familiar tasks, languages, and metaphors can facilitate understanding (Carroll, 1998). A three-pronged approach should be used: icons should be defined and acronyms and key phrases should be introduced early on (Fig. 12.10), just enough explanation should be provided (use of analogies is helpful), and a list of exception-oriented guidelines for common tasks should be supplied. In general, guidelines should not only explain how to perform the tasks, but provide action plans to follow if the computer does not work as expected. Seniors seem to prefer structured guidance (Tilley, 2003), and the absence of goal information, consequence information, and identification information in the instructions has a greater impact on older adults (van Horen et al., 2009). In some cases, it may be worthwhile to develop a special interface for seniors. For example, the National Institute of Health has developed a web site specifically for older adults: It includes on the home page obvious controls to adjust the font, adjust the contrast, and turn speech on or off (Fig. 12.11).

Users with disabilities   Computers have opened up the world to many users with disabilities that severely limited their communication capabilities. These users can now use alternative methods of input, such as switches, head tracking,

FIGURE 12.10

This figure is from the Palm Beach County, FL web site (http://www.pbcgov.com). Note the "breadcrumbs" near the top to explain how the user got to this page (Website Information), and the list of common icons provided on the right to familiarize novice users with the symbols used on the web site.

eye gazing, and voice. There are various screen-reader programs, such as Freedom Scientific JAWS, GW Micro's Window-Eyes, and IBM's Home Page Reader (Section 1.4.5). Documentation writers need to be aware that the material will be heard, not viewed. Long, wordy paragraphs will not be well understood in this environment. Writing in short sections and subsections is the preferred method.

Sometimes documentation may need to be used hands-free. This may be an environmental issue (when hands are busy) or one caused by a disability. Speech is the typical input modality supplied with these systems, and the output modality may be visual or auditory. The use of augmented-reality applications may have some potential (Ward and Novick, 2003). Some devices may not have a display, and speech may be the single output modality. This offers additional new challenges for designers (Kehoe and Pitt, 2006).

12.6 Online Tutorials and Animated Demonstrations

An online tutorial is an interactive training environment in which users can view explanatory descriptions of user-interface objects and actions, often tied to realistic task scenarios. There are many approaches to the use of electronic

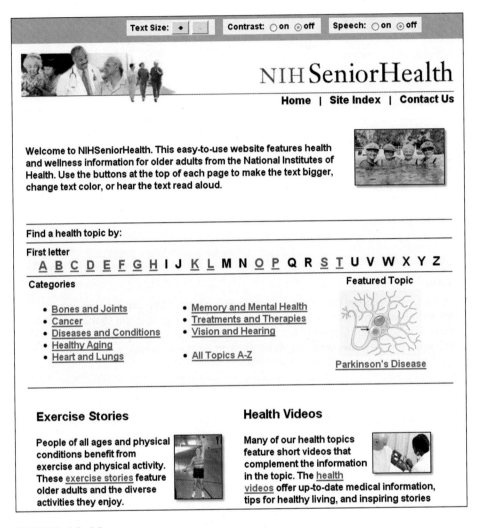

FIGURE 12.11
The National Institute for Health's site for seniors (http://www.nihseniorhealth.gov) has controls to adjust the text size, turn the contrast on or off, and turn speech on or off. The font used is a sans-serif font, and the font size is larger than the typical size used on the Web. Several ways are provided to navigate through the information (alphabetical, grouping by category, etc.).

media to teach users how to master an interface. Depending on the complexity of the interface and the amount of time users are ready to spend absorbing the tutorial materials, they might be served well by an extensive computer-based training module, an animated demonstration of features, or a recorded welcome message by a familiar person. The challenge often is to prepare materials that will satisfy users who want a three-minute introduction as well as those who need a one-hour in-depth treatment. This section reviews a range of online possibilities, from textual and graphical tutorials to fully animated demonstrations.

A more ambitious approach to training is based on a complex model of learning patterns tied to carefully designed educational tutorials that guide users and correct their mistakes. These have demonstrated impressive outcomes, but the success stories are based on years of development, testing, and refinement. The successful designs provide clear challenges, helpful tools, and excellent feedback (Section 7.4.5). They do not depend on natural-language interaction, but rather, they provide users with a clear context in which to work and control their learning experience.

12.6.1 Online tutorials

One introductory tutorial for the Adobe Photoshop® package displays the exact steps users must make, and then shows the actions being carried out using a recorded demonstration. Users just keep pressing the space-bar key to speed through the demonstration. Some users find this guided approach attractive; others are put off by the restrictive sequencing that prevents errors and exploration. Automated tutorials can be created using Autodemo® and Show Me How Videos™. Autodemo has arrangements with several worldwide companies and provides specific instructions on navigating the various web sites (Fig. 12.12).

The opportunity for carrying out *practice tasks* during online tutorials is one of their greatest strengths. Getting users to be active is one of the key tenets of the minimal-manual approach, and it applies especially well to online tutorials. One study of hands-on practice methods for learning software compared free exploration, exercises, and a combined format consisting of an exercise followed by free exploration. The type of practice did not affect the performance of the low-experience subjects, but the performance of high-experienced subjects significantly improved when they were trained using exercises (Wiedenbeck and Zila, 1997).

Creators of interactive tutorials must address the usual questions of instructional design and also the novelty of the computer environment. A library of common tasks for users to practice is a great help. Sample documents for word processors, slides for presentation software, and maps for geographic-information systems help users to experience the applications. Repeated testing and refinement is highly recommended for tutorials.

One attractive variant is the start-up tip: Each time users start the interface, they get a pop-up box displaying a brief explanation of a feature. Some systems monitor user behavior and show start-up tips only for features that are not used by this particular user. Of course, the user should always be given the option to turn off these tips at any time.

FIGURE 12.12
This is a screen capture from part of the priceline demo available from Autodemo (http://www.autodemo.com). The user can choose whether to listen to the demo or view the demo with explanatory text. This is Section 2 of 9 provided as part of the demo. On the right, there is a pop-up box with help and further explanation.

12.6.2 Animated demonstrations and multimedia

Animated demonstrations have become a modern high-tech art form. Manufacturers originally designed them mostly to attract potential users of software or hardware by showing off system features using the best animations, color graphics, sound, and information presentation that advertising agencies could produce. Those demonstrations focused on building a positive product image. More recently, demonstrations have become a standard technique to train users as they work. The focus in this case is on demonstrating step-by-step procedures and explaining the results of the actions (Woolf, 2008). Automatic pacing and manual control satisfy hands-off and hands-on users, respectively. Use of standard playback controls allows users to stop, replay, or skip parts and adds to their acceptability.

An animated demonstration can be prepared as a slide show, a screen-capture animation, or a video recording of a person using the device. A slide show might be appropriate for form fill-in or menu-based interfaces, but animation is preferable to demonstrate direct-manipulation interactions such as drag-and-drop operations, zoom boxes, or dynamic-query sliders. A screen-capture animation is easy to produce with standard tools such as Camtasia Studio® and Flash. These recordings can then be saved, possibly annotated or narrated, and replayed automatically by users. In our own explorations, we found that users appreciated recorded voice explanations, which make the demonstrations livelier and lead to more compact demonstrations; however, providing scripts and subtitles is necessary to address the needs of users with disabilities. Also, a video recording of a person using the interface can help clarify how special hardware is to be used—for example, to demonstrate the two-handed operation of a drawing system or the unfolding of a telephone keyboard accessory.

Animated demonstrations have been shown to be more effective at conveying the purpose and use of a tool than static explanations (Baecker et al., 1991; Sukaviriya and Foley, 1990). Users have also been shown to perform tasks faster and more accurately after being shown animated demonstrations rather than given textual explanations. Surprisingly, however, the time and error effect was reversed after a week, showing limitations to the benefits of using animations as teaching tools (Palmiter and Elkerton, 1991). The authors suggest reinforcing the animations (which were nonsegmented—that is, in one continuous execution) with textual explanations. Segmenting the animations may also help comprehension and retention. Other studies show that even when animations do not have clear benefits for learners, users usually enjoy this presentation style (Payne, et al., 1992; Harrison, 1995).

Novice users are sometimes overwhelmed by the complexity of today's interfaces. Supplying excellent documentation can aid their understanding, but sometimes the interface needs to be simplified. A *multi-layered interface design* that can unfold and further challenge and encourage users as they become more accomplished is a good approach (Kang et al., 2003). Allowing users to move through 3, 8, or more layers, which is a great success in game design, can help users gracefully learn the numerous features of productivity applications (Shneiderman, 2003). For example, the multi-layered design of Dynamap® allows novices to start with a simple interface consisting of only a map in Level 1 (Fig. 12.13) and to move up to Level 2 or Level 3 when they are ready, adding dynamic-query filters and a scatter plot, respectively. "Show me" demonstrations can be launched from within the live interface itself. This greater level of integration in the application permits users to alternate between watching a demonstration and trying other steps by themselves.

Computer-game designers deserve credit for advancing the art of the animated demonstration, with lively introductions that show samples of how the games are played. With public kiosk games, the motivation is clear: getting users to put their money in the machine. Demonstrations and previews have to explain the game and make it seem appealing and challenging, all within 30 seconds.

At the IBM Toronto Software Laboratory, a case study (Davison et al., 2005) culminated in the creation of an e-book to "explain" DB2 Universal Database®. The final product was a comic-book–like implementation including the

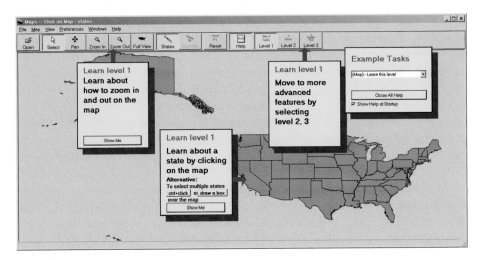

FIGURE 12.13

Dynamap is a multi-layered interface with three levels. Level 1, shown here, consists only of a map. Sticky notes introduce the main functions and example tasks. The "show me" buttons initiate animated demonstrations that activate the interface itself. Users can advance through the demonstration step by step or execute the commands themselves, following the directions. A sticky note also points to the buttons allowing users to move to Levels 2 and 3.

characters SuperDBA and DB2 Sidekick. It became the most downloaded e-book in *DB2 Magazine*'s history. Although this implementation was successful, there were some limitations that are being investigated further (e.g., although it could do screen captures, it lacked the ability to print).

A second part of Davison et al.'s research investigated static diagrams versus animation. Their results confirmed what others had found: that both forms have strengths and weaknesses. Another study (Hailey, 2004) made extensive use of animation and virtual reality in documentation with good success. The software tools used included: Maya® by Alias/Wavefront™, 3D Studio Max® by Discreet Software™, Virtools™ Dev 3.0, and GarageGames® Torque Game Engine™. Obviously, the gaming software development industry is heavily competing for this market.

12.7 Online Communities for User Assistance

Instead of natural-language conversations with computers to get help, interaction with other people online is proving to be effective and popular. This communal approach may employ e-mail, chat, or instant messaging for question

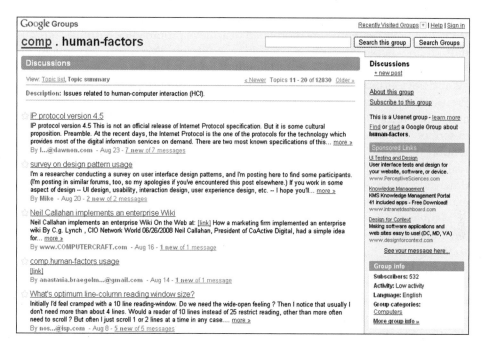

FIGURE 12.14

Using Google Groups (http://groups.google.com), users can post questions on discussion boards and get answers from other users. Each group has a list of threads, and a directory helps users find the most appropriate group. Related groups are also shown. The comp.human-factors group (http://groups.google.com/group/comp.human-factors/topics?lnk) contains links to over 12,800 topics related to human-computer interaction.

asking and responses (Novick et al., 2007). Questions can be sent to a designated help desk or staff member, or posted on a discussion board (Fig. 12.14 and Section 9.3.2). Responses can be received in seconds or, more typically, minutes or hours. In one simple but positive example, a broadcast message produced the answer to a user's query in 42 seconds:

```
Time: 18:57:10
From: <azir>
 after i change a list to a group, how long before I can use it?
Time: 18:57:52
From: starlight on a moonless night <clee>
 you can use it immediately
```

The communal broadcast approach is increasingly appealing because of the low cost to software maintenance organizations and help-desk staff. Many respondents get a sense of satisfaction from being able to help others and demonstrate their abilities. Some are motivated to achieve prominence within a community in the hope of gaining consulting contracts. Microsoft has made an ambitious effort to use online communities to provide assistance for professionals and novices (Smith, 2002). It rewards active contributors with a Most Valuable Professional citation on the web site, thereby steering consulting opportunities and other recognition towards these active contributors. Microsoft's web site describes the awardees as "exceptional technical community leaders from around the world who are awarded for voluntarily sharing their high quality, real world expertise in offline and online technical communities." Of course, the downside of broadcasting appeals for assistance is that users must publicly expose their lack of knowledge and risk getting incorrect advice.

Many web sites now provide e-mail contact information as opposed to written addresses or phone numbers. Also, to prevent basic questions from tying up staff resources, managers of help desks often record common questions and answers into files of FAQs. This enables newcomers to browse typical problems that have been discussed in the past. These files are often searchable and organized by type of issue or some other hierarchical scheme.

Today, going to the Web for information of all types is considered standard practice. The simple interface of the ubiquitous Google search screen (Fig. 1.12A) is commonly used. The online choices out there are many and varied, but users need to be aware that not all information is correct and valid.

Although companies may provide a host of online facilities for information and advice, people are still very comfortable with asking the office "guru" for help (Novick and Ward, 2006b). Human-to-human communication removes some of the barriers found with more traditional documentation: Lack of understanding can be handled quickly and without consequences of errors, and the human-to-human interface offers interactivity and other cues that enhance understanding.

12.8 The Development Process

Recognizing the difference between good and bad user documentation is necessary for producing successful documentation on time and within a reasonable budget. Production of any documentation, like any project, must be managed properly, handled by suitable personnel, and monitored with appropriate milestones (Box 12.3).

Getting started early is invaluable. If the documentation-writing process begins before the implementation, there will be adequate time for review, testing, and refinement. Furthermore, the user documentation can act as a more complete and comprehensible alternative to the formal specification for the software. Implementers may miss or misunderstand some of the design requirements when reading a formal specification; well-written user documentation may clarify the

BOX 12.3
Development process guidelines.

- Seek professional writers and copywriters.
- Prepare user documentation early (before implementation).
- Set up guidelines documents and coordinate and integrate across all involved departments.
- Review drafts thoroughly.
- Field-test early editions.
- Provide a feedback mechanisms for readers.
- Revise to reflect changes regularly.

design. The writer becomes an effective critic, reviewer, and question asker who can stimulate the implementation team. Early development of the documentation also enables pilot testing of the software's learnability even before the interface is built. In the months before the software is completed, the documentation may be the best way to convey the designers' intentions to potential customers and users, as well as to implementers and project managers.

Informal walkthroughs with users are usually an enlightening experience for software designers and writers. Potential users are asked to read through the documentation and to describe aloud what they are seeing and learning as well as what they think might be missing. Field trials with moderate numbers of users constitute a further process for identifying problems with the user documentation and the software. Field trials can range in scope from half an hour with a half-dozen people to several months with thousands of users. One effective and simple strategy is for field-trial users to mark up the documentation while they are using it, allowing them to rapidly indicate typos, misleading information, and confusing sections.

Software and its accompanying documentation are rarely truly completed. Rather, they undergo a continuous process of evolutionary refinement. Each version eliminates known errors, adds refinements, and extends the functionality. If the users can communicate with the writers, there is a greater chance of rapid improvement. When possible, keeping logs of the use of help materials and help-desk calls will determine which parts of the system need modification.

Quite often, this development work is performed by different groups of people that may be geographically dispersed in the same company, or some of the work may be "contracted out." However, it is important that the user sees a smooth and integrated view. This means attention to common colors, logos, terminology, and style. Standardized guidelines must be established and adhered to (Section 2.2), and the documentation, the associated software, and all the packaging must represent an integrated system.

Practitioner's Summary

Documentation (paper and online), online help, online communities for user assistance, and tutorials can determine the success or failure of a software product, mobile device, or web service. Sufficient personnel, money, and time should be allocated to producing these support materials. Documentation and online help should be developed before the implementation to help the development team to define the interface and to allow adequate time for testing. All documentation and online help should be tailored to specific user communities and to accomplishment of specific goals (for example, offering task instruction or describing interface objects and actions). Instructional examples should be realistic, encourage active exploration with exercises, use consistent terminology, and support error recognition and recovery. Animated demonstrations should be used when possible. Online guidance can lend a human touch if it contains presentations by real humans or appropriate animated characters. Social media participation through newsgroups, listservers, online communities, e-mail, chat, blogs, and instant messaging provides powerful low-cost support mechanisms. Where possible, explore a multilayer user interface that promotes graceful evolution as user skills increase.

Researcher's Agenda

The main advantage of online materials is the potential for rapid retrieval and traversal, but little is known about how to offer this advantage conveniently without overwhelming novice users. Cognitive models of how animated, integrated demos facilitate learning require better understanding to guide designers. Users' navigation of online help systems should be recorded and studied, so that we can gain a better understanding of what characterizes effective help strategies. Better strategies for integrating help directly in the user interface are needed. Multilayered designs in which users can select their level of expertise seem helpful, but further testing and refinement are necessary. Better understanding of reading patterns using electronic documents is also needed, as is further research and understanding regarding special populations and their specific design criteria.

WORLD WIDE WEB RESOURCES
http://www.aw.com/DTUI/

Online examples of tutorials and demonstrations that aid in the process of providing assistance to the users are given. In addition, samples from online communities for user assistance.

References

Alpert, Sherman R., Singley, Mark K., and Carroll, John M., Multiple multimodal mentors: Delivering computer-based instruction via specialized anthropomorphic advisors, *Behaviour & Information Technology* 14, 2 (1995), 69–79.

Baecker, Ronald, Small, Ian, and Mander, Richard, Bringing icons to life, *Proc. CHI '91 Conference: Human Factors in Computing Systems*, ACM Press, New York (1991), 1–6.

Carroll, J. M., *Minimalism Beyond the Nurnberg Funnel*, MIT Press, Cambridge, MA (1998).

Carroll, J. M. and Aaronson, A. P., Learning by doing with simulated intelligent help, *Communications of the ACM* 31, 9 (September 1988), 1064–1079.

Carroll, J. M. and Mack, R. L., Learning to use a word processor: By doing, by thinking, and by knowing, in Thomas, J. C. and Schneider, M. (Editors), *Human Factors in Computing Systems*, Ablex, Norwood, NJ (1984), 13–51.

Chimera, R. and Shneiderman, B., Evaluating three user interfaces for browsing tables of contents, *ACM Transactions on Information Systems* 12, 4 (October 1994), 383–406.

Cohill, A. M. and Williges, R. C., Computer-augmented retrieval of HELP information for novice users, *Proc. Human Factors Society—Twenty-Sixth Annual Meeting*, Human Factors Society, Santa Monica, CA (1982), 79–82.

Davison, Gord, Murphy, Steve, and Wong, Rebecca, The use of ebooks and interactive multimedia as alternative forms of technical documentation, *Proc. International Conference on Documentation*, ACM Press, New York (2005), 108–115.

Dong, Qiumin, Cross-cultural considerations in instructional documentation: Contrasting Chinese and U.S. home heater manuals, *Proc. International Conference on Documentation*, ACM Press, New York (2007), 221–228.

Frampton, Beth, Use as directed: Developing effective operations and maintenance manuals, *Intercom*, STC (June 2008), 6–9.

Galitz, Wilbert O., *The Essential Guide to User Interface Design, Third Edition*, John Wiley & Sons, New York (2007).

Grant, Allan, Homo quintadus, computers and ROOMS (repetitive ocular orthopedic motion stress), *Optometry and Vision Science* 67, 4 (1990), 297–305.

Hackos, J. T., *Information Development: Managing Your Documentation Projects, Portfolio, and People*, John Wiley & Sons, New York (2006).

Hackos, J. T. and Stevens, D. M., *Standards for Online Communication*, John Wiley & Sons, New York (1997).

Hailey, David E., A next generation of digital genres: Expanding documentation into animation and virtual reality, *Proc. International Conference on Documentation*, ACM Press, New York (2004), 19–26.

Harrison, Susan M., A comparison of still, animated, or non-illustrated on-line help with written or spoken instructions in a graphic user interface, *Proc. CHI '95 Conference: Human Factors in Computing Systems*, ACM Press, New York (1995), 82–89.

Hook, K., Steps to take before intelligent user interfaces become real, *Interacting with Computers* 12, 4 (2000), 409–426.

Hornbaek, Kasper and Frokjaer, Erik, Reading patterns and usability in visualizations of electronic documents, *ACM Transactions on Computer-Human Interaction* 10, 2 (June 2003), 119–143.

Horton, William K., *Designing and Writing Online Documentation: Hypermedia for Self-Supporting Products*, John Wiley & Sons, New York (1994).

Horvitz, E., Principles of mixed-initiative user interfaces, *Proc. CHI '99 Conference: Human Factors in Computing Systems*, ACM Press, New York (1999), 159–166.

Kang, H., Plaisant, C., and Shneiderman, B., New approaches to help users get started with visual interfaces: Multi-layered interfaces and integrated initial guidance, *Proc. Digital Government Research Conference*, Boston, MA (May 2003), 141–146.

Kehoe, Aidan and Pitt, Ian, Designing help topics for use with text-to-speech, *Proc. International Conference on Documentation*, ACM Press, New York (2006), 157–163.

Lannon, John M., *Technical Communication, Eleventh Edition*, Longman, New York (2007).

Lieberman, H., Autonomous interface agents, *Proc. CHI '97 Conference: Human Factors in Computing Systems*, ACM Press, New York (1997), 67–74.

Lieberman, H., Interfaces that give and take advice, in Carroll, John M. (Editor), *Human-Computer Interaction in the New Millennium*, ACM Press, New York (2001), 475–485.

Mager, Robert F., *Preparing Instructional Objectives: A Critical Tool in the Development of Effective Instruction*, Center for Effective Performance, Atlanta, GA (1997).

Magers, Celeste S., An experimental evaluation of on-line HELP for non-programmers, *Proc. CHI '83 Conference: Human Factors in Computing Systems*, ACM Press, New York (1983), 277–281.

Mandel, Theo, Quality technical information: Paving the way for usable print and web interface design, *ACM Journal of Computer Documentation* 26 (2002), 118–125.

Mao, J.-Y. and Leung, Y. W., Exploring the potential of unobtrusive proactive task support, *Interacting with Computers* 15, 2 (2003), 265–288.

Mehlenbacher, Brad, Documentation: Not yet implemented but coming soon, in Sears, Andrew and Jacko, Julie A. (Editors), *The Human-Computer Interaction Handbook: Fundamentals, Evolving Technologies and Emerging Applications*, Lawrence Erlbaum Associates, Mahwah, NJ (2008), 527–543.

Nielsen, Jakob, F-Shaped pattern for reading web content, Jakob Neilsen's Alertbox (April 17, 2006). Available at http://www.useit.com/alertbox/reading_pattern.html.

Novick, David G., Elizalde, Edith, and Bean, Nathaniel, Toward a more accurate view of when and how people seek help with computer applications, *Proc. International Conference on Documentation*, ACM Press, New York (2007), 95–102.

Novick, David G. and Ward, Karen, What users say they want in documentation, *Proc. International Conference on Documentation*, ACM Press, New York (2006a), 84–91.

Novick, David G. and Ward, Karen, Why don't people read the manual, *Proc. International Conference on Documentation*, ACM Press, New York (2006b), 11–18.

Palmiter, Susan and Elkerton, Jay, An evaluation of animated demonstrations for learning computer-based tasks, *Proc. CHI '91 Conference: Human Factors in Computing Systems*, ACM Press, New York (1991), 257–263.

Payne, S. J., Chesworth, L., and Hill, E., Animated demonstrations for exploratory learners, *Interacting with Computers* 4 (1992), 3–22.

Redish, Janice (Ginny), *Letting Go of the Words: Writing Web Content that Works*, Morgan Kaufmann, San Francisco, CA (2007).

Rieman, John, A field study of exploratory learning strategies, *ACM Transactions on Computer-Human Interaction* 3, 3 (September 1996), 189–218.

Robinson, Patricia and Etter, Ryn, *Writing and Designing Manuals, Third Edition*, CRC Press, Boca Raton, FL (2000).

Russell, John, Making it personal: Information that adapts to the reader, *Proc. International Conference on Documentation*, ACM Press, New York (2003), 160–166.

Shneiderman, Ben, Promoting universal usability with multi-layer interface design, *ACM Conference on Universal Usability*, ACM Press, New York (2003), 1-8.

Shroyer, R., Actual readers versus implied readers: Role conflicts in Office 97, *Technical Communication* 47, 2 (2000), 238–240.

Smart, Karl L., Whiting, Matthew, and DeTienne, Kristen Bell, Assessing the need for printed and online documentation: A study of customer preference and use, *Journal of Business Communication* 38, 3, (2001), 285–314.

Smith, Marc, Supporting community and building social capital: Tools for navigating large social cyberspaces, *Communications of the ACM* 45, 4 (2002), 51–55.

Strunk, Jr., William, White, E. B., and Angell, Roger, *The Elements of Style, Fourth Edition*, Allyn & Bacon, New York (2000).

Sukaviriya, Piyawadee "Noi" and Foley, James D., Coupling a UI framework with automatic generation of context-sensitive animated help, *Proc. UIST '90 Symposium on User Interface Software & Technology*, ACM Press, New York (1990), 152–166.

Tilley, Scott, Computer documentation for senior citizens, *Proc. International Conference on Documentation*, ACM Press, New York (2003), 143–146.

van der Meij, Hans and Carroll, John M., Principles and heuristics in designing minimalist instruction, *Technical Communication* (Second Quarter 1995), 243–261.

van Horen, Floor, Jansen, Carel, Noordman, Leo and Maes, Alfons, Manuals for the elderly: Text characteristics that help or hinder older users, in Hayhoe, George F. and Grady, Helen M. (Editors), *Connecting with Technology: Issues in Professional Communication*, Baywood Publishing Compnay, Inc., Amityville, NY (2009), 43–53.

Ward, Karen and Novick, David G., Hands-free documentation, *Proc. International Conference on Documentation*, ACM Press, New York (2003), 147–154.

Warren, Thomas L., *Cross-Cultural Communication: Perspectives in Theory and Practice*, Baywood, Amityville, NY (2006).

Wiedenbeck, S. and Zila, P. L., Hands-on practice in learning to use software: A comparison of exercise, exploration, and combined formats, *ACM Transactions on Computer-Human Interaction* 4, 2 (June 1997), 169–196.

Woolf, Beverly, *Building Intelligent Interactive Tutors: Student-Centered Strategies for Revolutionizing E-Learning*, Morgan Kaufmann, San Francisco, CA (2008).

Zinsser, William, *On Writing Well, Thirtieth Anniversary Edition*, Harper Collins, New York (2006).

CHAPTER 13

Information Search

> 66 The gods of the earth and sea
>
> Sought through nature to find this tree.
>
> But their search was all in vain:
>
> There grows one in the human brain. 99
>
> **William Blake**

13.1 Introduction

Information exploration should be a joyous experience, but many commentators talk of information overload and anxiety (Wurman, 1989). Still, there is promising evidence that the new generation of digital libraries and databases will enable convenient exploration of growing information spaces by a wider range of users. User-interface designers are inventing more powerful search methods, while offering smoother integration of technology with tasks (Hearst, 2009).

The terminology swirl in this domain is especially colorful. The older terms *information retrieval* (often applied to bibliographic and textual document systems) and *database management* (often applied to more structured relational database systems with orderly attributes and sort keys) are being pushed aside by newer notions of *information gathering, seeking, filtering, collaborative filtering, sensemaking,* and *visual analytics.* Computer scientists now focus on the huge volumes of available data and talk about *data mining* from *data warehouses* and *data marts,* while visionaries talk about *knowledge networks* or *semantic webs.* The distinctions are subtle; the common goals range from finding in a large collection a narrow set of items that satisfy a well-understood information need (a *known-item search*) to making sense of information or discovering unexpected patterns within a collection (Marchionini and White, 2007).

Exploring an information collection becomes increasingly difficult as the volume and diversity of the collection grows. A page of information is easy to explore, but when the source of information is the size of a book, a library, or even larger, it may be difficult to locate known items or to browse to gain an overview. The computer is a powerful tool for searching, but older user interfaces were often a serious hurdle for novice users (complex commands, Boolean operators, unwieldy concepts) and challenging even for experts (difficulty in repeating searches across multiple databases, weak methods for discovering where to narrow broad searches, poor integration with other tools). This chapter reviews interfaces appropriate for first-time or intermittent versus frequent computer users and also for task novices versus experts. Improvements on traditional text and multimedia searching seem possible as a new generation of strategies for query formulation and information presentation emerges (see also Chapter 14).

First-time users of an information-exploration system (whether they have little or much task knowledge) often struggle to understand what they see on the display while keeping in mind their information needs. They will be distracted if they have to learn elaborate query languages or master complex interactive controls. They need the low cognitive burdens of the simple keyword search functionality provided by menu and direct-manipulation designs. As users gain experience with the interface, they can request additional features by adjusting control panels or manipulating previews and overviews of the information available. Knowledgeable and frequent users want a wide range of search tools with many options that allow them to compose, save, replay, and revise increasingly elaborate query plans.

To facilitate discussion, we need to define a few terms. *Task objects*, such as movies for rent or sports-video segments from the Olympics, are stored in structured relational databases, textual document libraries, or multimedia document libraries. A *structured relational database* consists of *relations* and a *schema* to describe the relations. Relations have *items* (usually called *tuples* or *records*), and each item has multiple *attributes* (often called *fields*), which each have *attribute values*. In the relational model, items form an unordered set (although one attribute can contain sequencing information or be a unique key to identify or sort the other items), and attributes are *atomic*.

A *textual document library* consists of a set of *collections* (typically up to a few hundred collections per library) plus some *descriptive attributes* or *metadata* about the library (for example, name, location, owner). Each collection also has a name and some other descriptive attributes (for example, location, media type, curator, donor, dates, and geographic coverage), and a set of items (typically 10 to 100,000 items per collection). Items in a collection may vary greatly, but usually a superset of attributes exists that covers all the items. Attributes may be blank, have single values, have multiple values, or be lengthy texts. A collection is typically owned by a single library, and an item typically belongs to a single collection. A *multimedia document library* consists of collections of documents that can contain images, scanned documents, sound, video, animations, datasets, and so on. *Digital libraries* are generally sets of carefully selected and cataloged collections, while *digital archives* tend to be more loosely organized. *Directories* hold metadata about the items in a library and point users to the appropriate locations (for example, the NASA Global Change Master Directory helps scientists locate datasets in NASA's archives). Items in *unstructured collections* like the World Wide Web have fewer attributes: These may include the file format or date created. Tools are appearing that extract features automatically (e.g., topic or name entity extraction) or facilitate user tagging and annotation of items.

This dynamically created metadata becomes available to interface designers, but scalability and accuracy are often issues.

Task actions are decomposed into *browsing* or *searching* and are carried out by scrolling, zooming, joining, or linking. Structured tasks can range from specific fact finding, where there is a single readily identifiable outcome, to more extended fact finding with uncertain but replicable outcomes. Relatively unstructured tasks include exploration of the availability of information on a topic, open-ended browsing of known collections, or complex analysis of problems and are also referred to as *exploratory searches*. Here are some examples of task actions:

- Specific fact finding (known-item search)
  - Find the e-mail address of the President of the United States.
  - Find the highest-resolution LANDSAT image of College Park at 10 A.M. on July 26, 2008.
- Extended fact finding
  - What other books are by the author of *Jurassic Park*?
  - How do Maryland and Virginia counties compare on the Consumer Price Index in 2009?
- Exploration of availability
  - What genealogical information is available in the National Archives?
  - Is there new work on voice recognition in the ACM digital library?
- Open-ended browsing and problem analysis
  - Does the Mathew Brady Civil War photo collection show the role of women in that war?
  - Is there promising new research on fibromyalgia that might help my patient?

Once users have clarified their information needs, the first step towards satisfying those needs is deciding where to search. The conversion of information needs (stated in task-domain terminology) to interface actions is a large cognitive step. Once this is done, users can express these actions in a query language or via a series of mouse selections.

Supplemental *finding aids* can help users to clarify and pursue their information needs. Examples include tables of contents or indexes in books, descriptive introductions, and subject classifications. Careful understanding of the task, and of previous and potential future search requests, can improve search results by allowing the system to offer hot-topic lists and useful classification schemes. For example, the U.S. Congressional Research Service maintains a list of approximately 80 hot topics covering current bills before Congress and has 5,000 terms in its Legislative Indexing Vocabulary. The National Library of Medicine maintains the Medical Subject Headings (MeSH), with 24,000 items in a seven-level hierarchy, and the Gene Ontology Database has more than 15,000 genes organized in a 19-level hierarchy, with many genes appearing at multiple nodes.

Additional *preview and overview surrogates* for items and collections can be created to facilitate browsing (Greene et al., 2000). Graphical overviews indicate scope, size, or structure and help gauge the relevance of collections. Previews consisting of samples entice users and help them define productive queries.

Section 13.2 presents full-text search and database query strategies and introduces a five-stage search framework. Section 13.3 reviews the special case of multimedia documents, and Section 13.4 covers advanced search and filter interfaces.

13.2 Searching in Textual Documents and Database Querying

The way users conduct searches has undergone dramatic changes over the past decade. Once reserved for experts who had mastered cryptic languages, searching vast computer archives is now fully feasible for a broad spectrum of users, ranging from children preparing school reports to patients looking for possible medical treatments and researchers looking for up-to-date results or experts to consult.

World Wide Web search engines have greatly improved their performance by making use of statistical rankings and the information latent in the Web's hyperlink structure. For example, the search engine Google implements a link-based ranking measure called PageRank to compute a query-independent score for each document, taking into consideration the importance of the pages that point to a given page. Thanks to the redundancy of information on the Web, results almost always return some relevant documents, and they allow users to find answers by following hyperlinks. For example, to find an expert on information retrieval, users might first find papers on that topic, leading to identifying a major journal publication, the editors of the journal, and their personal web pages. However, empirical evaluation of the current algorithms shows that the quality of the relevant documents retrieved could still be improved (Agichtein et al., 2006).

Database searches have become widespread as the general public turns to the World Wide Web to reserve travel packages, shop for groceries, search digital libraries of children's books, and more. Specialized databases also help lawyers find relevant court cases and scientists locate the scientific data they need. The Structured Query Language (SQL) remains a widespread standard for searching such structured relational database systems and often is the underlying query mechanism hidden under a more accessible front end. Using SQL, expert users can write queries that specify matches on attribute values, such as author, date of publication, language, or publisher. Each document has values for the attributes, and database-management methods enable rapid retrieval, even with millions of documents. For example, an SQL-like command might be:

```
SELECT DOCUMENT#
FROM JOURNAL-DB
WHERE    (DATE >= 2004 AND DATE <= 2008)
   AND   (LANGUAGE = ENGLISH OR FRENCH)
   AND   (PUBLISHER = ASIST OR HFES OR ACM)
```

SQL has powerful features, but using it requires training (2 to 20 hours), and even then users make frequent errors for many classes of queries (Chapter 7).

Natural-language queries (for example, "please list the documents that deal with . . .") are meant to be appealing to users, but the computer's capacity for processing such queries is often limited to eliminating frequent terms or commands and searching for the remaining words, leading to user frustration (Section 7.4). Research continues on this topic.

Form fill-in queries (Section 6.7) have substantially simplified query formulation while still allowing some Boolean combinations to be made available (usually a conjunction of disjuncts, or ORs, within attributes, with ANDs between attributes). A more powerful approach that extends the form fill-in idea is *query by example* (QBE), in which users enter attribute values and some keywords in relational table templates. This approach has influenced modern systems but is no longer a major interface.

Other novel interface styles, such as faceted searching and searching by example, are discussed in Section 13.4. First, however, we'll discuss basic design principles that apply to search interfaces.

Providing powerful search capabilities without overwhelming novice users remains a challenge, usually addressed by providing both simple and advanced search interfaces: The simple interface allows users to specify phrases that are searched in all the fields, while the advanced interface allows users to specify more precise terms or restrict the search to specific fields (Fig. 13.1). Unfortunately, interfaces often either hide important aspects of the search (whether by poor design or to protect proprietary relevance-ranking schemes) or make the advanced query specification so difficult as to discourage its use. Evidence from empirical studies shows that users perform better and have higher subjective satisfaction when they can view and control the search (Koenemann and Belkin, 1996), but the lack of consistency between search interfaces means that users have to rediscover how to search each time they use a different system. An analogy to the evolution of automobile user interfaces might clarify the need for standardization of search interfaces. Early competitors offered a profusion of controls, and

FIGURE 13.1

The advanced search interface at the U.S. Library of Congress's web site (http://www. loc.gov/thomas/) helps users find bills—that is, proposed legislation—that were debated in Congress during current or past years. Controls are available to select the scope of the search and allow variants. Help buttons are provided for complex terms.

each manufacturer had a distinct design. Some designs—such as having a brake pedal that was far from the gas pedal—were dangerous. Furthermore, if you were accustomed to driving a car with the brake to the left of the gas pedal and your neighbor's car had the reverse design, it might be risky to trade cars. It took half a century to achieve good design and appropriate consistency in automobiles; let's hope we can make the transition faster for text-search user interfaces!

One design aspect that has reached the status of a standard is the provision of a simple search interface with a link to the advanced search interface. The simple interface consists of a single field in which to enter terms and a button to start the search (see, for example, Fig. 1.12A). In designing the advanced interface, a *five-stage framework* may help to coordinate design practices and satisfy the needs of first-time, intermittent, and frequent users. The five stages of action (extending the ideas in Shneiderman et al., 1997), illustrated more fully in Box 13.1, are:

1. *Formulation:* expressing the search
2. *Initiation of action:* launching the search
3. *Review of results:* reading messages and outcomes
4. *Refinement:* formulating the next step
5. *Use:* compiling or disseminating insight

The formulation stage includes identifying the *source* of the information, the *fields* for limiting the source, the *phrases,* and the *variants* (Fig. 13.1). Even if it's technically and economically feasible, searching all libraries or all collections in a library is not always the best approach. Users often prefer to limit the sources to a specific library or a specific collection in a library. They may also limit their searches to specific fields (for example, to the title or abstract of a scientific article), and the sources might be further restricted by structured fields such as year of publication, volume number, or language.

In textual databases, users typically seek items that contain meaningful phrases (`Civil War, Environmental Protection Agency, carbon monoxide`), and multiple-entry fields can be provided to allow for multiple phrases. Searches on phrases have proven to be more accurate than searches on individual words. Phrases also facilitate searching for names (for example, a search on `George Washington` should not turn up `George Bush` or `Washington, D. C.`). Since variations in wording may cause some relevant items to be missed by a phrase approach, though, users should have the option to expand a search by breaking the phrases into separate words. If Boolean operations, proximity restrictions, or other combining strategies are specifiable, users should also be able to express them. Users or service providers should additionally have control over stop lists (which typically filter out from the search terms common words, single letters, and obscenities).

When users are unsure of the exact value of the field (the terms to be searched for or the spelling or capitalization of a name), they may need to relax the search constraints by allowing variants to be accepted. In structured databases, the variants may include a wider range on a numeric attribute. In a textual-document search, interfaces should allow user control over variant capitalization (case sensitivity), stemmed versions (the keyword `teach` retrieves variant suffixes such as `teacher, teaching,` or `teaches`), partial matches (the keyword `biology` retrieves `sociobiology` and `astrobiology`), phonetic variants from soundex methods (the keyword `Johnson` retrieves `Jonson, Jansen,` and `Johnsson`),

BOX 13.1

Five-phase framework to clarify user interfaces for textual search.

1. **Formulation**
   - Provide access to the appropriate sources in libraries and collections.
   - Use *fields* for limiting the source: structured fields such as year, media, or language; and text fields such as titles or abstracts of documents.
   - Recognize *phrases* to allow entry of names, such as George Washington or Environmental Protection Agency, and concepts, such as abortion rights reform or gallium arsenide.
   - Permit *variants* to allow relaxation of search constraints, such as case sensitivity, stemming, partial matches, phonetic variations, abbreviations, or synonyms from a thesaurus.
   - Control the size of the result set.

2. **Initiation of action**
   - Include *explicit actions* initiated by buttons with consistent labels (such as "Search"), locations, sizes, and colors.
   - Include *implicit actions* initiated by changes to a parameter of the formulation phase that immediately produce new sets of search results.

3. **Review of results**
   - Present explanatory messages.
   - View an overview of the results and previews of items.
   - Manipulate visualizations.
   - Adjust the size of the result set and which fields are displayed.
   - Change the sequencing (alphabetical, chronological, relevance ranked, and so on).
   - Explore clustering (by attribute value, topics, and so on).
   - Examine selected items.

4. **Refinement**
   - Use meaningful messages to guide users in progressive refinement; for example, if the two words in a phrase are not found near each other, offer easy selection of individual words or variants.
   - Make changing of search parameters convenient.
   - Explore relevance feedback.

5. **Use**
   - Allow queries, parameter settings, and results to be saved and annotated, sent by e-mail, or used as input to other programs (such as visualization or statistical tools).

synonyms (the keyword cancer retrieves malignant neoplasm), abbreviations (the keyword IBM retrieves International Business Machines, and vice versa), and broader or narrower terms from a thesaurus (the keyphrase New England retrieves Vermont, Maine, Rhode Island, New Hampshire, Massachusetts, and Connecticut).

The second stage is the *initiation of action*, which may be explicit or implicit. Most current systems have a search button for explicit initiation or for delayed or regularly scheduled initiation. The button's label, size, and color should be consistent across versions. An appealing alternative is *implicit initiation*, in which each change to a component of the formulation stage immediately produces a new set of search results (Fig. 13.2). *Dynamic queries*, in which users adjust query widgets to produce continuous updates, have also proven to be effective and satisfying. They require adequate screen space and rapid processing, but their advantages are great (Section 13.4).

The third stage is the *review of results*, in which users read messages, view textual lists, or manipulate visualizations. Previews consisting of samples (e.g., the Google search results in Fig 1.13), human-generated abstracts, or

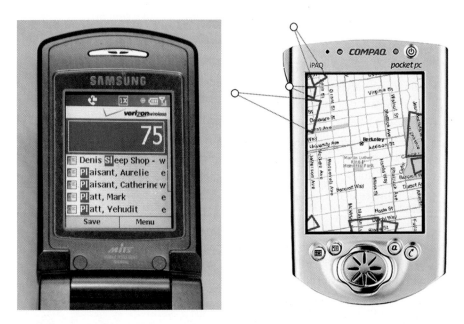

FIGURE 13.2

As users press keys on the keypad (left figure), the digits are shown and a search is implicitly initiated to display the list of names in the address book that match the series of keys pressed. On the right figure, red wedges at the edge of the screen hint at the locations of off-screen results on a map (Gustafson et al., 2008).

automatically generated summaries help users select a subset of the results for use and can help them define more productive queries as they learn about the contents of the items. Translations may also be proposed. If users have control over the result set size and which fields are displayed, they can better accommodate their information-seeking needs. While it is common practice to return only 10 or 20 results, larger result sets are preferable for those with high bandwidth and large displays. Allowing users to control how results are sequenced (e.g., alphabetical, chronological, relevance ranked, or by popularity) also contributes to more effective outcomes. One strategy used by Endeca® is to provide an overview of the results using attribute values; for example, providing the number of books, journal articles, or news articles (Fig. 13.3). Another strategy, used by Vivisimo® and Grokker™, involves automatic clustering and naming of the clusters. The automatic naming of clusters is problematic, though, and studies suggest that clustering according to more established and meaningful hierarchies might be more effective (Hearst, 2006). To help users identify items of interest, access to the full document is usually necessary, with highlighting of the keywords or keyphrases used in the search. For large documents, automatic scrolling to the first occurrence of the keyword is helpful, as are markers placed along the scrollbar to indicate the locations of other occurrences.

The fourth stage is *refinement*. Search interfaces should provide meaningful messages to explain search outcomes and to support progressive refinement. For example, users could be encouraged to provide fewer terms to allow partial matches. If two words in a search phrase are not found proximally, feedback should be given about the occurrence of the words individually. Corrections can be proposed; for example, asking "Did you mean fibromyalgia?" when the keyphrase is mispelled. If multiple phrases are input, items containing all phrases should be shown first and identified, followed by items containing subsets; if no documents are found with all phrases, that failure should be indicated. There is a fairly elaborate decision tree (perhaps 60 to 100 branches) of search outcomes and messages that needs to be specified. Another aspect of feedback is that, as searches are made, the system should keep track of them in a *search history* to allow review and reuse of earlier searches (Komlodi, 2002). Progressive refinement, in which the results of a search are refined by changing the search parameters, should be convenient.

The final stage, *use* of the results, is where the payoff comes. Results can be merged and saved, disseminated by e-mail, or used as input to other programs—for example, for visualization or statistical tools. Users may also want to activate an RSS feed in order to be notified when new results become available.

Designers can apply the five-stage framework to make the search process more visible, comprehensible, and controllable by users. This approach is in harmony with the general move towards direct manipulation, in which the state of

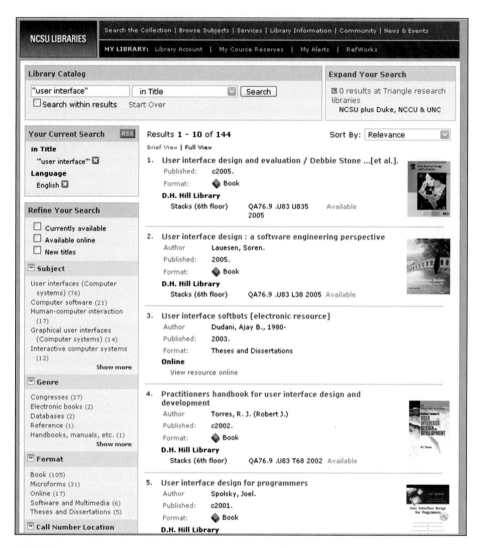

FIGURE 13.3

A search for "user interface" powered by Endeca (http://www.lib.ncsu.edu) returns 144 results grouped into 10 pages. The menu at the upper right allows users to sort results by relevance or by date, while on the left a summary of the results organized by Subject, Genre, or Format provides an overview of the results and facilitates further refinement of the search.

the system is made visible and is placed under user control. Novices may not want to see all the components of the five stages initially, but if they are unhappy with the search results, they should be able to view available options and change their queries easily.

13.3 Multimedia Document Searches

Interfaces to structured databases and textual-document libraries are good and getting better, but search interfaces in multimedia-document libraries are a greater challenge. To locate items such as images, videos, sound files, or animations, most systems depend on text searches in descriptive documents or searches on keywords, tags, and metadata. For example, searches in photo libraries can be done by date, photographer, medium, location, or text in captions, but without captioning and human annotation, finding a photo of a particular ribbon-cutting ceremony or horse race is very difficult. Collaborative tagging of multimedia documents is dramatically changing how users search for photos, videos, maps, and web pages (Section 9.3), but many important collections remain untagged. Even if completely automatic recognition is not possible, however, it is useful to have computers perform some filtering. Multimedia-document search interfaces have to integrate powerful annotation and indexing tools, search algorithms to filter the collections, and media-specific browsing techniques for viewing the results. Types of searches might include the following:

- *Image search*. Finding images of things such as the Statue of Liberty is a substantial challenge for image-analysis researchers, who describe this task as *query by image content*, or QBIC (Datta et al., 2008). Lady Liberty's distinctive profile might be identifiable if the orientation, lens focal length, and lighting were held constant, but the general problem is difficult in large and diverse collections of photos. Promising approaches are searching for distinctive local features, such as the torch or the seven spikes in the crown, or for distinctive textures or colors, such as red, white, and blue to locate an American flag. Of course, separating out the British, French, and other similarly colored flags is not easy! More success is attainable with searches based on similarily, where users can draw a desired profile and retrieve items with matching features (for example, with retrievr, illustrated in Fig. 13.4), or with restricted collections, such as images of glass vases or blood cells. For collections of personal photos, it is important to provide effective browsing and lightweight annotation mechanisms (Kang et al., 2007). Photo tagging first appeared in commercial tools such as Adobe Photoshop Album but is now widely used in online tools such as facebook, Flickr, or Google's Picasa™.

- *Map search*. Computer-generated maps are now widely used. While locating a point on a map by name or by specifying a latitude and longitude is the traditional solution, searching by features is now possible because geographical information systems preserve the structural aspects and the multiple layers in maps (Dykes et al., 2004). For example, users might specify a search for all port cities with a population greater than 1 million and an airport

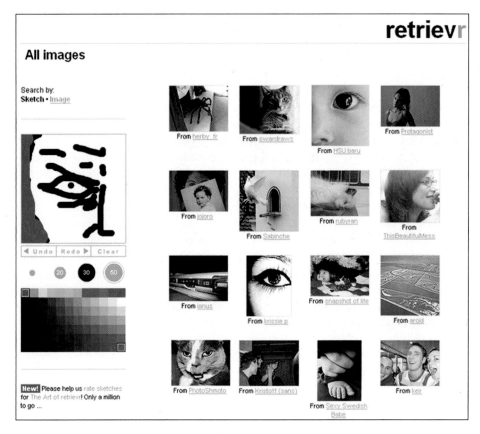

FIGURE 13.4

This search-by-example interface from retreivr (http://labs.systemone.at/retrievr/) allows users to upload an image or draw a sketch that will be used to find similar images. Each item in the result set is represented by a preview composed of a thumbnail and the name of the author. Results are presented in a compact grid to facilitate reviewing.

within 10 miles. Applications for mobile devices allow users to locate restaurants serving a certain type of cuisine within a given distance of their location (Fig 13.2)

- *Design or diagram search.* Some computer-assisted design packages offer users limited search capabilities within a single design or across design collections. Finding red circles inside blue squares may help in some cases, but more elaborate strategies, such as searching for engine designs with pistons smaller than 6 centimeters, could prove more beneficial. Document-structure recognition and search tools already exist that allow searching, for example, for newspaper front pages with headlines that span the front page and no advertisements (Doermann, 1998).

- *Sound search.* Music-information retrieval (MIR) systems can now use audio input, where users can query with musical content. Users can sing or play a theme, hook, or riff from the desired piece of music, and the system returns the most similar items (Downie, 2003). It is even becoming possible to recognize individual performers, such as "find Caruso." Finding a spoken word or phrase in databases of telephone conversations is still difficult, but it is becoming possible, even on a speaker-independent basis (Section 8.4).

- *Video search.* Searching a video or film involves more than simply searching through each of the frames. The video should be segmented into scenes or cuts and allow scene skipping. Gaining an overview of a two-hour video by a timeline of scenes enables better understanding, editing, and selection. Successful search tools use a variety of a visual scene features (for example, color, faces, or text superimpositions) as well as textual features such as speech-to-text transcripts to make a large volume of digital video retrievable (Luo et al., 2006; Wactlar et al., 1999).

- *Animation search.* Animation-authoring tools are becoming prevalent following the success of Flash, so it might soon become possible to specify searches for certain types of animations, such as spinning globes or morphing faces.

13.4 Advanced Filtering and Search Interfaces

Users have highly varied needs for advanced filtering features (Hearst, 2009). This section reviews a few alternatives to the form fill-in query interface:

- *Filtering with complex Boolean queries.* Commercial information-retrieval systems such as Dialog® and FirstSearch® permit complex Boolean expressions with parentheses, but their widespread adoption has been inhibited by their difficulty of use. Numerous proposals have been put forward to reduce the burden of specifying complex Boolean expressions, but a great part of the confusion stems from informal English usage. For example, a query such as "List all employees who live in New York and Boston" would typically result in an empty list, because the "and" would be interpreted as an intersection; only employees who live in both cities would qualify! In English, "and" usually expands the options; in Boolean expressions, AND is used to narrow a set to the intersection of two others. Similarly, in the English expression "I'd like Russian or Italian salad dressing," the "or" is exclusive, indicating that you want one or the other but not both; in Boolean expressions, however, an OR is inclusive and is used to expand a set. The desire to allow searching using *full Boolean expressions*, including nested parentheses and NOT operators, has led to novel metaphors for query specification. Venn diagrams, decision tables, and metaphors of water flowing through a series of filters have been used, but these representations become clumsy as query complexity increases.

- *Automatic filtering.* Another form of filtering is to apply a user-constructed set of keyphrases to dynamically generated information, such as incoming e-mail messages, newspaper stories, or scientific journal articles (Belkin and Croft, 1992). Users create and store their profiles, which are evaluated each time a new document appears. Users can be notified by electronic mail, RSS feed, voicemail, or text messaging that a relevant item has appeared, or the results can simply be collected into a file until users seek them out. These approaches are a modern version of a traditional information-retrieval strategy called *selective dissemination of information* (SDI), which was used in the earliest days of magnetic-tape distribution of document collections.

- *Dynamic queries.* The dynamic-queries approach of adjusting numeric range sliders, alphasliders for names or categories, or buttons for small sets of categories is appealing to many users for many tasks (Shneiderman, 1994). Dynamic queries might be called *direct-manipulation queries*, since they share the same concepts of visual display of actions (the sliders or buttons) and objects (the query results in the task-domain display); the use of rapid, incremental, and reversible actions; and the immediate (less than 100 milliseconds) display of feedback. Additional benefits are the prevention of syntax errors and an encouragement of exploration. A subset of Boolean queries are possible (ORs between attribute values and ANDs between attributes). Searching in online databases can also be done with dynamic queries (Fig. 13.5). To preserve the 100-millisecond reaction time of dynamic queries, however, data must be downloaded to and kept in the memory of the user's computer, which becomes problematic with large volumes of data. *Query previews* (Greene et al., 2000) address this issue by first providing an interactive overview of the data available. This overview allows users to gain useful information about the distribution of the data available over a few selected attributes and to rapidly eliminate undesired items. After rough selections have been made, the metadata of the remaining items can be downloaded for refinement of the query. While form fill-in interfaces often lead users to waste time posing queries that have zero-hit or mega-hit result sets, one user study showed that query previews made performance 1.6 to 2.1 times faster and led to higher subjective satisfaction (Tanin et al., 2000). Query previews used bar charts to show the frequency

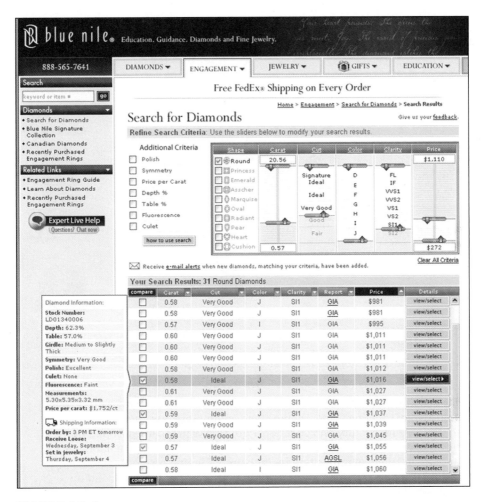

FIGURE 13.5

Blue Nile (http://www.bluenile.com/) uses dynamic queries to narrow down the results of searches. Here, the double-sided sliders were adjusted to show only lower-priced diamonds with very good cut and high carat ratings.

of attribute values for each facet, laying the foundation for faceted browsing that typically uses the more compact numeric counts.

- *Faceted metadata search.* This type of search interface integrates category browsing with keyword searching, as demonstrated in Flamenco (Yee et al., 2003; Fig. 13.6). This interface makes use of hierarchical faceted metadata presented as simultaneous menus (Section 6.4.1), and dynamically generated

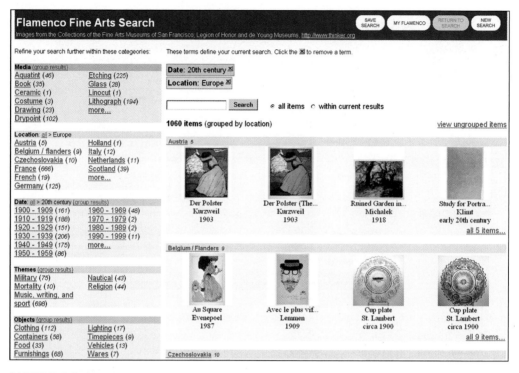

FIGURE 13.6

Flamenco (http://flamenco.berkeley.edu/) is an example of a faceted metadata search. Facets include Media, Location, Date, Themes, and so on. Here, two attribute values are selected (Date = 20th century and Location = Europe) with results grouped by location. The image previews are updated immediately as constraints are added or removed (another example of implicit query initiation). Clicking on a group heading such as "Belgium/Flanders" refines the query into that category, while clicking on "All" dates relaxes the date constraint.

numerical query previews. It allows users to navigate explicitly along multiple conceptual dimensions that describe the images and to progressively narrow or expand the scope of the query while browsing images. In the example of architectural photo browsing, users can look for photos of modern homes, narrow on front doors, narrow further on homes located in Virginia, then widen the query to show windows and doors, and then switch to homes in Maryland, all the while staying in the flow and focusing their attention on the images. Many search interfaces now offer multiple-menu selection, but they often allow refinements in only one menu at a time—this is the case, for example, with Epicurious (Fig. 6.9) and the International Children's Digital

Library (Fig. 1.16)—as opposed to more than one menu simultaneously, which is possible with Shopping.com (Fig. 6.14).

- *Query by example.* Using similarity-based algorithms, it is possible to find text or multimedia documents that are similar to the one submitted by users. For example, an image-search interface might allow users to upload their own example images and search for similar ones crop a feature of interest in an existing image, or draw a sketch of the type of image they wish to find (Fig 13.4). Results are often mixed but can also help users broaden the scope of their search. Rapid browsing of the results is important, and iterative refinement is necessary.

- *Implicit search.* Implicit search interfaces use similarity or context information to present items of potential interest. This strategy is commonly used by shopping web sites trying to encourage buyers to explore new products based on their purchasing history or to continue browing to look at products similar to the ones they just viewed. This type of search uses no query widgets, but users are more satisfied if they know what information was used to arrive at the recommendations.

- *Collaborative filtering.* This social form of filtering allows groups of users to combine their evaluations to help one another find interesting items in large collections (Herlocker et al., 2004). Each user rates items in terms of their interest. The system can then suggest unread items that may be close to users' interests, as determined by matches with other people's interests. This method can also be applied to movies, music, restaurants, and so on: For example, if you rate six restaurants highly, the algorithms will provide you with other restaurants that were rated highly by people who liked your six restaurants. This strategy has an inherent appeal, and many such systems have been built for shopping, news files, movies, or music.

- *Multilingual searches.* In some cases, users want to be able to search multilingual collections. Current web search engines merely provide rudimentary translation tools, but prototype systems allow users to search multilingual collections of speech and/or printed documents in languages they do not know and provide specialized browsers for iterative query refinement, select appropriate dictionaries, restrict keyword translations, etc. The goal of those powerful translation systems is often to identify documents that justify the cost of high-quality professional translation (Oard et al., 2008).

- *Visual field specification.* The specification of fields' values can sometimes be simplified by using specialized visual representations of the possible values (Figs. 6.12 and 6.13). For example, selecting dates on calendars or using an airplane layout to select among available seats is useful. For vacationers seeking tourist information about Marseilles who do not know its exact location, a scrolling alphabetical list is needed; but when a map of France or Europe is displayed, it becomes possible to point rapidly at hundreds of other locations, allowing the selection of other Mediterranean cities without having to know their names. When there are no natural graphical representations of the choices, information-visualization techniques can be used. For example, a treemap can be used to represent a product catalog (Fig. 13.7). Visual-search interfaces provide context and help users refine their needs. They are attractive and can reduce error messages such as "data out of range", while providing information about data availability and a feeling of thoroughness to users.

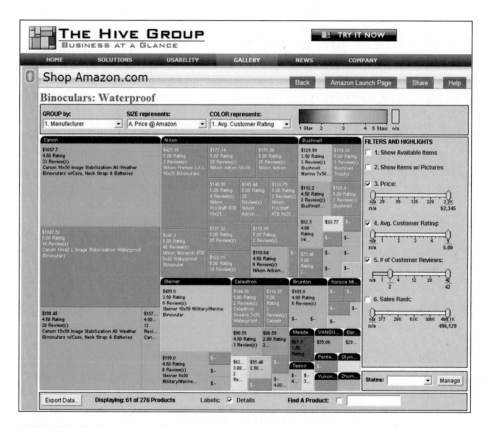

FIGURE 13.7

Using The Hive Group's treemap (http://www.hivegroup.com/), users can review all waterproof binoculars in the catalog of Amazon.com products and browse the items in the list, grouped by manufacturer. Each box corresponds to a pair of binoculars, and the size of the box is proportional to its price. Green boxes are best-sellers. Users can filter the results using the dynamic query sliders on the right. Here all the binoculars with less than three user reviews have been filtered out, leaving only 61 binoculars to consider.

There is much in common between visual-search interfaces and browsing interfaces that use combinations of menus (Section 6.4). Enhanced with implicit initiation and immediate feedback, visual-search interfaces can become powerful dynamic-query interfaces, while the addition of abstract data previews and overviews transforms visual-search interfaces into potent information-visualization and exploration tools that help users explore the data visually before any search is even specified.

Practitioner's Summary

While RSS feeds are changing how information reaches users, search interfaces remain a crucial component of many applications. Improved user interfaces to digital libraries and multimedia databases have spawned appealing new products. Flexible queries against complex text, sound, graphics, image, and video databases are emerging, while collaborative tagging of multimedia documents is transforming keyword searching. Novel graphical and direct-manipulation approaches to query formulation are now possible.

Researcher's Agenda

Although the computer contributes to the information explosion, it is potentially also the magic lens for finding, sorting, filtering, and presenting the relevant items. The need to search in complex structured documents, graphics or image libraries, and sound or video files presents grand opportunities for the design of advanced user interfaces. Powerful search engines will be able to find the needles in the haystacks and the forests beyond the trees.

WORLD WIDE WEB RESOURCES
http://www.aw.com/DTUI/

Search services such as those provided by Google or the Library of Congress provide always-improving access to the resources on the World Wide Web. You can find more information online about information-retrieval topics such as collaborative filtering, multimedia search and retrieval, and indexing methods.

References

Agichtein, E., Brill, E., and Dumais, S.T., Improving web search ranking by incorporating user behavior information, *Proc. 29th Annual ACM SIGIR Conference on Research and Development in Information Retrieval*, ACM Press, New York (2006), 19–26.

Belkin, N. J. and Croft, B. W., Information filtering and information retrieval: Two sides of the same coin?, *Communications of the ACM* 35, 12 (1992), 29–38.

Datta, R., Joshi, D., Li, J., and Wang, J. Z., Image retrieval: Ideas, influences, and trends of the new age, *ACM Computing Survey* 40, 2 (2008), 1–60.

Doermann, D., The indexing and retrieval of document images: A survey, *Computer Vision and Image Understanding* 70, 3 (1998), 287–298.

Downie, J. S., Music information retrieval, *Annual Review of Information Science and Technology* 37 (2003), 295–340.

Dykes, J., MacEachren, A. M., and Kraak, M. J. (Editors), *Exploring Geovisualization*, Elsevier, Amsterdam, The Netherlands (2004).

Greene, S., Marchionini, G., Plaisant, C., and Shneiderman, B., Previews and overviews in digital libraries: Designing surrogates to support visual information-seeking, *Journal of the American Society for Information Science* 51, 3 (March 2000), 380–393.

Gustafson, Sean, Baudisch, Patrick, Gutwin, Carl and Irani, Pourang, Wedge: clutter-free visualization of off-screen locations, *Proc. of CHI'08 Conference: Human factors in Computing Systems*, ACM Press, New York (2008), 787–796.

Hearst, M. Clustering versus faceted categories for information exploration, *Communications of the ACM* 49, 4 (2006), 59–61.

Hearst, Marti, *Search User Interfaces*, Cambridge University Press, NewYork (2009).

Herlocker, Jonathan, Konstan, Joseph, Terveen, Loren, and Riedl, John, Evaluating collaborative filtering recommender systems, *ACM Transactions on Information Systems* 22, 1 (2004), 5–53.

Kang, Hyunmo, Bederson, Benjamin B., and Suh, Bongwon, Capture, annotate, browse, find, share: Novel interfaces for personal photo management, *International Journal of Human-Computer Interaction* 23, 3 (2007), 315–337.

Koenemann, J. and Belkin, N., A case for interaction: A study of interactive information retrieval behavior and effectiveness, *Proc. CHI '96 Conference: Human Factors in Computing Systems*, ACM Press, New York (1996), 205–212.

Komlodi, A., The role of interaction histories in mental model building and knowledge sharing in the legal domain, *I-KNOW '02 2nd International Conference on Knowledge Management, Journal of Universal Computer Science* 8, 5 (2002), 557–566.

Luo, Hangzai, Fan, Jianping, Yang, Jing, Ribarsky, William, and Satoh, Shin'ichi, Exploring large-scale video news via interactive visualization, *Proc. IEEE Visual Analytics Science and Technology*, IEEE Computer Press, Los Alamitos, CA (2006), 75–82.

Marchionini, G. and White, R. W., Find what you need, understand what you find, *International Journal of Human-Computer Interaction* 23, 3 (2007), 205–237.

Oard, Douglas, He, Daqing, and Wang, Jianqiang, User-assisted query translation for cross-language information retrieval, *Information Processing and Management* 44, 1 (2008), 181–211.

Shneiderman, B., Dynamic queries for visual information seeking, *IEEE Software* 11, 6 (1994), 70–77.

Shneiderman, B., Byrd, D., and Croft, B., Clarifying search: A user-interface framework for text searches, *D-LIB Magazine of Digital Library Research* (January 1997). Available at http://www.dlib.org/.

Tanin, E., Lotem, A., Haddadin, I., Shneiderman, B., Plaisant, C., and Slaughter, L., Facilitating network data exploration with query previews: A study of user performance and preference, *Behaviour & Information Technology* 19, 6 (2000), 393–403.

Wurman, Richard Saul, *Information Anxiety*, Doubleday, New York (1989).

Wactlar, H. D., Christel, M. G., Yihong G., and Hauptmann, A. G., Lessons learned from building a terabyte digital video library, *IEEE Computer* 32, 2 (1999), 66–73.

Yee, K.-P., Swearingen, K., Li, K., and Hearst, M., Faceted metadata for image search and browsing, *Proc. CHI 2003 Conference: Human Factors in Computing Systems*, ACM Press, New York (2003), 401–408.

14

Information Visualization

" The real voyage of discovery consists not in seeking new landscapes but in having new eyes. "

Marcel Proust

14.1 Introduction

A picture is often said to be worth a thousand words, and for some tasks, a visual presentation—such as a map or photograph—is indeed dramatically easier to use or comprehend than is a textual description or a spoken report. Designers are discovering how to present and manipulate large amounts of information in compact and user-controlled ways, and we can now argue that an interface is worth a thousand pictures. *Information visualization* can be defined as the use of interactive visual representations of abstract data to amplify cognition (Ware, 2008; Card et al., 1999). The *abstract* characteristic of the data is what distinguishes information visualization from scientific visualization. For scientific visualization, three dimensions are necessary, because typical questions involve continuous variables, volumes, and surfaces (inside/outside, left/right, above/below). However, for information visualization, typical questions involve more categorical variables and the discovery of patterns, trends, clusters, outliers, and gaps in data, such as stock prices, patient records, or social relationships (Card, 2008; Spence, 2007; Henry et al., 2007; Grinstein et al., to appear).

Information visualization provides compact graphical presentations and user interfaces for interactively manipulating large numbers of items (10^2 to 10^6), possibly extracted from far larger datasets. Sometimes called *visual data mining*, it uses the enormous visual bandwidth and the remarkable human perceptual system to enable users to make discoveries, take decisions, or propose explanations about patterns, groups of items, or individual items. It may even allow users to answer questions they didn't know they had. In contrast, dashboards (Few, 2006; Fig. 5.9 and 5.10) and the few visualization applications designed for mobile devices tend to provide compact, automatically generated reports, usually summarizing business performance and offering limited interaction.

Perceptual psychologists, statisticians, and graphic designers offer valuable guidance about presenting static information (Tufte, 2006, 1983), but the opportunity for dynamic displays takes user-interface designers well beyond current wisdom (Ware, 2008). Humans have remarkable perceptual abilities that are greatly underutilized in most current interface designs. Users can scan, recognize, and recall images rapidly and can detect subtle changes in size, color, shape, movement, or texture. The core information presented in graphical user interfaces has remained largely text-oriented (even if enhanced with attractive icons and elegant illustrations), so as more visual approaches are explored, appealing new opportunities are emerging.

Some users resist visual approaches and prefer potent textual approaches, such as multiple menus and numerical query previews in faceted metadata searches (Fig. 13.6). Their choice may be appropriate, since these textual tools use compact presentations that are rich with meaningful information and comfortingly familiar. Successful information-visualization tools have to be more than "cool"; they have to provide measurable benefits for realistic tasks. They must be built to satisfy universal-usability principles of working on a variety of platforms while enabling access for all intended users, including users with disabilities.

As information visualization matures, guidelines, principles, and theories will emerge for this area. Among them will probably be this widely cited principle, usually known as the *visual-information-seeking mantra*:

> Overview first, zoom and filter, then details on demand.
> Overview first, zoom and filter, then details on demand.
> Overview first, zoom and filter, then details on demand.
> Overview first, zoom and filter, then details on demand.
> Overview first, zoom and filter, then details on demand.
> Overview first, zoom and filter, then details on demand.
> Overview first, zoom and filter, then details on demand.

The repetition suggests how often the principle has been applied and the recursive nature of the exploration process.

14.2 Data Type by Task Taxonomy

Information-visualization researchers and commercial developers may be able to sort the numerous tools and identify new opportunities by using a *data type by task taxonomy* (Box 14.1). As in the case of searches, users are viewing collections of items where items have multiple attributes. The data type by task taxonomy includes seven basic data types and seven basic tasks. The basic data types are one-, two-, three-, or multidimensional, followed by three more structured data types: temporal, tree, and network. This simplification is useful to describe the visualizations that have been developed and to characterize the classes of problems that users encounter. For example, with temporal data, users deal with events and intervals, and their questions are concerned with before, after, or during. With tree-structured data, users deal with labels on internal nodes and values at leaf nodes, and their questions are about paths, levels, and subtrees. The seven basic tasks are overview, zoom, filter, details-on-demand, relate, history, and extract. Our discussion begins with the seven data types, followed by the seven tasks.

BOX 14.1

Data type by task taxonomy to identify visualization data types
and the tasks that need to be supported.

Data Types	
1D Linear	Document Lens, Seesoft™, Information Mural, TextArc
2D Map	Geographic information systems, ESRI ArcInfo™, ThemeView™, newspaper layout, self-organizing maps
3D World	Desktops, WebBook™, VRML™, Web3D™, architecture, computer-assisted design, medicine, molecules
Multidimensional	Parallel coordinates, scattergram matrices, hierarchical clustering, Spotfire®, Tableau®, GGobi®, DataDesk®, TableLens®, InfoZoom®
Temporal	DataMontage, Palantir, Project Managers, LifeLines, TimeSearcher
Tree	Outliners, degree-of-interest trees, cone/cam trees, hyperbolic trees, SpaceTree, treemaps
Network	NetMap™, netViz™, Pajek, JUNG, UCINet, NetDraw, TouchGraph, SocialAction, NodeXL, Prefuse
Tasks	
Overview	Gain an overview of the entire collection
Zoom	Zoom in on items of interest
Filter	Filter out uninteresting items
Details-on-demand	Select an item or group and get details when needed
Relate	View relationships among items
History	Keep a history of actions to support undo, replay, and progressive refinement
Extract	Allow extraction of subcollections and of the query parameters

14.2.1 The seven data types

- *1D linear data*. Linear data types are one-dimensional; they include program source code, textual documents, dictionaries, and alphabetical lists of names, all of which can be organized in a sequential manner. For program source code, the substantial compressions of one pixel per character produce compact displays of tens of thousands of lines of program source code on a single display (Eick, 1998; Stasko et al., 1998; Fig. 14.1). The attributes, such as the date of most recent modification or the author name, may be used for color-coding. Interface-design issues include what colors, sizes, and layout to use, and what overview, scrolling, or selection methods to provide for users. User tasks might be to find the number of items, to see items that have certain attributes (for example, program lines that were changed from the previous version), to see the most common words in Chapter 3 of *Alice in Wonderland*

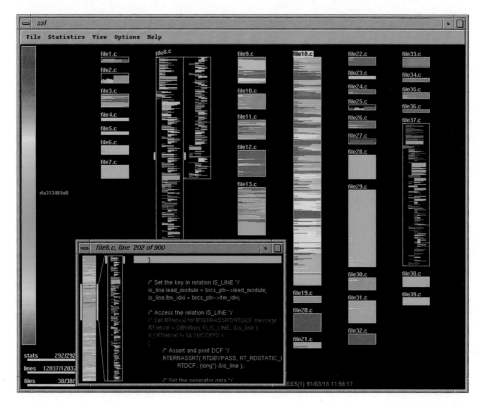

FIGURE 14.1

Seesoft shows a computer program with 4000 lines of code. The newest lines are in red; the oldest are in blue. The smaller browser window shows a code overview and detail window (Eick, 1998).

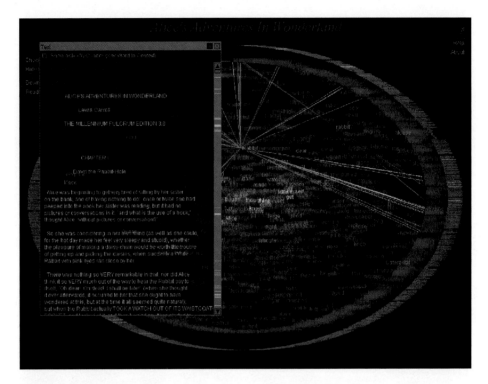

FIGURE 14.2

A TextArc (http://www.textarc.org/) showing the entire text of *Alice in Wonderland* arranged in an arc, stepping clockwise, starting at 12:00. Lines are drawn around the outside, words around the inside. Words that appear more often are brighter. Here, "Rabbit" is highlighted in the arc and in an overlay full-text window. Lines containing "Rabbit" are drawn in green around the arc, in the text window, and even in the scrollbar.

(Fig. 14.2), or to see an item with all its attributes. Tag clouds originated as displays of popular tags in collaborative tagging applications (Fig. 6.11) but have evolved into word clouds displaying statistics of word usage in texts (Viégas and Wattenberg, 2008). Examples include Many Eyes (Fig. 1.2) and Wordle (Fig. 14.3).

- *2D map data.* Planar data include geographic maps, floor plans, and newspaper layouts. Each item in the collection covers some part of the total area and may or may not be rectangular. Each item has task-domain attributes, such as name, owner, and value, and interface-domain features, such as shape, size, color, and opacity (Fig. 14.4). Many systems adopt a multiple-layer approach to dealing with map data, but each layer is two-dimensional. User tasks include finding adjacent items, regions containing certain items, and

FIGURE 14.3

While tag clouds summarize popular tags used in collaborative tagging applications, word clouds display statistics about word usage in a text collection. Here, a Wordle (http://www.wordle.net) shows in an elegant display the words that are over-represented in the most sentimental chapters of 80 mid-Victorian novels. (Courtesy of Sara Steger)

paths between items and performing the seven basic tasks. Examples include geographic information systems (Fig. 5.6), which are a large research and commercial domain (Dykes et al., 2004). Information-visualization researchers have used spatial displays of document collections organized proximally by term co-occurrences, such as ThemeView (Wise et al., 1995; Fig. 14.5). Such displays seem useful to give users an overview of the collection, but they may not necessarily be as useful as a representation to find documents, because relevance is difficult to judge without reading the text itself.

- *3D world data.* Real-world objects, such as molecules, the human body, and buildings, have volume and complex relationships with other items. Computer-assisted medical imaging, architectural drawing, mechanical design, chemical structure modeling, and scientific simulations are built to handle these complex three-dimensional relationships. Users' tasks typically deal with continuous variables such as temperature or density. Results are often presented as volumes and surfaces, and users focus on relationships of left/right, above/below, and inside/outside. In three-dimensional applications, users must cope with their position and orientation when viewing the objects and must handle the potential problems of occlusion and navigation.

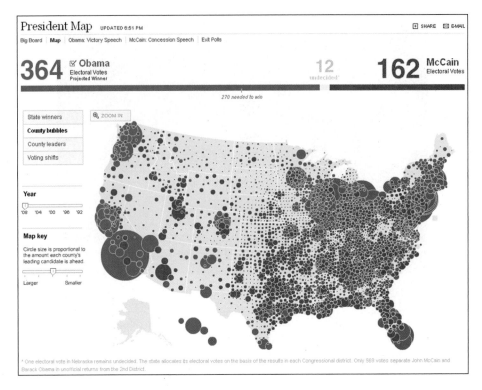

FIGURE 14.4

To present the results of the United States 2008 presidential election, the
New York Times used a variety of visualizations (http://elections.nytimes.com).
Here, a bubble map shows a circle for each county. The size of the circle is
proportional to the amount each county's leading candidate is ahead, colored blue
for Obama and red for McCain.

Solutions using enhanced 3D techniques, such as overviews, landmarks, teleportation, multiple views, and tangible user interfaces (Fig. 5.11), are finding
their way into research prototypes and commercial systems. Successes
include medical imagery from sonograms that helps doctors in planning
surgery and architectural walkthroughs or flythroughs that give home buyers an idea of what a finished building will look like.

Examples of three-dimensional computer graphics and computer-assisted
design tools are numerous, but information-visualization work in three dimensions is still controversial. Some virtual-environment researchers and business
graphics producers have sought to present information in three-dimensional
structures, but these designs seem to require more navigation steps and to make
the results harder to interpret (Section 5.4).

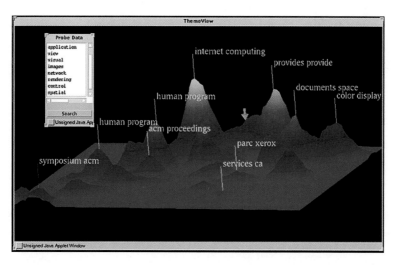

FIGURE 14.5

ThemeView (formerly ThemeScape™) shows a three-dimensional map representing the results of a search in a large corpus of documents. Proximity indicates similarity of the topics, while height reflects the number of documents and frequency of terms. Commercial applications are available from OmniViz, Inc. (Wise et al., 1995).

- *Multidimensional data.* Most relational- and statistical-database contents can be conveniently manipulated as multidimensional data, in which items with *n* attributes become points in an *n*-dimensional space. The interface representation may be a dynamic two-dimensional scattergram, with each additional dimension controlled by a slider (Ahlberg and Shneiderman, 1994). Buttons can be used for attribute values when the cardinality is small—say, less than 10. Tasks include finding patterns, such as correlations among pairs of variables, clusters, gaps, and outliers. Multidimensional data can also be represented by a three-dimensional scattergram, but disorientation (especially if the user's point of view is from inside the cluster of points) and occlusion (especially if close points are represented as being larger) can be problems. FilmFinder developed dynamic queries on zoomable, color-coded, user-controlled scattergrams of multidimensional data and laid the basis for the commercial product Spotfire (Fig. 12.2).
  Parallel coordinate plots are one of the few truly compact multidimensional techniques (Inselberg, 2009). Each parallel vertical axis represents a dimension, and each item becomes a line connecting values in each dimension. Training and practice are particularly helpful to become a "multidimensional detective." Other techniques include matrices that combine series of small bivariate representations (Fig. 14.6), using a spreadsheet metaphor (Fig. 14.7), and showing the

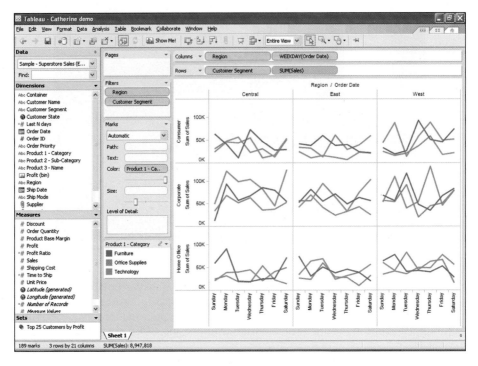

FIGURE 14.6

Tableau Software (http://www.tableausoftware.com/) allows users to interactively construct their displays by dragging variable names into elements of the display. Here, a small-multiple table of nine displays shows how sales vary over time for three regions and three customer segments. Tableau can also suggest new layouts (Mackinlay et al., 2007).

distribution of values for each dimension while allowing progressive filtering of the data by clicking on those values (for example, InfoZoom®). Finally, an increasingly common approach to looking at multidimensional data is to use hierarchical or k-means clustering algorithms to identify similar items. Hierarchical clustering identifies close pairs of items and forms ever-larger clusters until every point is included in a cluster. Clusters are typically represented as a tree structure. K-means clustering starts by users specifying how many clusters to create; the algorithm then places every item into the most appropriate cluster, and clouds of points represent the clusters. Surprising relationships and interesting outliers can be identified by these techniques, but results can be difficult to explain to novice users.

- *Temporal data*. Time series are very common (for example, electrocardiograms, stock market prices, or weather data) and merit a data type that is separate from one-dimensional data (Silva and Catarci, 2000). The distinc-

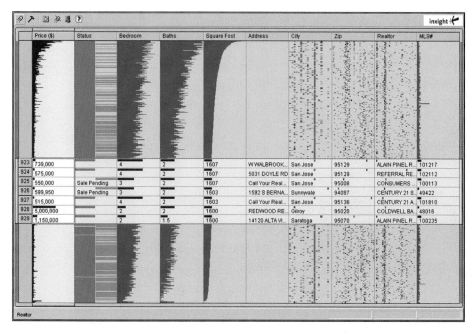

FIGURE 14.7

TableLens® (http://www.businessobjects.com/) provides a spreadsheet-like view of table data—here, a listing of houses for sale. The houses are ordered using the "Square Foot" attribute, which reveals that price is mostly related to the square footage, with some exceptions that are easy to spot in the Price column.

tions of *temporal data* are that items (events) have a start and finish time and that items may overlap (Fig. 14.8). Frequent tasks include finding all events before, after, or during some time period or moment, and in some cases comparing periodical phenomena, plus the seven basic tasks. Many project-management tools exist; novel visualizations of time include the Perspective Wall (Robertson et al., 1993) and LifeLines (Plaisant et al., 1998; Fig. 14.9). Space-time data have been a focus of great attention in geovisualization (Andrienko and Andrienko, 2005; Fig. 14.15). TimeSearcher combines multiple time series, such as representations of stock-market prices over time, or other linear data series, such as temperatures in an oil-well bore hole. Users draw boxes on the display to specify combinations of ranges, and Time-Searcher shows series whose data all fall within the specified ranges (Hochheiser and Shneiderman, 2004).

- *Tree data.* Hierarchies or tree structures are collections of items in which each item (except the root) has a link to one parent item. Items and the links between parents and children can have multiple attributes. The basic

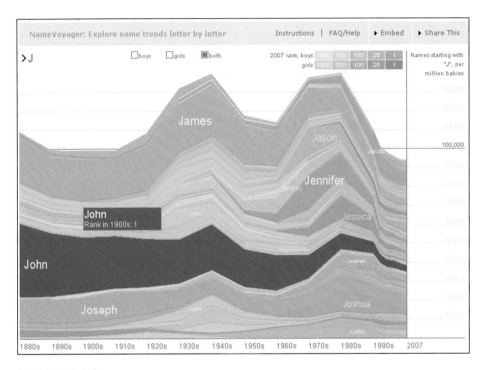

FIGURE 14.8

The Baby NameVoyager visualization (http://www.babynamewizard.com/voyager/) lets users type in a name and see a graph of its popularity over the past century. As you type the letters of the name, the visualization shows, letter by letter, the overall popularity of all the names starting with the letters you've entered so far (here, all the names that start with "J" revealing the decline of the use of the first name "John" since the 1960s).

tasks can be applied to items and links, and tasks related to structural properties become interesting—for example, for a company organizational chart, is it a deep or shallow hierarchy, and how many employees does each manager supervise? Interface representations of trees can employ the outline style of indented labels used in tables of contents or the Windows File Explorer or a node-and-link diagram; the latter approach is used by the Degree-Of-Interest Tree browser (Fig. 14.10), hyperbolic browsers and SpaceTree (Plaisant et al., 2002; Fig. 14.11). A space-filling approach, using treemaps shows arbitrary-sized trees in a fixed rectangular space (Shneiderman, 2009; Bederson et al., 2002). The treemap approach has been applied successfully to many applications, from stock-market data visualization (http://www.smartmoney.com/map-of-the-market/) to oil-production monitoring and searching in electronic product catalogs (Fig. 13.7).

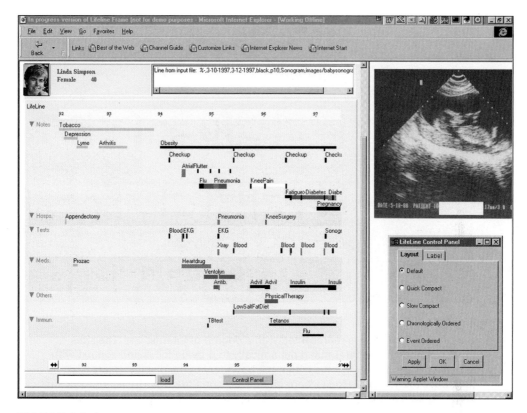

FIGURE 14.9

LifeLines (http://www.cs.umd.edu/hcil/lifelines/) present a summary of personal records—here, a medical record—on a zoomable timeline. LifeLines show multiple facets of the record, such as doctors' notes, hospitalizations, or tests, with line thickness and color used to map data attributes such as severity or drug dosage. A LifeLine acts as a giant menu; users click on events to display related information.

- *Network data.* When relationships among items cannot be captured conveniently with a tree structure, items can be linked to an arbitrary number of other items in a network. In addition to performing the basic tasks applied to items and links, network users often want to know about the shortest or least costly paths connecting two items or traversing the entire network. Node-and-link diagrams are one type of interface representation (Dodge and Kitchin, 2001), but layout algorithms are often so complex that user interaction is limited when large networks are shown, and filtering becomes important. Another option is to display matrices of items, with each cell representing a potential link and its attribute values (Henry et al., 2007). Network visualization is an old but still imperfect art, because of the

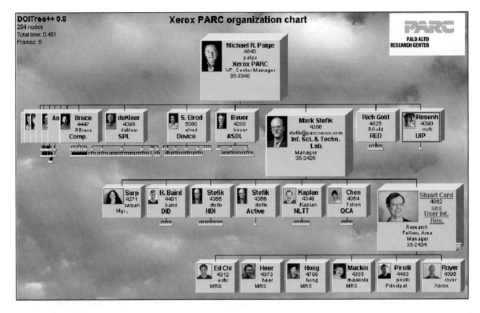

FIGURE 14.10

An organization chart is represented with a degree-of-interest tree. The sizes of the 341 nodes are determined dynamically to provide focus and context with a fisheye view that always fits within the boundary of the display. Users click on nodes to change the focus; here, the focus is on Stuart Card. His node appears larger as well as the nodes of his supervisors (Card and Nation, 2002).

complexity of relationships and user tasks (Herman et al., 2000). New interest in this topic has been spawned by the visualization of social networks (Fig. 14.12). Specialized visualizations can be designed to be more effective.

The seven data types discussed here reflect an abstraction of the reality. There are many variations on these themes (two-and-a-half- or four-dimensional data, multitrees, etc.), and many prototypes use combinations of these data types.

14.2.2 The seven basic tasks

The second framework for analyzing information visualizations covers seven basic tasks that users typically perform:

- *Overview task.* Users can gain an overview of the entire collection. Overview strategies include zoomed-out views of each data type that allow users to see

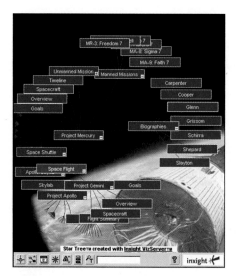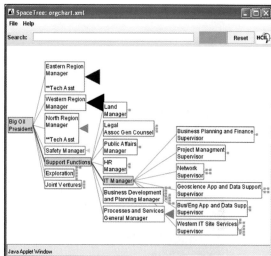

FIGURE 14.11

Two representations of the same tree. On the left, the StarTree™ hyperbolic tree browser (http://www.businessobjects.com/) allows 10 to 30 nodes near the center to be seen clearly, while branches are reduced gradually as they get closer to the periphery. As the focus is shifted among nodes, the display updates smoothly, producing a satisfying animation. On the right, SpaceTree (http://www.cs.umd.edu/hcil/spacetree/) shows an iconic representation of the branches that cannot be displayed, indicating the size of each branch. As users open and close the branches of the tree, the layout remains stable and predictable.

the entire collection, plus an adjoining detail view. The overview might contain a movable field-of-view box with which users control the contents of the detail view, allowing zoom factors of 3 to 30. Replication of this strategy with intermediate views enables users to reach larger zoom factors (Fig. 11.8). Another popular approach is the fisheye strategy, whose distortion magnifies one or more areas of the display (Fig. 11.9 and 8.23), but geometric zoom factors have to be limited to about 5, or different levels of representations must be used for the context to be usable (Figs. 14.7 and 14.10). Since most query-language facilities make it difficult to gain an overview of a collection, the provision of adequate overview strategies is a useful criterion to judge such interfaces (Hornbæk et al., 2002).

- *Zoom task.* Users can zoom in on items of interest. Users typically have an interest in some portion of a collection, and they need tools to enable them to control the zoom focus and the zoom factor. Smooth zooming helps users to preserve their sense of position and context. Users can zoom on one

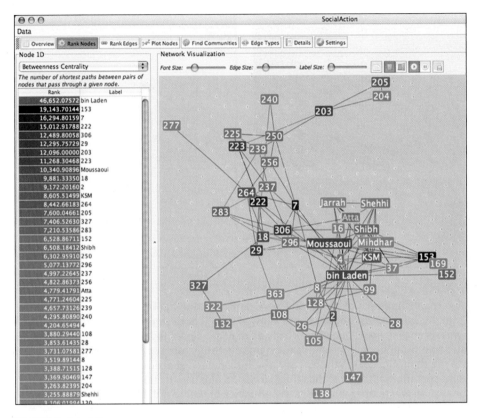

FIGURE 14.12

SocialAction allows users to analyze networks (here, a social network of suspected terrorists). Nodes are ranked and color-coded using a choice of social network analysis measures; in this case, the measure is "betweeness centrality," which highlights in red the gatekeepers in this network (Perer and Shneiderman, 2008).

dimension at a time by moving the zoom bar controls or by adjusting the size of the field-of-view box. A satisfying way to zoom in is to point to a location and to issue a zooming command, usually by holding down a mouse button. Zooming is particularly important in applications for small displays.

- *Filter task.* Users can filter out uninteresting items. Dynamic queries applied to the items in the collection constitute one of the key ideas in information visualization (Shneiderman, 1994). When users control the contents of the display, they can quickly focus on their interests by eliminating unwanted items. Sliders, buttons, or other control widgets coupled with rapid (less than 100 milliseconds) display update is the goal, even when there are tens of thousands of displayed items. Similarly, brushing and linking techniques allow users to dynamically highlight items of interest across displays.

- *Details-on-demand task.* Users can select an item or group to get details. Once a collection has been trimmed to a few dozen items, it should be easy to browse the details about the group or individual items. The usual approach is to simply click on an item and review details in a separate or pop-up window. The details-on-demand window may contain links to further information.

- *Relate task.* Users can relate items or groups within the collection. The attraction of visual displays when compared to textual displays is that they make use of the remarkable human perceptual ability for processing visual information. Within visual displays, there are opportunities for showing relationships by proximity, by containment, by connected lines, or by color-coding. Highlighting techniques can be used to draw attention to certain items in a field of thousands. Pointing to a visual display can allow rapid selection, and feedback is apparent. The eye, the hand, and the mind seem to work smoothly and rapidly as users perform actions on visual displays. In LifeLines (Fig. 14.9), for example, users can click on a medication and see the related visit notes or test results. However, designing user-interface actions to specify which relationship is to be manifested is still a challenge. Users may also want to combine multiple visualization techniques that are tightly coupled so that actions in one view trigger immediate changes in all other coupled views. Tools are being developed to allow users to specify what visualizations they need and how the interaction between the visualizations should be controlled (North et al., 2002).

- *History task.* Users can keep a history of actions to support undo, replay, and progressive refinement. It is rare that a single user action produces the desired outcome. Information exploration is inherently a process with many steps, so keeping a history of actions and allowing users to retrace their steps is important. However, most products fail to deal adequately with this requirement. Designers would do well to model information-retrieval systems, which typically preserve the sequence of searches so that these searches can be combined or refined.

- *Extract task.* Users can allow extraction of subcollections and of the query parameters. Once users have obtained the item or set of items that they desire, it is useful for them to be able to extract that set and to save it, send it by electronic mail, or insert it into a statistical or presentation package. They may also want to publish that data for others to view with a simplified version of the visualization tool.

14.3 Challenges for Information Visualization

The data type by task taxonomy helps organize our understanding of the range of problems, but there are still many challenges that information-visualization researchers need to face to create successful tools:

- *Importing and cleaning data.* Deciding how to organize input data to achieve a desired result often takes more thought and work than expected. Getting data into the correct format, filtering out incorrect items, normalizing attribute values, and coping with missing data can also be burdensome tasks.

- *Combining visual representations with textual labels.* Visual representations are potent, but meaningful textual labels have an important role. Labels should be visible without overwhelming the display or confusing users. Mapmakers have long wrestled with this problem, and their work offers valuable lessons. Often, user-controlled approaches such as ScreenTips and *excentric labels* can help (Fig. 14.13).

- *Finding related information.* Multiple sources of information are often needed to make meaningful judgments. Patent lawyers want to see related patents, other filings by the same people, and recent filings by competing companies. Genomics researchers want to see how clusters of genes work in harmony during the phases of cellular processes and then view similar genes in

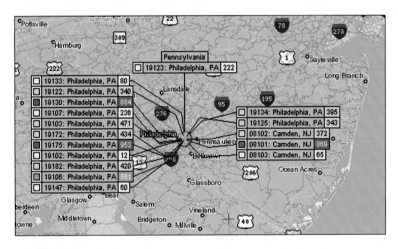

FIGURE 14.13

Dynamic labeling of items is still a challenge. Here, excentric labels in an NSpaceLab application (http://www.nspacelabs.com/) show all zip codes found inside the circle. The color hue indicates the region, and the intensity indicates the number of stores. Excentric labeling reveals hidden items, allowing their selection.

the Gene Ontology Database or read research papers on relevant biological pathways. The pursuit of meaning during discovery requires rapid access to rich sources of related information, which requires integration of data from multiple sources.

- *Viewing large volumes of data.* A general challenge to information visualization is the handling of large volumes of data. Many innovative prototypes can deal with only a few thousand items or have difficulty maintaining real-time interactivity when dealing with larger numbers of items. Dynamic visualizations showing millions of items (Fig. 14.14) demonstrate that information visualization is not yet close to reaching the limits of human visual abilities, and user-controlled aggregation mechanisms will push the envelope even

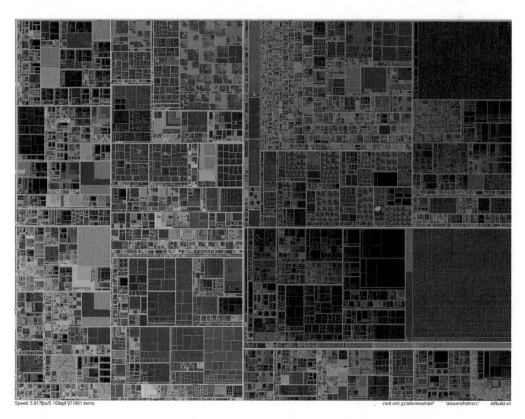

FIGURE 14.14

A treemap displaying a million files from a large file system, without aggregation (http://www. cs.umd.edu/hcil/millionvis/). Each rectangle is a file color-coded by file type. Files are grouped by directory. Careful examination of the high-resolution display reveals patterns, and special algorithms preserve the interactivity of the rich overviews and filtering tools (Fekete and Plaisant, 2002).

further (Shneiderman, 2008). Larger displays (Section 8.5.2) can help because additional pixels enable users to see more details while maintaining a reasonable overview.

- *Integrating data mining.* Information visualization and data mining originated from two separate lines of research. Information-visualization researchers believe in the importance of letting users' visual systems lead them to form hypotheses, while data-mining researchers believe that statistical algorithms and machine learning can be relied on to find interesting patterns. Some consumer purchasing patterns, such as spikes in demand before snowstorms or correlations between beer and pretzel purchases, stand out when properly visualized. However, statistical tests can be helpful in finding more subtle trends in consumer desires or demographic linkages for product purchases. Increasingly, researchers are combining the two approaches. Statistical summaries are appealing for their objective nature, but they can hide outliers or discontinuities (like freezing or boiling points). On the other hand, data mining might point users to more interesting parts of the data, which can then be visually inspected. For example, Spotfire's ViewTip suggests pairs of variables that show strong linear correlations, encouraging users to explore them.

- *Integrating with analytical reasoning techniques.* To support assessment, planning, and decision making, the field of visual analytics highlights the integration of information visualization with analytical reasoning tools (Fig. 14.15). Business and intelligence analysts use data and insights from searches and visualizations as evidence supporting or disclaiming competing hypotheses. They also need tools to rapidly produce summaries of their analyses and communicate their reasoning to decision makers, who may need to trace evidence back to the source (Thomas and Cook, 2005).

- *Collaborating with others.* Discovery is a complex process that depends on knowing what to look for, verifying assumptions by collaboration with others, noticing anomalies, and convincing others of the significance of a finding. Since support for social processes is critical to information visualization, software tools should make it easy to record the current state and send it to colleagues or post it to a web site with annotations and data (Chapter 9). The popular IBM web site called Many Eyes (Viégas et al., 2007; Fig. 1.2) allows users to upload their data, choose among various simple visualizations, and add a caption. Other users can then comment on the visualization or link to it from their blogs.

- *Achieving universal usability.* Making visualization tools accessible to diverse users regardless of their backgrounds, technical disadvantages, or personal disabilities is necessary when the tools are to be used by the public, but it remains a huge challenge for designers (Plaisant, 2004). For example, visually impaired users may need to use text-based alternatives to the visual display; a good example is provided by the National Cancer Institute's

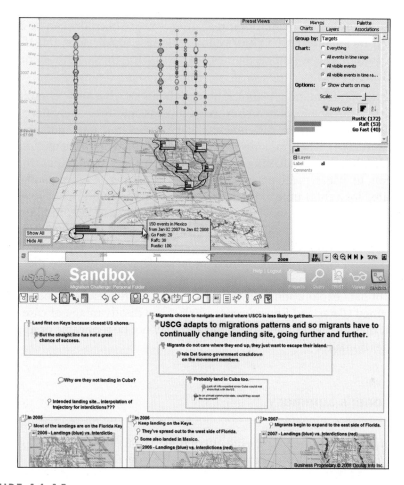

FIGURE 14.15

A visual-analytics user interface combines search, visualization, and the management of hypotheses. Here, the interface of GeoTime™ (top; http://www.oculusinfo.com/) shows geo-temporal patterns of immigrant boat landing, while the bottom frame shows examples of notes and hypotheses generated during the analysis. The green+ and red− icons indicate whether or not the evidence supports the hypothesis.

cancer atlas (http://www3.cancer.gov/atlasplus/). Encouraging results have been found with the sonification of graphs, scatterplots, and tables, and in the future, spatial sound might help sonify more complex data representations (Section 8.4.5). Tactile displays (Fig. 8.12) are still low resolution, but they may be useful when augmented with audio descriptions. Unfortunately, they are not widely available. Users with color deficiencies can be provided with alternative palettes or tools to customize the display colors. For example, the popular red/green palette of colors can be complemented by an alternative blue/yellow palette. ColorBrewer and VisCheck offer guidelines on color schemes that work for those with color vision impairment.

- *Evaluation.* Information visualization systems can be very complex. The analysis is rarely an isolated short-term process, and users may need to look at the same data from different perspectives over a long period of time (Plaisant, 2004). They may also be able to formulate and answer questions they didn't anticipate having before looking at the visualization (making it difficult to use typical empirical studies techniques), where subjects are recruited for a short time to work on imposed tasks. Finally, while discoveries can have a huge impact, they occur very rarely and are unlikely to be observed during a study. Insight-based studies, as described by Saraya, North, and Duca (2005), are one first step. Case studies report on users in their natural environments doing real tasks. They can describe discoveries, collaborations among users, frustrations of data cleansing, and the excitement of data exploration, and they can report on frequency of use and benefits gained (Perer and Shneiderman, 2008). The disadvantage of case studies is that they are very time-consuming and may not be replicable or applicable to other domains.

Practitioner's Summary

Information visualization is moving out of research laboratories, with a growing number of commercial products (such as those from TIBCO Spotfire, Tableau Software®, SAP Business Objects™, Gapminder, IBM Cognos®, ILOG®, and Macrofocus) and additions to statistical packages (SPSS®/ SigmaPlot®, SAS/GRAPH™, and DataDesk™) now available. Many other resources are also available to designers and developers, such as XmdvTool, GGobi, Common GIS, GeoVISTA Studio, the Indiana University InfoVis Repository, Jean-Daniel Fekete's InfoVis Toolkit, the University of Maryland's Piccolo toolkit for zooming user interfaces, and the Prefuse visualization toolkit. New products need to provide smooth integration with existing software and to support the full task list: overview, zoom, filter, details-on-demand, relate, history, and extract. These products will be attractive because they will present information rapidly and allow user-controlled exploration. If they are to be fully effective, they will require advanced data structures, high-resolution color displays, fast data retrieval, and novel forms of user training. Careful testing should be conducted to ensure that they go beyond the desire for "cool" interfaces and implement designs that have demonstrated benefits for realistic tasks.

Researcher's Agenda

The novel information-exploration tools—such as dynamic queries, treemaps, zoomable user interfaces, and parallel coordinates—are but a few of the inventions that user-interface researchers will have to tame and validate. A better integration with perceptual psychology (understanding preattentive processes and the impact of various coding or highlighting techniques), analytic reasoning, and business decision making (identifying tasks and procedures that occur in realistic situations) would accelerate progress. Similarly, theoretical foundations and practical benchmarks for choosing among the diverse emerging visualization techniques could guide researchers and developers. Since information exploration can result in complex interfaces that might overwhelm novice users, video demonstration and interactive training methods might be useful. Case studies and empirical studies using realistic data and tasks (e.g., from the Visual Analytics Science and Technology (VAST) Challenge) will help to sort out the specific situations in which visualization is most helpful. Finally, software toolkits for building visualizations will facilitate the exploration process.

WORLD WIDE WEB RESOURCES

http://www.aw.com/DTUI/

Information-visualization tools are growing more effective for a wider range of tasks, and commercial tools are now available.

References

Ahlberg, C. and Shneiderman, B., Visual information seeking: Tight coupling of dynamic query filters with starfield displays, *Proc. CHI '94 Conference: Human Factors in Computing Systems*, ACM Press, New York (1994), 313–321 and color plates.

Andrienko, Natalia and Andrienko, Gennady, *Exploratory Analysis of Spatial and Temporal Data, A Systematic Approach*, Springer-Verlag, New York (2005).

Bederson, B. B., Shneiderman, B., and Wattenberg, M., Ordered and quantum treemaps: Making effective use of 2D space to display hierarchies, *ACM Transactions on Graphics* 21, 4 (October 2002), 833–854.

Card, S., Information visualization, in Jacko, J. and Sears, A. (Editors), *The Human-Computer Interaction Handbook*, Lawrence Erlbaum Associates, Mahwah, NJ (2008), 544–582.

Card, S., Mackinlay, J., and Shneiderman, B., *Readings in Information Visualization: Using Vision to Think*, Morgan Kaufmann, San Francisco, CA (1999).

Card, S. and Nation, D., Degree-of-interest trees: A component of attention-reactive user interface, *Proc. Conference on Advanced Visual Interfaces (AVI 2002)*, ACM Press, New York (2002), 231–245.

Dodge, M. and Kitchin, R., *Atlas of Cyberspace*, Addison-Wesley, Reading, MA (2001).

Dykes, J., MacEachren A. M., and Kraak, M. J. (Editors), *Exploring Geovisualization*, Elsevier, Amsterdam, The Netherlands (2004).

Eick, Stephen, Maintenance of large systems, in Stasko, John, Domingue, John, Brown, Marc H., and Price, Blaine A. (Editors), *Software Visualization: Programming as a Multimedia Experience*, MIT Press, Cambridge, MA (1998), 315–328.

Fekete, J-D. and Plaisant, C., Interactive information visualization of a million items, *Proc. IEEE Symposium on Information Visualization*, IEEE Computer Press, Los Alamitos, CA (2002), 117–124.

Few, Stephen, *Information Dashboard Design: The Effective Visual Communication of Data*, O'Reilly Media, Sebastopol, CA (2006).

Grinstein, Georges, Keim, Daniel, and Ward, Matt, *Interactive Data Visualization: Foundations, Techniques, and Applications* (to appear).

Henry, N., Goodell, H., Elmqvist, N., and Fekete, J-D., 20 years of four HCI conferences: A visual exploration, *International Journal of Human-Computer Interaction* 23, 3 (2007), 239–285.

Herman, I., Melançon, G., and Marshall, M. S., Graph visualization and navigation in information visualization: A survey, *IEEE Transactions on Visualization and Computer Graphics* 6, 1 (2000), 24–43.

Hochheiser, H. and Shneiderman, B., Dynamic query tools for time series data sets: Timebox widgets for interactive exploration, *Information Visualization* 3, 1 (2004), 1–18.

Hornbæk, K., Bederson, B. B., and Plaisant, C., Navigation patterns and usability of zoomable user interfaces with and without an overview, *ACM Transactions on Computer-Human Interaction* 9, 4 (2002), 362–389.

Inselberg, A., *Parallel Coordinates: Visual Multidimensional Geometry and Its Applications*, Springer-Verlag, New York (2009).

Mackinlay, J.D., Hanrahan, P., and Stolte, C., Show me: Automatic presentation for visual analysis, *IEEE Transactions on Visualization and Computer Graphics* 13, 6 (2007), 1137–1144.

North, C., Conklin, N., and Saini, V., Visualization schemas for flexible information visualization, *Proc. IEEE Symposium on Information Visualization*, IEEE Computer Press, Los Alamitos, CA (2002), 15–22.

Perer, Adam and Shneiderman, Ben, Integrating statistics and visualization: Case studies of gaining clarity during exploratory data analysis, *Proc. SIGCHI Conference on Human Factors in Computing Systems*, ACM Press, New York (2008), 265–274.

Plaisant, C., Information visualization and the challenge of universal access, in Dynes, J., MacEachren, A. M., and Kraak, M. J. (Editors), *Exploring Geovisualization*, Elsevier, Amsterdam, The Netherlands (2004).

Plaisant, C., The challenge of information visualization evaluation, *Proc. Conference on Advanced Visual Interfaces (AVI 2004)*, ACM Press, New York (2004), 109–116.

Plaisant, C., Grosjean, J., and Bederson, B. B., SpaceTree: Supporting exploration in large node link tree, design evolution and empirical evaluation, *Proc. IEEE Symposium on Information Visualization*, IEEE Computer Press, Los Alamitos, CA (2002), 57–64.

Plaisant, C., Mushlin, R., Snyder, A., Li, J., Heller, D., and Shneiderman, B., LifeLines: Using visualization to enhance navigation and analysis of patient records, *American Medical Informatics Association Annual Fall Symposium*, AMIA, Bethesda, MD (1998), 76–80.

Robertson, George G., Card, Stuart K., and Mackinlay, Jock D., Information visualization using 3-D interactive animation, *Communications of the ACM* 36, 4 (April 1993), 56–71.

Saraiya, P., North, C., and Duca, K., An insight-based methodology for evaluating bioinformatics visualization, *IEEE Trans. Visualization and Computer Graphics* 11, 4 (2005), 443–456.

Shneiderman, B., Dynamic queries for visual information seeking, *IEEE Software* 11, 6 (1994), 70–77.

Shneiderman, B., Extreme visualization: Squeezing a billion records into a million pixels, *Proc. ACM SIGMOD 2008 International Conference on the Management of Data*, ACM Press, New York (June 2008), 3–12.

Shneiderman, B., Treemaps for space-constrained visualization of hierarchies (2009). Available at http://www.cs.umd.edu/hcil/treemap-history.

Silva, S. F. and Catarci, T., Visualization of linear time-oriented data: A survey, *Proc. First International Conference on Web Information Systems Engineering (WISE '00)*, IEEE Computer Press, Los Alamitos, CA (2000), 310–319.

Spence, Robert, *Information Visualization: Design for Interaction, Second Edition*, Prentice Hall, Upper Saddle River, NJ (2007).

Stasko, John, Domingue, John, Brown, Marc H., and Price, Blaine A. (Editors), *Software Visualization: Programming as a Multimedia Experience*, MIT Press, Cambridge, MA (1998).

Thomas, J., and Cook, K. (Editors), *Illuminating the Path—The Research and Development Agenda for Visual Analytics*, IEEE Computer Press, Los Alamitos, CA (2005).

Tufte, E., *The Visual Display of Quantitative Information*, Graphics Press, Cheshire, CT (1983).

Tufte, E., *Beautiful Evidence*, Graphics Press, Cheshire, CT (2006).

Viégas, Fernanda and Wattenberg, Martin, Tag clouds and the case for vernacular visualization, *ACM interactions* 15, 4 (2008), 49–52.

Viégas, Fernanda, Wattenberg, Martin, van Ham, Frank, Kriss, Jesse, and McKeon, Matt, Many Eyes: A site for visualization at Internet scale, *IEEE Transactions on Visualization and Computer Graphics* 13, 6 (2007), 1121–1128.

Ware, Colin, *Visual Thinking for Design*, Morgan Kaufmann, San Francisco, CA (2008).

Wise, J. A., Thomas, J., Pennock, K., Lantrip, D., Pottier, M., Schur, A., and Crow, V., Visualizing the non-visual: Spatial analysis and interaction with information from text documents, *Proc. IEEE Symposium on Information Visualization*, IEEE Computer Press, Los Alamitos, CA (1995), 51–58.

AFTERWORD

Societal and Individual Impact of User Interfaces

> **"** The machine itself makes no demands and holds out no promises: it is the human spirit that makes demands and keeps promises. In order to reconquer the machine and subdue it to human purposes, one must first understand it and assimilate it. So far we have embraced the machine without fully understanding it. **"**
>
> **Lewis Mumford**
> *Technics and Civilization*, 1934

A.1 Future Interfaces

Human-computer interaction (HCI) researchers and usability professionals can reflect proudly on three decades of accomplishments such as the development of graphical user interfaces, the World Wide Web, online communities, user-generated content, mobile devices, and much more. User interfaces are not perfect, but they have facilitated progress in many fields, including medical care, education, management, science, and engineering. They have also spawned consumer success stories in e-commerce, mobile communication, and entertainment.

This Afterword considers future directions (Section A.1) and cautions about some potential dangers (Section A.2). It then reviews continuing controversies over the design of user interfaces (Section A.3).

The natural question that journalists ask of HCI researchers is: What is the next big thing? One popular school of thought claims that future innovations emerge from advanced technology development, often based on Moore's Law (which described the rapid increase in chip densities, leading to the proliferation of faster and cheaper computers). Leaders of this view believe that advances will come by developing new devices, especially those that are ubiquitous and pervasive, suggesting that they can be everywhere, cheap, and small. A second theme is that these new devices will be wearable, mobile, personal, and portable, suggesting that they can be carried by users at all times. The third theme is that these new devices will be embedded, context-aware, and ambient, suggesting that they will be built into our surroundings (and thereby invisible) but available when needed and responsive to user needs. Finally, some of these new devices are labeled as perceptive and multimodal, suggesting that they can perceive user needs and allow interaction by visual, aural, tactile, haptic, gestural, and other stimuli. The students of this school of thought have generated clever innovations, such as tiny medical sensors that monitor health, hidden detectors that protect from dangers, and entertainment devices that enrich experiences. Technology development is a fertile source of new ideas and generates rich media attention for the compelling scenarios (Norman, 2007).

A second school of thought, centered on universal usability, suggests that the focus of the next decades will be on spreading the early successes to a broader community of users (Lazar, 2007; Shneiderman 2000). Proponents of this view believe that they can enable every person to benefit from information and communications technologies. Advocates of universal usability claim that this principle can stimulate innovative advances. Certainly, bringing cellphones to three billion users has advanced the infrastructure technologies and promoted novel business models. Broad use has also pushed cellphone user interfaces to be multilingual, usable in demanding conditions, and effective for a wide range of tasks. Progress towards universal usability is measured by the steadily increasing percentage of the world's population that has convenient, low-cost access to communication and Internet services.

There are still many forgotten users, especially low-income citizens in every country and many residents of developing nations. E-mail, web sites, and many services can be reshaped to accommodate weak writers and readers, while helping to improve their skills. Job training and searching can be organized to serve those people with poor employment skills and transient lifestyles. Services such as voting, motor vehicle registration, health information, or crime reporting can be enhanced if universal usability requirements are assumed. Designers can begin by improving interfaces for common tasks and then provide training and help methods so that using a computer becomes a satisfying opportunity, rather than a frustrating challenge. Evolutionary learning with multilayer interfaces would allow first-time users to succeed with common tasks and provide a clear, nonthreatening growth path to more complex features.

Tailoring of interfaces for diverse populations can be accomplished by improving dialog boxes to allow users to specify easily their national languages, preferred units of measurement, skill levels, and more. Portability to nonstandard hardware, accommodation of varying screen sizes or modem speeds, and design for physically challenged and older adult users can be common practices. Support for learning new interfaces with recorded demonstrations can be refined. Convenient semantic tagging of data and multimedia enables software designers to reformat their presentations to adjust to users' needs.

A third school of thought argues that the profound shift is from the traditional, introverted computer users to the new, eager-to-connect social users who employ communications technologies to build and maintain rich social networks. The supporters of this school of thought point to the enormous success of Facebook, MySpace, and LinkedIn and to the growing use of online communities, blogs, microblogs (e.g., Twitter), wikis, cellphones, text messaging, and instant messaging. They also see the rapid growth of user-generated content, such as videos, music, podcasts, photos, annotations, and reviews, as a sign of the desire for social media that weave people together. They are hopeful that the payoffs in terms of supportive neighborhoods, empathic communities, and collective intelligence will be large, but they realistically assess the dangers of distraction, multitasking, and fragmented attention (Shirky, 2008; Thompson, 2008; Maloney-Krichmar and Preece, 2005).

A fourth school of thought claims that those attending to individual and societal needs will generate appropriate socio-technical innovations more often (Whitworth and de Moor, 2009). Supporters of this view are most likely to discuss values, privacy, trust, empathy, and responsibility, while raising ethical issues of bias, disruption, and harmful side effects (Himma and Tavani, 2008; Hochheiser and Lazar, 2007; Friedman et al., 2006). Increasingly, the problems of modern society require interdisciplinary teams and novel research methods that blend traditional natural sciences with social sciences, ethics, and policy studies (Shneiderman, 2008).

These diverse schools of thought may all be needed in dealing with the difficult societal challenges that are likely to define the future of human-computer interaction research. Usability is increasingly seen as a key factor in successful professional tools, mobile devices, consumer electronics, games, and web sites for social media, e-commerce, and user-generated content. The strength of human-computer interaction lies in its integrative approach, which combines rigorous science, sophisticated technology, and sensitivity to human needs. This approach will be necessary for the complex socio-technical systems required for all of the following important purposes:

- *Terror prevention.* The aftermath of the terrorist attacks in New York City and Washington, D.C. on September 11, 2001 as well as subsequent attacks in Bali, London, Madrid, and Mumbai created many new needs for protective technologies. Some of these are tied to detecting terrorist activities in time to stop them, while others are intended to better protect potential targets. Ambitious efforts to collect extensive records from every resident have the serious risk of violating privacy and increasing discrimination. Worse still, such efforts may be an ineffective means to prevent terrorism. Alternatives are to focus analysts' attention on specific threats with data, such as visa applications, financial transfers among identified individuals, purchases of restricted materials, and hospital emergency room admissions. Biometric identification could be a valuable tool in reducing terrorist attacks and other criminal activity, but implementation, accuracy, and privacy problems must be addressed. Positive approaches are to increase understanding of other cultures through their history and languages, thereby building relationships that promote conflict resolution.

- *Disaster response.* The crucial role of communication among residents and with aid workers was highlighted by the disastrous tsunami in Aceh, Indonesia on December 26, 2004; by hurricane Katrina, which struck New Orleans, LA on August 29, 2005; and by later hurricanes, such as Rita, Gustav, and Ike. Communities can be increasingly resilient if they have effective communication that facilitates damage assessment, allocation of resources, restoration of services, rebuilding, job creation, and more. A different story of social media participation emerged following the tragedy at Virginia Tech on April 16, 2007, when a shooter killed 32 people. Students with cellphones were part of the reporting process, providing immediate photos and videos for CNN and other news media. Within hours, 1500 students self-organized to collaboratively write a factually accurate extensive Wikipedia article. In such crises, web sites that allow individual reporting of status ("I'm OK, and have gone to Susan's dorm for the night") would help friends and family to know the condition of their loved ones. Well-designed social networks could help communities prepare for disaster and even reduce damage.

- *International development.* In communities where adequate housing, sanitation, and food are still problems, information and communications technologies are not primary needs, but they can be helpful as part of an overall development plan. Community-networking technologies that are used in financially secure cities such as Singapore and Seattle are being adapted to mountainous Nepal, urban Rio de Janeiro, and rural Botswana. Multilingual designs and citizen participation will accelerate education and adoption. International efforts to create a global information society and promote development are coordinated by United Nations agencies, regional alliances, and many smaller nongovernmental organizations. The United Nations Millennium Development goals, to be achieved by 2015, include: eradicate extreme poverty and hunger; achieve universal primary education; promote gender equality and empower women; reduce child mortality; improve maternal health; combat HIV/AIDS, malaria, and other diseases; ensure environmental sustainability; and develop a global partnership for development.

- *Medical informatics.* The scientific exploration of genomics requires intense computer support to enable researchers to understand the biological pathways that govern cell processes. As researchers improve their understanding, new treatments will emerge, even for severe diseases such as cancer and HIV/AIDS. Medical care by physicians and nurses will also improve as interfaces enable refined diagnoses and treatment plans, as well as the basic recordkeeping necessary for hospitals and clinics. Improved search facilities for electronic health records could enable virtual clinical trials for each patient to choose treatment plans by studying outcomes with similar patients. Many of the deaths from medical errors—estimated at 98,000 each year in the United States alone—could be avoided with improved medical informatics. Web sites and online community discussions will help patients become better informed. Home medical devices will become important components of health monitoring and personal health care, although standard data formats and interfaces are necessary. Vigorous efforts with patient-controlled health records could lead to greater user responsibility for their medical information and create a remarkable resource for researchers.

- *Environmental protection and sustainable energy.* The dual issues of climate change and energy policies will have a profound effect in the coming decades (Blevis, 2007). The persuasive power of well-designed user interfaces will be part of any solution by providing feedback about environmental changes and energy consumption (Fogg, 2002; Hanks et al., 2008). Many drivers of the Toyota Prius carefully monitor their gas consumption through the innovative dashboard display that shows the state of the hybrid engine. Homeowners who get detailed visual displays of their energy consumption are more likely to use energy-conserving practices such as off-peak or reduced usage of appliances. Carbon calculators give users an understanding of how they might change their commuting, heating, or purchasing behaviors. Some users respond to simple numerical reports or bar charts, but other users may be more motivated by artistic approaches (Holmes, 2007).

- *E-commerce.* Advertising and shopping have become major applications of the World Wide Web, especially for products such as books, music, airline tickets, hotel accommodations, and auctions of personal goods. As universal usability expands markets, designers are fashioning convenient web sites and designing trust-management strategies that reduce fraud. Web-site optimization strategies are helping commercial clients make efficient web sites, while search engine optimization ensures that they reach their intended audiences. The targeted ads tied to search terms have been enormously successful, and the convenience of information gathering for product and price comparison facilitates commerce.

- *Government services.* Citizen access will continue to improve for services such as motor vehicle registration, business licenses, tax information, parks and recreation facilities, and much more. Well-designed voting technologies that are reliable, secure, and usable by all citizens could generate higher levels of participation and trust in public institutions. Local, state, and national services will grow over time as universal usability expands the number of users. Government reluctance to use social media participation and enable user-generated content is understandable, but innovative strategies and partnerships could facilitate innovative services from trusted government sources. Improved feedback from residents would help designers reshape their web sites.

- *Creativity support.* Technology has always been a part of creative endeavors in music, art, science, and engineering. Now user interfaces are enabling a more rapid pace of discovery through information visualization and easier consultation through collaboration technologies. Advanced tools smoothly integrate data mining and other statistical techniques to detect patterns, clusters, outliers, gaps, and anomalies. They support hypothesis generation as well as testing and allow users to see patterns that may surprise them. Advanced composition tools permit rapid exploration of alternatives in music, art, animation, and writing that support the explosion in user-generated content. Well-designed tools also allow users to make global changes, search for patterns, enforce useful constraints, and prevent errors. Having a large audience who comment and critique user-generated content encourages production and stimulates higher quality. The potential is growing to enable more people to be more creative more often (Shneiderman, 2007).

Undoubtedly, other opportunities and unexpected developments in human-computer interaction research will occur. Conducting research on these complex socio-technical systems requires fresh thinking as well. The traditional controlled experimental approaches will need to be complemented by rigorous and repeated in-depth case studies. These problems will require improved transdisciplinary methods that could form the basis of new forms of science (Shneiderman, 2008; Berners-Lee et al., 2006; Yin, 2003). Another way to gain ideas about future directions is to assess the serious problems that plague users, discussed in the next section.

A.2 Ten Plagues of the Information Age

66 The real question before us lies here: Do these instruments further life and enhance its values, or not? 99

Mumford
Technics and Civilization, 1934

It would be naïve to assume that widespread use of computers brings only benefits. There are legitimate reasons to worry that increased dissemination of information and communications technologies might lead to a variety of personal, organizational, political, or social oppressions. People who fear computers have good reason for their concerns. The disruption from unwanted e-mail (spam), malicious viruses, pornography, and other annoyances must be addressed if we desire to increase the beneficial uses of these technologies. Designers have an opportunity and a responsibility to be alert to the dangers and to make thoughtful decisions about reducing them. The following is a list of potential and real dangers from use of information and communications technologies:

1. *Anxiety.* Many people avoid the computer or use it with great anxiety; they experience *computer shock*, *web worry*, or *network neurosis*. Their anxieties include fear of breaking the machine, worry over losing control, trepidation about appearing foolish or incompetent ("computers make you feel so dumb"), or more general concern about facing something new. These anxieties are real, should be acknowledged rather than dismissed, and can often be overcome with positive experiences. Can we build improved user interfaces that will reduce the high level of anxiety experienced by many users?

2. *Alienation.* As people spend more time using computers and mobile devices, they may become less connected to other people. Computer users as a group are more introverted than others, and increased time with the computer may increase their isolation. The dedicated game player who rarely communicates with another person is an extreme case, but what happens to the emotional relationships of a person who spends eight hours per day dealing with e-mail instead of chatting with colleagues or family members? Can we build user interfaces that encourage more constructive human social interaction?

3. *Information-poor minority.* Although some utopian visionaries believe that information and communications technologies will eliminate the distinctions between rich and poor or will right social injustices, often these tools are just another way in which the disadvantaged are disadvantaged (NTIA, 2008). People who have weak computer skills may have a new reason for not succeeding in school or not getting a job. The well-documented differences in access by rich versus poor communities or nations can be overcome if we recognize them and make commitments to bridging the gap by offering appropriate access, training, support, and services. Can we build user interfaces that empower low-skilled workers to perform at the level of experts? Can we provide training and education for every member of society?

4. *Impotence of the individual.* Large organizations can become impersonal because the cost of handling special cases is great. Individuals who are frustrated in trying to receive personal treatment and attention may vent their anger at the organization, the personnel they encounter, or the technology that limits rather than enables. People who have tried to find out the current status of their social security accounts or have banks explain accounting discrepancies are aware of the problems, especially if they have language or hearing deficits, or other physical or cognitive handicaps. How can we design so that individuals will feel more empowered and self-actualized?

5. *Bewildering complexity and speed.* The tax, welfare, and insurance regulations developed by computer-based bureaucracies are so complex and fast-changing

that it is extremely difficult for individuals to make informed choices. Even knowledgeable technology users are often overwhelmed by the torrent of new software packages, mobile devices, and web services, each with hundreds of features and options. Speed dominates, and more features are seen as preferable. Simplicity is a simple, but too often ignored, principle. Stern adherence to basic principles of design may be the only path to a safer, more sane, simpler, and slower world where human concerns predominate.

6. *Organizational fragility.* As organizations come to depend on more complex technology, they can become fragile. When hardware breakdowns, security lapses, or virus attacks occur, they can propagate rapidly and halt the work of many people (Friedman et al., 2005). With computer-based airline services, telephone switching, or electricity grids, failures can mean rapid and widespread shutdowns of service. Since networks can cause concentration of expertise, a small number of people can disrupt a large organization. Can developers anticipate the dangers and produce robust, fault tolerant designs?

7. *Invasion of privacy.* The widely reported threat of invasion of privacy is worrisome because the concentration of information and the existence of powerful retrieval systems make it possible to violate the privacy of many people easily and rapidly. Of course, well-designed computer systems have the potential of becoming more secure than paper systems if managers are dedicated to privacy protection. Airline, telephone, bank, medical, legal, and employment records can reveal much about an individual if confidentiality is compromised. Can managers seek policies and systems that reduce privacy threats from commercial organizations and government agencies?

8. *Unemployment and displacement.* As automation spreads, productivity and overall employment may increase, but some jobs may become less valued or even eliminated. Retraining can help some employees, but others will have difficulty changing lifetime patterns of work. Especially in recessionary times, displacement may happen to low-paid clerks or highly paid automobile machinists whose work is outsourced overseas or automated. Can employers develop labor policies that ensure retraining and guarantee jobs?

9. *Lack of professional responsibility.* Faceless organizations may respond impersonally to, and deny responsibility for, problems. The complexity of technology and organizations provides ample opportunities for employees to pass the blame on to others or to the computer: "Sorry, the computer won't let us loan you the library book without your machine-readable card." Will users of medical diagnostic or defense-related user interfaces be able to escape responsibility for decisions? Will user interfaces become more trusted than a person's word or a professional's judgment? Complex and confusing user interfaces enable users and designers to blame the machine, but with

improved designs, users and designers will give and accept credit and responsibility where they are due.

10. *Deteriorating image of people.* With the development of *intelligent interfaces, smart machines,* and *expert systems,* it seems that the machines have indeed *taken over* human abilities. These misleading phrases not only generate anxiety about computers and robots, but also may undermine the image that we have of people and their abilities. Some behavioral psychologists suggest that we are little more than machines; some artificial intelligence workers believe that the automation of many human abilities is within reach. The rich diversity of human skills, the generative or creative nature of daily life, the emotional or passionate side of human endeavor, and the idiosyncratic imagination of each child seem lost or undervalued. Can robotic scenarios for medical services, elder care, and warfare be tempered with an appreciation for the role of human relationships and judgment (Asaro, 2008; Weizenbaum, 1976)?

Undoubtedly, more plagues and problems exist. Each situation is a small warning for the designer. Each design is an opportunity to apply technology in positive, constructive ways that avoid these dangers. There is no sure vaccine for preventing the ten plagues outlined here. Even well-intentioned designers can inadvertently spread them, but alert, dedicated designers whose consciousness is raised can reduce the dangers. Strategies for preventing the plagues and reducing their effects include the following:

- *Human-centered participatory design.* Concentrate attention on the users and the tasks they must accomplish. Make users the center of attention, include them in the design process, and build feelings of competence, mastery, clarity, and predictability. Construct well-organized menus, present specific and constructive instructions and messages, develop comprehensible displays, offer informative feedback, enable error prevention, ensure appropriate response times, and produce comprehensible learning materials.

- *Organizational support.* Beyond the interface design, the organization must also support the users. Apply participatory design strategies and elicit frequent evaluations and feedback from users. Techniques include personal interviews, focus groups, online surveys, paper questionnaires, online communities, online consultants, and suggestion boxes.

- *Job design.* European labor unions have been active in setting rules for computer users to prevent the exhaustion, stress, or burnout caused by *electronic shops.* Rules might be set to limit hours of use, guarantee rest periods, facilitate job rotation, and support education. Similarly, negotiated measures of productivity or error rates can help reward exemplary workers and guide training. Monitoring or metering of work must be done cautiously, but both managers and employees can be beneficiaries of a thoughtful plan.

- *Education.* The complexity of modern life and user interfaces makes education critical. Schools and colleges, as well as employers, all play a role in training. Special attention should be paid to continuing education, on-the-job training, and teacher education.

- *Feedback, recognition, and rewards.* User communities have become actively engaged in providing user-generated content and participating in governance. They can help set community norms that promote respectful behavior, encourage design improvements by communicating with managers and designers, and help fellow users to learn what they need. Constructive contributions should be acknowledged by recognition such as the ACM Awards for professional contributions and the Webby Awards for effective design.

- *Public consciousness raising.* Informed consumers and users of information and communications technologies can benefit the entire community. Professional societies such as the ACM, IEEE, HFES, and UPA and user groups can play a key role through public relations, consumer education, and professional standards of ethics.

- *Legislation.* Much progress has been made with legislation concerning privacy, right of access to information, and computer crime, but more work remains to be done. Cautious steps towards regulation, work rules, and standardization can be highly beneficial. Dangers of restrictive legislation do exist, but thoughtful legal protection will stimulate development and prevent abuses.

- *Advanced research.* Individuals, organizations, and governments can support research to develop novel ideas, minimize the dangers of technology, and spread the advantages of interactive systems. Improved theories of cognitive behavior, individual differences, community evolution, and organizational change would be helpful in guiding designers and implementers.

A.3 Continuing Controversies

66 Unlike machines, human minds can create ideas. We need ideas to guide us to progress, as well as tools to implement them. . . . Computers don't contain "brains" any more than stereos contain musical instruments. . . . Machines only manipulate numbers; people connect them to meaning. 99

Penzias
Ideas and Information, 1989

Many of the rapid advances in user interfaces have been shaped by the contrasting visions of researchers and designers, which have sometimes broken out into heated controversies. There have been continuing debates over which directions would be most fruitful. In each case, there is room for victory claims by all parties and reasons to believe that with more research funding the future will favor their positions. Informed discussion can lead to agreement, or at least ways to balance the dangers with greater protection. Issues at the center of the debates include:

- *Machine automation versus user control.* This fundamental issue remains a lively source of controversy, spawning many sub-debates about issues such as the degree of automation in cockpits, the utility of automatic indentation in word processors, and the dangers of autonomous agents in financial markets. While designers are often proud to enhance automation, users—some more than others—often want to be in control. Users' desire for mastery and a sense of accomplishment can be undermined by an overly enthusiastic interface that does more than they want. Making automation understandable, predictable, and controllable helps in many situations, especially if designers have built-in highlighting and other informative feedback to make the machine's state clear to users. Some examples may help clarify why users may desire control. Doctors do not want machines that make medical diagnoses; rather, they want machines that enable them to make more accurate, reliable diagnoses, to obtain relevant references to scientific papers or clinical trials, to gather consultative support rapidly, and to record that support accurately. Similarly, air-traffic or manufacturing controllers do not want machines that automatically do their jobs; rather they want machines that increase their productivity, reduce their error rates, and enable them to handle special cases or emergencies effectively. The argument for user control is tied to the belief that an increase in personal responsibility will result in improved service. Advocates of increased automation argue that in some complex fast-moving situations (such as NASA shuttle launchings), only a machine can make adequately fast and accurate decisions. In such cases, careful design and thorough testing are much needed, but launch failures and the long history of computer glitches should be cautionary tales for those who believe that automation can be made to be flawless.

- *Speech recognition versus visual interaction.* Early dreamers believed that speech was the "natural" way for humans to interact and therefore that speech recognition would be the "natural" way for users to operate computers. While speech-recognition technology has matured, it has proven to be only modestly effective in interfaces. Dictation and limited phone-based systems have shown steady improvements, but the huge success story has been visual interaction. Computers are not like people; they have large displays that can rapidly offer visual overviews, present large forms to fill in, and offer multiple choices in menus. Since the cognitive load of speaking is high, it makes good design sense to instead allow users to point and click (activities the human brain can process in parallel with planning). In addition to visual displays, well-designed interfaces allow operators of digital cameras, game computers, and fighter planes to rapidly slide switches, press buttons, and move joysticks.

- *Natural-language interaction versus direct manipulation.* The early fantasy of typing commands or speaking to computers in natural language to get answers to questions has thrived in Hollywood but languished on Wall Street and Main Street. The idea remains alive in scenarios of typing natural-language questions to web-based agents or speaking simple commands to household appliances, but the commercial markets have grown more rapidly for direct manipulation and graphical user interfaces. Natural-language interaction, whether by typing or talking, has usually proven to be more cumbersome and slower than pointing, dragging, and clicking on graphical representations. Devotees of natural-language interaction still believe that with further research improvements their approach could become attractive, but direct-manipulation strategies also continue to improve.

- *Anthropomorphic partners versus human operation.* The metaphors, images, and names chosen for user interfaces play a key role in the designers' and users' perceptions. It is not surprising that many user interface designers still mimic human or animal forms: Our first attempts at flight imitated birds, and the first designs for microphones followed the shape of the human ear. Such primitive visions may be useful starting points, but success comes most rapidly to people who move beyond these simple concepts. Except for purposes of amusement or for crash test dummies, the goal is rarely to accurately mimic the human form, but rather is to provide effective service to the users in accomplishing their tasks. Lewis Mumford, in his classic book *Technics and Civilization* (1934), characterized the problem of "dissociation of the animate and the mechanical" as the "obstacle of animism." He described Leonardo da Vinci's attempt to reproduce the motion of birds' wings, then Ader's batlike airplane (as late as 1897), and Branca's steam engine in the form of a human head and torso. Mumford wrote: "The most ineffective kind of machine is the realistic mechanical imitation of a man or another animal . . . for thousands of years animism has stood in the way of . . . development." Choosing human or animal forms as the inspiration for some projects is understandable, but significant advances will come more quickly if designers recognize the goals that serve human needs and the inherent attributes of the technology that is employed. Hand-held calculators do not follow human forms, but they serve effectively for doing arithmetic. Designers of championship chess-playing programs no longer imitate human strategies, but use hardware accelerators to explore billions of alternatives. Vision-systems researchers have realized the advantages of radar or sonar range finders and retreated from using human-like stereo depth-perception cues. Mature technologies such as industrial robots, clothes-washing machines, or robotic vacuum cleaners are not based on anthropomorphic designs. Still, in recent years, the belief in human-inspired robot design has been carried forward by a community of researchers who have shown some successes in helping autistic children, providing training, and offering robotic assistance for older adults.

- *Adaptive versus adaptable interfaces.* Designers who believe in their capacity to model and thereby anticipate user needs have proposed adaptive interfaces in which the layout and content change based on past user performance. Their goal of helping users by offering only relevant interface controls and content is admirable, but there are two problems: (1) users are not always predictable, so the changes based on past performance may not be helpful, and (2) changing interfaces can be surprising and disruptive to users who become familiar with a stable choice set. A successful compromise is to keep a stable display and then add one element—for example, a toolbar—that offers varying choices. Another useful adaptation might be in display areas that are already changing, such as a newspaper web site that has a box filled with topics predicted to be of interest to a specific user.

- *Media richness versus lean design.* Some communications theorists have argued that users will prefer and perform more effectively with richer media. They believe that videoconferencing would win over telephone conferencing, and that phone conversations are inherently more effective than typewritten messages. There are times when these beliefs are valid, but the surprising successes are often with leaner designs. Videoconferencing has the extra burden of requiring participants to give more attention to how they look and to show their interest in other speakers. By contrast, phone conferences allow participants to check e-mail or do something else during less interesting moments in the conversation. Similarly, text messaging and Twitter have become huge success stories because the messages exchanged are lightweight, take less time to read, are easily searched, saved, and re-sent. Both sides in this controversy have good claims for success, but over-generalizing leads to flawed predictions. While users often appreciate rich media with high-resolution video and high-quality audio, the high payoffs in rapid usage and low cognitive load for lean designs are also strong.

- *3D versus 2D interfaces.* The compelling success of Hollywood filmmakers in telling stories and showing the world through moving images is apparent. The three-dimensional video games from Electronic Arts®, Sony, Microsoft, Nintendo and others, as well as the animated films from Pixar®, Industrial

Light & Magic®, or Disney®, are stunning accomplishments for the graphics technology community. They offer users and viewers satisfying experiences that would be difficult to achieve in two-dimensional flat representations. However, in showing information, 2D strategies are almost always more effective: Users tend to initially favor 3D, but with regular use, well-designed 2D interfaces are perceived as more effective and preferred. Despite the attraction of 3D, immersive 3D interfaces and even 3D glasses to give stereo effects have not yet proven to be widely effective or popular. Here again, the controversy has led to refined understanding that higher dimensions and more immersive environments are not always better. Lower cognitive load, simplified navigation, less occlusion, and powerful actions are attractive goals.

- *Data gathering versus privacy.*   Technology advances have given corporations and governments the capacity to collect vast amounts of data about individuals to advance their commercial or security goals. However well intended the goals are, the loss of individual privacy because of rapid search capabilities is a dramatic change that is disturbing to many people. While radio-frequency identification (RFID) tags can speed drivers through toll booths or commuters through train stations, the detailed tracking of personal behaviors undermines traditional expectations. Credit databases facilitate loans, but they are a centralized collection of personal information that could be used by criminals or oppressive political groups. Terrorist-detection schemes may promote security, but data-mining strategies have been challenged as ineffective and potentially invasive of personal privacy (NAS, 2008), while other approaches might simultaneously increase security as well as privacy. Even social-networking and user-generated–content web sites raise concerns as individuals put personal information and photos in public spaces where they could be maliciously misused.

Controversies are an indicator of lively interest and emergent technologies. New controversies are arising about the benefits of ambient displays, strategies for motivating participation in social media participation, technologies to protect privacy, and much more. If controversies signal strength, our discipline is thriving.

Practitioner's Summary

Successful interactive user interfaces will bring ample rewards to their designers, but widespread use of effective tools is only the means to reach higher goals. A user interface is more than a technological artifact; interactive systems, especially when linked by computer networks, create human sociotechnical systems. As Marshall McLuhan pointed out, "The medium is the message," and therefore each interactive user interface is a message from the designer to the user. That message has often been a harsh one with the underlying implication that the designer does not care about the user. Nasty error messages are obvious manifestations; complex menus, cluttered screens, and confusing dialog boxes are also phrases in the unsympathetic message.

Most designers want to send a more kind and caring message. Designers, implementers, and researchers are learning to send warmer greetings to users, via effective and well-tested user interfaces. The message of quality is compelling to the recipients and can instill good feelings, appreciation for the designer, and the desire to excel in one's own work. The capacity for excellent systems to instill compassion and connection was noted by Sterling (1974) at the end of his guidelines for information systems: "In the long run what may be important is the *texture* of a system. By texture we mean the *quality* the system has to evoke in users and participants a feeling that the system increases the kinship among people." This prescient statement anticipated the enormous growth of social media participation and communications tools, and the desire of people to share their user-generated content. More than ever, user interface designers have a large challenge before them and a share in the responsibility for the development of human relationships. Let's use this opportunity well, to create a better world.

Researcher's Agenda

Interface designers can work towards furthering such high-level goals as world peace, excellent health care, energy efficiency, adequate nutrition, and safe transportation. In addition to these basic needs, designers should aspire to advance the causes of accessible education for all, improved communication, freedom of expression, support for creative exploration, and socially constructive entertainment. Computer technology can help us attain these high-level goals if we clearly state measurable objectives, obtain the participation of professionals, and design effective human-computer interfaces. Design considerations include adequate attention to individual differences among users; support of social and organizational structures; design for reliability and safety; provision of access by older adults, physically challenged, or illiterate users; and appropriate user-controlled adaptation.

The expectations that new devices will be universally usable, and support creativity imply enough ambitious research projects for a generation. Terror prevention, disaster response, international development, medical informatics, e-commerce, and government services are the most appealing candidates for early research, because the impact of changes could be so large. If we are to provide novel services to diverse users, we need effective theories and rigorous empirical research to achieve ease of learning, rapid performance, low error rates, and good retention over time, while preserving high subjective satisfaction.

WORLD WIDE WEB RESOURCES

http://www.aw.com/DTUI/

Organizations dealing with ethics, social impact, and public policy are doing their best to make computing and information services as helpful as possible. These organizations offer ways for you to become an activist.

References

Asaro, Peter, How just could a robot war be?, in Brey, Philip, Briggle, Adam, and Waelbers, Katinka (Editors), *Current Issues in Computing and Philosophy*, IOS Publishers, Amsterdam, The Netherlands (2008), 50–64.

Atkinson, Robert D. and Castro, Daniel D., *Digital Quality of Life: Understanding the Personal and Social Benefits of the Information Technology Revolution*, Information Technology and Innovation Foundation, Washington, D.C. (October 2008). Available at http://www.itif.org/files/DQOL.pdf.

Berners-Lee, T., Hall, W., Hendler, J., Shadbolt, N., and Weitzner, D., Creating a science of the Web, *Science* 313, 11 (August 2006), 769–771.

Blevis, Eli, Sustainable interaction design: Invention & disposal, renewal & reuse. *Proc. CHI 2007 Conference: Human Factors in Computing Systems*, ACM Press, New York (2007), 503–512.

Fogg, B.J., *Persuasive Technology: Using Computers to Change What We Think and Do*, Morgan Kaufmann, San Francisco, CA (2002).

Friedman, Batya, Kahn, Peter H., Jr., and Borning, Alan, Value sensitive design and information systems, in Zhang, P. and Galletta, D. (Editors), *Human-Computer Interaction in Management Information Systems: Foundations*, M. E. Sharpe, Armonk, New York (2006), 348–372.

Friedman, B., Lin, P., and Miller, J. K., In Cranor, L. and Garfinkel, S. (Eds.) Informed consent by design, in *Security and Usability: Designing Secure Systems That People Can Use*, O'Reilly Media, Sebastopol, CA (2005), 495–521.

Hanks, Kristin, Odom, William, Roedl, David, and Blevis, Eli, Sustainable millennials: Attitudes towards sustainability and the material effects of interactive technologies, *Proc. CHI 2008 Conference: Human Factors in Computing Systems*, ACM Press, New York (2008), 333–342.

Himma, Kenneth E. and Tavani, Herman T. (Editors), *The Handbook of Information and Computer Ethics*, John Wiley & Sons, Hoboken, NJ (2008).

Hochheiser, Harry and Lazar, Jonathan, HCI and societal issues: A framework for engagement, *International Journal of Human-Computer Interaction* 23, 3 (2007), 339–374.

Holmes, Tiffany, Eco-visualization: Combining art and technology to reduce energy consumption, *Proc. ACM Conference on Creativity and Cognition*, ACM Press, New York (2007), 153–162.

Lazar, Jonathan (Editor), *Universal Usability: Designing User Interfaces for Diverse Users*, John Wiley & Sons, New York (2007).

Maloney-Krichmar, Diane and Preece, Jennifer, A multilevel analysis of sociability, usability, and community dynamics in an online health community, *ACM Transactions on Computer Human Interaction* 12, 2 (June 2005), 201–232.

Mumford, Lewis, *Technics and Civilization*, Harcourt Brace and World, New York (1934).

National Academy of Sciences, *Protecting Individual Privacy in the Struggle Against Terrorists*, National Academies Press, Washington, D.C. (2008).

National Telecommunications and Information Administration, U. S. Dept. of Commerce, *Networked Nation: Broadband in America*, Washington, D.C. (January 2008). Available at http://www.ntia.doc.gov/reports/2008/NetworkedNationBroadbandin America2007.pdf.

Norman, Don, *The Design of Future Things*, Basic Books, New York (2007).

Penzias, Arno, *Ideas and Information*, Simon and Schuster, New York (1989).

Shirky, Clay, *Here Comes Everybody: The Power of Organizing Without Organizations*, Penguin Press, New York (2008).

Shneiderman, Ben, Creativity support tools: Accelerating discovery and innovation, *Communications of the ACM* 50, 12 (December 2007), 20–32.

Shneiderman, Ben, Science 2.0, *Science* 319, Issue 5868 (March 7, 2008), 1349–1350.

Shneiderman, Ben, Universal usability: Pushing human-computer interaction research to empower every citizen, *Communications of the ACM* 43, 5 (2000), 84–91.

Shneiderman, Ben and Preece, Jennifer, 911.gov, *Science* 315, Issue 5814 (February 16, 2007), 944.

Sterling, T. D., Guidelines for humanizing computerized information systems: A report from Stanley House, *Communications of the ACM* 17, 11 (November 1974), 609–613.

Thompson, Clive, Brave new world of digital intimacy, *New York Times Sunday Magazine* (14 September 2008), 42ff.

Weizenbaum, Joseph, *Computer Power and Human Reason*, W. H. Freeman, San Francisco, CA (1976).

Whitworth, Brian and De Moor, Aldo (Editors), *Handbook of Research on Socio-Technical Design and Social Networking Systems*, IGI Global, Hershey, PA (2009).

Yin, R. K., *Case Study Research: Design and Methods, Third Edition*, Sage Publications, Thousand Oaks, CA (2003).

Name Index

A

Aaronson, A. P., 495, 498, 509
Abowd, Gregory, 49, 304, 327, 352, 389, 401
Accot, J., 324, 352
Agichtein, E., 517, 534
Ahlberg, C., 234, 266, 545, 559
Ahmad, N., 368, 399
Alavi, M., 393, 402
Albert, William, 50, 154, 170
Allen, A., 426, 430
Allen, James, 287, 298
Allison, R. S., 214, 219
Alpert, Sherman R., 495, 509
Anderson, Ben, 201, 220
Anderson, J. R., 90
Anderson, T., 261, 268
Andre, E., 76, 91, 441, 472
Andrienko, Gennady, 547, 559
Andrienko, Natalia, 547, 559
Angell, Roger, 490, 511
Anshus, Otto J., 345, 357
Anson, Rob, 398
Ariel, Yaron, 377, 401
Arnheim, Rudolf, 194, 197, 219
Arnott, John L., 43
Asada, Minoni, 296, 299
Asaro, Peter, 572, 580
Ashcraft, Mark, H., 25, 49, 331, 334, 352
Atkins, D., 385, 400
Atkinson, Robert D., 579
Atlee, Joanne, 109, 127
Auden, W. H., 225
Ayer, A. J., 55

B

Babbage, Charles, 271
Badler, N., 76, 91, 441, 472
Badre, Albert, 51, 299, 355
Baecker, Ronald M., 51, 64, 92, 133, 170, 268, 389, 396, 399, 503, 509
Bailey, Robert W., 24, 47, 65, 90
Balakrishnan, Aruna, 367, 399
Balakrishnan, Ravin, 189, 220, 232, 267, 329, 353, 391, 402
Baldridge, Jason, 287, 299
Balentine, Bruce, 260, 266, 331, 352
Ball, R., 343, 355
Ballard, Barbara, 49, 348–349, 353
Bandlow, Alisa, 34, 42
Bangor, Aaron, 167
Banko, Michelle, 291, 298, 299
Barber, R. E., 421, 429
Barbesi, Alessandro, 418, 431
Barillot, E., 258, 268
Barnard, P. J., 281, 282, 298
Barnes, Julie, 110, 127
Barnum, Carol M., 149, 167

Barnwell, J., 265, 269
Bartram, Lyn, 461, 471
Basu, Sumit, 336, 353
Batsell, Richard R., 300
Batson, C. D., 368, 399
Batson, Trent, 392, 399
Baudel, T., 259, 266
Baudisch, Patrick, 265, 268, 269, 315, 324, 353, 357, 456, 461, 471, 472, 522, 534
Baumeister, L., 83, 90
Beale, Russell, 49
Bean, Nathaniel, 491, 505, 510
Beaudouin-Lafon, M., 324, 354
Becker, Sallie E. Gordon, 409, 431
Beckwith, L., 26, 42
Bederson, Ben B., 20, 34, 43, 349–350, 324–325, 350, 353, 354, 426, 431, 460, 461, 471, 472, 525, 534, 548, 551, 559, 560, 561
Belkin, N. J., 528, 534
Bellotti, Victoria, 371, 399
Benbasat, Izak, 284, 285, 299
Benford, Steve, 211, 217, 219
Benko, H., 324, 353
Bentley, R., 112, 125
Benyon, David, 49
Bergel, M., 452, 471
Bergman, Eric, 51, 261–262, 266, 441, 472
Berners-Lee, Tim, 76, 90, 569, 579
Bernoff, Josh, 362, 401
Bers, J., 260, 268
Bertran, A., 334, 353
Bessiere, K., 424–425, 430
Best, V., 356
Beyer, Hugh, 47, 109, 110, 125, 126
Bhatti, Nina, 409, 417–418, 429
Bi, Peng, 345, 357
Bias, Randolph, 15, 52, 100, 101, 125, 149, 168
Bibliowicz, Jacobo, 189, 200
Bier, E., 259, 266
Bilal, Dania, 53, 430
Billinghurst, Mark, 214, 222
Billings, Charles E., 75, 90
Bird, Steven, 287, 299
Birnholtz, J. M., 389, 396, 399
Bitan, Yuval, 414, 430
Bitter, Ingmar, 207, 221
Black, J., 283, 299
Blackmon, M. H., 136, 138
Blackwell, A., 308–309, 357
Blaedow, Karen, 296, 301
Blake, William, 513
Blanchard, Harry E., 331, 353
Blenkhorn, Paul, 30, 42
Blevis, Eli, 568, 579
Blum, Roger, 367, 400
Bodker, Susan, 117, 125
Bøegh, K., 327, 355
Boehm, Barry W., 103, 109–110, 125, 128
Boehner, Kirsten, 113, 125

Subject Index

A

Abbreviations in command languages, 283–285
ABCDE keyboard layout style, 307
Acceptable response time, 416–417
Acceptance tests, 154–156
Acoustic memory, 334
Acrobat, 231
Acyclic menu networks, 244
Adaptive menus, 247
Adaptive versus adaptable interfaces, 576
Adobe, 107, 178, 199, 231, 320, 482, 491, 501, 525
Adventure games, natural language and, 294
Affinity diagrams, 111
Alphasliders, 234
Amazon, 8, 77, 84, 99, 342, 343, 362, 412, 532
American Idol, 383
American Institute of Graphic Arts (AIGA), 48
American Society for Information Science & Technology (ASIST), 45
Android, 12
Animated demonstrations, 502–504
Animation searches, 527
Anthromorphic interfaces, 440–444, 575–576
    guidelines for avoidance of, 444
    interface design and, 440–444
    social impact of, 575–576
Anthropometry, study of, 23–24
Anxiety reduction, 38
Apple, 5, 7, 12, 31, 57, 76, 104, 105, 119, 178, 179, 182, 230, 311, 316, 329, 337, 457
Apple Human Interface Guidelines, 46
ArcGIS, 183
Artificial reality concepts, 211
Association for Computing Machinery (ACM), 45
Association of Computational Linguistics (ACL), 296
Association of Information Systems (AIS), 48
Attention-getting techniques, user-interface design for, 60
Audioconferencing, 387–389
Auditory interfaces, 60, 259–261, 331–341
    barge-in technique, 260–261
    continuous-speech recognition, 335–336
    discrete-word recognition, 333–335
    earcons, 340
    guidelines for design, 60
    head-related transfer function (HRTF), 340
    icons, 340
    menus, 259–261
    musical-instrument digital-interface (MIDI), 341
    out-of-turn interaction, 261
    sonification, 339–341
    speech generation, 331, 338–339
    speech systems, 331–333
    voice information systems, 337–338
Augmented reality interfaces, 191–193, 213–214
Automatic filtering, 528
Automation of designs, 73–79
    agent-like programming, 77–78
    closed system, 74
    control panels and, 78–79
    human judgement and, 74–76
    open system, 73–74
    user control and, 73–79
    user models for, 76–77
Auto-repeat keyboard features, 310

B

Between-subjects experimental design, 165
Bimanual device input, 326
Binary menus, 228–229
Bird's-eye-view evaluation, 138
Blackberry, 12, 308, 310, 335, 370
Blinking displays, design guidelines for, 60
Blogs, 374–378
Blogger, 362, 374, 375
Bookmarks, 251
Boolean queries, 527–528
Browsing, 516–517
    image, 460–463
    searches, 516–517
Bugzilla, 375
Bulletin boards, 372

C

Can-you-break-this approach, 148
Chat, 383–384
Chatterbots, 290
Check boxes, 229
Chief usability officer (CUO), 100
Children, universal usabilty requirements for, 33–36
Closed system, 74
Cognitive diversity, universal usabilty and, 25–26
Cognitive walkthrough, 136
Collaboration, 18–19, 217, 359–402
    asynchronous distributed interfaces, 368–383
    collaboratories, 365, 381–382
    conferences, 364
    cooperative work questions, 397
    decision support from meetings, 364
    electronic commerce, 364
    face-to-face interfaces, 389–396
    forced partnerships, 363–364
    goals of, 363–368
    groupware, 361

Acknowledgments

Section Openers: (clockwise, from top left) © Jeff Savge; © Alan Becker/The Image Bank/Getty Images ; © Bob Daemmrich/The Image Works; © Michael DeYoung/Aurora/Getty Images; AISPIX/Shutterstock; © Mel Yates/Cultura/Getty Images. Background: © Jason Reed/Photodisc/Getty Images.

Chapter Outline: AISPIX/Shutterstock.

Figure	Source
1.1	Mac OS X® © 2008 Apple, Inc. All Rights Reserved; Facebook © 2008. All Rights Reserved; eBay © 1995–2008 eBay Inc. All Rights Reserved. Designated trademarks and brands are the property of their respective owners.
1.2	Microsoft® Windows Vista® © 2008 Microsoft Corp. All Rights Reserved; Picasa™ © 2008 Google. All Rights Reserved; Many Eyes © IBM Corporation 1994, 2008. All Rights Reserved; University of Maryland © 2008 University of Maryland. All Rights Reserved.
1.3	iTunes® © 2008 Apple Inc. All Rights Reserved.
1.4	© 1996–2008 Amazon. All Rights Reserved.
1.5	© 2008 YouTube, LLC; Sony™ Playstation®3 Untold Legends™ © 2005-2009 Sony Online Entertainment LLC. SOE and the SOE logo are registered trademarks and Untold Legends is a trademark of Sony Online Entertainment LLC. "PlayStation," "PS" Family Logo and "PSP" are registered trademarks of Sony Computer Entertainment Inc. All other trademarks are properties of their respective owners. All rights reserved.
1.6	Courtesy United States Library of Congress.
1.7	Firefox® 3.0 © 1998–2008 Contributors. All Rights Reserved. Firefox and the Firefox logos are trademarks of the Mozilla Foundation. All Rights Reserved; Kayak.com © 2008 Kayak.com. All Rights Reserved; © 1995-2009 Alaska AirGroup Inc.; © United Airlines. All rights reserved.
1.8	Blackberry® Curve™ © 2009 Research In Motion® (RIM®) Limited; Apple® iPhone™ © 2009 Apple Inc. All Rights Reserved; HTC © 2009 HTC Corporation. All Rights Reserved; Android™ © Google Inc.
1.10	Guitar Hero™ © Activision Publishing, Inc. Activision™ is a registered trademark. All Rights Reserved.
1.11	© 2008 Yahoo! Inc. All Rights Reserved.
1.12A–B, 1.13	© 2008 Google. All Rights Reserved.
1.14	Autodesk® Inventor® © 2008 Autodesk, Inc. All Rights Reserved; Worm Gear Component Generator © 2008 Townsend Engineering. All Rights Reserved.
1.15	LeapFrog® Tag™ Reading Basics © LeapFrog Enterprises, Inc. All Rights Reserved.
1.16	Courtesy of International Children's Digital Library Foundation (http://www.childrenslibrary.org/).
3.2	© 2008 IBM Corporation. Reproduced by permission from International Business Machines Corporation (IBM) web site. All Rights Reserved.
Table 3.1	© 2005 by Elsevier Inc. All Rights Reserved. Morgan Kaufmann Publishers is an imprint of Elsevier.
3.3	Courtesy of Catherine Plaisant and University of Baltimore, KidsTeam (Nancy Kaplan).
3.4	© Dr. Allison Druin. Reprinted with permission.
Page 118	Courtesy of the National Digital Library of the Library of Congress.
Box 4.1	From Pinelle, Wong, and Stach. "Heuristic Evaluation for Games: Usability Principles for Video Game Design." Proc CH12008 Conference: Human Factors in Computing Systems. New York: ACM Press, 2008. 1453–1462. All Rights Reserved.
Box 4.2	© UPA, 2007, Reprinted from the *Journal of Usability Studies* 2, 4, (2007), 162–179; http://www.upassoc.org/upa_publications/jus/2007august/usefulusable.pdf.
4.1, 4.3	© CURE Center for Usability Research & Engineering.
4.2	Reproduced courtesy of U.S. Government.
4.4	© 1998–2009 Mangold International GmbH.
4.5	© Tracksys 2006–2007.
Box 4.3	From Dumas and Loring, *Moderating Useability Tests: Principles and Practices for Interacting*. © 2008 Kaufmann Publishers. Reprinted with permission Elsevier.
4.6	© 2006 UserWorks, Inc.
Table 4.1	© University of Maryland. All Rights Reserved.
4.7	Google's Chrome™ browser © 2008 Google. All Rights Reserved.
4.8	Reprinted by permission of ACM and Guimbretiére, Dixon, and Hinckley. "Experiscope: An Analysis Tool for Interaction Data. CHI 2007 Conference: Human Factors in Computing Systems. New York: ACM Press 2007, 1333–1342. All Rights Reserved."
5.1	From Wang et al., Aligning temporal data by sentinel events: discovering patterns in electronic health records. In *Proceeding of the Twenty-Sixth Annual SIGCHI Conference on Human Factors in Computing Systems* (Florence, Italy, April 05–10, 2008). CHI '08. ACM, New York, NY, 457–466. © 2008 ACM, Inc. All Rights Reserved.
5.4	Xerox Star 8010 with the ViewPoint™ system courtesy of Steven Miller, University of Maryland.
5.6	The ArcVier® Graphical User Interface is the intellectual property of ESRI and is used herein by permission. © ESRI. All Rights Reserved. Content used by permission of Tarracon. All Rights Reserved.
5.7	Courtesy of Catherine Plaisant.
5.8	Spore™ © 2008 Electronic Arts Inc. Electronic Arts, EA, the EA logo and Spore are trademarks or registered trademarks of Electronic Arts Inc. in the U.S. and/or other countries. All Rights Reserved.
5.9, 5.10	© 2008 The Dashboard Spy. This reproduction courtesy of The Dashboard Spy (http://dashboardspy.com).
5.11	© 2003 A. Olson, The Scripps Research Institute (TSRI).
5.12	Ambient™ Energy Joule © 2008 Ambient Devices, Inc. All Rights Reserved.
5.13	Jitterbug® OneTouch™ © GreatCall, Inc.

About the Authors

Ben Shneiderman is a Professor in the Department of Computer Science, Founding Director (1983–2000) of the Human-Computer Interaction Laboratory (http://www.cs.umd.edu/hcil), and Member of the Institute for Advanced Computer Studies and the Institute for Systems Research, all at the University of Maryland at College Park. He is a Fellow of the ACM and AAAS and received the ACM CHI (Computer Human Interaction) Lifetime Achievement Award. His books, research papers, and frequent lectures have made him an international leader in this emerging discipline. For relaxation he likes biking, hiking, skiing, and travel.

Catherine Plaisant is Associate Research Scientist at the Human-Computer Interaction Laboratory of the University of Maryland Institute for Advanced Computer Studies. She earned a Doctorat d'Ingénieur degree in France in 1982 and has been conducting research in the field of human-computer interaction since then. In 1987, she joined Professor Shneiderman at the University of Maryland, where she has worked with students and members of the lab throughout the growth of the field of human-computer interaction. Her research contributions range from focused interaction techniques to innovative visualizations validated with user studies to practical applications developed with industrial partners.

Written in collaboration with . . .

Maxine S. Cohen is a Professor in the Graduate School of Computer and Information Sciences at Nova Southeastern University in Fort Lauderdale, Florida, where she teaches graduate courses in Human-Computer Interaction (HCI). Before joining NSU, she worked at IBM in the User Centered Design department. Prior to IBM, she was a faculty member in the Computer Science department in the Watson School of Engineering at the State University of New York at Binghamton. She has been teaching and working in the HCI field for over 20 years. She received a B.A. in Mathematics from the University of Vermont, an M.S. (specialization Computer Science) and a Ph.D. (specialization Systems Science) from the State University of New York at Binghamton.

Steven M. Jacobs recently retired from the University of Southern California and the aerospace industry and is now Adjunct Faculty at Northern Arizona University at Flagstaff, Arizona. He was formerly with Northrop Grumman Mission Systems in Carson, California. Mr. Jacobs managed engineers developing user interface and web applications software for various government and commercial applications. He was also Adjunct Assistant Professor at the University of Southern California for 17 years, where he developed and taught their graduate computer science courses in user interface design and human performance engineering. He has also taught short courses in similar topics for UCLA Extension and ACM. He received his M.S.C.S. from UCLA and his B.A. in Mathematics from Monmouth University (New Jersey).